Instructor's Resource

Modern Carpentry
Essential Skills for the Building Trades

by

Willis H. Wagner
Professor Emeritus
Industrial Technology
University of Northern Iowa, Cedar Falls

Howard Bud Smith
Technical Author and Editor
Lee Howard Associates
Black River Falls, WI

Publisher
The Goodheart-Willcox Company, Inc.
Tinley Park, Illinois
www.g-w.com

Copyright © 2008
by
The Goodheart-Willcox Company, Inc.

Previous editions copyright 2003, 2000, 1996, 1992, 1987, 1983, 1979, 1976, 1973, 1969

All rights reserved. No part of this work may be reproduced, stored, or transmitted in
any form or by any electronic or mechanical means, including information
storage and retrieval systems, without the prior written permission of
The Goodheart-Willcox Company, Inc.

Manufactured in the United States of America.

ISBN 978-1-59070-650-3 (Instructor's Manual)

ISBN 978-1-59070-651-0 (Instructor's Resource Binder)
ISBN 978-1-59070-652-7 (Instructor's Resource CD)

3 4 5 6 7 8 9 – 08 – 11 10 09

The Goodheart-Willcox Company, Inc. Brand Disclaimer: Brand names, company names, and illustrations for products and services included in this text are provided for educational purposes only and do not represent or imply endorsement or recommendation by the author or the publisher.

The Goodheart-Willcox Company, Inc. Safety Notice: The reader is expressly advised to carefully read, understand, and apply all safety precautions and warnings described in this book or that might also be indicated in undertaking the activities and exercises described herein to minimize risk of personal injury or injury to others. Common sense and good judgment should also be exercised and applied to help avoid all potential hazards. The reader should always refer to the appropriate manufacturer's technical information, directions, and recommendations; then proceed with care to follow specific equipment operating instructions. The reader should understand these notices and cautions are not exhaustive.

The publisher makes no warranty or representation whatsoever, either expressed or implied, including but not limited to equipment, procedures, and applications described or referred to herein, their quality, performance, merchantability, or fitness for a particular purpose. The publisher assumes no responsibility for any changes, errors, or omissions in this book. The publisher specifically disclaims any liability whatsoever, including any direct, indirect, incidental, consequential, special, or exemplary damages resulting, in whole or in part, from the reader's use or reliance upon the information, instructions, procedures, warnings, cautions, applications, or other matter contained in this book. The publisher assumes no responsibility for the activities of the reader.

Contents

Introduction

Using the Textbook 7
Introduction 8
Text Body 8
End-of-Chapter Materials 8
Appendix A: Carpentry Math Review 9
Appendix B: Technical Information 9
Glossary of Technical Terms 9
Index 9

Using the Workbook 9

Using the Instructor's Resource 10
Introduction 10
Pedagogical Charts 10
Course Outlines 11
Supplementary Activities 11
Chapter Resources 11
Section Exams 12
Color Transparencies (Binder/CD only) 12

Teaching Carpentry 13
Setting Up an Advisory Council 13
Teaching Methods 13
Teaching Carpentry with Limited Facilities 15
Student Outcomes 15
Varying Student Abilities 15
Additional Student Experiences and Resources 16

Evaluation 17
Chapter Quizzes 17
Section Exams 17
Procedure Checklists 17

Employability Skills 18

Supplemental Reading and Professional Resources ... 19

Copyright by Goodheart-Willcox Co., Inc.

Pedagogical Charts

Basic Skills Chart 25
Scope and Sequence Chart 37
SkillsUSA Competencies 45

Course Outlines

Eighteen-Week Course of Study 49
Thirty-Six Week Course of Study 51
Seventy-Two Week Course of Study 53

Supplementary Activities

Activity 4-1—Hand Tool Exercise 59
Activity 4-2—Constructing a Small-Parts Storage Box 61
Activity 4-3—Constructing an Octagonal Frame 62
Activity 4-4—Laying Out and Cutting 63
Activity 4-5—Building a Stool 65
Activity 4-6—Building a Sawhorse 67
Activity 5-1—Power Tool Exercise 68
Activity 6-1—Figuring Shop Elevations with the Level 69
Activity 6-2—Squaring a Building 70
Activity 7-2—Volume Proportioning 72
Activity 10-1—Roof Framing Computations 74
Activity 10-2—Common Rafter Layout 77
Activity 10-3—Calculating Common Rafters 78
Activity 11-1—Wall Framing with Steel and Drywall Installation ... 80
Activity 12-1—Building a Doghouse 82
Activity 14-1—Concrete and Masonry Assignment 84
Activity 14-2—Block Wall Setup 85

Chapter Resources

Section 1—Preparing to Build
Chapter 1—Building Materials 87
Chapter 2—The Carpenter's Workplace 103
Chapter 3—Plans, Specifications, and Codes 111
Chapter 4—Hand Tools 123
Chapter 5—Power Tools 133
Chapter 6—Building Layout 143

Section 1 Exam 153

Section 2—Footings, Foundations, and Framing
Chapter 7—Footings and Foundations 157
Chapter 8—Floor Framing 175
Chapter 9—Wall and Ceiling Framing 199
Chapter 10—Roof Framing 215
Chapter 11—Framing with Steel 233

Section 2 Exam 243

Section 3—Closing In
Chapter 12—Roofing Materials and Methods 247
Chapter 13—Windows and Exterior Doors 269
Chapter 14—Exterior Wall Finish 281

Section 3 Exam 297

Section 4—Finishing
Chapter 15—Thermal and Sound Insulation 301
Chapter 16—Interior Wall and Ceiling Finish 315
Chapter 17—Finish Flooring 329
Chapter 18—Stair Construction 343
Chapter 19—Doors and Interior Trim 353
Chapter 20—Cabinetry 367
Chapter 21—Painting, Finishing, and Decorating 379

Section 4 Exam 393

Section 5—Special Construction
Chapter 22—Chimneys and Fireplaces 399
Chapter 23—Post-and-Beam Construction 407
Chapter 24—Systems-Built Housing 417
Chapter 25—Passive Solar Construction 423
Chapter 26—Remodeling, Renovating, and Repairing 431
Chapter 27—Building Decks and Porches 441

Section 5 Exam 451

Copyright by Goodheart-Willcox Co., Inc.

Section 6—Mechanical Systems
Chapter 28—Electrical Wiring 455
Chapter 29—Plumbing Systems 463
Chapter 30—Heating, Ventilation, and Air Conditioning............................. 473

Section 6 Exam... 481

Section 7—Scaffolds and Careers
Chapter 31—Scaffolds and Ladders 485
Chapter 32—Carpentry—A Career Path 493

Section 7 Exam... 499

Answers to Section Exams... 501

Transparency Captions 505

Transparency Packet (Binder/CD Only)

Introduction

Modern Carpentry provides up-to-date information about equipment, methods, and materials used in residential and light commercial construction. Although most of the examples are related to residential construction, the procedures and techniques detailed in this text may also be applied to a wide range of other frame buildings. The text is designed to provide fundamental information and instruction; however, the content has sufficient depth that it can be effectively used in advanced courses. This text addresses an industry need for persons who are able to understand and apply their skills and techniques.

Modern Carpentry also serves as an introduction to other building trades. Section 6 of the text, *Mechanical Systems,* presents technical information and know-how on house wiring; plumbing; and heating, ventilation, and air conditioning (HVAC). While these systems are normally installed by other tradespeople, knowledge of the processes employed is helpful to the carpenter or homeowner.

Each topic is addressed in clear and simple language. Tasks that require a series of steps to complete are set off from the text with a *Procedure* heading and the title of the task.

Nearly all of the more than 1700 illustrations are presented in color. Clear and concise drawings illustrate current carpentry techniques and standards.

Modern Carpentry places emphasis on the importance of safety on the work site—whether it is on a job, at school, or at home. Students, do-it-yourselfers, and even experienced carpenters must be able to recognize and correct unsafe conditions and practices.

Chapter 2, *The Carpenter's Workplace* covers what is expected of an apprentice carpenter, and also provides basic safety procedures and rules for the different topics covered in the text.

Safety-related items throughout the text have been printed in red for emphasis.

Using the Textbook

The chapters in **Modern Carpentry** are arranged in sequence with the phases of construction performed on a typical structure. Student abilities, available facilities, and time constraints often determine the number of chapters your class will be able to cover. You may choose to include only those chapters (or series of chapters) appropriate for a particular course. As each chapter is complete by itself, the content flow is not disturbed.

An outstanding feature of the **Modern Carpentry** textbook is the description of complicated processes in easy-to-understand terms. Explanations are clarified with carefully selected photographs, diagrams, and drawings. The textbook's detailed descriptions of construction processes make it an excellent out-of-classroom resource. Completing out-of-classroom reading assignments will prepare students for in-class discussions. Students will also be able to better comprehend additional content presented through discussions, lectures, demonstrations, and other classroom resources.

Out-of-class study is especially important in vocational courses where students spend most of their in-class time working on construction activities. It not only saves valuable classroom time, but also provides students with the experience of researching and securing answers to questions. This out-of-class experience will also minimize the tendency of some students to depend on the instructor for direct assistance and help in finding solutions to every problem.

The textbook is divided into seven sections and 32 chapters. Section 1, *Preparing to Build* includes information that needs to be mastered before beginning any carpentry project. Topics covered in Section 1 include building materials; wood identification; what the beginning carpenter should know on his or her first job; safety rules; plans, specifications, and codes; hand tools; power tools; and building layout. Section 2, *Footings, Foundations, and Framing* details topics involved in the preliminary stages of construction. A chapter on steel framing is included in this section. Section 3, *Closing In* deals with installation of roofing and wall coverings, windows, and exterior doors.

Section 4, *Finishing* discusses such topics as insulation, wall and ceiling finishing, floor finishing, stair building, trim, and cabinetry. Section 5, *Special Construction* involves topics such as chimneys, fireplaces, solar construction, remodeling, and painting. A chapter devoted to deck and porch building is included in this section. Section 6, *Mechanical Systems* provides basic information and methods for installing wiring, plumbing, and HVAC. Section 7, *Scaffolds and Careers* contains technical information on safe scaffolding, ladders, and an insight into career opportunities in carpentry.

Each chapter includes many features, including learning objectives, technical vocabulary, end-of-chapter reinforcement questions, curricular connections activities, and outside assignments. At the back of the textbook, you will find a math review section, technical information, a glossary, and an index. These are included for easy reference.

Introduction

Chapter topics are introduced in the opening paragraphs of each chapter, immediately following the learning objectives. In some cases, the introduction relates the new information to material that was discussed in the previous chapter. Heighten the students' interest in the chapter by having them read the introduction in class and then asking them to list topics they feel might be included in the chapter.

Text Body

Technical vocabulary terms are listed alphabetically at the beginning of each chapter and appear in ***bold italics*** on their first occurrence in the text. They are also defined in a running glossary at the bottom of the page where they appear and are more extensively defined in the *Glossary of Technical Terms* at the back of the textbook.

Headings within each chapter are organized in a numeric system as an aid to locating material and making reading assignments. Major headings are preceded by the chapter number, then numbered in sequence. Major headings for each chapter are also displayed in the textbook's expanded table of contents, making it easy to identify, at a glance, the topics covered in that chapter.

Many trade tips are integrated throughout the body of the text. These are identified with the heading *Working Knowledge* and presented on a color background. In many cases, the tips reinforce concepts presented in the text. In other cases, they provide additional information about a topic discussed in the text body. Safety material is presented under the heading *Safety Note*.

Numerous step-by-step procedures are included in the book, providing students with detailed instruction for important tasks in preparing, building, and finishing residential and light commercial structures. These procedures are set off from the text body with special graphic treatment.

Occupational information features, under the heading *On the Job*, appear at the end of most chapters. Each feature concentrates on a particular building trades occupation, describing the nature of the job, the training required, and the long term outlook for employment. More general career material is presented in Chapter 32, *Carpentry—A Career Path*.

End-of-Chapter Materials

At the end of each chapter are reinforcement questions in the *Test Your Knowledge* section, integrated academic activities in the *Curricular Connections* section, and more advanced research, problem-solving, and group activities in the *Outside Assignments* section.

Research and development in building construction has resulted in a tremendous number of new and improved materials and assembly systems. It is impractical, if not impossible, to adequately cover the field of carpentry in a single textbook. Thus, it is important that students spend some of their out-of-class time studying reference books, trade magazines, and manufacturer literature.

Curricular Connections questions provide students with an opportunity to extend and enrich their learning experiences by applying skills from other disciplines. These activities involve language arts, math, science, and social studies. They vary in complexity and form to match varying student interests and provide opportunities for using higher-order thinking skills.

Outside Assignments may be adapted to either individual or group work. Some activities are "paper and pencil" type while others require hands-on involvement. Although completion of these assignments is not vital to accomplishing the objectives, it allows students to further their knowledge of the carpentry field. *Outside Assignments* are not designed to replace the regular construction activities being carried out in the laboratory. However, when the use of tools and materials is required, it may be appropriate to provide laboratory time to complete the projects.

To maintain some measure of control over the *Outside Assignments*, have students submit a brief written statement describing the problem and procedure they plan to follow. This is especially important for projects that require materials and equipment. At this point, you can assist the student(s) in finalizing plans and make it possible to carry out the project in a practical and safe manner. Have students set the projects up as though they are "doing a job." Instruct them to keep records, including a bill of materials, billable work hours, and any other applicable records. These records and a written summary should be included in the student notebooks for evaluation at the close of the term.

Appendix A: Carpentry Math Review

An understanding of basic mathematics is a tool a carpenter will find as useful as any saw, drill, or hammer. Effective use of math skills ensures that roofs slope properly, stairs rise evenly, and studs fit correctly. Appendix A, *Carpentry Math Review* provides a refresher course covering the following topics:
- The use of rules, tapes, and squares.
- Working with fractions and decimals.
- Knowing and using formulas.
- Volume computation.

Appendix B: Technical Information

This part of the text includes technical information and specifications used in the carpentry trade. The following items are included:
- Standard abbreviations.
- Metrics in construction.
- Measurement conversions.
- Material specifications and grading information.
- Fastener specifications.
- Span tables.
- Truss types.
- Construction details.
- Insulation specifications and material types.
- Pipe sizes and specifications.
- Electrical specifications.

Glossary of Technical Terms

The glossary provides detailed descriptions of technical terms commonly used in the trade. Although many of these terms are defined in the text, the glossary provides a convenient reference.

Index

Modern Carpentry contains a comprehensive index of all the concepts and topics presented in the text. The index allows the student to find information on a specific subject quickly and easily.

Using the Workbook

The workbook for **Modern Carpentry** is designed to measure student achievement and comprehension of the material presented in the chapter. The workbook reinforces the concepts and techniques described in the text. By using a variety of questions, you are able to fairly evaluate the students' progress. For the student, the workbook is a study guide and reference tool.

Copyright by Goodheart-Willcox Co., Inc.

The workbook correlates with the content of the textbook. Objectives, questions, and problems in the workbook are listed in the same sequence as the information in the textbook.

You will find that the workbook provides an efficient method of checking on the students' progress. Selected items from the workbook can be used to develop periodic or final examinations. Informing the students of this procedure will likely stimulate their efforts to fully understand the information in the textbook, rather than simply copying answers.

Answers to the questions and problems consist of words, letters, numbers, and simple drawings. Instruct students that words should be spelled correctly and letters and numbers should be carefully formed. It is highly recommended that the letters and words be printed, rather than written in cursive. Stress to students that most tradespeople follow this same practice, since the information is easier to read and the possibility of errors is greatly reduced.

Estimating amounts of material required for a building is an important part of carpentry. Procedures and examples are covered in various sections of the textbook, and estimating problems are included in the workbook. Extra space has been provided in the workbook for making the calculations. Students should organize their computations so that they can check through their work. This will also make it easier for you to evaluate a student's procedure.

Numbers should be rounded off and calculations factored as shown in the sample problems in various sections of the textbook. Simple diagrams and sketches are often helpful when solving complex problems. These could be made on a separate sheet of paper or included in the space provided for calculations in the workbook.

Using the Instructor's Resource

The instructor's resource is a useful teaching tool alongside the **Modern Carpentry** textbook. The instructor's resource is offered in three different formats:

- **Instructor's Manual.** Printed resource including all the materials described in this section.
- **Instructor's Resource Binder.** Printed resource packaged in a loose-leaf binder. The binder includes the content of the Instructor's Manual plus a set of full-color transparencies.
- **Instructor's Resource CD:** Electronic resource on disc. The CD includes the entire content of the resource binder (including transparencies), plus Exam*View*® Assessment Suite, electronic lesson plans, and links to related Web sites. The Exam*View*® Assessment Suite offers a test bank of more than 2000 questions.

Introduction

The instructor's resource facilitates the development of a carpentry curriculum by offering suggestions on course content and providing resource material for the novice, as well as the experienced, instructor. It details methods of implementing a carpentry curriculum in your own classroom. The chapter resources provide detailed information regarding the instructional process for the course. In some chapters, procedure checklists are provided for evaluating students' psychomotor skills. A quiz is included for each of the 32 chapters, and comprehensive exams are included for each of the seven sections.

Answers to all questions in the text and workbook are also provided along with answers to chapter quizzes and section exams. Reproducible masters, used to reinforce major concepts, are included for each chapter.

Pedagogical Charts

This instructor's resource includes three pedagogical charts: a *Basic Skills Chart*, a *Scope and Sequence Chart*, and a *SkillsUSA Competencies* chart. These charts can serve as an aid in aligning the content of **Modern Carpentry** with your specific curricular requirements.

Basic Skills Chart

The *Basic Skills Chart* is designed to identify those activities in the **Modern Carpentry** text, workbook, and instructor's resource that specifically encourage the development of basic skills. These interdisciplinary activities are an integral part of most vocational programs. Academic areas addressed in the chart include reading, writing, mathematics, communication (other than reading and writing), science, and social studies.

- **Scope and Sequence Chart**

  The *Scope and Sequence Chart* identifies the major concepts presented in each chapter of the text. Refer to the chart to select those chapters and sections that meet your curriculum needs.

SkillsUSA Competencies

A correlation chart for the SkillsUSA Championships corresponds to the skill competency outline included in the organization's carpentry contest instructions. The instructions are contained in the association's book of contest rules used by clubs preparing for the annual SkillsUSA Championship. The *SkillsUSA Competencies* chart correlates to the **Modern Carpentry** text by page numbers.

Course Outlines

The instructor's resource contains sample course outlines for 18-week, 36-week, and 72-week programs. These outlines include course descriptions and objectives. The outlines can be modified to suit high school, post-high vocational, and technical college levels. Once you determine what material will best serve your students and how that material should be presented, you can modify the outlines accordingly.

Supplementary Activities

Seventeen supplementary activities, developed by carpentry instructors from around the country, are included in the instructor's resource. For your convenience, they are numbered according to the chapters with which they best correspond. Each activity includes a list of objectives and a step-by-step procedure. They can be used accordingly or adapted to fit the unique needs of your program. The activities can be modified to suit your classroom facilities and assigned as either group or individual projects. Answers, where applicable, are also included.

Chapter Resources

Chapter resources provide activities and teaching suggestions. They also provide answers to all questions, exercises, and activities in the textbook and workbook. Reproducible masters, procedure checklists (where applicable), and chapter quizzes are also included.

Objectives

Objectives are listed for each of the 32 chapters. The goals presented involve basic concepts, skills, and understandings students should derive from their study. You will want to adapt these goals to your particular teaching situation and student composition. Preparation for instruction with these objectives in mind will lend direction to the use of **Modern Carpentry** in your course.

Instructional Materials

The instructional materials section lists all of the resources provided for teaching the chapter. Prepare the majority of the instructional materials prior to teaching the chapter. This will allow you to review the material while you are duplicating it. Chapter quizzes should not be copied until just prior to giving the evaluation. This will allow you to maintain confidentiality of the quiz.

Trade-Related Math

This section of the chapter resources includes one or two basic math concepts that can be related to the text information. The math concepts can be integrated into the chapter presentation or used as a follow-up at the conclusion of the chapter.

Instructional Concepts and Student Learning Experiences

This section provides teaching suggestions and strategies for using the textbook, workbook, and reproducible masters. Information and teaching suggestions should be tailored to fit the needs of the curriculum. Other activities and strategies can be developed from ideas that are presented in the chapter resources. Maintain a file of ideas for future use.

In selecting and developing your instructional resources, look for opportunity to reinforce, extend, enrich, and reteach.

- **Reinforce.** It is generally accepted that the more ways a student is exposed to a given concept, the greater the chances for his or her understanding and retention

of the material. A variety of learning experiences are designed to meet the reinforcement needs of students.
- **Extend.** The teaching suggestions in the instructor's resource are directed to students at a variety of ability levels. You may choose some of the assignments to encourage highly motivated students to extend their learning experience outside of the classroom. These types of activities allow students to relate text information to other experiences, particularly life skills.
- **Enrich.** Enrichment activities are designed to help students learn more about topics introduced in the text. These types of activities, such as research and survey activities, give students the opportunity to enrich their learning through more in-depth study.
- **Reteach.** Studies have shown that students respond differently to different teaching methods and techniques. Therefore, these materials provide suggestions for several strategies that can be used to teach the concepts in the text. This allows you to choose a different strategy to reteach students who showed a low response to a previous strategy.

In applicable chapters, safe work practices are stressed. In the text, safety considerations are highlighted in a red *Safety Note* feature. The instructor's resource calls your attention to these safety considerations so they will not be overlooked in your presentation. Stress the need for adequate personal protective equipment during all shop work.

Procedure Checklists

As the instructor, you would fill out a procedure checklist as a student performs certain tasks. A range of scores (1–5) is listed for each measurable objective. You can circle the score appropriate for each task performed. Since the checklists are general in nature, you may modify them to evaluate more specific tasks.

Some of the tasks involved in carpentry must be performed by several people working together. In these cases, write all students' names at the top of the procedure checklist and evaluate them as a group.

Reproducible Masters

Reproducible masters are designed to be used in several ways—duplicating masters, overhead transparencies, and test masters. Duplicating masters are designed to be copied and used by the students. You can make a transparency from the same master and project it while the students work on a copy of the duplicating master. The reproducible masters can also be projected using an opaque projector.

The reproducible masters can also be used for periodic tests and examinations. A test master can be prepared by masking out selected information and using a number or letter to identify the item.

Section Exams

Exams for each of the seven sections of the text are included in the instructor's resource. The section exams follow the chapter resources for the last chapter in the section. The answers to all sections exam follow the final section exam. A variety of question types are included on each exam. Section exams should be administered to students for evaluation after they have completed the textbook and workbook questions and the quizzes for all chapters of the section. Students should prepare for the section exam by reviewing the appropriate chapter materials and quizzes.

Color Transparencies (Binder/CD only)

The transparency package is intended to be used as an additional resource when teaching from **Modern Carpentry.** The transparencies are designed to assist your carpentry students in understanding principles and practices of carpentry. Transparencies can be used to help illustrate uses of carpentry products, show details of construction, and build additional interest in the subject. They may be coordinated with and worked into your daily lesson plans.

Additionally, the transparencies may also be used as reproducible handouts and as worksheets or quizzes (with the callouts covered and replaced with letters or numbers).

The identification number found at the bottom of each transparency indicates the chapter number and the material's position in the chapter. For example: CT 1-1 is the first color transparency in Chapter 1; CT 1-2 is the second; etc. The included list of corresponding captions offer a brief description, list callouts where applicable, and offer useful suggestions for using the transparencies.

Teaching Carpentry

Teaching carpentry, like teaching many technical subjects, requires a multifaceted approach in order to be successful. The combination of lectures, demonstrations, and other related activities may pose special problems for an instructor.

Every carpentry course should follow the overall goals and objectives that have been established for the curriculum. These, in turn, are determined by expected student outcomes, labor needs in the community, and career applications. Only when goals and objectives have been set should you begin to design a carpentry course. Several factors must be considered in course design, including:
- Related academic skills.
- Varying student abilities.
- Budget limitations.
- Safety and liability.

There are more teaching curricula and materials available than most instructors could review. Many state boards of education and organizations such as the Associated General Contractors have funded curriculum projects. Check with your regional and state boards of education, state department of vocational and technical education, or other related agencies.

Setting Up an Advisory Council

A carpentry advisory council is a committee of construction industry experts that advises the school department on course content, trends, and local labor needs. Invite members from a number of different fields. This panel helps you, as an instructor, identify the requirements of a carpentry program and keep up-to-date.

For a carpentry program, an advisory council might be formed with several general contractors (both commercial and residential) and carpenters. The course curriculum is based on their knowledge of the industry and your knowledge of teaching methodology and curriculum. The combination should allow you to present practical, up-to-date information to the students.

Teaching Methods

Learning does not take place until the pupil *wants* to learn. Getting your students interested in learning is one of the most difficult parts of teaching. Motivation, therefore, is the first step in effective teaching. You need to stimulate your students so they want to learn.

Decide how you want to motivate your class. Make it interesting! You can use human curiosity or the competitive nature of people to your advantage. If you pique their curiosity, most students will be interested in seeing, hearing, and *learning* about new and different things. Challenge your students—create an atmosphere where students will want to advance themselves. Make some projects a competition between groups.

Reward your students for a job well done. A word or two of praise can often change a person or class into success seekers. Emphasize a reward or personal gain. A reward could be something as simple as a free period or a field trip. Stress to your students that with true effort on their part and the proper training, the opportunity to secure a better job with greater earnings is much more likely to present itself.

Above all, *you* must be interested in what you are doing. Lack of interest on your part will convey itself to your students.

One of the quickest ways to lose students' interest is to be unprepared and present a meandering lesson. For effective teaching, you must carefully prepare the material, the learning environment, and the students.

Prepare yourself by becoming familiar with the material and having all of the necessary teaching aids readily available and in good working condition. A variety of teaching methods and materials should be used to make topics clear to all students. Materials and methods that may be used include textbooks, workbooks, videos, lectures, demonstrations, overhead transparencies, interactive group discussions, hands-on activities, and field trips.

Copyright by Goodheart-Willcox Co., Inc.

Visual Aids

Short lectures supported with visual aids work best for conveying a large amount of information in a short amount of time. Avoid lecturing for an entire class session. Student comprehension and attention decrease drastically beyond a certain point. Vary the teaching methods to add variety to the class. The unit resources outline various teaching methods that can be used in the classroom.

Balance the instruction by combining lectures with exercises and hands-on activities. Students need hands-on activities to apply what they have learned. Get your students involved! With available equipment, make videos of standard techniques and procedures. These can then be used for future classes. Each following class then can improve the video. Encourage students to solve problems on their own by using other available resources.

Safety

A feature of the textbook is the special attention devoted to safety. Chapter 2 covers the basic rules and regulations for construction work. At appropriate intervals throughout the text, safety considerations are included with instructions for performing specific operations. Safety-related instructions are highlighted in red *Safety Note* features.

As the instructor of the course, you should continually emphasize the importance of safety in construction. Try to include further explanations related to the various safety rules and regulations as they apply to a specific situation. Students are more likely to develop a responsible attitude toward safety and follow recommended practices when they understand the reasoning behind the rules and regulations.

Construction Activities

The carpentry student should have the opportunity to perform as many construction operations as practical. In an ideal situation, the advanced student will have the opportunity to participate in work on a regular construction site.

In many vocational schools, project houses are constructed over a two- to three-year time span. Initially, financing problems may be encountered. The initial costs of the property and materials may seem tremendous. However, when the house is sold, the profit can be reinvested into a new project house for the following years.

In many cases, a qualified contractor completes the site preparation and foundation work for a project house. This allows the students to begin with the rough framing of the structure. Small work groups (three to six students) should be formed to work as teams. Group the students and reassign them, as necessary, a few weeks into the project.

If your program cannot afford to finance a project house, research other possibilities. There are many government programs and not-for-profit groups that need and welcome help. Some carpentry programs contract directly with homeowners for remodeling or small construction jobs. Use your library resources and make contact with these programs. Offer the assistance of your student workers in exchange for a valuable learning experience.

When it is not possible to work on a project house, full-scale construction of small buildings can often be carried out in the school shop or an outside area adjacent to the shop. Get the students involved in the community. Contact your local municipalities and offer the assistance of your student workers.

Construction uses a broad range of component structures and prefabricated units, some of which may be built in the school shop and then removed for outdoor assembly or erection. Wall panels, roof trusses, stairs, and kitchen cabinet units are examples of this type of construction. Completed units may be disassembled and some of the materials reclaimed for other work. These units may also be designed and built for use in a structure being erected by the class or a local contractor.

Considerable experience can be gained by the student through the construction of scale models. Since this work is time-consuming, it may be best to erect only a wing or portion of a given structure. Since the model may be viewed from any angle, it shows how the finished structure will look in all three dimensions. This stimulates and motivates the students throughout the activity.

For model framing, the scale should be large enough to make work practical (minimum 1 1/2″ = 1′-0″). Cut the framing members to match the nominal size of lumber, not the dressed dimensions. Use white pine, sugar pine, basswood, or other soft-textured woods that are free of heavy grain. Since the strips are usually too small for regular machine surfacing operations, rip them to size with a hollow-ground combination blade or with a thin-kerf, carbide-tipped blade.

In addition to model framing, various sections of a structure can be built using a larger scale (quarter-size, half-size, or even full-size). These constructions might consist of sill sections, cornice sections, rake sections, or such inside work as door frames, stairs, finished flooring, and wall sections.

Models of the various components previously mentioned could be fabricated at a scale similar to framing structures. Also, special experimental designs of stressed-skin panels or box beams might serve as visual aids or as specimens that could be subjected to certain controlled testing.

Samples and Specimens

Throughout a building construction course, samples of materials should be available for the student to examine. Materials that are commonly used in a given area are easily obtained from local contractors and building supply dealers. Usable samples can also be obtained from most construction sites. Obtain permission from the contractor before entering the site. A partial list of samples includes species of lumber used locally; brick, stone, and concrete block; concrete forms; metal studs; sheathing lumber and boards; insulation materials; various types of shingles; finished flooring; ceiling tile; and inside molding and trim.

When storage space is available, various millwork items might be obtained. For example, a standard double-hung window unit, mounted upright on a base to permit operation and inspection, may be especially valuable. Also, sections of prefabricated kitchen cabinets or other building units provide examples of design, methods of construction, and appropriate materials.

Teaching Carpentry with Limited Facilities

Squeezing needed equipment out of a limited budget is not easy. If budget constraints pose a problem, try to improvise. Use the best possible means to get your message across to the students. In some cases, the large classes of students can be addressed using one of the two methods described in the next sections.

Pairing Students

After demonstrating a procedure or technique, pair more advanced students with beginners for hands-on activities to reinforce the concept(s) previously presented. The advanced student has the knowledge and initiative to work through the activity and then act as a teacher. This person should answer questions and provide training to his or her partner.

The help should not extend too far beyond answering questions and demonstrating some techniques. The advanced student should not do the work for the partner. A disadvantage may occur when a behavioral-problem student inhibits the study of his or her partner. If necessary, remedy this problem by pairing different partners at different times during the course.

Rotating Assignments

In many cases, the amount of time required to complete a certain phase of the project allows you to rotate student assignments for particular tasks. When roofing a house, for example, allow one group of students to complete the first few courses and then rotate other students into their positions. However, rotate only one or two students at a time. This allows the "experienced" roofers to become the teachers.

Student Outcomes

Knowledge is the most important tool you can provide to your students. You must form a solid base in the fundamentals in order to build your students' carpentry skills. Emphasize the importance of developing reading, writing, mathematics, and communication skills. Stress that in addition to carpentry skills, employers often list the abilities to follow proper procedures, work with others, and communicate clearly as the deciding factors as to which job applicants will be hired.

Varying Student Abilities

Students entering your classroom will undoubtedly possess a variety of skills. Some students may have extensive exposure to the carpentry trade. Some may possess basic woodworking skills, while others will not. Students will also have a wide variety of career goals. Some students take a carpentry course for exploratory purposes, while others intend to use the skills throughout their careers.

Students entering your classroom also possess a wide range of potential abilities. In many high school programs, special-needs students are regularly mainstreamed into vocational-technical programs. Special-needs students generally include mentally or physically impaired students. Gifted students may also enroll in technical courses.

Identifying Special-Needs Students

Ideally, special-needs students will be identified by the school psychologist. The instructor is then informed of the situation. If the special-needs students have not been identified, you must assume the responsibility of doing so. Once the students are identified, specialized learning programs and teaching methods may be implemented.

Characteristics of special-needs students are included in the following list. An infrequent occurrence of one or more of these characteristics does not necessarily denote a special-needs student.
- Inability to communicate effectively (reading, writing, oral expression, and questioning).
- Short attention span or lack of interest.
- Frequent disruptive behavior.
- Lack of motivation.
- Poor computational skills.
- High rate of absenteeism.
- Impaired speech, hearing, or sight.
- Lack of self-confidence.

A variety of special-needs students are commonly found in any classroom. Some may have limited mobility; others may have vision or hearing problems. Always remember that a special-needs student must be challenged just like any other student. The type of challenge should be based on each student's potential. You may need to modify your teaching methods, allowing the special-needs students to reach their goals.

Identifying the Gifted Student

The gifted student may be more difficult to identify and just as challenging to instruct as the special-needs student. In some cases, an instructor is informed of a gifted student by a counselor. In many cases, however, gifted students have not been identified. Vocational instructors should be familiar with gifted students' characteristics and modify teaching methods accordingly. Common characteristics of gifted students include:
- When properly motivated, displays more interest and a longer attention span.
- May be more inclined to question or comment on the subject.
- May seem restless, bored, or disinterested.
- Consistently completing work ahead of others.
- Consistently scores high on assessments.
- Pays close attention to detail on a procedure or technique that is generally taken for granted.

A gifted student should be constantly challenged to maintain interest in the subject matter. Assign tasks with greater complexity, such as calculating rafter angles. A gifted student might also be used as a classroom assistant. He or she might be able to estimate materials that are needed for upcoming projects or other similar activities.

Additional Student Experiences and Resources

A variety of supplemental materials may be used to help students further develop their interest in carpentry. Not all learning occurs in the classroom. Students should be encouraged to read supplemental material and participate in field trips. In either case, the activity should be followed up by some means of discussion and evaluation.

Curricular Connections and Outside Assignments

Students should thoroughly study assigned textbook chapters. Time may be given in class for review or questions, but the reading and *Test Your Knowledge* questions should be completed on the students' own time. Stress to them that the technical and instructional information must be thoroughly studied for complete comprehension.

Extensive programs of research and development in all areas of building construction have resulted in an "explosion" of knowledge, which makes it impractical to adequately cover the field of carpentry in a single textbook. Thus, it is essential that students spend some of their out-of-class time in the study of reference books, trade magazines, and manufacturer literature. A number of suggested activities that may provide topics and ideas for outside assignments of this nature are included at the end of each unit.

Field Trips

Teachers of building construction classes have found field trips to be highly effective. Every community, large or small, offers opportunities in this area. Field trips should be carefully planned and arrangements made ahead of the actual visit. More than one trip can be made to a particular project. Several trips in close sequence during the rough framing phase may be followed by additional visits spaced further apart during finishing stages. The greatest instructional gains can be made when the work in progress at the construction site is in phase with the content being covered in regular class sessions.

Students should be briefed prior to the trip. They will then know what to look for and can better understand what they observe. If possible, have a representative from the project give a presentation to your class. A follow-up evaluation and discussion session is extremely valuable, especially when it can be held shortly after returning. You might choose to have students write a brief report on the field trip.

Cooperative Training

A cooperative training program, or internship, is an agreement between a school and a local contractor. This agreement allows a student to work part-time for the contractor. The program is designed to help mature, advanced students pursue career goals. The student earns money while gaining valuable experience. The employer gains a worker at minimum cost. In addition, that student may move into the company once his or her studies are finished. Assist students in determining their goals and objectives so they can look for a job that holds the same focus.

Organizations

Encourage students to get involved in recognized organizations such as SkillsUSA. These organizations promote vocational-technical education and provide worthwhile experiences for the students. Organizations also help to develop interpersonal communication skills. A person, regardless of his or her career, must be able to communicate effectively with coworkers.

Evaluation

Students learn in a variety of ways. Many are very visual; others learn better from lectures and demonstrations. In a similar manner, a variety of techniques must be used to fairly evaluate student progress. The instructor's resource for **Modern Carpentry** provides several means of evaluating students in a carpentry course. Chapter quizzes, section exams, and procedure checklists are included in the form of reproducible masters.

In a broad view of evaluation, give students credit for work well done. Provide frequent reports showing each student's accomplishments. Hold the students responsible for their progress and offer motivation to reach their goals. Adjust your teaching methods and emphasis as needed.

Chapter Quizzes

The chapter resources include a short quiz for each chapter. The quiz should be used to verify the student's comprehension of the information presented in the unit. You may also use the quizzes to identify any shortcomings of the instruction. You can record the class results of each question. Questions that are often incorrectly answered may denote shortcomings of the instruction on a particular subject. You may use the results to modify the instruction when the chapter is presented again.

Section Exams

The instructor's resource includes exams for each of the seven sections of the text. Each exam provides an overall evaluation of the material contained in the chapters of that section. A variety of question types are used, including true-false, multiple choice, identification, matching, completion, and short answer.

Procedure Checklists

Procedure checklists are used to evaluate common procedures or techniques. Productivity plays a major role on the job and should be evaluated in the classroom as well. Procedure checklists are included in many of the chapter resources.

Employability Skills

Employability skills are a vital part of career and technical education programs. They should be included in any occupation-focused course. Incorporate some of the following learning outcomes into your program:

Identifying Employment Opportunities
- Identify requirements for a job.
- Investigate educational opportunities.
- Investigate occupational opportunities.
- Locate resources for finding employment.
- Confer with prospective employers.
- Identify job trends.

Applying Employment Seeking Skills
- Locate job openings.
- Document skills and abilities.
- Prepare for interview.
- Participate in interview.
- Complete required forms.
- Write application letter.
- Write follow-up letter.
- Evaluate job offer.
- Evaluate job rejection.

Interpreting Employment Capabilities
- Match interest to job area.
- Match aptitudes to job area.
- Verify abilities.
- Identify immediate work goal.
- Develop career plan.

Demonstrating Appropriate Work Behavior
- Exhibit dependability.
- Demonstrate punctuality.
- Follow rules and regulations.
- Recognize the consequences of dishonesty.
- Control emotions.
- Assume responsibility for decisions and actions.
- Exhibit pride and loyalty.
- Exhibit ability to handle pressure and stress.
- Demonstrate ability to set priorities.
- Demonstrate problem-solving skills.

Maintaining Safe and Healthy Environment
- Comply with safety and health rules.
- Select correct tools and equipment.
- Use equipment correctly.
- Use personal protective equipment properly.
- Use appropriate action during emergencies.
- Maintain clean and orderly work area.
- Demonstrate personal hygiene and cleanliness.

Maintaining Businesslike Image
- Participate in company or agency orientation.
- Demonstrate knowledge of company or agency products and services.
- Exhibit positive behavior.
- Read current job-related publications.
- Support and promote employer's company image and purpose.
- Maintain appearance to comply with company standards.

Maintaining Working Relationships with Others
- Work productively with others.
- Show empathy, respect, and support for others.
- Demonstrate procedures and assist others when necessary.
- Recognize, analyze, and solve problems.
- Minimize occurrence of problems.
- Channel emotional reactions constructively.

Communicating on the Job
- Read and comprehend written communications and information.
- Speak effectively with others.
- Use job-related terminology.
- Listen attentively.
- Write legibly.
- Follow written and oral directions.
- Ask questions.
- Locate information in order to accomplish tasks.

Adapting to Change
- Recognize need to change.
- Demonstrate willingness to learn.
- Demonstrate flexibility.
- Participate in continuing education.
- Adjust career goals as needed.

Understanding How a Business Works
- Recognize the role of business in the American enterprise system.
- Identify general responsibilities of employees.

- Investigate opportunities and options for business ownership.
- Identify the planning processes needed to open a business.
- Participate in meetings.

Supplemental Reading and Professional Resources

An in-house library of current magazines, catalogs, journals, brochures, user's manuals, advertisements, and other informative publications is an excellent investment. Many publications are free for the asking. The task of acquiring literature can be given as student projects.

In addition to current periodicals, have other trade references pertaining to the carpentry field on hand. This might include OSHA manuals, *Architectural Graphics Standards, Machinery's Handbook,* and texts on carpentry, construction, manufacturing, materials and processes, welding, electronics, etc.

Resources for Carpentry Education

Various resources are available for additional carpentry information. The following is a list of periodicals that provide information pertaining to the carpentry trade and woodworking in general.

Web Sites for Periodicals	
Periodical	Web Site
Builder	www.builderonline.com
Builder & Contractor	www.abc.org
Building Design and Construction	www.bdcnetwork.com
Construction Digest	www.acppubs.com/community/837.html
Construction Equipment	www.constructionequipment.com
Constructor	www.constructoragc.construction.com
Fine Homebuilding	www.taunton.com/finehomebuilding
Fine Woodworking	www.taunton.com/finewoodworking
Historic Preservation	www.nationaltrust.org/magazine
Interior Construction	www.cisca.org/publications
Interior Design	www.interiordesign.net
The Journal of Light Construction	www.jlconline.com
Residential Construction Guidelines	www.steel.org
Journal of Research of the National Bureau of Standards	www.nist.gov
Multi-Housing News	www.multi-housingnews.com
Nation's Building News	www.nbnnews.com
Professional Builder	www.housingzone.com/probuilder
Qualified Remodeler	www.qualifiedremodeler.com/
Wood and Wood Products	www.iswonline.com
Woodshop News	www.woodshopnews.com
Woodsmith	www.woodsmith.com

Manufacturer and supplier catalogs and the various forms of descriptive literature these companies distribute are a valuable resource for building construction courses. Some of this material is available from local building supply dealers, while other items may be secured by writing directly to the company. Single copies are usually available free of charge when the letter of request is written on official school stationery.

A word of caution: do not secure these materials unless you plan to make good use of them. Some companies have stopped making their literature available because it is often wasted. In your letter, assure the organization that the materials they send will be effectively used.

Trade associations are formed when a number of manufacturers in a related field join together and pool their efforts in such areas as research and development, product standards and inspection, public information, and sales promotion. These associations usually have a wide range of literature. In an initial letter, you should simply request a listing of the items they have available and would be willing to furnish. When this list is received, requests for specific items can be made.

Several companies and trade associations make a selection of DVDs available for school use. They show the fabrication of various building materials and products.

The following table lists building material manufacturer associations and related groups, along with their Web sites.

Web Sites for Construction Associations	
Manufacturers' Associations and Related Groups	**Web Site**
Acoustical Society of America (ASA)	http://asa.aip.org
Adhesive and Sealant Council, Inc. (ASC)	www.ascouncil.org
Allied Construction Employers Association (ACEA)	www.buildacea.org
Aluminum Association (AA)	www.aluminum.org
American Arbitration Association (AAA)	www.adr.org
American Association of State Highway and Transportation Officials (AASHTO)	www.transportation.org
American Concrete Institute (ACI)	www.concrete.org
American Hardware (AHMU)	www.ahma.org
American Institute of Architects (AIA)	www.aia.org
American Institute of Constructors (AIC)	www.aicnet.org
American Institute of Timber Construction	www.aitc-glulam.org
American Lumber Standards Committee (ALSC)	www.alsc.org
American National Standards Institute (ANSI)	www.ansi.org
American Plywood Association (APA)	www.apawood.org
American Society for Testing and Materials (ASTM)	www.astm.org
American Society for Interior Designers (ASID)	www.asid.org

(continued)

Web Sites for Construction Associations *(continued)*	
Manufacturers' Associations and Related Groups	**Web Site**
American Society of Professional Estimators (ASPE)	www.aspenational.com
American Subcontractors Association (ASA)	www.asaonline.com
Architectural Aluminum (AAMA)	www.aamanet.org
Architectural Woodwork Institute (AWI)	www.awinet.org
Asphalt Roofing Manufacturers Association (ARMA)	www.asphaltroofing.org
Associated Builders and Contractors, Inc. (ABC)	www.abc.org
Associated General Contractors of America (AGC)	www.agc.org
Associated Specialty Contractors (ASC)	www.assoc-spec-con.org
Association of the Wall and Ceiling (AWCI)	www.awci.org
Builder's Hardware (BHMA)	www.buildershardware.com
Building Officials and Code Administrators International (BOCA)	www.iccsafe.org
Building Systems Council (BSC)	www.nahb.org/councils
California Redwood Association (CRA)	www.calredwood.org
Canadian Forest Products Ltd.	www.canfor.com
Canadian Wood Council	www.cwc.ca
Carpet and Rug Institute (CRI)	www.carpet-rug.com
Ceilings and Interior Systems Construction Association (CISCA)	www.cisca.org
Ceramic Tile Institute of America (CTIOA)	www.ctioa.org
Concrete Reinforcing Steel Institute (CRSI)	www.crsi.org
Construction Employers Association (CEA)	www.cea-ca.org
Construction Specifications Institute (CSI)	www.csinet.org
Council of American Building Officials (CABO)	www.iccsafe.org
Door and Hardware Institute (DHI)	www.dhi.org
Environmental Protection Agency (EPA)	www.epa.gov
Federal Housing Administration (FHA)	www.fha.gov
Forest Products Research Society (FPRS)	www.forestprod.org

(continued)

Web Sites for Construction Associations *(continued)*	
Manufacturers' Associations and Related Groups	**Web Site**
General Building Contractors Association (GBCA)	www.gbca.net
Gypsum Association (GA)	www.gypsum.org
Industrial Fasteners Institute (IFI)	www.industrial-fasteners.org
Insulation Contractors Association of America (ICAA)	www.insulate.org
International Council of Building Officials (ICBO)	www.icbolabc.org
International Institute for Lath and Plaster (IILP)	www.iilp.org
Laborers' International Union of North America (LIUNA)	www.liuna.org
Manufactured Housing Institute	www.manufacturedhousing.org
Maple Flooring Manufacturers Association (MFMA)	www.maplefloor.org
North American Association of Floor Covering Distributors (NAFCD)	www.nafcd.org
National Association of Home Builders (NAHB)	www.nahb.org
National Association of Housing Redevelopment Officials (NAHRO)	www.nahro.org
National Association of Reinforcing Steel Contractors (NARSC)	www.narsc.com
National Association of Women in Construction (NAWIC)	www.nawic.org
National Building Code American Insurance Association	www.aiadc.org
North American Building Material Distributors Association	www.nbmda.org
National Conference of States on Building Codes and Standards (NCSBCS)	www.ncsbcs.org
National Council of Radiation Protection and Measurement (NCRPM)	www.ncrponline.org
National Fire Protection Association (NFPA)	www.nfpa.org
National Forest Products Association, renamed American Forest and Paper Association	www.afandpa.org
National Kitchen Cabinet Association (NKCA) renamed Kitchen Cabinet Manufacturers Association	www.kcma.org

(continued)

Web Sites for Construction Associations *(continued)*	
Manufacturers' Associations and Related Groups	**Web Site**
National Lumber and Building Material Dealers Association (NLBMDA)	www.dealer.org
National Oak Flooring Manufacturers Association (NOFMA)	www.nofma.org
National Paint and Coatings Association (NPCA)	www.paint.org
National Roofing Contractors Association (NRCA)	www.nrca.net
Window and Door Manufacturers Association	www.wdma.com
Operative Plasterers' and Cement Masons' International Association of the United States and Canada	www.opcmia.org
Sustainable Buildings Industry Council (SBIC)	www.sbicouncil.org
Red Cedar Shingle and Handsplit Shake Bureau (RCSHSB)	www.cedarbureau.org
Scaffolding, Shoring, and Forming Institute, Inc.	www.ssfi.org
Screen Manufacturers Association (SMA)	www.smacentral.org
Sealant and Waterproofers Institute (SWI)	www.swrionline.org
Southern Building Code Congress International, Inc. (SBCCI)	www.iccsafe.org
Southern Forest Products Association (SFPA)	www.sfpa.org
Steel Door Institute (SDI)	www.steeldoor.org
Steel Joist Institute (SJI)	www.steeljoist.org
Steel Window Institute (SWI)	www.steelwindows.com
Stucco Manufacturers Association (SMA)	www.stuccomfgassoc.com
Systems Builders Association (SBA)	www.systemsbuilders.org
Tile Contractors Association of America, Inc. (TCAA)	www.tcaainc.org
Tile Council of North America	www.tileusa.com
Truss Plate Institute	www.tpinst.org
United Brotherhood of Carpenters and Joiners of America (UBC)	www.carpenters.org
U.S. Department of Labor/Occupational Safety and Health Administration	www.osha.gov

(continued)

Copyright by Goodheart-Willcox Co., Inc.

Web Sites for Construction Associations *(continued)*	
Manufacturers' Associations and Related Groups	**Web Site**
U.S. Forest Products Laboratory	www.fpl.fs.fed.us
United Union of Roofers, Waterproofers and Allied Workers (UURWAW)	www.roofersunion.org
Vinyl Siding Institute	www.vinylsiding.org
Western Wood Products Association (WWPA)	www2.wwpa.org
Wood Truss Council of America	www.sbcindustry.com

Feedback

Goodheart-Willcox welcomes your input. If you have comments, corrections, or suggestions regarding the textbook or its supplements, please send them to:

Managing Editor–Technical
Goodheart-Willcox Publisher
18604 West Creek Drive
Tinley Park, IL 60477

Basic Skills Chart

The *Basic Skills Chart* has been designed to identify those activities in the **Modern Carpentry** textbook and instructor's resource that specifically encourage the development of basic academic skills. The academic areas addressed in the chart include reading, writing, verbal (other than reading and writing), math, science, and analytical.

- *Reading* activities include assignments designed to improve comprehension of information presented in the chapter. Some are designed to improve understanding of vocabulary terms.
- *Writing* activities allow students to practice composition skills, such as letter writing and informative writing.
- *Verbal* activities encourage students to organize ideas, develop interpersonal and group speaking skills, and respond appropriately to verbal messages. Activities include oral reports and interviews.
- *Math* activities require students to use basic principles of math, as well as computation skills, to solve typical problems.
- *Science* activities call for students to use fundamental principles of science to solve typical problems.
- *Analytical* activities involve the higher-order skills needed for thinking creatively, making decisions, solving problems, visualizing information, reasoning, and knowing how to learn.

Activities are broken down by chapter, and a page number is given to locate the activity.

	Chapter 1	Chapter 2
Reading	**Text:** Lumber (18); wood structure and growth (18); kinds of wood (19); cutting methods (20); moisture content and shrinkage (21); lumber defects (23); softwood grades (25); hardwood grades (27); lumber stress values (27); lumber sizes (27); panel materials (29); wood treatments (37); handling and storing lumber (39); engineered lumber (40); nonwood materials; metal structural materials (44); concrete (51); adhesive bonding agents (51). **IR:** Reproducible Master 1-1, *Basic House Parts* (93); Reproducible Master 1-2, *Typical Grade Stamps* (94); Reproducible Master 1-3A, *Nail Types* (95); Reproducible Master 1-3B, *Nail Types* (96); Reproducible Master 1-4, *Nail Sizes* (97); Reproducible Master 1-5A, *Framing Connectors and Ties* (98); Reproducible Master 1-5B, *Framing Connectors and Ties* (99).	**Text:** Skill development and job competency (59); conduct on the job (60); general safety rules (62); decks and floors (66); excavations (66); scaffolds and ladders (66); fall protection (66); falling objects (68); handling hazardous materials (68); lifting and carrying (69); fire protection (69); first aid (69); Activity 2 (72). **IR:** Reproducible Master 2-1, *Safety: Fall Protection* (107); Reproducible Master 2-2, *Skills/Behaviors Contractors Value Most in Beginning Carpenters* (108).
Writing	**Text:** 🖉Activity 1 (56); 🖉Activity 3 (56).	**Text:** 🖉Curricular Connections (72).
Verbal	**Text:** 🖉Activity 2 (56).	**Text:** 🖉Activity 3 (72).
Math	**Text:** Calculating board footage (27); metric lumber measure (29); 🖉Curricular Connections (55).	
Science		**Text:** 🖉Curricular Connections (72).
Analytical		**Text:** 🖉Activity 1 (72).

	Chapter 3	Chapter 4
Reading	**Text:** Set of plans (74); changing plans (92); specifications (92); modular construction (92); building codes (95); Activity 1 (100). **IR:** Reproducible Master 3-1, *Architectural Symbols, Parts A and B* (115, 116); Reproducible Master 3-2, *Symbols for Openings* (117); Reproducible Master 3-3, *Appliance/Fixture Symbols* (118).	**Text:** Measuring and layout tools (104); saws (109); planing, smoothing, and shaping tools (111); fastening tools (113); prying tools (115); gripping and clamping tools (116); tool belts and storage (118); care and maintenance of tools (118). **IR:** Reproducible Master 4-2, *Parts of a Plane* (128); Reproducible Master 4-3, *Parts of a Claw Hammer* (129).
Writing	**Text:** ✏Activity 2 (100).	**Text:** Activity 2 (120).
Verbal	**Text:** ✏Curricular Connections (100); ✏Activity 3 (100).	**Text:** ✏Curricular Connections (120).
Math	**Text:** How to scale a drawing (90); metric measurement (95); ✏Curricular Connections (100).	**Text:** ✏Curricular Connections (120). **IR:** Reproducible Master 4-1, *Saw Tooth Shapes* (127).
Science		**Text:** ✏Activity 1 (120).
Analytical		

	Chapter 5	Chapter 6
Reading	**Text:** Power tool safety (122); portable circular saws (124); saber saws (127); chain saws (129); portable electric drills (130); rotary hammer drills (131); power planes (132); portable routers (133); portable sanders (135); staplers and nailers (136); radial armsaws (138); table saws (140); special saws (142); jointers (143); specialty tools (144); power tool care and maintenance (146); ✏Activity 3 (147). **IR:** Reproducible Master 5-1, *Portable Power Circular Saw* (139); Reproducible Master 5-2, *Parts of an Electric Drill* (140).	**Text:** Plot plan (149); measuring tapes (151); laying out with leveling instruments (152); laser systems (164).
Writing		**Text:** ✏Activity 2 (167).
Verbal	**Text:** ✏Curricular Connections (147); ✏Activity 2 (147).	
Math		**Text:** Establishing building lines (151); using the instruments (157); ✏Curricular Connections (167). **IR:** Reproducible Master 6-1, *Laying Out Building Lines* (147); Reproducible Master 6-2, *Transit Graduated Circle* (148).
Science	**Text:** ✏Curricular Connections (147).	
Analytical	**Text:** ✏Activity 1 (147).	**Text:** ✏Activity 1 (167).

	Chapter 7	Chapter 8
Reading	**Text:** Clearing the site (170); excavation (172); foundation systems (173); erecting wall forms (181); concrete (188); ordering concrete (192); placing concrete (193); concrete block foundations (194); insulating block walls (200); backfilling (202); ICF foundation and wall systems (203); slab-on-grade construction (205); basement floors (209); entrance platforms and stairs (211); sidewalks, steps, and drives (212); wood foundations (213); cold weather construction (215); insect protection (216); Activity 3 (221). **IR:** Reproducible Master 7-2, *Foundation Elements* (164); Reproducible Master 7-3, *Foundation Types* (165); Reproducible Master 7-7, *Four Types of Insulated Concrete Forms (ICFs)* (169); Reproducible Master 7-8, *Wood Foundation Design* (170).	**Text:** Types of framing (224); girders and beams (227); sill construction (232); joists (235); special framing problems (243); open-web floor trusses (244); solid-web trusses (245); subfloors (247). **IR:** Reproducible Master 8-1, *Platform Framing Details* (181); Reproducible Master 8-3, *Using Joist Hangers* (183).
Writing	**Text:** Curricular Connections (221); ✏Activity 1 (221).	**Text:** Curricular Connections (251); ✏Activity 1 (251).
Verbal	**Text:** ✏Activity 3 (221).	**Text:** ✏Curricular Connections (251).
Math	**Text:** Laying out building lines (170); estimating materials (218); ✏Activity 2 (221). **IR:** Reproducible Master 7-1, *Using Batter Boards* (163); Reproducible Master 7-4, *Laying Out Footing Forms* (166); Reproducible Master 7-5, *Locating Footing Forms* (167); Reproducible Master 7-6, *Concrete Blocks* (168).	**Text:** Estimating materials (250); ✏Curricular Connections (251).
Science	**Text:** ✏Curricular Connections (221).	
Analytical		**Text:** ✏Activity 2 (251). **IR:** Reproducible Master 8-2, *Framing Methods at Sill* (182); Reproducible Master 8-4, *Framing over Girders/Beams, Parts A, B,* and *C* (184, 185, 186); Reproducible Master 8-5, *Laying Out Joists Parts A and B* (187, 188); Reproducible Master 8-6, *Floor Frame* (189); Reproducible Master 8-7, *Assembling Floor Frame, Parts A and B* (190, 191); Reproducible Master 8-8, *Truss Construction* (192); Reproducible Master 8-9, *Placing Subflooring* (193).

Copyright by Goodheart-Willcox Co., Inc.

	Chapter 9	**Chapter 10**
Reading	**Text:** Parts of the wall frame (254); plate layout (258); wall sections (261); erecting wall sections (263); partitions (265); tri-level and split-level framing (271); special framing (271); wall sheathing (273); multistory floor framing (273);strongbacks (277); housewrap and building paper (277); 🔨Curricular Connections (281); 🔨Activity 3 (282).	**Text:** Roof types (284); roof supports (284); parts of a roof frame (286); layout terms and principles (287); erecting jack rafters (306); special problems (307); roof openings (308); roof anchorage (308); collar ties (308); dormers (310); framing flat roofs (311); gambrel roof (312); mansard roof (312); special framing (313); roof truss construction (314); bracing of truss rafters (317); roof sheathing (318). **IR:** Reproducible Master 10-1, *Roof Types* (221); Reproducible Master 10-3, *Rafter Layout Parts and Terms, Parts A and B* (223, 224); Reproducible Master 10-5, *Truss Rafter Construction, Parts A and B* (227, 228).
Writing		**Text:** 🔨Activity 1 (327).
Verbal	**Text:** 🔨Curricular Connections (271); 🔨Activity 3 (282).	
Math	**Text:** Estimating materials (279); 🔨Activity 1 (281); 🔨Activity 2 (282).	**Text:** Unit measurements (289); framing plans (289); rafter sizes (290); laying out common rafters (290); erecting a gable roof (294); gable end frame (296); hip and valley rafters (298); estimating materials (324); model and small-scale construction (325); 🔨Curricular Connections (326); 🔨Activity 2 (327). Reproducible Master 10-4, *Rafter Layout, Parts A and B* (225, 226).
Science		**Text:** 🔨Curricular Connections (327).
Analytical	Reproducible Master 9-1, *Framing Corners* (205); Reproducible Master 9-2, *Framing Wall Intersections* (206); Reproducible Master 9-3, *Framing Wall Openings* (207); Reproducible Master 9-4, *Framing with Patterns, Parts A, B, and C* (208, 209, 210).	Reproducible Master 10-2, *Plan View of Rafters* (222); Reproducible Master 10-5, *Truss Rafter Construction, Parts A and B* (227, 228).

Basic Skills Chart **29**

	Chapter 11	**Chapter 12**
Reading	**Text:** Steel framing (329); framing floors (333); framing walls and ceilings (336); framing roofs (339).	**Text:** Types of materials (344); roofing terminology (345); preparing the roof deck (346); asphalt roofing products (346); flashing (350); strip shingles (356); hips and ridges (361); wind protection (361); individual asphalt shingles (362); low-slope roofs (362); roll roofing (362); reroofing (365); built-up roofing (366); ridge vents for asphalt roofing (368); wood shingles (369); wood shakes (375); tile roofing (378); metal roofing (383); gutters (387); Curricular Connections (394). **IR:** Reproducible Master 12-2, *Vent Stack Flashing* (258); Reproducible Master 12-5, *Metal Gutter System* (261).
Writing		**Text:** ⫸Activity 1 (394); ⫸Activity 2 (394).
Verbal	**Text:** Curricular Connections (341); Activity 1 (341); Activity 2 (341).	
Math		**Text:** Estimating material (388); ⫸Curricular Connections (394).
Science	**Text:** ⫸Curricular Connections (341).	
Analytical	**Text:** ⫸Activity 1 (341). **IR:** Reproducible Master 11-1, *Fastening Steel Sills to a Foundation* (237); Reproducible Master 11-2, *Fasteners Used on Metal Beams* (238); Reproducible Master 11-3, *Installing X Bridging on Steel Joists* (239); Reproducible Master 11-4, *Attaching Steel Ceiling Joist to Wall Plate* (240).	**Text:** Reroofing (365); ⫸Curricular Connections (394). **IR:** Reproducible Master 12-1, *Shingling Valleys, Parts A, B, and C* (255, 256, 257); Reproducible Master 12-3, *Six-Inch Shingling Method* (259); Reproducible Master 12-4, *Four-Inch Shingling Method* (260).

Copyright by Goodheart-Willcox Co., Inc.

	Chapter 13	**Chapter 14**
Reading	**Text:** Manufacture (396); parts of windows (397); types of windows (398); window glass (401); energy-efficient windows (403); screens (404); windows in plan and elevation drawings (404); detail drawings (406); jamb extensions (410); installing windows (410); installing fixed units (412); glass blocks (413); replacing windows (416); skylights (417); installing bow and box bay windows (418); exterior doors and frames (420); sliding glass doors (426); garage doors (429); ⚒Activity 1 (434).	**Text:** Cornice designs and terms (436); prefabricated cornice materials (440); wall finish (442); wall sheathing and flashing (442); horizontal wood siding (444); vertical siding (451); wood shingles (453); plywood siding (458); hardboard siding (460); fiber-cement siding (463); aluminum and vinyl siding (463); stucco (470); exterior insulation and finish systems (471); brick or stone veneer (476); shutters (480). **IR:** Reproducible Master 14-1, *Typical Cornice Details, Parts A and B* (287, 288); Reproducible Master 14-3, *Typical Exterior Insulation and Finish System* (291); Reproducible Master 14-4, *Brick Veneer Construction* (292).
Writing	**Text:** ⚒Curricular Connections (434); ⚒Activity 2 (434).	**Text:** ⚒Activity 2 (482).
Verbal	**Text:** ⚒Activity 2 (434).	**Text:** ⚒Activity 2 (482).
Math	**Text:** Window heights (401); window sizes (404); jamb extensions (410); aligning tops of windows (410).	**Text:** Aluminum and vinyl siding (463); ⚒Curricular Connections (482).
Science	**Text:** ⚒Curricular Connections (434).	**Text:** ⚒Curricular Connections (482).
Analytical	**Text:** ⚒Activity 2 (434). **IR:** Reproducible Master 13-1, *Window Framing Detail* (275).	**Text:** ⚒Activity 1 (482). **IR:** Reproducible Master 14-2, *Siding Application, Parts A and B* (289, 290).

	Chapter 15	**Chapter 16**
Reading	**Text:** Building sequence (486); thermal insulation (488); terminology (488); how much insulation? (492); types of insulation (492); where to insulate (498); condensation (502); vapor barriers (502); ventilation (503); safety with insulation (507); installing batts and blankets (507); installing loose and foamed insulation (511); installing rigid installation (513); insulating basement walls (514); insulating existing structures (514); stopping air infiltration (515); acoustics and sound control (517); noise reduction within a space (524); ⌁Curricular Connections (528); ⌁Activity 2 (529).	**Text:** Drywall construction (533); single-layer construction (535); double-layer construction (542); special backing (543); moisture-resistant (MR) wallboard (545); veneer plaster (545); predecorated wallboard (546); wallboard on masonry walls (547); installing plywood paneling (547); hardboard (551); plastic laminates (551); solid lumber paneling (551); plaster (555); plastering materials and methods (560); ceiling tile (561); suspended ceilings (564); Curricular Connections (570); ⌁Activity 3 (570). **IR:** Reproducible Master 16-1A, *Drywall Application* (321); Reproducible Master 16-1B, *Drywall Application—Fasteners* (322); Reproducible Master 16-1C, *Double-Layer Drywall Application* (323); Reproducible Master 16-2, *Suspended Ceiling System* (324).
Writing	**Text:** ⌁Curricular Connections (528); ⌁Activity 2 (529); ⌁Activity 3 (529).	**Text:** ⌁Curricular Connections (570); ⌁Activity 3 (570); ⌁Activity 4 (570).
Verbal		**Text:** ⌁Curricular Connections (570); ⌁Activity 1 (570).
Math	**Text:** Estimating thermal insulation materials (515). **IR:** Reproducible Master 15-1, *Typical Insulating Values* (307).	**Text:** Estimating materials (566); ⌁Curricular Connections (570); ⌁Activity 2 (570).
Science	**Text:** How heat is transmitted (487); how acoustical materials work (524); ⌁Curricular Connections (529); ⌁Activity 1 (529).	
Analytical	**IR:** Reproducible Master 15-2, *Insulating Band Joists at Sills* (308); Reproducible Master 15-3, *Insulating Band Joists at Ceiling* (309); Reproducible Master 15-4, *Insulating to Prevent Ice Dams* (310).	

Copyright by Goodheart-Willcox Co., Inc.

	Chapter 17	**Chapter 18**
Reading	**Text:** Wood flooring (572); installing wood strip flooring (573); wood block (parquet) flooring (580); prefinished wood flooring (581); laminated wood strip flooring (582); underlayment for nonwood floors (584); resilient floor tile (586); self-adhering tiles (588); sheet vinyl flooring (589); ceramic floor tile (590). **IR:** Reproducible Master 17-1A, *Installing Strip Flooring* (333); Reproducible Master 17-2, *Strip Flooring Sequence* (336).	**Text:** Types of stairs (598); stair parts (600); stairwell framing (600); types of stringers (608); winder stairs (609); open stairs (611); using stock stair parts (611); spiral stairways (614); disappearing stair units (615). **IR:** Reproducible Master 18-1A, *Stair Terminology* (347); Reproducible Master 18-1B, *Stair Designs* (348); Reproducible Master 18-3, *Stringer Types* (350).
Writing	**Text:** ✐Activity 1 (596).	
Verbal	**Text:** ✐Activity 2 (596).	
Math	**Text:** Estimating wood strip flooring (580); estimating tile flooring and adhesive (589). **IR:** Reproducible Master 17-3, *Laying Out Parquet Flooring* (337)	**Text:** Stair design (602); stair calculations (604); stairwell length (605); stringer layout (606); treads and risers (607); ✐Activity 1 (616); ✐Activity 2 (616). **IR:** Reproducible Master 18-2, *Calculating Sizes of Stair Treads and Risers and Layout Out Stringers* (349).
Science	**Text:** ✐Curricular Connections (596).	
Analytical	**IR:** Reproducible Master 17-1B, *Nailing Strip Flooring* (334); Reproducible Master 17-1C, *Laying Strip Flooring around Barriers* (335).	**Text:** ✐Curricular Connections (616).

	Chapter 19	**Chapter 20**
Reading	**Text:** Mouldings (619); interior door frames (621); panel doors (625); flush doors (627); sizes and grades (628); door installation (629); door locks (632); thresholds and door sweeps (633); sliding pocket doors (635); sliding bypass doors (637); bifold doors (638); multifold doors (639); window trim (639); baseboard and base shoe (642); installing baseboard and base shoe (642). **IR:** Reproducible Master 19-1, *Typical Mouldings, Parts A and B* (357, 358); Reproducible Master 19-2, *Casing Interior Doors* (359); Reproducible Master 19-3, *Installing Baseboard and Base Shoe, Parts A and B* (360, 361).	**Text:** Drawings for cabinetwork (648); standard sizes (650); types of construction (651); factory-built cabinets (652); cabinet materials (654); cabinet installation (654); cabinets for other rooms (658); building cabinets (659); doors (666); counters and tops (669); cabinet hardware (672); other built-in units (672). **IR:** Reproducible Master 20-2, *Cabinet Styles* (372).
Writing	**Text:** ✏Curricular Connections (645).	
Verbal	**Text:** ✏Curricular Connections (645); ✏Activity 1 (646).	**Text:** ✏Curricular Connections (674).
Math	**Text:** ✏Activity 3 (646).	**Text:** ✏Curricular Connections (675); ✏Activity 1 (675); ✏Activity 2 (675); ✏Activity 3 (675); ✏Activity 4 (675). **IR:** Reproducible Master 20-1, *Standard Cabinet Dimensions* (371).
Science	**Text:** ✏Curricular Connections (646).	
Analytical	**Text:** ✏Activity 2 (646).	**IR:** Reproducible Master 20-3, *Installing Factory-Built Cabinets* (373).

	Chapter 21	Chapter 22
Reading	**Text:** Painting and finishing tools (678); painting, finishing, and decorating materials (683); color selection (685); preparing surfaces for coating (686); choosing paint applicators (687); using proper brushing technique (688); roller and pad application (688); spray painting (689); painting wood exteriors (689); problems with coatings (690); interior painting (691); working with stains and clear finishes (694); wallcoverings (696). **IR:** Reproducible Master 21-1, *Safety Rules for Painting and Finishing* (383); Reproducible Master 21-2, *Parts of a Paintbrush* (384); Reproducible Master 21-3, *Types of Brushes* (385); Reproducible Master 21-4, *Parts of a Spray Gun* (386); Reproducible Master 21-7, *Wallpapering Tools* (389).	**Text:** Masonry chimneys (706); masonry fireplaces (708); prefabricated chimneys (714); prefabricated fireplaces (716); glass enclosures (718); Curricular Connections (720). **IR:** Reproducible Master 22-1, *Masonry Fireplace Components* (403); Reproducible Master 22-2, *Parts of a Prefabricated Chimney* (404).
Writing	**Text:** ✏Curricular Connections (702); ✏Curricular Connections (703); ✏Activity 1 (703).	**Text:** ✏Curricular Connections (720); ✏Activity 1 (720).
Verbal	**Text:** ✏Curricular Connections (702); ✏Curricular Connections (703); ✏Activity 2 (703).	**Text:** ✏Activity 1 (720); ✏Activity 2 (720).
Math	**Text:** Wallcoverings (696); ✏Curricular Connections (703); ✏Activity 3 (703).	
Science	**Text:** ✏Curricular Connections (702).	
Analytical	**Text:** ✏Curricular Connections (703). **IR:** Reproducible Master 21-5, *Identifying Sprayer Heads* (387); Reproducible Master 21-6, *Efficient Method of Painting a Paneled Door* (388).	

	Chapter 23	Chapter 24
Reading	**Text:** Advantages of post-and-beam construction (721); floor beams (725); beam descriptions (726); roof beams (726); fasteners (726); partitions (730); planks (730); stressed-skin panels (731); box beams (732); laminated beams and arches (734); prefabricating pot-and-beam structures, (735); ✏Activity 1 (739). **IR:** Reproducible Master 23-1, *Post-and-Beam Framing Details Parts A and B* (411,412).	**Text:** Factory-built components (742); types of systems-built homes (744); modular homes (745); panelized homes (746); precut homes (747); log homes (748); on-site building erection (748); assembling a panelized home (750); manufactured homes (754); ✏Curricular Connections (756). **IR:** Reproducible Master 24-1, *Panelized Construction* (419); Reproducible Master 24-2, *Typical Closed Panels for Systems-Built Housing* (420).
Writing	**Text:** ✏Activity 1 (739).	**Text:** ✏Curricular Connections (756).
Verbal	**Text:** ✏Curricular Connections (738); ✏Activity 1 (739).	**Text:** ✏Activity 1 (756); ✏Activity 2 (756).
Math		
Science		
Analytical	**IR:** Reproducible Master 23-2, *Plank-and-Beam Roof Construction* (413).	

	Chapter 25	Chapter 26
Reading	**Text:** Types of solar energy systems (759); passive solar construction (761); passive solar advantages (763); passive solar disadvantages (764); solar heat control (764); building passive solar structures (768); passive thermosiphon system (773); insulating passive solar buildings (773).	**Text:** Design of old structures (780); replacing rotted sills (783); hidden structural details (784); removing old walls (785); providing shoring (787); framing openings in a bearing wall (788); small remodeling jobs (792); building additions onto homes (797); solar retrofitting (797); responsible renovation (798). **IR:** Reproducible Master 26-1, *Remodeling Post-and-Beam Construction* (435); Reproducible Master 26-2, *Replacing Rotted Sills* (436).
Writing		**Text:** Curricular Connections (801); 🔨Activity 1 (802); 🔨Activity 2 (802).
Verbal	**Text:** 🔨Activity 1 (776).	
Math	**Text:** Sizing thermal storage systems (769); 🔨Curricular Connections (776).	**Text:** 🔨Curricular Connections (802). **IR:** Reproducible Master 26-3, *Guidelines for Sizing Headers* (437).
Science	**Text:** How radiation and heat act (757); 🔨Curricular Connections (775).	
Analytical	**Text:** Designing an isolated-gain system (771); 🔨Activity 2 (776); 🔨Activity 3 (776). **IR:** Reproducible Master 25-1, *Trombe Wall Section* (427); Reproducible Master 25-2, *Cross Section of a Well-Insulated Dwelling* (428).	**Text:** What comes first? (777).

	Chapter 27	Chapter 28
Reading	**Text:** Structural materials (805); decking materials (806); fasteners and connectors (807); constructing the deck (810); pergolas (816); porches (817). **IR:** Reproducible Master 27-1, *Softwoods Suited for Decks* (445); Reproducible Master 27-2, *Deck Fasteners and Connectors* (446); Reproducible Master 27-3 Cutting Dadoes for Trends (447).	**Text:** Tools and equipment (822); electrical system components (824); installing the service (828); grounding and ground faults (829); reading prints (832); running branch circuits (833); device wiring (835); home security and automation wiring (839). **IR:** Reproducible Master 28-1, *Basic Tool List for Electricians* (459); Reproducible Master 28-2, *Electrical Symbols* (460).
Writing		**Text:** 🔨Activity 3 (842).
Verbal		**Text:** 🔨Activity 3 (842).
Math	**Text:** Deck planning and layout (808); 🔨Curricular Connections (819).	
Science		**Text:** Basic electrical wiring theory (826); 🔨Curricular Connections (842).
Analytical	**Text:** 🔨Activity 1 (819); 🔨Activity 2 (819); 🔨Activity 3 (819).	**Text:** Electrical troubleshooting (838); 🔨Activity 1 (842); 🔨Activity 2 (842); 🔨Curricular Connections (842).

	Chapter 29	**Chapter 30**
Reading	**Text:** Plumbing codes (845); two separate systems (846); tools (848); plumbing supplies (850); fixtures (854); sealing plumbing systems (854); reading prints (855); installing plumbing (855); replacing plumbing parts (862); other drain problems (867); wells and pumps (867). **IR:** Reproducible Master 29-2, *Parts of a Globe Valve* (468); Reproducible Master 29-3, *Components of a Toilet* (469).	**Text:** Heating and cooling principles (871); heating systems (874); air cooling systems (881); ducts (882); controls (882); air exchangers (884); heat pumps (884).
Writing	**Text:** ✓Curricular Connections (870); ✓Activity 1 (870).	
Verbal	**Text:** ✓Curricular Connections (870).	**Text:** ✓Activity 1 (888); ✓Activity 2 (888).
Math		
Science		**Text:** Conservation measures (872); ✓Curricular Connections (888).
Analytical	**Text:** ✓Activity 2 (870). **IR:** Reproducible Master 29-1, *Typical Plumbing System* (467).	**Text:** ✓Activity 3 (888). **IR:** Reproducible Master 30-1, *Fundamentals of a Gas Furnace* (477); Reproducible Master 30-2, *Basic Hydronic Heating System* (478).

	Chapter 31	**Chapter 32**
Reading	**Text:** Types of scaffolding (891); brackets, jacks, and trestles (895); ladders (899). **IR:** Reproducible Master 31-2, *Metal Scaffold Assembly* (489); Reproducible Master 31-3, *Ladder Handling and Care* (490).	**Text:** Economic outlook for construction (904); employment outlook (904); working conditions (906); job opportunities (906); training (907); personal qualifications (909); entrepreneurship (911); teaching as a construction career (912); related occupations (912); organizations promoting construction training (914); Activity 3 (916). **IR:** Reproducible Master 32-1, *Apprenticeship Training and Related Groups* (495)
Writing	**Text:** ✓Activity 1 (901).	**Text:** ✓Activity 3 (916).
Verbal	**Text:** ✓Curricular Connections (901); ✓Activity 2 (901).	**Text:** ✓Activity 1 (916); ✓Activity 2 (916).
Math		**Text:** ✓Curricular Connections (916).
Science		
Analytical	**Text:** ✓Activity 2 (901). **IR:** Reproducible Master 31-1, *Wooden Scaffold Designs, Parts A and B* (487,488).	**Text:** ✓Curricular Connections (916); ✓Activity 1 (916).

Scope and Sequence Chart

The *Scope and Sequence Chart* identifies the major concepts presented in each chapter of the **Modern Carpentry** textbook. The chart is divided into the seven textbook sections.

Section 1 (Chapters 1–6)

Safe and Efficient Work Practices, Construction Techniques, and Methods

- **1:** Cutting methods (20); handling and storing lumber (39).
- **2:** Skill development and job competency (59); conduct on the job (60); general safety rules (62); scaffolds and ladders (66); decks and floors (66); excavations (66); fall protection (67); falling objects (68); handling hazardous materials (68); lifting and carrying (69); fire protection (69); first aid (69).
- **3:** How to scale a drawing (90).
- **4:** Care and maintenance of tools (118).
- **5:** Power tool safety (122).
- **6:** Establishing building lines (151); laying out with leveling instruments (152); using the instruments (157); laser systems (164).

Use and Care of Tools and Equipment

- **2:** General safety rules (62); scaffolds and ladders (66); decks and floors (66); excavations (66); fall protection (67); falling objects (68); fire protection (69).
- **4:** Measuring and layout tools (104); saws (109); planing, smoothing, and shaping tools (111); fastening tools (113); prying tools (115); gripping and clamping tools (116); tool belts and storage (118); care and maintenance of tools (118).
- **5:** Power tool safety (122); portable circular saws (124); saber saws (127); chain saws (129); portable electric drills (130); rotary hammer drills (131); power planes (132); portable routers (133); portable sanders (135); staplers and nailers (136); radial arm saws (138); table saws (140); special saws (142); jointers (143); specialty tools (144); power tool care and maintenance (146).
- **6:** Laying out with leveling instruments (152); using the instruments (157).

Selection and Use of Materials

- **1:** Lumber (18); lumber defects (23); softwood grades (25); hardwood grades (27); lumber stress values (27); lumber sizes (27); panel materials (29); wood treatments (37); engineered lumber (40); nonwood materials (43); metal structural materials (44); concrete (51); adhesive bonding agents (51).

Industry Standards and Practices, Model Codes, and Building Codes

- **1:** Softwood grades (25); hardwood grades (27); lumber stress values (27); lumber sizes (27).
- **3:** Modular construction (92); building codes (95).
- **6:** Plot plan (149).

Copyright by Goodheart-Willcox Co., Inc.

Math and Measurement

1: Moisture content and shrinkage (21); lumber stress values (27); calculating board footage (27); metric lumber measure (29).
3: How to scale a drawing (90); modular construction (92); metric measurement (95).
6: Measuring tapes (151); using the instruments (157).

Estimating

1: Moisture content and shrinkage (21); lumber stress values (27); calculating board footage (27); metric lumber measure (29).

Print Reading and Interpretation

3: Set of plans (74); how to scale a drawing (90); changing plans (92); specifications (92).

Career Information and Employable Skills

1: Calculating board footage (27).
2: Skill development and job competency (59); conduct on the job (60).
3: How to scale a drawing (90); changing plans (92).
6: Laying out with leveling instruments (152); using the instruments (157).

Section 2 (Chapters 7–11)

Safe and Efficient Work Practices, Construction Techniques, and Methods

7: Clearing the site (170); laying out building lines (170); excavation (172); foundation systems (173); erecting wall forms (181); concrete (188); placing concrete (193); concrete block foundations (194); insulating block walls (200); backfilling (202); ICF foundation and wall systems (203); slab-on-grade construction (205); basement floors (209); entrance platforms and stairs (211); sidewalks, steps, and drives (212); wood foundations (213).
8: Types of framing (224); girders and beams (227); sill construction (232); joists (235); special framing problems (242); open-web floor trusses (244); solid-web trusses (245); subfloors (247); estimating materials (250).
9: Parts of the wall frame (254); plate layout (258); wall sections (261); erecting wall sections (263); partitions (265); tri-level and split-level framing (271); special framing (271); wall sheathing (273); multistory floor framing (273); strongbacks (277); estimating materials (279).
10: Laying out common rafters (290); erecting a gable roof (294); gable end frame (296); hip and valley rafters (298); erecting jack rafters (306); special problems (307); roof openings (308); roof anchorage (308); collar ties (308); dormers (310); framing flat roofs (311); gambrel roof (312); mansard roof (312); special framing (313); roof truss construction (314); bracing of truss rafters (317); roof sheathing (318).
11: Steel framing (329); framing floors (333); framing walls and ceilings (336); framing roofs (339).

Use and Care of Tools and Equipment

10: Laying out common rafters (290).
11: Steel framing (329)

Selection and Use of Materials

 7: Concrete (188); ordering concrete (192); placing concrete (193); concrete block foundations (194); wood foundations (213); cold weather construction (215); insect protection (216).
 8: Subfloors (247).
 9: Wall sheathing (273); housewrap and building paper (277).
 10: Roof sheathing (318); model and small-scale construction (325).

Industry Standards and Practices, Model Codes, and Building Codes

 7: ICF foundation and wall systems (203); wood foundations (213).
 10: Roof types (284); roof supports (285); parts of a roof frame (286).

Math and Measurement

 7: Laying out building lines (170); estimating materials (217).
 8: Girders and beams (227); estimating materials (250).
 9: Plate layout (258); estimating materials (279).
 10: Layout terms and principles (287); unit measurements (289); rafter sizes (290); laying out common rafters (290); hip and valley rafters (298) model and small-scale construction (325).

Estimating

 7: Ordering concrete (192); estimating materials (217).
 8: Girders and beams (227); estimating materials (250).
 9: Estimating materials (279).
 10: Estimating materials (324).

Print Reading and Interpretation

 8: Joists (235).
 10: Framing plans (289).

Career Information and Employable Skills

 7: Concrete block foundations (194); estimating materials (217).
 8: Estimating materials (250).
 9: Erecting wall sections (263); estimating materials (279).
 10: Laying out common rafters (290).
 11: Framing floors (333); framing walls and ceilings (336); framing roofs (339).

Section 3 (Chapters 12–14)

Safe and Efficient Work Practices, Construction Techniques, and Methods

 12: Preparing the roof deck (346); flashing (350); strip shingles (356); wind protection (361); individual asphalt shingles (362); low-slope roofs (362); roll roofing (362); reroofing (365); built-up roofing (366); ridge vents for asphalt roofing (368); wood shingles (369); wood shakes (375); tile roofing (378); metal roofing (383); gutters (387).
 13: Jamb extensions (410); aligning tops of windows (410); installing windows (410); installing fixed units (412); replacing windows (416); skylights (417); installing bow and box bay windows (418); exterior doors and frames (420); sliding glass doors (426); garage doors (429).
 14: Wall finish (442); wall sheathing and flashing (442); horizontal wood siding (444); vertical siding (451); wood shingles (453); plywood siding (458); hardboard siding (460); fiber-cement siding (463); aluminum and vinyl siding (463); stucco (470); exterior insulation and finish systems (471).

Use and Care of Tools and Equipment

12: Strip shingles (356); wood shingles (369); wood shakes (375).
14: Fiber-cement siding (463); aluminum and vinyl siding (463); brick or stone veneer (476).

Selection and Use of Materials

12: Types of materials (344); asphalt roofing products (346); hips and ridges (361); wood shingles (369); wood shakes (375); tile roofing (378); metal roofing (383); gutters (387).
13: Manufacture (396); types of windows (398); window glass (401); energy-efficient windows (403); screens (404); glass blocks (413); garage doors (429).
14: Cornice designs and terms (436); prefabricated cornice materials (440); wall sheathing and flashing (442); horizontal wood siding (444); wood shingles (453); plywood siding (458); hardboard siding (460); fiber-cement siding (463); aluminum and vinyl siding (463); stucco (470); exterior insulation and finish systems (471); brick or stone veneer (476); shutters (480).

Industry Standards and Practices, Model Codes, and Building Codes

12: Roofing terminology (345); low-slope roofs (362).
13: Manufacture (396).
14: Cornice designs and terms (436).

Math and Measurement

12: Strip shingles (356).
13: Window heights (401); window sizes (404); aligning tops of windows (410).
14: Horizontal wood siding (444); wood shingles (453); hardboard siding (460).

Estimating

12: Estimating material (388).
14: Horizontal wood siding (444); wood shingles (453); aluminum and vinyl siding (463).

Print Reading and Interpretation

13: Parts of windows (397); windows in plan and elevation drawings (404); window sizes (404); detail drawings (406).

Career Information and Employable Skills

12: Preparing the roof deck (346); estimating material (388).
13: Installing windows (410); installing fixed units (412); replacing windows (416); installing bow and box bay windows (418).
14: Horizontal wood siding (444); wood shingles (453); aluminum and vinyl siding (463).

… Scope and Sequence Chart 41

Section 4 (Chapters 15–21)

● **Safe and Efficient Work Practices, Construction Techniques, and Methods**

15: Building sequence (486); where to insulate (498); ventilation (503); safety with insulation (507); installing batts and blankets (507); installing loose and foamed insulation (511); installing rigid insulation (513); insulating basement walls (514); insulating existing structures (514); stopping air infiltration (515).
16: Single-layer construction (535); double-layer construction (542); wallboard on masonry walls (547); installing plywood paneling (547); solid lumber paneling (551); plaster (555); plastering materials and methods (560); suspended ceilings (564).
17: Installing wood strip flooring (574); wood block (parquet) flooring (580); prefinished wood flooring (581); laminated wood strip flooring (582); underlayment for nonwood floors (584); resilient floor tile (586); sheet vinyl flooring (589).
18: Stairwell framing (600); treads and risers (607); winder stairs (609); open stairs (611); disappearing stair units (615).
19: Door installation (629); door locks (632); window trim (639); installing baseboard and base shoe (642).
20: Cabinet installation (654); building cabinets (659); doors (666); counters and tops (669); cabinet hardware (672).
21: Preparing surfaces for coating (686); using proper brushing technique (688); roller and pad application (688); spray painting (689); painting wood exteriors (689); problems with coatings (690); interior painting (691).

● **Use and Care of Tools and Equipment**

16: Single-layer construction (535).
21: Painting and finishing tools (678); choosing paint applicators (687); interior painting (691); working with stains and clear finishes (694).

Selection and Use of Materials

15: How heat is transmitted (487); thermal insulation (488); types of insulation (492); ventilation (503); noise reduction within a space (524); how acoustical materials work (524).
16: Drywall construction (533); single-layer construction (535); double-layer construction (542); special backing (543); moisture-resistant (MR) wallboard (545); veneer plaster (545); predecorated wallboard (546); hardboard (551); plastic laminates (551); solid lumber paneling (551); plaster (555); plastering materials and methods (560); ceiling tile (561).
17: Wood flooring (572); wood block (parquet) flooring (580); prefinished wood flooring (581); laminated wood strip flooring (582); underlayment for nonwood floors (584); resilient floor tile (586); self-adhering tiles (588); ceramic floor tile (590).
18: Using stock stair parts (611).
19: Mouldings (619); panel doors (625); flush doors (627); door locks (632); thresholds and door sweeps (633); sliding pocket doors (635); sliding bypass doors (637); bifold doors (638); multifold doors (639).
20: Factory-built cabinets (652); cabinet materials (654); counters and tops (669).
21: Painting, finishing, and decorating materials (683); painting wood exteriors (689); problems with coatings (690); working with stains and clear finishes (694).

●

Industry Standards and Practices, Model Codes, and Building Codes

15: Terminology (488); how much insulation? (492); where to insulate (498); ventilation (503); acoustics and sound control (517).
16: Plaster (555).
17: Wood flooring (572); wood block (parquet) flooring (580).
18: Types of stairs (598); stair parts (600); stairwell framing (600); stair design (602); treads and risers (607); types of stringers (608); winder stairs (609); spiral stairways (614).
19: Mouldings (619); interior door frames (621); sizes and grades (628).
20: Standard sizes (650); types of construction (651); counters and tops (669).

Math and Measurement

18: Stair design (602); stair calculations (604); stairwell length (605); stringer layout (606).

Estimating

15: Estimating thermal insulation materials (515).
16: Estimating materials (566).
17: Estimating strip flooring (580); estimating tile flooring and adhesive (589); ceramic floor tile (590).
21: Working with stains and clear finishes (694); wallcoverings (696).

Print Reading and Interpretation

18: Stair design (602).
20: Drawings for cabinetwork (648).

Career Information and Employable Skills

15: Installing batts and blankets (507); installing loose and foamed insulation (511); installing rigid insulation (513).
16: Installing plywood paneling (547); solid lumber paneling (551); plaster (555); plastering materials and methods (560).
17: Installing wood strip flooring (574); estimating strip flooring (580); estimating tile flooring and adhesive (589).
18: Stairwell framing (600).
19: Door installation (629).
20: Cabinet installation (654); building cabinets (659).
21: Interior painting (691).

Scope and Sequence Chart **43**

Section 5 (Chapters 22–27)

● **Safe and Efficient Work Practices, Construction Techniques, and Methods**

22: Masonry chimneys (706); masonry fireplaces (708); prefabricated fireplaces (716).
23: Advantages of post and beam construction (721); foundations and posts (723); fasteners (726); partitions (730); planks (730).
24: On-site building erection (748); assembling a panelized home (750).
25: Types of solar energy systems (759); passive solar construction (761); passive solar advantages (763); passive solar disadvantages (764); sizing thermal storage systems (769); insulating passive solar buildings (773).
26: Hidden structural details (784); removing old walls (785); providing shoring (787); framing openings in a bearing wall (788); small remodeling jobs (792); solar retrofitting (797); responsible renovation (798).
27: Deck planning and layout (808); constructing the deck (810); pergolas (816); porches (817).

Selection and Use of Materials

22: Prefabricated chimneys (714); prefabricated fireplaces (716); glass enclosures (718).
23: Foundations and posts (723); floor beams (725); beam descriptions (726); roof beams (726); fasteners (726); planks (730); stressed-skin panels (731); box beams (732); laminated beams and arches (734).
25: Solar heat control (764); building passive solar structures (768); designing an isolated-gain system (771).
26: Responsible renovation (798).
27: Structural materials (805); decking materials (806); fasteners and connectors (807).

● **Industry Standards and Practices, Model Codes, and Building Codes**

22: Masonry chimneys (706); masonry fireplaces (708); prefabricated chimneys (714); prefabricated fireplaces (716).
23: Foundations and posts (723); beam descriptions (726); prefabricating post-and-beam structures (735).
24: Factory-built components (742); types of systems-built homes (744); modular homes (745); panelized homes (746); precut homes (747); log homes (748); manufactured homes (754).
26: Building additions onto homes (797).
27: Deck planning and layout (808).

Math and Measurement

25: Sizing thermal storage systems (769); passive thermosiphon system (773).
26: Framing openings in a bearing wall (788).

Print Reading and Interpretation

27: Deck planning and layout (808).

Career Information and Employable Skills

24: Assembling a panelized home (750).
25: Building passive solar structures (768); designing an isolated-gain system (771).
26: Removing old walls (785); providing shoring (787); framing openings in a bearing wall (788); small remodeling jobs (792); solar retrofitting (797); building additions onto homes (797).
27: Deck planning and layout (808); constructing the deck (810).

Copyright by Goodheart-Willcox Co., Inc.

Section 6 (Chapters 28–30)

Safe and Efficient Work Practices, Construction Techniques, and Methods

28: Grounding and ground faults (829); running branch circuits (833); device wiring (835); electrical troubleshooting (838); home security and automation wiring (839)
29: Installing plumbing (855); replacing plumbing parts (862); other drain problems (867); wells and pumps (867).
30: Conservation measures (872).

Use and Care of Tools and Equipment

28: Tools and equipment (822).
29: Tools (848); installing plumbing (855).

Selection and Use of Materials

29: Plumbing supplies (850); sealing plumbing systems (854); installing plumbing (855).
30: Heating systems (874); air cooling systems (881); ducts (882); air exchangers (884); heat pumps (884).

Industry Standards and Practices, Model Codes, and Building Codes

28: Electrical system components (824); basic electrical wiring theory (826); running branch circuits (833); device wiring (835).
29: Plumbing codes (845); two separate systems (846).

Math and Measurement

29: Installing plumbing (855).

Print Reading and Interpretation

28: Reading prints (832).
29: Reading prints (855).

Career Information and Employable Skills

28: Running branch circuits (833); device wiring (835); electrical troubleshooting (838).
29: Installing plumbing (855).

Section 7 (Chapters 31–32)

Safe and Efficient Work Practices, Construction Techniques, and Methods

31: Types of scaffolding (891); brackets, jacks, and trestles (895); ladders (899).

Use and Care of Tools and Equipment

31: Types of scaffolding (891); brackets, jacks, and trestles (895); ladders (899).

Career Information and Employable Skills

32: Economic outlook for construction (904); employment outlook (904); working conditions (906); job opportunities (906); training (907); personal qualifications (909); entrepreneurship (911); teaching as a construction career (912); related occupations (912); organizations promoting construction training (914).

SkillsUSA Competencies

In selecting the competencies that carpentry trainees should attain, you might review the outline that SkillsUSA includes in their contest instructions for carpentry. The instructions are contained in the association's book of contest rules used by clubs preparing for the annual SkillsUSA Championship.

"Contestants," the instructions read in part, "will demonstrate their ability to perform jobs and skills selected from the following list of competencies considered essential by the SkillsUSA Championships technical committee. Committee membership include Associated General Contractors of America, Inc.; Home Builders Institute; National Association of Home Builders; and Steel Framing Alliance."

The outline, reproduced here in chart form to correlate with the **Modern Carpentry** textbook, covers eleven areas. Specific text page numbers have been provided for added convenience to your planning.

Correlation to SkillsUSA Carpentry Contest	
Contest Task	**Textbook Page(s)**
A. Blueprints and Specifications	
1. Interpret and determine dimensions from multiview drawings.	73–74, 96
2. Interpret specifications and drawing notes.	88, 90–93
3. Identify plot plan information such as reference points and bench marks.	149–154
4. Interpret oral and written changes.	77–92
5. Understand common abbreviations and symbols.	89–91, 94, 926, 927
6. Interpret door, window, and finish schedules.	402, 405–409, 413, 415, 422–428
B. Building Site	
1. Use builder's level and transit properly for layout and elevation.	150, 154, 157–164
C. Building Materials	
1. Identify, receive, and inspect materials.	17–39
2. Store lumber and other materials properly.	39–43
D. Foundations and Forms	
1. Construct and align various footing forms to include keyways, bulkheads, dowels, and anchorages.	171–181
2. Construct and align foundation wall and wall forms to include pilasters and beam pockets.	181, 187
3. Construct and align column and pier forms.	185
4. Maintain form materials properly.	185

(continued)

Correlation to SkillsUSA Carpentry Contest *(continued)*	
Contest Task	**Textbook Page(s)**
E. Rough Framing	
1. Identify framing members and select materials.	223–280
2. Frame and install sill plate, girders, floor joists, and bridging.	223–250
3. Frame floor opening and subfloor.	239–241
4. Build or erect safe scaffolding.	891–894
5. Frame and brace walls to include corners, openings, trimmers, cripples, partitions, plumbing partitions, fixture backing, and sheathing.	253–280
6. Frame stair stringer, horse, and other components.	597–615
F. Roof Framing	
1. Identify types and components of roof construction.	284–288
2. Determine rafter lengths from a rafter scale.	293
3. Calculate and use the rise and run of a common roof.	289
4. Lay out a common roof plan.	290–292
5. Lay out, cut, and install common rafters, ridge board, collar ties, gambrel rafters, valley rafters, valley jack rafters, hip rafters, hip jack rafters, and cripple jack rafters.	290–307
6. Frame roof openings, dormers, and saddles.	307–323
7. Build roof trusses and lay out, cut, and install purlins.	309–310, 313–317
8. Install roof sheathing.	323
G. Exterior Finish	
1. Construct, install, and trim window and door frames.	410–413
2. Install corner boards, moulding, or metal corners.	443–444, 447–449
3. Install wood bevel and lap siding, and aluminum or vinyl siding.	442–451, 463–470
4. Install wood shingles and miter corners.	453–457
5. Exterior finish rake, open cornice, and box cornice.	435–442
H. Interior Finish	
1. Install gypsum board.	533–543
2. Cut and install paneling and trim.	547–561
3. Fit and hang doors and trim to include swinging, sliding, folding, and pocket doors.	531–567
4. Construct closets and built-in units and install accessories.	651–669, 672–673
5. Cut and install crown moulding or other mouldings.	619–621
I. Stairs	
1. Lay out a straight run stringer and a two-flight stringer set with landing using a carpenter square.	600–606
2. Calculate rise, run, and tread width.	605–607
3. Cut and install stair treads and stair skirt.	608

(continued)

Correlation to SkillsUSA Carpentry Contest *(continued)*	
Contest Task	**Textbook Page(s)**
J. Lumber	
1. Match letters designating uses in plywood or composition board to their current application.	29–37
2. Match common hardwoods and softwoods to their uses.	26, 28, 39
3. Identify types of trim and mouldings.	619–621
4. Identify common defects in lumber.	23–25
5. Write a request for ordering lumber.	25–39
6. Compute board feet.	26–29
K. 1. A. Tools. Safely Use and Maintain Hand Tools	
1. Sliding T-bevel.	106
2. Tape measure.	104–105
3. Combination square/speed square.	104–106
4. Coping saw.	110
5. Keyhole saw.	110
6. Folding rule.	104
7. Hammer.	113–114
8. Punch.	104–108
9. Hand saw.	109–111
10. Nail set.	113
11. Wood chisel.	112
12. Carpenter's level.	108
13. Framing square.	104
14. Hand plane.	111–113
K. 1. B. Tools. Safely Use and Maintain Power Tools	
1. Reciprocating (jig) saw.	128–129
2. Miter saw.	143–144
3. Hand drill.	130–132
4. Belt sander.	135–136
5. Circular band saw.	124–126
6. Saber saw.	127–129
7. Table saw.	140–141
8. Hand plane.	132–133
9. Finish sander.	136
10. Hand router.	133–134
11. Pneumatic nailers.	136–137

Copyright by Goodheart-Willcox Co., Inc.

Course Outlines

Introduction

The following course outlines suggest various ways for organizing your building trades program using the **Modern Carpentry** text. Each outline includes a course description and objectives provided by the contributor. The outlines can be applied to the high school, post-high vocational, and technical college levels. The outlines can also be modified to suit your program and its facilities as well as covering technological advances, and new practices in the building trades.

Eighteen-Week Course of Study Construction Technology

Course Description

This eighteen-week course covers the building trades from codes and permits on to handling concrete and masonry units, and through framing and finishing. Electrical wiring and plumbing are also included. Students will become familiar with carpentry tools, construction tools, and instruments as well as with the processes involved in carpentry. Safety is stressed throughout the eighteen-week course.

Course Objectives

After completing this course of study, students will be able to:
- Use hand tools to measure, cut, and assemble wooden pieces of a specific dimension.
- Use power tools (handsaw, drill, reciprocating saw, circular saws, etc.) to fabricate construction materials.
- Set up the builder's level and rod to check different elevations.
- Lay out a building with batter boards and strings using the 3-4-5 method.
- Lay up a short sample wall section with concrete blocks and mortar.
- Mix concrete to various specifications and test its strength.
- Experiment with different parting compounds for form work.
- Mix, place, finish, and cure a small concrete slab.
- Cast a small concrete wall section.
- Do a small precast concrete project using reusable forms.
- Wire up a simple circuit with a switch, light, and outlet.
- Cut and assemble plastic pipe, cut and solder copper tubing, and flare copper tubing.
- Select and build a personal project or work on a group project such as a *mini-bam, shed,* or similar project.

Course Outline

1. Construction Materials
   A. Sawed Lumber and Engineered Lumber
   B. Timbers
   C. Sheet Materials
   D. Concrete and Concrete Blocks
   E. Fasteners and Metal Framing Materials
   F. Miscellaneous Materials
2. Safety
   A. Personal Protective Equipment
   B. Working Safely
   C. Handling Hazardous Materials
   D. Fire Protection
   E. First Aid
3. Hand Tools
   A. Identification
   B. Hand Tool Safety
   C. Common Uses
   D. Care and Maintenance
4. Power Tools
   A. Identification
   B. Power Tool Safety
   C. Common Uses
   D. Care and Maintenance
5. Leveling Instruments
   A. Set Up
   B. Reading the Rod
   C. Calculations
   D. Applications
6. Laying Out Buildings
   A. Getting Started
   B. Squaring Using the 3-4-5 Method
   C. Batter Boards and Stakes
7. Footings and Foundations
   A. Codes and Specifications
   B. Block Laying
   C. Cast Concrete Walls
   D. Types of Foundations
   E. Pole Construction
   F. Concrete Technology
   G. Concrete Flatwork
   H. Special Treatments
8. Wall Framing
   A. Conventional
   B. Post Construction
9. Roof Framing
   A. Roof Types
   B. Roof Math
   C. Laying Out and Cutting Common Rafters
   D. Making and Setting Truss Rafters
   E. Sheathing
10. Exterior Wall Sidings and Enclosures
    A. Types of Sidings
    B. Vertical Steel Siding
    C. Enclosing Overhangs
11. Roof Finishing
    A. Types of Coverings
    B. Asphalt Shingles and Roll Roofing
    C. Wood Shingles and Shakes
    D. Metal Roofing
    E. Flashings
    F. Gutters
12. Insulation—Thermal and Sound
    A. Types of Materials
    B. R-Values
    C. Vapor Barriers
    D. Ventilation
    E. Special Construction Needs
13. Electrical Wiring
    A. Service Entrance
    B. Single-Phase and Three-Phase Power
    C. Simple Circuits
    D. Conduit and Romex
    E. Basic Wiring Procedures
14. Plumbing
    A. Well and Pump Troubleshooting
    B. Outdoor Hydrants and Valves
    C. Connecting Fixtures to Pipe and Tubing
    D. Drains and Traps
15. Building Codes and Permits
    A. Electrical
    B. Plumbing
    C. General Construction
    D. Area Plan Commission/Board of Zoning Appeals (BZA)

Outline materials provided by:
James Geise, Instructor
Rushville Consolidated High School
Rushville, Indiana

Thirty-Six Week Course of Study Construction Technology

Course Description
This thirty-six week course introduces students to the construction industry. It surveys the construction field as a career and explains its importance to the community. The course also covers and explains the processes involved in residential construction and lists other types of construction. Both model construction and live work are used to provide students with hands-on experience.

Course Objectives
After completing this course of study, you will be able to:
- Identify major technology systems and list types of construction.
- Practice safety in use of tools and carrying out of processes.
- Show basic skill in use of various carpentry tools.
- Perform carpentry tasks at a satisfactory level of skill.
- Demonstrate a knowledge of job opportunities in construction.
- Complete small construction projects with supervision.
- Demonstrate desirable on-the-job interpersonal relationship skills.

Course Outline

1. Overview of Construction Industry
   A. Identify major systems of technology
   B. Define construction technology
   C. Review the history of construction technology
   D. Identify types of construction
   E. Describe community planning
2. Safety Program
   A. General safety tests
   B. Machine and portable power tool safety instruction and tests
3. Structure Evaluation
   A. Build model project of wood frame structure
   B. Destructive testing of structural members
   C. 2 × 4 simulated destruction tests
   D. Laminates testing
4. Trusses
   A. Truss construction
   B. Truss and bridge building
   C. Destructive testing and evaluation
5. Foundations
   A. Footing types
   B. Foundations
   C. Reinforcement
6. Site Preparation
   A. What is a *lot*?
   B. Building location and orientation to lot
   C. Transit use and elevations
7. Insulation
   A. Principle of heat transfer
   B. Dead air space
   C. R-Values
   D. Moisture barriers
   E. Radon gas testing and information
8. Mechanical Systems
   A. Electrical installations
   B. Plumbing installations
   C. Heating and cooling
   D. What is HVAC?
9. Plot Planning
   A. Reading a plat map

Copyright by Goodheart-Willcox Co., Inc.

    B. Lot layout and offset restrictions
    C. Zoning
10. Masonry Skills
    A. Laying out square corners
    B. Block/brick wall layout and set up
    C. Mixing and pouring concrete
11. Career Investigation
    A. Construction opportunities
    B. Report on areas of interest
    C. Skills and schooling needed
    D. What should I be doing now?
12. Building Kit Activities
    A. Bridge building kit
    B. Truss building kit
    C. Geodesic dome structure kit
13. Superstructures
    A. What holds the roof up?
    B. Framing
    C. Two-story structures
    D. Multi-story structures
    E. Bridges, towers, arches
14. Human Relation Exploration
    A. Getting along with people your age
    B. Getting along with adults
    C. Being a desirable employee
    D. Job interviews
    E. Problem mediation
15. Construction Projects
    A. Structure layout
    B. Marking procedures
    C. Squaring structures and procedures
    D. Sheet material used to square structures
    E. Squaring concepts
    F. Doghouse
    G. Playhouse
    H. Wishing well
    I. Sawhorse

Outline materials provided by:
Roy Gerdes, Instructor
Santa Rita High School
Tucson, Arizona

Seventy-Two Week Course of Study Building Trades

Course Description

The purpose of this course is to provide training on-the-job and in the classroom to junior and senior students from member high schools who show an interest in the building trades. On-the-job work will consist of building mock-ups and homes, which, upon completion will be sold. This experience will be supplemented by classroom instruction and reading assignments.

Course Objectives

After completing this course, the student will be able to:
- Perform framing and finishing work necessary for entry-level carpentry work.
- Apply paint, stain, and other finishes properly.
- Do layout and installation work necessary for entry-level electrical work.
- Demonstrate entry-level skills in laying out and installing plumbing and heating.
- Demonstrate knowledge of apprenticeships, working conditions, unions, opportunities, and related careers that use building trades skill and experience.
- Work efficiently on work assignments in house construction.
- Demonstrate desirable work attitudes by accepting assignments willingly, and following instructions with proper safety procedures.
- Demonstrate the ability to work well with other students, workers, supervisors, and teacher on the job.

Course Outline

1. Layout
    A. Leveling Instruments
        1. Care and Use
        2. Types
        3. Leveling
        4. Horizontal Angles
        5. Contour Lines
        6. Running Straight Lines
        7. Vertical Planes and Lines
    B. Batter Boards, Placement
        1. Building Code
        2. Level
        3. Square
2. Excavation
    A. Equipment
    B. Methods
3. Footings and Foundations
    A. Types
    B. Sizes
    C. Water and Moisture Problems
    D. Soil and Settlement
    E. Anchorage
    F. Decay and Termite Protection
    G. Ventilation of Closed Spaces
4. House Framing
    A. Floor Systems
        1. Sill Sealer
        2. Girder and Posts
        3. Sill and Allied Parts
        4. Joists
        5. Bridging
        6. Subfloor
    B. Walls and Partitions
        1. Corner Posts
        2. Exterior Walls
        3. Window Framing
        4. Door Framing
        5. Interior Partitions
        6. Types and Sizes
        7. Construction Methods

Copyright by Goodheart-Willcox Co., Inc.

            8. Garage Sidewalls
        C. Ceiling Joists
            1. Materials and Sizes
            2. Construction Methods
            3. Placement
            4. Hip Roof and Gable Roof Designs
            5. Cutting Angles at Outside Ends
        D. Roof Framing
            1. Rafters Types
            2. Placement
            3. Ridge Board
            4. Roof Trusses
            5. Cornice
            6. Gable Ends
5. Sheathing
    A. Sidewalls
        1. Materials
        2. Construction Methods
        3. Building Codes
    B. Roofs
        1. Materials
        2. Construction Methods
        3. Placement
6. Roof Coverings
    A. Materials
        1. Felt Paper and Ice and Water Barrier
        2. Drip Strip
        3. Shingles and Roll Roofing
        4. Metal Roofing
7. Electrical Wiring
    A. Terminology and Codes
    B. Boxes, Receptacles, and Switches
    C. Outlet Locations
        1. Exterior
        2. Interior
    D. Circuit Installations
        1. Branch Circuits
        2. Feeder Circuits
    E. Service Installations
    F. Special Considerations
        1. Entrance Signals
        2. Communication
        3. Fire Alarms
        4. Television and Radio
        5. Telephone
8. Plumbing
    A. Septic Tanks
        1. Size
        2. Materials
        3. Location
        4. Hook-up
    B. Drain Field
        1. Materials
        2. Location
        3. Inspection
    C. Soil Pipe
        1. Materials
        2. Sizes
        3. Connections
    D. Drain Lines
        1. Materials
        2. Sizes
        3. Installation
        4. Connections
    E. Vent Pipes
        1. Materials
        2. Sizes
        3. Purpose
        4. Connections
        5. Flashing
    F. Water Supply Piping
        1. Materials
        2. Sizes
        3. Connectors
        4. Installation Methods
    G. Water Heater
        1. Types
        2. Sizes
        3. Installation
    H. Plumbing Fixtures/Supplies
        1. Sinks
        2. Tubs
        3. Shower Enclosures
        4. Traps
        5. Faucets
        6. Sump Pump
        7. Stool
9. Heating and Air Conditioning
    A. Furnaces and Boilers
        1. Types and Sizes
        2. Installation Methods
        3. Fuel Lines
        4. Electrical Circuits
        5. Flues
    B. Heat Distribution Systems
        1. Duct Work (Forced Air Systems)
        2. Pipe Work (Hydronic Systems)
        3. Resistance Heat Grids and Units (Electrical Systems)
        4. Thermostats
        5. Registers
        6. Safety
    C. Air Conditioning Units
        1. Types and Sizes

       2. Installation Methods
    D. Large Appliances
       1. Ranges and Ovens
       2. Washers and Dryers
       3. Vent Hoods
       4. Installation Methods
    E. Exhaust Fans
       1. Types
       2. Uses
       3. Location
       4. Installation Methods
10. Insulation, Interior Trim, and Wall Covering
    A. Windows
       1. Types
       2. Sizes
       3. Hardware
       4. Installation Methods
    B. Doors
       1. Types
       2. Sizes
       3. Hardware
       4. Installation Methods
    C. Insulation
       1. Types
       2. Uses
       3. Sizes
       4. Installation
    D. Interior Wall Coverings
       1. Materials
       2. Uses
       3. Codes
       4. Installation Methods
    E. Trim
       1. Types
       2. Finishes
       3. Uses
       4. Installation Methods
    F. Cabinets
       1. Types
       2. Layout
       3. Styles
       4. Sizes
11. Decorating
    A. Painting
       1. Purpose
       2. Types
       3. Paint Selection
       4. Application Methods
    B. Staining
       1. Purpose
       2. Types
       3. Surface Preparation
       4. Stain Selection
       5. Application Methods
    C. Varnishes
       1. Purpose
       2. Kinds
       3. Surface Preparation
       4. Selection
       5. Application Methods

Outline materials provided by:
H. Enervold, Instructor
Grundy Area Vocational Center
Morris, Illinois

Copyright by Goodheart-Willcox Co., Inc.

Supplementary Activities

This section contains seventeen supplementary activities developed by carpentry instructors from around the country. For your convenience, they are numbered according to the **Modern Carpentry** text chapters with which they correspond. Each activity includes a list of objectives and a step-by-step procedure. They can be used accordingly or adapted to fit the unique needs of your program. The activities can be modified to suit your classroom facilities and assigned as either group or individual projects. Answers, where applicable, are also included.

Activities

4-1 — Hand Tool Exercise.. 59

4-2 — Constructing a Small-Parts Storage Box 61

4-3 — Constructing an Octagonal Frame 62

4-4 — Laying Out and Cutting.. 63

4-5 — Building a Stool.. 65

4-6 — Building a Sawhorse.. 67

5-1 — Power Tool Exercise 68

6-1 — Figuring Shop Elevations with the Level.................... 69

6-2 — Squaring a Building 70

7-1 — Volume Proportioning (with answer key)................... 72

10-1 — Roof Framing Computations (with answer key)........ 74

10-2 — Common Rafter Layout 77

10-3 — Calculating Common Rafters (with answer key)...... 78

11-1 — Wall Framing with Steel and Drywall Installation 80

12-1 — Building a Doghouse 82

14-1 — Concrete and Masonry Assignment........................ 84

14-2 — Block Wall Setup... 85

Copyright by Goodheart-Willcox Co., Inc.

Exercise 4-1
Hand Tool Exercise

Name _____ Date _____ Score _____

Objectives
- To develop skill in using layout tools such as the compass, steel tape, T-bevel, square, and combination square.
- To practice using various hand or power tools accurately to shape or cut wood.

Procedure
1. Study the accompanying drawing of the hand/power tool exercises before continuing.
2. On the board supplied by your instructor, measure 15 1/4″ from the left end and draw a line using a square. Make a crosscut to the right of this line, being careful not to cut off the line.
3. Using the combination square, draw a line at a 45° angle upward from the lower-left corner.
4. Use the sliding T-bevel to lay out an angle of 67.5° from the lower-left corner. Make a crosscut, leaving the line.
5. Lay out a parallel line 3 3/8″ from the bottom edge of the workpiece and hand plane to the line.
6. Measure over 3 1/2″ from the right end and 1 3/8″ up from the bottom edge. Bore a 7/8″ hole with a brace and auger bit.
7. Measure 7″ from the right end and up 1 1/4″. Drill a 7/32″ hole using a hand "crank-type" drill.
8. Measure over 7″ and up 2 3/8″. Using a push drill, drill a pilot hole for a #8 × 3/4″ screw. Also, use the hand drill and a countersink to recess the top of the hole.
9. Measure over 10 5/8″ from the right end and up 1 1/2″. Scribe an arc (using a compass) with a 1 7/8″ radius from that point.
10. Turn the piece to work on the bottom face. Measure over 2″ from the right end and down 5/8″ and drive an 8d nail.
11. Measure over 4″ from the right edge and down 7/8″. Drive a 16d nail.
12. Measure over 5 1/2″ from the right end and up 3/4″. Drive a 16d nail. Using a nail claw, lift the nail to make it ready for pulling.
13. Measure over from the right end 7 1/4″ and up 5/8″. At this point, drive a 4d finishing nail. Set it 1/16″ to 3/32″ below the surface.
14. Use the door hinge provided and trace around it after positioning the right end 9 1/2″ from the right edge of the workpiece. Recess the hinge so it will be flush with the edge of the workpiece. Use flat chisels to remove material.
15. Turn the workpiece over and snap a chalkline from corner to corner at the longest points.

Exercise 4-2
Constructing a Small-Parts Storage Box

Name _____ Date _____ Score _____

Objectives
- To practice making several types of common joints.
- To develop skill in cutting dadoes accurately.

Procedure
1. Construct a box with the four joints as shown in the drawing below, using either hand or power tools. Select four suitable pieces of softwood for the sides and two ends, and a piece of 1/4" plywood for the bottom and dividers.
2. Plane your pieces of softwood to finish height, checking often with your tape measure and square. Consider cutting and fitting your corner joints before cutting one of the end pieces and one of the side pieces to length to allow a little room for adjusting and resawing the mitered joint. After the mitered joint fits well, cut the affected pieces to length.
3. Dado the four sides to accept the 1/4" plywood bottom. Then cut dadoes for the dividers as shown in the drawing. Both the bottom and dividers extend 3/8" into each side.
4. Trial fit all pieces before gluing. Apply a thin film of glue to all corner joints. Assemble the sides and bottom and clamp. Check for square.
5. Allow the glued joints to dry.
6. Install the dividers, checking height so they do not extend above the box. Adjust as needed.
7. Check your work and have the instructor grade your project.

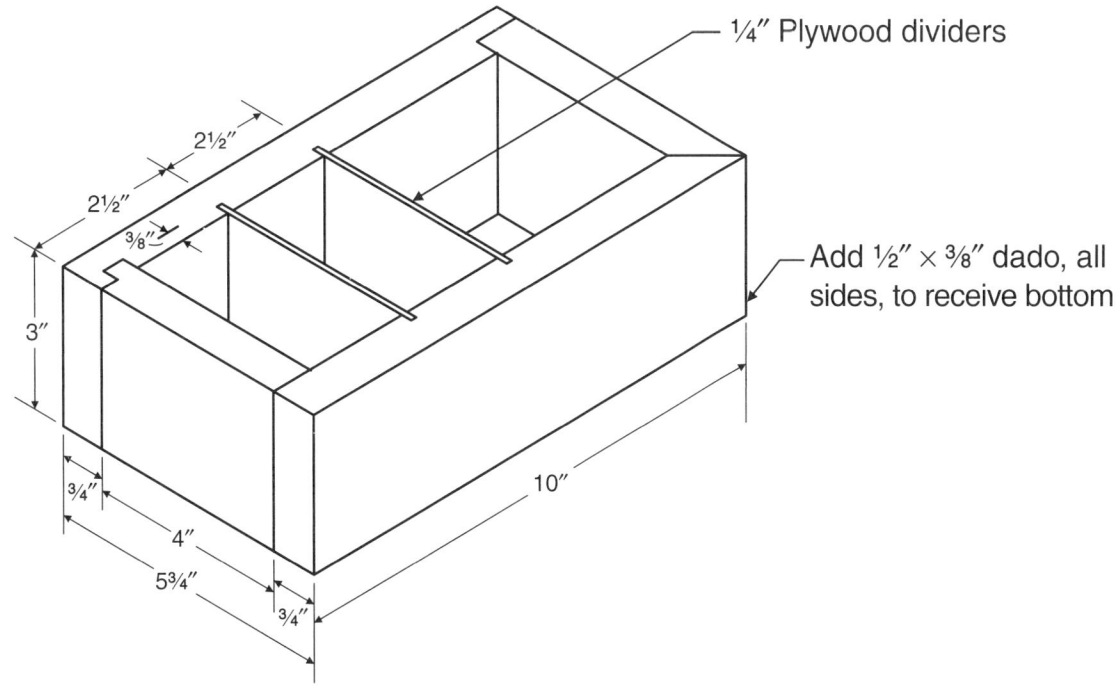

James Maddox
St. Paul Technical College
St. Paul, Minnesota

Exercise 4-3
Constructing an Octagonal Frame

Name _____ Date _____ Score _____

Objectives
- To develop skill and accuracy in producing a rabbet in a board.
- To develop skill and accuracy in constructing angles.
- To develop skill in securing joints with brads.

Procedure
1. Using your hand tools and the hand miter box, construct an octagon, as shown in the drawing.
2. Rabbet one edge to 1/2" × 1/2".
3. Cut pieces to correct length and angle with the hand miter box. Refer to the drawing.
4. Apply a thin film of glue to each surface to be joined. Secure joints with brads and a brad pusher.
5. Use paper to protect the benchtop when gluing. A damp rag also helps clean up fingerprints before they stain the wood.

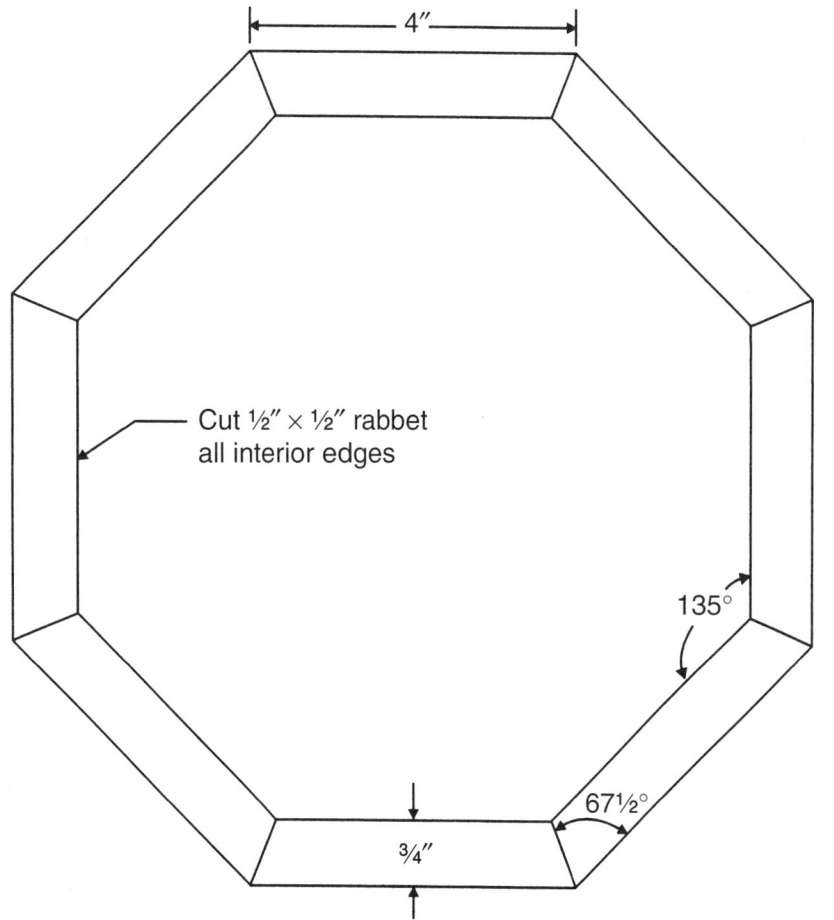

James Maddox
St. Paul Technical College
St. Paul, Minnesota

Exercise 4-4
Laying Out and Cutting

Name _____ Date _____ Score _____

Objectives
- To learn to accurately lay out straight lines.
- To practice cutting square straight cuts using a handsaw or a power saw.
- To measure accurately within 1/16" and make cuts with a handsaw to that tolerance.
- To practice driving 12d nails straight and at an angle.
- To learn the basic use of a speed square.
- To accurately transfer a line to an adjoining surface.

Procedure

1. Measure in 43 1/2" from the end of a 2 × 4 and mark it. Using a speed square, draw a square line across the board at the mark. Continue the same line on the facing edge and around the board until the line meets the starting point. They should match up. Cut next to your line, leaving the line or half the line on the 43 1/2" board that you are going to use.

    Instructor Check: _____

2. Measure in from one end 1" and, at that point, draw a square line all the way around the workpiece again (A). Measure 20 1/4" up from the first line and draw another square line all the way around (B). Measure 1" from that line and draw another line all the way around (C). Now measure another 20 1/4" from your last line and draw another square line around the board again (D). You should have four lines around the board.

    Instructor Check: _____

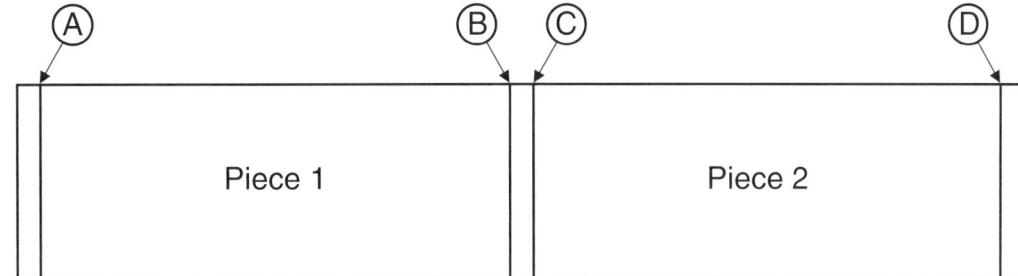

3. Using an 8-point handsaw, make two 20 1/4" workpieces by cutting at the four lines. You will have to decide which cuts to make first. IMPORTANT—Leave the marked lines on the ends of the 20 1/4" pieces. You must cut next to the lines, *not* on them. It takes concentration—you are learning a basic but very important skill. Put your name in ink on both 20 1/4" pieces.

    Instructor Check: _____

4. Measure and mark out three 3 1/2" boxes on the face of Piece 1. Locate two of the boxes 2" in from each end. Using a steel rule, locate the center of the workpiece and mark it. Place the third box in the middle of the workpiece. The vertical lines at the ends of the boxes will be drawn all the way around the board. It is important they transfer precisely.

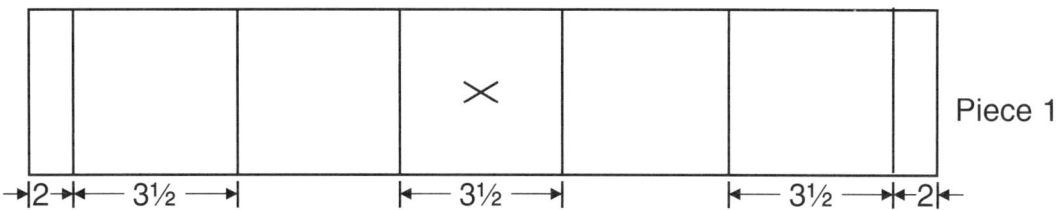

5. On one face of the workpiece (Face 1), draw a line 1/2" from each edge. On the opposite face (Face 2), for the left and center boxes, draw a line across the center of the face and a line 1/2" from the bottom edge. On the right box, place horizontal lines 1/2" from each edge.

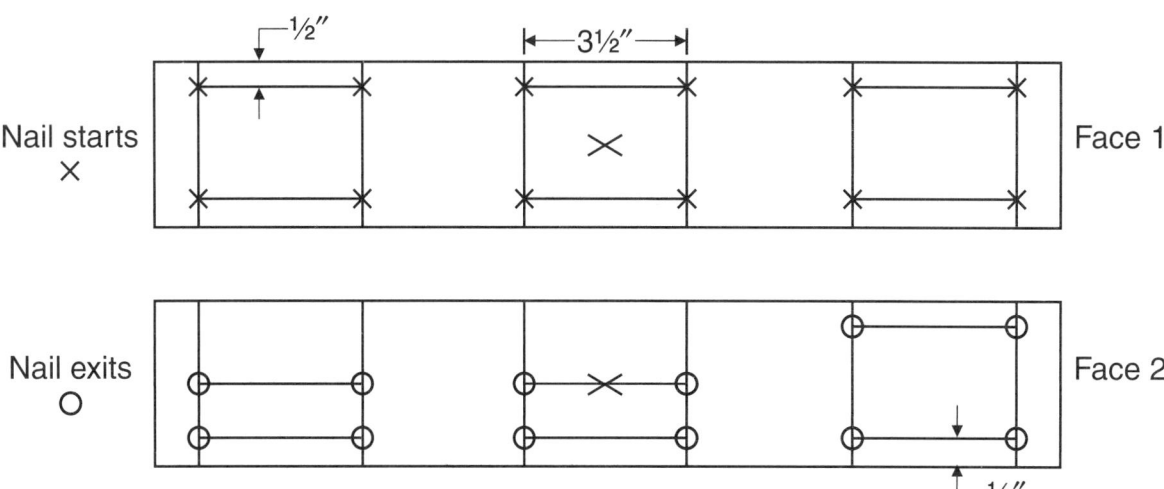

6. Turn the workpiece over in preparation for nailing. Place the board on the floor and use your other board to keep the exiting nails off the floor. Start four 12d nails at the top corners of the first two squares from the left. Angle them to exit the board at the center on the opposite face. Drive them until they begin to exit the opposite face. Do *not* drive them through. Next, start 12d nails at the four corners of the third square and drive them straight through so that they will begin to exit at the corners of the square on the opposite face. Finally, drive the last four 12d nails straight into the 2 × 4. Do not drive the nails through. *Never* leave nail points sticking out of any board at any time.

Instructor Check: _____

7. Remove the nails using a claw hammer and a block of wood. (It is important to use the block to pull the nails straight.) Try using both a straight claw and a curved claw to see the difference.

Instructor Check: _____

Exercise 4-5
Building a Stool

Name _____ Date _____ Score _____

Objectives
- To improve print reading skills.
- To develop skill in measuring stock.
- To develop proficiency in the use of hand and power tools.

Procedure
1. Review the accompanying working drawings.
2. Select materials from stock as provided by your instructor.
3. Determine your own procedures for measuring, cutting, and assembly.
4. Review your procedures with your instructor.

Instructor Check: _____

5. Use a protractor and T-bevel to determine angles for workpieces.
6. Use a T-bevel to transfer angles to workpieces.
7. Mark, cut, and assemble the stool according to your procedures.
8. A nice finish is recommended, but optional.

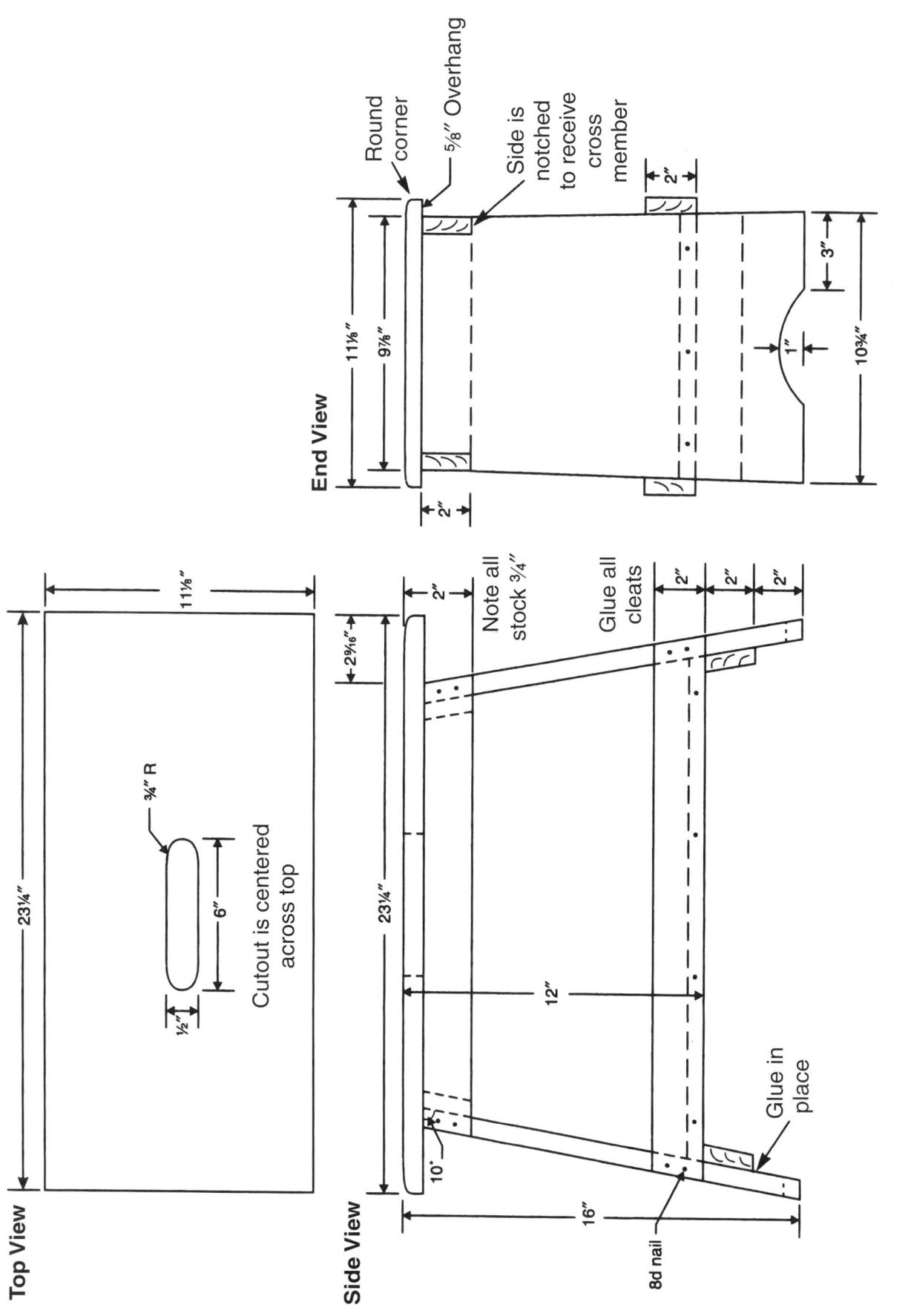

James Maddox
St. Paul Technical College
St. Paul, Minnesota

Exercise 4-6
Building a Sawhorse

Name _____ Date _____ Score _____

Objectives
- To develop skills in the use of hand and power tools.
- To improve print reading skills.
- To develop skill in cutting angles.

Procedure
1. Mark and cut a 2 × 6 to 3'-5 3/4" length.
2. Measure and mark each end of the 2 × 6 for the location of the legs. Place marks on the edge 4" and 7 1/2" in from the end of the 2 × 6.
3. Set the blade of a T-bevel to 99°. Mark the angle of the legs at each mark on the edges of the 2 × 6.
4. Set the T-bevel at 81°. Use this angle to mark crosscuts on four 1 × 4 legs. Be sure the angle is running in the right direction.
5. Since all crosscutting of legs will be at compound angles, set the T-bevel at 76°. Mark the edges of all leg cuts to 76°. Make the legs 29 1/4" long.
6. Cut legs to length along the compound angles just marked.
7. Set the T-bevel to 14° and mark the bevel at the top of each leg.
8. Make the bevel cuts.
9. Cut braces, tray, and stretchers to dimensions and angles shown on the drawing.
10. Drill pilot holes and assemble the sawhorse using glue and #8 × 2" wood screws.

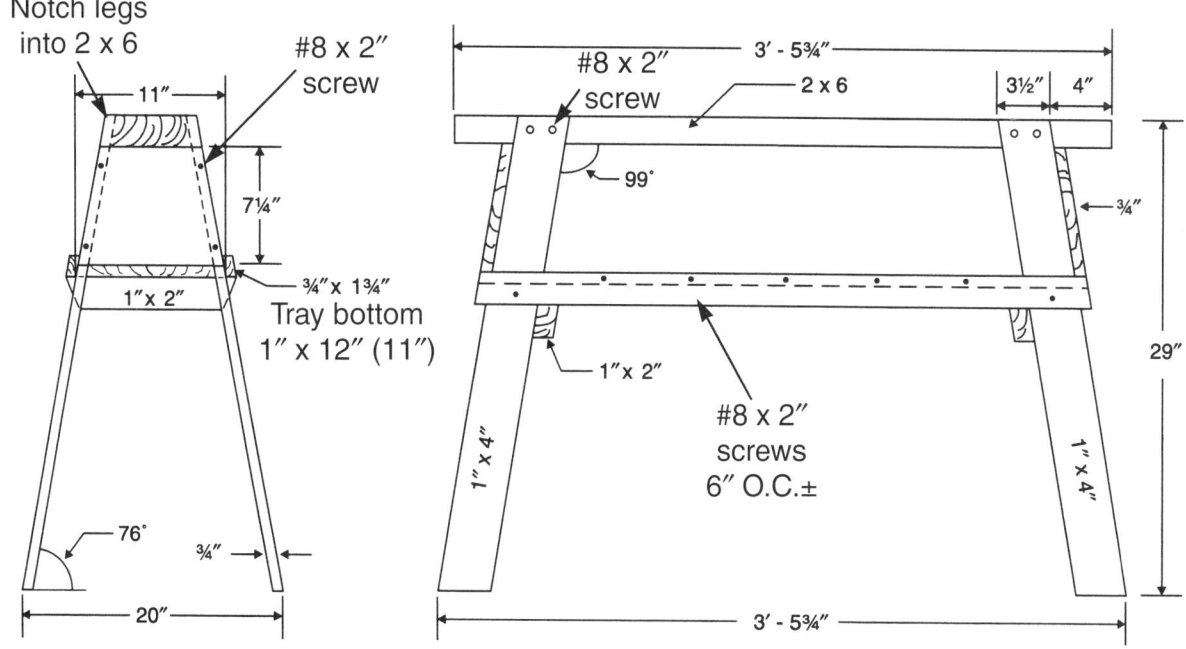

James Maddox
St. Paul Technical College
St. Paul, Minnesota

Exercise 5-1
Power Tool Exercise

Name _____ Date _____ Score _____

Objectives
- To make accurate cuts using various power tools.
- To make accurate setups on power tools.
- To practice making accurate measurements.

Procedure
1. Using a circular saw, make a crosscut to square one end of the 1 × 4 workpiece.
2. Crosscut the other end square using the radial arm saw, making the workpiece 13" long.
3. Use the power miter saw to cut a 45° angle cut starting halfway down the left end, with the cut angling to the upper edge. (For accuracy, measure and mark the middle of the workpiece width before making the cut.)
4. Set up the table saw to rip the top edge so the workpiece width is 3 1/16".
5. Measure 1 1/2" from the left end and upward 1 11/16" from the bottom edge. Drill a 1/4" hole using a twist drill in a 3/8" power hand drill.
6. Measure 2 3/16" from the left end and up 1 7/8". Drill an 11/16" hole with a spade bit in the power hand drill.
7. Measure 5 1/8" from the left end and up 2 1/8" from the bottom. At that point, drive a 1 1/4" drywall screw using a 3/8" variable speed electric drill and a #2 Phillips tip.
8. Measure 4 5/8" from the top-right corner and scribe an arc with a 2" radius. With a jigsaw, cut the arc one-half way around, as shown on the drawing.
9. Draw a line 1 1/2" from the right end and down 1 1/4". Using a reciprocating saw, make a plunge cut along the right side of this line its full length.

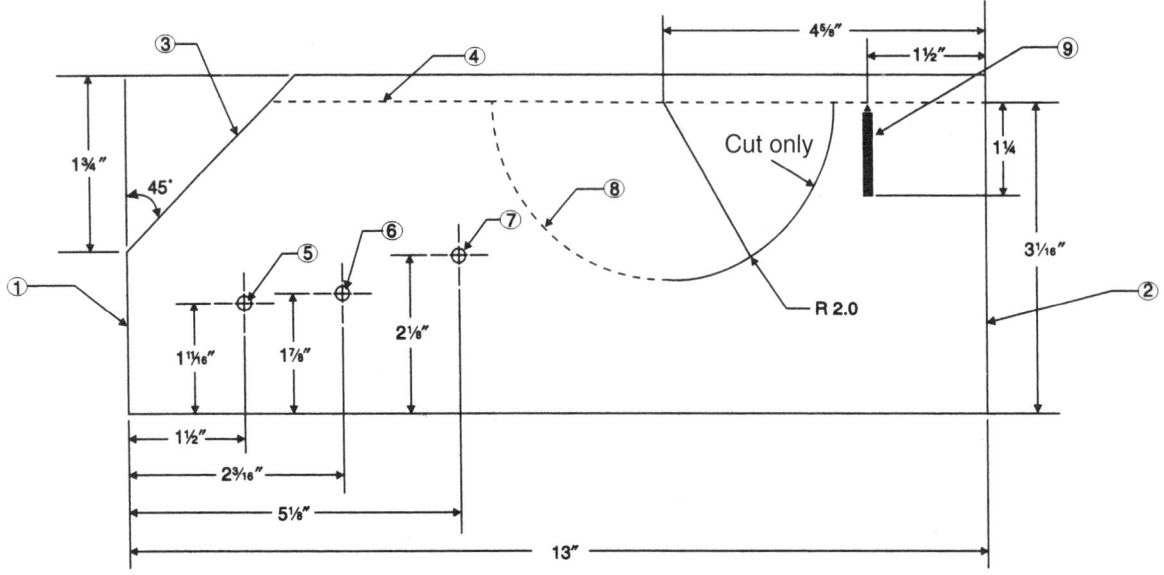

Jim Geise
Rushville Consolidated High School
Rushville, Indiana

Exercise 6-1
Figuring Shop Elevations with the Level

Name _____ Date _____ Score _____

Objectives
- To gain experience in the use of the level.
- To locate and establish a benchmark.
- To establish the height of the instrument in relation to the level.

Procedure
1. In this exercise with the level, you will determine the elevation of ten targets located in the shop area.
2. Locate the benchmark by measuring up 24" on the shop wall. Place a piece of tape on the wall at this point.
3. From the benchmark, establish the height of your instrument and determine the following elevations. You may need to move your instrument. Be sure to compute your new instrument height each time you move.
4. Targets are marked by your instructor. Compute the elevations to the nearest hundredth foot.

Target 1: _____   Target 6: _____
Target 2: _____   Target 7: _____
Target 3: _____   Target 8: _____
Target 4: _____   Target 9: _____
Target 5: _____   Target 10: _____

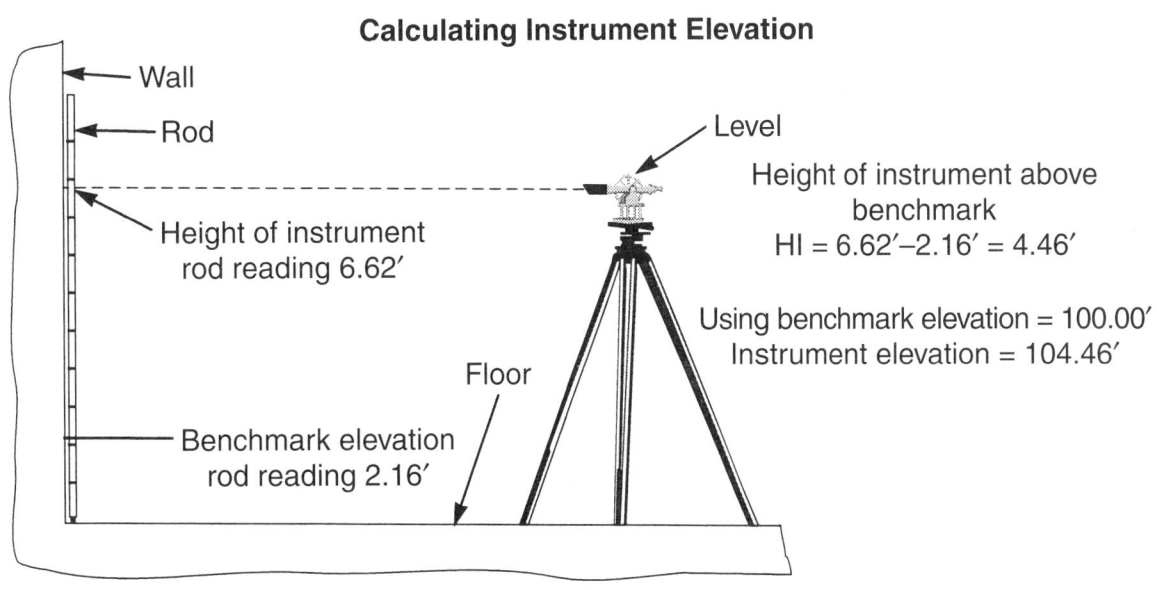

Calculating Instrument Elevation

Height of instrument above benchmark
HI = 6.62' – 2.16' = 4.46'

Using benchmark elevation = 100.00'
Instrument elevation = 104.46'

James Maddox
St. Paul Technical College
St. Paul, Minnesota

Exercise 6-2
Squaring a Building

Name _____ Date _____ Score _____

Objectives
- To use a transit or builder's level to set the corners of a structure.
- To learn to read a vernier scale on a transit.
- To accurately measure from a given point.
- To occupy a given point with a transit or builder's level using a plumb bob.
- To learn to check a building for square by using a corner-to-corner measurement.

Procedure
1. Before setting up in the field and doing this activity, review the textbook section on reading a vernier degree scale.
2. Select a point approximately 5′ behind a corner of the building line. Drive a temporary 2 × 2 stake in the ground.
3. Set up the transit or level over the temporary stake so the plumb bob will be centered over the top of the stake. (It is not necessary to level the instrument.)
4. Drive an 8d nail in the top of the stake so the head is exactly under the point of the plumb bob.
5. At this point, have the instructor check your setup and see if you can read the vernier degree scale on the transit or level.

Instructor Check: _____

6. Place the first corner stake on a line of sight about 5′ from the temporary stake and drive a nail in its top. This is Stake #1. Now, on a line of sight, measure exactly 15′ from the nail in Stake #1, and place Stake #2. Drive a nail in this stake exactly 15′ from the nail in Stake #1.
7. Place the vertical crosshair on the nail head of Stake #2. There is a fine adjustment knob to move the crosshairs just slightly. Record the reading on the vernier scale.
8. Center and level the transit or builder's level over the nail head of Stake #1.
9. Loosen the instrument head and swing it exactly 90° to locate Stake #3. Measure 15′ from Stake #1 under the transit/level. Using the vertical crosshair and your tape measure, drive Stake #3 in the ground.
10. Measure exactly 15′ from the nail head in Stake #1, and draw a pencil line on the top of Stake #3. Using the crosshairs, place your third nail in the top of that stake.
11. Move the instrument and center it over the top of Stake #3, so the plumb bob is located on top of the nail head.

Instructor Check: _____

12. Put the vertical crosshairs on the nail on Stake #1. Locate Stake #4. This stake must be located exactly 15′ from the point that you are occupying and also 15′ from Stake #2. If your measurements and angles are accurate, you should be on the vertical crosshairs when you measure 15′ from Stake #2.
13. If your measurements are off, begin your corrections by measuring between Stake #1 and Stake #3. Set Stake #4 exactly 15′ from Stake #3, then go back to Stake #1 and reset Stake #2 from there.
14. Measure diagonally from corner-to-corner across the 15′ square to check if the two diagonal measurements are exactly the same distance.

Instructor Check: _____

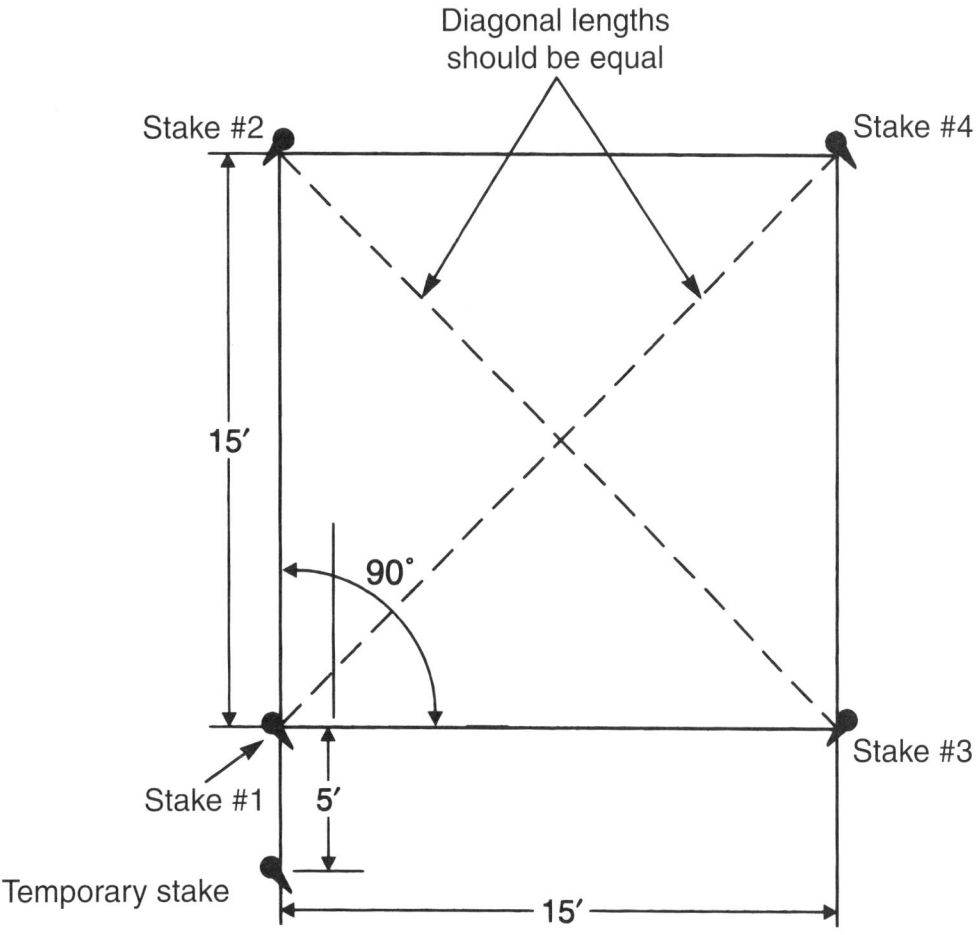

Roy Gerdes
Santa Rita High School
Tucson, Arizona

Exercise 7-1
Volume Proportioning

Name _____ Date _____ Score _____

Objectives
- To develop skill and accuracy in reading prints.
- To determine quantities of material needed for a job.

Procedure
1. Study the drawing. Note the dimensions.

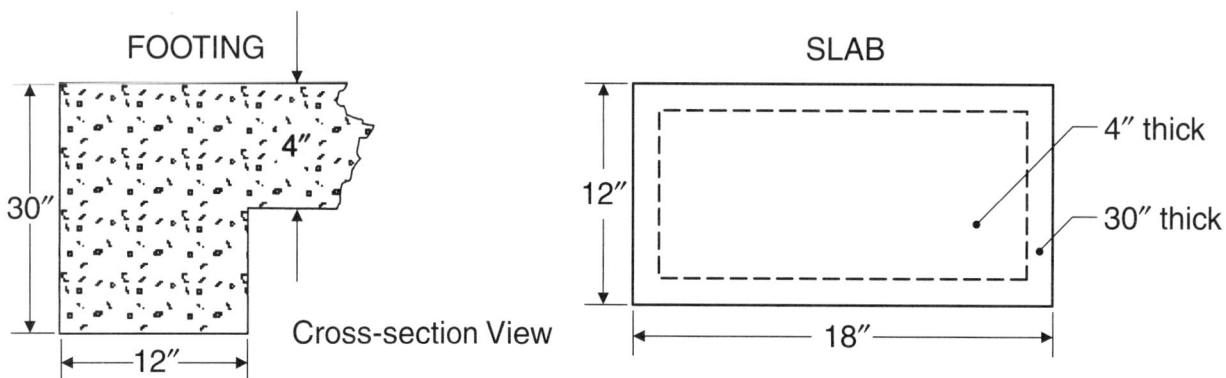

2. Answer the questions below regarding quantity of concrete required.
3. Before answering the batching questions, discuss the appropriate mixture with the instructor.
4. If the instructor does not provide a different mixture, assume a six-bag mixture. (Four bags of cement, 9 ft³ of sand, and 12 ft³ of gravel are needed to produce one cubic yard of concrete.)

Quantity
How many cubic yards of concrete are in the slab and footing pictured above?

1. Actual amount: _____

2. Rounded up to the next full yard: _____

Use this amount in figuring the following problems.

Batching
How much material is needed to mix the "rounded" amount if you were to mix it yourself?

	Per one cu. yd.	Total cu. yd.	Total
Bags of cement:	_____ ×	_____ =	_____ bags
Sand:	_____ ft³ ×	_____ =	_____ ft³
Gravel:	_____ ft³ ×	_____ =	_____ ft³

Jim Geise
Rushville Consolidated High School
Rushville, Indiana

Answer Key—Exercise 7-1

1. Actual amount: **7.16 yd³**
2. Rounded up to the next full yard: **8 yd³**

	Per one cu. yd.		Total cu. yd.		Total	
Bags of cement:	4	×	8	=	32	bags
Sand:	9 ft³	×	8	=	72	ft³
Gravel:	12 ft³	×	8	=	96	ft³

Exercise 10-1
Roof Framing Computations

Name _____ Date _____ Score _____

Objectives
- To practice calculating rafter length from runs and rises.
- To study the difference between the terms "rise" and "run."

Procedure
Using the formulas and the figures provided, complete the chart on the following page.
  Pitch = Rise ÷ Span   **OR**   Pitch = Rise ÷ (2 × Run)
  Rise = Pitch × Span   **OR**   Rise = Pitch × (2 × Run)
  Run = Span ÷ 2
  Span = 2 × Run
  Inches of rise per foot of run = Total inches of rise ÷ Total feet of run

Line length procedure (rafter length):
1. Find the inches of rise per foot of run. This is the unit rise.
2. The unit rise is used to locate the corresponding number on the rafter square table.
3. Find the number under the rafter square table number that will represent the line length per foot of run. Multiply this number times the total feet of run.

Cut: The cut is the same thing as the inches of rise per foot of run but expressed in a different way.

Example: If you had a roof with 4" of rise per foot of run, the cut would be 4/12. It may also be expressed as the following symbol on a drawing.

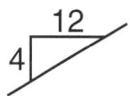

Total Rafter Length: This is found by taking the total line length, subtracting one half the thickness of the ridge board, then adding on the amount of overhang you want to use. (If you want 1' of overhang, you add one unit of line length to the rafter length, rather than adding 12".)

Example: Calculate total rafter length if line length is 127.58", ridge thickness is 1 1/2", and unit length for the 1' overhand is 12.65".
1. Subtract one-half ridge thickness from the line length:
   127.58" − 0.75" = 126.83"
2. Add line length for overhang:
   126.83" + 12.65" = 139.48"

Jim Geise
Rushville Consolidated High School
Rushville, Indiana

Exercise 10-1 (continued)
Roof Framing Computations

Name _____ Date _____ Score _____

(Take decimals to two places, e.g. 115.67".)

Specs.	1	2	3	4	5	6	7	8	9	10
Rise	3'		5'		6'			3'	10'	
Run		7'		16'	18'		8'			12'
Span	24		40'		36'	12'			48'	
Pitch		1/2		1/4						1/6
Inches of rise per foot of run										
Cut	12	12	12	12	12	12 / 8	12 / 9	12 / 6	12	12
Line length per foot of run	in.	in.	in.	in.	in.	in.	in.	in.	in.	in.
Total line length in inches	in.	in.	in.	in.	in.	in.	in.	in.	in.	in.
Total rafter length w/ 1 1/2" ridge and 1' overhang	in.	in.	in.	in.	in.	in.	in.	in.	in.	in.

Answer Key—Exercise 10-1

Specs.	1	2	3	4	5	6	7	8	9	10
Rise	3'	7'	5'	8'	6'	4'	6'	3'	10'	4'
Run	12'	7'	20'	16'	18'	6'	8'	6'	24'	12'
Span	24'	14'	40'	32'	36'	12'	16'	12'	48'	24'
Pitch	1/8	1/2	1/8	1/4	1/6	1/3	3/8	1/4	5/24	1/6
Inches of rise per foot of run	3"	12"	3"	6"	4"	8"	9"	6"	5"	4"
Cut	12/3	12/12	12/3	12/6	12/4	12/8	12/9	12/6	12/5	12/4
Line length per foot of run	12.37 in.	16.97 in.	12.37 in.	13.42 in.	12.65 in.	14.42 in.	15.00 in.	13.42 in.	13.00 in.	12.65 in.
Total line length in inches	148.44 in.	118.79 in.	247.40 in.	214.72 in.	227.70 in.	86.52 in.	120.00 in.	80.52 in.	312.00 in.	151.80 in.
Total rafter length w/ 1 1/2" ridge and 1' overhang	160.06 in.	135.01 in.	259.02 in.	227.37 in.	239.60 in.	100.19 in.	134.25 in.	93.19 in.	324.25 in.	163.70 in.

Exercise 10-2
Common Rafter Layout

Name _____ Date _____ Score _____

Objectives
- To practice figuring rafter length from runs and rises.
- To learn the difference between the terms "rise" and "run."

Procedure
1. Using the step-off method as described in the textbook, lay out a common rafter. The pitch for your rafter will be 1/4. The run for your rafter will be 12′. The overhang on your rafter will be 2′.
2. Mark all cuts that will be made, but do *not* make the cuts.
3. After your instructor has checked your layout, sand out pencil marks with a belt sander and restock the material.

Exercise 10-3
Calculating Common Rafters

Name _____ Date _____ Score _____

Objectives
- To calculate lengths of common rafters.
- To develop skill in laying out common rafters.
- To demonstrate an understanding of roof framing geometry.

Procedure
Using the appropriate formulas, complete the following chart. Note the overhang dimension. The ridge board is a 2 × 8 (1 1/2" wide).

	#1	#2	#3
Overhang	12"	16"	18"
Rise	3'	7'	4'
Run		7'	6'
Span	12'		
Pitch			
Inches of rise per foot of run			
Cut	12	12	12
Line length per foot of run			
Total line length			
Total rafter length			
Purchase length			

Jim Geise
Rushville Consolidated High School
Rushville, Indiana

Answer Key—Exercise 10-3

	#1	#2	#3
Overhang	12"	16"	18"
Rise	3'	7'	4'
Run	6'	7'	6'
Span	12'	14'	12'
Pitch	1/4	1/2	1/3
Inches of rise per foot of run	6"	12"	8"
Cut	6/12	12/12	8/12
Line length per foot of run	13.42"	16.97"	14.42"
Total line length	80.52"	118.79"	86.52"
Total rafter length	93.19"	140.67"	107.40"
Purchase length	94"	142"	108"

Exercise 11-1
Wall Framing with Steel and Drywall Installation

Name _____ Date _____ Score _____

Objectives
- To experience cutting and assembling steel wall framing.
- To demonstrate skill and improve drywalling technique.
- To improve skill in attaching electrical boxes to wall studs.

Procedure
1. Build two intersecting walls with steel studs as indicated in the sketch. Make each wall 10' long.

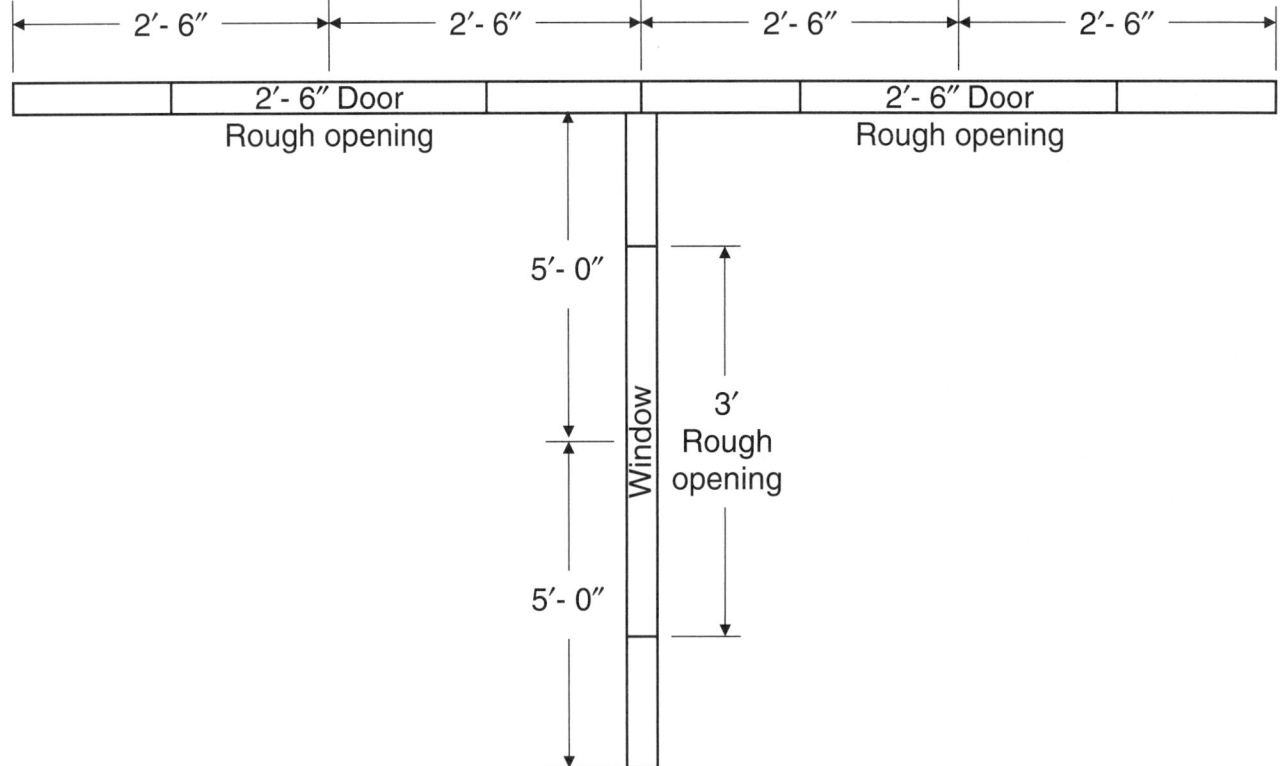

2. Refer to the textbook to review proper dimensions for rough openings for doors and windows.
3. Space studs 24" O.C., and attach them with 1/2" pan head screws to steel track at top and bottom. Be sure that the walls are squared and plumbed before bracing is attached. These screws are only an aid in building a temporary wall and serve no structural purpose.
4. Frame in rough openings for two 2'-6" doors and a window with a rough opening of 3'-0" × 3'-0", as shown in the drawing. The door openings will be lined with a wood 2 × 4 to provide a nailing base for the door frame and trim. Be sure to allow for the 2 × 4 when calculating your rough opening. The window opening will not be lined with the 2 × 4 material.
5. Check with your instructor for guidance when making the headers and sills for the openings.

Instructor Check: _____

6. Choose ten electrical boxes from the selection available and mount them somewhere in your framed walls. Check with your instructor for proper location of switch and receptacle boxes.
7. Mount the boxes so their openings will be flush with the finished surface of the 1/2" drywall.
8. Before installing the drywall, locate the position of each box and transfer its location to the appropriate drywall panel. Have your instructor check your measurements before continuing.

Instructor Check: _____

9. Cut out each box opening before installing the panel. You should practice cutting openings if a drywall cutter is to be used.
10. Apply the drywall vertically with the 1 1/4" screws. Do not go more than 8' high and do not fill in above the full sheets. Apply drywall to both sides of the wall with the door openings. Joints should be staggered, not back to back. Drywall one side of the wall with the window opening. Door and window openings should be cut away after the full sheets are in place. Use a drywall cutter or a drywall saw.

James Maddox
St. Paul Technical College
St. Paul, Minnesota

Exercise 12-1
Building a Doghouse

Name _____ Date _____ Score _____

Objectives
- To plan and lay out the structural members of a doghouse.
- To use print reading skills to formulate a plan
- To use measuring and marking skills to lay out structural members to be cut out for assembly.
- To use table and radial arm saws to rip and cut off 2 × 4 and plywood material to exact lengths and widths.
- To use squaring techniques while properly nailing and assembling component parts.
- To learn a truss building method and the techniques needed to build a gambrel-type roof system with overhang and installing outlookers (lookouts) and fascia.
- To learn to properly cut and apply three-tab shingles.
- To identify and use various types of nails.

Procedure
1. Lay out, cut, and assemble floor joists and headers (rim joists) using 2 × 4s. Cut a floor panel from 1/4″ plywood to 23 1/4″ × 36″. Nail the panel to the floor joists. Use 16d sinkers to assemble the joists and 6d cement-coated nails for flooring every 6″ on the flooring panel.

   Instructor Check: _____

2. Referring to dimensions and features on the drawings, cut materials and lay out walls with sole plate, upper plate, and studs (12″ centers for studs). Notch the top plates on both side walls and end wall to form lap joints when wall frames are assembled. Assemble all four (4) walls completely before attaching studded walls to the floor. Position the walls and nail sole plates to the floor, using 16d sinkers. Position nails over floor frame members for strength. Square up all four walls and nail together. Do not nail on the siding yet.

   Instructor Check: _____

3. Cut out siding material. Plan carefully to avoid wasting siding material. Siding should cover at least half of the sides of the top and bottom plates. Square up sides with a framing square and plumb with a level before nailing on the siding. Nail the siding using 6d coated or galvanized nails with 6″ spacing on the siding.

   Instructor Check: _____

4. After the sides are completed, lay out the four 2 × 2 rafter trusses. Make the miter cuts using the power miter box. Cut the small gussets from scrap 1/4″ plywood. Assemble the trusses and end fascia.

   Instructor Check: _____

5. Toenail the trusses to the upper plate directly above the wall studs. Be sure that the peaks of the trusses are in line. *NOTE:* It is easier to notch your end trusses for attaching lookouts

before nailing trusses to the top plate. Locate 1/2" deep notches toward the ends of each leg of the gable end rafters. Cut lookouts 6" long and notch one end to fit flush to the top of the rafter notches. Assemble the trusses and lookouts and then attach 1 × 2 fascia to gable end lookouts.

Instructor Check: _____

6. Cut and attach the roof decking. Use either sheet material or boards as directed by your instructor. Make sure the decking is even, so the shingles will lie flat. If drip edge is to be used, cut and attach it at this time.

Instructor Check: _____

7. Apply the roofing material with 3/8" of the shingle extending over the edge of the roof boards. Put on the ridge cap. Install screening, if required, to gable ends. Check all appearance items and paint as required.

Instructor Check: _____

Floor

Side Wall Frame

Front and Rear Wall Frame

Roy Gerdes
Santa Rita High School
Tucson, Arizona

Permission granted to reproduce for educational use only.

Exercise 14-1
Concrete and Masonry Assignment

Name _____ Date _____ Score _____

Objectives
- To measure form material accurately and construct the form for a small concrete slab.
- To mix concrete to proper ratios and make a slump test.
- To finish placed concrete to a specified surface.

Procedure
1. Students will work in teams of two or three in completing this assignment. Each team member will be equally responsible for completing the work.
2. Select 2 × 4 lumber from stock.
3. Cut pieces for a rectangular form with inside dimensions measuring 2′ × 4′ × 3 1/2″ deep.
4. Mix enough concrete to fill the form using a cement-sand-coarse aggregate ratio of 1:1 3/4:2. Coarse aggregate should be no larger than 1 1/2″. Use air-entrained concrete. Add water until mixture is plastic.
5. Make a slump test and record the results.
6. Pour the mixture into the form and strike off.
7. Using a groover, make grooves between all sections (see illustration).
8. Use an edger to round all outside edges. Leave the edger marks in the smooth troweled segment and keep all edges the same size.
9. Finish all surfaces according to the illustration.

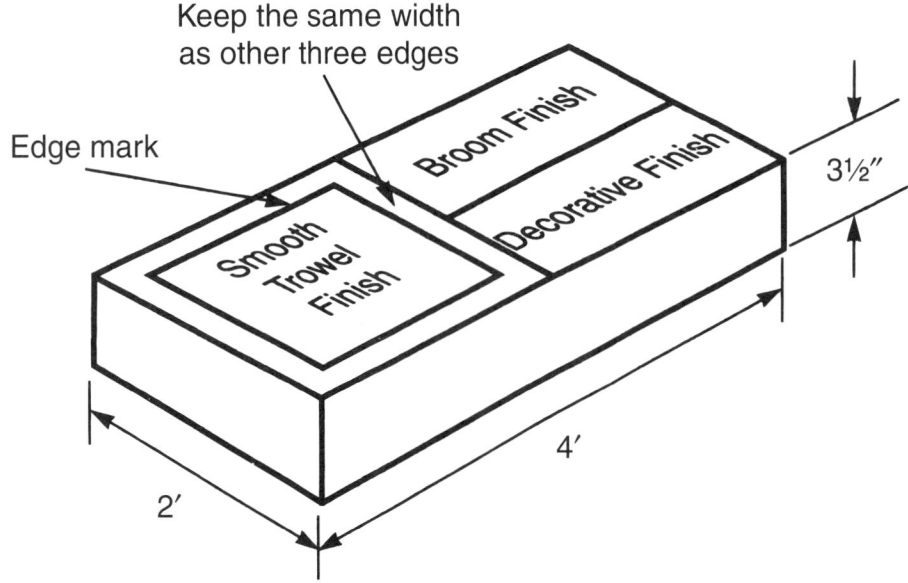

Jim Geise
Rushville Consolidated High School
Rushville, Indiana

Exercise 14-2
Block Wall Setup

Name _____ Date _____ Score _____

Objectives
- To use a chalk line for layout work.
- To use the 6-8-10 method to establish square corners of a layout.
- To learn to plan ahead for block lengths.
- To learn to allow for mortar joints.

Procedure

1. Using a chalk line and a tape measure, lay out a footing on the shop floor for a cement block wall. The size is a 6' × 8' rectangle that will be seven courses high. When chalking your lines, be sure to extend them at least 1' past the corners so once the blocks are laid, you will be able to tell where the lines are. Use the 6-8-10 check method to keep your corners square.

    Instructor Check: _____

2. Check layout by placing unmortared blocks around your building lines. Form the corners by placing two blocks in each of the four corners. Begin filling in the space between the corners by placing blocks next to each other just as you would set them. Allow an even space between each block as though you were using the mortar. This is done to help you understand the spacing that is needed between the blocks to keep the joints even and to come out on the correct dimensions of the wall. When the first course is laid down, have your instructor check your work.

    Instructor Check: _____

3. When the first course is complete, build up only the corners to seven courses high. You must keep them spaced evenly for mortar joints and also plumb on the outside. (You will learn how to keep them level when you start to use mortar in the joints.) When you have completed building up the corners, have your instructor check your work.

    Instructor Check: _____

Roy Gerdes
Santa Rita High School
Tucson, Arizona

Building Materials

Objectives

After studying this chapter, students will be able to:
- Describe the hardwood and softwood classifications.
- Define moisture content (M.C. and E.M.C.).
- Identify common defects in lumber.
- Define lumber grading terms.
- Calculate lumber sizes according to established industry standards.
- Explain plywood, hardboard, and particleboard grades and uses.
- Identify nail types and sizing units.
- List precautions to observe while working with treated lumber.
- Identify types of engineered lumber and list their uses and advantages.
- Discuss the uses of metal structural materials and describe their advantages/disadvantages.
- Identify a variety of metal framing connectors and indicate where each is used.

Instructional Materials

Text: Pages 17–58
  Technical Vocabulary, page 17
  Test Your Knowledge, page 55
  Curricular Connections, page 55
  Outside Assignments, page 56
Workbook: Pages 5–10
Instructor's Resource:
  Reproducible masters:
    RM 1-1 *Basic House Parts*
    RM 1-2 *Typical Grade Stamps*
    RM 1-3A *Nail Types*
    RM 1-3B *Nail Types*
    RM 1-4 *Nail Sizes*
    RM 1-5A *Framing Connectors and Ties*
    RM 1-5B *Framing Connectors and Ties*
  Transparencies (binder/CD only):
    CT 1-1 *Reading a Typical Plywood Trademark*
  Chapter Quiz

Instructional Concepts and Student Learning Experiences

This section provides teaching suggestions and strategies for using the textbook, workbook, and instructor's resources. Information and teaching suggestions should be tailored to fit the needs of the curriculum. The trade-related math concepts can be integrated into the chapter presentation or used as a follow-up at the conclusion of the chapter.

Trade-Related Math

1. The board foot is the standard unit of measure for lumber. One board foot is equivalent to a piece of lumber measuring 1″ thick by 12″ square. To calculate board feet, use the following formula:

   Bd. ft. = No. pcs. × T × W × L / 12

   Note that T and W are the nominal thickness and width in inches, while L is the length of the board in feet.

Lumber

1. Identify types of materials that are considered to be lumber. Also identify materials that are not considered to be lumber. Have different types of materials available for student inspection. Ask them to identify each.

Wood Structure and Growth

1. Using a cross-sectional piece of a log, ask students to identify the following parts and their purpose(s): heartwood, sapwood, pith, wood rays, annular rings, wood rays, cambium, and bark.
2. Discuss the growth of a tree. Explain how the parts of the tree must interact for proper growth.

Types of Wood

1. List the differences between hardwood and softwood. Stress that the physical hardness of a wood does not necessarily indicate

whether a wood is classified as a hardwood or softwood.
2. Using the full-color wood samples at the end of Chapter 1 of the text, have students identify the wood by color. Discuss other means for identifying wood, such as weight and material properties.
3. Using unlabeled wood specimens, have students identify various types of wood. Ask them to list the criteria that they used to determine the type of wood.

Cutting Methods
1. Discuss the methods of cutting lumber at a sawmill, including plain-sawed (softwoods) and quarter-sawed (hardwoods). List the advantages and disadvantages of each type of cutting.

Moisture Content and Shrinkage
1. Describe the method used to determine the moisture content of wood.
2. If an oven is available, demonstrate the procedure for determining moisture content outlined in the text. Use various specimens of wood to conduct the demonstration.
3. Have the students define the term *equilibrium moisture content*. Cite examples where the relative humidity of the air affects the carpentry trade. Identify parts of the country where more or less humidity can be expected.
4. Using reproducible master RM 1-1 *Basic House Parts*, have students identify parts of the house where particular attention must be paid to the moisture content of lumber.

Seasoning Lumber
1. Identify the primary means of seasoning lumber: air drying and kiln drying. Discuss the type of preparation necessary before lumber can be seasoned.
2. Review the procedure for determining moisture content by drying a sample in an oven.
3. Identify the two basic types of moisture meters. If possible, demonstrate the use of a moisture meter. Allow students to determine the moisture content of various wood samples.

Lumber Defects
1. Discuss the problems associated with wood defects in lumber, including loss of strength, durability, and usefulness.
2. Display several pieces of lumber that have various wood defects. Have students identify the defects and list the causes. Stress the importance of using good-quality lumber on a construction project.

Softwood Grades
1. Identify the principal organizations involved in grading lumber, including the American Lumber Standards Committee, Western Wood Products Association, Southern Forest Products Association, and California Redwood Association.
2. Using the charts in text Figure 1-15 and reproducible master RM 1-2 *Typical Grade Stamps*, discuss the various grades of softwood lumber.
3. Obtain price lists from a local lumberyard. Compare the costs of the different grades of softwood lumber. Stress the importance of obtaining good-quality lumber for a construction project, but balancing construction costs versus lumber quality.

Hardwood Grades
1. Identify the three major classifications of hardwood lumber: FAS, selects, and No. 1 common. Obtain samples of the different grades and discuss the methods used to grade the lumber. Reproducible master RM 1-2 *Typical Grade Stamps* may also be used to enhance the discussion.

Lumber Stress Values
1. Discuss the means for assigning lumber stress values.

Lumber Sizes
1. Review the charts in text Figure 1-16, stressing the difference between nominal and dressed sizes. List the various nominal sizes of lumber and have students identify the respective dressed sizes.

Figuring Board Footage
1. Define the term *board foot*. Discuss how board feet are determined.
2. Select several pieces of lumber with different measurements and label each A, B, C, and so on. Have students work in pairs to determine the number of board feet in each piece.

Metric Lumber Measure
1. Review the table in text Figure 1-18 regarding metric lumber sizes. Refer to Appendix B, **Technical Information** in the text for additional inch to millimeter conversions used in carpentry.

Panel Materials
1. Display a variety of panel materials, including plywood (both hardwood and softwood), hardboard, particleboard, waferboard, and oriented strand board. Have students determine the composition and construction of each.
2. Have students identify the parts of plywood, including the plies, crossbands, faces, and core. Discuss the differences between exterior and interior plywood.
3. Identify the common thicknesses of plywood and the possible uses of each thickness.
4. Using Figure 1-21, discuss the groups of softwood plywood panels that are available. Have the students list the species that fit into each group.
5. Discuss the various plywood veneer grades. Ask students to list applications for the various veneer grades. Once again, stress the importance of using good-quality materials in construction, but not to use material that is too high of a grade for the application.
6. Identify the components of a typical grade-trademark for plywood. Using hypothetical information, have the students place the information in the correct position in the grade-trademark using a template that you have drawn on the chalkboard.
7. Discuss the term *exposure durability* classification. Describe how this classification is important in determining the correct type of plywood for a construction project.
8. Discuss the differences between softwood plywood and hardwood plywood grading. Describe how hardwood plywood grades are determined.
9. Using specimens of softwood and hardwood plywood, compare and contrast the construction of each type.

Composite Board
1. Discuss the differences between plywood and composite board. Have students cite different types of composite board.
2. Differentiate between the construction of hardboard, particleboard, waferboard, and oriented strand board. Have students cite applications of each type.
3. Obtain samples of different types of composite board. Have students identify each type.

Wood Treatments
1. Identify different types of wood treatments that are on the market. Determine whether the wood treatments can be classified as waterborne, oilborne, or creosote.

Handling and Storing
1. Stress the importance of proper handling and storage of building materials. Discuss the steps that should be taken for the storage of lumber, panel materials, and interior and exterior finish materials.
2. Discuss precautions for handling of treated lumber.

Engineered Woods
1. Display samples of engineered lumber. Discuss the makeup, applications, and advantages of the samples you have displayed.

Nonwood Materials
1. Identify various types of nonwood materials that are used in building construction, including structural steel members, metal lath, wallboard and sheathing, shingles, fasteners, flashing, caulking materials, and adhesives.
2. Cite recent developments of materials in the construction trades. Discuss the types of materials that were originally developed for the commercial trades and are now being used in residential construction, such as metal structural members. Have examples on hand for inspection.
3. Using reproducible masters RM 1-3A and RM 1-3B *Nail Types*, discuss different nail types used in construction. Discuss the similarities and differences between the types.
4. Obtain a variety of nails and have students identify each type. Include examples of fasteners used with pneumatic nailers and staplers. Have students cite applications of each type of nail.
5. Using reproducible master RM 1-4 *Nail Sizes*, discuss the size system used for nails.

6. Explain the differences between round, oval, and flat head screws. Identify the dimensions that are used to size screws.
7. Have students list various types of adhesives that are used in the carpentry field, including polyvinyl resin emulsion adhesive, urea-formaldehyde resin glue, contact cement, and casein glue. Identify similarities and differences between the types.
8. Discuss the methods for applying adhesives and mastics.
9. Using reproducible masters RM 1-5A and RM 1-5B *Framing Connectors and Ties*, discuss how metal connectors can strengthen framing parts and speed up construction.

Chapter Review

1. Review the chapter objectives. Be sure that the students are fully competent in the task identified by each objective.
2. Review the terms in the *Technical Vocabulary* section and make certain students are clear on each definition.
3. Assign the *Test Your Knowledge* questions, *Curricular Connections,* and *Outside Assignments* for Chapter 1 of the text. Review the answers to test questions in class. Also, have students report on the *Curricular Connections* and *Outside Assignments* activities as appropriate.
4. Assign Chapter 1 of the workbook. Review the answers in class.

Evaluation

This chapter provides three methods for evaluating student performance. Students should complete the *Test Your Knowledge* section using the book as reference. Students should also be allowed to use the book for reference when completing the workbook material. Use the Chapter 1 Quiz in the instructor's resources for in-class evaluation. Correct the quizzes, return them to the students, and review the quiz questions in group discussion.

Answers to Test Your Knowledge
Text Page 55

1. lignin
2. cambium
3. willow
4. edge-grained
5. 15%
6. 30%
7. equilibrium
8. 1 1/2
9. B and better
10. FAS (firsts and seconds)
11. 128 bd. ft.
12. Instances where plywood may be exposed to the weather for an extended period before being protected.
13. Span rating is the maximum recommended center-to-center distance in inches between the supports when the long dimension of the panel is at right angles to the supports.
14. They harden as the wood absorbs their moisture. Under heat they will soften. They should not be used in constructions where the temperature may rise above 165°F (75°C).
15. They absorb moisture from the air or wood and expand (foam) as they set up.

Answers to Workbook Questions
Pages 5–10

1. lignin
2. A. heartwood
   B. sapwood
   C. wood rays
   D. cambium
   E. bark
   F. annular rings
3. spring; summer
4. conifers
5. ash, basswood, birch, willow
6. eastern red cedar
7. D. edge-grained
8. D. equilibrium
9. 13%
10. C. 30%
11. B. 8%
12. oven; electronic moisture meter
13. A. 2
    B. 1
    C. 3
    D. 4
14. splits; checks; shakes
15. A. crook
    B. bow
    C. twist or wind

16. dimension
17. B and better, or supreme
18. FAS
19. A. nominal width.
    B. dressed width.
20. A. 7 1/4"
21. 832
22. composite panel
23. B. Southern pine.
24. Span rating
25. A. Panel grade.
    B. Span rating.
    C. Exposure durability classification.
    D. Mill number.
26. B. 40 lb.
27. B. 5/16"
28. False.
29. open-web truss
30. A. common
    B. box
    C. casing
    D. finish
31. C. 3 1/2"
32. A. round
    B. oval
    C. flat
33. B. The glue has a high resistance to moisture.
34. more
35. A. contact cement

Answers to Chapter Quiz

1. False.
2. True.
3. False.
4. False.
5. True.
6. C. plain-sawed
7. D. Particleboard; G. Waferwood.
8. D. softwood
9. C. 3.33
10. B. Cement, sand, gravel, and water.
11. B
12. C
13. A
14. more
15. Open time

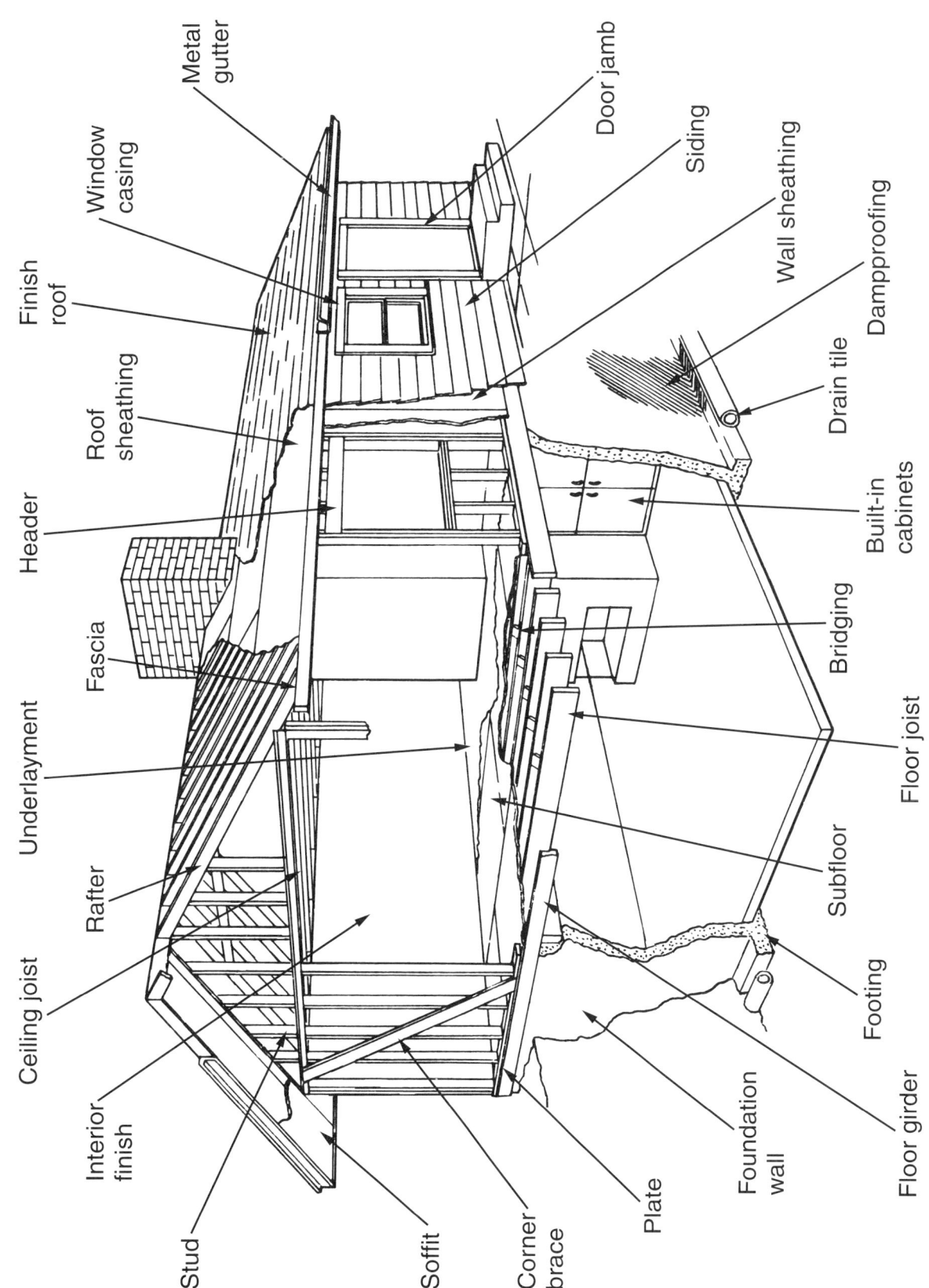

Typical Grade Stamps

Dimension Grades

Commons

Glued Products

Machine Stress-Rated Products

Finish & Select Grades

Finish Grade—Graded Under WCLIB Rules

Cedar Grades

Decking

Species Identification

Some WWPA grade stamps identify an individual western lumber species.

- Douglas Fir
- Western Red Cedar
- Douglas Fir South*
- Incense Cedar
- Englemann Spruce
- Sugar Pine
- Ponderosa Pine
- Idaho White Pine

*Lumber manufactured from Douglas fir grown in Arizona, Colorado, New Mexico and Utah.

A number of western lumber species have similar performance properties and are marketed with a common species designation.

- DOUG. FIR-L — Douglas Fir and Larch
- HEM FIR — California Red Fir, Grand Fir, Noble Fir, Pacific silver Fir, White Fir, and Western Hemlock
- PP SP — Ponderosa Pine and Sugar Pine
- WESTERN CEDAR — Incense and Western Red Cedar
- ES-AF — Engelmann Spruce and Alpine Fir

Because of timber stand composition, some mills market additional species combinations.

- ES LP — Engelmann Spruce, Lodgepole Pine
- WESTERN WOODS — Western Woods (any combination of western softwood species except redwood)
- WW — White Woods (Engelmann Spruce and true firs, any hemlocks, and pines)
- PP-LP — Ponderosa Pine, Lodgepole Pine
- ES-AF-LP — Engelmann Spruce-Alpine Fir-Lodgepole Pine

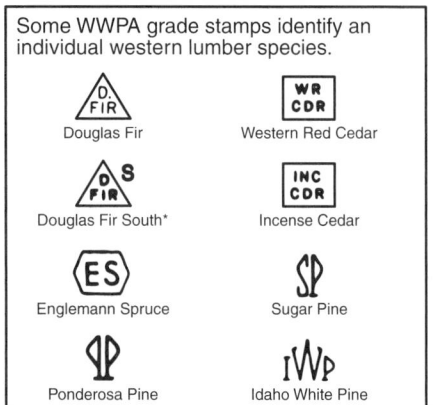

RM 1-2

Permission granted to reproduce for educational use only.
Copyright by Goodheart-Willcox Co., Inc.
Western Wood Products Association

Nail Types

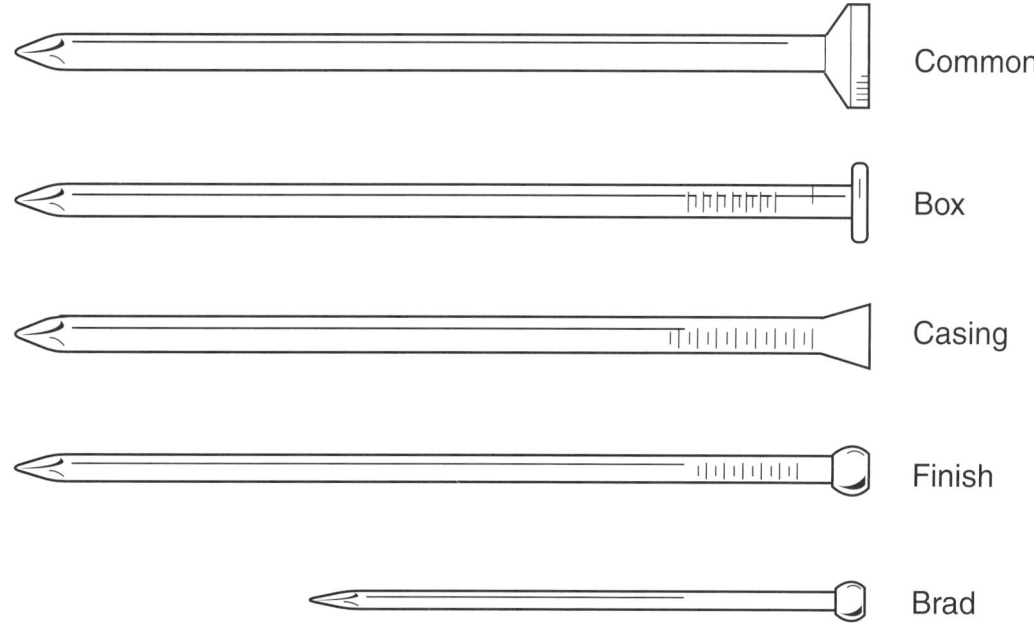

RM 1-3A

Nail Types

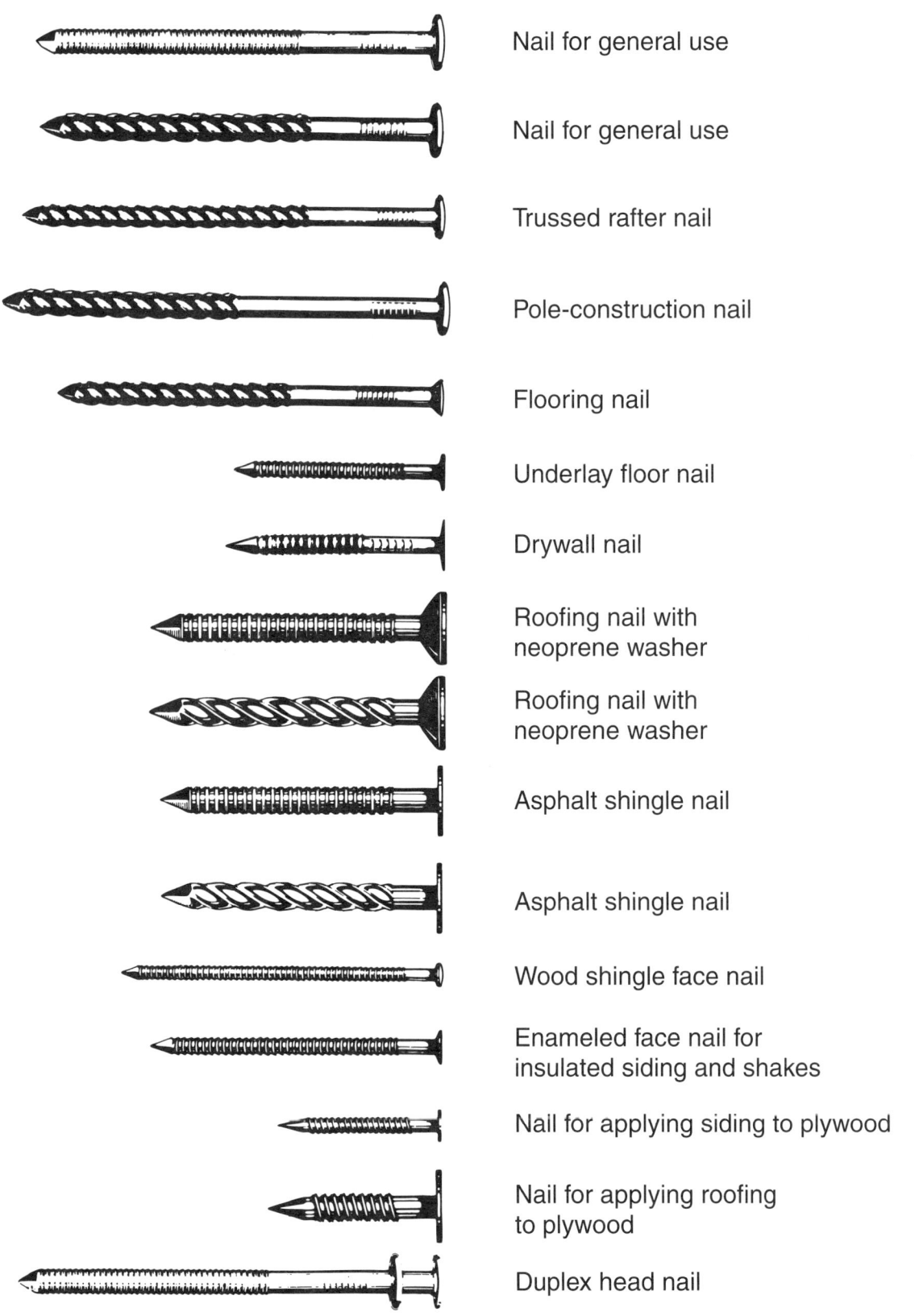

Nail Sizes

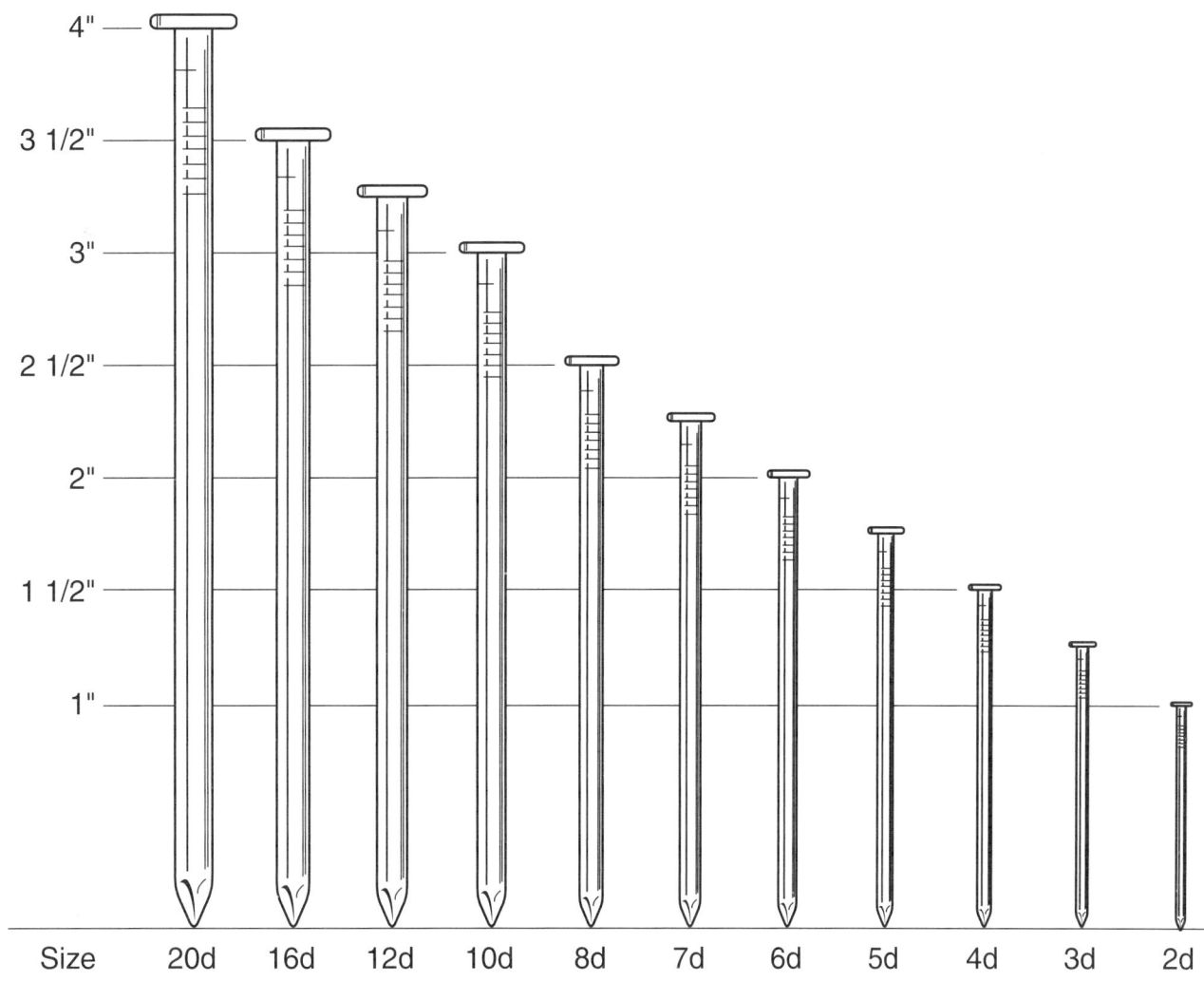

RM 1-4

Framing Connectors and Ties

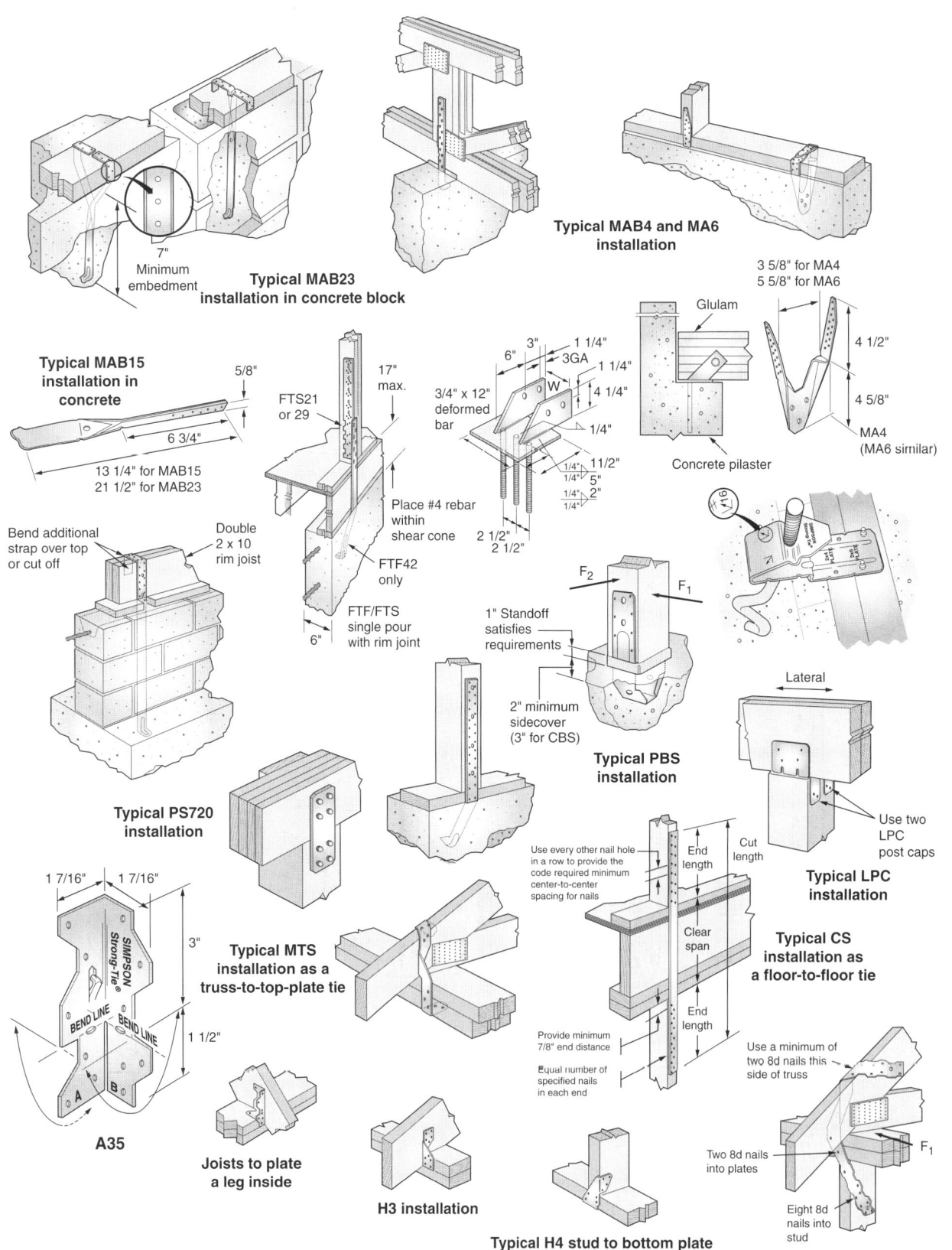

Framing Connectors and Ties

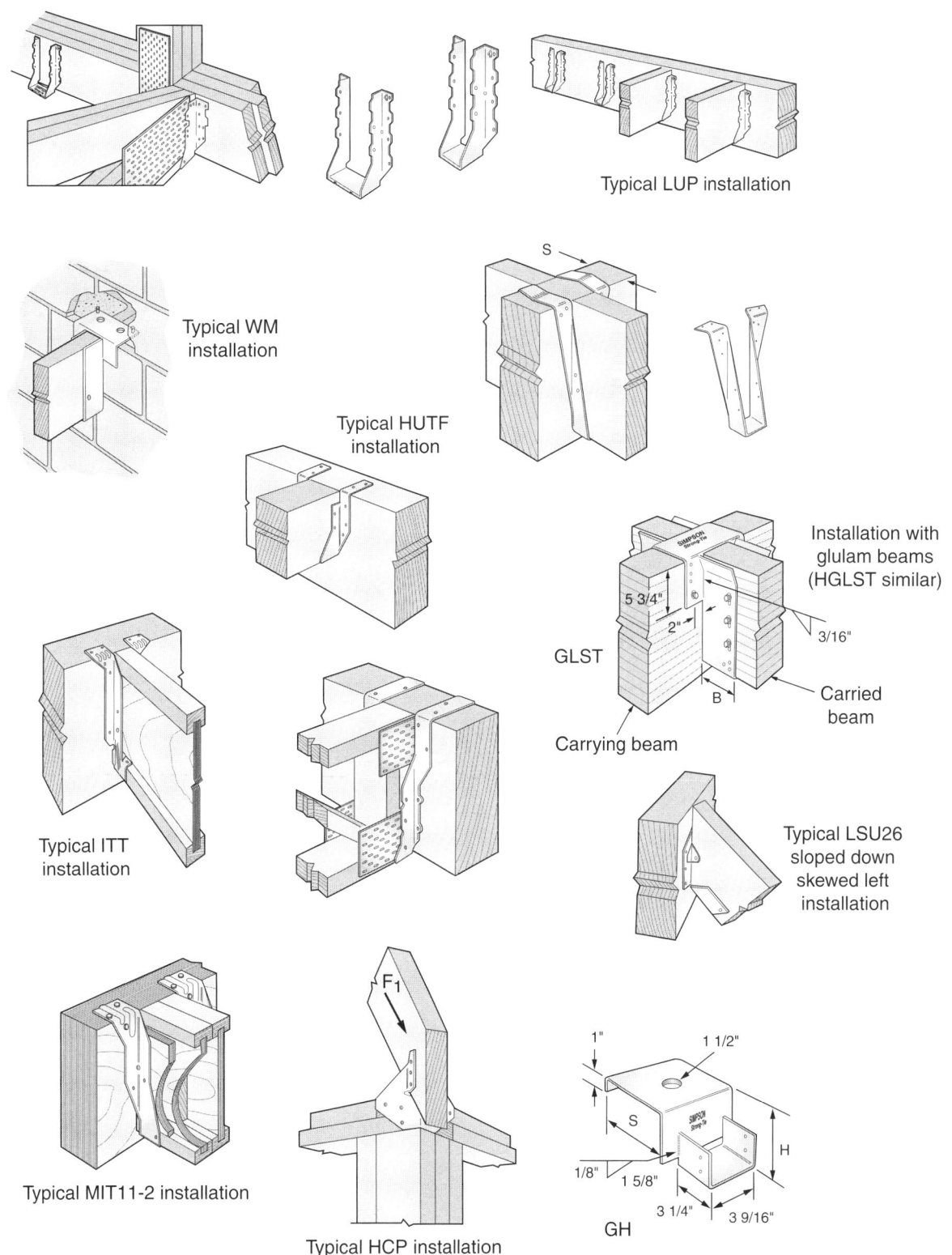

Chapter 1 Quiz
Building Materials

Name _____ Date _____ Score _____

True-False
Circle T if the answer is true or F if the answer is false.

T F 1. Knots are separations along the grain and between the annular growth rings.

T F 2. FAS is the best grade of hardwood lumber.

T F 3. Plywood always contains an even number of layers.

T F 4. Nail size is measured in a unit called the *penny,* which is abbreviated with the lower-case letter p.

T F 5. Hardboard is made of refined wood fibers, pressed together to form a hard, dense material.

Multiple Choice
Choose the answer that correctly completes the statement. Write the corresponding letter in the space provided.

_____ 6. Hardwood lumber that is cut so the annular rings form an angle less than 45° with the surface is called _____ lumber.
  A. edge-grained
  B. quarter-sawed
  C. plain-sawed
  D. flat-grained

_____ 7. Which of the following are *not* included in the group known as engineered lumber?
  A. Laminated-veneer lumber.
  B. Wood I-beams.
  C. Glulams.
  D. Particleboard.
  E. Open-web truss.
  F. Parallel-strand lumber.
  G. Waferwood.
  H. Laminated-strand lumber.

_____ 8. Basic classifications of _____ grading include boards, dimension, and timbers.
  A. hardwood plywood
  B. softwood plywood
  C. hardwood
  D. softwood

_____ 9. A piece of stock measuring 1″ × 10″ × 4′ contains _____ board feet.
   A. 40
   B. .83
   C. 3.33
   D. 4

_____ 10. Concrete is a combination of:
   A. Cement, sand, and water.
   B. Cement, sand, gravel, and water.
   C. Cement, gravel, and water.
   D. Sand, gravel, and water.

Identification
Identify the following types of warp.

_____ 11. Twist.

_____ 12. Bow.

_____ 13. Crook.

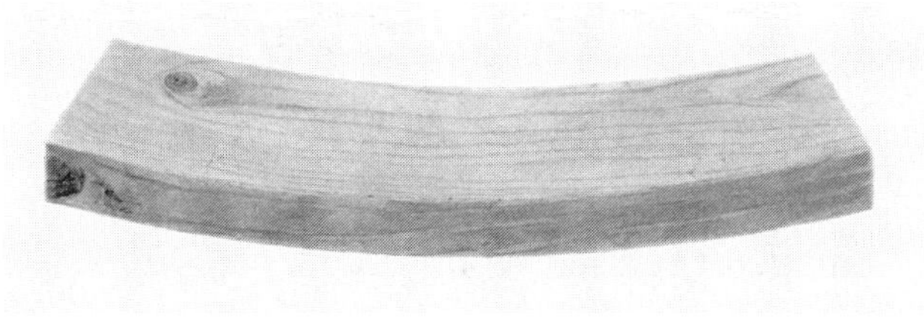

A

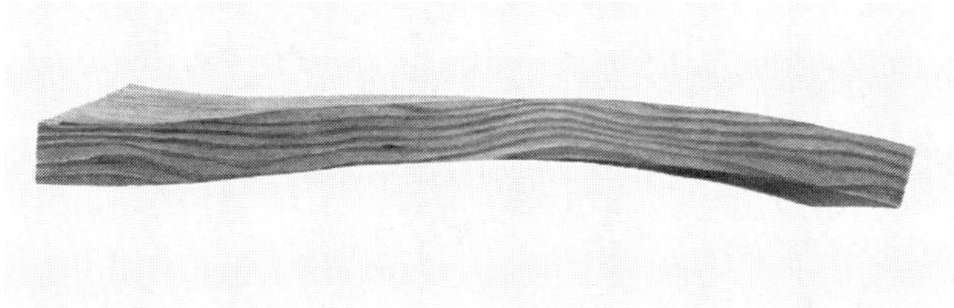

B

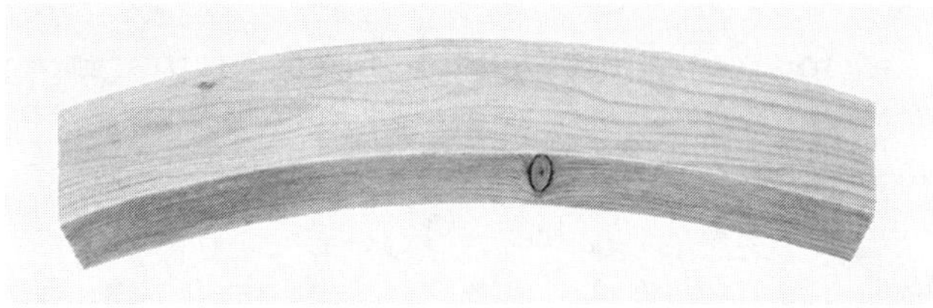

C

Completion
Write the answer that correctly completes the statement in the space provided.

_____ 14. Thermoset adhesives are (*more, less*) resistant to water and heat than polyvinyl adhesives.

_____ 15. _____ is the time elapsed from the spreading of adhesive and when parts must be clamped.

2 The Carpenter's Workplace

Objectives

After studying this chapter, students will be able to:
- Describe the qualities employers value in a beginning carpenter.
- List advantages of maintaining a proper relationship with other members of the crew.
- List and describe clothing safety as it applies to carpenters.
- List other personal safety equipment recommended for carpenters to use.
- Cite safety measures relating to hand and power tools.
- Explain housekeeping measures that promote safe working conditions.
- List safety measures relating to shoring and scaffolding.
- Describe proper methods of lifting and carrying to avoid personal injury.
- Describe the classes of fires.

Instructional Materials

Text: Pages 59-72
  Technical Vocabulary, page 59
  Test Your Knowledge, page 72
  Curricular Connections, page 72
  Outside Assignments, page 72
Workbook: Pages 11–12
Instructor's Resource:
  Reproducible masters:
    RM 2-1 *Safety: Fall Protection*
    RM 2-2 *Traits and Skills Builders Value Most in Apprentices*
  Transparencies (binder/CD only):
    CT 2-1 *Top Employer Expectations for Beginning Carpenters*
    CT 2-2 *General Safety Rule*
    CT 2-3 *Fire Extinguishers and Fire Classifications*
  Chapter Quiz

Instructional Concepts and Student Learning Experiences

This section provides teaching suggestions and strategies for using the textbook, workbook, and instructor's resources. Information and teaching suggestions should be tailored to fit the needs of the curriculum. The trade-related math concepts can be integrated into the chapter presentation or used as a follow-up at the conclusion of the chapter.

Trade-Related Math

1. It is a fact that objects in a free fall accelerate at the rate of 32 feet per second for each second elapsed from their resting height to the ground. For example, if a hammer dropped from the roof of a two-story building takes six seconds to reach the ground, how fast will it be falling at the point of impact? The answer may be found by adding:

   32 + 32 + 32 + 32 + 32 + 32 = 192 ft./sec

   or by multiplying:

   32 × 6 = 192 ft./sec

2. If a carpenter is paid at the rate of $28 per hour and works eight hours each day for five days, what is the gross amount of the carpenter's pay for the week?
   Gross amount of pay = $28 × 8 × 5 = $1120

Conduct on the Job

1. Stress the importance of developing good reading and comprehension skills in advancing on the job.
2. Review reproducible master RM 2-2 *Traits and Skills Builders Value Most in Apprentices* with your students. Cite comments from contractors of your own acquaintance as proof of desired qualities for apprentice carpenters.
3. Invite a local builder to address your class on the traits he or she values in an apprentice.

4. Review the definition of sexual harassment as it relates to the workplace and relationship with other workers.

Clothing
1. Discuss the reasons for special clothing requirements and the possible consequences of ignoring these rules.
2. Have students evaluate their fellow students' clothing with respect to safety rules.
3. Demonstrate a hard hat's effectiveness in preventing injury from falling objects by dropping a tool on it from different heights.

Personal Protective Equipment
1. Display a pair of approved safety glasses. Discuss the properties and effectiveness of safety glasses. Suggest the types of flying objects that carpenters might encounter while working.
2. Discuss the effectiveness of reinforced-toe safety shoes in preventing crushing injuries.
3. Display a pair of gloves that could be worn to avoid injuries from rough materials.

Hand and Power Tool Safety
1. Set up a demonstration to show the merits of using tools with sharp blades versus dull blades.
2. Demonstrate the proper way to use various hand tools common to the carpentry trade.
3. Demonstrate the safe and proper method of operating various power tools.
4. Refer students to the safety sections of Chapter 5. Suggest that they study these rules in preparation for later use of the power tools.

Good Housekeeping
1. Review the rules of good housekeeping on the job site. Point out the dangerous consequences of stumbling over or slipping on debris.
2. If possible, visit a construction site and have students note any housekeeping problems. Ask students to write down their evaluation of the job site and how problems might be remedied. In the classroom, discuss the findings and solutions.

Excavations
1. Explain the dangers of working in excavations that are not properly sloped or shored up.
2. Show photos of properly sloped or shored excavations.

Scaffolds and Ladders
1. Explain the factor of four to students and show pictures of appropriate, approved scaffolds.
2. Using reproducible master RM 2-1 *Safety: Fall Protection*, discuss the OSHA regulations regarding avoidance of falls and the safeguards required on scaffolds.
3. When on a job site, make sure students check the safety of any scaffolds and ladders used.
4. Refer to Chapter 31 **Scaffolds and Ladders** and have students review the safety information it contains.

Falling Objects
1. Stress the need for good housekeeping on scaffolds and on upper levels of buildings.
2. Demonstrate the force of a falling object and suggest the injury that could result from being struck.
3. Stress the need for vigilance in walking underneath carpenters at work on an upper level.

Handling Pressure-Treated Lumber
1. Discuss the toxic properties of waterborne and oilborne preservatives used on lumber.
2. Demonstrate the proper safeguards to use in working with pressure-treated lumber.

Lifting and Carrying
1. Demonstrate the proper method for lifting and carrying heavy loads.
2. Suggest that assistance should be sought for lifting and carrying very heavy objects.
3. Have students practice proper lifting and carrying techniques.

Fire Protection
1. Review the types of fires. Relate this review to the proper extinguisher to be used for each type of fire. Demonstrate the use of each type.
2. Explain the relationship of fire prevention to good housekeeping.
3. Show examples of approved containers for storing of combustible materials.
4. Make certain that students know the locations of fire extinguishers and that they know how to use them.

First Aid
1. Maintain a fully-equipped first aid kit. Drill students on basic first aid procedures.
2. Keep the kit available at all times and make certain students know its location.

Chapter Review
1. Review the chapter objectives. Be sure that the students are fully competent in the task identified by each objective.
2. Review the terms in the *Technical Vocabulary* section and make certain students are clear on each definition.
3. Assign the *Test Your Knowledge* questions, *Curricular Connections*, and *Outside Assignments* for Chapter 2 of the text. Review the answers to test questions in class. Also, have students report on the *Curricular Connections* and *Outside Assignments* activities as appropriate.
4. Assign Chapter 2 of the workbook. Review the answers in class.

Evaluation
This chapter provides three methods for evaluating student performance. Students should complete the *Test Your Knowledge* section using the book as reference. Students should also be allowed to use the book for reference when completing the workbook material. Use the Chapter 2 Quiz in the instructor's resources for in-class evaluation. Correct the quizzes, return them to the students, and review the quiz questions in group discussion.

Answers to Test Your Knowledge
Text Page 72
1. B. Have respect for customers and owners
2. A. Work is more likely to get done on time;
   B. It promotes good attitudes among workers.
3. B. Trousers or overalls without cuffs.
4. Whenever work involves even the slightest hazard to the eyes.
5. C. Wherever there is a danger of falling objects.
6. C. 2500 lb.
7. True.
8. D. stored in panels or chests
9. four
10. turn or twist
11. False

Answers to Workbook Questions
Pages 11-12
1. E. All of the above.
2. True.
3. VII
4. True.
5. knowledge; skill; care; concern
6. leather
7. C. 1/8" diameter ball dropped from 50"
8. B. 80 lb. ball; 5'
9. neatness
10. True.
11. B. day
12. 200; 42"
13. B. special
14. C. Class C
15. A. Wearing safety glasses.
    B. Wearing a hard hat.
    C. Using push sticks.
    D. Using a guard over the blade.

Answers to Chapter Quiz
1. False.
2. True.
3. False.
4. True.
5. False.
6. False.
7. C. When the ground is cracked or a cave-in is likely to occur.
8. A. turn or twist
9. flammable
10. Housekeeping

Safety: Fall Protection

OSHA's fall protection regulations cover seven different job site areas.

Floor Framing	Do not stand on sill or top plates while placing joists or floor trusses. Work from the ground, ladders, or sawhorse staging.
Subfloor	Install the first course from the ground, ladders, or staging, then work from the deck. Paint a warning line six feet from the edges that are unprotected.
Working on Decks	Workers not doing leading-edge work (including those cutting material) must stay six feet in from the edges or other fall hazards.
Working on Decks	Complete as much work as possible away from the edge of the deck. Try to store materials within the six foot warning perimeter.
Trussing and Rafter Framing	Set first two trusses or rafters from ladders or staging. Brace trusses and rafters before using them for support. If they cannot safely work from staging, workers can then work from the top plate using stabilized roof framing for support.
Roof Sheathing	Install bottom course of sheathing while standing in the truss webs. Then, install slide guards at least 4" high across the roof at intervals 13'. Steeper roofs require higher guards and closer intervals.
Guardrails and Openings	Block floor and wall openings with guardrails. Set top rail of guard 42" off the subfloor and a midrail at around 21". Install a toe guard on the deck. Window openings lower than 39" also require a rail.

RM 2-1

Traits and Skills Builders Value Most in Apprentices

Skills/Behaviors Contractors Value Most in Beginning Carpenters		
Name of skill or behavior	Value (5 = crucial; 4 & 3 important)	Type
Have respect for customers and owners	4.77	Affective
Able to measure material accurately	4.73	Cognitive
Carries basic tools (pencil, tape, knife)	4.68	Affective
Notify superior when unable to report for work due to personal emergency	4.62	Affective
Cooperate with coworkers	4.59	Affective
Observe safety rules	4.58	Affective
Use safe lifting/carrying techniques	4.49	Affective
Take proper care of power tools	4.49	Affective
Follow company rules/procedures	4.49	Affective
Operate skilsaw	4.49	Psychomotor
Report for work properly rested/ready to work	4.49	Affective
Use leveling instruments	4.25	Cognitive
Keep work area clean	4.24	Affective
Attend to details	4.23	Affective
Operate pneumatic nailer	4.07	Psychomotor
Exhibit fall protection procedures	4.04	Cognitive
Use the right nail for the application	3.97	Cognitive
Report for work 10 or more minutes early	3.91	Affective
Wear suitable clothing	3.88	Affective
Recognize fire hazards	3.87	Cognitive
Perform first aid	3.86	Psychomotor
Volunteer for undesirable jobs	3.81	Affective
Record number of hours on the job	3.80	Cognitive
Absent from work no more than four days per year	3.80	Affective
Care for electrical extension cords	3.75	Affective
Toe-nail with minimum splitting of lumber	3.70	Psychomotor
Read blueprints	3.65	Cognitive
Operate screw gun	3.62	Psychomotor
Use telephone etiquette	3.54	Affective
Apply adhesives	3.51	Psychomotor
Scale dimensions from a blueprint	3.48	Cognitive
Operate powder-actuated tool	3.44	Psychomotor
Use job site sanitation facilities	3.41	Affective
Apply caulk	3.41	Psychomotor
Install door hardware	3.35	Psychomotor
Install doors	3.25	Psychomotor
Install moulding	3.17	Psychomotor
Operate radial arm saw	3.17	Psychomotor
Establish building lines	3.15	Cognitive
Install cabinets	3.13	Psychomotor
Lay out stairways	3.07	Cognitive
Install metal studs	3.01	Psychomotor

RM 2-2

Permission granted to reproduce for educational use only.   Copyright by Goodheart-Willcox Co., Inc.

Chapter 2 Quiz
General Safety Rules

Name _____ Date _____ Score _____

True-False
Circle T if the answer is true or F if the answer is false.

T   F   1. Skill in using hand and power tools is the most important trait for a beginning carpenter.

T   F   2. A willingness to follow the safety rules is a fundamental of safely working on the job site.

T   F   3. It is permissible and safe to wear lightweight canvas shoes when doing carpentry work in a very warm climate.

T   F   4. Class C fires are caused by electrical wiring and equipment.

T   F   5. On arriving at the job site, it is good practice to set out all of your tools so they will be close at hand. This makes the carpenter safer and more productive.

T   F   6. It is not advisable to keep a first aid kit on the job site because of dirt, dust, and generally unsanitary conditions.

Multiple Choice
Choose the answer that correctly completes the statement. Write the corresponding letter in the space provided.

_____   7. Under which conditions is shoring required for excavating?
   A. When the hole is more than 5' deep.
   B. If the sides are less than the angle of repose of the material being excavated.
   C. When the ground is cracked or a cave-in is likely to occur.
   D. Where soil is rain-soaked.

_____   8. When carrying a heavy load, do not _____ your body, rather make adjustments in position by shifting your feet.
   A. turn or twist
   B. bend
   C. straighten
   D. None of the above.

Completion

Write the answer that correctly completes the statement in the space provided.

_____ 9. Always keep containers of _____ materials closed when not in use.

_____ 10. _____ refers to the neatness and good order of the construction site.

3 Plans, Specifications, and Codes

After studying this chapter, students will be able to:
- Identify the elements commonly included in a set of house plans.
- Demonstrate the use of scale in architectural drawings.
- Identify architectural symbols.
- Explain the use of building specifications.
- Summarize the concept of modular construction.
- Describe the application of building codes, standards, and permits.

Instructional Materials

Text: Pages 73–102
  Technical Vocabulary, page 73
  Test Your Knowledge, page 100
  Curricular Connections, page 100
  Outside Assignments, page 100
Workbook: Pages 13–18
Instructor's Resource:
  Reproducible masters:
    RM 3-1 *Architectural Symbols*
    RM 3-2 *Symbols for Openings*
    RM 3-3 *Appliance/Fixture Symbols*
  Transparencies (binder/CD only):
    CT 3-1 *Getting Measurements from Scaled Drawings*
  Procedure Checklist: *Reading a Set of Working Drawings*
  Chapter Quiz

Instructional Concepts and Student Learning Experiences

This section provides teaching suggestions and strategies for using the textbook, workbook, and instructor's resources. Information and teaching suggestions should be tailored to fit the needs of the curriculum. The trade-related math concepts can be integrated into the chapter presentation or used as a follow-up at the conclusion of the chapter.

Trade-Related Math

Foot and inch values are the most common units of measurement used in construction. In many instances, foot and inch values must be added or subtracted to obtain a final dimension. When performing any type of calculation using foot and inch values, treat the foot value and inch value separately. Then, combine the results to obtain the final answer.

1. When adding, if the sum (result) of the inch value computation is more than 12″, convert the sum to a foot value by dividing by 12 and using the remainder as the new inch value. For example:

   6′-9″ + 2′-4″ + 1′-6″ = X

   $$\begin{array}{r} 6'\text{-}\ 9'' \\ 2'\text{-}\ 4'' \\ +\ 1'\text{-}\ 6'' \\ \hline 9'\text{-}19'' = 10'\text{-}7'' \end{array}$$

   X = 10′-7″

2. When subtracting foot and inch values, you may need to borrow 12″ (1′) from the left column. Then, subtract as you would any other whole numbers. For example:

   7′-6″ − 4′-9″ = X

   Since 9″ cannot be subtracted from 6″, 12″ is borrowed from the foot value. The 7′-6″ value is equal to 6′-18″. Now, subtract the two values.

   $$\begin{array}{r} 6'\text{-}18'' \\ -\ 4'\text{-}\ 9'' \\ \hline 2'\text{-}\ 9'' \end{array}$$

   X = 2′-9″

Set of Plans

1. Using the plans shown in the chapter or another complete set of plans, review the

primary drawings, including the plot plan, foundation plan, floor plans, elevations drawings, and mechanical and electrical layouts.
2. Discuss the reasons for scaling drawings for structures. Explain what notations such as 1″ = 1′-0″ represent on a plan. Discuss why a 1/4″ = 1′-0″ scale is commonly used for residential plans.
3. Review the purpose of a plot plan. Ask students to list the major components of the plan.
4. Using Figure 3-6 or another floor plan, reproducible master RM 3-1 *Architectural Symbols*, RM 3-2 *Symbols for Openings*, and RM 3-3 *Appliance/Fixture Symbols*, have students identify the symbols commonly used on floor plans. Discuss the importance of readily identifying and interpreting symbols in becoming a productive carpenter.
5. Have students develop a floor plan for a simple, one-story structure. Emphasize the use of appropriate symbols on the floor plan. Ask students to write a thorough description of the floor plan using only words. Discuss the advantages of using symbols on plans over a written description.
6. Using Figures 3-6 and 3-7 or another comparable floor plan and foundation plan, ask students to locate features that are common to both plans such as the stairs, building walls, and so on.
7. Review the elevation drawings shown in Figures 3-9 and 3-10 or another comparable set of elevations. Ask students to identify any symbols they recognize. Using reproducible master RM 3-1 *Architectural Symbols*, compare the symbols used on floor plans and elevations.
8. Describe the relationship between floor plans and elevations. Ask students to correlate features shown on the floor plan with the respective symbols on an elevation. Stress that features shown on an elevation will likely be located by dimensions given on a floor plan.
9. Using Figures 3-11 through 3-13, discuss the use of framing plans for a house. Ask students to describe how the placement of framing members is determined if framing plans are not included with the set of plans. Discuss where dimensions are found that can help determine the placement of the framing members if framing plans are not included.
10. Discuss the importance of using sections and detail drawings to provide additional information about the construction of a house. Using Figures 3-14 and 3-15 and reproducible master RM 3-1 *Architectural Symbols*, ask students to interpret the sections and details.
11. Using the set of plans that were used for the previous discussions, explain the importance of accurately reading and interpreting dimensions on a drawing. Stress that dimensions greater than one foot are usually shown in feet and inches, such as 1′-8″, rather than 20″.
12. Review the trade-related math concepts to illustrate the addition and subtraction of dimensions. Using the floor plan of a structure, add and/or subtract the overall dimensions with other feature dimensions to verify accuracy.
13. Review the items commonly found on a materials list, including quantity, name of the material, description, and size. Have students develop an abbreviated materials list for the simple, one-story structure they developed in item 5.

How to Scale a Drawing
1. Discuss the means for determining missing dimensions on a drawing, including using an architect's scale or a folding rule to scale a plan.
2. Hand out architect's scales to the class. Ask students to draw lines of varying lengths and measure each line using the 1/4″ = 1′-0″ and 1/8″ = 1′-0″ scales. Place the measurements next to each line. Have the students exchange their drawings with each other for verification.

Changing Plans
1. Explain the ramifications of changes made in plans.
2. Discuss possible scenarios that may occur if plans are changed without notifying other tradespeople.

Specifications
1. Explain the purpose of developing a list of specifications in addition to a set of plans. Have students list the headings generally

included in the specifications for a residential structure. Discuss the importance of having a thorough set of specifications.

Modular Construction
1. Discuss the concept of modular construction. Emphasize that many construction materials are based on the modular system, including plywood panels and concrete blocks. Explain the advantages of using modular construction.
2. Define the terms *minor module* and *major module*.
3. Discuss how the modular construction concept is applied in the metric system.

Building Codes
1. Describe the purpose of building codes. Obtain a copy of the local building code and discuss the importance of conforming to the code.
2. Secure copies of a variety of model codes including the International Building Code, BOCA Basic Building Code, ICBO Uniform Building Code, and SBBCI Standard Building Code. Have students locate similar items in the codes and compare the requirements of each code. Note: The International Code Council introduced the *International Residential Code for One- and Two-Family Dwellings* in 2000. This new model code was developed from the codes published by BOCA, ICBO, and SBCCI and is intended to replace the older codes. Although BOCA, ICBO, and SBCCI ceased to exist as separate organizations in 2002, their codes are still in use in a number of states and municipalities.
3. Assign a particular topic that is addressed in all of the major model codes. Ask students to research the topic using at least two of the model codes and the local building code as references.
4. Discuss the organizations and associations that play a key role in the development of model codes. Ask students to explain why they think these organizations or associations are involved in the development of standards.
5. Invite a local building inspector to discuss the process of obtaining a building permit in your community. Allow students to ask questions related to the building permit and inspection process.

Chapter Review
1. Review the chapter objectives. Be sure that the students are fully competent in the task identified by each objective.
2. Review the terms in the *Technical Vocabulary* section and make certain students are clear on each definition.
3. Assign the *Test Your Knowledge* questions, *Curricular Connections*, and *Outside Assignments* for Chapter 3 of the text. Review the answers to test questions in class. Also, have students report on the *Curricular Connections* and *Outside Assignments* activities as appropriate.
4. Assign Chapter 3 of the workbook. Review the answers in class.

Evaluation
This chapter provides four methods for evaluating student performance. Students should complete the Test Your Knowledge section using the book as reference. Students should also be allowed to use the book for reference when completing the workbook material. Use the Chapter 3 Quiz in the instructor's resources for in-class evaluation. Correct the quizzes, return them to the students, and review the quiz questions in group discussion. A procedure checklist is also provided.

Procedure Checklist
Using the procedure checklist *Reading a Set of Working Drawings*, have students identify symbols, perform math computations for missing dimensions, and interpret the working drawings of a residential structure.

Answers to Test Your Knowledge
Page 100
1. Plot plan; foundation or basement plan; floor plans; elevation drawings; drawings of electrical, plumbing, heating, and air conditioning layouts; section drawings; and detail drawings.

2. 1/4″ = 1′-0″
3. size
4. footprint of the building and its location on the building site
5. outside
6. cut by a vertical plane
7. distance
8. See Figures 3-21 to 3-23 in text.
9. architect's
10. specifications (or specs)
11. 4
12. Computer-aided drafting and design/computer-aided manufacturing
13. millimeters
14. True.
15. Usually, the contractor or building owner files a formal application with the appropriate local agency along with one or two sets of plans.
16. False.

Answers to Workbook Questions
Pages 13–18
1. A. 2 × 10, 2 × 8, 2 × 6
   B. 2 × 6
   C. 16″ O.C.
   D. 2 × 10
   E. collar ties
   F. 1 3/4″ × 11 7/8″ LVL beams
   G. 32″ O.C.
2. A. 28′-8″
   B. 6″–8″
   C. 15′-5″
   D. 20′-2″
   E. 9′-6″
   F. linoleum
   G. 2″ × 6″
   H. 16″ O.C.
   I. 20″ × 20″
   J. 1′-8″
   K. one
   L. 4″
   M. hardwood (oak)
3. A. wood
   B. brick
   C. stone
   D. concrete
   E. concrete block
   F. earth
   G. glass
4. 38′-2″
5. A. double hung window
   B. casement window
   C. sliding doors (exterior)
   D. bifold doors
   E. pocket sliding door
   F. arch
   G. bypass sliding door
   H. interior door
6. A. shower (built-in)
   B. lavatory (built-in)
   C. stool
   D. tub (recessed)
   E. refrigerator (free standing)
   F. built-in cooking top
   G. kitchen sink
   H. range
7. D. Number of painters to be used on the job.
8. Commerce; CS
9. owner
10. C. inspector

Answers to Chapter Quiz
1. False.
2. True.
3. True.
4. True.
5. False.
6. B. Floor plans
7. C. erasures
8. D. Room size.
9. B. 4″
10. F
11. A
12. D
13. B
14. C
15. E

Architectural Symbols

Material	Plan	Elevation	Section
Wood	Floor areas left blank	Siding; Panel	Framing; Finish
Brick	Face; Common	Face or common	Same as plan view
Stone	Cut; Rubble	Cut; Rubble	Cut; Rubble
Concrete	(aggregate pattern)	(stippled pattern)	Same as plan view
Concrete block	(diagonal hatch)	(stippled block pattern)	Same as plan view
Earth	None	None	(diagonal hatched pattern)

RM3-1A

Architectural Symbols

Material	Plan	Elevation	Section
Glass	—	(glass elevation symbol)	Large scale / Small scale
Insulation	Same as section	Insulation	Loose fill or batt / Board
Plaster	Same as section	Plaster	Stud / Lath and plaster
Structural steel	– – –	Indicated by note	(I-beam and angle shapes)
Sheet metal flashing	Indicated by note	(horizontal lines)	Show contour
Tile	Floor	Wall	(hatched section)

RM3-1B

Symbols for Openings

Openings in frame wall

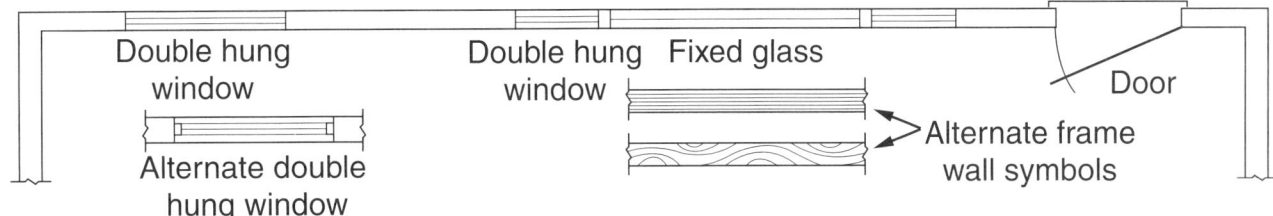

Openings in brick veneer wall

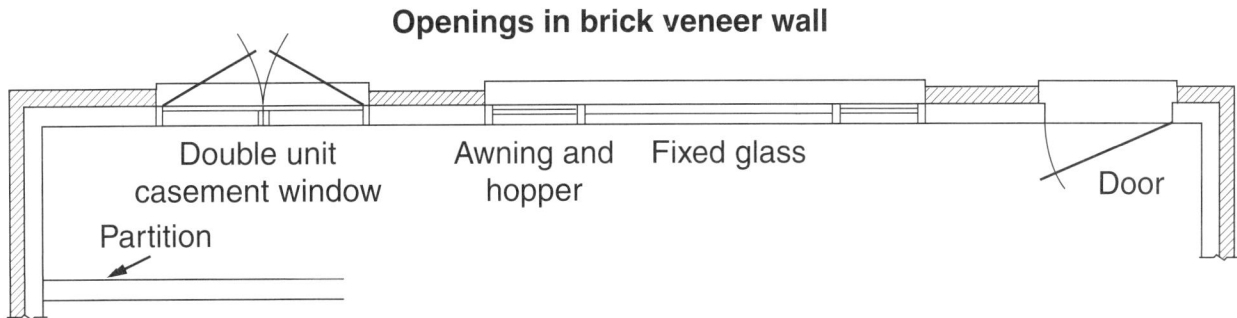

Openings in masonry wall

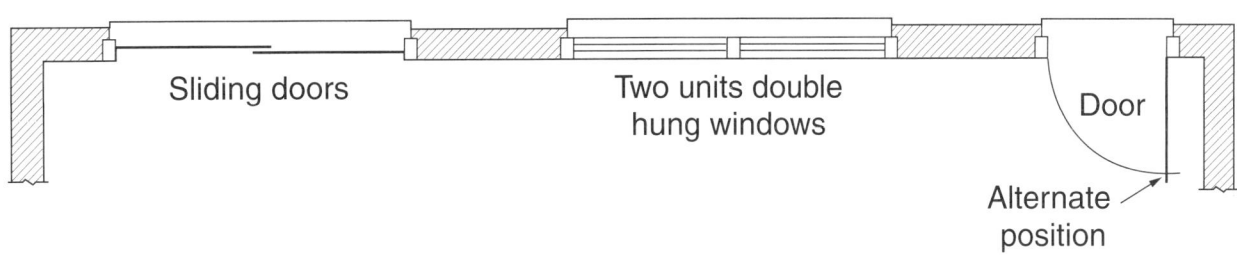

Openings in interior partitions

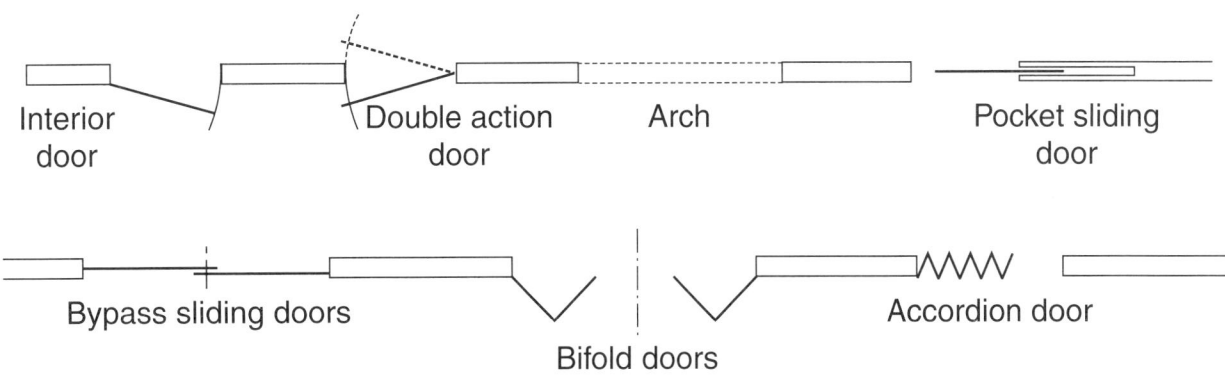

RM 3-2

Appliance/Fixture Symbols

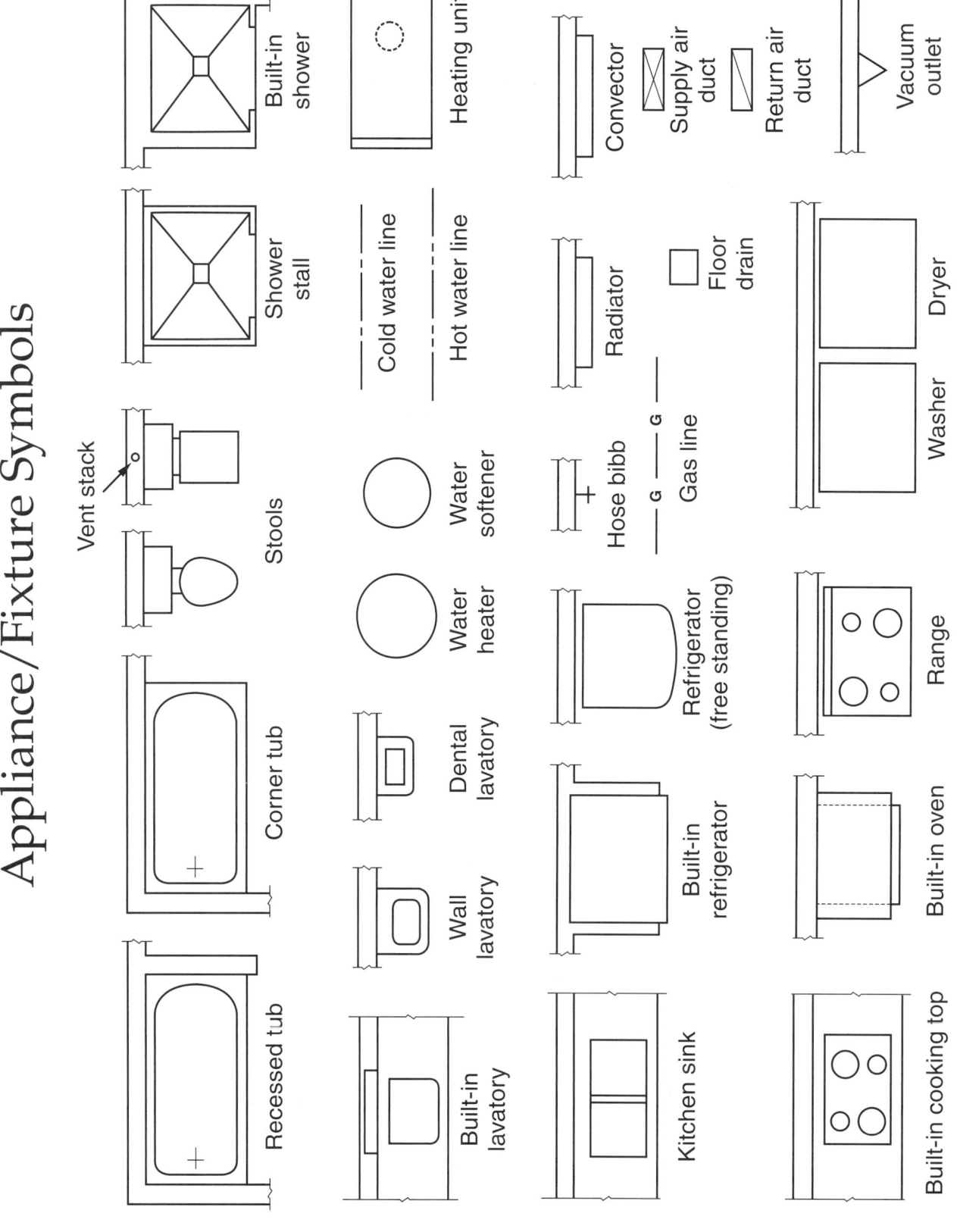

RM3-3

Chapter 3 Procedure Checklist
Reading a Set of Working Drawings

Name _____ Total _____

❏	Identifies the scale of a drawing and explains its meaning.	5	4	3	2	1	Unable to identify the scale; cannot explain the importance of a scale on a drawing.
❏	Readily identifies drawings in a set without reading the title; explains the purpose of the drawing.	5	4	3	2	1	Unable to differentiate between types of drawings in a set; cannot explain the purpose of the drawings.
❏	Interprets drawings when instructor requests dimensions for particular feature of the plan.	5	4	3	2	1	Cannot identify appropriate dimensions; unable to correctly read dimensions for particular features.
❏	Readily identifies symbols of materials and other architectural items.	5	4	3	2	1	Unable to identify symbols when requested by instructor.
❏	Properly scales a drawing.	5	4	3	2	1	Cannot read an architect's scale.
❏	Reads and understands specifications included with a set of drawings; states the purpose of specifications.	5	4	3	2	1	Cannot locate specifications in a set; unable to state purpose of specifications.

Chapter 3 Quiz
Plans, Specifications, and Codes

Name _____ Date _____ Score _____

True-False
Circle T if the answer is true or F if the answer is false.

T F 1. The window and door schedule always specifies the manufacturer of the window or door.

T F 2. The Unicom system makes it possible to apply mass production methods to building construction.

T F 3. Dimension lines on architectural drawings show distance and size.

T F 4. The full-size length of a line that measures 4′-0″ using a 1/4″ = 1′-0″ scale is longer than the full-size length of a line that measures 4′-0″ using a 1/8″ = 1′-0″ scale.

T F 5. The modular system in the SI metric system is based on a grid made of 100 meter squares.

Multiple Choice
Choose the answer that correctly completes the statement. Write the corresponding letter in the space provided.

_____ 6. ____ show the size and outline of a building and its rooms.
  A. Elevation drawings
  B. Floor plans
  C. Plot plans
  D. Section drawings

_____ 7. A major advantage of CADD is that a drawing can be changed without making ____ on drafting paper.
  A. symbols
  B. notes
  C. erasures
  D. clippings

_____ 8. Which of the following cannot be determined from an elevation drawing?
  A. Floor level.
  B. Window and door heights.
  C. Roof slopes.
  D. Room size.

_____ 9. All dimensions in modular construction are based on multiples of _____.
   A. 3″
   B. 4″
   C. 5″
   D. 6″

Identification
Identify the following door symbols.

_____ 10. Accordion door.

_____ 11. Interior door.

_____ 12. Bypass sliding doors.

_____ 13. Double action door.

_____ 14. Pocket sliding door.

_____ 15. Bifold doors.

Openings in interior partitions

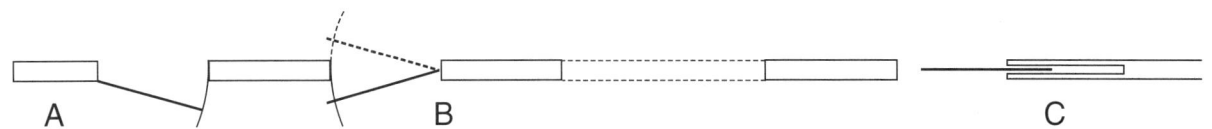

4 Hand Tools

Objectives

After studying this chapter, students will be able to:
- Identify the most common hand tools.
- Select the proper hand tool for a given job.
- Identify the main parts of each major hand tool.
- Explain proper methods of tool maintenance and storage.

Instructional Materials

Text: Pages 103–120
- *Technical Vocabulary,* page 103
- *Test Your Knowledge,* page 120
- *Curricular Connections,* page 120
- *Outside Assignments,* page 120

Workbook: Pages 19–22

Instructor's Resource:
- Reproducible masters:
  - RM 4-1 *Saw Tooth Shapes*
  - RM 4-2 *Parts of a Plane*
  - RM 4-3 *Parts of a Claw Hammer*
- Transparencies (binder/CD only):
  - CT 4-1 *Parts of a Plane*
  - CT 4-2 *Parts of a Claw Hammer*
- Chapter Quiz

Instructional Concepts and Student Learning Experiences

This section provides teaching suggestions and strategies for using the textbook, workbook, and instructor's resources. Information and teaching suggestions should be tailored to fit the needs of the curriculum. The trade-related math concepts can be integrated into the chapter presentation or used as a follow-up at the conclusion of the chapter.

Trade-Related Math

Working with fractions is required in almost every aspect of carpentry, from rough layout to finish work. The most common fractional increment is the sixteenth of an inch. In order to do math computations with fractions, a common denominator must be first obtained.

1. A common denominator is determined by multiplying the upper (numerator) and lower (denominator) part of the fraction by the same number. For example:

   $1/2 = X/8$
   $1/2 \times 4/4 = 4/8$

   or:

   $3/8 = X/16$
   $3/8 \times 2/2 = 6/16$

   Once a common denominator has been determined for the fractions in the problem, computation may begin.

2. When adding fractions, a common denominator must first be determined. The denominator remains the same, while the numerator is added. For example:

   $1/2 + 1/4 = X$
   $1/2 \times 2/2 = 2/4$
   $2/4 + 1/4 = 3/4$

2. When subtracting fractions, a common denominator must first be determined. The denominator remains the same, while the numerators are subtracted. For example:

   $9/16 - 1/4 = X$
   $1/4 \times 4/4 = 4/16$
   $9/16 - 4/16 = 5/16$

Measuring and Layout Tools

1. Review the layout tools commonly used by a carpenter. Compare and contrast these to

tools that the students may have used in a woodworking or cabinetmaking course. Explain why it is important for a carpenter to use good-quality tools.
2. If necessary, review the markings on a tape rule or a folding rule. Compare a conventional inch-foot tape with an metric tape. Explain the division marks as necessary.
3. Demonstrate the use of layout tools that students are not accustomed to using, such as a framing square, marking gauge, level, and plumb bob. Ask the students to show the proper use of the tools after the demonstration.

Saws
1. Identify the handsaws commonly used by a carpenter. Review the applications of each by demonstrating its use.
2. Using reproducible master RM 4-1 *Saw Tooth Shapes,* compare and contrast the saw tooth shapes of the crosscut saw and ripsaw. Have the students explain why different types of teeth are necessary on crosscut and ripsaws.
3. Have students list the types of saws commonly used for rough cutting and finish work. Ask the students to explain their categorization.
4. Discuss the different types of set used for hacksaw blades.
5. Stress the importance of safely using saws.

Planing, Smoothing, and Shaping
1. Review the types of planing and smoothing tools used by a carpenter.
2. Identify the parts of the tools. Use reproducible master RM 4-2 *Parts of a Plane* and color transparency CT 4-1 *Parts of a Plane.*
3. Emphasize the importance of using proper terminology when discussing tools.
4. Demonstrate the proper use of planing and smoothing tools with which students are not familiar. Stress the importance of using the tools safely.

Fastening Parts Together
1. Review the types of tools that carpenters commonly use to fasten parts together.
2. Distinguish between the curved claw and rip claw hammers. Ask the students if there are any applications where one type of hammer should be used.
3. Review the parts of a hammer using reproducible master RM 4-3 *Parts of a Claw Hammer* and color transparency CT 4-2 *Parts of a Claw Hammer.* Discuss the proper procedure for driving and pulling nails with the hammer.
4. Have the students check the condition of each hammer in the shop. With instructor supervision, ask the students to repair any tools that are in disrepair.
5. Identify tools that students may not be familiar with, such as hatchets, ripping bars, tackers, staplers, and nailers. Discuss applications of these tools. Demonstrate their proper, safe use.
6. Discuss the criteria (width and thickness of the blade) that should be used to select an appropriate screwdriver for a given application.

Clamping Tools
1. Identify the two types of clamping tools that are commonly used by a carpenter: C-clamps and hand screws. Ask students to demonstrate the proper use of these tools.

Tool Storage
1. Discuss the importance of having some type of chest or cabinet to store tools.
2. Have students design some type of storage chest for their tools. Have students evaluate each other's designs based on organization of the tools and preventing damage to the cutting edges.

Care and Maintenance
1. Discuss the methods of properly maintaining tools.
2. Demonstrate the proper method used to hone edge tools on an oilstone.
3. Have the students identify tools in the shop that may need maintenance. With instructor supervision, have students repair or perform maintenance on these tools.

General Safety Rules
1. Discuss the general safety rules in Chapter 2 of the text. Stress the importance of safely

working in class and on the job site. Using statistics obtained from the Occupational Safety and Health Administration (OSHA), emphasize the fact that a person safely working with lower productivity is of more value to a company than a worker who is injured on the job due to unsafe work habits.

Chapter Review

1. Review the chapter objectives. Be sure that the students are fully competent in the task identified by each objective.
2. Review the terms in the *Technical Vocabulary* section and make certain students are clear on each definition.
3. Have students develop their own lists of hand tools that they feel should be included in a carpenter's toolbox. Make sure they understand the importance of having enough tools, but not every tool that is available. Have the students explain their tool selections.
4. Assign the *Test Your Knowledge* questions, *Curricular Connections,* and *Outside Assignments* for Chapter 4 of the text. Review the answers to test questions in class. Also, have students report on the *Curricular Connections* and *Outside Assignments* activities as appropriate.
5. Assign Chapter 4 of the workbook. Review the answers in class.

Evaluation

This chapter provides three methods for evaluating student performance. Students should complete the *Test Your Knowledge* section using the book as reference. Students should also be allowed to use the book for reference when completing the workbook material. Use the Chapter 4 Quiz in the instructor's resources for in-class evaluation. Correct the quizzes, return them to the students, and review the quiz questions in group discussion.

In addition, give the students a set of tools in need of repair. Have the students identify the problems with the tools. Then, have students identify ways to correct the problems.

Answers to Test Your Knowledge
Text Page 120

1. 6
2. Check or square lines across boards; check squareness of corners; make a 45° angle across wide boards; find length and angles of rafters; lay out stairs.
3. B. 1/12″
4. On the face. They can be used in determining the length of rafters.
5. Level.
6. D. 14-16 points per inch
7. A. up
8. False.
9. D. weight of the head
10. Curved claw—claw used to pull nails. Ripping (straight claw)—claw used to pry apart fastened pieces.
11. To cut light sheet metal and asphalt shingles.
12. Slotted—by length of the blade. Phillips—as a point number ranging from No. 0 (smallest) to No. 4 (largest).
13. jointing

Answers to Workbook Questions
Pages 19–22

1. A. folding wood rule; E. flexible measuring tape
2. speed square, quick square, or super square
3. A. backsaw
   B. crosscut saw
   C. drywall saw
4. Seven.
5. D. 14″
6. block plane
7. A. head
   B. face
   C. neck
   D. cheek
   E. claw
   F. handle
8. shingling hatchet
9. B. 1/32″
10. A. ferrule

Copyright by Goodheart-Willcox Co., Inc.

11. A. Torx
    B. Phillips
    C. slotted or flat blade
12. A. hand screw
13. A. 45°
    B. 30°–35°
14. D. Jointing
15. honing a chisel

Answers to Chapter Quiz
1. False.
2. True.
3. False.
4. True.
5. True.
6. False.
7. True.
8. False.
9. C. rafter square
10. B. T-bevel
11. D. face
12. B. rounded
13. A. 30″
14. A. hand screws
15. D. five-gallon buckets fitted with a pocketed fabric holder

Saw Tooth Shapes

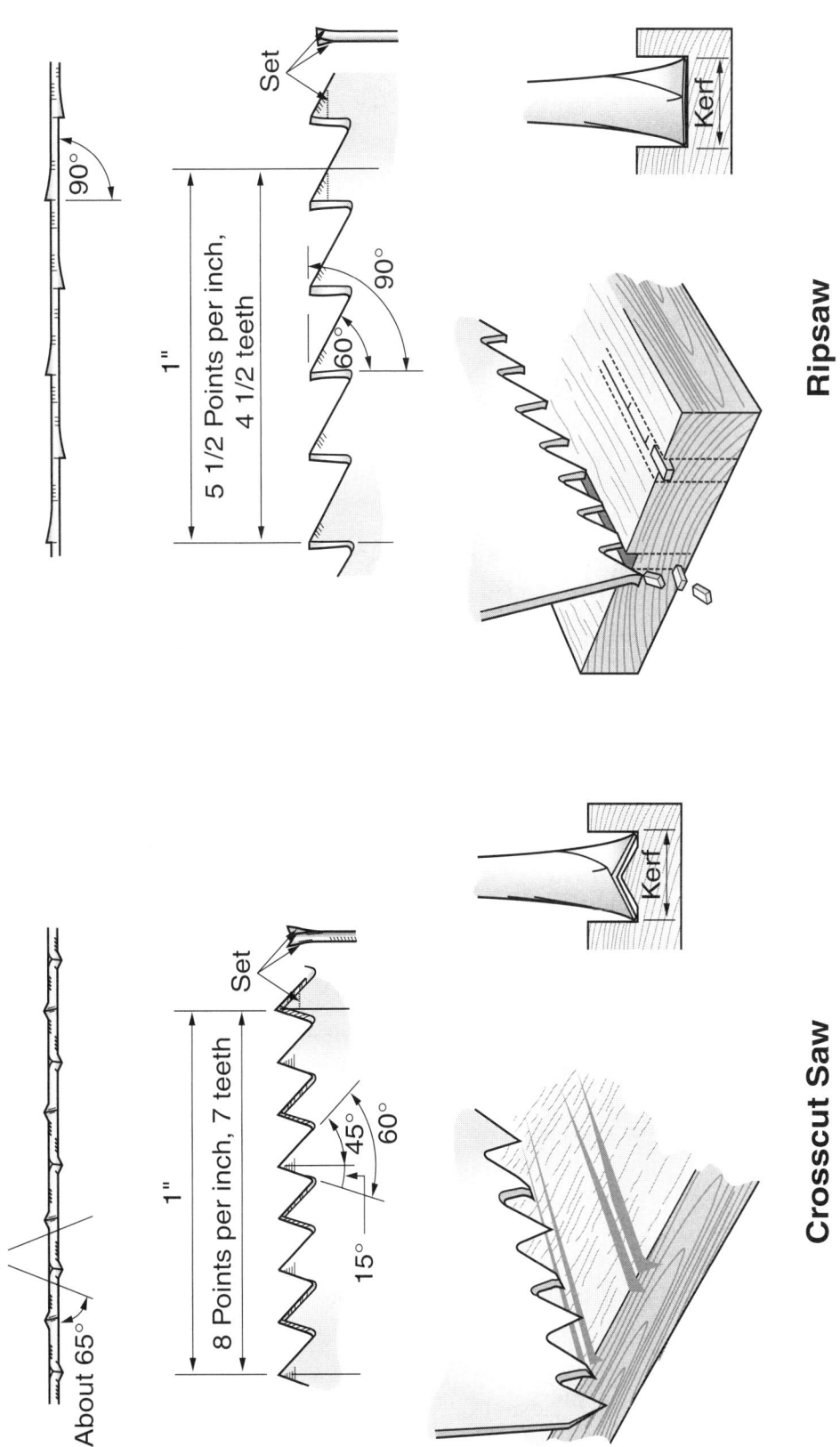

RM4-1

Parts of a Plane

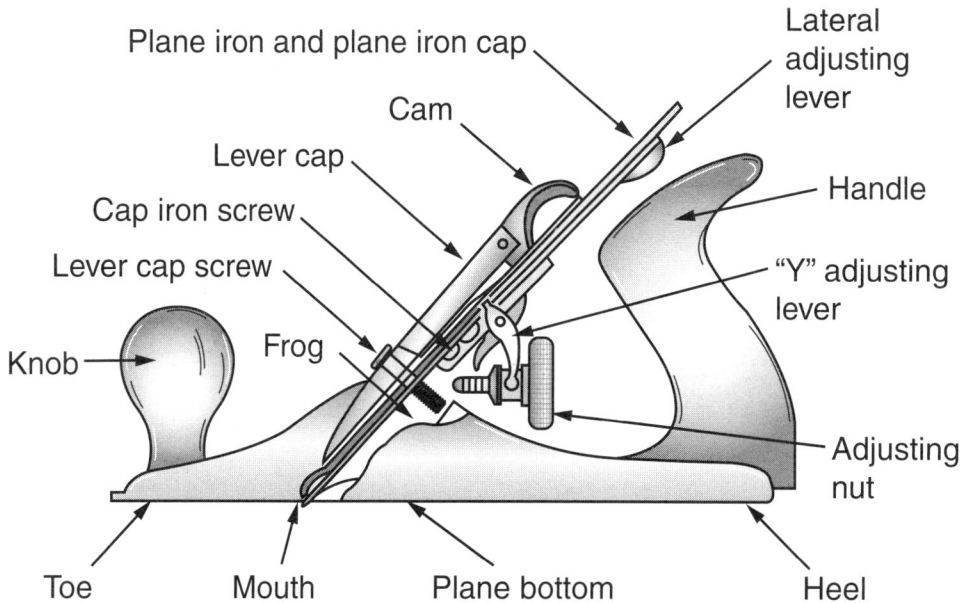

RM 4-2

Parts of a Claw Hammer

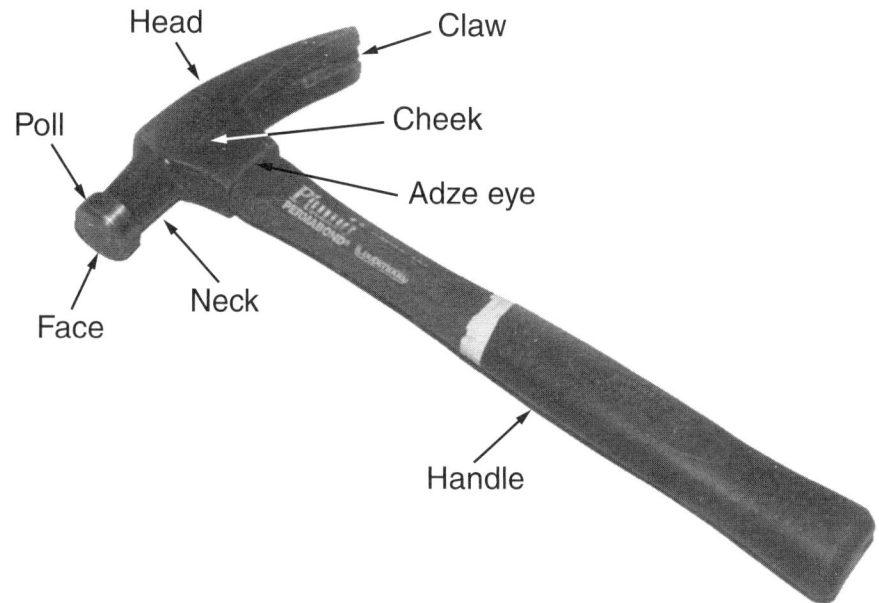

Chapter 4 Quiz
Hand Tools

Name _____ Date _____ Score _____

True-False
Circle T if the answer is true or F if the answer is false.

T   F   1. A saw used for finishing work should have fewer teeth per inch than one used for general-purpose applications.

T   F   2. A plumb bob can be used to establish a vertical line.

T   F   3. A nail set is used to drill holes for casing or finishing nails.

T   F   4. Sizes of Phillips screwdrivers range from No. 0 to No. 4, with No. 4 being the largest.

T   F   5. The ripping claw hammer has a straight claw.

T   F   6. The blade of a block plane is set at a higher angle than a jack plane to produce a finer cut.

T   F   7. Hacksaw blades should be installed so the teeth point away from the handle.

T   F   8. A super square is shaped like a conventional framing square, but is larger.

Multiple Choice
Choose the answer that correctly completes the statement. Write the corresponding letter in the space provided.

_____ 9. The framing square is also called a _____.
   A. combination square
   B. try square
   C. rafter square
   D. T-bevel

_____ 10. The _____ has an adjustable blade and is used to transfer angles from one place to another.
   A. try square
   B. T-bevel
   C. wing dividers
   D. combination square

_____ 11. The part of a hammer that contacts a nail when driving it is the _____.
   A. poll
   B. cheek
   C. neck
   D. face

_____ 12. Gullets of a sheetrock-drywall saw are _____ to prevent their clogging from the gypsum material.
   A. squared off
   B. rounded
   C. tapered
   D. All of the above.

_____ 13. The _____ pry bar is the most-used size because it fits into a standard carpenter's toolbox.
   A. 30″
   B. 36″
   C. 48″
   D. 56″

_____ 14. Wood clamps are also known as _____.
   A. hand screws
   B. wood screws
   C. C screws
   D. clamp screws

_____ 15. For storing tools and transporting them to the job site, most carpenters today prefer:
   A. folding tool panels
   B. backpacks
   C. carts
   D. five-gallon buckets fitted with a pocketed fabric holder

5 Power Tools

Objectives

After studying this chapter, students will be able to:
- Recognize common power tools.
- Explain the function and operation of the principle power tools.
- Identify the parts of common power tools.
- Apply safety rules.

Instructional Materials

Text: Pages 121–147
    Technical Vocabulary, page 121
    Test Your Knowledge, page 147
    Curricular Connections, page 147
    Outside Assignments, page 147
Workbook: Pages 23–28
Instructor's Resource:
    Reproducible masters:
        RM 5-1 *Portable Power Circular Saw*
        RM 5-2 *Parts of an Electric Drill*
    Transparencies (binder/CD only):
        CT 5-1 *Parts of a Table Saw*
        CT 5-2 *Parts of a Radial Arm Saw*
        CT 5-3 *Parts of a Circular Saw*
    Chapter Quiz

Trade-Related Math

In some instances, a carpenter may need to use decimals. Measurements on a plot plan, for example, may be shown in a decimal format. To add or subtract decimal values, always make sure that the decimal points align, no matter how many numbers are shown on either side of the decimal points. Mention that as many zeros as desired can be added after the last number to the right of the decimal point, without altering its value. To add decimal values, simply align the decimal points and add as shown in the following example:

$$400.26 + 25.7 = X$$

$$\begin{array}{r} 400.26 \\ +\ 25.70 \\ \hline 425.96 \end{array}$$

$$X = 425.96$$

To subtract fractions, once again align the decimal points, but this time subtract the values.

$$345.76 - 221.52 = X$$

$$\begin{array}{r} 345.76 \\ -221.52 \\ \hline 124.24 \end{array}$$

$$X = 124.24$$

In some cases, numbers must be carried over (for addition) or borrowed from (subtraction) in order to add or subtract.

Instructional Concepts and Student Learning Experiences

Power Tool Safety

1. Review the general safety rules for the use of power tools in Chapter 2 of the text. Emphasize the importance of working safely in class and on the job site.
2. Stress the fact that many of the tasks performed by a carpenter require the use of power tools. Instruct students to think through an operation before performing it. Demand that students have their total focus placed on the operation they are about to perform. Discourage students from distracting others during an operation.

Electrical Safety

1. Describe the function of magnetic starters on power tools. Stress that power tools should

be in the *off* position while in storage and before they are plugged into a live circuit.
2. Emphasize the importance of using grounded (three-wire) cords and plugs with power tools.
3. Identify potential electrical problems that may be evident in a power tool including frayed cords, grounding plugs that have been broken off, etc. Have students identify possible fixes for these problems. Stress that a cheap repair is not necessarily the best type of repair.
4. Define the term *ground fault circuit interrupter* as it relates to electrical safety.
5. Have the students inspect the electrical cords of the power equipment. With instructor supervision, have students make any necessary repairs.

Portable Circular Saws
1. Using reproducible master RM 5-1 *Portable Power Circular Saw,* list the types of portable circular saws and then identify the parts. Have the students note the location and function of each part on both types of saws.
2. Discuss the different types of blades that can be used on a portable circular saw, identifying the applications of each type. Stress the importance of selecting the proper blade for the task being performed.
3. Review the safety rules for using and servicing portable circular saws.
4. Demonstrate the proper use of a portable circular saw. Use the saw to cut different types of materials, making straight and angled cuts.

Saber Saws
1. Identify the parts of a saber saw. Have the students cite applications where a saber saw might be used.
2. Show the students a variety of saber saw blades. Have them describe possible applications of each.
3. Review the safety rules for using and servicing saber saws.
4. Demonstrate the proper, safe use of a saber saw. Have students note where splintering occurs (on the topside of the work). Show the students the proper methods of cutting internal openings.

Portable Electric Drills
1. Using reproducible master RM 5-2 *Parts of an Electric Drill,* identify the parts of a portable electric drill. Discuss how speeds vary and how chuck capacity determines the size of a drill.
2. Identify the different types of drill bits that may be used with electric drills.
3. Review the safety rules for using and servicing electric drills.
4. Demonstrate the safe use of an electric drill. Stress that the pressure required to operate a drill will vary with the drill size, type of wood, and the diameter of the drill bit.

Power Planes
1. Identify the parts of a power plane. Compare the parts of a power plane with those of a hand plane.
2. Review the safety rules for using and servicing power planes.
3. Demonstrate the safe use of a power plane. Show the students how to plane chamfers and make square cuts.

Portable Routers
1. Identify the parts of a portable router.
2. Review the safety rules for using portable routers.
3. Demonstrate the safe use of a router. Stress the importance of moving the router from left to right when making a cut along an edge. Show the students how to use bits with and without pilot tips.

Portable Sanders
1. Identify the three basic types of portable sanders: belt, disc, and finish. Discuss the advantages and disadvantages of each.
2. Name the parts of a portable sander and have students identify the location of each.
3. Differentiate between orbital and oscillating finish sanders.
4. Demonstrate the safe use of portable sanders.

Staplers and Nailers
1. Cite advantages of using power staplers and nailers over using hand tools to fasten materials. Stress the safety concerns that must be recognized.

2. Review the safety rules for power staplers and nailers.
3. Demonstrate the proper use of power nailers and staplers. Stress the importance of making sure that the nail or staple "hits its mark" in the material, thus eliminating the possibility of stray nails or staples.

Radial Arm Saws
1. Identify the parts of the radial arm saw. Cite applications where a radial arm saw might be used.
2. Review the safety rules for using radial arm saws. Emphasize that the saw may tend to "feed itself" into the stock, and that the saw handle should be firmly grasped to control the tool.
3. Demonstrate the safe use of a radial arm saw. In addition to demonstrating crosscutting and ripping operations, show the students how to cut miters and bevels.

Table Saws and Jointers
1. Review the parts of a table saw. Have students identify operations that can be performed on the table saw other than crosscutting and ripping operations.
2. Discuss preparations that must be made to the stock before cutting it on the table saw.
3. Review the safety rules for using and servicing the table saw. Stress the importance of using the guard for cutting operations.
4. Have students design their own push sticks. Emphasize the margin of safety that should be maintained between the saw operator's hands and the saw blade.
5. Identify the parts of the jointer. Compare the parts and operation of a jointer to those of a power plane.
6. Review the safety rules for using a jointer. Emphasize the minimum dimensions of stock that can be safely jointed.
7. Demonstrate the safe use of the jointer. Point out the importance of "stepping" hands along the stock to avoid bearing down on the stock while it passes over the cutter head.

Special Saws
1. Identify special saws that are commonly used by a carpenter. Include the power miter saw, plate joiner, frame and trim saw, and chain saw. Discuss why these saws are now often found among the carpenter's tools.
2. Identify the principle parts of the power miter box and the frame and trim saw. Discuss the function of each part.
3. Review the safety rules for using special saws. In addition, refer to the operator's manuals for specific operating and safety instructions.

Specialty Tools
1. Identify tools designed for special carpentry operations. Include tools such as drywall screw guns, plate joiners, panel saws, and powder-actuated tools.
2. If possible, demonstrate the use of several specialty tools.

Power Tool Care and Maintenance
1. Emphasize the importance of properly maintaining power tools.
2. Have the students identify power tools in the shop that need repairing. With instructor supervision, have students make any necessary repairs.

Chapter Review
1. Review the chapter objectives. Be sure that the students are fully competent in the task identified by each objective.
2. Review the terms in the *Technical Vocabulary* section and make certain students are clear on each definition.
3. Have students develop their own lists of hand tools that they feel should be included in a carpenter's toolbox. Make sure they understand the importance of having enough tools, but not every tool that is available. Have the students explain their tool selections.
4. Assign the *Test Your Knowledge* questions, *Curricular Connections,* and *Outside Assignments* for Chapter 5 of the text. Review the answers to test questions in class. Also, have students report on the *Curricular Connections* and *Outside Assignments* activities as appropriate.
5. Assign Chapter 5 of the workbook. Review the answers in class.

Evaluation

This chapter provides three methods for evaluating student performance. Students should complete the *Test Your Knowledge* section using the book as reference. Students should also be allowed to use the book for reference when completing the workbook material. Use the Chapter 5 Quiz in the instructor's resources for in-class evaluation. Correct the quizzes, return them to the students, and review the quiz questions in group discussion.

In addition, give the students a set of tools in need of repair. Have the students identify the problems with the tools. Then, have students identify ways to correct the problems.

Answers to Test Your Knowledge
Text Page 147

1. Check the plate attached to the power tool's case.
2. Ground continuity involves the third or ground conductor, which will bleed off current resulting from a short in a tool's housing or case. It protects the operator from electrical shock.
3. Units that can be installed in a circuit or plugged into an outlet that is grounded. These units sense when a short has occurred and turn off power to the tool.
4. blade diameter
5. 10
6. up
7. False.
8. front shoe
9. collet
10. belt width
11. It is faster and it allows working in close quarters.
12. False.
13. overhead arm
14. toward
15. outfeed table

Answers to Workbook Questions
Pages 23-28

1. stationary
2. grounded
3. A. Circular saw.
   B. Pneumatic stapler.
   C. Router.
   D. Saber saw.
   E. Power plane.
4. The saw could kick back.
5. A. Switch.
   B. Handle.
   C. Shoe or base.
   D. Telescoping guard.
   E. Arbor and locking bolt.
   F. Upper guard.
6. shoe
7. A. 1/8"
8. A. Crosscut.
   B. Rip.
   C. Hollow ground combination.
   D. Carbide-tipped.
9. upward
10. B. 1/2"
11. C. capacity of the chuck
12. B. Place the base of the drill firmly on the stock before starting motor.
13. D. 20,000 rpm
14. A. front shoe
15. Straight
16. clockwise
17. B. belt width
18. B. compressed air
19. C. overhead arm
20. A. Saw feed.
    B. Stock.
    C. Table.
    D. Thrust.
    E. Fence.
21. C. 6"
22. toward
23. A. Guard and splitter.
    B. Fence.
    C. Raising and lowering handwheel.
    D. Arbor tilt wheel and scale.
    E. Safety switch.
    F. Table.
24. B. When ripping stock freehand, do not use the fence.
25. A. Infeed table.
    B. Depth scale.
    C. Power switch.
    D. Base.
    E. Outfeed table.
    F. Fence.

26. B. outfeed table is slightly higher than the cutter head
27. 10″, 20″
28. screw shooter, screw gun
29. plate joiner, biscuit cutter

Answers to Chapter Quiz
1. True.
2. False.
3. False.
4. True.
5. False.
6. D
7. A
8. B
9. C
10. E
11. F
12. A. portable jig
13. D. All of the above.
14. C. 90 psi

Portable Power Circular Saw

RM 5-1

Parts of an Electric Drill

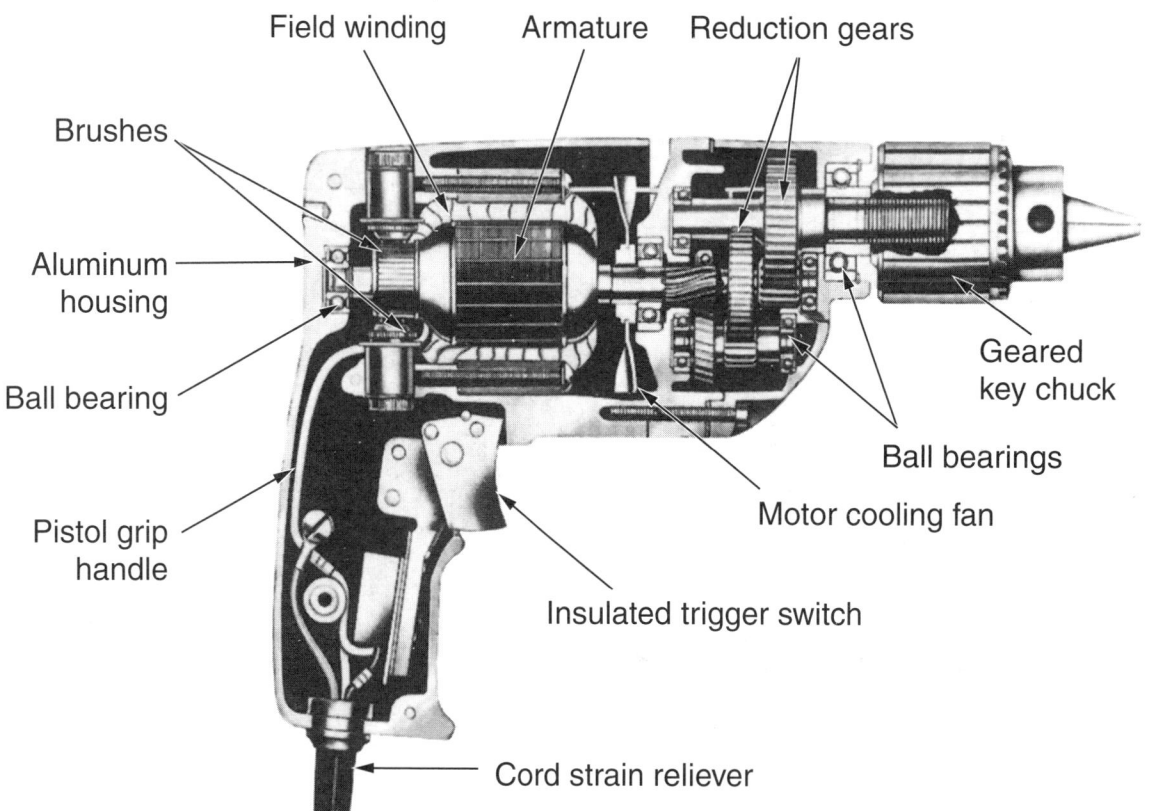

RM 5-2

Chapter 5 Quiz
Power Tools

Name _____ Date _____ Score _____

True-False
Circle T if the answer is True or F if the answer is False.

T   F   1. The size of a circular saw is determined by the diameter of the largest blade it will accept.

T   F   2. Electrical power tools operate only on 120 V electric power.

T   F   3. A router bit, viewed from above, revolves in a counterclockwise direction.

T   F   4. A power nailer that carries nails in a round canister is called a coil-fed nailer.

T   F   5. Routers cannot be used to cut through material.

Identification
Identify the parts of the portable circular saw.

_____ 6. Tilt adjustment.

_____ 7. Switch.

_____ 8. Upper guard.

_____ 9. Arbor and locking bolt.

_____ 10. Shoe or base.

_____ 11. Telescoping guard.

Multiple Choice

Choose the answer that correctly completes the statement. Write the corresponding letter in the space provided.

_____ 12. A saber saw is also referred to as a(n) _____ saw.
   A. portable jig
   B. builder's
   C. drywall
   D. None of the above.

_____ 13. A _____ sander is considered a portable power sander.
   A. belt
   B. disc
   C. finish
   D. All of the above.

_____ 14. Air pressure for an air-powered nailer should seldom exceeds _____.
   A. 30 psi
   B. 60 psi
   C. 90 psi
   D. 120 psi

6 Building Layout

Objectives

After studying this chapter, students will be able to:
- Explain the operation of the builder's level and level-transit.
- Explain the basic operation of a laser level system.
- Demonstrate proper setup, sighting, and leveling procedures.
- Measure and lay out angles using leveling equipment.
- Read the vernier scale.
- Use a plumb line.

Instructional Materials

Text: Pages 149–167
  Technical Vocabulary, page 149
  Test Your Knowledge, page 167
  Curricular Connections, page 167
  Outside Assignments, page 167
Workbook: Pages 29–32
Instructor's Resource:
  Reproducible masters:
    RM 6-1 *Laying Out Building Lines*
    RM 6-2 *Transit Graduated Circle*
  Transparencies (binder/CD only):
    CT 6-1 *Laser Leveling Unit*
    CT 6-2 *Parts of a Builder's Level*
    CT 6-3 *Parts of a Transit*
  Procedure Checklist: *Setting Up and Leveling a Builder's Level*
  Chapter Quiz

Trade-Related Math

When using a builder's level or level-transit, a good understanding of angular divisions is necessary. A graduated circle contains 360 degrees (°). Each degree can be divided into 60 minutes ('). Each minute can be further divided into 60 seconds ("). In order to convert the number of degrees in a given number of minutes, or the number of minutes in a given number of seconds, divide the given number by 60. For example:

90 minutes = X degrees
90 ÷ 60 = 1.5
90 minutes = 1.5 degree

120 seconds = X minutes
120 ÷ 60 = 2
120 seconds = 2 minutes

To find the number of minutes in a given number of degrees, or the number of seconds in a given number of minutes, multiply the number by 60. For example:

5 degrees = X minutes
5 × 60 = 300
5 degrees = 300 minutes

8 minutes = X seconds
8 × 60 = 480
8 minutes = 480 seconds

Instructional Concepts and Student Learning Experiences

1. Using a plot plan obtained from a contractor, identify the primary components of the plan. These items might include: length and bearing of each property line, location and size of buildings on the site, contour of the lot, elevation of the property corners, streets, drives, and other means of access, utility easements, and scale of the drawing.

Establishing Building Lines

1. Stress the importance of accurately establishing the building lines on a site. Discuss possible scenarios that may occur if the building lines are not properly located.
2. Review the markings found on a measuring tape. Have students take turns in measuring

long distances and accurately reading the tape.
3. Emphasize the importance of measuring perpendicular to the boundary lines when locating the building lines. Demonstrate methods of ensuring perpendicularity, such as swinging arcs or using the 6-8-10 method.
4. Divide the students into pairs and have them establish building lines for a hypothetical plot plan. Have students check the measurements of the building lines established by other students.

Laying Out with Leveling Instruments

1. Using reproducible master RM 6-1 *Laying Out Building Lines*, discuss the tools that may be used to lay out building lines for small structures. Once again, stress the importance of accurately locating the building lines.
2. Identify the parts of the builder's level and level-transit. Discuss the similarities and differences between the two instruments.
3. Demonstrate the proper methods for setting up a builder's level and level-transit. Describe possible obstacles that may be encountered when setting up these instruments in different types of terrain (i.e. sandy or extremely hard and rocky soil).
4. Emphasize the importance of properly leveling the instruments when setting them up. Have students take turns leveling the instruments. Change the location of the leveling instruments after each attempt.
5. Show students the correct procedures for sighting a builder's level or level-transit over long and short distances. Describe how the leveling rod is used when sighting over long distances. Most people tend to close their less-dominant eye when sighting a leveling instrument. Stress that both eyes should be kept open when sighting the instrument.
6. Demonstrate the procedures for using the laserplane system as a leveling device. If possible, invite a manufacturer's sales representative to give a demonstration.
7. Stress the importance of proper care and maintenance of all leveling systems. Emphasize the importance of following correct storage and maintenance procedures when setting up, using, and storing the instruments.

Using the Instruments

1. Using reproducible master RM 6-2 *Transit Graduated Circle*, define the terms commonly associated with the graduated circle. Be sure that the students fully understand these terms before progressing to reading the graduated horizontal circle of a transit.
2. Set the horizontal circle and vernier scales at different locations on a transit. Have the students read the scales and correctly state the measurements.
3. Demonstrate the proper procedure for laying out and staking a house. As a class, lay out the building lines for a hypothetical building site. Use 90° corners for this class exercise. When this has been completed, divide students into pairs and have each pair lay out another building site. Use angles other than 90° for this exercise.
4. Define the term *grade leveling*. Cite applications for grade leveling a building site.
5. Describe the means for indicating cuts and fills on a building site.
6. Define *contour lines* and have students identify contour lines on a plot plan. Ask them to interpret the meanings of several contour lines found on a plot plan.
7. Discuss the means for using a level-transit to measure vertical angles and for laying out and checking walls.
8. Demonstrate the use of a level-transit to establish vertical angles.

Chapter Review

1. Review the chapter objectives. Be sure that the students fully understand each objective.
2. Assign *Technical Vocabulary, Test Your Knowledge* questions, *Curriculum Connections,* and *Outside Assignments* for Chapter 6 of the text. Review the answers in class.
3. Assign Chapter 6 of the workbook. Review the answers in class.

Evaluation

This chapter provides three methods for evaluating student performance. Students should complete the *Test Your Knowledge* section using the book as reference. Students should also be allowed to use the book for reference when completing the workbook material. Use the Chapter 6 Quiz in the instructor's resources for in-class evaluation. Correct the quizzes, return them to the students, and review the quiz questions in group discussion.

In addition, give the students a set of tools in need of repair. Have the students identify the problems with the tools. Then, have students identify ways to correct the problems.

Procedure Checklist

Using the procedure checklist *Setting Up and Leveling a Builder's Level*, evaluate the techniques students use to perform these tasks.

Answers to Test Your Knowledge
Text Page 167
1. decimal parts of a foot
2. Building lines are the lines marking where the walls of a structure are to be located on a building site.
3. See Figure 6-4 in text.
4. line of sight
5. circular
6. leveling
7. focusing knob
8. True.
9. plumb bob
10. central
11. True.

Answers to Workbook Questions
Pages 29–32
1. plot plan
2. straight
3. A. Checking plumb lines.
4. A. Focusing knob.
   B. Instrument level vial.
   C. Eyepiece.
   D. Leveling screw.
   E. Horizontal graduated circle.
5. C. tripod
6. A. 6'-3 1/4"
   B. 0.70'
7. A.
8. benchmark
9. 7'-1"
10. 47° 5'
11. 21,600'
    54,000"
12. line of sight
13. level-transit
14. B. both eyes be kept open
15. leveling rod
16. The operator places the bucket or blade cutting edge on the benchmark or the finished elevation. Then, the receiver is adjusted up or down on the machine and the operator tightens the clamp when the on-grade point is reached. The receiver catches the laser beam from the rotating transmitter and signals the operator whether the measured surface is above, below, or on grade.

Answers to Chapter Quiz
1. False.
2. False.
3. True.
4. True.
5. D. 90°
6. A. your left thumb moves
7. B. 60
8. C. grade leveling
9. E.
10. F.
11. B.
12. C.
13. D.
14. G.
15. A.
16. D.
17. I.
18. A.
19. E.
20. B.
21. G.
22. F.
23. C.
24. H.

Laying Out Building Lines

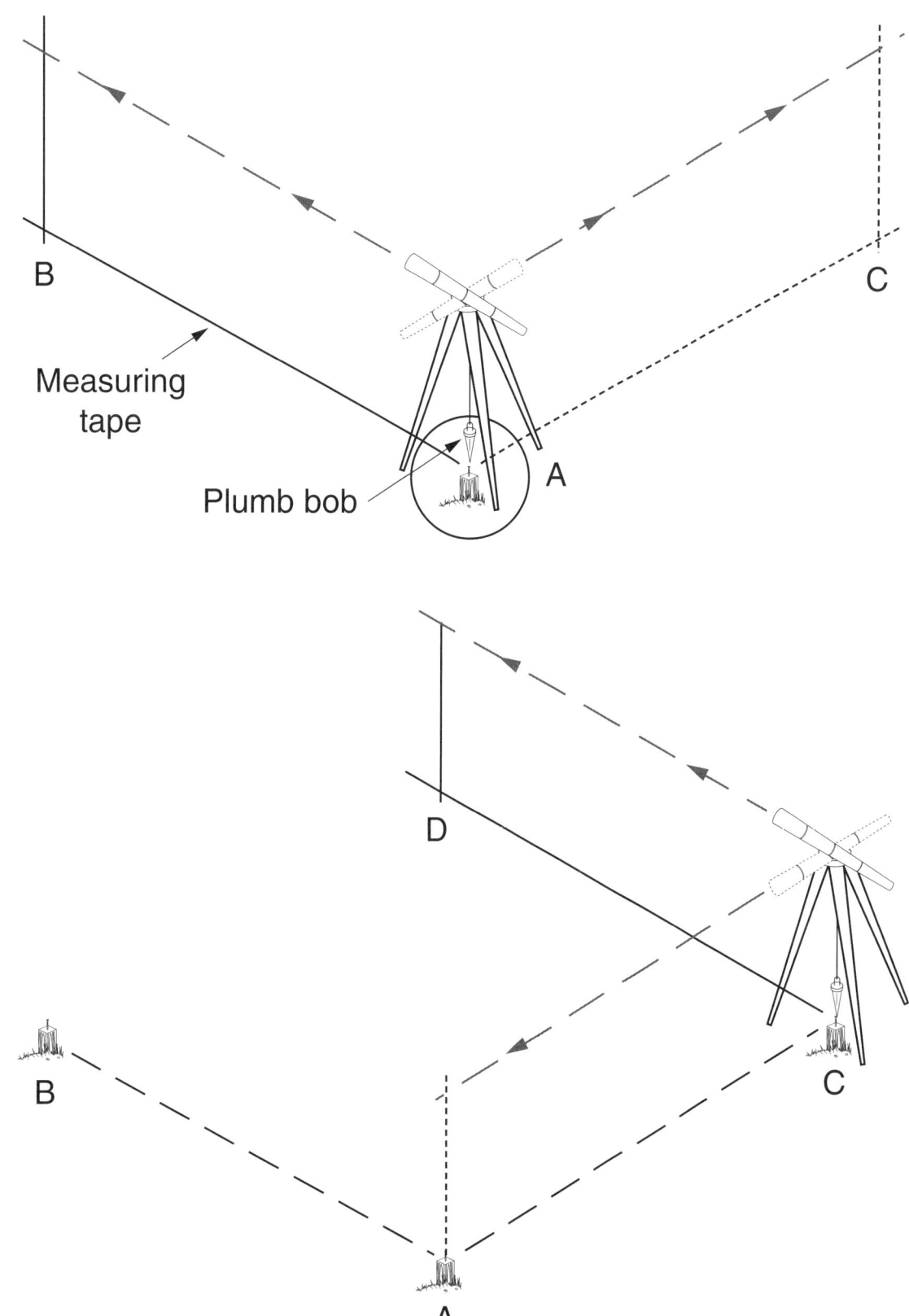

RM 6-1

Transit Graduated Circle

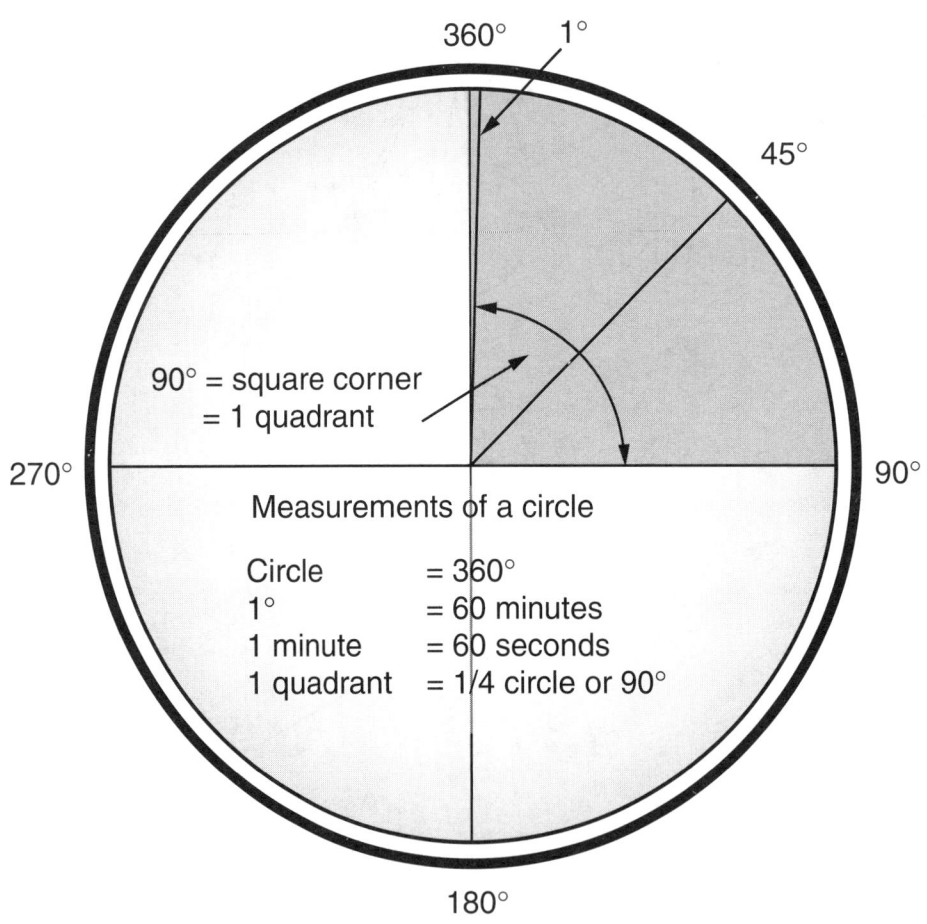

RM 6-2

Chapter 6 Procedure Checklist
Setting Up and Leveling a Builder's Level

Name _____   Total _____

❏	Properly sets up tripod; makes sure points are secure; properly adjusts tripod legs.	5	4	3	2	1	Treats tripod with little respect; legs are unstable; narrow box formed by tripod legs.
❏	Properly mounts instrument on tripod, taking care not to damage it.	5	4	3	2	1	Reckless use of instrument; damage to instrument.
❏	Correctly levels the instrument in one direction using both thumbs to adjust levelness.	5	4	3	2	1	Cannot level instrument; unable to move the level bubble toward center of vial.
❏	Turns level 90° over other set of leveling screws; properly adjusts levelness.	5	4	3	2	1	Neglects to level instrument in other direction.
❏	Rotates level in complete circle and checks for bubble movement.	5	4	3	2	1	Neglects to verify levelness.

Chapter 6 Quiz
Building Layout

Name _____ Date _____ Score _____

True-False
Circle T if the answer is True or F if the answer is False.

T F 1. Building lines are the lines indicating where the walls of the structure will be constructed.

T F 2. The laser plane receiver requires two people to carry out any layout operation.

T F 3. Both eyes should be kept open when sighting with a leveling instrument.

T F 4. A reference point where a leveling instrument is located is called a station mark.

Multiple Choice
Choose the answer that correctly completes the statement. Write the corresponding letter in the space provided.

_____ 5. The 6-8-10 method can be used to verify _____ corners.
   A. 30°
   B. 45°
   C. 60°
   D. 90°

_____ 6. When adjusting a builder's level for levelness, the bubble in the level vial will travel in the direction that _____.
   A. your left thumb moves
   B. your right thumb moves
   C. the telescope is pointed
   D. None of the above.

_____ 7. One degree contains _____ minutes.
   A. 30
   B. 60
   C. 90
   D. 120

_____ 8. Finding the difference in the grade level between several points is called _____.
   A. grading
   B. calibrating
   C. grade leveling
   D. grade staking

Identification

Identify the parts of the builder's level.

_____ 9. Horizontal clamp screw.

_____ 10. Leveling screws.

_____ 11. Instrument level vial.

_____ 12. Eyepiece.

_____ 13. Horizontal tangent screw.

_____ 14. Horizontal graduated circle.

_____ 15. Telescope lens.

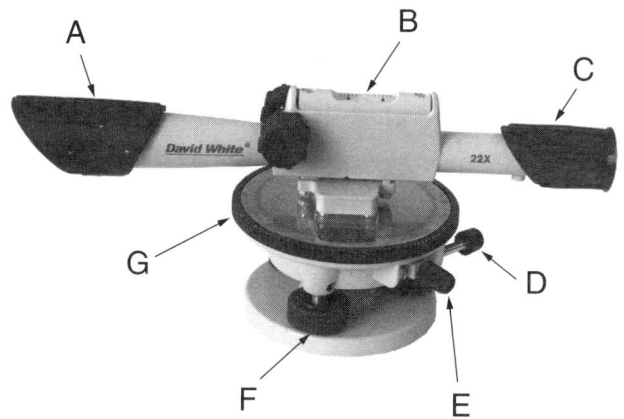

Identify the parts of the level-transit.

_____ 16. Eyepiece.

_____ 17. Focusing knob.

_____ 18. Telescope lens.

_____ 19. Horizontal clamp screw.

_____ 20. Vertical clamp screw.

_____ 21. Horizontal graduated circle.

_____ 22. Index vernier.

_____ 23. Vertical tangent screw.

_____ 24. Vertical arc.

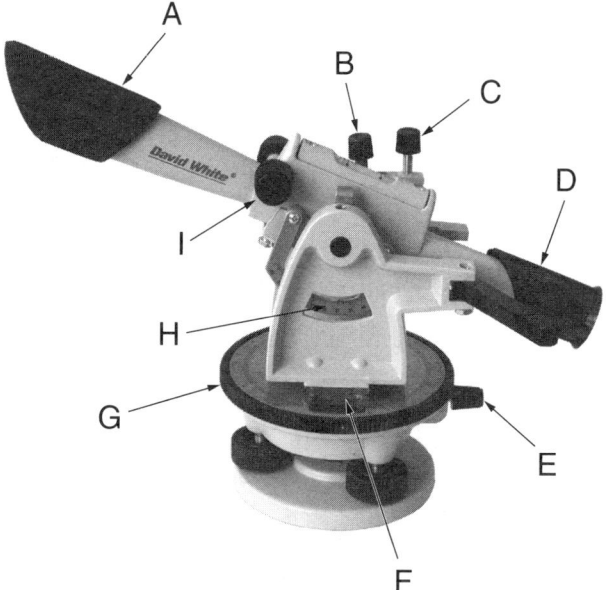

Section 1 Exam
Preparing to Build

Name _____ Date _____ Score _____

True-False
Circle T if the answer is True or F if the answer is False.

T F 1. Open grain woods generally do not require additional preparation during finishing.

T F 2. The best grade of softwood lumber is Select.

T F 3. Engineered lumber does not warp; however, it is not as strong as sawed lumber.

T F 4. Nominal dimensions of lumber are always greater than the dressed dimensions.

T F 5. A set of house plans includes five different types of drawings.

T F 6. A small backsaw should be used to cut curves.

T F 7. The blade rotation of a radial arm saw is in the direction of the saw feed.

T F 8. A transit is like a builder's level but pivots downward at a 45° angle.

Multiple Choice
Choose the answer that correctly completes the statement. Write the corresponding letter in the space provided.

_____ 9. Steel framing members are available in several gauges and often replace wood ____.
   A. subflooring
   B. bracing
   C. studs, joists, rafters, and wall plates
   D. trim

_____ 10. The moisture content of a piece of wood weighing 45 lb. before it is dried and 40 lb. after it is dried is ____.
   A. 1%
   B. 5%
   C. 7.5%
   D. 12.5%

_____ 11. The ____ of a hammer should strike the nail head when driving a nail.
   A. cheek
   B. face
   C. neck
   D. handle

_____ 12. The size of a belt sander is determined by the _____.
   A. width of the belt
   B. length of the belt
   C. size of the sander motor
   D. None of the above.

_____ 13. When using a radial arm saw, a _____ margin of safety should be maintained between operator's hands and the path of the saw blade.
   A. 1″
   B. 6″
   C. 1′
   D. 1′-6″

_____ 14. When using a jointer, the stock must be no less than _____ long.
   A. 2″
   B. 4″
   C. 8″
   D. 12″

_____ 15. Wood cells are formed in the _____.
   A. tracheids
   B. phloem
   C. lignin
   D. cambium layer

Matching
Select the correct answer from the list on the right and place the corresponding letter in the blank on the left.

_____ 16. Laminated veneer lumber.

_____ 17. Glue-laminated beams.

_____ 18. Wood I-beams.

_____ 19. Open-web trusses.

_____ 20. Parallel-strand lumber.

_____ 21. Laminated-strand lumber.

A. Four or more layers of 1 1/2″ thick stock glued under pressure.

B. Fabricated of solid 2 × 4 chords with webbing of steel.

C. Made of solid lumber chords between a web of plywood or oriented strand board.

D. Veneer laid up parallel and glued under pressure.

E. Manufactured in billets 66′ long and cut to various lengths and widths.

F. Laid up from 1/32″ × 1″ × 12″ strands bonded with polyurethane adhesive.

Name _____

Completion
Place the answer that correctly completes the statement in the space provided.

_____ 22. A piece of lumber measuring 2″ × 12″ × 48″ contains ____ board feet.

_____ 23. A(n) ____ plan indicates the location of the structure and the distances from it to the property lines.

_____ 24. One quadrant contains ____ degrees.

_____ 25. The operating principle of a leveling instrument is that a(n) ____ is always a straight line.

_____ 26. The officially established elevation that can be used for a number of building sites in a given location is called the ____.

_____ 27. The dressed dimensions of a 2 × 4 stud are ____.

_____ 28. Ten 2 × 6s that are 12′ long contain a total of ____ board feet.

_____ 29. Plastic laminates are usually bonded to a base material with ____.

_____ 30. A(n) ____d nail is 3″ long.

_____ 31. The size of a portable circular saw is determined by the ____ of the largest blade it will take.

Identification
Identify the parts of the log cross section.

_____ 32. Cambium.

_____ 33. Sapwood.

_____ 34. Heartwood.

_____ 35. Pith.

_____ 36. Bark.

_____ 37. Annual rings

_____ 38. Wood rays.

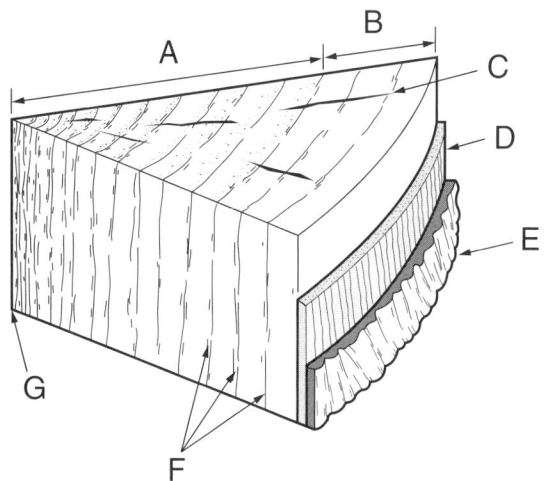

Identification

Identify the parts of the grade-trademark.

_____ 39. Thickness.

_____ 40. Panel grade.

_____ 41. Exposure durability classification.

_____ 42. Mill number.

_____ 43. Span rating.

_____ 44. Product standard.

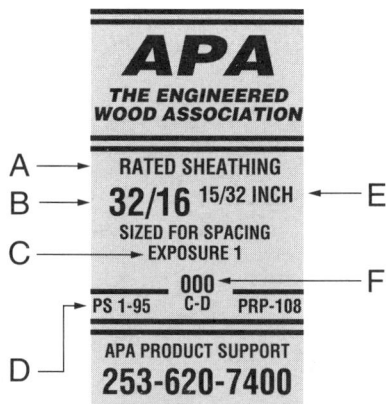

7 Footings and Foundations

Objectives

After studying this chapter, students will be able to:
- Lay out building lines and set up batter boards.
- Describe excavation procedures.
- Explain footing requirements and how to build footing forms.
- Define the terms *concrete*, *cement*, and *aggregate*.
- Describe the building, erecting, and use of forms for poured foundation walls.
- Discuss the types of foundation systems used for residential buildings.
- List steps and professional practices for laying up concrete block foundation walls.
- Explain foundation insulating and waterproofing procedures.
- Discuss design factors that apply to sidewalks and driveways.
- Estimate concrete materials required for a specific area.

Instructional Materials

Text: Pages 169–221
  Technical Vocabulary, page 169
  Test Your Knowledge, page 220
  Curricular Connections, page 221
  Outside Assignments, page 221
Workbook: Pages 33–40
Instructor's Resource:
  Reproducible masters:
    RM 7-1 *Using Batter Boards*
    RM 7-2 *Foundation Elements*
    RM 7-3 *Foundation Types*
    RM 7-4 *Laying Out Footing Forms*
    RM 7-5 *Locating Footing Forms*
    RM 7-6 *Concrete Blocks*
    RM 7-7 *Four Types of Insulated Concrete Forms (ICFs)*
    RM 7-8 *Wood Foundation Design*
  Transparencies (binder/CD only):
    CT 7-1 *Forming Up for a Slab-on-Grade Foundation in a Warm Climate*
    CT 7-2 *Proper Bracing of a Poured Basement*
    CT 7-3 *Pile Foundation*
    CT 7-4 *Prefabricated Plastic Footing Form*
    CT 7-5 *Preparing to Pour a Footing for a Foundation*
    CT 7-6 *Traditional Foundation Form*
    CT 7-7 *New Types of Foundation Forms*
  Procedure Checklist: *Setting Up Batter Boards*
  Procedure Checklist: *Constructing Footing Forms*
Chapter Quiz

Trade-Related Math

Concrete is measured and sold by the cubic yard. A cubic yard measures $3' \times 3' \times 3'$. It contains 27 cu. ft. ($3 \times 3 \times 3 = 27$). To determine the number of cubic yards needed for a square or rectangular area, multiply the width by the length by the height (or thickness), and then divide by 27. For example, if you want to determine the number of cubic yards of concrete needed for a concrete slab measuring $20' \times 15' \times 4''$ (.33') thick, calculate it as follows:

width × length × thickness ÷ 27 = cubic yards

$20 \times 15 \times .33 \div 27 = 3.66$

3.66 cubic yards of concrete are required

Tables are available for determining the number of concrete blocks and the bags per 100 sq. ft. of wall. Refer to the table, Estimating Concrete Block and Mortar in Appendix B Technical Information in the text.

Suppose that you wish to determine the amount of block and cement needed for a basement 8' high and 24' square $8'' \times 8'' \times 16''$. The chart, Number of Block/Course for Solid Walls, in Appendix B Technical Information in the text shows that 70 blocks are needed for each course. According to the chart, Concrete Masonry Courses by Heights, also found in Appendix B Technical Information in the text, shows that 12 courses are needed. Thus:

Number of Blocks in a Course × Number of Courses = Number of Blocks Needed = 70 × 12 = 840.

Number of blocks needed: 840; however, since there is some waste, estimators usually increase this total by 2%:

840 × 1.02 = 856.8, which is rounded off to the next larger whole number: 857 blocks are needed.

Instructional Concepts and Student Learning Experiences

Clearing the Site
1. Describe typical operations performed when clearing a building site. Discuss the advantages of retaining conifers and deciduous trees on the property when clearing the site.

Laying Out Building Lines
1. Discuss the process of establishing lot lines. Explain why a registered engineer or licensed surveyor should verify them.
2. Review the laying out of building lines by use of measuring tapes and then by use of a builder's level or transit. This is discussed in text Chapter 6. Describe the means of checking for squareness of building lines.
3. Explain the purpose of corner stakes and their uses.
4. Explain the purpose of setting up batter boards. Using reproducible master RM 7-1 *Using Batter Boards*, have the students list the materials necessary to construct batter boards.
5. Given the floor plan of a residential structure, have the students indicate where they would position the batter boards.
6. Demonstrate the correct procedure for setting up batter boards. As a class, lay out the building lines for a small residential structure and construct batter boards. Emphasize the importance of constructing the batter boards accurately.

Excavation
1. Describe the different operations that may occur when excavating the building site.
2. Discuss why foundations must be located below the frost line in cold climates. Explain what might happen if a foundation is not located deep enough.
3. Define the term *control point* and explain how to find it.
4. Describe factors that should be considered when determining the depth of an excavation.

Foundation Systems
1. Using reproducible master RM 7-2 *Foundation Elements*, identify the components of a foundation. Ask the students to briefly describe the purpose of each component.
2. Using reproducible master RM 7-3 *Foundation Types*, discuss the various types of foundations used in residential construction.
3. Refer to Figure 7-10. Have the students identify the different types of footings. Compare and contrast each of these types of footings and describe situations where each might be used.
4. Discuss the different types of slab foundations, including structurally supported, ground supported, and monolithic. Describe applications and advantages of each type.

Footing Design
1. Discuss the typical dimensions for standard footings, footings located under columns and posts, and chimney footings.
2. Describe the applications of reinforced footings in residential construction. Identify the types of materials commonly used for reinforcement.
3. Explain the purpose of forming a key in the footings when cast-in-place concrete walls are to be used. Describe how the key is formed in the concrete.

Forms for Footings
1. Discuss the importance of checking the placement of the batter boards after the excavation.
2. Using reproducible master RM 7-4 *Laying Out Footing Forms*, describe the proper procedure for laying out footing forms. Emphasize the importance of checking footing forms for levelness. Note that if the footing is not level, the rest of the structure will not

be level. Stress the importance of accurate measurements and layout techniques. Identify the types of materials that are commonly used to construct footing forms. Emphasize the importance of having an adequate excavation slope to avoid cave-ins.
3. Review reproducible master RM 7-5 *Locating Footing Forms*. Demonstrate the construction of footing forms for a residential structure. Have students assist you in laying out the proper position of the forms and actually constructing the forms. When this has been completed, divide the students into pairs and have each pair lay out and construct a small section of footing forms. Use nontypical dimensions for the footings so that students must make adjustments to the width and height of the forms.

Concrete
1. Identify the primary ingredients of concrete and briefly describe each. Discuss the importance of using good quality materials and being able to recognize unsuitable materials.
2. Obtain samples of different types of aggregate. Have the students list characteristics of each.
3. Demonstrate the proper techniques for mixing concrete. Emphasize the correct order of adding materials to the mix.

Erecting Wall Forms
1. Identify the different types of wall forms that are used in residential construction, including site built and prefabricated forms. Discuss the advantages of each type.
2. Calculate the amount of pressure that is created by concrete at the bottom of wall forms. Compare the amount of pressure that is created at the bottom of a 4′ wall versus a 10′ wall. Stress the importance of using materials that can withstand this pressure.
3. Discuss the procedure for setting up foundation wall forms. Emphasize that correct placement and bracing of wall forms is vital to the remainder of the building construction.
4. Obtain a variety of form hardware including snap ties, taper ties, coil ties, and corner clamps. Allow the students to inspect the hardware.
5. As a class, have the students construct a scale model of a site-built wall form. Be sure to include all bracing and form hardware.

Stress the importance of carefully checking the dimensions of the formwork prior to pouring concrete.
6. Discuss the advantages of using panel forms. Explain that panel forms are designed to be used many times and, thus, should be removed and handled carefully to avoid damaging them.
7. Discuss the methods used to form frame openings in foundation walls.
8. Using the scale model of the site-built wall form, add formwork for a window opening. Once again, stress the importance of accurate placement of the formwork.
9. Define the term *pilaster*. Describe situations where pilasters may be necessary.

Placing Concrete
1. Describe methods commonly used to deliver concrete to the forms, such as ready-mix trucks, concrete buckets, concrete buggies, and wheelbarrows.
2. Define *segregation* and list causes of it.
3. Demonstrate methods used to vibrate and compact concrete in forms. Stress that excessive vibration creates additional pressure in the forms and causes segregation.
4. Identify different types of anchors used to secure wall plates to the top of a concrete or concrete block foundation wall.
5. Using the scale model of the site-built wall form, demonstrate the correct procedure for placing concrete and vibrating it. When the placement of the concrete is complete, set anchor bolts to accept a 2 × 4 wall plate.

Concrete Block Foundations
1. Discuss the design and composition of concrete block.
2. Using reproducible master RM 7-6 *Concrete Blocks*, identify the various types of concrete blocks and cite applications for each. Have the students take note that the actual size of a block is 3/8″ less than the nominal size to allow for a 3/8″ mortar joint.
3. Discuss the materials used in mortar and important properties that create a strong bond between the blocks.
4. Explain procedures for laying block. Discuss the proper tools for getting a level, plumb wall.

5. Explain the use and installation of anchors.
6. Define the term *lintel*. Discuss how lintels play an important part in supporting masonry across the tops of door and window openings. Identify various techniques used to form lintels.

Insulating Foundation Walls
1. Describe the means of insulating concrete block walls. Cite examples of where one method or another might be advantageous.
2. Explain why waterproofing is necessary. Discuss the methods used to waterproof concrete and concrete block walls.
3. Demonstrate the proper procedure for waterproofing concrete and concrete block foundation walls. Allow students to assist you in applying the waterproofing materials.

Backfilling
1. Stress the importance of bracing foundation walls before backfilling.
2. Discuss the other three elements for an approved grading operation.
3. Stress the need to avoid certain damaging operations, such as burying construction debris and damaging perimeter drains during backfilling.

ICF Foundation and Wall Systems
1. Explain the acronym *ICF*. Detail the advantages of polystyrene (plastic foam) as to construction ease and energy conservation.
2. Explain code restrictions on ICF use under certain conditions, especially regarding areas infested with termites.
3. Discuss reproducible master RM 7-7 *Four Types of Insulated Concrete Forms (ICFs)*.
4. Discuss the proper procedure for erecting and bracing ICFs.
5. Explain proper method of pouring an ICF foundation wall.

Slab-on-grade Construction
1. While referring to Figure 7-58, describe the three types of slab-on-grade foundations. Discuss applications for each type.
2. List preparations that must be made before placing a slab-on-grade. Emphasize the importance of insulation and moisture control when creating the subgrade.
3. Discuss the use of perimeter insulation for slab-on-grade construction in cold climates.

Basement Floors
1. Describe where in the construction sequence concrete is placed for a basement floor. Discuss the type of preparation that is necessary before placing the concrete.

Entrance Platforms and Steps
1. Describe the construction of formwork for steps. Cite obstacles that may be encountered when constructing the forms, such as building forms between two existing walls.
2. Demonstrate the construction of the formwork for steps. Stress the importance of adequate bracing to avoid a concrete blowout.

Sidewalks and Drives
1. Have students summarize the general dimensions for walks. Discuss the materials required to construct the formwork.
2. Describe how a piece of asphalt-impregnated composition board is placed between a walk and other structure such as foundation walls or entrance platforms. Ask the students to explain why this is necessary.
3. Discuss the general dimensions of driveways. Have students contrast the differences between the dimensions for walks and driveways. Ask them to explain why they think these differences occur.
4. Define the terms *screeding* and *floating*. Discuss the proper procedure for screeding and floating a walk or driveway.
5. Explain the purpose of using control joints in a walk or driveway. Discuss how control joints are made.
6. Describe the final steps that should be taken to finish a concrete walk or driveway, including edging and brushing. In addition, discuss how concrete should be protected against extreme heat, rain, and cold.

Wood Foundations
1. Describe why all-weather wood foundations have gained in popularity. Discuss the type of preparation that must be made to the wood components.

2. Explain the type of preparation that must be made to the grade before constructing an all-weather wood foundation.
3. Using reproducible master RM 7-8 *Wood Foundation Design*, have the students list the types of materials that might be used in constructing an all-weather wood foundation.

Cold Weather Construction
1. Discuss the methods used to protect concrete in cold weather.
2. Cite techniques that might be used to ensure the integrity of concrete and masonry materials.
3. Define *admixture*. Describe how admixtures can be used to change the working properties of concrete.

Estimating Materials
1. Discuss the method used to determine the amount of concrete needed for a particular project. Make sure that an extra 5%–10% is added for waste.
2. Discuss the method used to determine the number of concrete masonry units (concrete blocks) needed for a particular construction project. Be sure to add 2% for waste.

Chapter Review
1. Review the chapter objectives. Be sure that the students are fully competent in the task identified by each objective.
2. Review the terms in the *Technical Vocabulary* section and make certain students are clear on each definition.
3. Assign the *Test Your Knowledge* questions, *Curricular Connections,* and *Outside Assignments* for Chapter 7 of the text. Review the answers to test questions in class. Also, have students report on the *Curricular Connections* and *Outside Assignments* activities as appropriate.
4. Assign Chapter 7 of the workbook. Review the answers in class.

Evaluation
This chapter provides three methods for evaluating student performance. Students should complete the *Test Your Knowledge* section using the book as reference. Students should also be allowed to use the book for reference when completing the workbook material. Use the Chapter 7 Quiz in the instructor's resources for in-class evaluation. Correct the quizzes, return them to the students, and review the quiz questions in group discussion.

Procedure Checklist
Using the procedure checklists *Setting Up Batter Boards* and *Constructing Footing Forms*, have students evaluate the techniques used to perform these tasks.

Answers to Test Your Knowledge
Text Page 220
1. True.
2. False.
3. three to four
4. True.
5. B. Control point.
6. A slab that is supported directly by the ground. Also called ground-supported slab.
7. Thickened reinforced portion of a slab foundation.
8. 18
9. stepped
10. twice
11. 2
12. False.
13. cement
14. Thickened section of a concrete or masonry wall that strengthens the wall or provides extra support for beams.
15. hydration
16. Covering with burlap, straw, or any material that will hold water and keep material wet. Covering with plastic and sealing laps with tape or planking. Using liquid-membrane compound to seal in moisture. Flooding with water or using sprinklers to keep concrete wet.
17. slump
18. 94
19. smooth
20. bolts
21. 7 5/8 × 7 5/8 × 15 5/8
22. Corners

23. Closure
24. insulated
25. 8
26. vapor barrier
27. To level surface by removing the excess concrete.
28. Makes a smoother finish, fills hollows, and compacts the concrete.
29. Will bring too many fines to the surface; this will produce fine cracks in the cured concrete.
30. 4″
31. 1/4″ per foot
32. porous gravel or crushed stone
33. False.
34. False.
35. 112.5 (purchase 113)

Answers to Workbook Questions Page 33–40

1. lot lines
2. A. 90°
   B. 8′-0″
   C. 6′-0″
   D. 10′-0″
3. diagonals
4. D. ledger
5. A. 2′
6. B. 8″
7. A. 5″
   B. 5″
   C. 10″
   D. 20″
8. A. 12″
   B. 6″
9. D. 5/8″
10. A. Grade stake.
    B. Level.
    C. Corner stake.
    D. Outside form for footing.
11. hydration
12. D. 94 lb.
13. D. 1 1/2″
14. A. Wales.
    B. Sheathing.
    C. Tie rods/wall ties.
    D. Studs.
15. D. sill
16. A. anchor bolt
    B. 4
17. A. Face shell.
    B. Concave end.
    C. Ear.
    D. Cells or cores.
    E. Cross web.
18. B. 3/8″
19. A. Stretcher (3 core).
    B. Corner.
    C. Double-corner/pier.
    D. Bull nose.
    E. Beam/lintel.
    F. Half-cut header.
    G. Jamb.
20. areaway
21. See Figure 7-48 in text.
22. A. Tack strip.
    B. Metal reinforcement.
    C. Rigid insulation.
    D. Membrane dampproofing.
    E. Granular fill.
23. A. 18 hours
24. C. pressure-treated with chemicals
25. C. sump pump
26. D. 40°F
27. B. admixtures
28. 16 cu. yd.
29. 7 1/2 cu. yd.
30. 5 2/3 cu. yd.
31. 1944
32. 112.5

Answers to Chapter Quiz

1. False.
2. False.
3. True.
4. True.
5. False.
6. A. 8″
7. B. Segregation
8. B. 1800–2500
9. C. Hydration
10. E.
11. B.
12. C.
13. D.
14. F.
15. A.
16. G.

Using Batter Boards

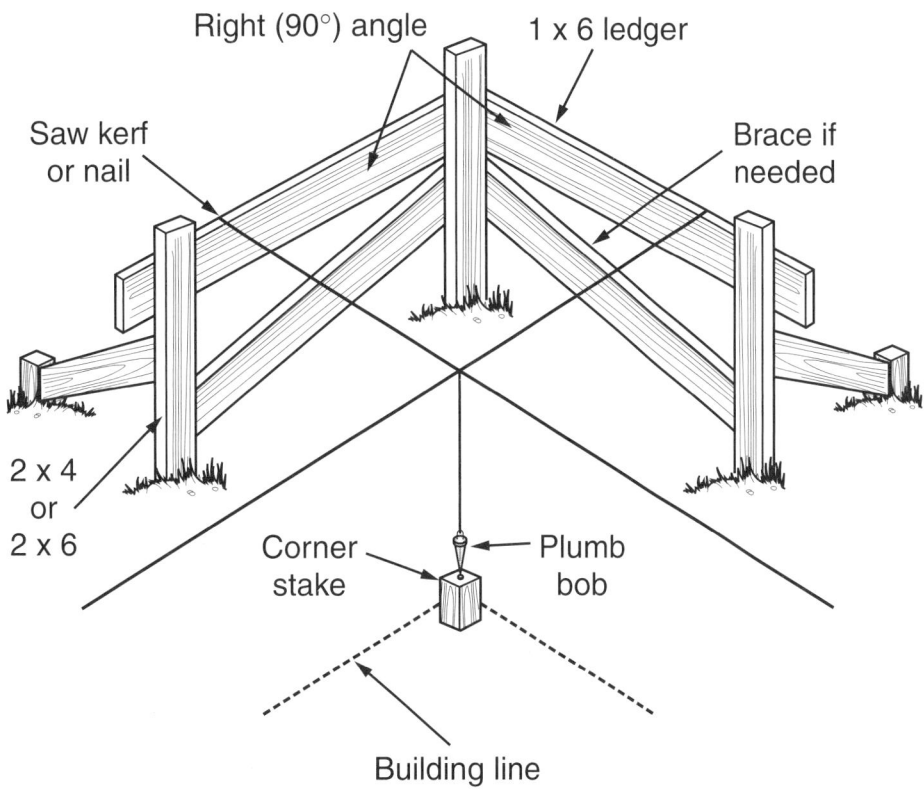

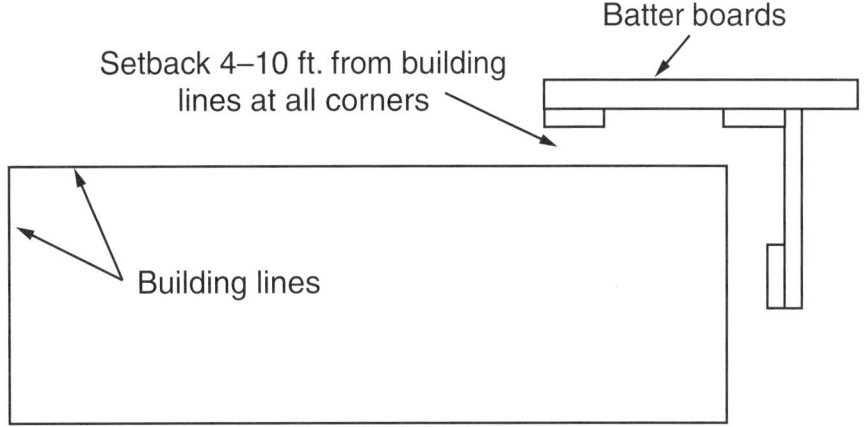

RM 7-1

Foundation Elements

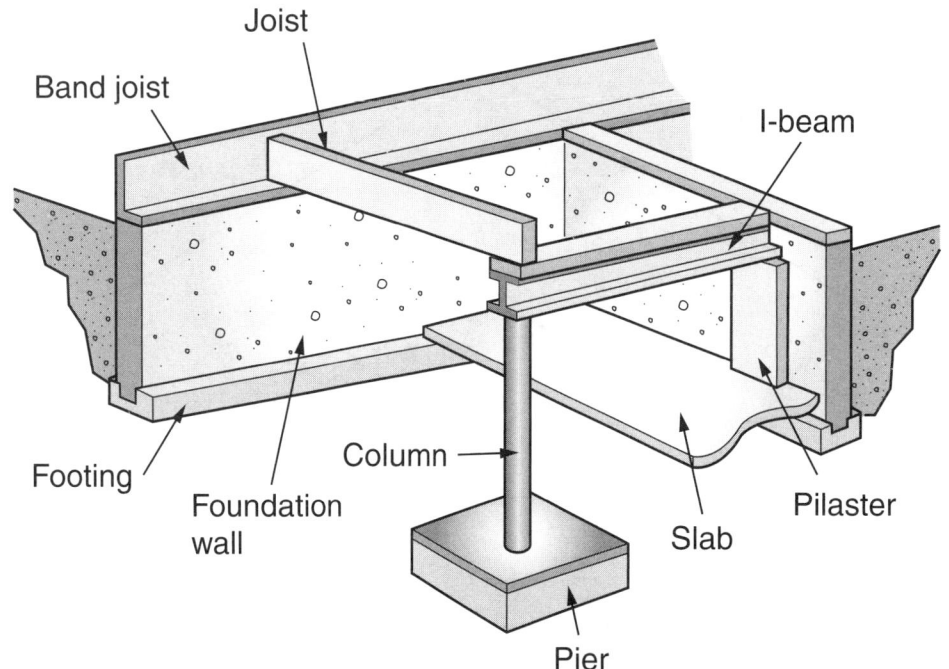

RM 7-2

Foundation Types

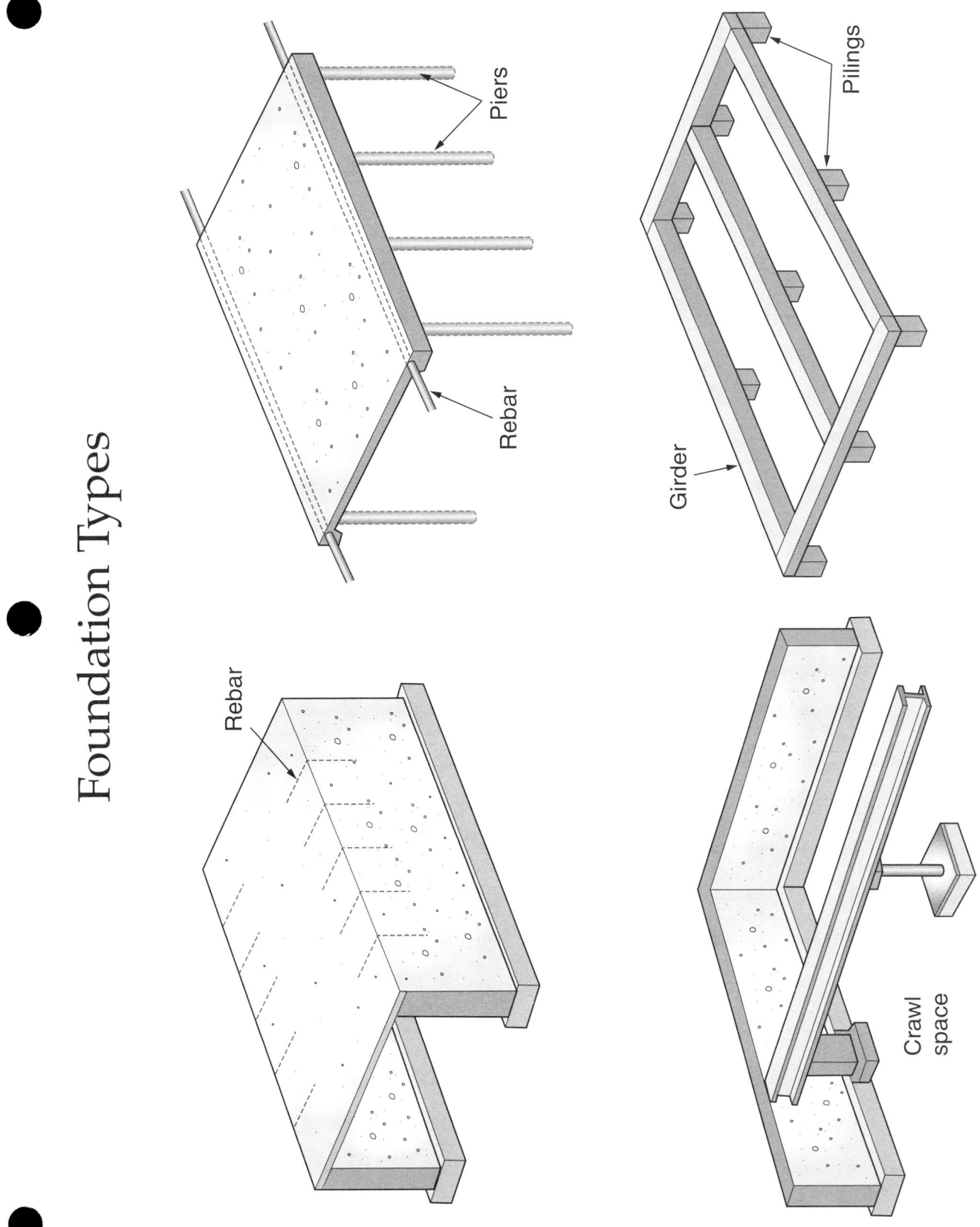

RM7-3

Laying Out Footing Forms

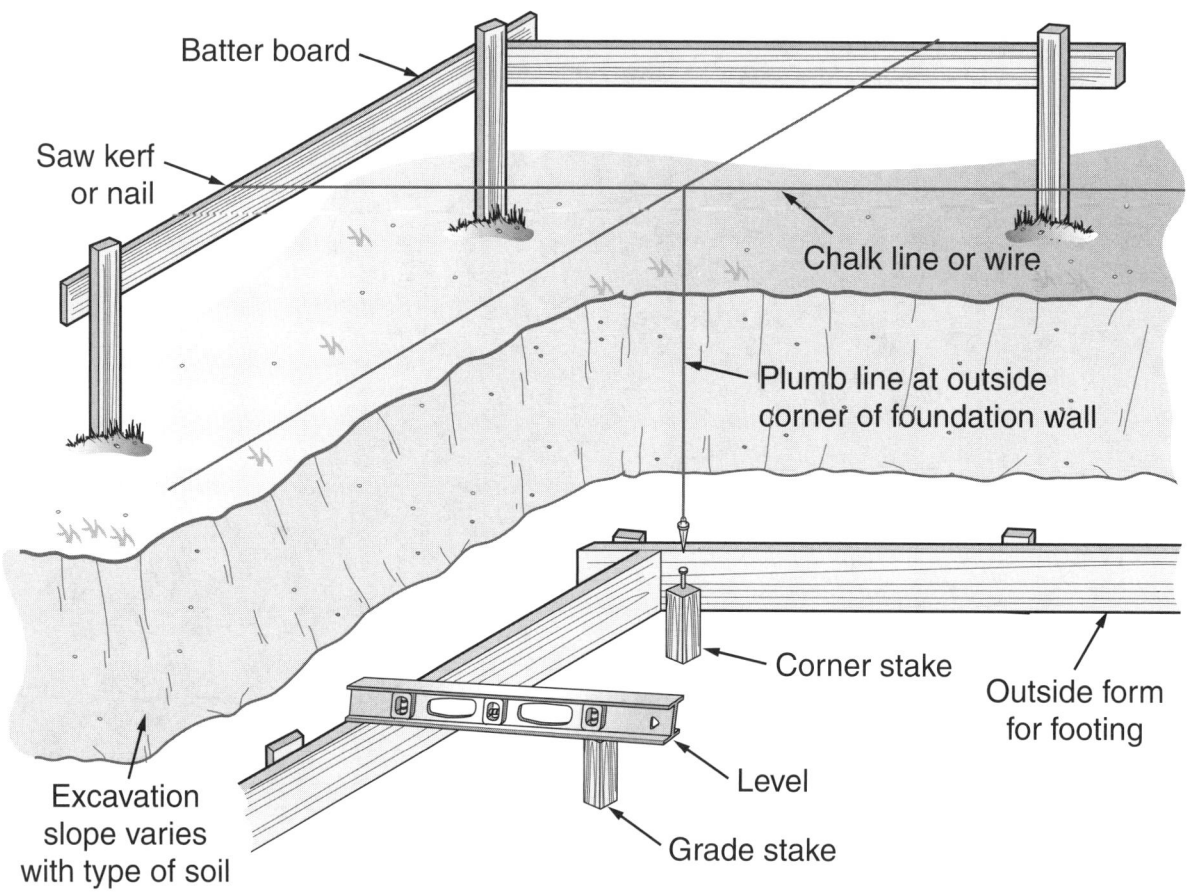

RM 7-4

Locating Footing Forms

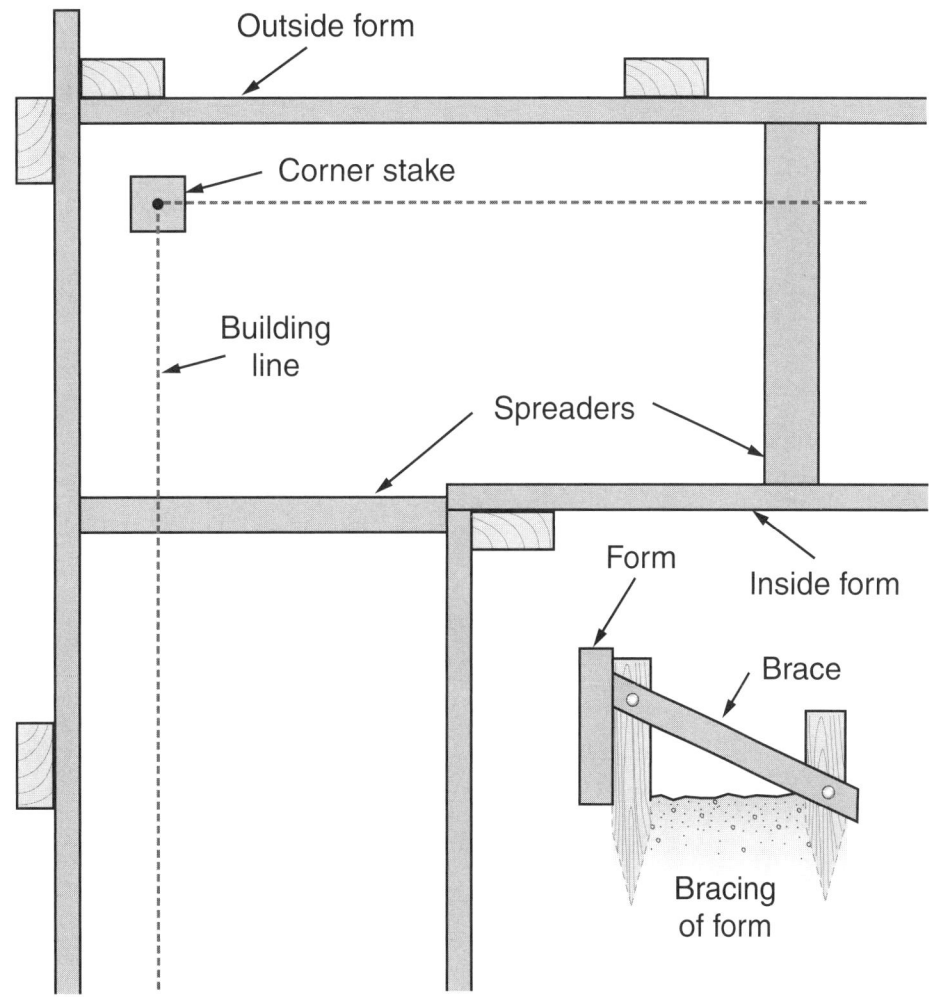

RM 7-5

Concrete Blocks

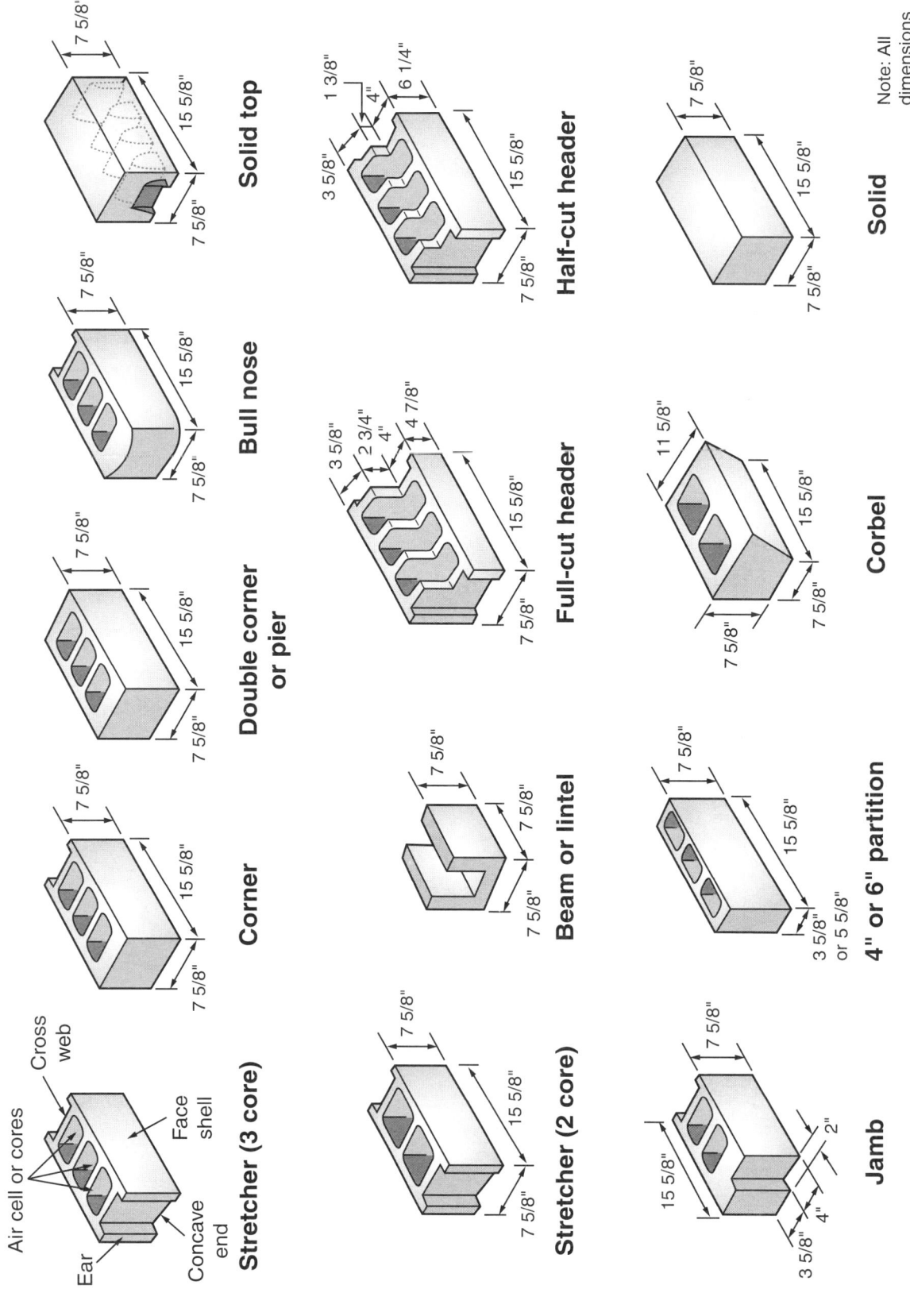

RM 7-6

Four Types of Insulated Concrete Forms (ICFs)

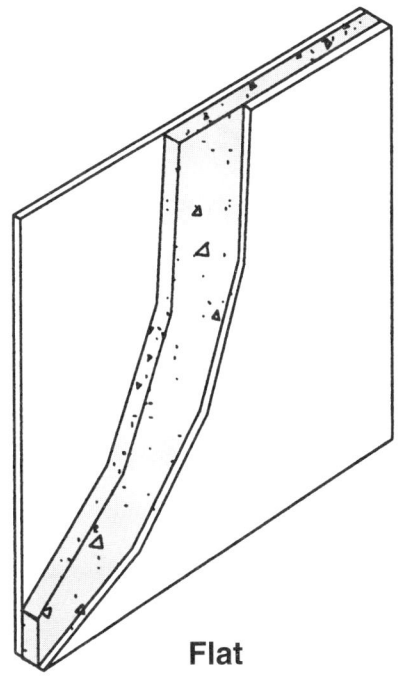
Flat

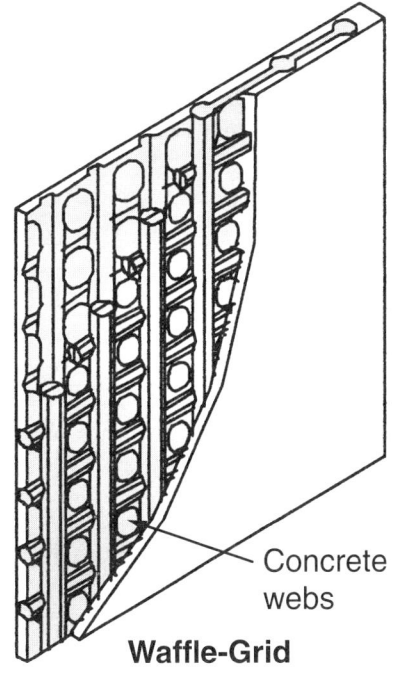
Concrete webs
Waffle-Grid

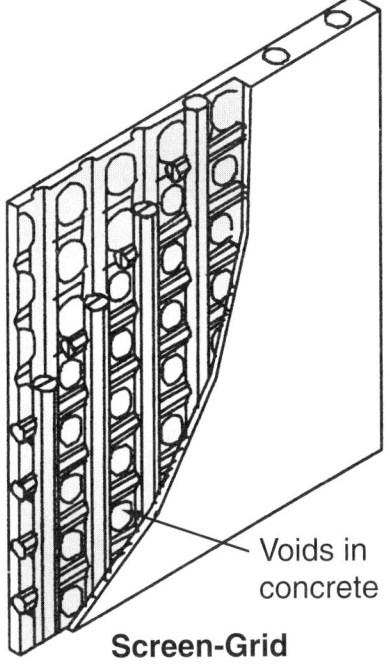
Voids in concrete
Screen-Grid

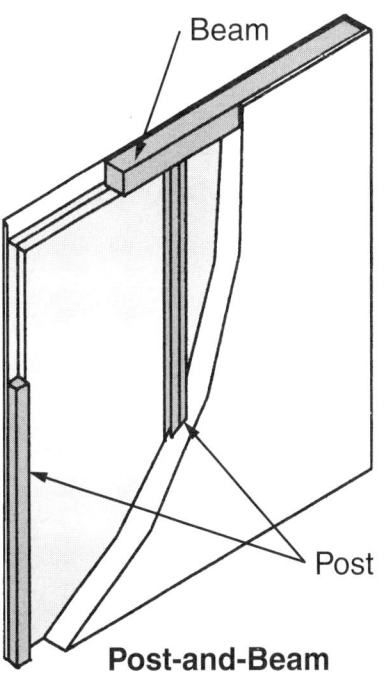
Beam
Post
Post-and-Beam

RM 7-7

Wood Foundation Design

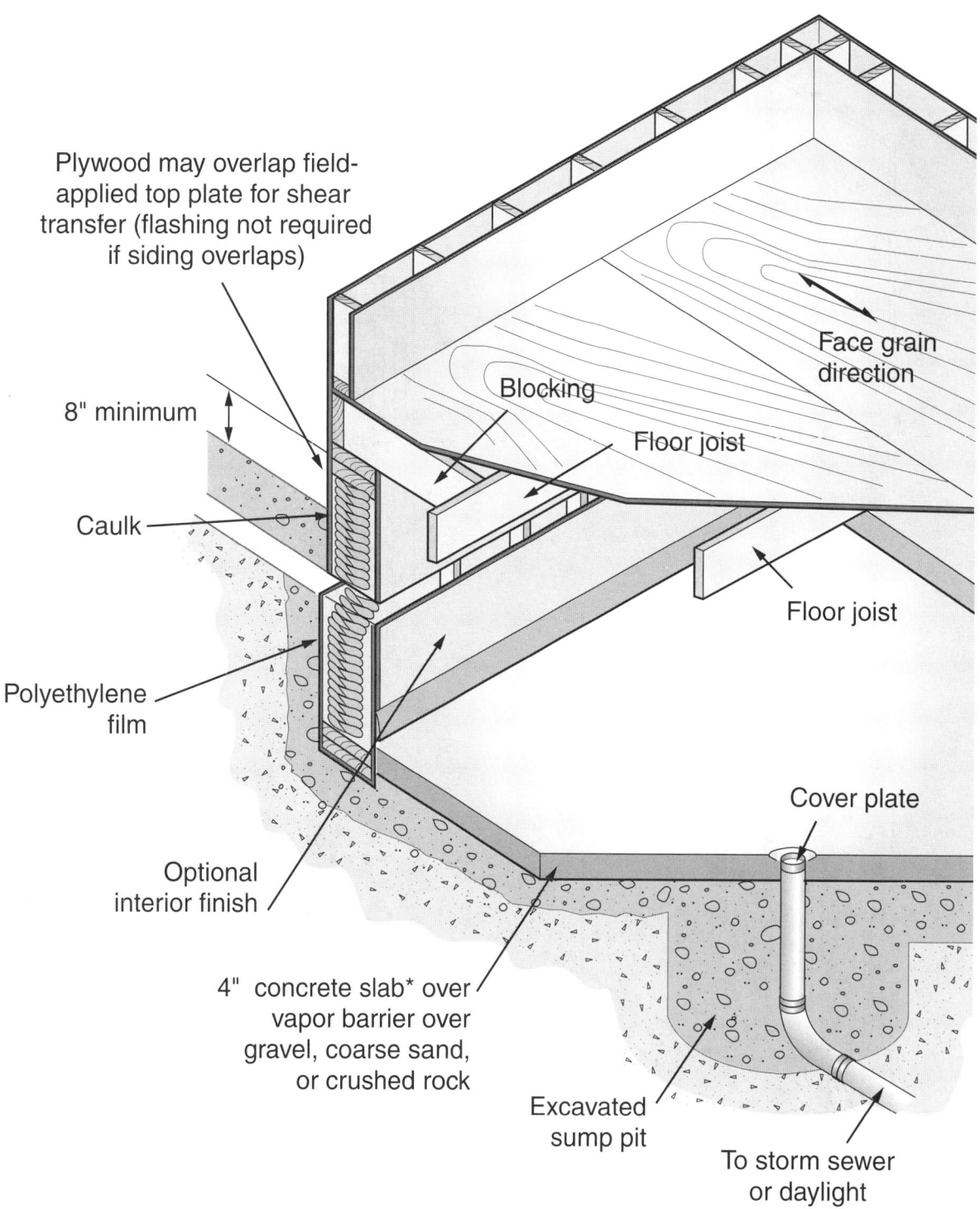

*A wood basement floor system is available; write APA for details

Chapter 7 Procedure Checklist
Setting Up Batter Boards

Name _____ Total _____

❏	Selects proper materials for stakes, ledgers, and braces.	5	4	3	2	1	Must be told the appropriate materials to use for batter boards.
❏	Properly locates positions of stakes (approximately 4′ from intersection of building line).	5	4	3	2	1	Places stakes directly in line with building lines.
❏	Nails ledger boards in place and checks levelness; verifies levelness with other ledger boards.	5	4	3	2	1	Nails ledger boards at inconvenient height, disregarding levelness. Does not check levelness with other ledger boards.
❏	Properly runs lines and plumbs corner over corner stake; takes care in making sure alignment is accurate.	5	4	3	2	1	Cannot run or adjust building lines; recklessly places lines.

Permission granted to reproduce for educational use only. Copyright by Goodheart-Willcox Co., Inc.

Chapter 7 Procedure Checklist
Construction Footing Forms

Name _____ Total _____

- ❏ Accurately re-establishes building lines.   5 4 3 2 1   Neglects to re-establish building lines.

- ❏ Sets up builder's level and accurately locates grade and corner stakes; connects corner stakes with lines.   5 4 3 2 1   Sets up grade and corner stakes randomly without verifying location with leveling instrument.

- ❏ Determines footing width and accurately lays it out.   5 4 3 2 1   Must be told the footing width; unable to determine proper placement of footing boards.

- ❏ Efficiently sets up outside footing boards, then the inside ones using spacers or spreaders; determines whether bracing will be required and installs it if necessary.   5 4 3 2 1   Must be assisted when setting up footing form boards; does not use spacers or spreaders; does not realize importance of bracing in necessary situations.

Permission granted to reproduce for educational use only.   Copyright by Goodheart-Willcox Co., Inc.

Chapter 7 Quiz
Footings and Foundations

Name _____ Date _____ Score _____

True-False
Circle T if the answer is True or F if the answer is False.

T   F   1. Batter boards should be 6″ away from the corners created by the building lines.

T   F   2. Reinforced footings gain their strength from aggregate and concrete.

T   F   3. Monolithic concrete is constructed in one continuous pour.

T   F   4. When mixing concrete, first combine the aggregate and cement before adding water.

T   F   5. In most areas, concrete sidewalks are at least 12″ thick.

Multiple Choice
Choose the answer that correctly completes the statement. Write the corresponding letter in the space provided.

_____ 6. Foundations should extend about _____ above finished grade.
  A. 8″
  B. 16″
  C. 24″
  D. 32″

_____ 7. _____ is a condition in which the large aggregate gets separated from the cement paste and smaller aggregate.
  A. Separation
  B. Segregation
  C. Vibration
  D. None of the above.

_____ 8. Mortar used in concrete block foundations, according to ASTM standards, must withstand pressures from _____ psi.
  A. 1000–1500
  B. 1800–2500
  C. 2000–2700
  D. 2700–3400

_____ 9. _____ is the chemical reaction of cement and water during concrete hardening.
  A. Setting
  B. Segregation
  C. Hydration
  D. None of the above.

Permission granted to reproduce for educational use only.   Copyright by Goodheart-Willcox Co., Inc.

Identification

Identify the parts of the following foundation.

_____ 10. Slab.

_____ 11. Foundation wall.

_____ 12. Column.

_____ 13. Pier.

_____ 14. Pilaster.

_____ 15. Footing.

_____ 16. I-beam.

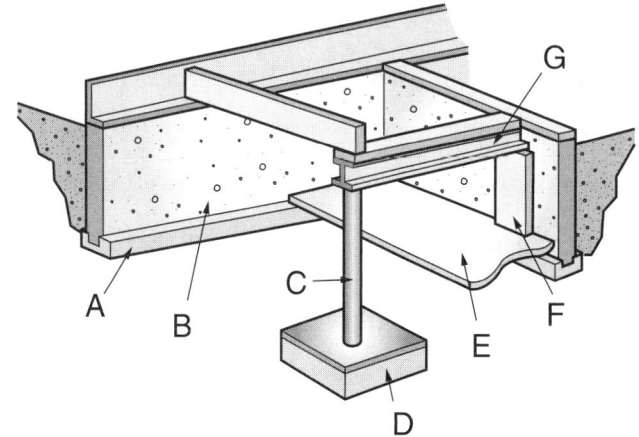

8 Floor Framing

Objectives

After studying this chapter, students will be able to:
- Explain the difference between platform and balloon framing.
- Identify the main parts of a platform frame.
- Calculate the load on girders and beams used in residential construction.
- Lay out and install sills on a foundation wall.
- Describe how layouts are made on a header joist.
- Explain the correct procedure to follow when assembling a floor frame.
- Identify the parts of a floor truss.
- Prepare a sketch that shows how overhangs and projections are framed.
- Describe materials used for subflooring.
- Estimate materials (sizes and amounts) required to construct a specific floor frame.

Instructional Materials

Text: Pages 223–252
  Technical Vocabulary, page 223
  Test Your Knowledge, page 251
  Curricular Connections, page 251
  Outside Assignments, page 251
Workbook: Pages 41–48
Instructor's Resource:
  Reproducible masters:
    RM 8-1 *Platform Framing Details*
    RM 8-2 *Framing Methods at Sill*
    RM 8-3 *Using Joist Hangers*
    RM 8-4A *Framing over Girders/Beams*
    RM 8-4B *Framing over Girders/Beams*
    RM 8-4C *Framing over Girders/Beams*
    RM 8-5A *Laying Out Joists*
    RM 8-5B *Laying Out Joists*
    RM 8-6 *Floor Frame*
    RM 8-7A *Assembling Floor Frame*
    RM 8-7B *Assembling Floor Frame*
    RM 8-8 *Truss Construction*
    RM 8-9 *Placing Subflooring*
  Transparencies (binder/CD only):
    CT 8-1 *Basic Components of a House*
    CT 8-2 *Second-Story Floor Framing*
  Procedure Checklist: *Installing Sills*
  Procedure Checklist: *Installing Joists*
  Chapter Quiz

Trade-Related Math

A carpenter may be required to estimate the number of floor joists used for a job. First, use a plan to scale the length of joists needed. Be sure to allow additional length so the joists rest properly on girders and partitions. Then, multiply the length of the wall by 3/4 for 16" O.C., 3/5 for 20" O.C. or 1/2 for 24" O.C. and add one. Be sure to add extra pieces for doubled joists. The formula looks like this:

length of wall $\times$ 3/4 + 1 + extras = Number of joists

For example, if the wall length is 28′, the joists are spaced 16″ O.C., and four extra joists are required, the number of joists is figured as follows:

length of wall $\times$ 3/4 + 1 + extras = Number of joists

$28 \times 3/4 + 1 + 4 = 21 + 1 + 4 = 26$
26 joists will be required

Instructional Concepts and Student Learning Experiences

Types of Framing
1. Discuss the use of platform framing, why it is used, and what advantages it offers.
2. Discuss the major advantages of balloon framing and why its use has been abandoned.
3. Using reproducible master RM 8-1 *Platform Framing Details,* discuss the construction procedures used for platform framing.

4. Using reproducible master RM 8-2 *Framing Methods at Sill*, discuss the framing methods shown in an architectural plan. Discuss what part of the plans contain details showing the framing. Have the students note the differences.
5. Discuss modern applications for balloon framing. Explain why balloon framing is now used on a limited basis.

Girders and Beams
1. Discuss the reasons for using girders and beams in a residential structure. Have students identify the types of materials commonly used as girders or beams.
2. Describe the procedure used to determine the size of girders or beams needed for support in a structure.
3. List and discuss the advantages and disadvantages of using steel beams in a house.
4. Explain the difference between S and W steel beams.
5. Discuss the procedure for constructing a built-up girder. Stress that the lumber should be securely nailed together and that the joints should rest directly over columns or posts.

Posts and Columns
1. Discuss the sizes of beams that are generally used to support beams or girders. Emphasize that, as a rule of thumb, it is safe to assume that a post or column whose greatest dimension is equal to the width of the girder it supports will adequately carry the imposed loads.
2. Describe the types of footings that must be provided to support girder posts and columns. Stress that some forethought must be used to make sure that reinforcing rod or iron bolts are embedded into the concrete footing before the concrete sets.
3. Have students identify the types of materials used for posts and columns. If possible, set up a steel adjustable post and demonstrate its use.

Framing over Girders and Beams
1. Show how joist hangers are placed using reproducible master RM 8-3 *Using Joist Hangers*. Discuss the advantages of using joist hangers.
2. Demonstrate how joist hangers are attached to a girder or beam.
3. Using reproducible masters 8-4A, B, and C *Framing over Girders/Beams*, discuss the common methods of framing joists over girders and beams. Discuss the means for raising or lowering the ceiling height by using different methods of framing joists.

Sill Construction
1. Discuss the purpose of a sill. Have students list other names that are commonly used for a sill.
2. Describe why 2 × 6 lumber is typically used for sills. Explain that in the past, 2 × 4 lumber was commonly used for sills.
3. Ask the students to describe any type of preparation (such as a sill sealer) that should be used prior to attaching the sill.

Termite Shields
1. Have students identify the parts of the United States that are susceptible to termites. Discuss the destruction that may be caused by termites.
2. Describe techniques that may be used to guard against termite damage, including termite shields, treated lumber, and poisoning the soil around the structure.

Installing Sills
1. Discuss the importance of accurately laying out the holes in a sill when it is to be attached with anchor bolts. Using reproducible master RM 8-5A *Laying Out Joists*, describe the procedures that can be used to attach a sill to a foundation wall. Stress that the sill will be set back from the outside of the foundation wall and that this measurement must be taken into consideration when laying out the anchor bolt holes.
2. Using the scale model of the foundation wall constructed in Chapter 6, have the students attach a sill to it. Be sure to include sill sealer.
3. Describe what should be done when an uneven foundation wall is encountered.

Joists
1. Discuss the purpose of floor joists. Explain that joists are usually placed 16″ O.C., but that other spacing may be used in some circumstances.

2. Using a complete set of plans for a residential structure, have the students locate information that should be used to determine the type and direction of the floor joists. Have the students pay close attention to dimensions and other notes that relate to other superstructure members.
3. Using reproducible master RM 8-5B *Laying Out Joists*, discuss where joist positions are usually located. Mention that in platform framing, joist position is generally marked on the joist header, not on the sill. Stress the importance of marking an X on the sill or joist header to indicate on which side of the line the joist should actually be located.
4. Have students list areas where they feel that joists should be doubled, such as under load-bearing partitions and around openings in the floor frame for stairways, chimneys, and fireplaces.
5. Discuss the proper procedure for installing joists. Emphasize that joists should be placed with the crown facing up.
6. Using reproducible master RM 8-6 *Floor Frame*, point out the framing members that must be installed in a finished floor assembly.
7. Explain that header and tail joist cuts must be made square and that they must fit tightly together with other framing members. Stress that considerable strength will be lost if members do not fit tightly together.
8. Using Figure 8-33, describe the procedure for assembling frames for floor openings.
9. Using reproducible masters RM 8-7A and B *Assembling Floor Frame*, describe a good nailing pattern to use when assembling a floor frame. Emphasize that a good nailing pattern will provide good support for concentrated loads.

Special Framing Problems
1. Describe special framing problems that may be encountered in residential construction.
2. Using Figure 8-40, discuss the problems that may be encountered when floor joists run parallel to the foundation wall.
3. Identify areas of a house that may pose special framing problems, such as bathrooms and areas where tile or stone is to be laid.

4. Demonstrate the concepts of tension and compression with regard to floor joists. Secure a thin piece of stock in two vises (one at each end) along the edge of a shop table. Hang weights along the bottom of the stock to represent the loads of a floor, furniture, and appliances. Note the deflection of the stock. Drill a hole along the top edge of the strip, hang the weights, and note the deflection. Make a cut three-quarters of the way through a similar piece of stock. Hang weights from the bottom (as done in the previous examples) and note the deflection and/or damage. Use this demonstration to stress the importance of properly placing cuts or drilling holes in joists.
5. Discuss precautions that should be considered when cutting joists for plumbing runs.
6. Explain the advantages of using a crawl space in a residential structure. Discuss the construction of a crawl space that can be used as a heating/cooling plenum.

Floor Trusses and Wood I-Beams
1. Discuss the purpose of floor trusses and wood I-beams in residential construction. Cite advantages of using floor trusses.
2. Using reproducible master RM 8-8 *Truss Construction*, identify the various types of truss construction. Discuss the purpose of a subfloor.
3. Have students identify the types of materials commonly used for subfloors.
4. Describe the advantages of using plywood as a subflooring.
5. Using reproducible master RM 8-9 *Placing Subflooring*, discuss the proper spacing and nailing procedures for plywood subflooring.

Other Sheet Materials
1. Have students identify other sheet materials that can be used as subflooring.

Glued Floor System
1. Discuss the advantages of using a glued floor system. Describe the correct procedure for applying glue for subflooring.

Bridging
1. Discuss the purpose of bridging. Cite examples of places where bridging can be eliminated.

2. Describe the various types of bridging used for residential structures, including wood cross bridging, solid bridging, and prefabricated steel bridging. If possible, obtain samples of different types of bridging and allow students to inspect each type.
3. Demonstrate how wooden cross bridging is laid out using a framing square. Also, have students demonstrate the proper layout procedure.

Estimating Materials
1. Demonstrate the method used to estimate the number and size of floor joists for a residential structure.
2. Discuss the means for estimating the amount of subflooring required.

Chapter Review
1. Review the chapter objectives. Be sure that the students are fully competent in the task identified by each objective.
2. Review the terms in the *Technical Vocabulary* section and make certain students are clear on each definition.
3. Assign the *Test Your Knowledge* questions, *Curricular Connections*, and *Outside Assignments* for Chapter 8 of the text. Review the answers to test questions in class. Also, have students report on the *Curricular Connections* and *Outside Assignments* activities as appropriate.
4. Assign Chapter 8 of the workbook. Review the answers in class.

Evaluation
This chapter provides three methods for evaluating student performance. Students should complete the *Test Your Knowledge* section using the book as reference. Students should also be allowed to use the book for reference when completing the workbook material. Use the Chapter 8 Quiz in the instructor's resources for in-class evaluation. Correct the quizzes, return them to the students, and review the quiz questions in group discussion.

Procedure Checklist
Using the procedure checklists *Installing Sills* and *Installing Joists,* have students evaluate the techniques used to perform these tasks.

Answers to Test Your Knowledge
Text Page 251
1. platform
2. sill
3. builtup, engineered, steel
4. sheathing thickness
5. 1/360
6. tail
7. doubled
8. two
9. chords
10. parallel

Answers to Workbook Questions
Page 41–48
1. floor frame
2. A. Band joist.
   B. Subfloor.
   C. Joist.
   D. Sole plate.
   E. Sill.
   F. Girder.
3. western
4. C. ribbon
5. C. 40
6. B. 12″
7. A. Girder.
   B. Ledger.
   C. Joist.
   D. Solid bridging.
   E. Steel beam.
   F. Steel post.
8. C. attach the sill to foundation walls
9. A. Width.
   B. Depth.
   C. Flange.
   D. Web.
10. 1/3″
11. A. 16″
    B. 16″
    C. 15 1/4″
12. B. 3-16d
13. C. one-half
14. A. Header/band joist.
    B. Regular joist.
    C. Tail joist.
    D. Double header.

E. Double trimmer.
   F. Tail joist.
15. D. 12'-0".
16. A. Make each joist stronger.
17. doubled
18. B. approximately in the middle
19. B. 1/2"
20. A. 25%
21. See Figure 8-44 in text.
22. A. 10"
    B. 6"
23. Headers: 4, 2 × 8 × 16
    Joists: 25, 2 × 8 × 12
    Total bd. ft.: 486
24. 12 pcs.
    384 sq. ft.
25. 80 pcs.
26. 162'
    162 bd. ft.
27. 48 pcs.
    1536 sq. ft.
28. Use smaller joists, doubling them up or spacing them closer together.

Answers to Chapter Quiz
1. True.
2. True.
3. False.
4. True.
5. C. S and W
6. B. engineered
7. D. All of the above.
8. A. trimmers
9. C.
10. B.
11. A.
12. G.
13. E.
14. D.
15. F.

Platform Framing Details

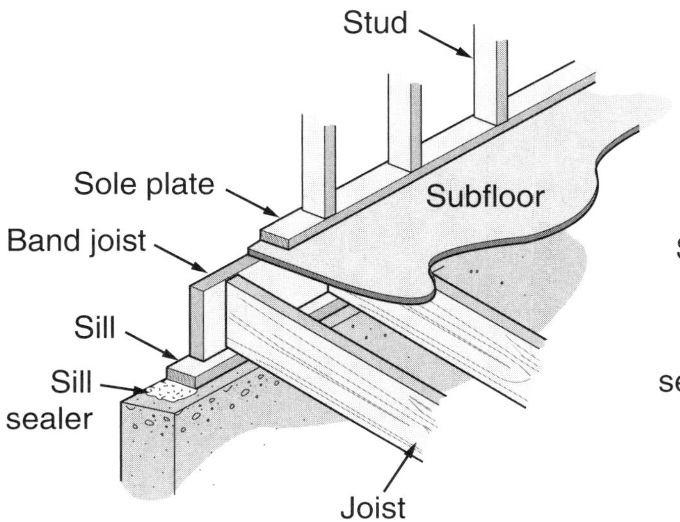

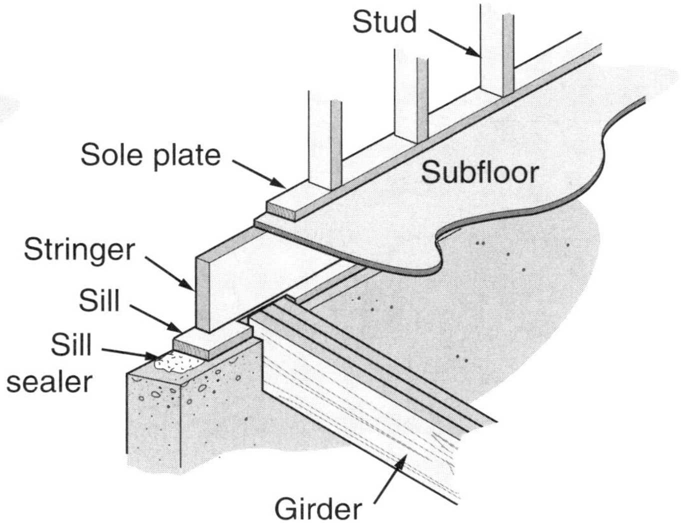

Exterior wall at girder
- Stud
- Sole plate
- Subfloor
- Stringer
- Sill
- Sill sealer
- Girder

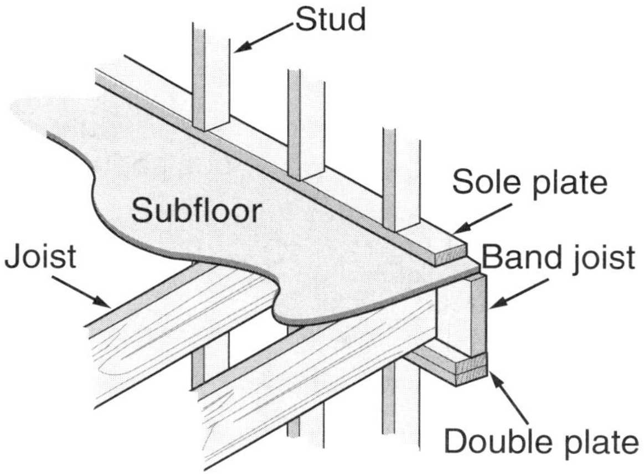

Exterior wall
- Stud
- Sole plate
- Subfloor
- Band joist
- Sill
- Sill sealer
- Joist

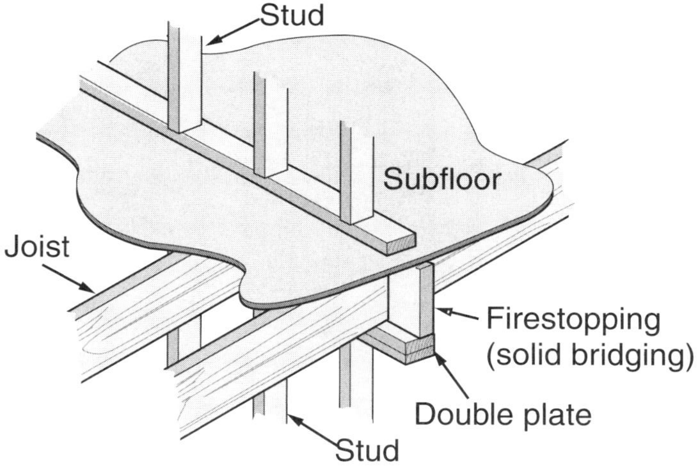

Bearing partition
- Stud
- Subfloor
- Firestopping (solid bridging)
- Double plate
- Stud
- Joist

Exterior wall
- Stud
- Sole plate
- Band joist
- Double plate
- Subfloor
- Joist

RM 8-1

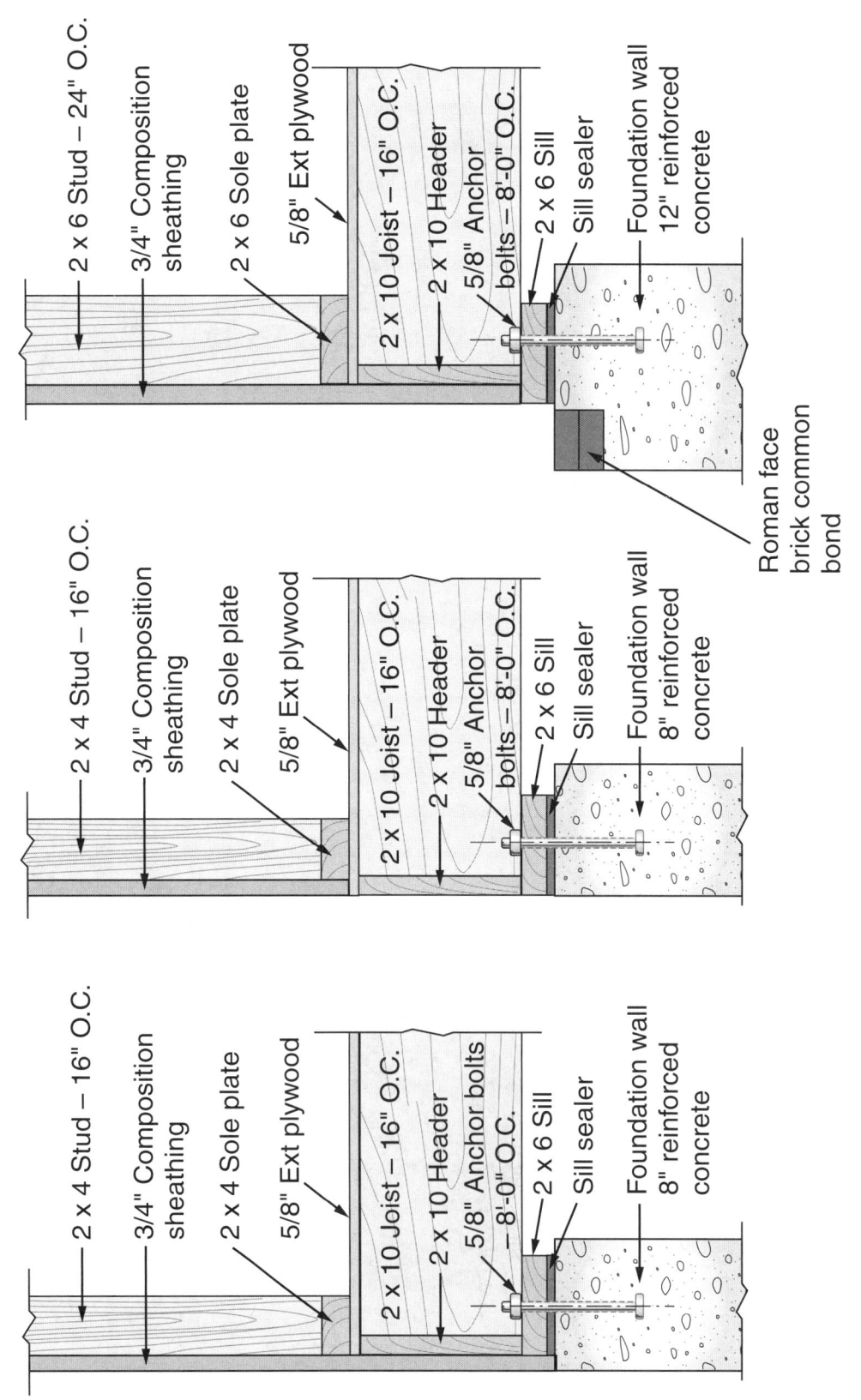

Using Joist Hangers

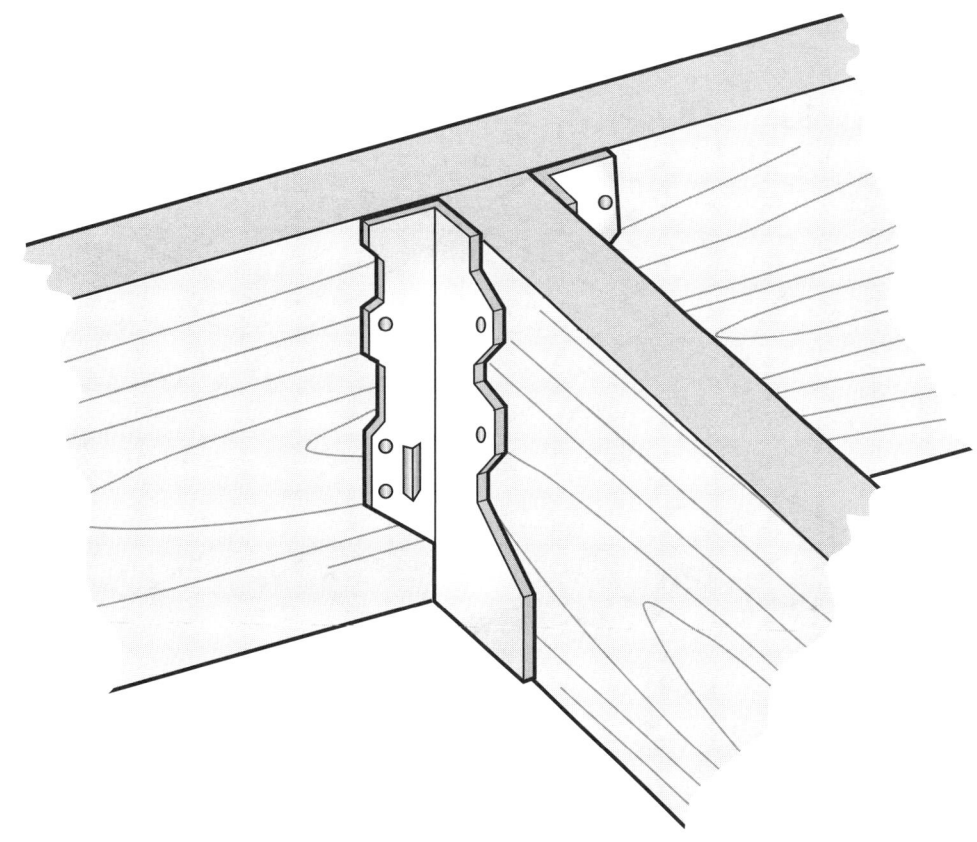

RM 8-3

Framing over Girders/Beams

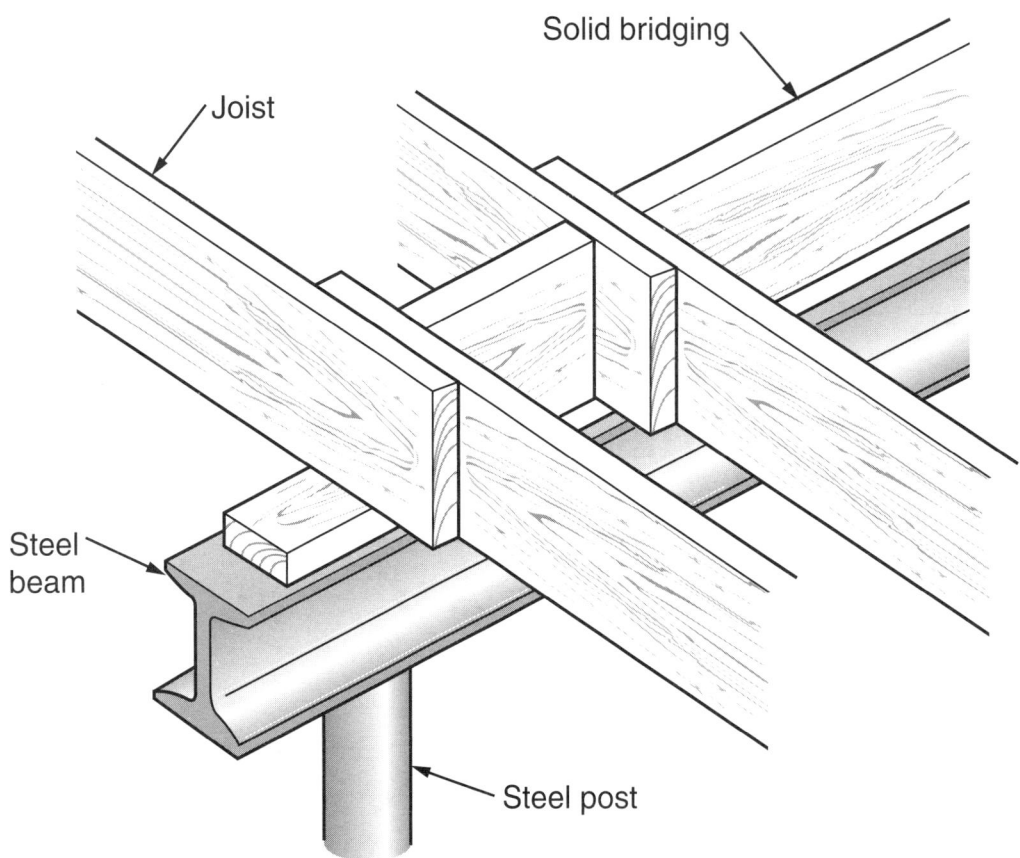

RM 8-4A

Framing over Girders/Beams

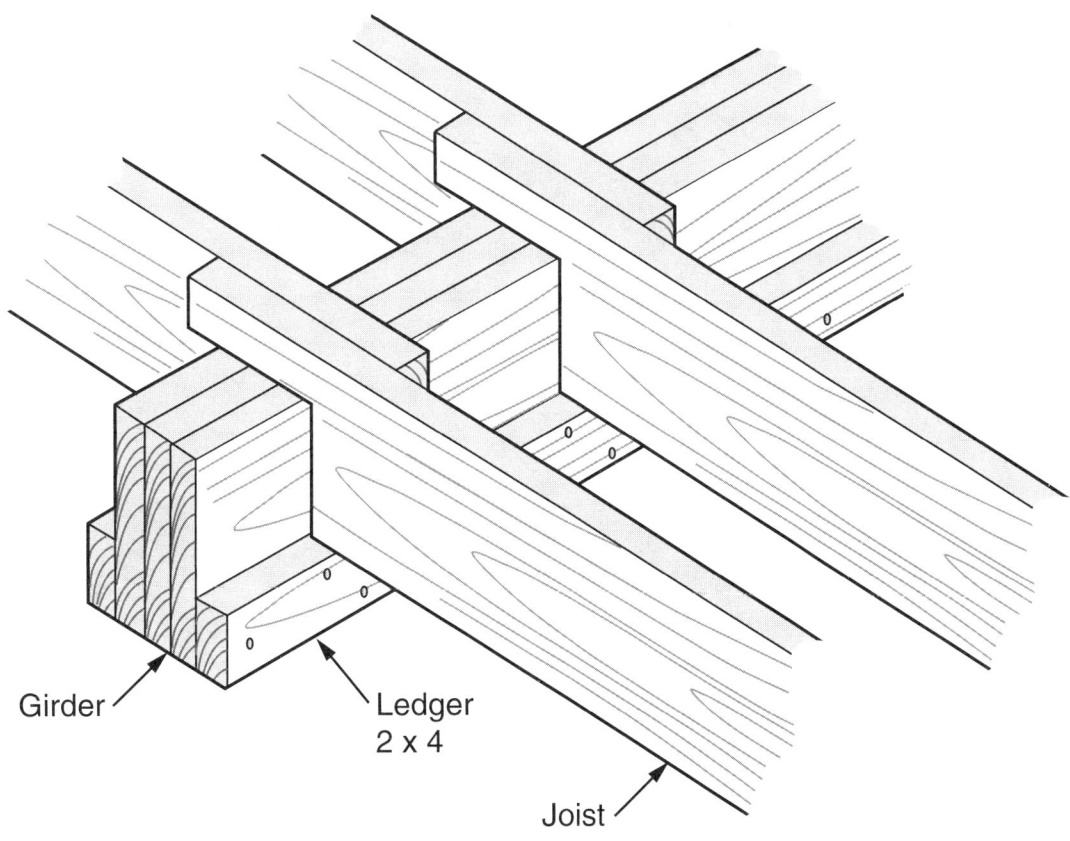

RM 8-4B

Framing over Girders/Beams

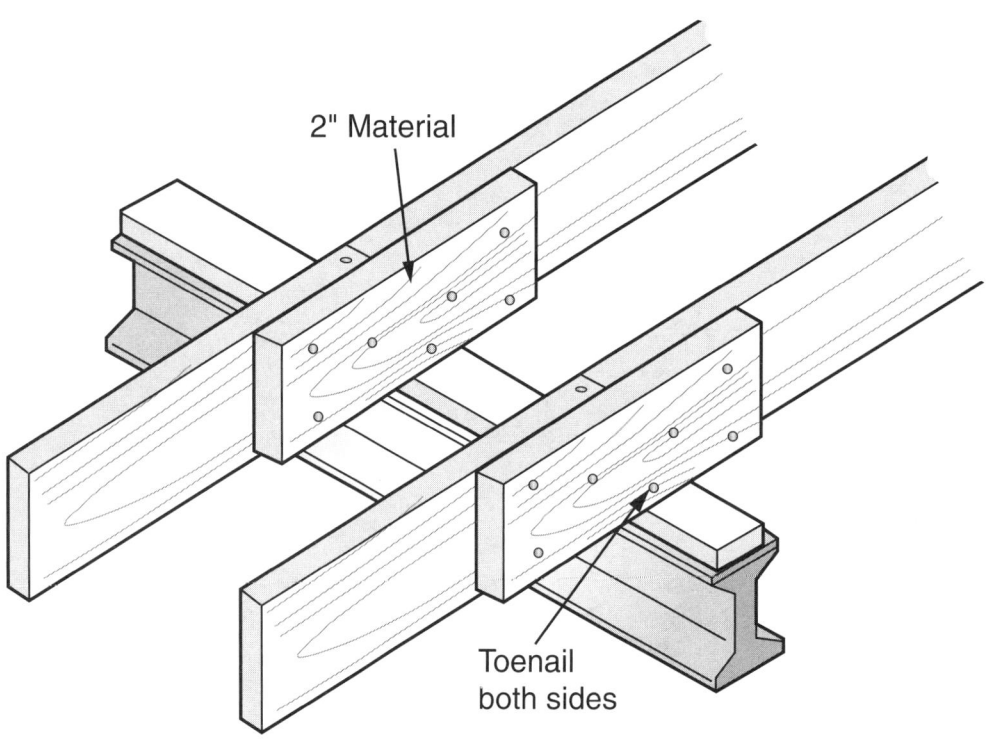

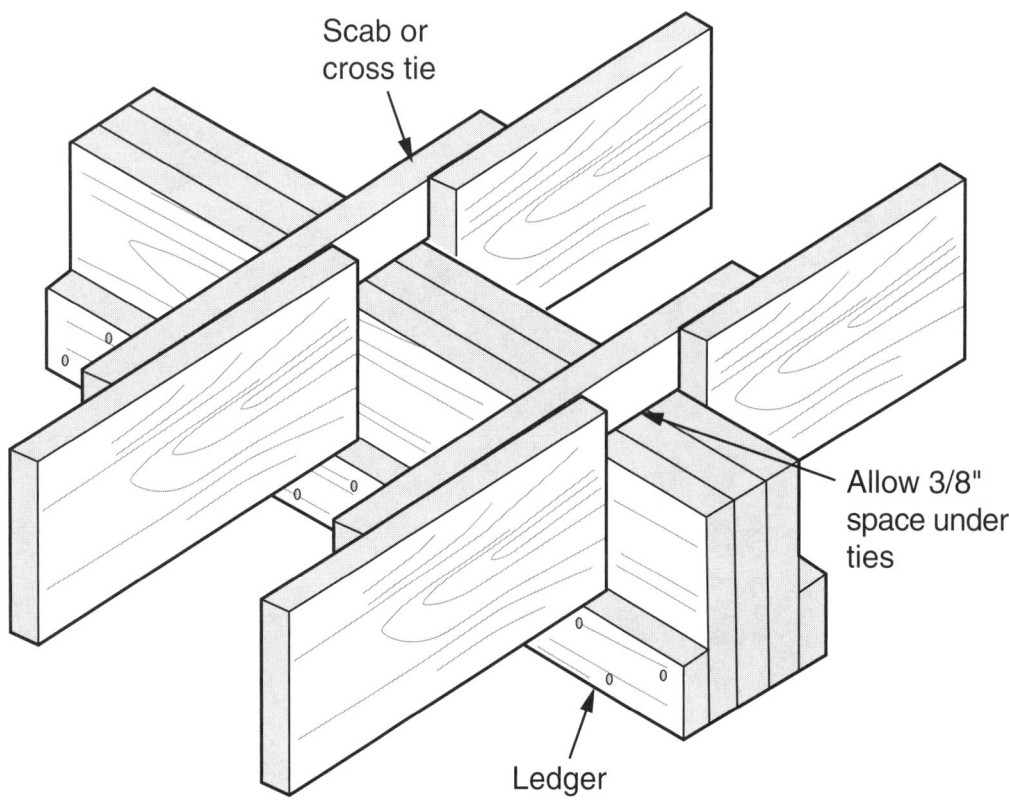

Laying Out Joists

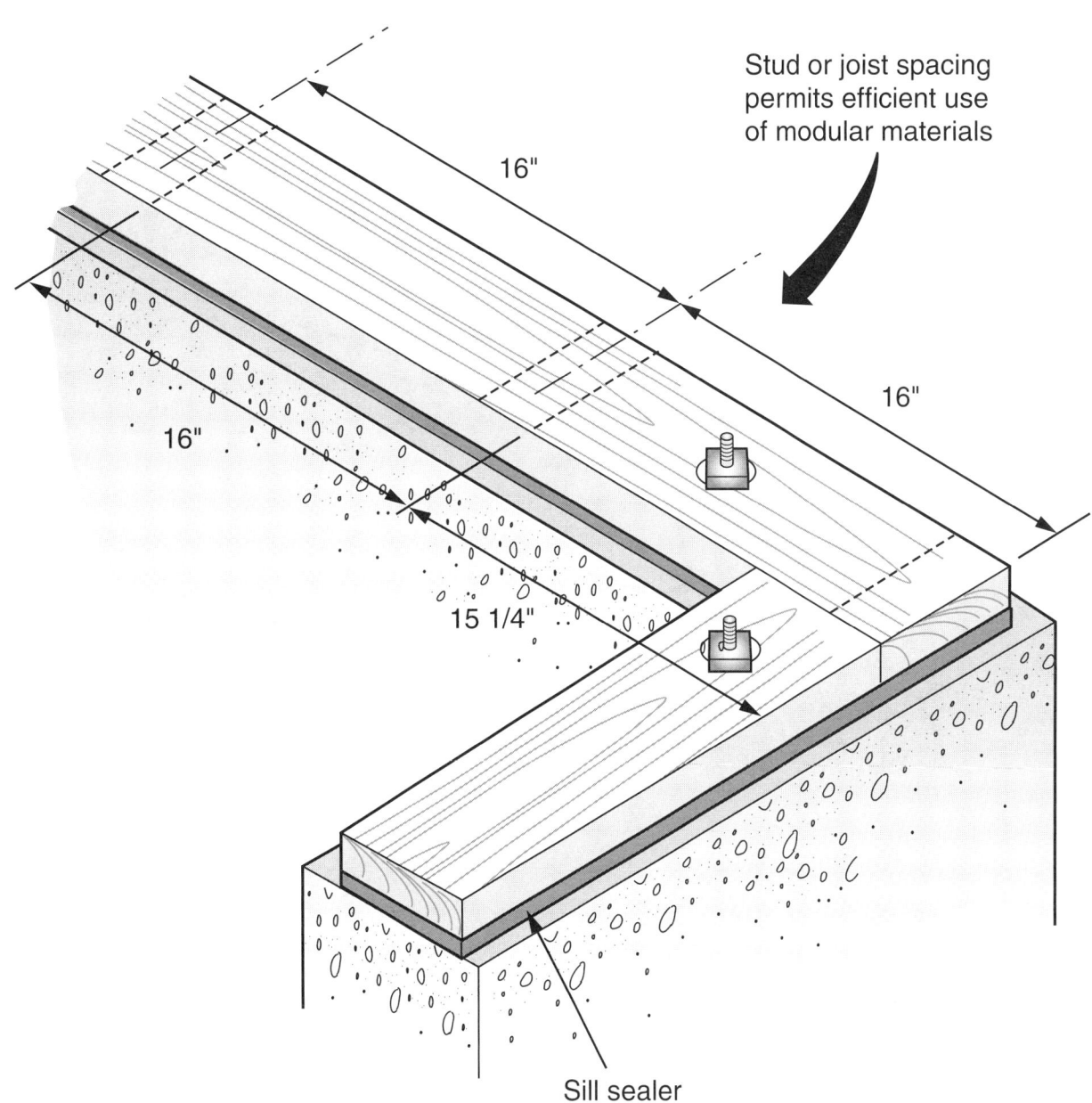

Sill sealer

Stud or joist spacing permits efficient use of modular materials

RM 8-5A

Laying Out Joists

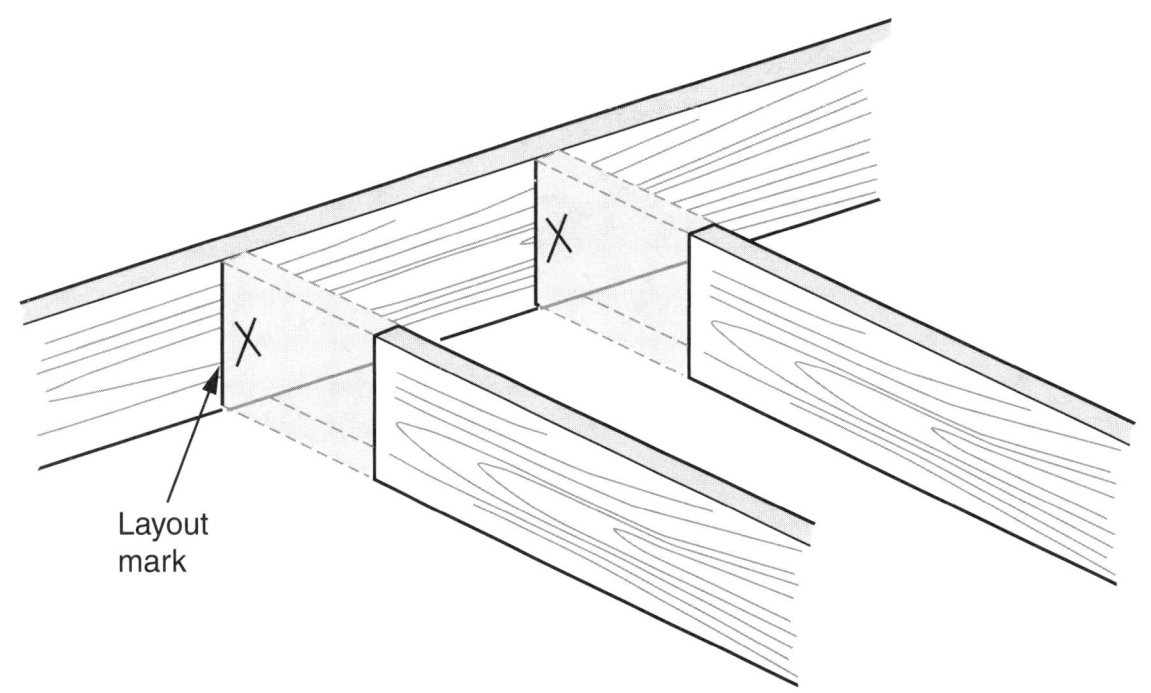

Layout mark

RM 8-5B

Floor Frame

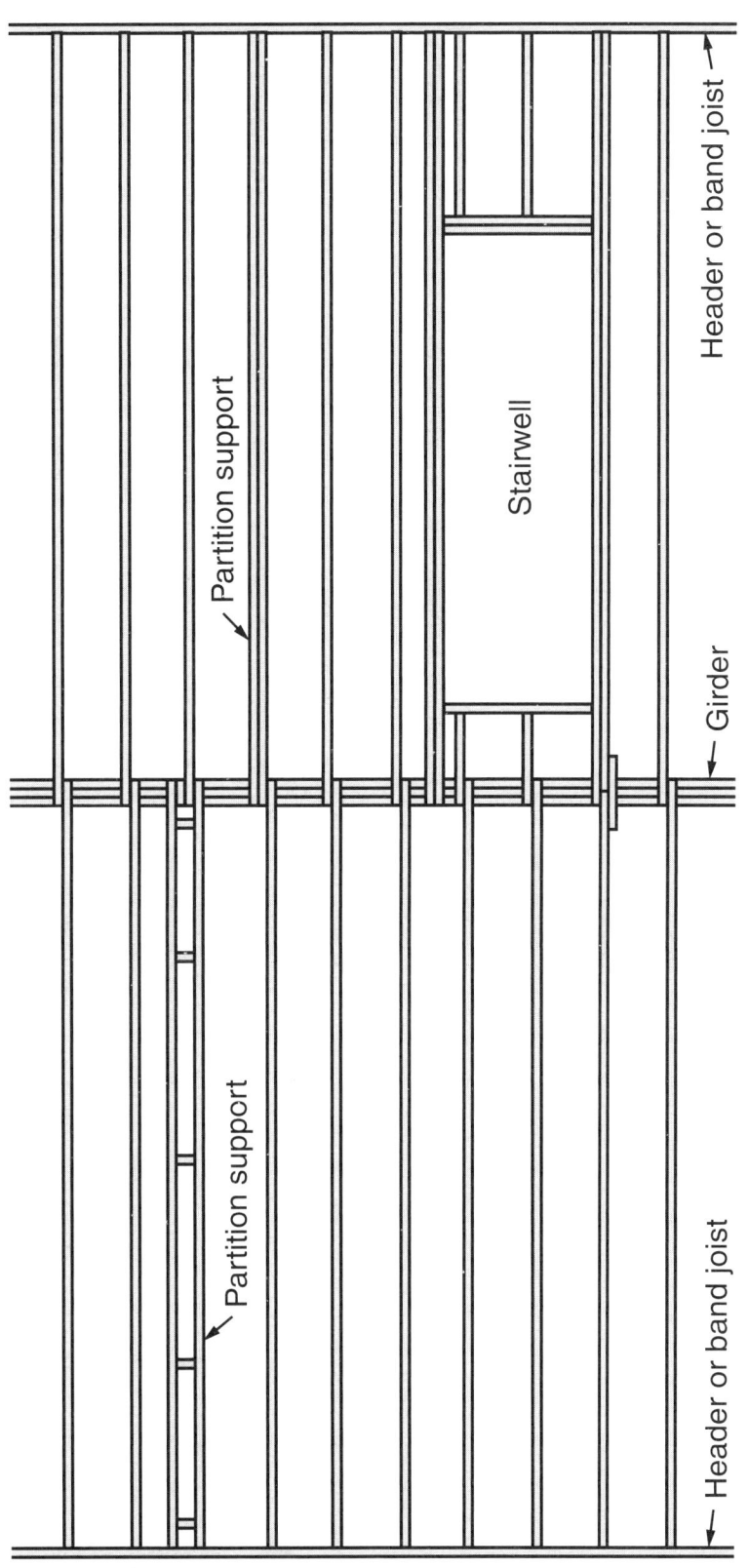

RM 8-6

Assembling Floor Frame

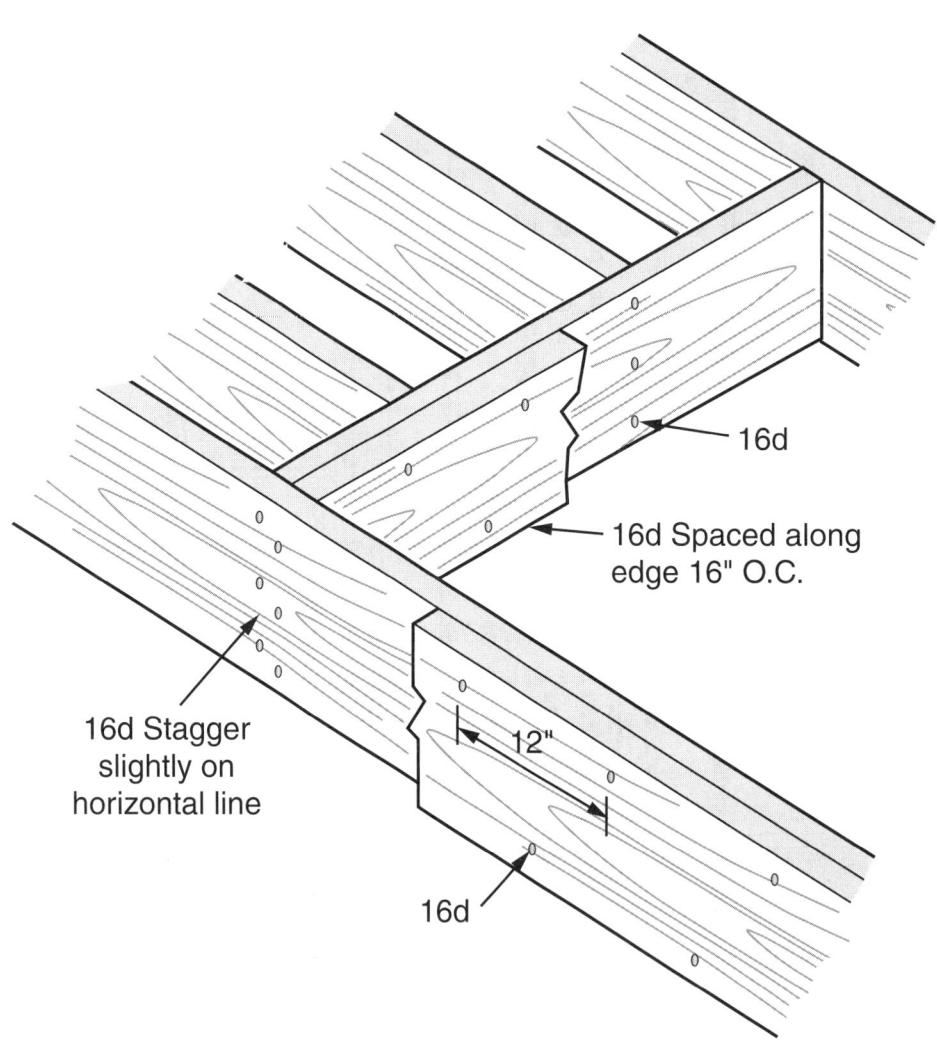

RM 8-7A

Assembling Floor Frame

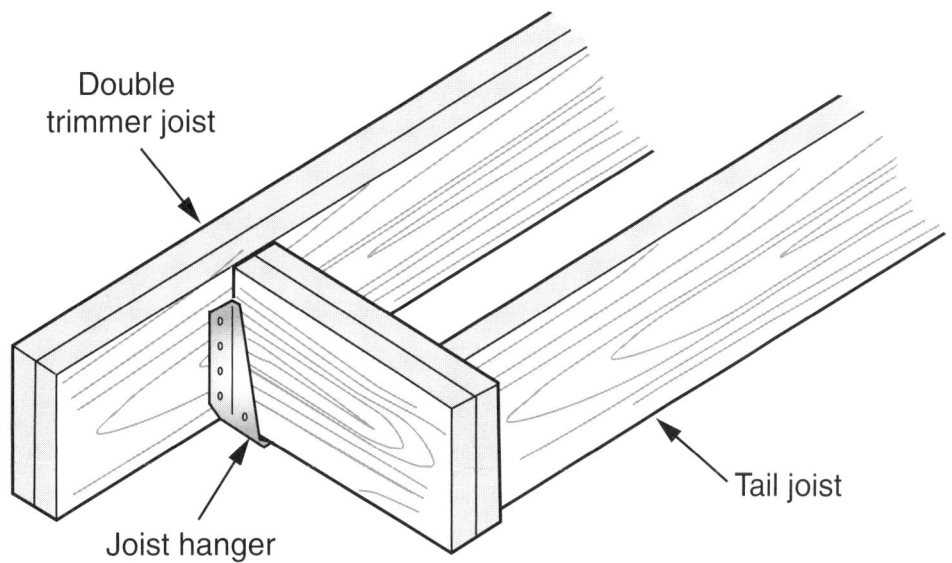

RM 8-7B

Truss Construction

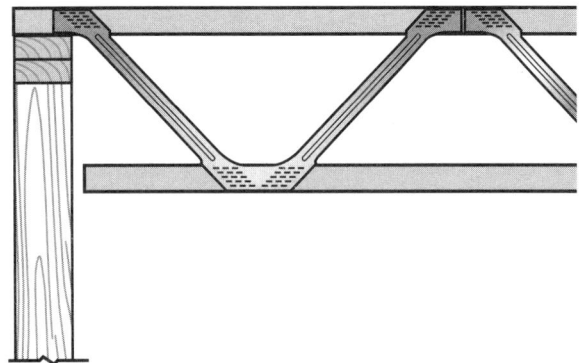

Top chord

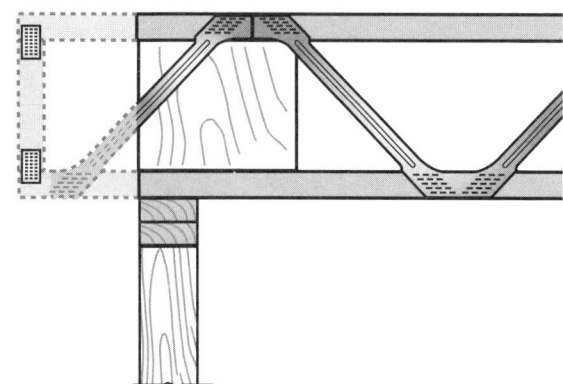

Field cut truss detail

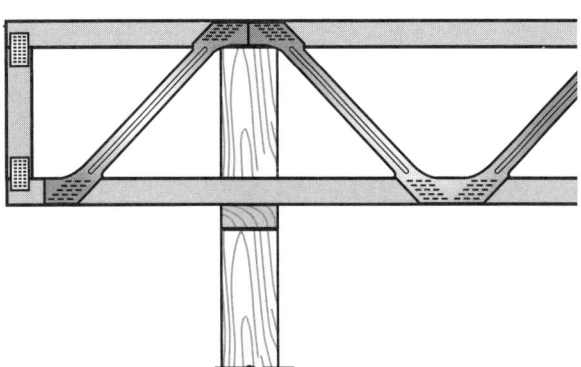

Bottom chord cantilever

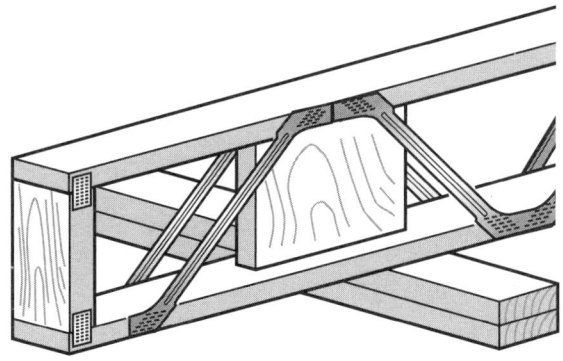

Bottom chord without banding block

RM 8-8

Placing Subflooring

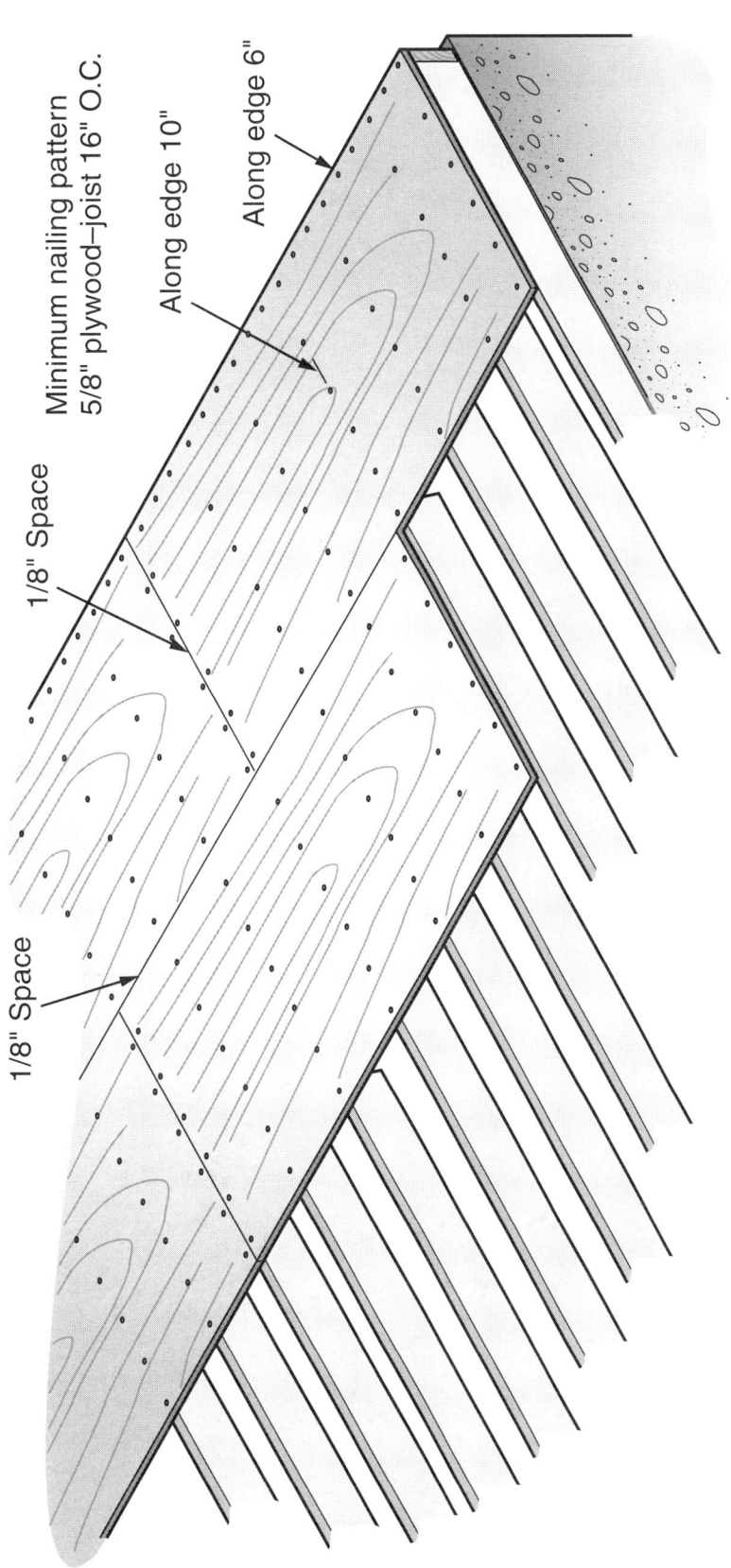

RM8-9

Chapter 8 Procedure Checklist
Installing Sills

Name _____ Total _____

❏	Removes nuts and washers; lays sill along foundation wall for anchor bolt placement.	5	4	3	2	1	Tries to measure position of anchor bolt holes.
❏	Lays out lines across sill for anchor bolt placement; accurately measures distance from center of the bolt to the outside of foundation wall and then subtracts sheathing thickness; accurately lays out this dimension on the sill.	5	4	3	2	1	Guesses at placement of anchor bolt holes; forgets to compensate for sheathing thickness.
❏	Snaps line on foundation wall to accurately align sill.	5	4	3	2	1	Neglects to snap line on foundation wall.
❏	Bores anchor bolt holes at one time for maximum productivity using the proper size drill bit (approximately 1/4" larger than bolt diameter).	5	4	3	2	1	Bores anchor bolt hole as each is laid out, thus reducing productivity; bores holes that are the same size as the bolts.
❏	Dry fits sills on foundation wall; removes sills; installs sill sealer and replaces sill; tightens sills down using washers and nuts.	5	4	3	2	1	Places sills on foundation wall without sill sealer; neglects to use washers when tightening down sills.
❏	Verifies proper placement of sill on foundation wall; levels sill and shims where necessary.	5	4	3	2	1	Neglects to check placement of sill; forgets to level the sill.

Chapter 8 Procedure Checklist
Installing Joists

Name _____ Total _____

❏	Toenails header joist to the sill.	5	4	3	2	1	Tries to balance the header joist on the sill.
❏	Positions full length joists with crowns turned up; nails joists into position using three 16d nails.	5	4	3	2	1	Does not check crown on joists; uses fewer or more nails than required.
❏	Fastens joists along the opposite wall into position; properly joins joists that butt or overlap.	5	4	3	2	1	Neglects to fasten joists along opposite wall into position; does not join butting or overlapping joists.
❏	Interprets plans; accurately locates areas where doubled joists are required.	5	4	3	2	1	Neglects installation of doubled joists.

Chapter 8 Quiz
Floor Framing

Name _____ Date _____ Score _____

True-False
Circle T if the answer is True or F if the answer is False.

T F 1. Platform framing is also referred to as western framing.

T F 2. In balloon framing, studs extend from the sill to the rafter plate.

T F 3. When cutting openings in joists, cuts should be made along the bottom edge.

T F 4. Floor joists carry the weight of the floor between the sills and girders.

Multiple Choice
Choose the answer that correctly completes the statement. Write the corresponding letter in the space provided.

_____ 5. The two types of steel beams commonly used in residential construction are _____ beams.
  A. I and S
  B. I and W
  C. S and W
  D. None of the above.

_____ 6. Units such as open truss joists, wood I-beams, and laminated veneer lumber are known collectively as _____ lumber.
  A. manufactured
  B. engineered
  C. laminated
  D. span-rated

_____ 7. The subfloor _____.
  A. adds rigidity to the structure
  B. provides a base for finish flooring material
  C. provides a surface on which the carpenter can lay out and construct framing
  D. All of the above.

_____ 8. Joists that are doubled around openings in the floor frame are called _____.
  A. trimmers
  B. headers
  C. footers
  D. sills

Identification

Identify the parts of the platform framing detail.

_____ 9. Joist.

_____ 10. Subfloor.

_____ 11. Stud.

_____ 12. Sole plate.

_____ 13. Sill.

_____ 14. Sill sealer.

_____ 15. Band joist.

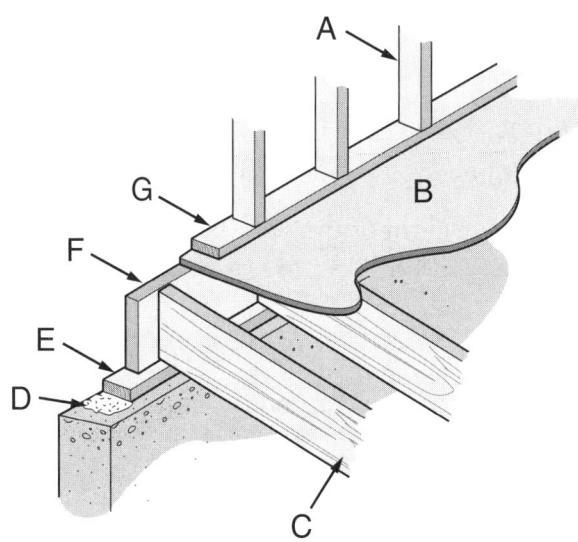

9 Wall and Ceiling Framing

Objective

After studying this chapter, students will be able to:
- Identify the main parts of a wall frame.
- Explain methods of forming the outside corners and partition intersections of wall frames.
- Show how rough openings are handled in wall construction.
- Explain plate and stud layout.
- Describe the construction and erection of wall sections and partitions.
- List the materials commonly used for sheathing.
- Demonstrate the process of ceiling frame construction.
- Estimate materials required for wall frames, ceiling frames, and sheathing.

Instructional Materials

Text: Pages 253–282
 Technical Vocabulary, page 253
 Test Your Knowledge, page 281
 Curricular Connections, page 281
 Outside Assignments, page 281
Workbook: Pages 49–54
Instructor's Resource:
 Reproducible masters:
  RM 9-1 *Framing Corners*
  RM 9-2 *Framing Wall Intersections*
  RM 9-3 *Framing Wall Openings*
  RM 9-4A *Framing with Patterns*
  RM 9-4B *Framing with Patterns*
  RM 9-4C *Framing with Patterns*
 Transparencies (binder/CD only):
  CT 9-1 *Using Metal Strapping to Strengthen Joists*
 Procedure Checklist: *Constructing Wall Sections*
 Procedure Checklist: *Erecting Wall Sections*
 Chapter Quiz

Trade-Related Math

To determine the amount of sheathing, first measure the perimeter of the structure. Multiply this by the wall height when sheathing extends over the foundation wall. Then, subtract the square footage of the openings in the wall to determine the area of the walls. Divide this number by the area per sheet of sheathing. The following formula is used:

Perimeter × Height − Wall openings ÷ Area of one sheet of sheathing = Number of sheathing panels

Assume that 4 × 8 sheets of sheathing are used. The perimeter of the structure measures 20′ × 25′, with window and door openings amounting to 105 square feet. The wall height is 8′. The number of sheets of sheathing that are required is calculated as follows (round the answer to the next highest whole number):

(25 + 20 + 25 + 20) × 8′ − 105 ÷ (4 × 8) = Number of sheathing panels

20 sheets of sheathing will be required

Instructional Concepts and Student Learning Experiences

Parts of the Wall Frame

1. Refer to Figure 9-1. Identify the parts of a typical wall frame including the sole plates, top plates, studs, and headers. List the type of materials that are used for each of these parts. Have students note where additional studs are used.

2. Using reproducible master RM 9-1 *Framing Corners,* discuss the various methods used to frame wall corners. Demonstrate the methods used to frame corners by building scale models. Follow up the demonstration by having the students construct scale models of corner framing.

Copyright by Goodheart-Willcox Co., Inc.

3. Using reproducible master RM 9-2 *Framing Wall Intersections,* discuss the methods used to construct partition intersections. Explain the importance of creating a square inside corner to provide a nailing surface for wall-covering materials.
4. Review a house plan to determine the location of rough openings in a wall. Stress that rough opening measurements are usually made from the corners to the centerlines of the openings.
5. Discuss the purpose of headers in wall construction. Have students identify places where headers will be installed.
6. Discuss the construction of window and door headers. Show the students how to determine the length of the header by adding the rough opening plus two headers. Demonstrate the construction of a header.
7. Using reproducible master RM 9-3 *Framing Wall Openings,* review the parts of a wall frame. Stress the importance of using the proper terminology when referring to the parts of the wall frame.
8. Discuss alternate methods of header construction. Caution students about the disadvantages of using a header that extends completely to the top plate.

Plate Layout
1. Discuss different methods of laying out the plates. Stress that they should be laid out along the outside wall to minimize the necessity of moving the completed wall around the structure.
2. Refer to reproducible master RM 9-4A *Framing with Patterns.* Describe the meaning of the Xs, Ts, and Cs on the plates. Emphasize that markings made during layout will help to eliminate confusion when constructing the wall plate.
3. Using a set of drawings from a small residential structure, have a group of students interpret the drawings and lay out the sole and top plates. Have another group of students check the accuracy of their measurements.
4. Explain and demonstrate why it is sometimes necessary to adjust placement of the first stud on an outside wall according to the thickness of the sheet material used for wall sheathing.

Story Pole
1. Describe the purpose of a story pole. Discuss the advantages of using a story pole over laying out all the measurements individually. Stress the importance of making sure that the measurements on the story pole are accurate.
2. Using reproducible master RM 9-4B *Framing with Patterns,* show how the story pole is used. Lay out a story pole using measurements from the plans used in the previous step.

Master Stud Layout
1. Compare the story pole in the previous step to the layout of the master stud in reproducible master RM 9-4C *Framing with Patterns.*

Constructing Wall Sections
1. Discuss the advantages of using P.E.T. (precision end-trimmed) lumber in constructing a wall section.
2. Have students list the steps involved in the construction of a common wall section. Use the listed steps to construct a wall section. Use the measurements from previously used plans.
3. Review the safety procedures that should be followed when constructing wall sections using a power nailer.
4. Attach the sheathing to the wall section. Make certain that the wall frame is square before attaching it. Mention that the same procedure for checking the squareness of a building site (measuring diagonals) can be used to check the squareness of a wall section.

Erecting Wall Sections
1. Discuss different methods that can be used to erect a wall section. If wall jacks are to be used, demonstrate their use before raising the wall section.
2. Stress the importance of plumbing the wall section after erecting it. Demonstrate the use of a straightedge with lugs at each end to check plumb if the framing member or surface is warped.

Partitions

1. Discuss the next stage of construction, erecting bearing partitions. Using the set of plans from the previous steps, have students determine which partitions are bearing walls and their locations. Review the use of a chalk line at this point.
2. Stress the importance of getting the structure closed in before erecting nonbearing partitions. Discuss possible problems that may occur if the structure does not get closed in quickly.
3. Identify special framing considerations that may need to be addressed when constructing walls and partitions. Include openings for the heating ducts and extra bracing for the bathtub and wall-mounted stool.
4. Discuss special construction that is required for electrical runs and plumbing and venting pipes.
5. Referring to Figure 9-28, identify special reinforcement methods for studs when notched for plumbing or wiring.
6. Have students refer to the local building code to determine the wall bracing requirements. Identify various types of wall bracing that can be used, including wood let-in braces and metal strap bracing. Stress that bracing cannot simply be attached to the outside of the wall sections because it interferes with sheathing.
7. Quiz students on why nonbearing walls do not require headers over openings.

Double Plate

1. Describe why a double top plate is used.
2. Bring up the use of steel strapping and connectors for reinforcing joints and explain their importance in areas that experience earthquakes and high winds.

Special Framing

1. Discuss special framing problems encountered in residential construction.
2. Using a set of plans for a small residential structure, have students identify special framing problems that may be encountered. Have the students sketch possible framing configurations for each of the problems they identify.

Wall Sheathing

1. Identify materials that are commonly used for wall sheathing. Discuss the advantages or disadvantages of installing wall sheathing after the wall sections have been erected.
2. Describe how fiberboard, plywood, and insulating panels are attached to the wall section. Have students explain additional factors that should be considered, such as use of plywood at corners as bracing (or letting in of angle braces at corners) when fiberboard or insulating board is used as sheathing.

Ceiling Frame

1. Discuss the similarities between ceiling framing and floor framing. Identify the factors that should be considered when determining the length of span and spacing used for ceiling joists. Mention that this information is usually found in the set of plans.
2. Refer to Figure 9-43 and discuss the construction of the ceiling frame. If time and materials allow, construct a scale model of a ceiling frame. Identify problems that may be encountered when constructing the frame.
3. Define *stub joists*. Explain how to lay out the ends of stub ceiling joists to match the roof pitch.
4. Discuss the methods for fastening partitions that run parallel to the joists to the ceiling frame. Stress that the primary purpose of fastening the partitions to the ceiling frame is to provide support.
5. Have students refer to the local building code to determine the minimum size of the attic scuttle hole. Ask the students to provide ideas on how to frame the scuttle hole.

Strongbacks

1. Discuss the purpose of a strongback. Demonstrate how strongbacks are constructed.

Housewrap and Building Paper

1. Explain the difference between housewrap and building paper and explain their common purpose.

2. Using a previously constructed wall, demonstrate the installation of housewrap. Repeat the demonstration using building paper.

Estimating Materials

1. Using a stock plan, determine the wall and ceiling framing members that are required. Suggest that the students mark each wall and partition that they are adding to make sure that all of the walls and partitions are included.
2. Using the same stock plan, determine the number of studs required if studs are spaced 16″ on center.
3. Estimate the amount of wall sheathing required for the house shown in the stock plan.

Chapter Review

1. Review the chapter objectives. Be sure that the students are fully competent in the task identified by each objective.
2. Review the terms in the *Technical Vocabulary* section and make certain students are clear on each definition.
3. Assign the *Test Your Knowledge* questions, *Curricular Connections,* and *Outside Assignments* for Chapter 9 of the text. Review the answers to test questions in class. Also, have students report on the *Curricular Connections* and *Outside Assignments* activities as appropriate.
4. Assign Chapter 9 of the workbook. Review the answers in class.

Evaluation

This chapter provides three methods for evaluating student performance. Students should complete the *Test Your Knowledge* section using the book as reference. Students should also be allowed to use the book for reference when completing the workbook material. Use the Chapter 9 Quiz in the instructor's resources for in-class evaluation. Correct the quizzes, return them to the students, and review the quiz questions in group discussion.

Procedure Checklist

Using the procedure checklists, *Constructing Wall Sections* and *Erecting Wall Sections,* have students evaluate the techniques used to perform these tasks.

Answers to Test Your Knowledge
Text Page 281

1. The outside and inside walls of a structure, upper floors, ceilings, and the roof.
2. header
3. They bear the direct weight of a header.
4. regular stud
5. A long measuring stick made up by the carpenter on the job, which represents the actual wall frame with markings made at the proper height for every horizontal member of the wall frame.
6. sole plate
7. A wooden block.
8. 4′
9. False.
10. rafters
11. length
12. E. All of the above.
13. A thin, tough, plastic sheet material that is applied to side walls and prevents movement of air into or out of a building.
14. Building paper.
15. Seven.

Answers to Workbook Questions
Page 49–54

1. C. sheathing
2. B. 16″
3. A. Top plate.
   B. Header (lintel).
   C. Trimmers.
   D. Rough sill.
   E. Sole plate.
   F. Cripple or jack studs.
   G. Stud.
4. B. 10d
5. C. 4′-9″
6. C. 1/2″
7. C. 2 × 10
8. D. Lay out two stud positions at each side of all openings.
9. story pole
10. C. distance from rough floor to ceiling

11. C. bottom of header to top of rough sill
12. A. 16d.
    B. 16d.
    C. 10d.
    D. 8d.
13. plumb line
14. A. P.E.T.
15. wall backing
16. B. 1 × 4
17. B. 16″
18. See Figure 9-33 in text.
19. A. 25/32″
    B. 1 1/2″
20. A. 2″
    B. 8d.
21. polystyrene
22. ceiling joists
23. See Figure 9-46 in text.
24. When it is not load-bearing or when roof trusses are used to carry the roof load.
25. lineal ft.: 891
    bd. ft.: 594
26. studs: 305
27. pcs.: 39
28. See Figure 9-6B.
29. See Figure 9-6A.

Answers to Chapter Quiz

1. True.
2. False.
3. B. 2 × 4
4. D. story pole
5. D. All of the above.
6. C. strongback
7. B. Trimmer
8. E
9. B
10. C
11. F
12. A
13. D
14. Provides backing for mounting of fixtures and appliances.
15. 25%

Framing Corners

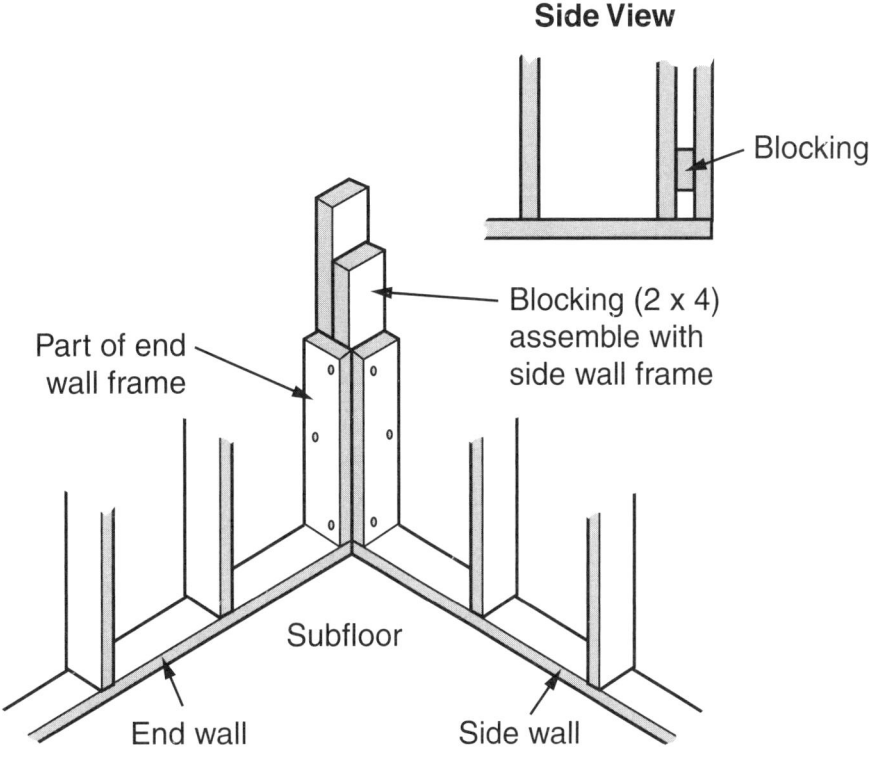

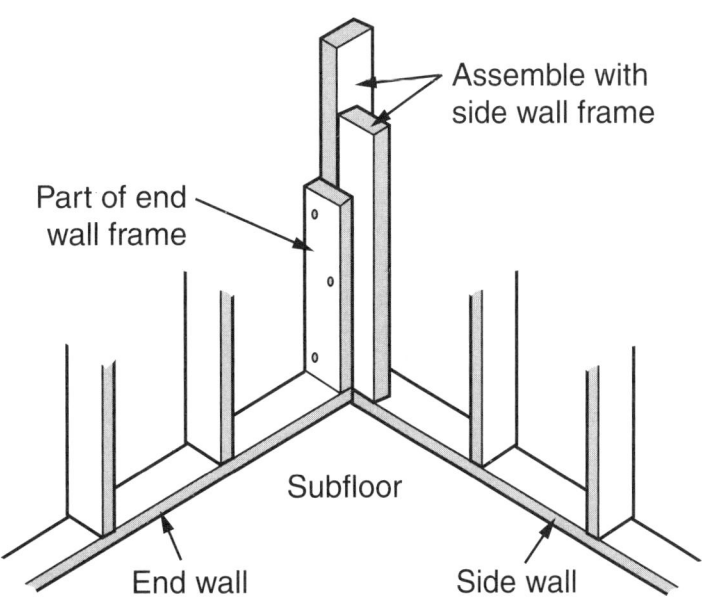

RM 9-1

Framing Wall Intersections

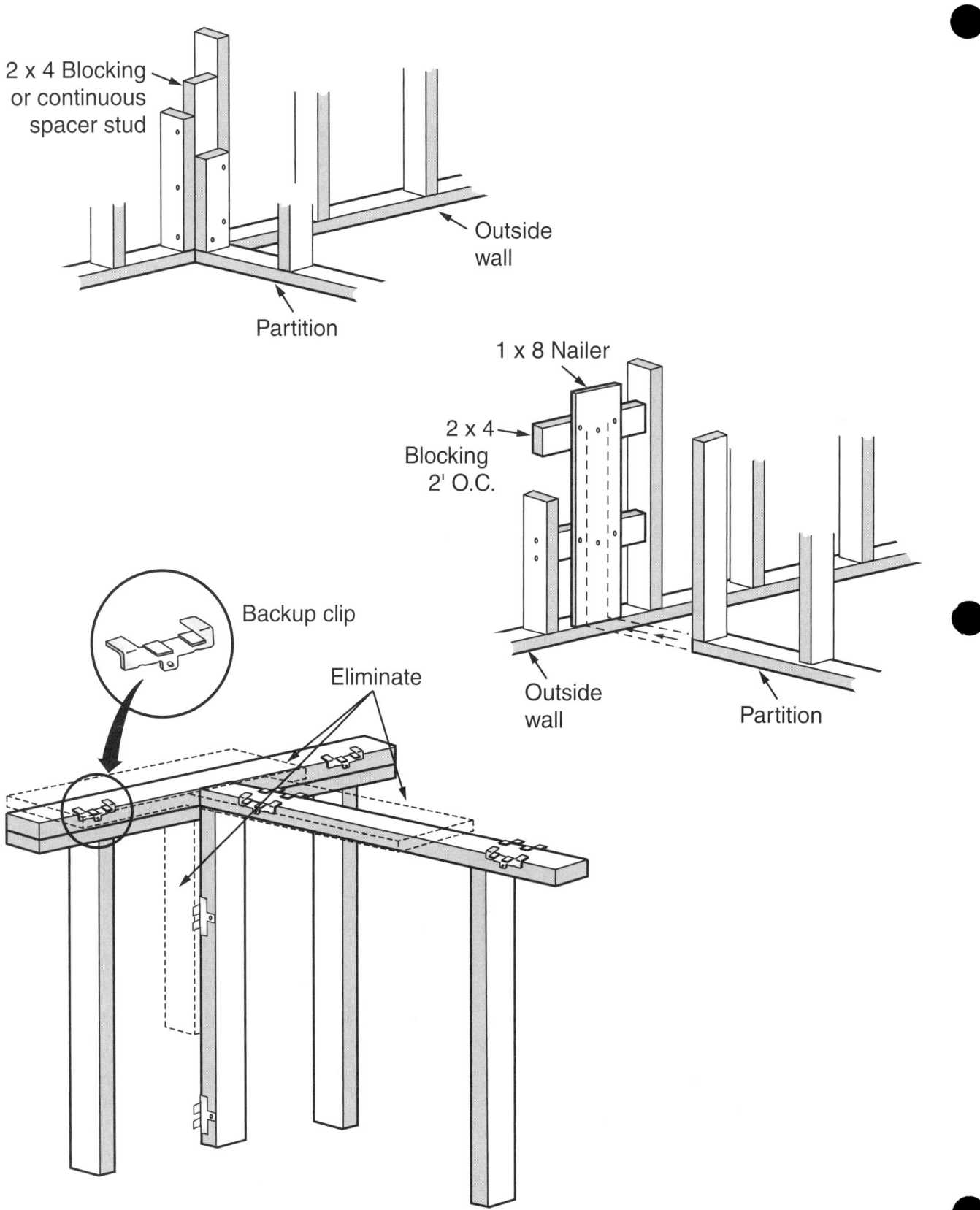

Framing Wall Openings

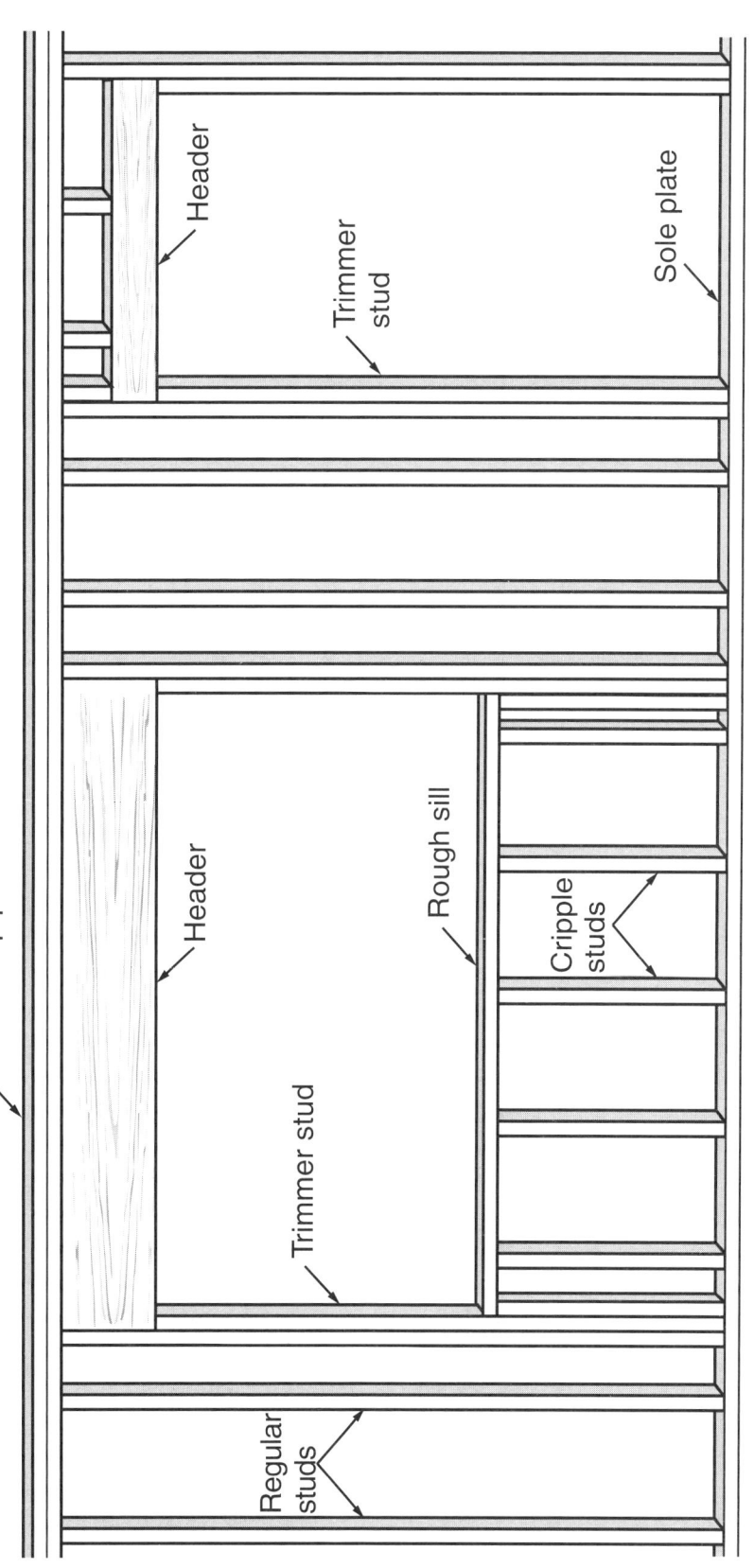

RM 9-3

Framing with Patterns

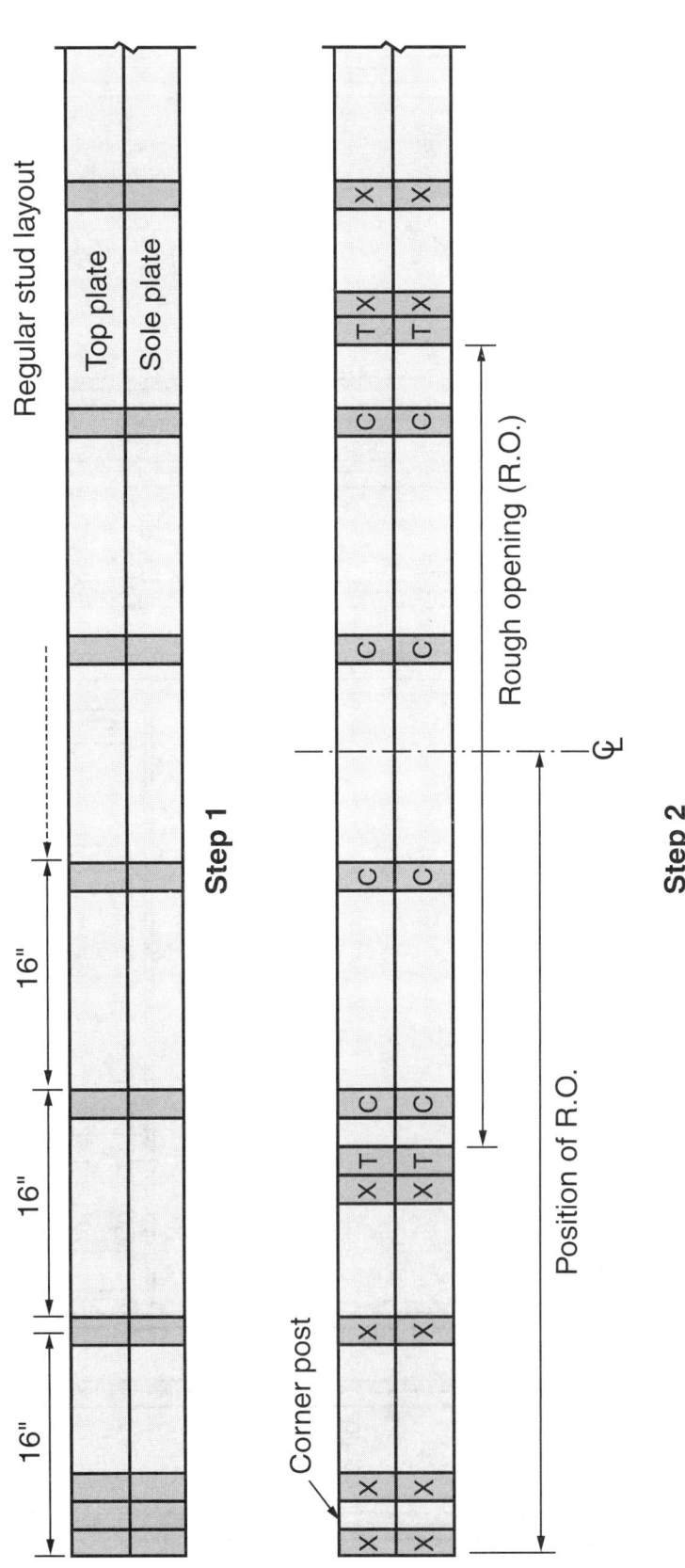

RM 9-4A

Framing with Patterns

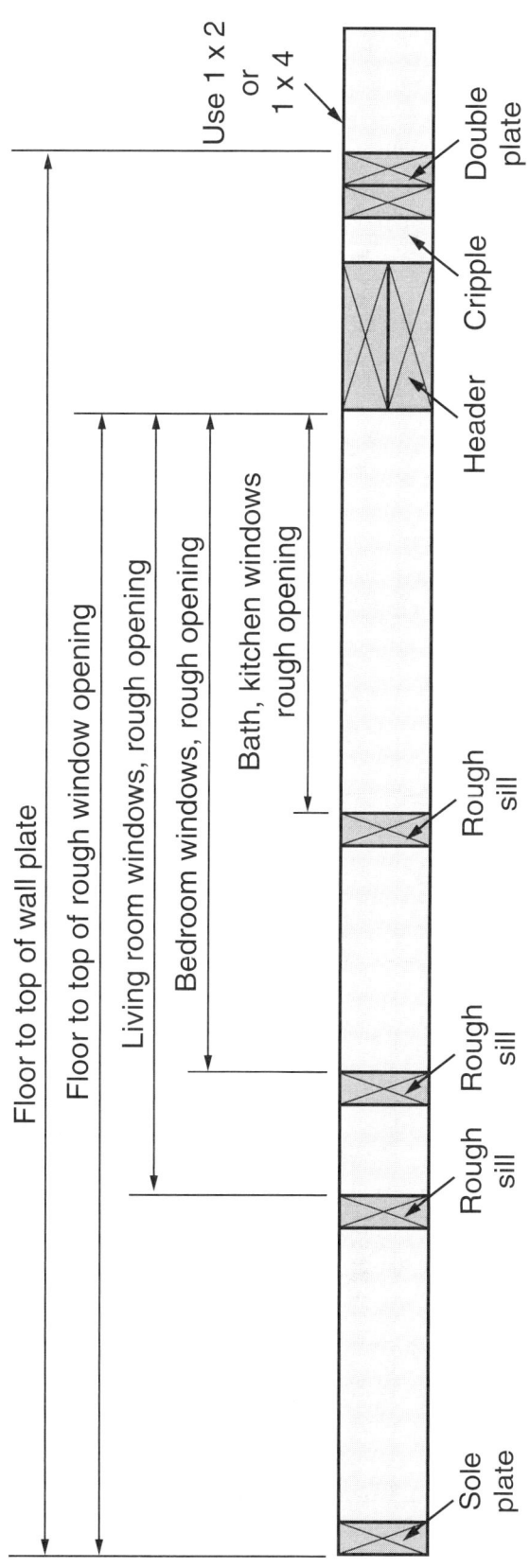

RM 9-4B

Framing with Patterns

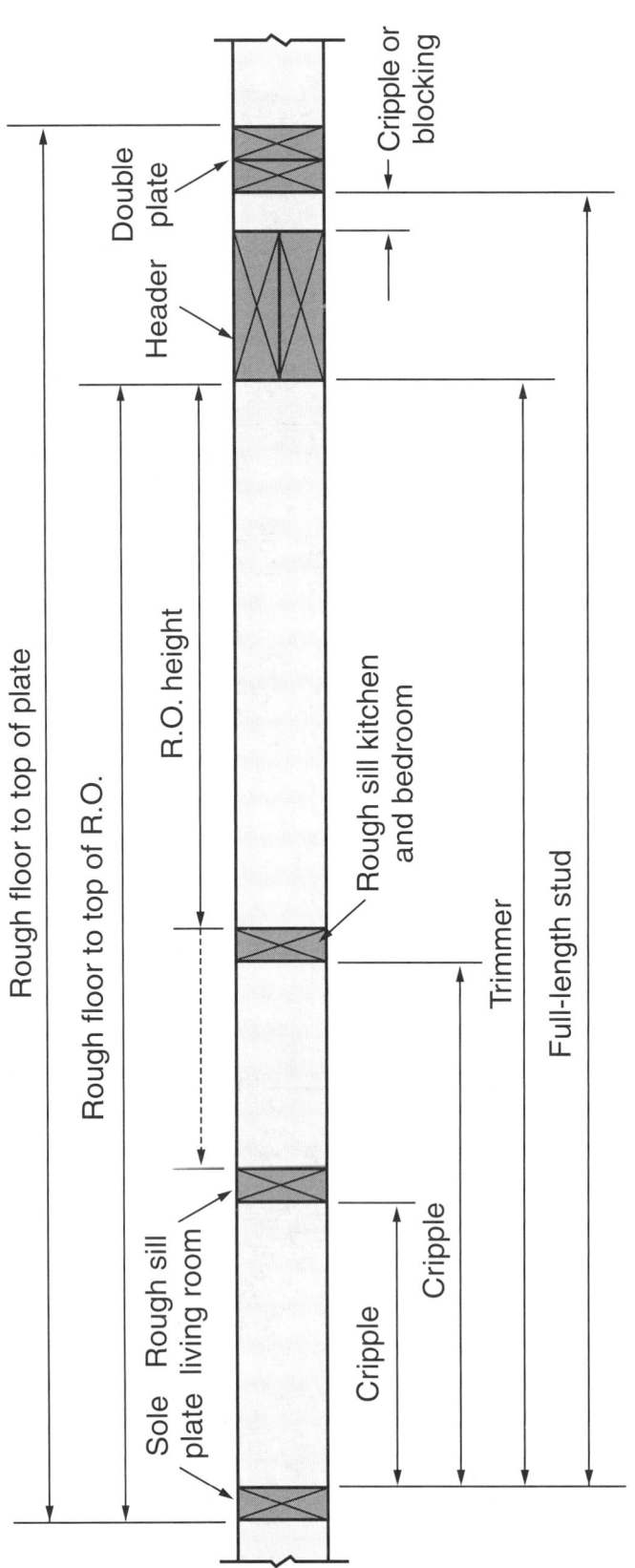

RM 9-4C

Chapter 9 Procedure Checklist
Constructing Wall Sections

Name _____ Total _____

❏	Easily selects the appropriate materials for the wall section after referring to the prints.	5	4	3	2	1	Must be told the appropriate materials to use for wall sections.
❏	Readily determines the size of the headers, and cuts and assembles them efficiently.	5	4	3	2	1	Cannot determine the size of the headers; needs help assembling them.
❏	Properly constructs wall section; accurately places studs, making sure crowns are facing up.	5	4	3	2	1	Miscalculates position of studs; disregards position of crowns.
❏	Positions trimmer studs on correct side of full length studs; installs header solidly.	5	4	3	2	1	Places trimmer studs on wrong side of full length studs; header loosely attached.
❏	Accurately lays out position of window openings; determines best time to install cripple studs.	5	4	3	2	1	Cannot determine the position of window openings; not able to install the rough sills and cripple studs.
❏	Determines placement of studs or blocking at partition intersections; installs wall bracing when necessary.	5	4	3	2	1	Not able to determine locations of partition intersections; forgets to check for bracing installation.
❏	Checks squareness of wall section; applies sheathing efficiently and in the correct direction.	5	4	3	2	1	Neglects to check wall squareness; applies sheathing in the wrong direction.

Permission granted to reproduce for educational use only.   Copyright by Goodheart-Willcox Co., Inc.

Chapter 9 Procedure Checklist
Erecting Wall Sections

Name _____ Total _____

- ❏ Determines the best means for raising wall section; readies bracing; makes sure enough workers are available; prepares platform so section does not fall off.   5   4   3   2   1   Neglects to properly prepare work area for raising wall section; tries to erect wall section by self or with too few workers.

- ❏ Erects wall section; immediately secures it with braces; adjusts sole plate and nails it into floor frame.   5   4   3   2   1   Carelessly erects wall section; neglects to brace wall section when erected; does not properly attach sole plate to floor frame.

- ❏ Carefully loosens braces one at a time and plumbs wall.   5   4   3   2   1   Loosens bracing all at once; does not plumb wall section.

Permission granted to reproduce for educational use only.   Copyright by Goodheart-Willcox Co., Inc.

Chapter 9 Quiz
Wall and Ceiling Framing

Name _____ Date _____ Score _____

True-False
Circle T if the answer is True or F if the answer is False.

T   F   1. When listing the size of a rough opening, the width dimension is given first.

T   F   2. Nonbearing partitions require headers.

Multiple Choice
Choose the answer that correctly completes the statement. Write the corresponding letter in the space provided.

_____ 3. Studs are generally _____ stock.
    A. 1 × 4
    B. 2 × 4
    C. 1 × 6
    D. 2 × 6

_____ 4. A _____ is a measuring stick that represents the actual wall frame, with markings made at the proper height for every horizontal member of the wall frame.
    A. trimmer
    B. master stud
    C. double header
    D. story pole

_____ 5. Which of the following are used as wall sheathing?
    A. Plywood.
    B. Fiberboard.
    C. Composite board.
    D. All of the above.

_____ 6. A _____ is an L-shaped support that is attached to the top of joists to strengthen them.
    A. joist hanger
    B. girder
    C. strongback
    D. header

_____ 7. _____ studs stiffen the sides of an opening and bear the direct weight of the header.
   A. Cripple
   B. Trimmer
   C. Header
   D. Master

Identification
Identify the parts of the wall frame.

_____ 8. Stud.

_____ 9. Rough sill.

_____ 10. Header.

_____ 11. Sole plate.

_____ 12. Cripple stud.

_____ 13. Trimmer.

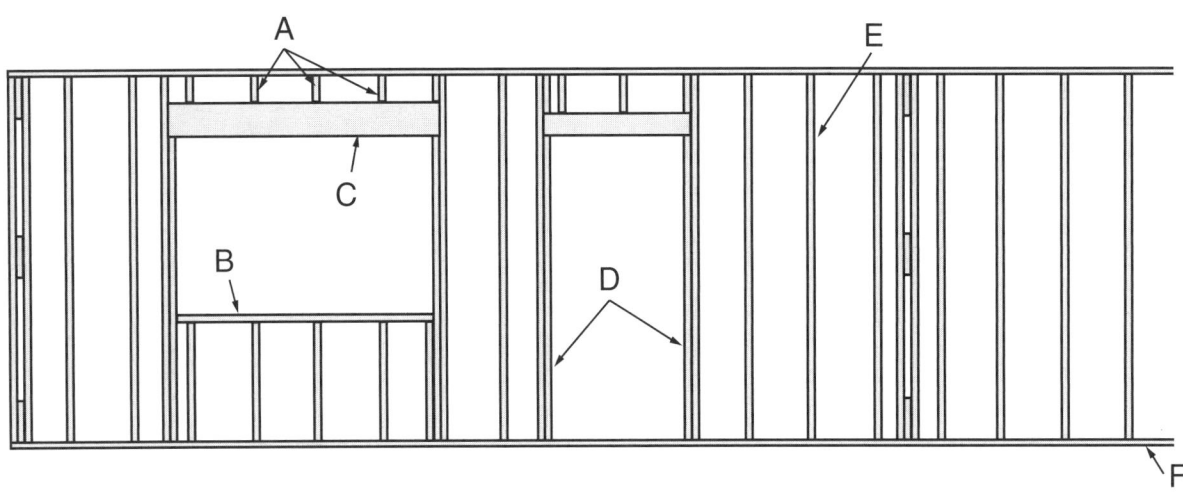

_____ 14. Refer to the drawing below and explain the purpose of the special backing let into the studs.

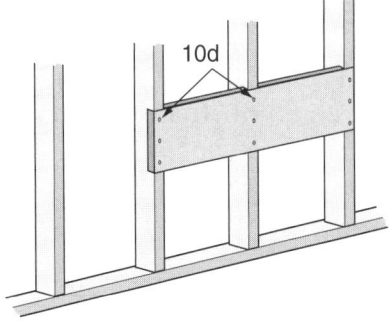

_____ 15. What percentage of the stud can be removed on a bearing wall?

10 Roof Framing

Objectives

After studying this chapter, students will be able to:
- List and describe the various types of roofs.
- Identify the parts of a common rafter.
- Define the terms *slope* and *pitch*.
- Use a framing square, speed square, and rafter tables.
- Lay out common rafters.
- Describe the layout and erection of a gable roof.
- Explain the design and erection of trusses.
- Describe the procedure for sheathing a roof.
- Estimate roofing materials.

Instructional Materials

Text: Pages 283–327
  Technical Vocabulary, page 283
  Test Your Knowledge, page 326
  Curricular Connections, page 326
  Outside Assignments, page 327
Workbook: Pages 55–64
Instructor's Resource:
  Reproducible masters:
    RM 10-1 *Roof Types*
    RM 10-2 *Plan View of Rafters*
    RM 10-3A *Rafter Layout Parts and Terms*
    RM 10-3B *Rafter Layout Parts and Terms*
    RM 10-4A *Rafter Layout*
    RM 10-4B *Rafter Layout*
    RM 10-5A *Truss Rafter Construction*
    RM 10-5B *Truss Rafter Construction*
  Transparencies (binder/CD only):
    CT 10-1 *Rafter Layout Terminology*
    CT 10-2 *Allowable Rafter Span*
    CT 10-3 *Length of Common Rafters*
    CT 10-4 *Standard Fink Truss*
    CT 10-5 *Truss Rafter Designs*
    CT 10-6 *Bracing Truss Rafters*
  Procedure Checklist: *Erecting a Gable Roof*
  Procedure Checklist: *Erecting Jack Rafters and Installing Fascia*
  Chapter Quiz

Trade-Related Math

The Pythagorean theorem is used to calculate rafter length. The Pythagorean theorem states that if the lengths of any two sides of a right triangle are known, the other side can be determined mathematically. The formula is:

$$A^2 + B^2 = H^2$$

where A is the altitude (height), B is the base length, and H is the hypotenuse.

This formula can be applied to rafter layout. The altitude can be compared to the rise, or the distance the rafter extends upward above the wall plate. The base length is called the run, or the distance from the outside of the plate to a point directly below the center of the ridge. The hypotenuse can be compared to the line length of the rafter. To determine the line length of the rafter using the previous formula when the rise is 5′ and run is 12′, the following computation is performed:

$$A^2 + B^2 = H^2$$
$$(5)^2 + (12)^2 = H^2$$
$$25 + 144 = H^2$$
$$169 = H^2$$
$$\sqrt{169} = H$$

13 feet is the line length of the rafter

Instructional Concepts and Student Learning Experiences

Roof Types

1. Using reproducible master RM 10-1 *Roof Types*, identify the different roof types found in residential construction. Have students identify the types of roofs on their houses and/or apartment buildings.

215

2. Discuss the advantages or disadvantages of each type of roof.
3. Have students research the different types of roofs and explain their histories.

Roof Supports
1. Review the construction that was discussed in the last chapter. Have students identify the parts of the structure that support the roof.

Parts of Roof Frame
1. Using reproducible master RM 10-2 *Plan View of Rafters*, discuss the various components of a roof frame. Once again, stress the importance of using the proper terminology to communicate efficiently with workers in other related trades.
2. Using reproducible master RM 10-3A *Rafter Layout Parts and Terms*, identify the parts of a rafter and its associated terms. Describe the purpose of each part.

Layout Terms and Principles
1. Cut a piece of plywood into the shape of a right triangle. Label the hypotenuse, altitude, and base. Describe how you can solve for the third value using the Pythagorean theorem if the other two values are known.
2. Compare the right triangle to the rafter parts shown in reproducible master RM 10-3B *Rafter Layout Parts and Terms*.
3. Discuss the difference between the terms *slope* and *pitch*. Given the rise and run of several roofs, have the students calculate the slope and pitch for each.

Unit Measurements
1. Review the parts of the framing square and its use.

Framing Plans
1. Discuss how carpenters lay out roof framing on simple structures.
2. Using a framing plan from a house, have the students determine the type of roof framing that is required.
3. Using the floor plan of a house, have students develop a roof framing plan. Be sure that the students include ridges, overhangs, and all rafters. Stress that the sketch should be as accurate as possible.

Rafter Sizes
1. Have students refer to the local building code to determine whether rafter sizes are included. If they are included, use the information to determine the rafter sizes for a small residential structure. If they are not included, use the table in Figure 10-8 and a stock plan. Determine the necessary rafter sizes for the structure.

Laying Out Common Rafters
1. Have the students identify the two methods used to lay out common rafters. Briefly discuss both methods.
2. Using reproducible masters RM 10-4A and B *Rafter Layout*, discuss the use of the framing square or quick square. When students understand the concepts you have presented, demonstrate their application using an actual framing square or quick square. Stress the importance of accurately measuring the dimensions.
3. Have students cut rafters for one side of a small mock-up of a gable roof.

Using the Rafter Table
1. Demonstrate the use of rafter tables on a framing square. Identify the various numbers in the rafter table and explain their meaning.
2. Divide the students into groups and give each group a framing square during this activity. Read off the unit rise and rafter length and have the students determine the run.
3. Using the results from one of the previous activities, have the students use these numbers to layout a pattern rafter. Stress that measurements must be accurate since the pattern rafter will be used to lay out other rafters.

Using the Speed Square
1. Explain the speed square and demonstrate its use.
2. Show students the instruction manual supplied by the speed square manufacturer.
3. From the manual, prepare and duplicate a handout of simple instruction and pass it out to the students. Be sure to have the manufacturer's permission to do this.
4. Using the handout, have students solve a hypothetical problem in determining rafter

length. Collect their papers and check their answers.
5. Use their answers to determine if more instruction is required.

Erecting a Gable Roof
1. Discuss the procedure for assembling a roof frame. Emphasize the importance of teamwork when assembling the frame.
2. Obtain a few framing anchors and clips and pass them out to the students. Explain how the anchors or clips are attached to rafters and plates.
3. Demonstrate the proper procedure for erecting a gable roof. Emphasize that the rafters should be cut and installed with the crown turned upward. Identify places where the rafters should be nailed.
4. Have students build a mock-up using rafters cut in a previous session.
5. Review steps for installing site-built rafters.

Gable End Frame
1. Describe the procedure for constructing the gable-end frame of a structure. Demonstrate this procedure by constructing a scale model at ground level. This allows all students to get a close look at the construction techniques.
2. Discuss the various techniques used to construct a gable overhang (shown in Figure 10-23). With the scale model completed in the previous step, construct a gable overhang using one of the methods common in your area.
3. Explain the risk factors involved when working at heights. Stress the importance of using fall protection and solid scaffolding and avoiding working directly over someone.
4. Demonstrate use of the framing square to find the common difference.

Hip and Valley Rafters
1. Identify the types of rafters that are generally included in hip roofs or intersecting gable roofs. Make sure that the students understand the terms *common, hip, valley, jack,* and *valley rafters* before proceeding.
2. Discuss a common procedure for constructing a hip roof. If possible, demonstrate this procedure.
3. Have the students determine the unit run of the hip rafters for a given plan. Explain that 17″ can be used as the unit run for the hip rafters while the unit run of the common rafters is 12″.
4. Have the students explain what is meant by the term *hip jack rafter* and where these rafters are used. Emphasize that if hip jack rafters are evenly spaced, then the change in length is consistent from one rafter to another (otherwise known as the common difference).
5. Using a framing square or a speed square, demonstrate how the common differences can be determined from rafter tables. Give different slopes of roofs spaced at different standard intervals and have students determine the common differences.
6. Discuss how jack rafters are laid out and demonstrate this procedure.
7. Have the students explain the procedure for laying out a valley jack rafter. Make sure that their layout begins at the building line.
8. Demonstrate how jack rafters are cut. Review the safe use of the radial arm saw and the advantages of using it for cuts of this nature. Stress the importance of tight-fitting joints when constructing a roof frame.

Erecting Jack Rafters
1. Discuss the procedure for erecting jack rafters. Explain different techniques that can be used to ensure that rafters are not bowed when applying the sheathing.
2. Have the students explain the purpose of fascia. Discuss different techniques used to attach fascia to the vertical ends of the rafters.

Special Problems
1. Describe special problems that may occur when framing intersecting roofs. Have the students determine the length of valley cripple jacks.

Roof Openings
1. Have students identify applications for roof openings. Discuss the procedures for framing both large and small openings.

Roof Anchorage
1. Identify various means of anchoring a roof. Discuss advantages or disadvantages of each anchoring device.

Collar Beams
1. Discuss the purpose of collar beams. Stress that they do not provide any support, but rather stiffen the roof frame and provide bracing to counteract the force rafters exert on walls. Point out that not every pair of rafters requires a collar beam.

Purlins
1. Describe the purpose of purlins in residential construction. Explain how purlins are attached to the roof frame.

Dormers
1. Define the term *dormer* and discuss its purpose(s).
2. Describe the different types of dormers, including the shed dormer and gable dormer. Explain how each is constructed.

Framing Flat Roofs
1. Compare the construction of a flat roof frame to a floor frame. Discuss possible problems that may occur in cold weather locations with a roof that is perfectly flat.
2. Describe the construction of a flat roof. Have students take note of the increased size of the roof joists due to the increase in combined load.

Framing Gambrel Roof
1. Discuss the advantages of a gambrel roof in residential construction. Identify the angles commonly used for the upper roof surface (20°) and the lower roof surface (70°).
2. Have the students make a full-size section drawing of the intersection between the two slopes. Stress the advantage of taking the time to draw this section drawing, rather than trying to construct the roof without it.

Mansard Roof
1. Point out the similarities of the mansard roof and the gambrel roof.
2. Discuss the advantages of the mansard roof.
3. Have students review the history of the mansard roof.

Special Framing
1. Using Figures 10-56 and 10-57, discuss some of the special framing problems that may be encountered.

Roof Truss Construction
1. Discuss with the students the purpose of a roof truss. List the advantages of using roof trusses for standard roof frames.
2. Using reproducible master RM 10-5A *Truss Rafter Construction,* identify the common parts of a truss rafter. Emphasize that the carpenter is seldom, if ever, responsible for determining the sizes of truss members, but that every carpenter should understand the principles involved in their construction.
3. Obtain plates and connectors that are commonly used in truss construction. Using reproducible master RM 10-5B *Truss Rafter Construction,* identify each of the plates or connectors.
4. Discuss the most efficient method of constructing truss rafters. Demonstrate their construction by creating a scale model of a pattern. When the pattern has been completed and checked for accuracy, have the students construct other scale model trusses.
5. Have students obtain information about portable truss assembly units and discuss the advantages of using such equipment.
6. Describe the means used to install roof trusses. Stress that carpenters are usually responsible for installing the trusses and that much of the work involves working at heights.
7. Discuss the types of bracing that are commonly used to support roof trusses.

Roof Sheathing
1. Discuss the purpose of roof sheathing. Identify the various materials used for roof sheathing.
2. List the steps necessary to prepare for applying roof sheathing, including setting up scaffolding and moving the sheathing materials into a position where they can be easily reached.
3. Discuss the application of board sheathing when the finish roofing material is to be wood shingles, metal sheets, or tile. Stress that the joints must be made over the center of rafters.
4. Have the students identify the advantages of using structural panels for roof sheathing. Identify the thicknesses commonly used

for the different types of finish roofing material.
5. Discuss problems that may occur when using panel materials. As a class, design a ladder rack that can be used to hold roof sheathing.

Panel Clips
1. Obtain panel clips to show to the students. Have them describe where these clips should be used.

Estimating Materials
1. Discuss the method used to determine the number of rafters required for a plain gable roof.
2. Discuss the method used to estimate the number of rafters required for a hip roof.
3. Discuss the means for estimating the amount of sheathing needed for a roof. Mention that a waste factor should always be included to make sure that there is enough material on the job site.

Model Construction
1. Throughout the chapter, it has been suggested that scale models be used to demonstrate the construction concepts used for roof framing of a typical residential structure. Scale models can be constructed to save money, yet still convey the construction methods used on the job. The most important concepts that students should gain from the scale models are the techniques used to construct them.

Chapter Review
1. Review the chapter objectives. Be sure that the students fully understand each objective.
2. Assign *Technical Vocabulary*, *Test Your Knowledge questions*, *Curriculum Connections*, and *Outside Assignments* for Chapter 10 of the text. Review the answers in class.
3. Assign Chapter 10 in the workbook. Review the answers in class.

Evaluation
This chapter provides three methods for evaluating student performance. Students should complete the *Test Your Knowledge* section using the book as reference. Students should also be allowed to use the book for reference when completing the workbook material. Use the Chapter 10 Quiz in the instructor's resources for in-class evaluation. Correct the quizzes, return them to the students, and review the quiz questions in group discussion.

Procedure Checklist
Using the procedure checklists *Erecting a Gable Roof* and *Erecting Jack Rafters and Installing Fascia*, have students evaluate the techniques used to perform these tasks.

Answers to Test Your Knowledge
Text Page 326
1. live
2. dead
3. False.
4. hip
5. span
6. 16
7. 16'-9 7/8", 21'-10 5/8"
8. center
9. The difference between the two stud lengths.
10. intersection
11. common
12. pairs
13. The main trim member attached to the plumb-cut ends of the rafters.
14. purlin
15. shed
16. camber
17. strength/rigidity
18. rafter spacing
19. common rafter
20. 66

Answers to Workbook Questions
Page 55–64
1. A. Shed.
   B. Hip.
   C. Gable.
   D. Flat.
   E. Gambrel.
2. mansard

3. common
   hip
   valley
4. A. Plumb cut.
   B. Ridge.
   C. Bird's mouth.
   D. Tail cut.
5. A. Line length of rafter.
   B. Overhang.
   C. Run.
   D. Span.
   E. Rise.
6. A. rise
   B. run
7. 24
8. face
9. D. 1/12
10. C. setting the rise and run
11. 8'-11 1/2"
12. pitch
13. rafter tables
14. 7"
15. See Figure 10-17 in text.
16. A. Roof slope.
17. C. 17"
18. 14'-9 1/4"
19. B. ledger
20. A. hip rafters
    B. valley rafter
21. C. one-half of 45° thickness of ridge
22. A. Common difference.
    B. Unit rise.
    C. Rafter spacing.
23. A. common rafter pattern
24. C. fifth
25. equal
26. 2"
27. dormer
28. collar beams
29. roof joists
30. A. Top chord.
    B. Bottom chord.
    C. Compression web.
    D. Tension web.
31. C. 1/2"
32. A. Kingpost.
    B. Scissors.
33. A. Ceiling joist.
    B. Cantilevered support.
    C. Ribbon.
    D. Lookout.
34. nailing base
35. A. Rafter.
    B. 2 × 4 or 2 × 6 Purlin.
    C. 2 × 4 Brace.
    D. Ceiling joist.
    E. Bearing partition.
36. B. 2"
37. 74
38. A. 14'
    B. 44
    C. 616 bd. ft.
39. A. 48 pcs.
    B. 20'
40. A. 54 pcs.
    B. 1705 sq. ft.
41. A. 78 pcs.
    B. 2485 sq. ft.

Answers to Chapter Quiz

1. False.
2. True.
3. True.
4. F.
5. C.
6. E.
7. D.
8. G.
9. A.
10. B.
11. H.
12. C.
13. D.
14. A.
15. B.
16. B. Hip
17. C. 1/8
18. A. Hip jack

Roof Types

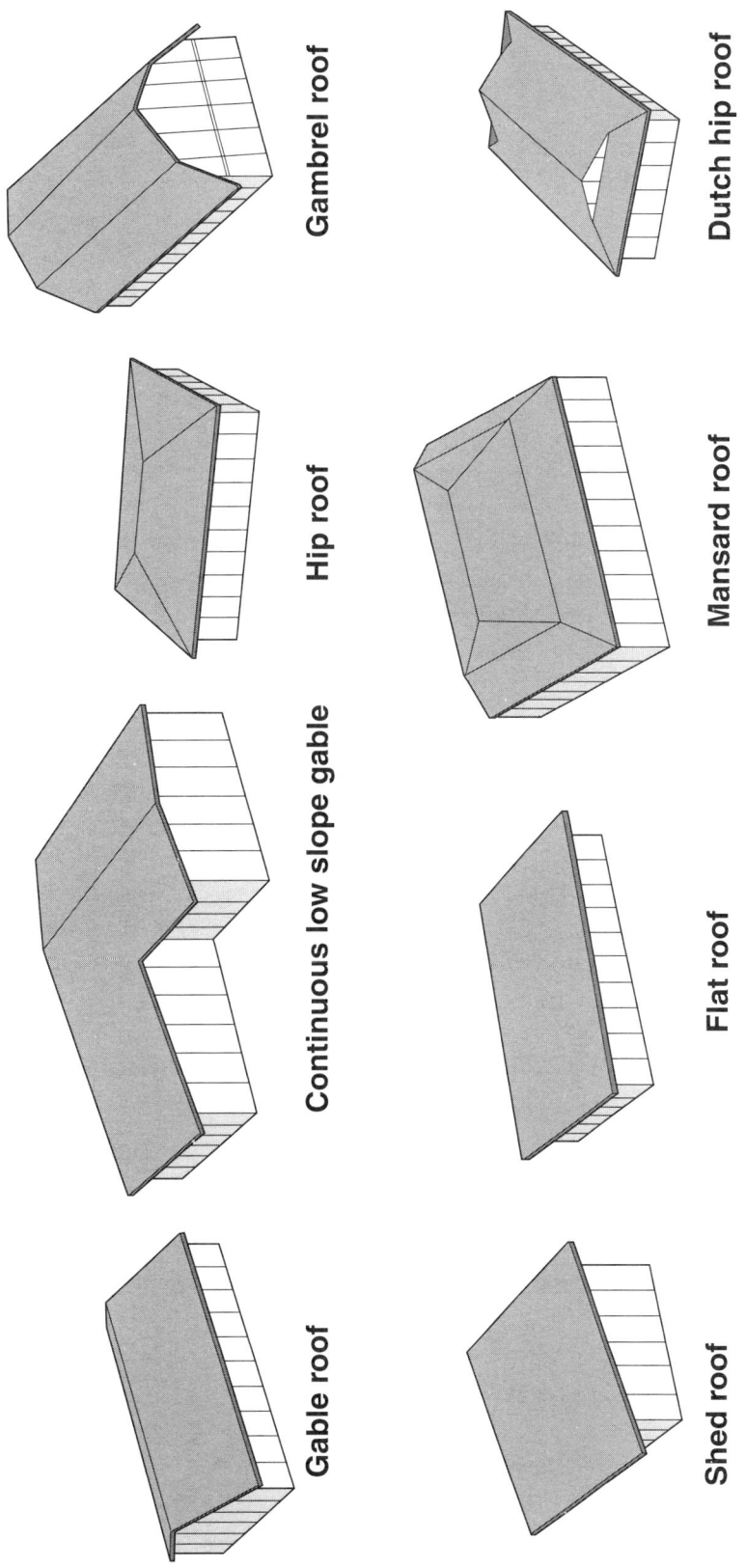

RM 10-1

Plan View of Rafters

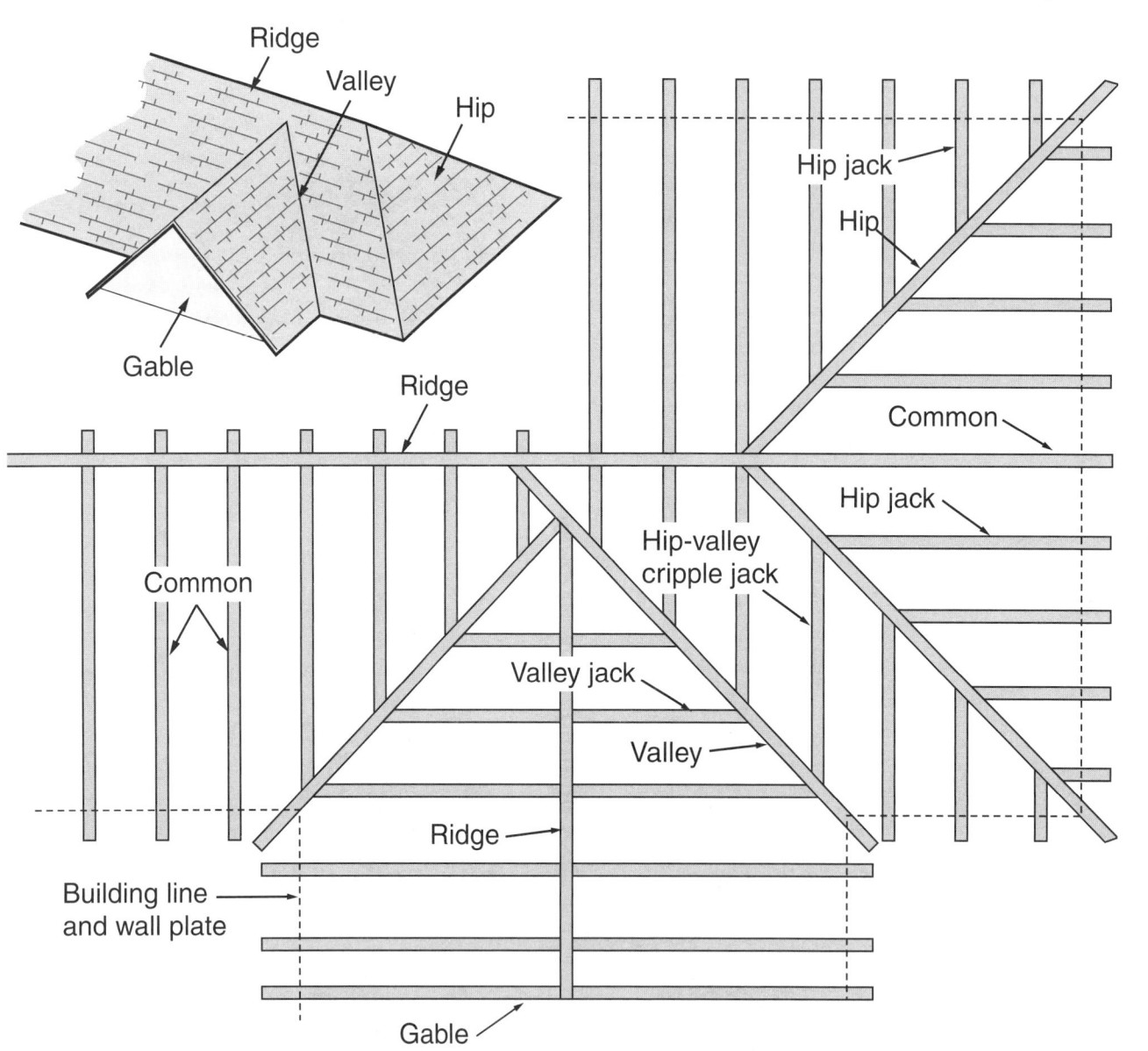

RM 10-2

Rafter Layout Parts and Terms

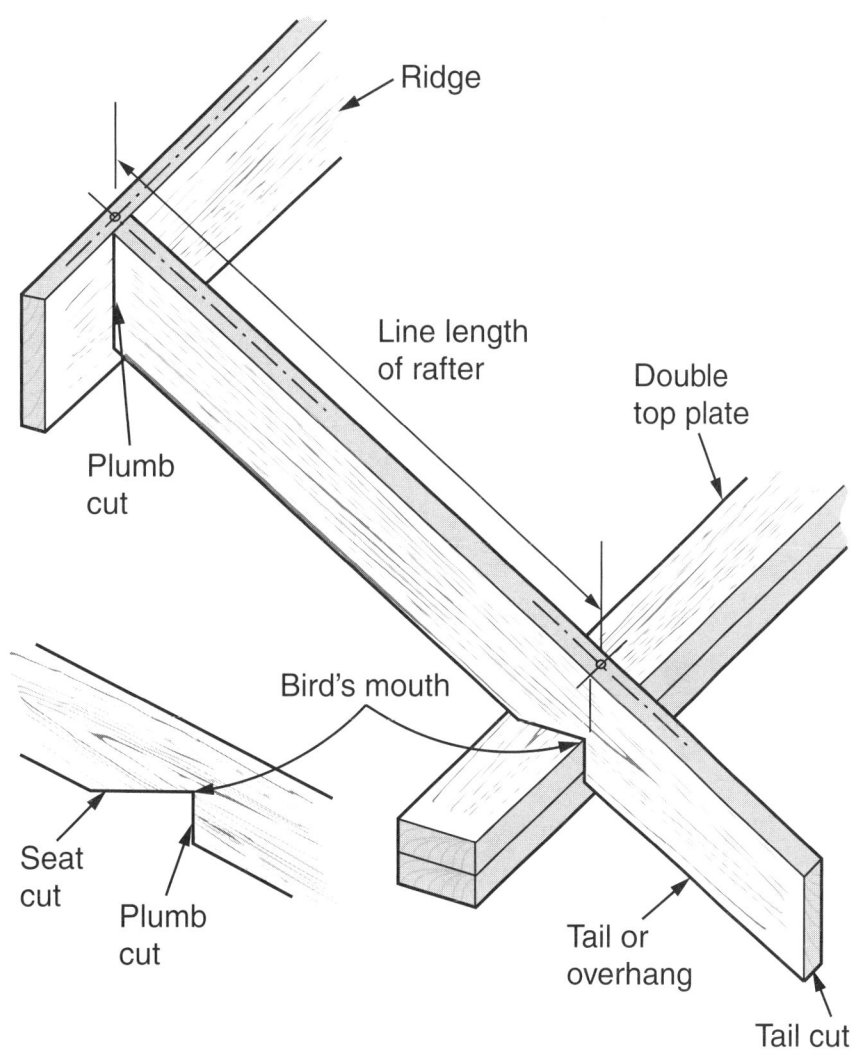

Rafter Layout Parts and Terms

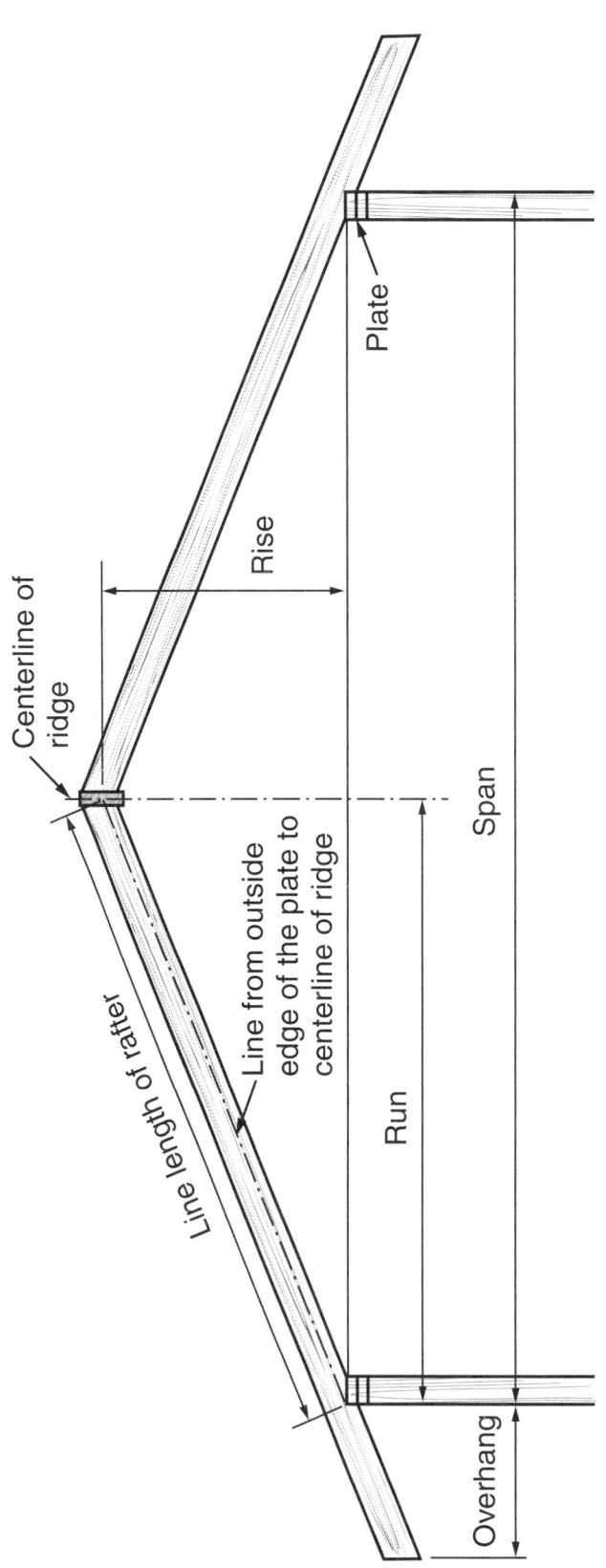

RM 10-3B

Rafter Layout

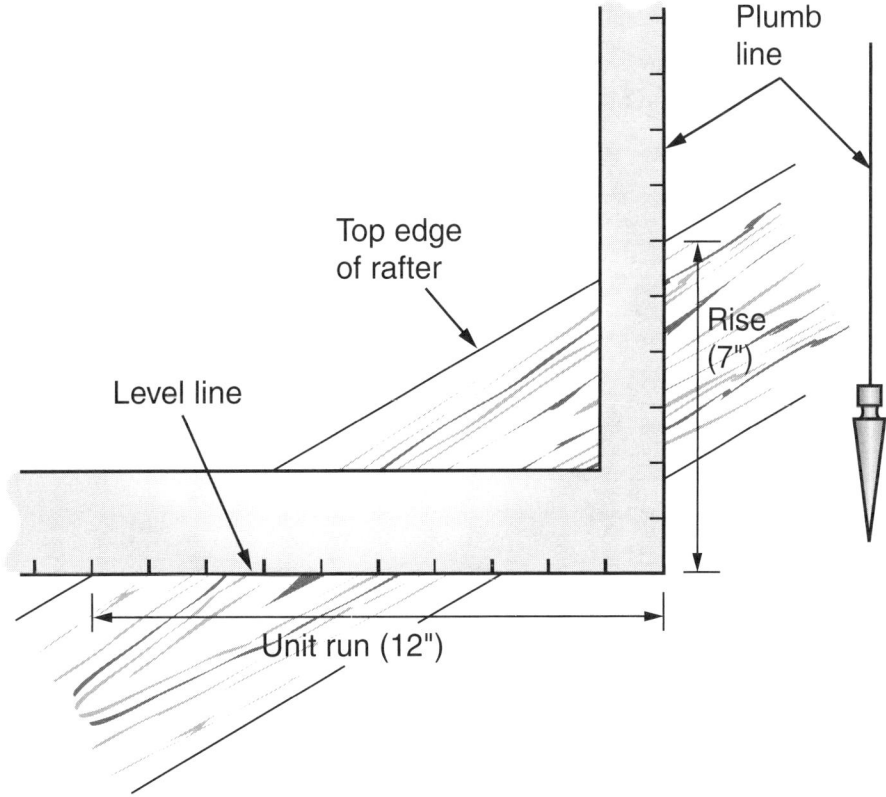

RM 10-4A

Rafter Layout

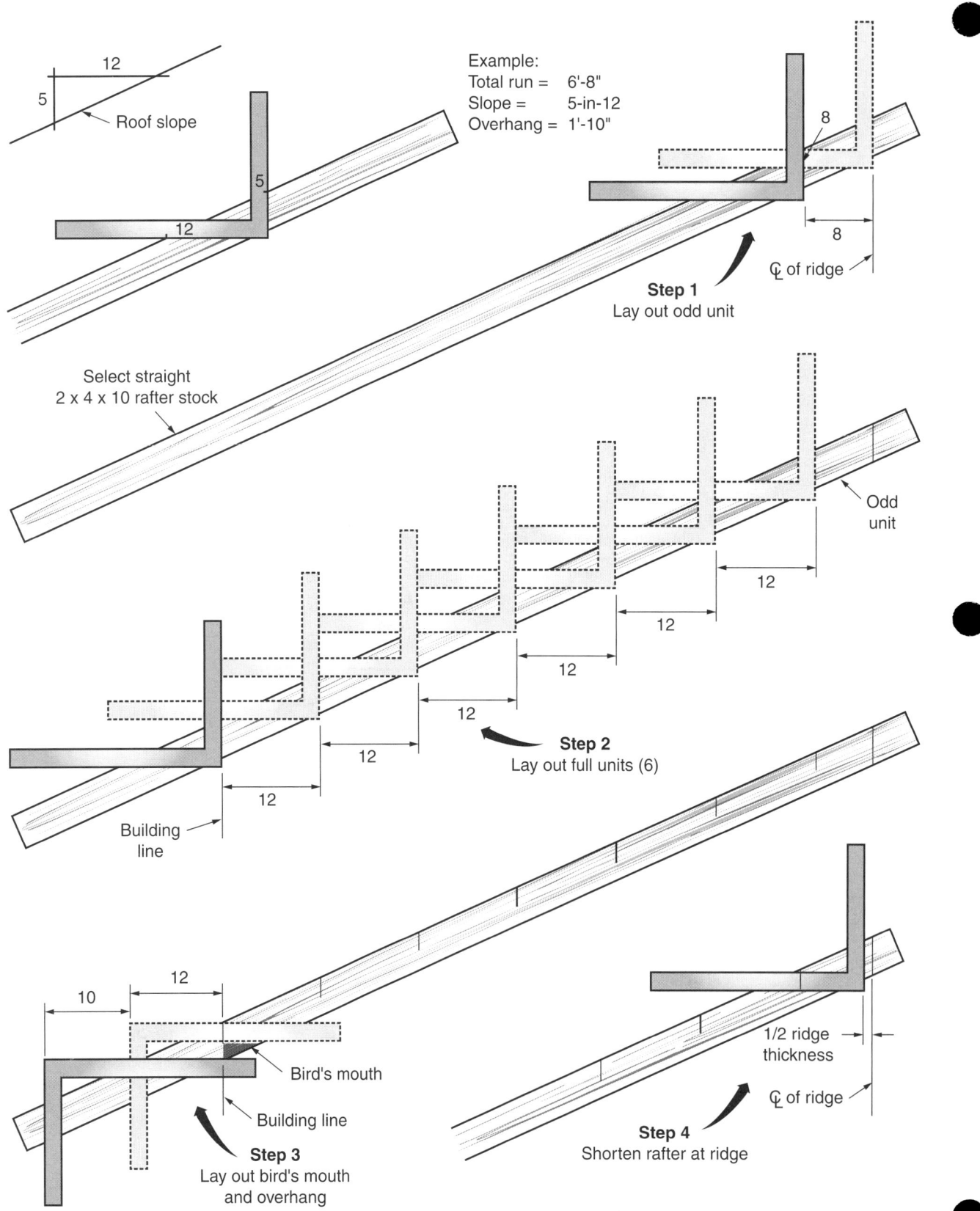

RM 10-4B

Truss Rafter Construction

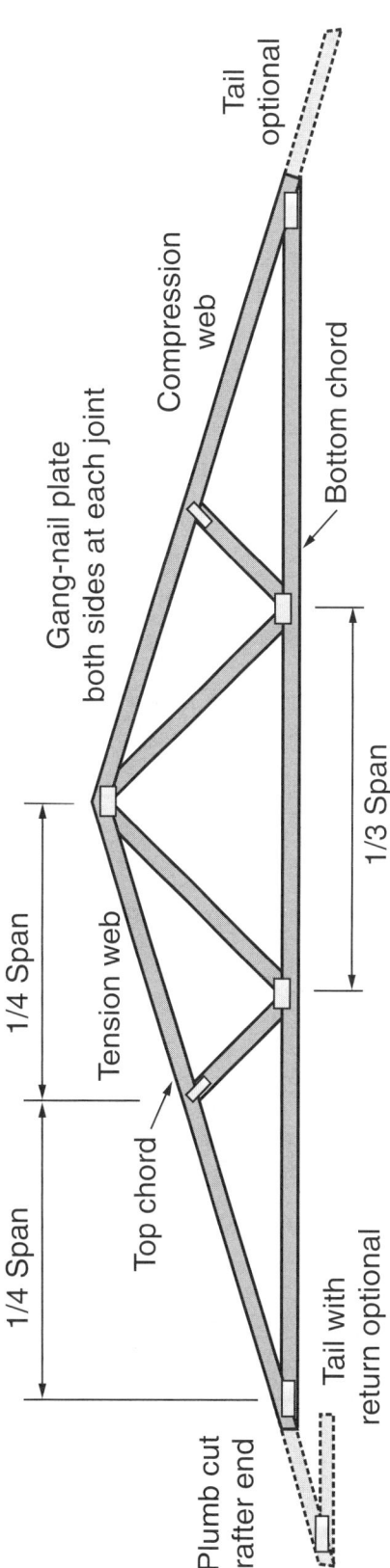

RM 10-5A

Truss Rafter Construction

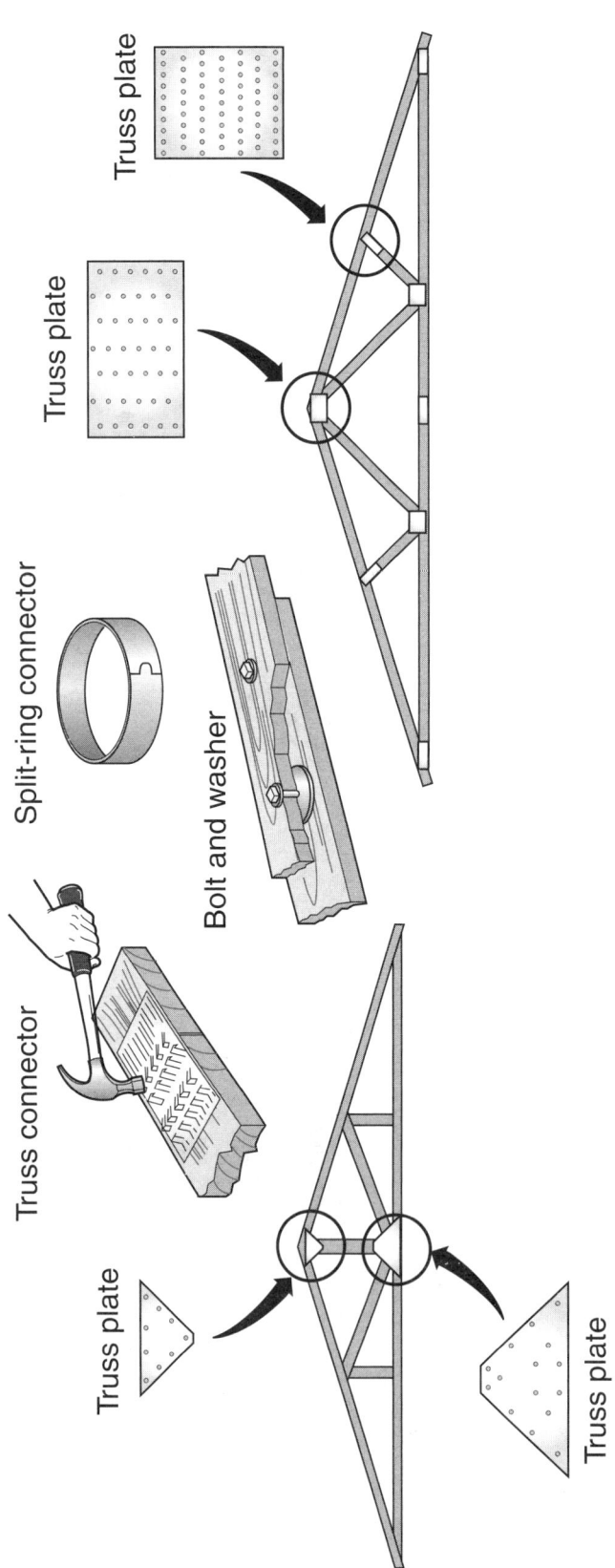

RM 10-5B

Chapter 10 Procedure Checklist
Erecting a Gable Roof

Name _____ Total _____

- [ ] Selects appropriate materials for ridge; accurately lays out rafter spacing by transferring markings from the plate or layout rod; makes sure that joints in the ridge will occur at the center of a rafter; carefully cuts ridge members and lays them across ceiling joists.   5   4   3   2   1   Disregards stock's condition when selecting material for the ridge; measures rafter spacing rather than transferring it; neglects to have ridge joints occur at centers of rafters; tries to cut ridge members after moving stock to the ceiling joists.

- [ ] Makes sure that rafters, ridge boards, and bracing are at hand; recruits other workers to help erect gable; temporarily nails rafter at plate first, then at ridge; moves about five rafters down and installs next rafter, making sure the ridge is level.   5   4   3   2   1   Must constantly locate materials for the roof frame while it is being erected; tries to erect frame alone; installs rafter adjacent to the end rafter; neglects to level ridge.

- [ ] Installs rafters between main supporting rafters using 16d nails; places only a few rafters on one side before installing matching rafters; installs additional sections of the ridge and assembles the rafters sections; adds bracing where required.   5   4   3   2   1   Uses inappropriate nails when installing rafters; erects rafters all on one side before erecting matching rafters; neglects to use bracing.

Chapter 10 Procedure Checklist
Erecting Jack Rafters and Installing Fascia

Name _____ Total _____

❏	Accurately cuts jack rafters; erects jack rafters in pairs to prevent jack and valley rafters from being pushed out of line; nails stock using an appropriate size nail; uses bracing where necessary.	5	4	3	2	1	Miscalculates rafter dimensions, resulting in poor joints or new stock being cut; erects all jack rafters on one side, pushing the jack and valley rafters out of line; uses too small or too large nails; neglects to use bracing if necessary.
❏	Checks over entire roof frame; corrects bows; sights rafters and shims where necessary.	5	4	3	2	1	Neglects to check over roof frame and correct problems.
❏	Determines best method of attaching fascia; accurately cuts the fascia, matching the angle of the upper edge of the fascia to the roof angle; cuts miters on corners; carefully installs fascia using correct size nails.	5	4	3	2	1	Miscalculates length of fascia; neglects to cut upper edge of fascia to match roof angle; uses butt joints for corners; uses too small or too large nails to attach the fascia.

Permission granted to reproduce for educational use only. Copyright by Goodheart-Willcox Co., Inc.

Chapter 10 Quiz
Roof Framing

Name _____ Date _____ Score _____

True-False
Circle T if the answer is True or F if the answer is False.

T   F   1. A gable roof has four sloping sides.

T   F   2. In a plan view, common rafters run at a right angle from the wall plate to the ridge.

T   F   3. Collar beams tie rafters and the ridge together, reinforcing the roof frame.

Identification
Identify the parts of the rafter illustrated to the right.

_____ 4. Plumb cut.

_____ 5. Double top plate.

_____ 6. Tail or overhang.

_____ 7. Tail cut.

_____ 8. Seat cut.

_____ 9. Ridge.

_____ 10. Line length of rafter.

_____ 11. Bird's mouth.

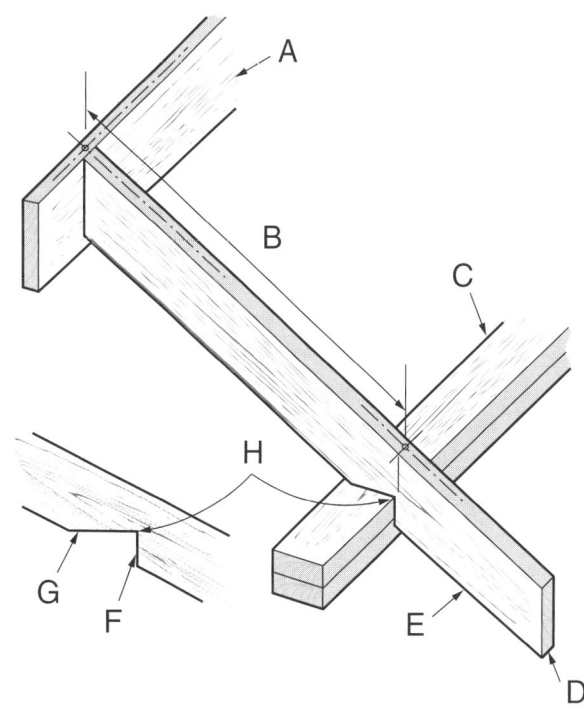

Permission granted to reproduce for educational use only.   Copyright by Goodheart-Willcox Co., Inc.

Identify the parts of the rafter illustrated to the right.

_____ 12. Bottom chord.

_____ 13. Tail with return optional.

_____ 14. Top chord.

_____ 15. Tail optional.

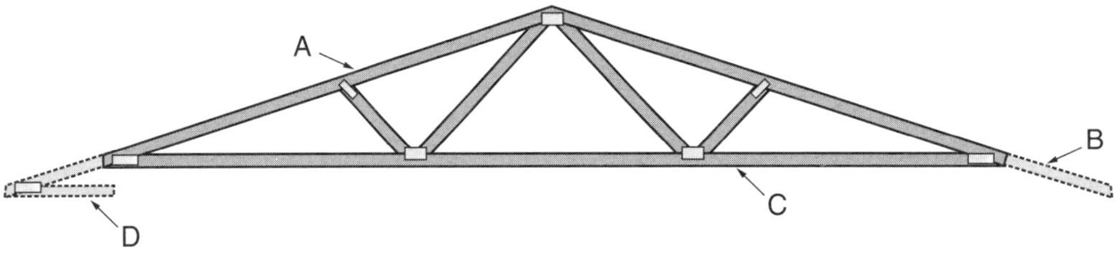

Standard W (Fink) Truss

Multiple Choice
Choose the answer that correctly completes the statement. Write the corresponding letter in the space provided.

_____ 16. _____ rafters run from the wall plate to the ridge at a 45° angle.
   A. Common
   B. Hip
   C. Valley
   D. None of the above.

_____ 17. If the total roof rise is 4′ and the total span is 32′, the pitch is _____.
   A. 1/2
   B. 1/6
   C. 1/8
   D. 1/10

_____ 18. _____ rafters run between the wall plate and a hip rafter.
   A. Hip jack
   B. Valley
   C. Common
   D. None of the above.

11 Framing with Steel

Objectives

After studying this chapter, students will be able to:
- List the advantages and disadvantages of steel framing.
- Describe the fastening methods used with steel framing components.
- Explain how wood and steel structural components are combined in floor framing.
- Demonstrate construction of walls using metal studs.
- Explain the use of a jig for fabricating steel roof trusses on the job site.
- Describe the safety precautions that must be used when working with steel framing components.

Instructional Materials

Text: Pages 329–341
Technical Vocabulary, page 329
Test Your Knowledge, page 341
Curricular Connections, page 341
Outside Assignments, page 341

Workbook: Pages 65–66

Instructor's Resource:
Reproducible masters:
RM 11-1 *Fastening Steel Sills to a Foundation*
RM 11-2 *Fasteners Used on Metal I-Beams*
RM 11-3 *Installing X Bridging on Steel Joists*
RM 11-4 *Attaching Steel Ceiling Joist to Wall Plate*
Transparencies (binder/CD only):
CT 11-1 *Framing with Steel*
CT 11-2 *Steel Framing Assembly Details*
Chapter Quiz

Trade-Related Math

Often, the decision to build with either wood or steel rests on comparative costs of wood versus steel. Load-bearing steel studs are generally more expensive than a standard wood 2 × 4, while non-load-bearing steel studs may be cheaper than a wood stud. Other considerations enter into and complicate the equation, however. Consider the following: steel members come in standard measurements that eliminate waste and mistakes; fewer work hours are needed, since fewer workers are required due to the lightweight assemblies; and termite-proofing, such as shields and poisoning of soil, can be eliminated. Have teams of students research these costs, and come up with a recommendation on which material to use.

Instructional Concepts and Student Learning Experiences

Steel Framing

1. Discuss the manufacture of steel framing members, noting that steel studs are made in several gages from 14 to 26 and studs are offered in five widths, 1 5/8", 2 1/2", 3 5/8", 4", and 6". Explain that the higher the gage number, the thinner the metal.
2. Show students a metal stud, pointing out the cutouts for running mechanical systems in the wall.
3. Show samples of self-tapping screws, which are the simplest fastening devices for metal framing.
4. Be sure to mention the advantages as well as the disadvantages of framing in steel. Stress the absence of warping, crooking, and knots. Point out the superiority of metal for walls where cabinets must be installed. Point out other instances where metal framing saves time or energy.
5. Display the different tools required when working with metal.

Framing Floors

1. Using reproducible master RM 11-1 *Fastening Steel Sills to a Foundation,* describe and discuss

both typical and alternate methods of fastening the mud sill to concrete.
2. Using reproducible master RM 11-2 *Fasteners Used on Metal I-Beams,* explain that different methods can be used to install and fasten joists to beams. The reproducible master illustrates when the joists must be flush with the top of the I-beam and the joist resting on top of the beam.
3. If a powder-actuated tool is available, demonstrate its use as a fastening device.

Framing Walls and Ceilings
1. Make inquiries about metal framing being done in your area and try to arrange a field trip to observe framing methods used.
2. Secure enough materials to construct a wall with steel studs. Have students lay out and build the wall. Demonstrate running of wiring and plumbing through the cutouts. Have students repeat the demonstration.
3. Using reproducible master RM 11-3 *Installing X Bridging on Steel Joists,* show the similarity in installing metal or wood bridging.
4. Use reproducible master RM 11-4 *Attaching Steel Ceiling Joist to Wall Plate* to explain approved assembly and fastening system for ceiling joists. If a Shielded Metal Arc Welding unit is available, produce a mockup to be used as a teaching tool.

Framing Roofs
1. Point out that most steel roof trusses, like their wood counterparts, come engineered and prefabricated.
2. Construct a jig and have students fabricate a small truss rafter.

Chapter Review
1. Review the chapter objectives. Be sure that the students are fully competent in the task identified by each objective.
2. Review the terms in the *Technical Vocabulary* section and make certain students are clear on each definition.
3. Assign the *Test Your Knowledge* questions, *Curricular Connections,* and *Outside Assignments* for Chapter 11 of the text. Review the answers to test questions in class. Also, have students report on the *Curricular Connections* and *Outside Assignments* activities as appropriate.
4. Assign Chapter 11 of the workbook. Review the answers in class.

Evaluation
This chapter provides three methods for evaluating student performance. Students should complete the *Test Your Knowledge* section using the book as reference. Students should also be allowed to use the book for reference when completing the workbook material. Use the Chapter 11 Quiz in the instructor's resources for in-class evaluation. Correct the quizzes, return them to the students, and review the quiz questions in group discussion.

Answers to Test Your Knowledge
Text Page 341
1. thousands of lineal feet
2. brake, punching
3. B. nails
4. False.
5. True.
6. 25
7. steel pins
8. SMAW
9. screws
10. True.

Answers to Workbook Questions
Pages 65–66
1. D. All of the above.
2. Use care in handling components and wear leather gloves.
   Welded joints should be allowed to cool before handling.
3. insulators
4. See Figure 11-15 in text.
5. A. 3/4" weld.
   B. Joist.
   C. 3/4" weld.
   D. Stud.
6. color code

7. B. sometimes engineered by specialty companies.
   C. sometimes build on-site to code specifications.
   D. required to follow engineering specifications.
8. Variable speed drill, screw gun, hearing protectors, clamping pliers, metal snips, metal punch, metal cutoff blade for portable saw, magnetic level, metal cutoff saw, right angle drill, and sometimes welding equipment.
9. Install structural sheathing to both sides of the wall. Apply type II OSB with the long side parallel to the studs. Install X bracing extending from the top plate to the bottom track.
10. track

Answers to Chapter Quiz
1. False.
2. False.
3. True.
4. False.
5. B.
6. C.
7. A.
8. B. wood
9. B. thermal break

Fastening Steel Sills to a Foundation

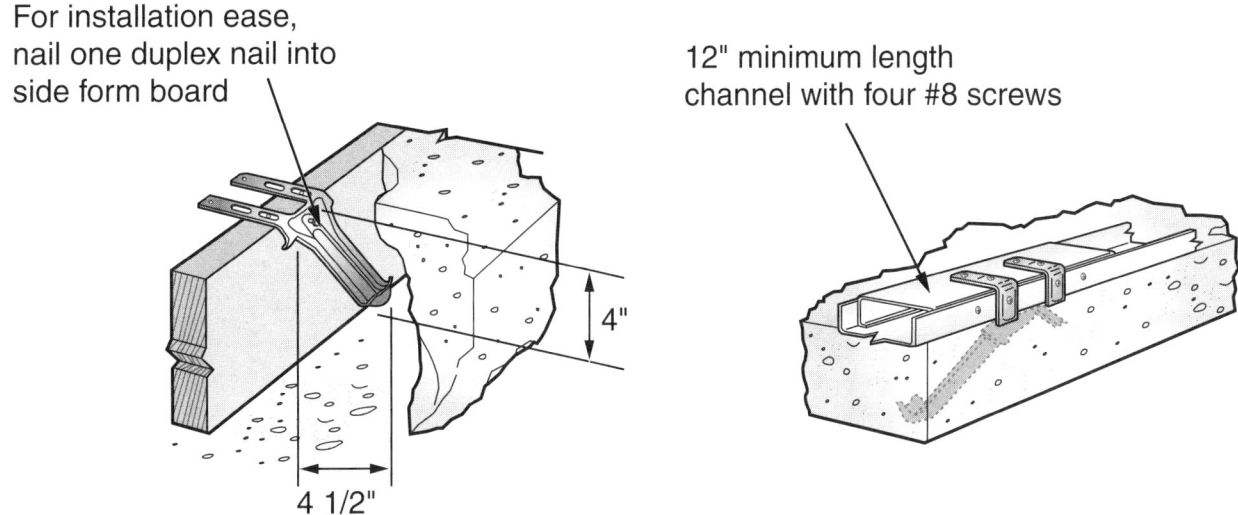

Typical installation

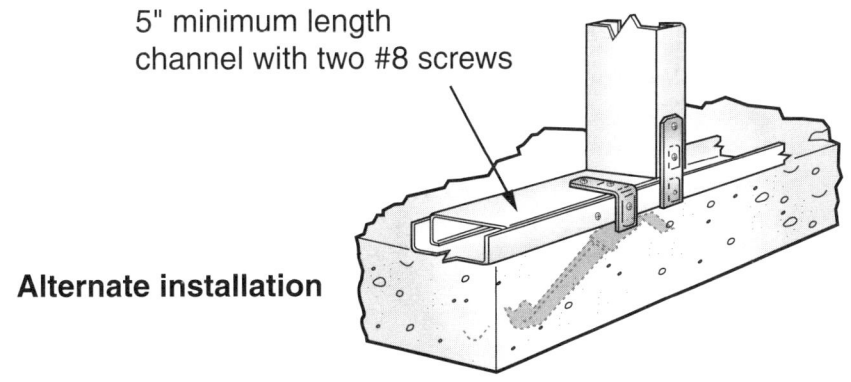

Alternate installation

RM 11-1

Fasteners Used on Metal I-Beams

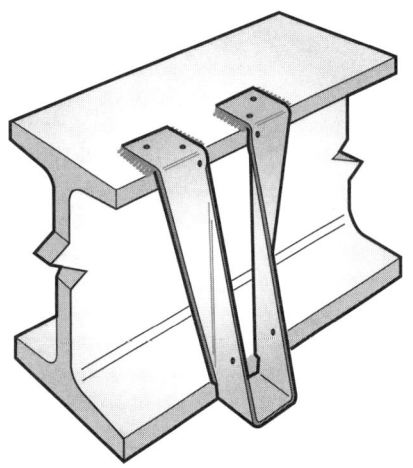

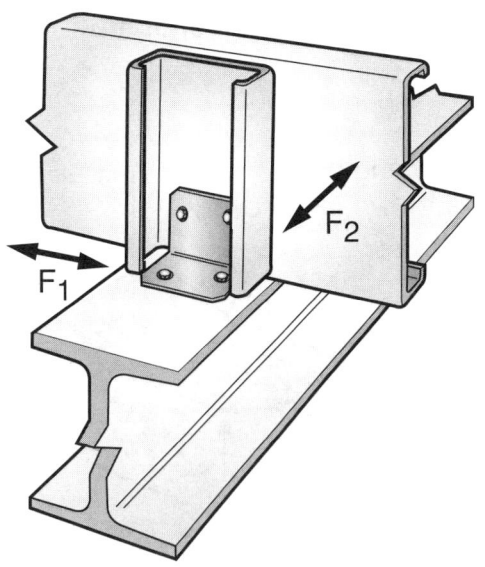

RM 11-2

Installing X Bridging on Steel Joists

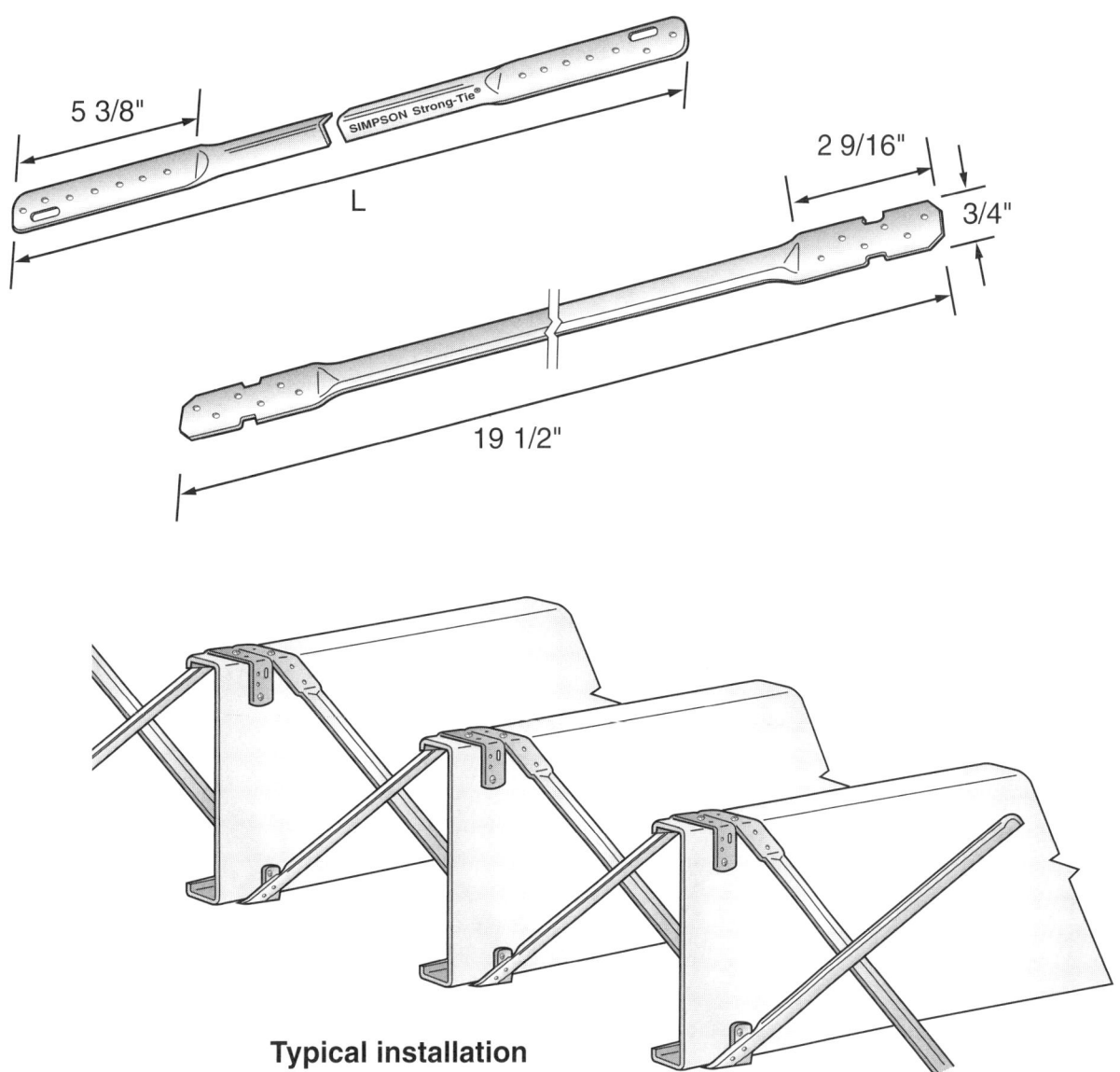

Typical installation

RM 11-3

Attaching Steel Ceiling Joist to Wall Plate

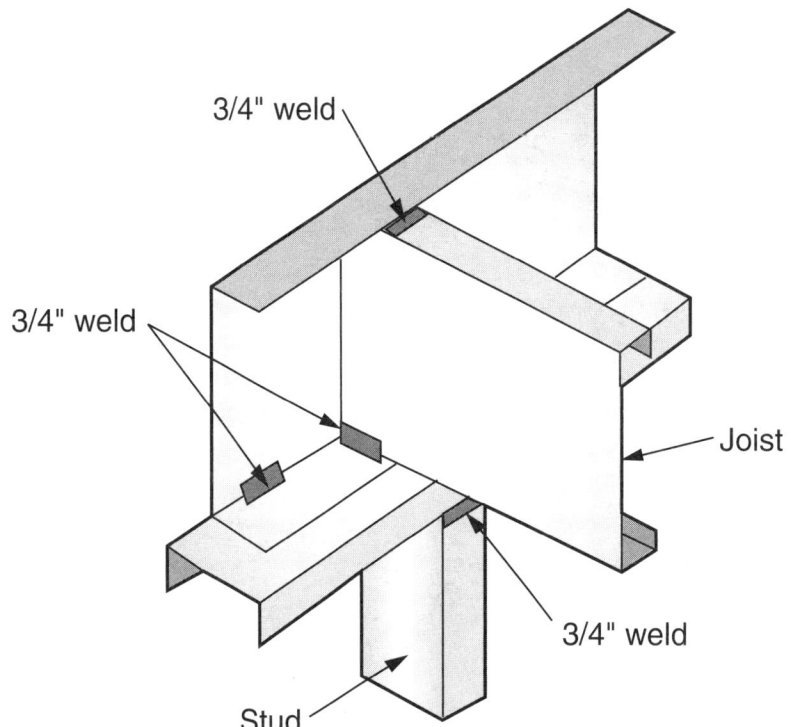

RM 11-4

Chapter 11 Quiz
Framing with Steel

Name _____ Date _____ Score _____

True-False
Circle T if the answer is true or F if the answer is false.

T F 1. All metal studs and joists have a gap in their edges that receive and hold nails.

T F 2. The cost of metal framing pieces is based on 100 lineal feet.

T F 3. Steel joists are available in lengths up to 40 feet.

T F 4. Studs 2 1/2" wide and 25 GA. are suitable for load-bearing walls.

Identification
Identify the details for the wall frame.

_____ 5. 1 1/2" CRC horizontal bridging.

_____ 6. Clip angle.

_____ 7. CS stud.

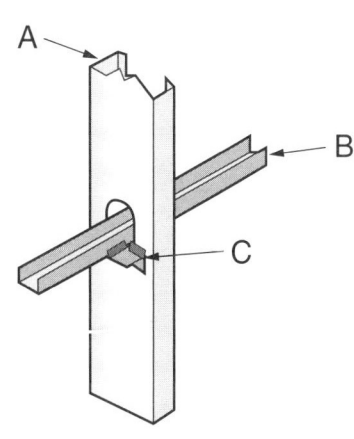

Multiple Choice

Choose the answer that correctly completes the statement. Write the corresponding letter in the space provided.

_____ 8. Metal studs can be used with either metal or _____ plates.
   A. plastic composite
   B. wood
   C. fiberglass

_____ 9. When steel studs are used for exterior walls, a(n) _____ must be installed to reduce heat loss.
   A. electric heat panel
   B. thermal break
   C. sprayed on insulation between studs

Section 2 Exam
Footing, Foundations, and Framing

Name _____ Date _____ Score _____

True-False
Circle T if the answer is True or F if the answer is False.

T F 1. Platform framing is also referred to as balloon framing.

T F 2. If large holes are to be cut in a joist for a plumbing run, they should be cut along the bottom edge.

T F 3. In cold climates, footings should be located above the frost line so that freezing can be avoided.

T F 4. A key is formed in a foundation wall by cutting it in with a concrete saw.

T F 5. A first course of concrete block should first be strung out dry (without mortar) to check the layout.

T F 6. The compressive strength of concrete is high, while its tensile strength is relatively low.

T F 7. Perimeter insulation is not required for slab-on-grade construction in cold climates.

T F 8. Screeding is the process of leveling off concrete slabs or plastering on interior walls.

T F 9. When positioning joists, the crowns should always be turned upward.

T F 10. Interior, non-load-bearing walls are called partitions.

Multiple Choice
Choose the answer that correctly completes the statement. Write the corresponding letter in the space provided.

_____ 11. The chemical action that occurs when cement, aggregate, and water are added together is called _____.
   A. setting
   B. hydration
   C. thermosiphoning
   D. leaching

_____ 12. The steel or masonry structure that provides space around basement windows located below finished grade is a(n) _____.
   A. window well
   B. window buck
   C. areaway
   D. lintel

Permission granted to reproduce for educational use only.   Copyright by Goodheart-Willcox Co., Inc.

_____ 13. A _____ mortar joint is commonly used with standard concrete blocks.
   A. 1/16"
   B. 1/8"
   C. 1/4"
   D. 3/8"

_____ 14. _____ cubic yards of concrete are required for a slab measuring 6" × 20' × 25'. Round your answer to the nearest half cubic yard.
   A. 6
   B. 7.5
   C. 9.5
   D. 11

_____ 15. In most areas of the country, sidewalks are _____ thick.
   A. 4"
   B. 6"
   C. 8"
   D. 10"

_____ 16. _____ are not a type of admixture.
   A. Accelerators
   B. Air-entraining agents
   C. Corrosion inhibitors
   D. All of the above are admixtures.

_____ 17. Subfloors _____.
   A. add rigidity to the structure
   B. provide a base for finish flooring material
   C. provide a layout surface for carpenters when constructing additional framing
   D. All of the above.

_____ 18. _____ stiffen the sides of a rough opening and bear the direct weight of the header.
   A. Cripple studs
   B. Trimmer studs
   C. Columns
   D. Posts

_____ 19. The ceiling of a one-story structure is supported by a framework consisting of members called _____.
   A. trusses
   B. ceiling joists
   C. rafters
   D. stretchers

Matching
Select the correct answer from the list on the right and place the corresponding letter in the blank on the left.

_____ 20. ICFs.

_____ 21. Reinforced footings.

_____ 22. Stepped footings.

A. Changes grade levels at intervals to accommodate for a sloping lot.

B. Forms for concrete made of light polystyrene foam or other rigid insulating material types.

C. Steel rebar is used for added strength against cracking.

Name _____

_____ 23. Joist.
_____ 24. Ribbon.
_____ 25. Sill.
_____ 26. Tail joist.
_____ 27. Girder.

A. Provides support for joists when long spans are necessary.
B. Horizontal framing members used to support floor and ceiling loads.
C. Narrow board let into a stud or other vertical member of a frame and adds support.
D. Wall studs are usually tied into this framing member.
E. Runs from the band joist to the header of the opening.

_____ 28. Common rafter.
_____ 29. Hip jack.
_____ 30. Valley rafter.
_____ 31. Valley jack rafter.
_____ 32. Cripple jack rafter.

A. Runs at 90° (in the plan view) from the wall plate to the ridge.
B. Extends diagonally from the wall plate to the ridge in the hollow formed by the intersection of two roof sections.
C. Intersects neither the plate nor the ridge and is terminated at each end by hip and valley rafters.
D. Same as the upper end of the common rafter, but intersects a valley rafter rather than the plate.
E. Same as the lower part of a common rafter, but intersects a hip rafter rather than the ridge.

Completion
Place the answer that correctly completes the statement in the space provided.

_____ 33. A batter board assembly consists of stakes and at least one horizontal member called a(n) ____.

_____ 34. Foundations should generally extend at least ____ inches above finished grade.

_____ 35. Intersecting concrete block walls should be tied into each other every ____ course.

_____ 36. A special water collection basin used to ensure good drainage around a foundation is called a(n) ____.

_____ 37. A slab measuring 4″ × 15′ × 20′ requires ____ cubic yards of concrete. Add 5% waste to allow for waste and slab thickness variations. Round your answer to the nearest half cubic yard.

_____ 38. Headers are formed by nailing two members together with a ____ inch spacer between.

_____ 39. In construction, studs are usually cut to length at the mill and are designated with the letters ____.

_____ 40. Steel framing is fastened with either ____ or ____.

Identification

Identify the types of concrete blocks.

_____ 41. Stretcher.

_____ 42. Corner.

_____ 43. Bull nose.

_____ 44. Jamb.

_____ 45. Double corner or pier.

_____ 46. 4″ or 6″ partition.

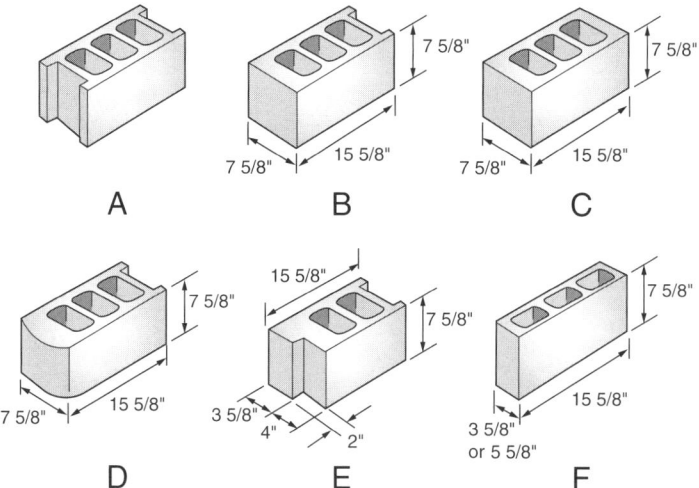

Identify the types of roofs.

_____ 47. Gable roof.

_____ 48. Shed roof.

_____ 49. Hip roof.

_____ 50. Gambrel roof.

_____ 51. Dutch hip roof.

_____ 52. Mansard roof.

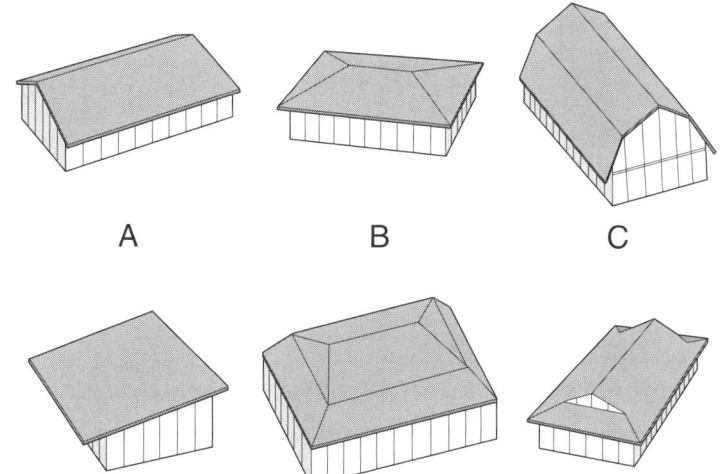

12 Roofing Materials and Methods

Objectives

After studying this chapter, students will be able to:
- List the covering materials commonly used for sloping roofs.
- Define roofing terms.
- Describe how to prepare the roof deck.
- Describe reroofing procedures for both asphalt and wood shingles.
- Demonstrate correct nailing patterns.
- Select appropriate roofing materials for various slopes and conditions.
- Describe the application procedure for a built-up roof.
- Explain how various roofing products are applied.
- Demonstrate the proper positioning of gutters.
- Estimate materials needed for a specific roofing job.

Instructional Materials

Text: Pages 343–394
  Technical Vocabulary, page 343
  Test Your Knowledge, page 393
  Curricular Connections, page 394
  Outside Assignments, page 394
Workbook: Pages 67–74
Instructor's Resource:
  Reproducible masters:
    RM 12-1A *Shingling Valleys*
    RM 12-1B *Shingling Valleys*
    RM 12-1C *Shingling Valleys*
    RM 12-2 *Vent Stack Flashing*
    RM 12-3 *Six-Inch Shingling Method*
    RM 12-4 *Four-Inch Shingling Method*
    RM 12-5 *Metal Gutter System*

Transparencies (binder/CD only):
  CT 12-1 *Opening up Attics for Proper Ventilation*
Procedure Checklist: *Applying Wood Shingles*
Procedure Checklist: *Installing Asphalt Shingles*
Chapter Quiz

Trade-Related Math

One method of estimating roofing material is to calculate the total surface area to be covered. In new construction, the figures used to estimate the sheathing can also be used to estimate the underlayment and finished roofing material.

Another method to estimate roof area is to determine the total ground area of the structure, including the eaves and cornice overhang. The ground area is converted to roof area by adding a percentage. These percentages are shown in Section 12.20 of the text. In either case, the roof area is then divided by 100 to determine the number of squares of roofing material to be used. The following formula can be used:

$$\frac{\text{Roof area}}{100} = \text{number of squares}$$

In the following example, the total ground area is 1650 square feet and the slope of the roof is 5 in 12.

$$\text{Roof area} = 1650 + (1650 \times 8.5\%)$$
$$= 1650 + (1650 \times .085)$$
$$= 1650 + 140.25$$
$$\text{Roof area} = 1790.25$$
$$\frac{\text{Roof area}}{100} = \text{number of squares}$$
$$\frac{1790.25}{100} = 17.9$$

18 squares of roofing material should be purchased

Instructional Concepts and Student Learning Experiences

Types of Materials
1. Discuss the factors to consider when selecting roofing materials. Emphasize that a carpenter should always check the local building code before installing any type of roofing material to make sure that a particular type of material is not prohibited.
2. If the job is a reroof, explain that it is good to check local codes regarding the number of layers of shingles allowed before a tearoff is necessary.
3. Have the students identify various types of roofing materials including: shingles (made of a variety of materials), slate, tile, and sheet materials (of metal and other materials).

Roofing Terminology
1. Have the students define the following roofing terms: square, coverage, exposure, head lap, side lap, and shingle butt. Refer to Figure 12-3 to illustrate each term.

Preparing the Roof Deck
1. Discuss the necessary preparation for a roof deck. Identify various things that a carpenter should be aware of when inspecting a roof deck in preparation for the roofing material.
2. Explain the purpose of using louvered openings for an attic.

Asphalt Roofing Products
1. Have the students list the three general categories of asphalt roofing products and discuss the purpose of each.
2. Discuss the composition of saturated felts. Mention that saturated felts are commonly used under shingles for sheathing paper.
3. Discuss the composition of ice-and-water barrier. Be sure to cover its purpose and uses.
4. Discuss the composition of roll roofing and shingles. Explain the purpose of the mineral granules embedded in the surface.
5. Examine the charts in Figure 12-4 of the text regarding shingles and roll roofing. Have students note the weight and size of each.
6. Using a standard three-tab asphalt strip shingle, measure its dimensions. Dimensions can be written on duct tape placed directly on the shingle.
7. Discuss the advantages of applying self-sealing shingles during the summer.
8. Emphasize the risks involved in roofing a structure. Stress the importance of using solid scaffolding when applying shingles.

Underlayment
1. Discuss the purpose of underlayment. Identify materials commonly used as underlayment in your specific location. Also, identify materials that should *not* be used as underlayment.
2. Describe the proper application of underlayment materials.

Drip Edge
1. Describe the purpose and proper application of a drip edge.

Flashing
1. Discuss the purpose of an eaves flashing strip or ice-and-water barrier in cold climates.

Installing Open Valley Flashing
1. Define *flashing* and identify materials that are commonly used as flashing.
2. Using reproducible master RM 12-1A *Shingling Valleys*, describe the proper application of open valley flashing.
3. Discuss the purpose of snapping a chalk line along the edges and down the center of the valley.

Woven and Closed-Cut Valleys
1. Discuss the purpose of using woven or closed-cut valleys.
2. Using reproducible masters RM 12-1B and 12-1C *Shingling Valleys*, discuss the preparations necessary for installing a woven or closed-cut valley. Compare and contrast the two types.

Flashing at a Wall
1. Discuss the purpose of using metal flashing at a wall and roof intersection. Describe the size of flashing that should be used. Stress that the flashing should not be nailed to the

wall since the settling of the roof frame may damage the seal.

Chimney Flashing
1. Identify the two parts of chimney flashing and discuss why both are required.
2. Describe the correct procedure for applying flashing around a chimney that does not have a saddle.

Chimney Saddle
1. Discuss the construction of a chimney saddle. Identify the materials commonly used for the covering of chimney saddles (sheet metal or roll roofing).

Vent Stack and Skylight Flashing
1. Using reproducible master RM 12-2 *Vent Stack Flashing*, discuss the procedure for installing flashing around a vent stack.
2. Remove a portion of the shingles on the simulated roof used to show shingling methods. Drill or cut a hole in this roof to accept a vent stack. Secure the vent stack into position on the underside of the plywood. Demonstrate the correct procedure for installing vent stack flashing.

Strip Shingles
1. Explain the difference in laying shingles for a small roof and a large roof (over 30′ long).
2. Discuss the need for snapping chalk lines to aid inexperienced carpenters or roofers. Describe where the chalk lines should be snapped.
3. Since shingles may vary from manufacturer to manufacturer, stress that a carpenter should always read the manufacturer's recommendations before applying shingles.
4. Obtain various types of nails used for installing asphalt shingles and have the students identify each type. Discuss the length of nail that should be used.
5. Describe the number and placement of nails for the correct application of roofing materials. Mention that the shingle should be nailed from one edge to the other to avoid buckling it.
6. Review the safety precautions for using a pneumatic stapler for shingle application. Whether using nails or staples, stress that they should be driven square and flush to the shingle and not sunken into the shingle.
7. Explain the purpose of a starter strip and how it should be applied.
8. Using reproducible master RM 12-3 *Six-Inch Shingling Method*, describe the procedure for laying shingles. Stress the importance of accurate cuts and exactly aligning the cutouts in every other course to secure a neat appearance.
9. Using reproducible master RM 12-4 *Four-Inch Shingling Method*, compare the four and six inch methods. Point out the differences between the two methods.
10. Demonstrate the six and four inch shingling methods using a 4′ × 8′ sheet of plywood mounted on an angled support setup at table-top level. This will allow all students to see the techniques involved in laying shingles without exposing them to heights. Be sure to treat the sheet of plywood as if it is an entire roof section. Apply underlayment, drip edges, and a starter strip for realism.

Hips and Ridges
1. Describe how hip and ridge shingles can be fabricated from common square-butt shingle strips or from mineral surfaced roll roofing. Demonstrate this procedure as well. Discuss how the hip or ridge shingles are attached to the roof.

Wind Protection
1. Review the purpose of the adhesive strips found on some shingles. Stress that self-sealing shingles are generally satisfactory only for roofs with slopes up to 60°.
2. Discuss procedures that should be followed for installing roofing materials on steep roofs, such as mansard roofs.

Individual Asphalt Shingles
1. Refer to Figure 12-29 and discuss the use of individual asphalt shingles for roofing. Cite advantages and disadvantages of using this type of shingle.

Low-Slope Roofs
1. Discuss special procedures that should be followed for low-slope roofs.

Roll Roofing
1. Point out the two parts of typical roll roofing—the granular surfaced area and the selvage.
2. Describe the proper procedure for applying roll roofing.
3. Remove the asphalt shingles installed on the simulated roof. Demonstrate how roll roofing is applied to a roof and cemented into place.

Reroofing
1. Discuss the two primary factors involved in determining whether old roofing should be removed before applying new roofing. Discuss the means for removing old shingles if it is determined that they must be taken off.
2. Explain the steps taken to reroof over old wood shingles. Emphasize the importance of repairing and renailing existing shingles if necessary.
3. Discuss the preparation necessary for re-roofing over old asphalt shingles.
4. Describe steps that should be taken to seal the joint between a vertical wall and roof surface in a reroofing operation.

Built-Up Roofing
1. Describe situations in which built-up roofing is advantageous over asphalt shingles.
2. Discuss the procedure for applying built-up roofing materials. Explain the purpose of spreading slag, gravel, crushed stone, or marble chips over the surface of the built-up roof.
3. Compare the terms *dead-flat asphalt* and *steep asphalt*. Discuss the importance of using the correct type of asphalt for the situation.
4. Describe the purpose of a gravel stop and discuss its installation on a built-up roof.
5. Identify the types of precautions that must be taken around chimneys, vents, and the intersections of the walls and the roof. Describe the basic construction commonly used at the intersection of a flat roof and wall.

Wood Shingles
1. Discuss the advantages and disadvantages of using wood shingles for roofing.
2. Have the students identify the types of wood commonly used for wood shingles. Explain why these types of wood are more widely used than other types.
3. Explain that the exposure of wood shingles depends on the slope of the roof. List different exposures that are used for different sizes of shingles.
4. Identify the types of sheathing that are commonly used for wood shingles. Discuss why one type of sheathing might be used rather than another.
5. Describe the types of underlayment that can be used for wood shingles, including fire-resistant underlayment.
6. Explain that flashing may be required in areas where temperatures drop below 0°F (–19°C). Identify the types of flashing, including ice-and-water barrier. Describe the proper application of each.
7. Discuss why only rust-resistant nails should be used with wood shingles. Identify the types of nails commonly used for wood shingles by referring to Figure 12-44.
8. Discuss the proper use of a shingler's hatchet when installing wood shingles and shakes. Stress safety precautions since the blade and heel are sharp.
9. Describe the procedure for applying the first course of shingles. Stress the nailing pattern that should be used and that the shingles should not be crushed when installing the nails. Also mention that the shingles should be spaced about 1/4″ apart to allow for expansion.
10. Explain the installation of the second and successive rows of wood shingles. Describe why a straightedge is used when installing wood shingles.
11. Demonstrate the installation of wood shingles on the simulated roof. Emphasize that alignment of the shingles should be checked every fifth or sixth course to ensure that the courses run parallel with the ridge. Show the proper means of installing a piece of beveled siding along the roof edge to tilt the shingles inward.
12. Discuss the procedure of installing wood shingles at hips and ridges using prefabricated units and common wood shingles.
13. Discuss the types of special effects that can be obtained with wood shingles. However,

stress that the basic procedure for installing wood shingles should be accomplished before trying to create special effects.
14. Discuss the preparation necessary for reroofing with wood shingles. Describe how new wood shingles are installed over an existing wood shingled roof.

Wood Shakes
1. Discuss the similarities and differences between wood shakes and wood shingles.
2. Point out that the recommended minimum slope for roofs on which shakes are to be applied is 4-in-12. Discuss the exposure necessary for various sizes of wood shakes.
3. Describe the preparation necessary for wood shakes.
4. Discuss the installation of wood shakes. Stress that there should be 1/4" to 3/8" of space between shakes and that the joints of successive courses should be offset at least 1 1/2".
5. Review the types of nails that are used for wood shingles. Mention that these are the same types of nails used for wood shake installation.
6. Compare the installation of wood shingles to that of wood shakes.
7. Remove the wood shingles from the simulated roof and then apply wood shakes. Point out any differences between the procedures.
8. Explain that wood shakes are also available in 8' panels. Discuss the preparation necessary for these panels and the proper procedure for applying them.

Tile Roofing
1. Identify the types of roofing tile that are commonly used. Have students list advantages of using roofing tile over other types of roofing products.
2. Discuss the weight of tile and the need for strong roof framing to support the weight.

Application of Tile
1. Explain the underlayment requirements for installing tile roofs as they relate to roof pitch.
2. Explain what battens are and their use in the installation of tile.
3. Discuss lugs and their purpose.

4. Compare valley, hip, and ridge installations of tile with other types of roofing material.
5. Explain the term *sweat sheet* and discuss its proper application.
6. Discuss how cuts may be made on tile.
7. Identify materials required for installation at hips, ridges, and rakes.
8. Discuss methods of installation. Go over installation of tile in areas with severe weather conditions or on tall structures.

Metal Roofing
1. Emphasize the need to use either galvanized sheets or those coated with aluminum-zinc alloy for permanent structures. Explain that sheets with thinner coatings will likely need to be painted every few years.
2. Discuss the proper means of lapping galvanized sheets to ensure water tightness. Stress that sheets should overlap a minimum of 1 1/2 corrugations for sufficient effectiveness.
3. Obtain a few lead-headed nails and galvanized nails with lead washers. Discuss the importance of using the correct type of nail for this type of roofing.

Aluminum Roofing
1. Identify areas of the country where aluminum roofing should not be used. Explain the effects of salt-laden spray on aluminum.
2. Stress the importance of not allowing aluminum roofing material to come into contact with other types of metals. Describe what should be done if there are places where this contact cannot be avoided.
3. Identify the type of preparation that is necessary for aluminum roofing. Discuss the type of nails that should be used to install aluminum roofing.

Terne Metal Roofing
1. Describe the composition and manufacture of terne metal roofing.
2. Discuss the grades and sizes of terne metal roofing that are available.

Gutters
1. Describe the relationship between gutters or eaves troughs and downspouts. Explain

the difference between a gutter and eaves trough.
2. Have students list the types of wood commonly used for wood gutters and have them explain why they think these are good materials to use.
3. Using reproducible master RM 12-5 *Metal Gutter System*, identify the parts of such a system.
4. Discuss how sizes of gutters are determined for different sizes of roofs.

Estimating Materials
1. Discuss how the amount of roofing materials for a structure can be determined from the figures obtained in estimating the sheathing.
2. Describe an alternative method of estimating the roof area by determining the total ground area of the structure and then multiplying by a percentage factor of the roof slope.
3. Explain how the number of squares of roofing material can be obtained from the total square footage of roof surface.

Chapter Review

1. Review the chapter objectives. Be sure that the students fully understand each objective.
2. Assign *Technical Vocabulary*, *Test Your Knowledge* questions, *Curricular Connections*, and *Outside Assignments* for Chapter 12 of the text. Review the answers in class.
3. Assign Chapter 12 in the workbook. Review the answers in class.

Evaluation

This chapter provides three methods for evaluating student performance. Students should complete the *Test Your Knowledge* section using the book as reference. Students should also be allowed to use the book for reference when completing the workbook material. Use the Chapter 12 Quiz in the instructor's resources for in-class evaluation. Correct the quizzes, return them to the students, and review the quiz questions in group discussion.

Procedure Checklist

Using the procedure checklists *Applying Wood Shingles* and *Installing Asphalt Shingles*, have students identify symbols, perform calculations for missing dimensions, and interpret the working drawings of a residential structure.

Answers to Test Your Knowledge
Text Page 393

1. durability
2. exposure
3. The weight of the felt needed to cover 100 sq. ft. of the roof deck in a single layer.
4. 15 lb. roofer's felt
5. Ice-and-water barrier
6. 1/8
7. base
8. A saddle is an auxiliary roof deck placed on high side of chimney to divert flow of water and prevent ice and snow buildup behind the chimney.
9. four
10. A. install the fasteners 5/8" below adhesive strips
    B. adjust the gun for proper staple application
    C. if a fastener must be removed, repair hole with asphalt cement
11. 2-in-12
12. Roofing shovel, pitchfork, and standard shovel.
13. Slag, gravel, crushed stone, or marble chips.
14. gravel stop
15. To help dissipate heat and moisture.
16. perpendicular
17. 1/4, 3/8
18. wood shakes
19. 3-in-12. A minimum of two plies of Type 15 felt, hot-mopped between layers.
20. False.
21. Snow accumulations slide off easily.
22. Terne metal
23. downspouts
24. 1/4, 4
25. 100

Answers to Workbook Questions
Pages 67–74

1. Shingles of asphalt, wood, metal, mineral fiber, slate, tile, membrane, roll roofing, galvanized iron, aluminum, tin, and copper.

2. 640 sq. in.
3. fascia
4. square
5. A. Side lap.
   B. Head lap.
   C. Exposure.
6. A. 4″ side lap.
   B. 2″ top lap.
   C. Metal drip edge.
   D. Underlayment.
7. B. 24″
8. 1/8
9. A. step-flashing
10. A. Annular thread.
    B. Plain barbed.
    C. Spiral thread.
11. A. 12″
    B. 36″
    C. 5 5/8″
12. B. a strip from which one-half tab has been cut away
13. cap flashing
14. A. 1″
    B. 5 1/2″
15. B. 24″
16. A 1″
17. B. 19″
18. A. Metal gravel stop.
    B. Built-up roofing.
    C. Sheathing.
    D. Exterior plywood soffit.
    E. Slanted fascia.
19. A. 8″ (minimum).
    B. Cant strip.
    C. Metal flashing.
20. A. 24″
    B. 25 sq. ft.
21. B. three
22. A. 1 1/2″
    B. 1″–2″
    C. 1/4″–3/8″
23. A. 4-in-12
24. A. Straight split.
    B. Handsplit and resawn.
    C. Taper split.
25. 30 lb. felt
26. A. 5.8
    B. 10.25
27. A. battens
    B. 24
28. C. 1 1/2
29. A. lead and tin
30. A. Gutter.
    B. Downspout.
    C. Outside miter.
    D. Outlet tube.
    E. Elbow.
    F. Fascia hanger.
    G. Strap hanger.
    H. Pipe band.
31. Squares: 23
32. Bundles: 37
33. Bundles: 86
34. Squares: 22
35. Pitch: 1/2
    Slope: 12

Answers to Chapter Quiz

1. False.
2. True.
3. False.
4. False.
5. D. All of the above.
6. B. drip edge
7. B. 24″
8. D. All of the above.
9. B.
10. A.
11. D.
12. C.

Shingling Valleys

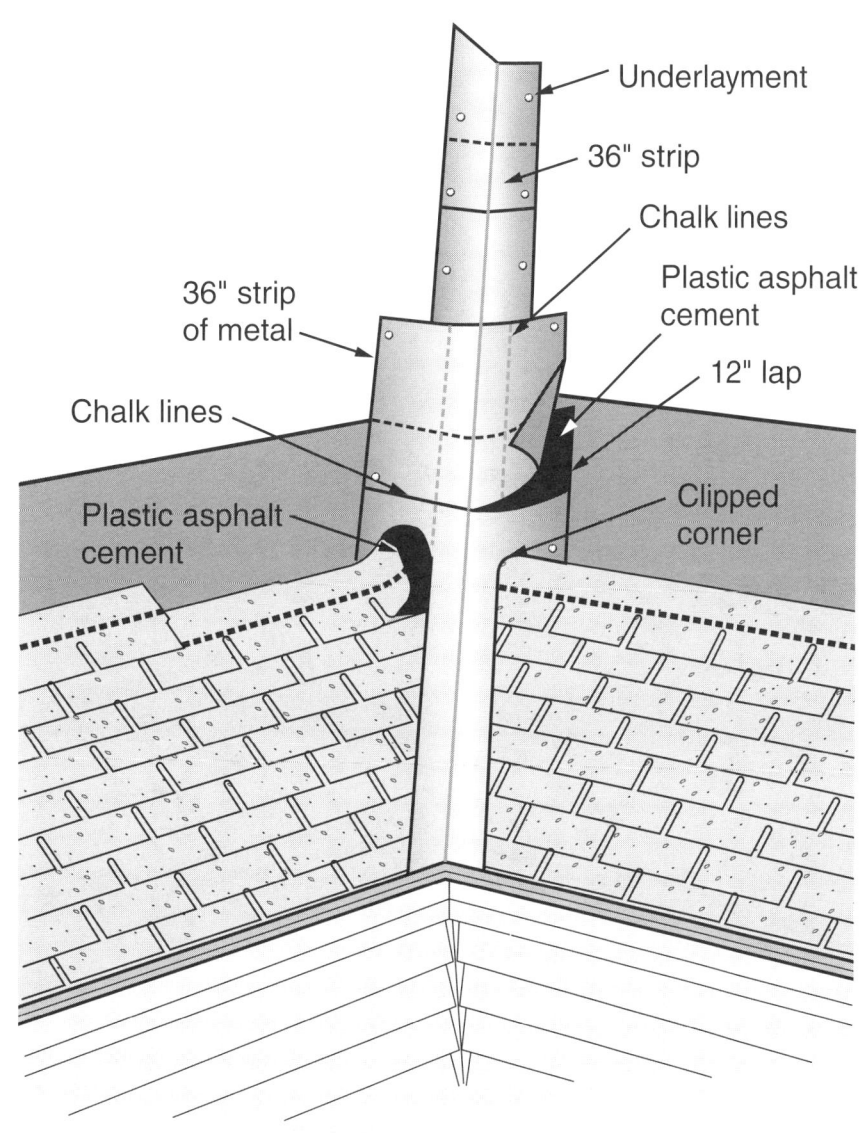

RM 12-1A

Shingling Valleys

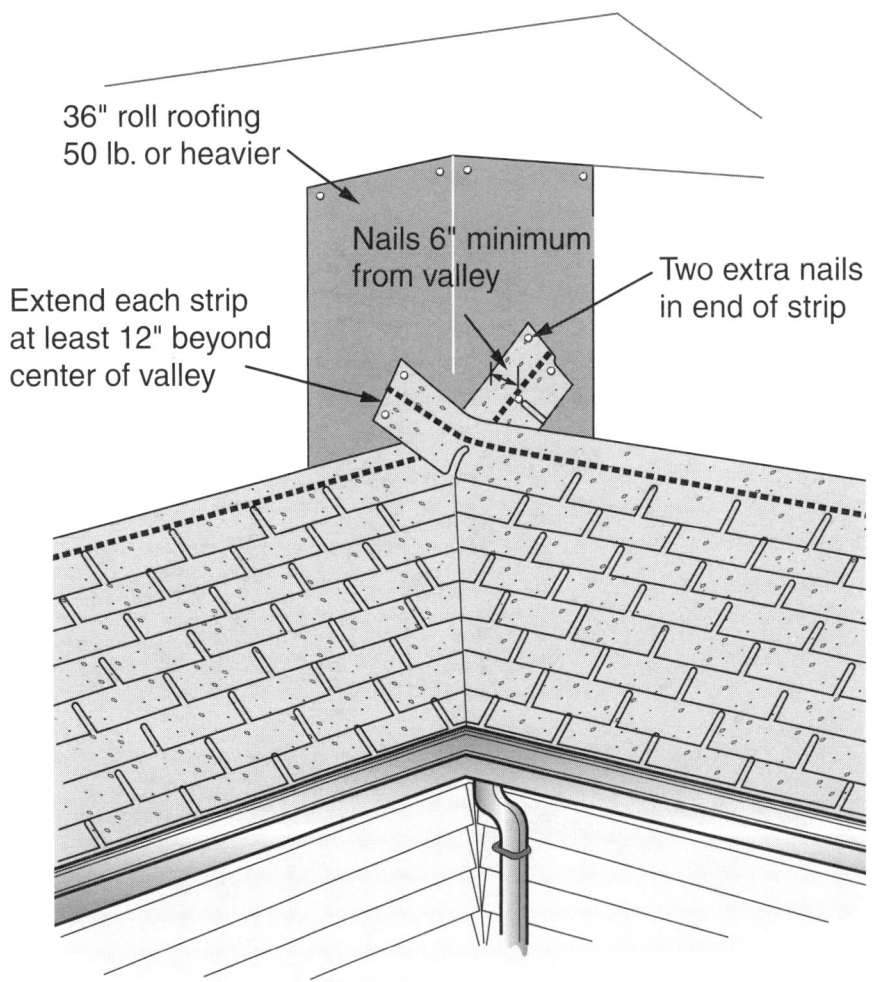

RM 12-1B

Shingling Valleys

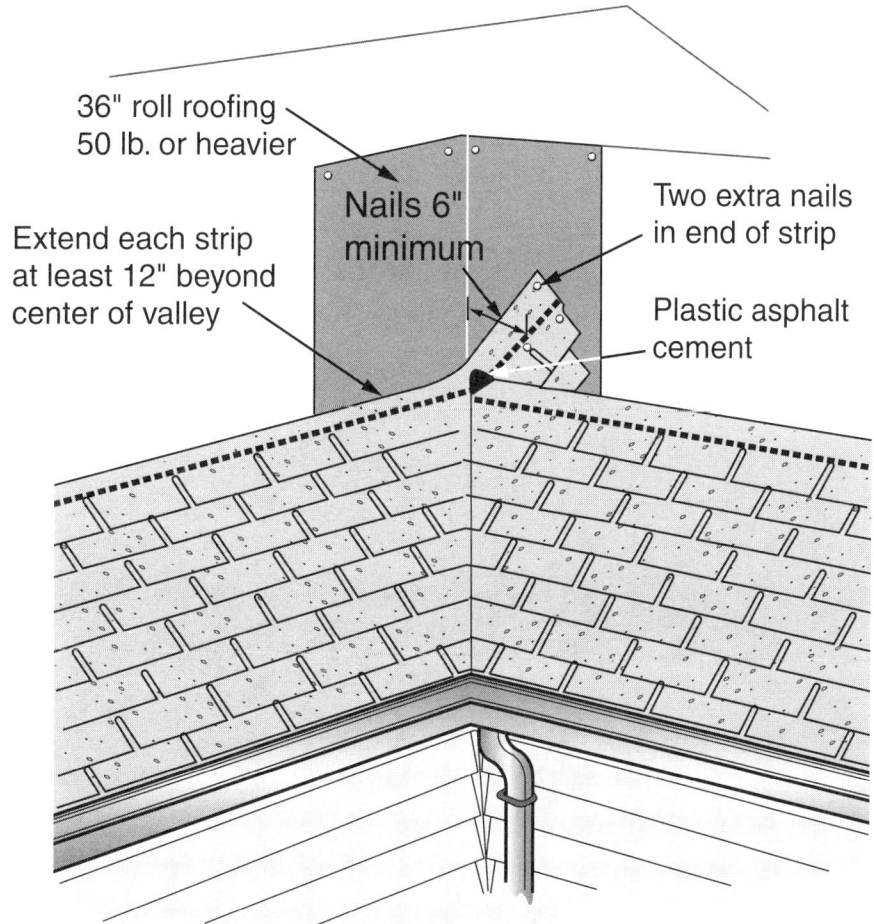

RM 12-1C

Vent Stack Flashing

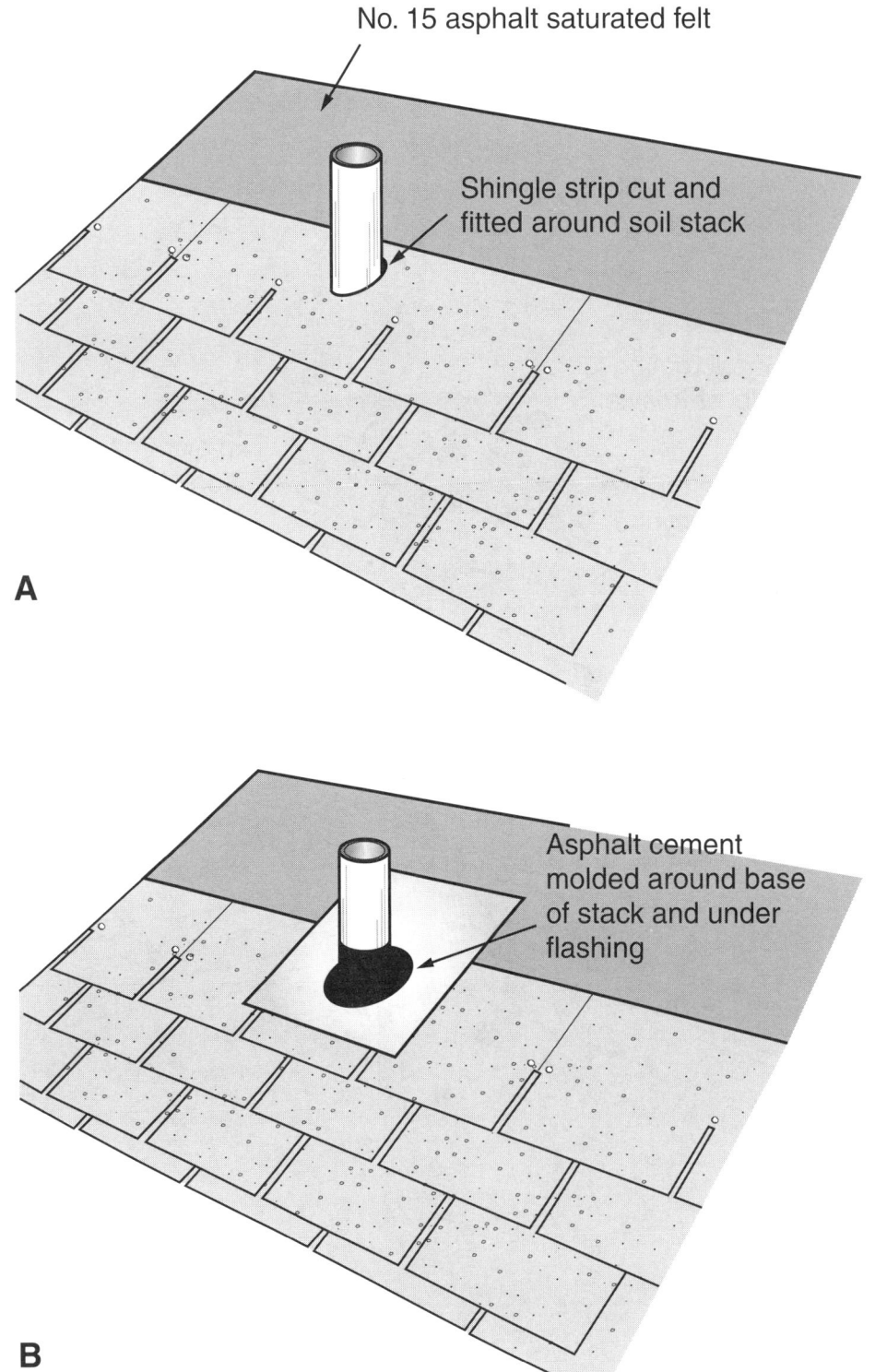

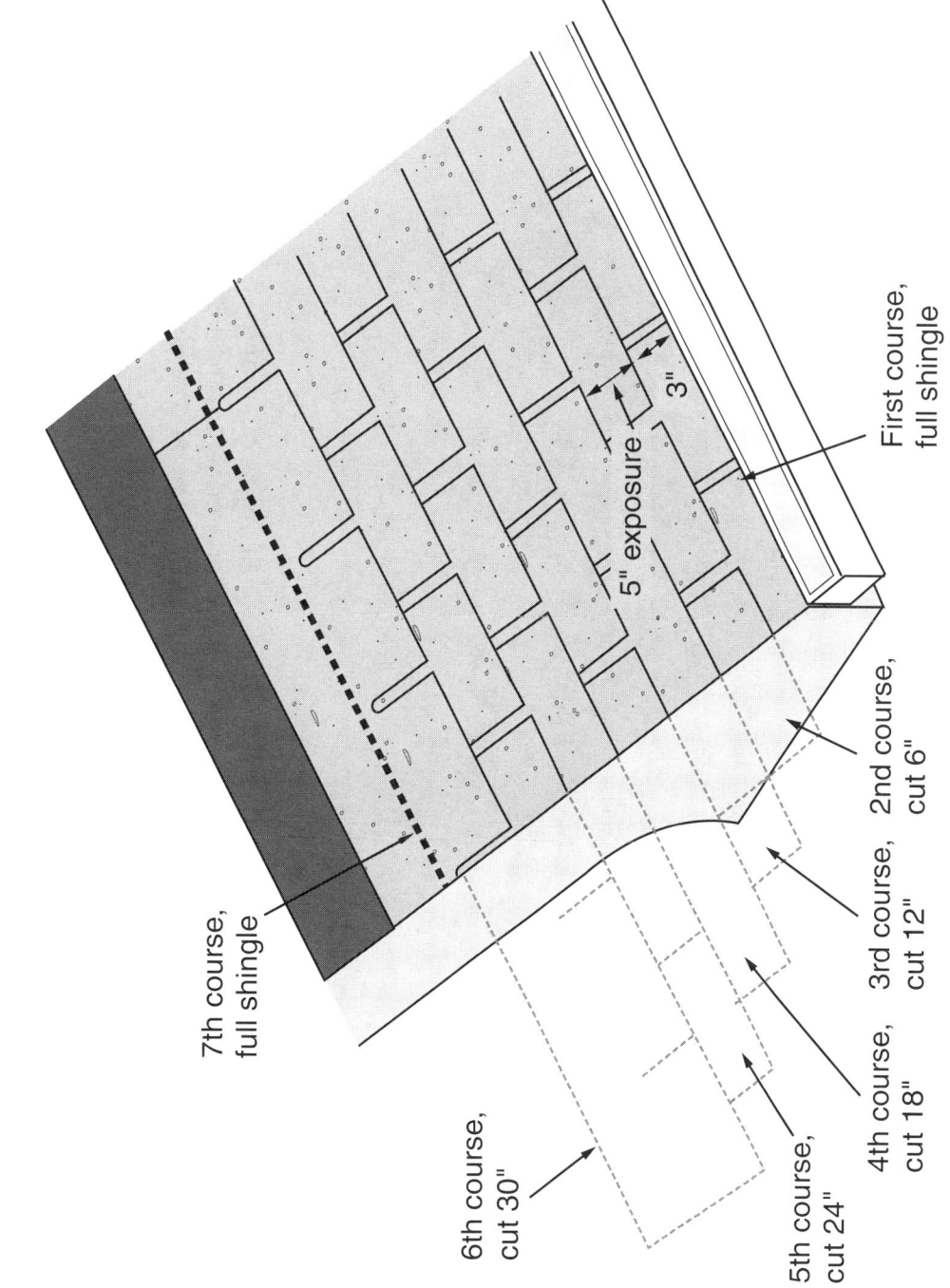

Four-Inch Shingling Method

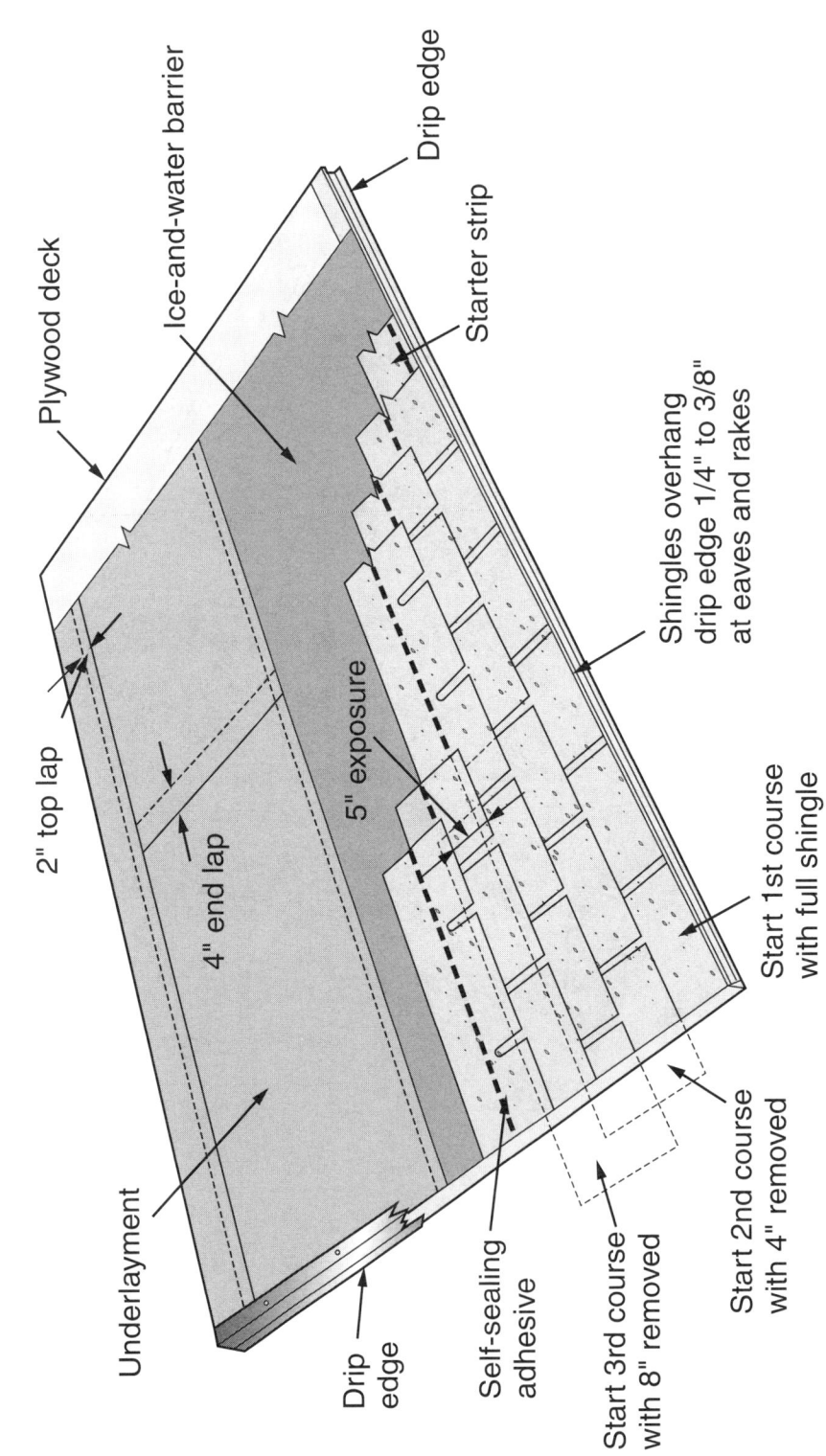

RM 12-4

Metal Gutter System

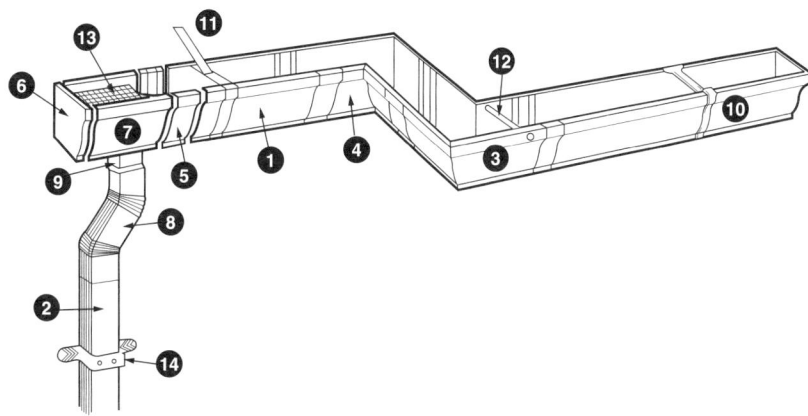

Key	Description	Key	Description
1	5" K gutter	9	K Outlet tube (with flange)
2	3" Square corrugated downspout	10	5" K Fascia hanger
3	5" K Miter (outside)	11	5" K Strap hanger
4	5" K Miter (inside)	12	7" Spike (aluminum) / 5" Ferrule (aluminum)
5	5" K Slip joint connector	13	5" K Strainer
6	5" K End cap left or right	14	3" Pipe band (ornamental)
7	5" x 3" K End section with outlet tube		Touch-up paint
8	A B — 3" Square corrugated 75° elbow or 60° elbow style a and b		Gutter seal (tube or cartridge)

RM 12-5

Chapter 12 Procedure Checklist
Applying Wood Shingles

Name _____ Total _____

❏	Installs proper type of sheathing to roof deck, making sure it is adequate to hold the roofing materials and fasteners; cleans off any chips or other scrap material.	5	4	3	2	1	Neglects to prepare roof deck; does not clean off roof prior to installing underlayment.
❏	Properly applies underlayment using proper top and side laps.	5	4	3	2	1	Neglects to install underlayment.
❏	In cold climates, installs flashing at eaves; installs flashing at valleys (if necessary); installs flashing at vertical wall lines (if necessary).	5	4	3	2	1	Neglects to install any flashing.
❏	Selects the correct type and length of nail for the roofing material being used.	5	4	3	2	1	Selects the wrong type of nail for roofing.
❏	Doubles or triples the first course of shingles; uses appropriate number of nails per shingle with the correct nailing pattern; starts the second course offset with the joints in the first course; uses a straightedge to align rows of shingles; places pieces of beveled siding along gable ends to prevent water from dripping off edge.	5	4	3	2	1	Neglects to use doubled or tripled shingles for the first course; neglects to follow nailing pattern; does not offset second course of shingles; "eyeballs" straightness of rows; neglects to use beveled siding along edge.

Permission granted to reproduce for educational use only. Copyright by Goodheart-Willcox Co., Inc.

Chapter 12 Procedure Checklist Applying Wood Shingles (continued)

❏ Installs wood cap shingles along hips and ridges, making sure not to expose nails.   5   4   3   2   1   Neglects to install hip or ridge shingles; if cap shingles were installed, no attention was paid to concealing nail heads.

Chapter 12 Procedure Checklist
Installing Asphalt Shingles

Name _____ Total _____

❏	Properly prepares the roof deck, making sure it is adequate to hold the roofing materials and fasteners; repairs any large knot holes with sheet metal; cleans off any chips or other scrap material.	5	4	3	2	1	Neglects to prepare roof deck, forgets to cover large knot holes; does not clean off roof prior to installing underlayment.
❏	Properly applies underlayment using proper top and side laps	5	4	3	2	1	Neglects to install underlayment.
❏	Determines the correct shape of drip edge; accurately cuts the drip edge to length; properly positions drip edge over the underlayment at the rake and under the underlayment along the eaves.	5	4	3	2	1	Must be told the correct length of drip edge; does not correctly measure length of drip edge resulting in poor fit; does not properly install drip edge.
❏	In cold climates, installs flashing at eaves; installs flashing at valleys (if necessary); installs flashing at vertical wall lines (if necessary).	5	4	3	2	1	Neglects to install dry flashing.
❏	Determines best means for installing shingles; snaps chalk lines; carefully places shingles at locations along the roof.	5	4	3	2	1	Neglects to snap chalk lines; stacks all shingles in one pile, resulting in more work later.

Permission granted to reproduce for educational use only. Copyright by Goodheart-Willcox Co., Inc.

Chapter 12 Procedure Checklist Installing Asphalt Shingles (continued)

❏	Selects the correct type and length of nail for the roofing material being used; properly installs starter strip.	5	4	3	2	1	Selects the wrong type of nail for roofing; forgets to install starter strip.
❏	Starts first course with full shingle; uses appropriate number of nails per shingle with the correct nailing pattern; cuts and starts the second course with a cut strip; follows a uniform laying pattern.	5	4	3	2	1	Uses cut shingle for first course; neglects to follow nailing pattern; lays shingles in irregular pattern.
❏	Flashes around chimney (if necessary); constructs chimney saddle (if necessary); flashes vent stack projections; carefully installs shingles around these obstructions.	5	4	3	2	1	Neglects to install flashing around roof obstructions; carelessly installs shingles around these obstructions.
❏	Determines whether to use special hip or ridge shingle or to make them from standard shingles; properly installs hip and ridge shingles.	5	4	3	2	1	Neglects to install hip or ridge shingles.

Chapter 12 Quiz
Roofing Materials and Methods

Name _____ Date _____ Score _____

True-False
Circle T if the answer is True or F if the answer is False.

T F 1. One square of asphalt shingles covers 150 square feet.

T F 2. Saturated felts are used for sheathing paper under shingles.

T F 3. One ply is generally sufficient for a built-up roof on a residential structure.

T F 4. When driving nails into wood shingles, the heads should be driven about 3/16″ below the surface.

Multiple Choice
Choose the answer that correctly completes the statement. Write the corresponding letter in the space provided.

_____ 5. Materials commonly used for pitched roofs include ____.
  A. asphalt shingles
  B. slate and tile
  C. roll roofing
  D. All of the above.

_____ 6. The ____ is bent downward over the edge of the roof, causing rainwater to drip free of the cornice construction.
  A. flashing
  B. drip edge
  C. underlayment
  D. starter strip

_____ 7. It is recommended that an ice-and-water barrier be installed at the eaves and extend ____ inside the building's outside wall line.
  A. 12″
  B. 24″
  C. 30″
  D. 36″

_____ 8. Wood shingles are made from ____.
  A. cypress
  B. western red cedar
  C. redwood
  D. All of the above.

Identification

Identify recommendations for types of roofing according to pitch.

_____ 9. All styles of shingles.

_____ 10. Slope.

_____ 11. Roll roofing (at least 3″ top lap or double coverage 19″ selvage).

_____ 12. Roll roofing (exposed nails).

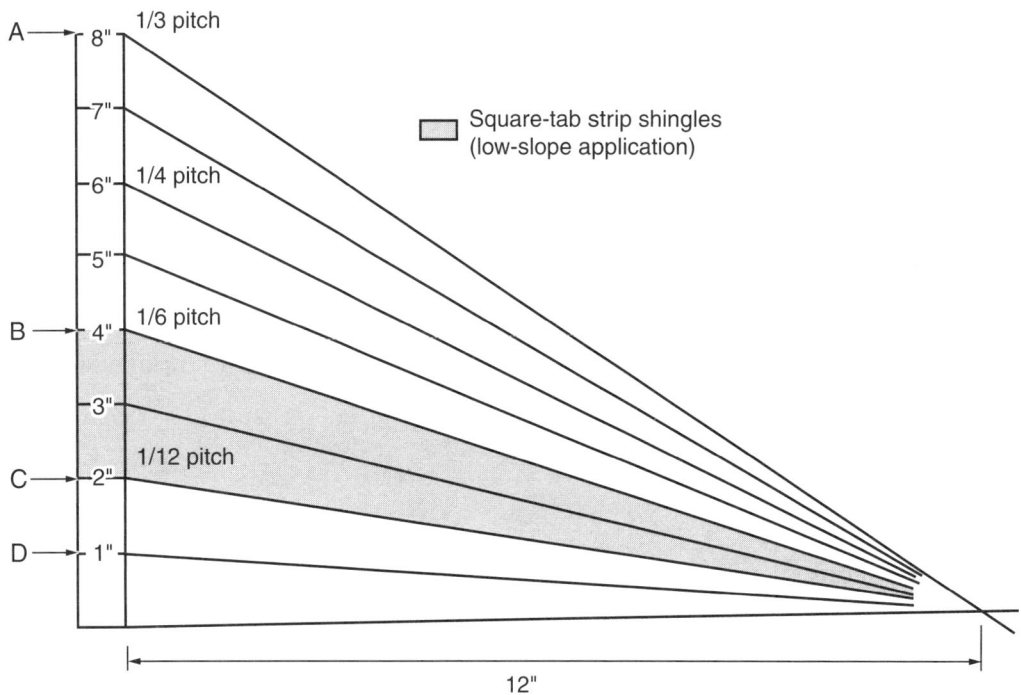

13 Windows and Exterior Doors

Objectives

After studying this chapter, students will be able to:
- Discuss standards for window and door fabrication.
- Identify the various types of windows.
- Calculate required rough openings.
- Interpret a window schedule.
- Explain how window frames are adjusted for wall thickness.
- Summarize procedures for installing a standard window.
- Describe procedures for installing a replacement window.
- Prepare a rough opening for installation of a door frame.
- Describe the procedure for sliding glass door installation.
- Explain the correct construction of garage door frames.
- Select appropriate garage door hardware.
- Describe the procedure for installing a bow or box bay window unit.

Instructional Materials

Text: Pages 395–434
  Technical Vocabulary, page 395
  Test Your Knowledge, page 433
  Curricular Connections, page 434
  Outside Assignments, page 434
Workbook: Pages 75-80
Instructor's Resource:
  Reproducible masters:
    RM 13-1 *Window Framing Detail*
  Transparencies (binder/CD only):
    CT 13-1 *Wall Framing for Windows*
    CT 13-2 *Window Design*
  Procedure Checklist: *Installing Movable Windows*
  Procedure Checklist: *Installing Door Frames*
  Chapter Quiz

Trade-Related Math

Glass blocks are commonly used for interior decorative work as well as exterior windows. The widths and heights of the openings can be determined by multiplying the number of units horizontally and vertically, multiplying each by the nominal block size, and then adding 3/8″. For example, to determine the size opening required for a panel of 6″ blocks that is to be five units wide by eight units high, the following calculations are:

width = 5 × 6 + 3/8 = 30 3/8″ = 2′–6 3/8″
height = 8 × 6 + 3/8 = 48 3/8″ = 4′–3/8″

Instructional Concepts and Student Learning Experiences

Manufacture
1. Describe the manufacture of window and door units. Ask the students to list the materials commonly used for windows and doors. Discuss advantages and disadvantages of using these materials.

Parts of Windows
1. Identify the following parts of a window: mullion, drip cap, head, sill, and jamb. Stress the importance of using the correct terminology when referring to windows so that they can communicate effectively with members of other trades.

Types of Windows
1. Identify the three general categories of windows: sliding, swinging, and fixed. List the basic window designs that are included in each category.
2. Describe the basic components and operation of a double-hung window.
3. Describe the basic components and operation of a horizontal sliding window.

4. Describe the basic components and operation of a casement window.
5. Define the term *crank operator* and discuss its use with a casement window. Describe the basic components and operation of an awning window.
6. Describe the basic components and operation of a hopper window. Contrast its operation to that of an awning window. Discuss some of the inconveniences caused by hopper windows.
7. Have the students describe the purpose of a multiple-use window.
8. Describe the basic components and operation of a jalousie window. Explain why they find limited use in the northern climates.
9. Describe the basic components and operation of a fixed window.

Window Heights
1. Refer to Figure 13-10. Have students note the different size windows that are used for different rooms of the house. Also, have them note that the standard window height from the finished floor to the bottom side of the window head is 6'-8". Explain why a standard height is generally used.

Window Glass
1. Discuss the manufacture of window glass. Have the students refer to Figure 13-12 for a list of standard thicknesses that are manufactured.

Energy-Efficient Windows
1. Define the term *R value* and how it relates to windows. Stress the importance of using windows with high R values for energy conservation.
2. Have students state reasons why two or three layers of glass might be used in a window unit. Discuss the advantages of double and triple glazing.
3. Define *emissivity* and how it relates to windows. Describe how low-e windows help to conserve energy.

Screens
1. Discuss the purpose of a window screen. Identify materials that are commonly used for screens.

Windows in Plan and Elevation Drawings
1. Discuss how windows and exterior doors are shown in working drawings. Emphasize that these items are generally dimensioned to the middle of the opening for frame construction and to the edge of the opening for masonry construction.
2. Have students identify the direction of swing using a stock plan for a house. Mention that sliding windows will probably be noted as such so as to distinguish them from fixed windows.

Window Sizes
1. Explain that in addition to the type and position of the window, the carpenter should also know the glass size, sash size, rough frame opening, and masonry or unit opening. Given a stock plan, have the students identify these measurements. Stress that the horizontal measurement is always listed first.
2. Describe the items that are usually found in a window and door schedule. Explain how letters found on a plan for a structure are generally cross-referenced to a window and door schedule.

Detail Drawings
1. Using manufacturer's literature or Figure 13-18, ask the students to note how different types of construction affect window installation.

Jamb Extensions
1. Discuss how a jamb extension can be used to compensate for different wall thicknesses.

Story Pole
1. Review the use of a story pole when installing doors and windows. Discuss the advantages of using a story pole. Mention that even though the heads of the windows and doors are at the same height, the bottoms will vary.
2. Using reproducible master RM 13-1 *Window Framing Detail,* have the students note the other dimensions that should be added to a story pole when checking the height of certain parts of the window frame.

Installing Windows

1. Describe the proper means of storing windows on a job site. Note that they should be allowed to acclimate to the humidity of the locality before being installed.
2. Discuss the preparation that should be made before installing a window unit such as checking the rough opening for the correct size and priming the window if necessary.
3. Explain the proper procedure for installing a window. Stress the importance of properly leveling and plumbing the window unit before permanently fastening it into position.
4. Discuss steps that might be taken after the installation of the window units to protect them against damage and dirt.
5. Explain the installation of large fixed window units. Emphasize that larger units generally require extra precautions in handling and installation.
6. Refer to Figure 13-35. Stress the need for clearance between sealed insulating glass and its frame.

Glass Blocks

1. Have the students list advantages of using glass block for interior and exterior wall applications.
2. List the three nominal sizes of glass blocks. Mention that even though a carpenter usually will not make the actual installation, it is helpful for him or her to have knowledge of the design requirements.
3. Discuss the procedure for installing small glass block panels. Refer to Figure 13-31 for illustrations of this procedure.
4. Compare the installation of a small glass block panel to that of a large glass block panel. Emphasize that wall tie and anchors must be used for larger panels to add stability to the panel.
5. Explain how to determine the opening required for a glass block installation.

Replacing Windows

1. Cite reasons for replacing older window units. Discuss the information needed to order new window units. Mention that some newer replacement window units are made to size and thus made to fit the rough opening for existing windows.
2. Describe the procedure for removing the older units and installing new units.
3. Discuss reasons for installing skylights.

Installing Bow and Box Bay Windows

1. Discuss differences between stick-built bay windows and the prefabricated units known as bow and box bay windows.
2. Explain the procedure for installing a typical prefabricated unit.

Exterior Doors and Frames

1. Identify the sizes of exterior doors commonly used in residential construction. Note that rear entrance and service doors are usually narrower than front entrance doors.
2. Have the students refer to the local building code to determine the minimum exterior door width.
3. Discuss why the door head and jambs are made of 5/4″ stock.
4. Explain that exterior doors in residential construction swing inward and the rabbets for the head and jambs must be located on the inside.
5. Have the students list materials that are commonly used for sills.

Installing Door Frames

1. Identify the preparation necessary before installing the door frame.
2. Describe the procedure for installing the door frame. Impress upon your students the reason why nails used to secure the frame should not be driven in all the way until a final check has been made.

Installing Prehung Door Units

1. Discuss the advantages of using prehung door units.
2. Describe the procedure for installing prehung doors. Stress the importance of following the manufacturer's recommendations when installing a prehung door unit.

Sliding Glass Doors

1. Have students list reasons why sliding glass doors have become so popular in residential construction.

2. Explain how sliding and fixed doors are indicated on working drawings and manufacturers' literature.
3. Describe the procedure used to install sliding glass doors. Stress that an X made with tape or washable paint should be placed on the sliding glass doors and fixed doors to prevent anyone from walking into the doors.

Garage Doors
1. Have the students list the three types of garage doors. Mention that roll-up doors are the most common type in residential construction.

Garage Door Frames
1. Identify the most common garage door widths and heights.
2. Discuss the procedure for installing garage doors. Emphasize that the frame construction is very similar to frame construction for regular door frames.
3. Discuss the purpose of garage door hardware and counterbalances.

Chapter Review

1. Review the chapter objectives. Be sure that the students fully understand each objective.
2. Assign *Technical Vocabulary*, *Test Your Knowledge* questions, *Curricular Connections*, and *Outside Assignments* for Chapter 13 of the text. Review the answers in class.
3. Assign Chapter 13 in the workbook. Review the answers in class.

Evaluation

This chapter provides three methods for evaluating student performance. Students should complete the *Test Your Knowledge* section using the book as reference. Students should also be allowed to use the book for reference when completing the workbook material. Use the Chapter 13 Quiz in the instructor's resources for in-class evaluation. Correct the quizzes, return them to the students, and review the quiz questions in group discussion.

Procedure Checklist

Using the procedure checklists, *Installing Movable Windows* and *Installing Door Frames*, have students evaluate the techniques used to perform these tasks.

Chapter 13

Answers to Test Your Knowledge
Text Page 433
1. millwork
2. 6, 12
3. jamb
4. drip cap
5. casement
6. 6'-8"
7. 0.88, 2.00
8. 3'-5"
9. jamb extension
10. B. Align the top to the proper height.
11. 1/4"
12. 3 7/8
13. 3/8"
14. wood bracing, cable suspension
15. lintel
16. 16
17. fixed
18. roll-up
19. False.
20. torsion

Answers to Workbook Questions
Pages 75-80
1. millwork
2. C. National Woodwork Manufacturers
3. double-hung
4. A. Height to R.O.
   B. Rough opening.
   C. Sash opening.
5. awning
6. B. 6'-8"
7. B. 2.00
8. C. float
9. B. 3/16"

10. C. 3′-4″
11. B. edge
12. A. Sill.
    B. Jamb.
    C. Head.
13. B. 3/4″
14. B. jamb extension
15. C. raise frame to correct height as marked on story pole
16. A. 3 7/8 × 11 3/4 × 11 3/4
17. Width: 4′-6 3/8″
    Height: 5′-6 3/8″
18. B. remove inside stops and lift out lower sash
19. C. 3-in-12
20. A. 6′-8″
    B. 2′-6″
21. A. Head.
    B. Sill.
    C. Jamb.
22. D. 2 1/2″
23. hinges
24. C. 16d
25. B. a bead of sealing compound be applied
26. swing-up
27. C. 7′-0″
28. torsion
29. Clear outer pane. An air space. A special coating on the air-gap side of the inner pane.

Answers to Chapter Quiz

1. False.
2. False.
3. True.
4. True.
5. D. Both B and C.
6. B. 6′-8″
7. A. hopper
8. B. 1/2″
9. B.
10. E.
11. C.
12. A.
13. D.

Window Framing Detail

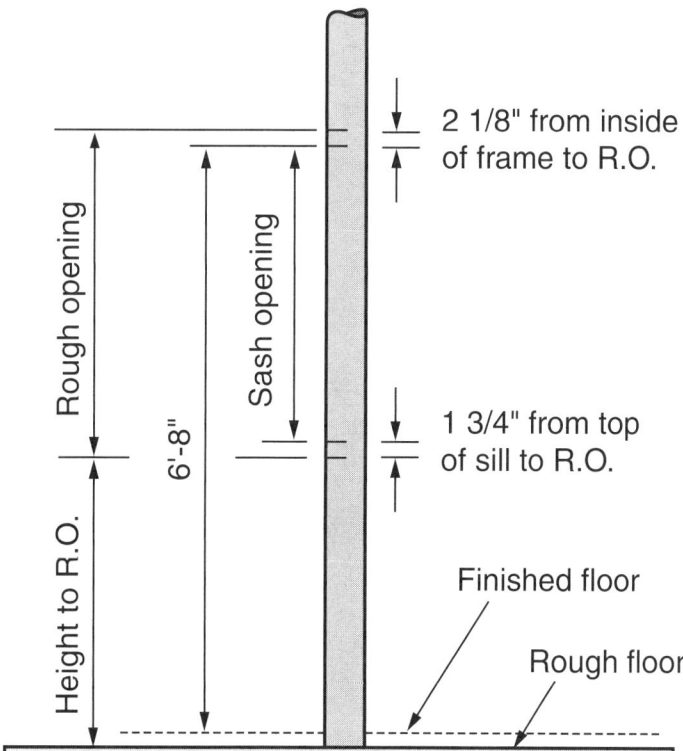

RM 13-1

Chapter 13 Procedure Checklist
Installing Movable Windows

Name _____   Total _____

❏	Moves all windows to vicinity of installation; unpacks and checks for damage (does not remove brace); checks plumb and level of rough openings; checks size of rough opening.	5	4	3	2	1	Moves only one window to needed location, then begins installing it; neglects to check for damage (removes bracing); forgets to check size of rough opening.
❏	Refers to manufacturer's recommendations and primes windows (if necessary).	5	4	3	2	1	Primes windows when it is not needed, or neglects to prime windows if it is needed.
❏	Installs window from the outside; temporarily secures window in opening.	5	4	3	2	1	Tries to install window from the inside; neglects to secure window in opening.
❏	Places wedge blocks under sill and raises it to proper height; levels window; plumbs the side jambs; checks squareness in window corners.	5	4	3	2	1	Rests window on sill (does not raise it to proper height); neglects to plumb or level window; neglects to square window.
❏	Drives nails into bottom, then top, of side casing; levels and plumbs again; checks window to make sure it works properly.	5	4	3	2	1	Nails into top and bottom casing (possibly breaking window); neglects to plumb or level window; does not check window to make sure it works properly.
❏	Nails window permanently into place using appropriate types of nails; uses nail set to drive nail heads below surface; covers window with plastic if interior wall surface materials are to be applied.	5	4	3	2	1	Forgets to permanently nail window into position; does not use proper type of nail; neglects to cover window with plastic.

Permission granted to reproduce for educational use only.   Copyright by Goodheart-Willcox Co., Inc.

Chapter 13 Procedure Checklist
Installing Door Frames

Name _____ Total _____

❏	Checks size of rough opening; cuts out sill area (if necessary); installs flashing (if necessary).	5	4	3	2	1	Neglects to check size of rough opening; does not make adjustments to allow for larger door; forgets to install flashing (if required).
❏	Places frame in opening, centering it horizontally; secures door frame with temporary brace; levels the sill using wedges and blocking; makes sure the sill is well supported.	5	4	3	2	1	Pushes frame to one side of opening; neglects to support frame with brace; forgets to level sill; does not provide adequate support for sill.
❏	Drives nail through casing and into wall frame; inserts wedges or blocking between studs and jambs; adjusts wedges until frame is plumb.	5	4	3	2	1	Neglects to drive nails into casing (or misses wall frame); does not plumb frame.
❏	Places additional wedges and blocks between the jamb and studs; drives nails through the jamb wedge and into the stud.	5	4	3	2	1	Does not support frame with additional wedges and blocks.
❏	Nails casing in place; installs a piece of plywood over sill to protect it during further construction work.	5	4	3	2	1	Neglects to place casing in position; forgets to place plywood over sill.

Permission granted to reproduce for educational use only. Copyright by Goodheart-Willcox Co., Inc.

Chapter 13 Quiz
Windows and Exterior Doors

Name _____ Date _____ Score _____

True-False
Circle T if the answer is True or F if the answer is False.

T   F   1. A building material with a high R-value has a low resistance to heat passage.

T   F   2. When specifying window sizes, the vertical dimension is always listed first.

T   F   3. Glass blocks have good insulating properties.

T   F   4. Emissivity is the relative ability of a material to absorb or radiate heat.

Multiple Choice
Choose the answer that correctly completes the statement. Write the corresponding letter in the space provided.

_____ 5. A(n) _____ window is classified as a swinging window.
- A. double hung
- B. casement
- C. awning
- D. Both B and C.

_____ 6. In residential construction, the standard height from the bottom of the window head to the finished floor is _____.
- A. 6'-4"
- B. 6'-8"
- C. 7'-0"
- D. 7'-6"

_____ 7. A(n) _____ window is hinged along the bottom and swings inward.
- A. hopper
- B. awning
- C. casement
- D. jalousie

_____ 8. The rough opening for a window should allow at least _____ clearance on the sides and 3/4" clearance above the head.
- A. 1/4"
- B. 1/2"
- C. 3/4"
- D. 1"

Identification

Identify the parts of the double-glazed window unit.

_____ 9. Jamb.

_____ 10. Sill.

_____ 11. Head.

_____ 12. Stile.

_____ 13. Sash.

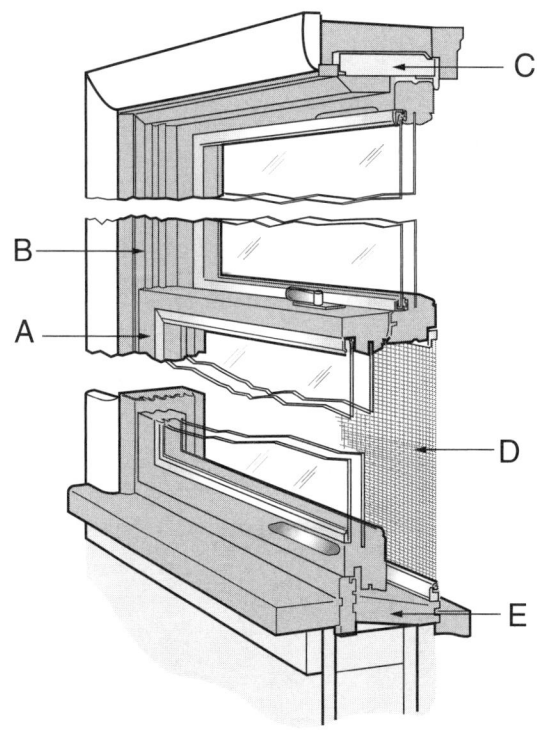

14 Exterior Wall Finish

Objectives

After studying this chapter, students will be able to:
- Identify the parts of a cornice and rake.
- Describe cornice and rake construction.
- Illustrate approved methods of flashing installation.
- Describe how wood siding and shingles are applied.
- Estimate the amount of siding or shingles required for a specific structure.
- Discuss the proper application of bevel siding.
- List the most common siding choices and their characteristics.
- Discuss exterior insulation and finish systems (EIFS) and their application.
- Demonstrate installation techniques for various siding materials.

Instructional Materials

Text: Pages 435–483
Technical Vocabulary, page 435
Test Your Knowledge, page 481
Curricular Connections, page 482
Outside Assignments, page 482

Workbook: Pages 81–88

Instructor's Resource:
Reproducible masters:
RM 14-1A *Typical Cornice Details*
RM 14-1B *Typical Cornice Details*
RM 14-2A *Siding Application*
RM 14-2B *Siding Application*
RM 14-3 *Typical Exterior Insulation and Finish System*
RM 14-4 *Brick Veneer Construction*
Transparencies (binder/CD only):
CT 14-1 *Stucco Exterior Wall Finish*
CT 14-2 *Exterior Insulated Finish System (EIFS)*
CT 14-3 *Brick Veneer Construction*

Procedure Checklist: *Installing Horizontal Wood Siding*
Chapter Quiz

Trade-Related Math

When determining the amount of horizontal siding required for a structure, the net wall surface must be multiplied by a factor. The factor is used to compensate for cutting of joints, overlap in bevel siding, and other considerations. The factors are shown in Figure 14-23 of the text.

First, determine the net wall surface area by subtracting the areas of the openings from the gross wall area (height × perimeter). For example, if the wall height is 8′, the perimeter of the house is 140′, and door and window openings amount to 210 square feet, determine the net area.

Net area = gross area – area of openings
= (8 × 140) – 210 = 1120 – 210
Net area = 910 square feet

Next, multiply the net area by the appropriate factor from Figure 14-23. If 1 × 6 rustic shiplapped siding is to be used, the factor is 1.19. Multiply the factor by the net wall area.

Siding needed = net area × factor = 910 × 1.19
Siding needed = 1083 square feet

Instructional Concepts and Student Learning Experiences

1. Using reproducible masters RM 14-1A and 14-1B *Typical Cornice Details*, discuss the various cornice designs. Mention that most residential structures have boxed cornices.
2. Define each of the following terms associated with a boxed cornice, making sure that the students understand their relationship to the other terms: *fascia, ledger strip, frieze, soffit,* and *lookout.* Have the students identify the

types of materials that are used for each of these parts.
3. Discuss the properties that the exterior members should have, including good painting and weathering characteristics, easy workability, freedom from warp, and decay resistance.

Cornice and Rake Construction
1. Describe the procedure used to construct a cornice with a horizontal soffit. Emphasize that since this is finish work, the joints should be mitered to hide unsightly end grain. Mention that rust-resistant nails or screws should be used to secure the soffit into position. If regular casing or finish nails are used, they must be countersunk and the holes filled with putty.
2. Discuss the procedure used to construct the rake so that it matches the cornice.
3. Discuss the advantages of using prefabricated cornice materials.
4. Describe the purpose of screened vents in a soffit.
5. Explain the procedure used to construct a cornice from prefabricated cornice materials.
6. Identify the three basic components of soffit systems made of prefinished metal panels.
7. Discuss the procedure for constructing and hanging metal soffits.

Wall Finish
1. Explain that the upper level of finish material is usually applied to gable ends first so that scaffolding can be attached directly to the wall frame along the lower section.
2. Identify the five most common types of horizontal siding and discuss their sizes. Mention that bevel siding is most commonly used. Discuss advantages and disadvantages of all the types.
3. Describe the steps that should be taken to protect the siding when it is delivered to the construction site. Once again, stress that since this is finish material, it should be handled carefully.
4. Introduce stucco and exterior insulation finish systems (EIFS) as alternatives to wood, fiber-cement, aluminum, or vinyl siding.

Wall Sheathing and Flashing
1. Discuss preparations that should be made prior to applying siding. Mention that, depending on the type of sheathing, the use of building paper may or may not be required. Stress that coated papers or laminated papers should not be used because they have a high moisture resistance and will act as a vapor barrier.
2. Using reproducible master RM 14-2A *Siding Application,* illustrate how flashing should be used over drip caps of doors and windows.
3. Discuss the minimum lap that should be used for horizontal siding.
4. Explain the procedure for laying out the position of the siding using a story pole. Mention that a carpenter should try to adjust the courses of siding to come out even with the tops and bottoms of windows, if possible.
5. Using reproducible master RM 14-2B *Siding Application*, describe the procedure for installing horizontal siding. Emphasize that nails should be driven into the studs.
6. Discuss the finishing techniques used at the inside and outside corners.

Estimating Siding
1. Discuss the method used to estimate the amount of siding required for a residential structure. Make sure to include the waste factor.

Vertical Siding
1. Identify the types of materials commonly used for vertical siding.
2. Describe how vertical wood siding is attached to a structure. Discuss the type of preparation (if any) that might be required prior to installation.
3. Discuss the use of battens. Describe how the board and batten effects can be simulated using large sheets of wood paneling.

Wood Shingles
1. Explain the recommendations for maximum exposure of 16", 18", and 24" wood shingles.
2. Define *double coursing* and describe how it can be used effectively as a wall covering. Describe how shingles are applied using the single-coursing method.

3. Discuss the difference between applying shingles for a roof and a sidewall. Describe the application of wood shingles using the single-coursing method.
4. Explain how quantities of wood shingles are estimated for sidewalls.

Shingle and Shake Panels
1. Discuss the advantages of using shingle or shake panels over using individual shingles or shakes.

Applying Wood Shingles over Old Siding
1. Describe the preparation necessary to install wood shingles over existing siding or other wall coverings.

Plywood Siding
1. Describe how plywood siding can be used to enhance the appearance of other exterior finish materials.
2. Have the students identify the types of wood that are commonly used for exterior plywood siding. Ask them to describe the types of finishes that may be used.
3. Identify the different thicknesses of plywood siding that are available and describe situations where each type can be used.
4. Discuss the application of plywood siding to a residential structure. Emphasize that since plywood and hardboard provide tight, draft-free wall construction, it is important to have an effective vapor barrier between the insulation and warm surface of the wall.
5. Refer to Figure 14-37. Discuss the different means of treating joints between plywood panels.
6. Have the students refer to the local building code to see if it includes any requirements regarding plywood or hardboard siding.

Hardboard Siding
1. Compare installation of hardboard siding to that of plywood siding. Emphasize that some types of hardboard siding may expand more than plywood siding and this factor should be considered when installing the panels.
2. Identify the common dimensions of hardboard siding.

3. Discuss the advantages of using a siding system over installing panels or individual shingles.

Aluminum Siding
1. Describe the advantages of using aluminum siding.
2. Emphasize that the manufacturer's recommendations should be followed when installing aluminum siding.
3. Since aluminum is an electrical conductor, stress the possibility of an electrical hazard. Emphasize that the Aluminum Siding Association recommends connecting a No. 8 wire or larger from the aluminum siding to the electrical service ground or cold water service.

Vinyl Siding
1. Discuss the type of backing that should be used beneath vinyl siding.
2. Refer to Figure 14-47 for an illustration showing the types of accessories commonly used with vinyl siding.

Stucco
1. Have students explain why balloon framing is the preferred framing method when applying a stucco finish.
2. Identify the types of bases used for stucco.
3. Briefly explain the procedure used to apply stucco.

Exterior Insulation and Finish Systems (EIFS)
1. Using reproducible master RM 14-3 *Typical Exterior Insulation and Finish System*, introduce this siding system and discuss its components.
2. Explain the EIFS insulating qualities.
3. Explain steps for applying EIFS siding materials.

Brick or Stone Veneer
1. Using reproducible master RM 14-4 *Brick Veneer Construction*, have the students note features of brick veneer construction including the base flashing, weep holes, and air space between the plywood sheathing and brick veneer. Have the students explain why these features are incorporated into brick veneer construction.

Shutters

1. Describe the historical significance of blinds and shutters along the sides of windows and doors. Discuss their purpose in this day and age.

Chapter Review

1. Review the chapter objectives. Be sure that the students fully understand each objective.
2. Assign *Technical Vocabulary, Test Your Knowledge* questions, *Curricular Connections,* and *Outside Assignments* for Chapter 14 of the text. Review the answers in class.
3. Assign Chapter 14 in the workbook. Review the answers in class.

Evaluation

This chapter provides three methods for evaluating student performance. Students should complete the *Test Your Knowledge* section using the book as reference. Students should also be allowed to use the book for reference when completing the workbook material. Use the Chapter 14 Quiz in the instructor's resources for in-class evaluation. Correct the quizzes, return them to the students, and review the quiz questions in group discussion.

Procedure Checklist

Using the procedure checklist *Installing Horizontal Wood Siding,* have students evaluate the techniques used to perform these tasks.

Answers to Test Your Knowledge
Text Page 481

1. A. An entry door.
2. ledger strip
3. lookouts
4. wall hanger strips (frieze strips or runner guides), soffit panels, fascia covers
5. one-fourth
6. drop
7. edge
8. 1 1/2
9. before
10. batten
11. 24
12. A second layer is applied over the first layer.
13. 3/8
14. exterior primer, aluminum paint, oil paint
15. warm
16. 7/16
17. galvanized
18. wood, stucco, concrete block
19. polyvinyl chloride compound
20. False.
21. square (100 sq. ft.)
22. three, base or scratch coat, brown coat, color or finish coat
23. Application of housewrap or other water barrier materials to the sheathing, placing grooves on one surface of the foam panel to channel incidental water that has entered the wall to the outside through weep holes, installation of a drainage mat between the exterior insulation board and the water barrier, careful application of flashing at points where leakage is likely to occur.
24. foundation
25. weep holes

Answers to Workbook Questions
Pages 81–88

1. A. exterior finish
   B. doors
   C. windows
2. rafters
3. A. Fascia.
   B. Soffit.
   C. Vent.
   D. Lookout.
   E. Molding.
   F. Sheathing.
4. nailing strip/fascia backer, false fascia
5. soffit
6. A. through the center
7. Insulation
8. A. Lookout.
   B. Rake soffit.
   C. Fascia.
   D. Trim moulding.
9. A. Bevel or bungalow.
   B. Dolly Varden.
   C. Drop.
   D. Tongue and groove (T&G).
   E. Channel rustic.
   F. Log cabin.

10. D. 24″
11. B. Rigid polystyrene insulating board.
    C. Housewrap.
12. A. Flashing.
    B. Drip cap.
13. B. 1 1/2″
14. story pole
15. metal corner
16. before
17. above
18. 280
19. 1597
20. D. 7 1/2″
21. A backing block that is horizontally installed at 16″ to 24″ intervals between studs if the siding is directly applied to the building frame to provide a good nailing surface.
22. False.
23. B. 4′
24. B. temperature changes
25. C. 7/16″
26. Aluminum Siding Association
27. A. No. 8
28. B. extrusion
29. B. 1/4″
30. A. Stud.
    B. Sheathing.
    C. Floor frame.
    D Spacer strip.
    E. Bevel siding.
31. D. 48″
32. B. Shutters are usually attached with special, concealed hinges.

Answers to Chapter Quiz

1. True.
2. False.
3. False.
4. True.
5. C. fascia
6. A. 1 1/2″
7. C. 8′
8. B. Four
9. B. 4–6
10. D.
11. C.
12. B.
13. E.
14. F.
15. A.

Typical Cornice Details

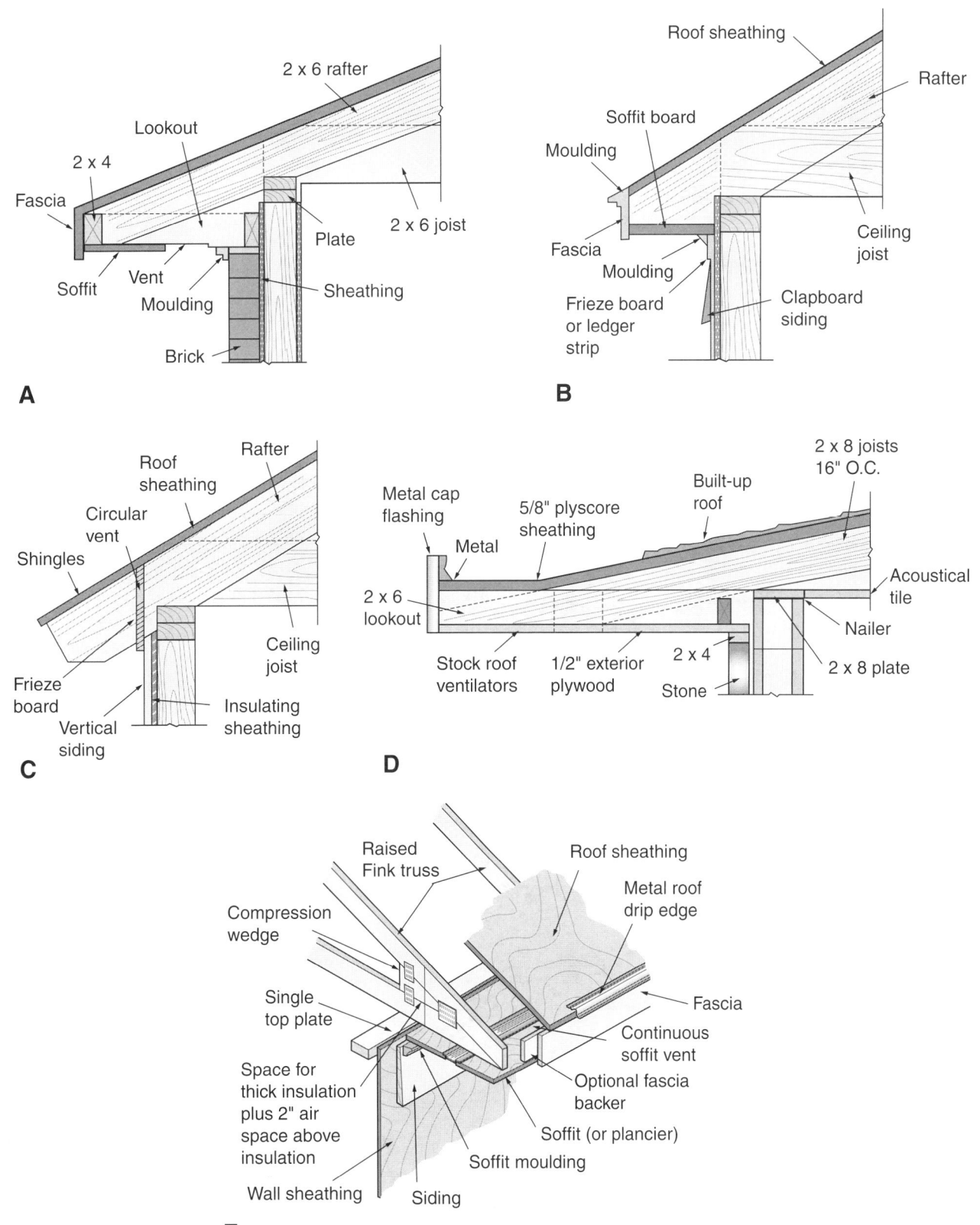

Typical Cornice Details

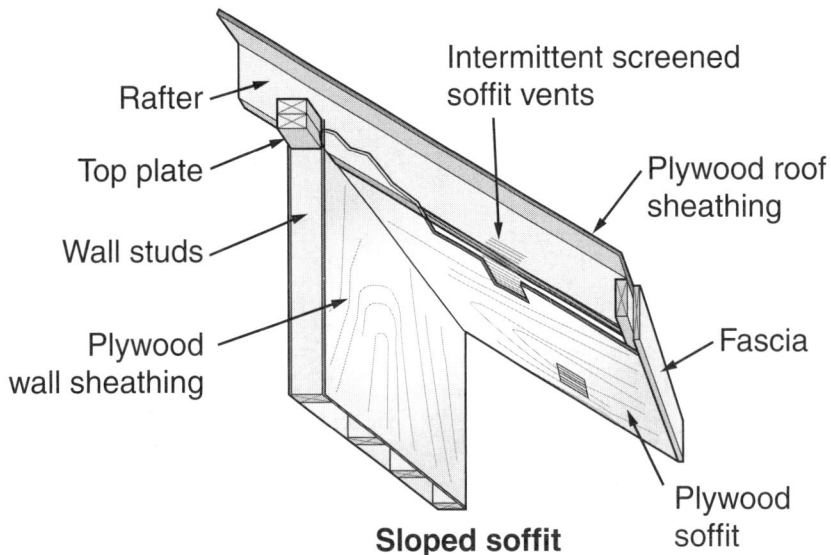

Sloped soffit

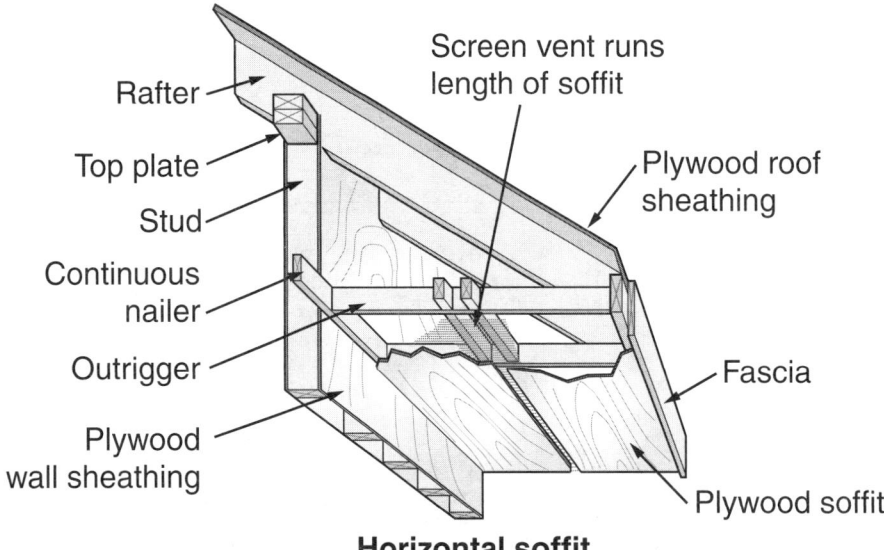

Horizontal soffit

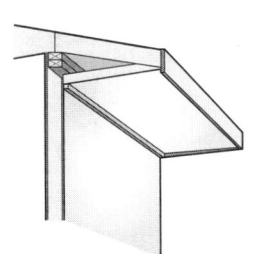

Standard horizontal soffit—sloping roof

Standard sloping soffit and roof

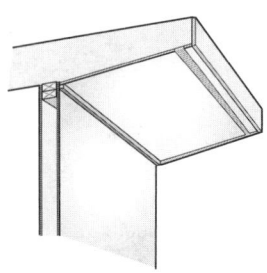

Flat roof with sloping soffit—note vent strip

RM 14-1B

Siding Application

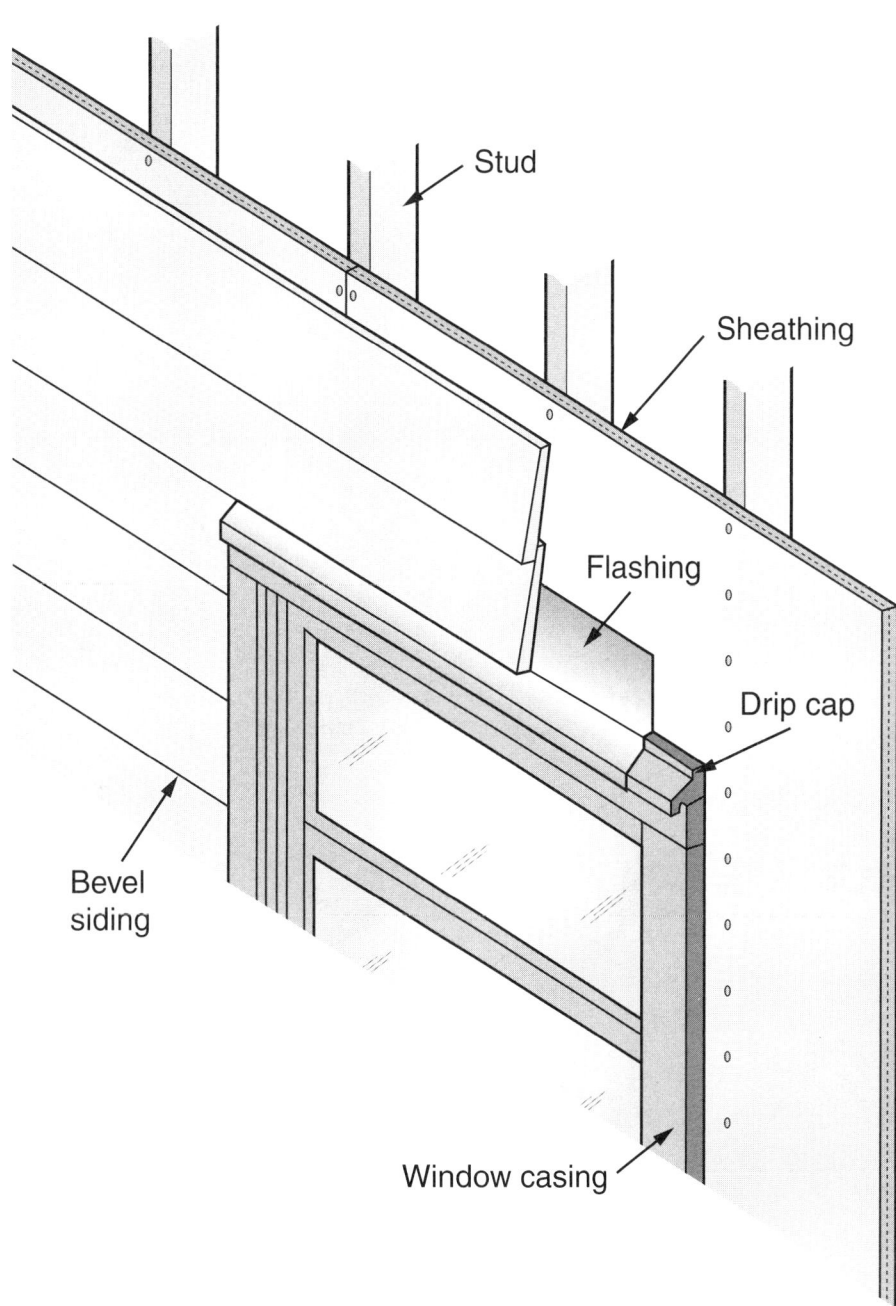

RM 14-2A

Siding Application

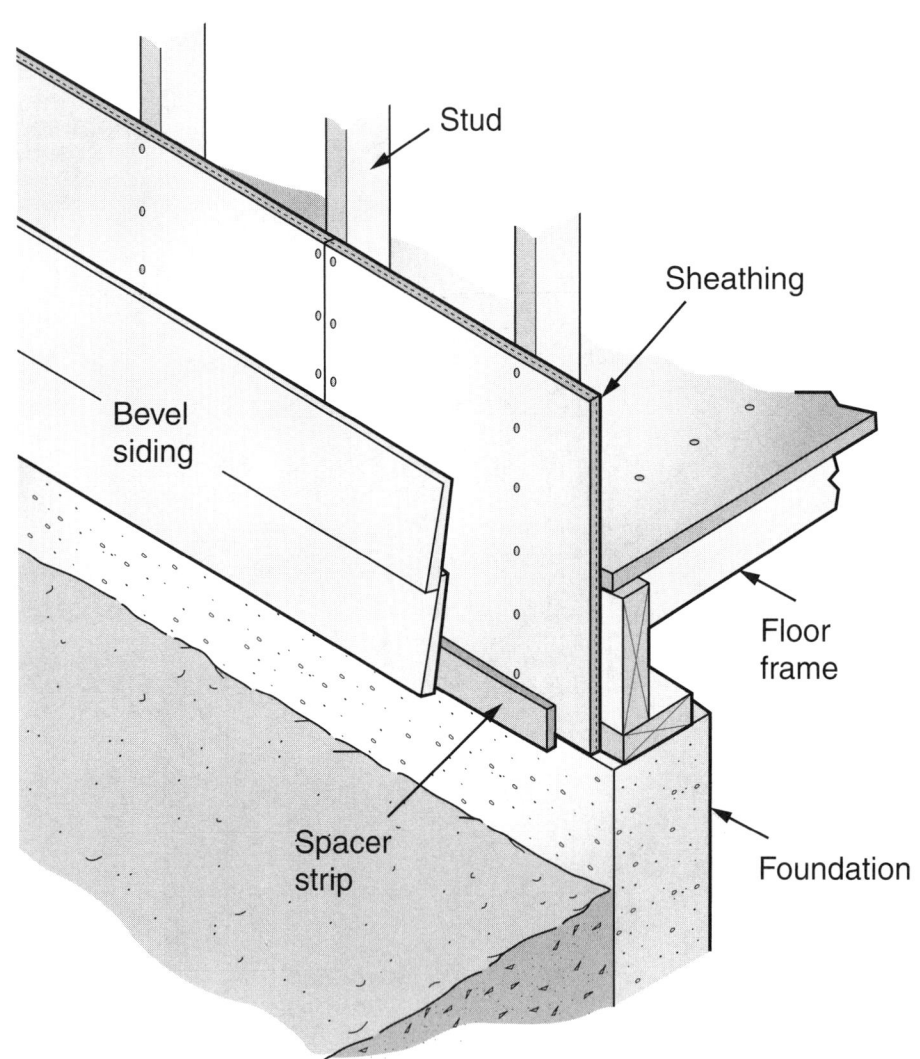

RM 14-2B

Typical Exterior Insulation and Finish System

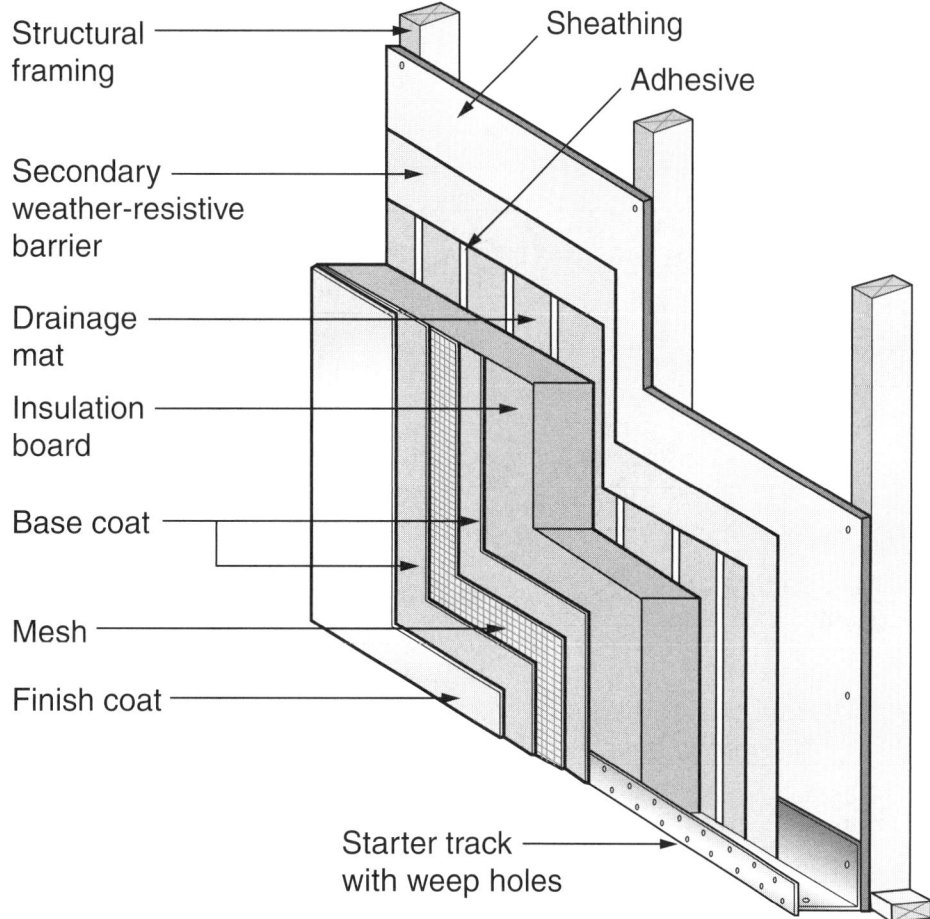

RM 14-3

Brick Veneer Construction

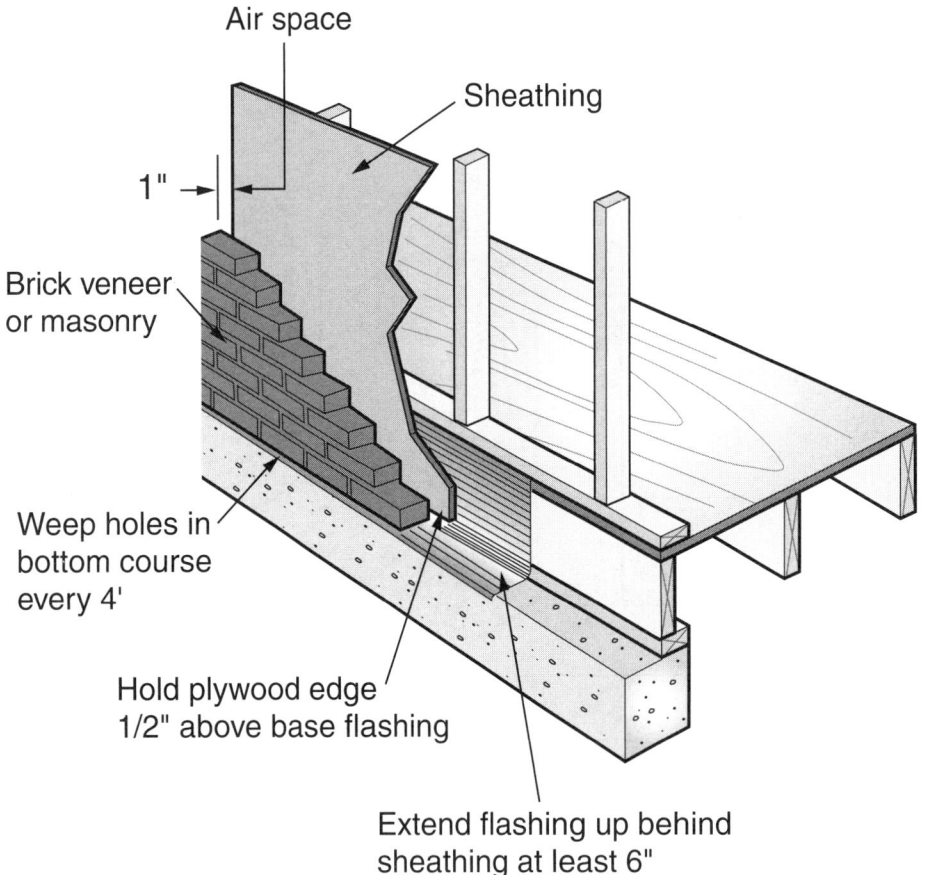

RM 14-4

Chapter 14 Procedure Checklist
Installing Horizontal Wood Siding

Name _____ Total _____

❏	Properly prepares the wall surface with sheathing material; installs flashing where required.	5	4	3	2	1	Neglects to install sheathing material and flashing.
❏	Prepares story pole with appropriate measurements; transfers these measurements to corners; lays out measurements around doors and windows.	5	4	3	2	1	Tries to lay out measurements with tape measure, possibly resulting in inaccurate measurements.
❏	Installs spacer strip along the foundation wall; installs first course of siding, allowing lower edge to extend below spacer strip.	5	4	3	2	1	Neglects to install a spacer strip; installs first course with lower edge even with or above the spacer strip.
❏	Determines method to be used for inside corners; carefully cuts and installs additional sections of siding.	5	4	3	2	1	Neglects to make adjustments for inside corners; raggedly cuts additional sections of siding.
❏	Completes installation of wood siding with coat of water-repellent preservative.	5	4	3	2	1	Fails to coat structure with preservative.

Permission granted to reproduce for educational use only.   Copyright by Goodheart-Willcox Co., Inc.

Chapter 14 Quiz
Exterior Wall Finish

Name _____ Date _____ Score _____

True-False
Circle T if the answer is True or F if the answer is False.

T   F   1. Most shingles are made in random widths.

T   F   2. Plywood siding is made from interior-grade plywood.

T   F   3. Hardboard siding panels are available in standard 4′ lengths.

T   F   4. Balloon framing should be used if a stucco finish is to be applied.

Multiple Choice
Choose the answer that correctly completes the statement. Write the corresponding letter in the space provided.

_____ 5. The _____ is the main trim member along the edge of a roof.
    A. cornice
    B. rake
    C. fascia
    D. None of the above.

_____ 6. Eight- or ten-inch wood siding should overlap about _____.
    A. 1 1/2″
    B. 2″
    C. 3 1/2″
    D. 5″

_____ 7. The standard length for shingle panels is _____.
    A. 4′
    B. 6′
    C. 8′
    D. 10′

_____ 8. _____ bundles of shingles equal one square.
    A. Two
    B. Four
    C. Six
    D. Eight

Permission granted to reproduce for educational use only.   Copyright by Goodheart-Willcox Co., Inc.

9. The weather-resistive barrier installed over the sheathing in an EIFS installation must be lapped ____ inches.
   A. 3–5
   B. 4–6
   C. 2–4

Identification
Identify the parts of the EIFS structure.

_____ 10. Mesh.

_____ 11. Base coat.

_____ 12. Insulation board.

_____ 13. Finish coat.

_____ 14. Adhesive.

_____ 15. Secondary weather-resistive barrier.

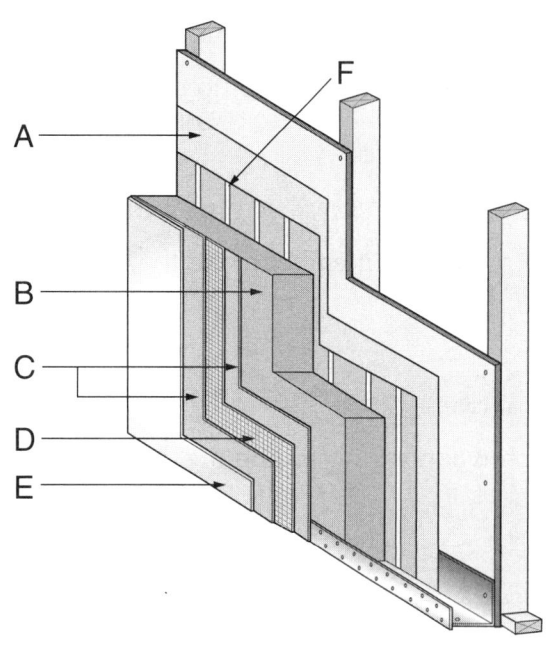

Section 3 Exam
Closing In

Name _____ Date _____ Score _____

True-False
Circle T if the answer is True or F if the answer is False.

T　F　1. For shingle installation, most manufacturers recommend 12 gauge galvanized nails with barbed shanks.

T　F　2. One-piece flashing is required around chimneys.

T　F　3. Any type of finish nail can be used when installing wood shakes.

T　F　4. A material with a high R-value has a great amount of resistance to heat passage.

T　F　5. When listing the dimensions of windows, always state the horizontal dimension first.

T　F　6. Most window units are installed from the outside.

T　F　7. Sheathing paper is applied directly to the wall frame to resist air and moisture infiltration.

T　F　8. Ice-and-water barrier should extend 24″ inside the building's outside wall line.

T　F　9. In residential construction, exterior doors usually swing inward.

T　F　10. Less than 1/4″ clearance should be allowed for windows.

Multiple Choice
Choose the answer that correctly completes the statement. Write the corresponding letter in the space provided.

_____ 11. The trim board applied to the lower edge of a sloping roof before applying the surface material is called the ____.
　　A. gutter
　　B. drip edge
　　C. fascia
　　D. starter strip

_____ 12. The amount of roofing material needed to provide 100 square feet of coverage is called a ____.
　　A. square
　　B. bundle
　　C. lot
　　D. lift

_____ 13. In frame construction, the horizontal location of windows is measured to the _____ of the window unit.
   A. left side
   B. centerline
   C. right side

_____ 14. The purpose of a _____ is to divert the flow of water and prevent ice and snow buildup behind the chimney.
   A. saddle
   B. fascia
   C. drip edge
   D. starter strip

_____ 15. The acronym EIFS stands for _____.
   A. Ecologically Friendly Fiberboard Siding
   B. Exterior Insulation Finishing Systems
   C. Extra-insulated Finished Siding
   D. Easily Installed Flooring Systems

_____ 16. Main entrance doors are generally _____ wide.
   A. 2′-6″
   B. 3′-0″
   C. 3′-6″
   D. 4′-0″

_____ 17. Underlayment _____.
   A. protects the sheathing from moisture until shingles are laid
   B. provides additional weather protection by preventing the entrance of wind-driven rain and snow
   C. prevents contact between shingles and resinous areas in the sheathing
   D. All of the above.

_____ 18. Three-tab shingles require a minimum of _____ nails per strip.
   A. 2
   B. 3
   C. 4
   D. 6

_____ 19. _____ is often used for base flashing around chimneys.
   A. Asphalt-impregnated sheathing
   B. Sheet metal
   C. Cap flashing
   D. Fiberglass

Name _____

Matching

Select the correct answer from the list on the right and place the corresponding letter in the blank on the left.

_____ 20. Coverage.

_____ 21. Exposure.

_____ 22. Head lap.

_____ 23. Side lap.

_____ 24. Shingle butt.

A. The lower, exposed edge of a shingle.

B. The distance (in inches) between the edges of one course and the next higher course.

C. The amount of weather protection provided by the overlapping of shingles.

D. The distance (in inches) from the lower edge of an overlapping shingle to the top edge of the shingle beneath.

E. The overlap length (in inches) for side-by-side roofing elements.

_____ 25. Double-hung window.

_____ 26. Casement window.

_____ 27. Awning window.

_____ 28. Hopper window.

_____ 29. Jalousie window.

A. Sash is hinged on the side and swings outward.

B. Sash is hinged at the top and swings out at the bottom.

C. Consists of two sashes that slide up and down in the window frame.

D. Consists of a series of horizontal glass slats held at each end by a movable metal frame.

E. Sash is hinged along the bottom and swings inward.

Completion

Place the answer that correctly completes the statement in the space provided.

_____ 30. _____ flashing is commonly used to waterproof joints between sloping roofs and vertical walls.

_____ 31. The minimum roof slope for wood shakes is _____-in-12.

_____ 32. Concrete roofing tile usually weighs from _____ to _____ pounds per square foot.

_____ 33. Common sheet glass is produced by the _____ process.

_____ 34. In residential construction, the standard height of windows measured from the bottom of the window head to the finished floor is _____.

Identification

Identify the parts of exterior wall finish.

_____ 35. Bevel siding.

_____ 36. Drip cap.

_____ 37. Stud.

_____ 38. Window casing.

_____ 39. Sheathing.

_____ 40. Flashing.

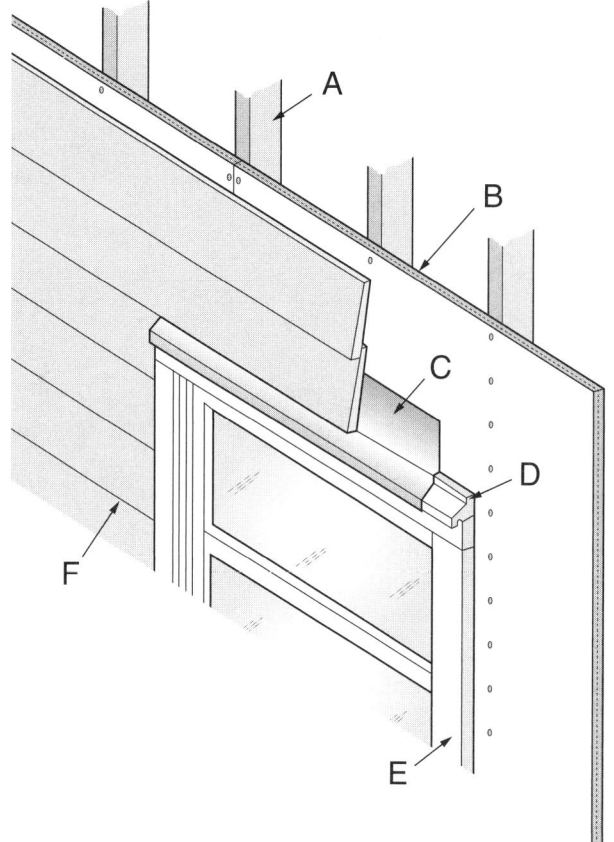

15 Thermal and Sound Insulation

Objectives

After studying this chapter, students will be able to:
- Summarize the principles of conduction, convection, and radiation.
- Define technical terms relating to thermal and acoustical properties of construction materials.
- Interpret thermal ratings charts.
- Describe the types of insulation.
- Select appropriate areas for insulation in a given structure.
- Explain the principle of condensation.
- Describe methods of controlling moisture problems.
- List general procedures for installing batt and blanket, fill, and rigid insulation.
- Define acoustical terms.
- Describe methods of construction that raise STC ratings in desired areas.

Instructional Materials

Text: Pages 485-529
  Technical Vocabulary, page 485
  Test Your Knowledge, page 528
  Curricular Connections, page 528
  Outside Assignments, page 529
Workbook: Pages 89–98
Instructor's Resource:
  Reproducible masters:
    RM 15-1 *Typical Insulating Values*
    RM 15-2 *Insulating Band Joists at Sills*
    RM 15-3 *Insulating Band Joists at Ceilings*
    RM 15-4 *Insulating to Prevent Ice Dams*
  Transparencies (binder/CD only):
    CT 15-1 *Where to Insulate*
  Procedure Checklist: *Installing Batts and Blankets*
  Chapter Quiz

Trade-Related Math

The amounts of insulating materials are calculated on the basis of the area to be filled. To determine the amount of insulating material needed for exterior walls, first calculate the perimeter of the structure. Then, multiply by the ceiling height. Subtract the area of any window or door openings. This net area is then divided by the number of square feet in a roll or batt. For example, if the perimeter of the house is 400′, the ceiling height 8′, and windows and doors comprise 96 sq. ft., determine the net wall area:

Net wall area = (perimeter × ceiling height) − area of openings
 = (400 × 8) − 96
 = 3200 − 96
Net wall area = 3104 sq. ft.

If 3″ blanket insulation (70 square feet per roll) is used, how many rolls will be required?

Number of rolls = net wall area ÷ sq. ft./roll
 = 3104 ÷ 70
Number of rolls = 45 (44 1/3 approximately)

Instructional Concepts and Student Learning Experiences

Building Sequence
1. Have the students list some of the tradespeople who other than carpenters are involved in building a residential structure. Have them explain what types of construction activities the tradespeople perform. Stress that a carpenter should check to see if additional reinforcing of the framing members is needed after their activities on a job site have been completed.

How Heat is Transmitted
1. Discuss the three methods used to transfer heat: conduction, convection, and radiation.
2. Describe the concept of conduction as it relates to building materials.
3. Describe the concept of convection, stressing that this type of heat transfer only occurs in fluids or gases.
4. Describe the concept of radiation as it relates to building components.

Thermal Insulation
1. Have students list materials that they feel are good or poor insulators. Explain that the materials they listed as good insulators should be fairly porous materials and materials they listed as poor insulators should be fairly dense. Discuss the molecular composition of these materials and how it affects insulating qualities.
2. Cite the types of materials that are commonly used as insulators, including glass fibers, glass foam, mineral fibers, organic fibers, and foamed plastic.
3. Describe the characteristics of good insulating materials.

Heat Loss Coefficients
1. Define the following terms: *Btu, k, C, R,* and *U values* as they relate to building materials.
2. Using reproducible master RM 15-1 *Typical Insulating Values*, discuss the R-values and U-values of the materials that are shown.
3. Refer to Figure 15-5 and have students note the improved insulating values as they progress down the chart.
4. Referring to Figure 15-6, discuss insulating qualities of different types of materials and the implications for construction.

How Much Insulation
1. List factors that should be considered when determining the amount of insulation required for a structure.
2. Refer to Figure 15-8 and have students determine the amount of insulation required for ceilings, walls, and floors in your specific region. Emphasize that insulation not only provides protection against the cold, but also helps to keep the heat out in the summer.
3. Define *degree day* and discuss how it is calculated. Have the students find out the number of degree days per year in your area of the country.
4. Review the relationship between U-values and R-values. Emphasize that heat transmission decreases as the thickness of insulation increases, but not in a direct relationship. It is important for the students to understand that at some point, additional insulation will not make a significant difference in the amount of heat transmission.

Types of Insulation
1. Identify the five major classifications of insulation: flexible, loose fill, rigid, foamed, and reflective. Obtain samples of these types of insulation for student inspection.
2. Describe the composition of blanket and batt insulation.
3. Distinguish between blanket and batt insulation.
4. Discuss the composition of loose fill insulation and describe its purpose in building construction.
5. Describe the composition of rigid insulation. List places where rigid insulation is commonly installed in houses.
6. Discuss the advantages and disadvantages of blown-in and foamed-in-place insulation materials.
7. Discuss the use of reflective insulation in residential construction. Emphasize that it is only effective when the reflective material is exposed to an air gap of 3/4″ or more.

Other Types of Insulation
1. Discuss other types of insulation that are used in residential construction. If possible, have samples of these types of insulation on hand for student inspection,

Where to Insulate
1. Identify areas of a house that should be insulated. Emphasize that the insulation should be placed as close to the heated area as possible.
2. Have students explain the advantages of insulating a basement area.
3. Using reproducible master RM 15-2 *Insulating Band Joists at Sills*, discuss the advantages of

insulating along a band joist and placing a seal between the foundation and sills.
4. Describe how crawl spaces should be insulated.
5. Explain how the ground in a crawl space should be covered with a vapor barrier to control the amount of moisture.
6. Discuss the insulation requirement for a slab-on-grade structure. Mention that only the perimeter needs to be insulated, since very little heat is lost through the ground under the center of the structure.
7. Using Figures 15-21 and 15-22, describe how insulation is added to slab-on-grade and existing foundation walls. Point out the use of flashing in adding insulation to the outside of existing foundation walls.

Condensation
1. Discuss the problems that may occur because of condensation in a residential structure.
2. Define the term *dewpoint* and explain how it relates to the construction of a house.

Vapor Barriers
1. Emphasize the proper location and placement of a vapor barrier to avoid condensation in walls.
2. Identify types of materials that are used as vapor barriers. Mention that many insulating materials already have a vapor barrier applied to one of the surfaces.
3. Discuss when vapor barriers should be applied. Stress that any punctures or cuts in a vapor barrier reduce its effectiveness.

Ventilation
1. Explain the importance of having good ventilation in a structure. Cite possible scenarios that may occur if ventilation is less than adequate.
2. Emphasize the importance of maintaining airways near the soffit in an attic when installing thicker insulation. Describe possible means to ensure that the airways are not blocked.

Safety with Insulation
1. Emphasize the importance of wearing appropriate clothing—gloves, long-sleeve shirt, and long pants—when installing any type of insulation. In addition, stress wearing a mask covering the mouth and nose to avoid inhaling fibers.
2. Stress the need for good housekeeping in reference to proper disposal of fiberglass scraps.

Installing Batts and Blankets
1. Describe how blankets or batts can be laid out and cut on the floor.
2. Explain how batts are installed in wall sections. Mention that if batts must be joined, there should be at least a 1″ overlap between the pieces. Describe the three ways that flanges might be stapled to hold the insulation in place. If possible, demonstrate these methods.
3. Describe how insulation is installed in a situation where drywall will be placed over it.
4. Discuss how insulation is installed around electrical boxes and plumbing pipes. Demonstrate the correct procedures.
5. Using reproducible master RM 15-3 *Insulating Band Joists at Ceilings*, describe how insulation is installed in a ceiling's perimeter in a multistory structure.
6. Using reproducible master RM 15-4 *Insulating to Prevent Ice Dams*, explain how batt insulation is extended over a wall plate to prevent heat from escaping at this point. This heat loss causes the melting that results in ice damming on a roof. Have students note that the insulation must not block airflow between soffits and vents in the roof. Explain how this is accomplished through raising rafters at the eaves and by use of plastic airways to allow sufficient room for airflow.
7. Discuss the importance of insulating around window and door frames. Mention that cuttings left over from other pieces can be installed in these places and then covered with a vapor barrier.

Installing Fill Insulation
1. Discuss the two methods used to install fill insulation.
2. Describe the procedure used to pour fill insulation. Emphasize that a vapor barrier should be installed prior to installing the

insulation. Demonstrate this procedure if time and space allows.
3. Explain the purpose of installing batt insulation around the perimeter of a ceiling prior to installing fill insulation.
4. Discuss the procedure used to blow-fill insulation. Stress the importance of using protective equipment such as a face mask, goggles, and gloves.

Installing Rigid Insulation
1. Discuss applications for rigid insulation.
2. Explain the purpose of applying a plaster coat or other protective covering after installing rigid insulation to an exterior masonry wall.

Insulating Basement Walls
1. Describe the preparation necessary before installing batt insulation on basement walls. Stress the importance of checking local codes to avoid possible violations. Emphasize the importance of installing a vapor barrier on the warm side of the insulation.

Insulating Existing Structures
1. Discuss the concerns that should be addressed when insulating an existing structure. Describe materials that can be used instead of a conventional vapor barrier.

Stopping Air Infiltration
1. Discuss the locations on a structure that should be caulked or sealed. List the materials that can be used to caulk these locations. Emphasize the importance of sealing such places as electrical conduit and plumbing runs that enter from the attic or basement.

Estimating Thermal Insulation Materials
1. Describe how to estimate the amount of insulation for exterior walls.
2. Describe how to estimate the amount of insulation for floors and ceilings.

Acoustics and Sound Control
1. Have the students identify the possible sources of noise in a residential structure.

Sound Intensity
1. Define the acoustical terms *sound* and *decibel* as they relate to sound control in a residential structure.
2. Using Figure 15-52, have students identify the decibel levels of sounds and noises that are familiar to them.

Sound Transmission
1. Define the acoustical terms *sound transmission loss (STL)*, *sound absorption*, *noise reduction coefficient (N-RC)*, and *sound transmission class (STC)* as they relate to sound control in a residential structure.
2. Describe the action of sound when it is generated within a room. Discuss the diaphragm action that occurs, allowing sound to be transmitted through a wall.
3. Define the term *masking sounds* as it relates to designing a sound-insulating panel.

Wall Construction
1. Referring to Figure 15-56, explain the methods of constructing interior walls and the sound transmission classes assigned to them.
2. Describe the composition of sound deadening board and how it can be used to increase the STC of a partition. Explain how sound deadening board is identified.
3. Discuss the use of double walls to increase the STC. Describe the construction of double walls using resilient channels.
4. Compare the methods used for sound-proofing walls to floors and ceilings.
5. Describe the use of spring clips to attach the ceiling material.
6. Describe a method used to soundproof an existing floor using sleepers and glass wool. Emphasize that the sleepers float on the glass wool and are not actually tied into the existing floor.
7. Identify materials that can be used to reduce the amount of sound transmitted around a door.
8. Have students identify the rooms of a house in which sound control is most important. Describe materials that can be used to reduce the amount of sound transmission.
9. Discuss how acoustical materials, such as acoustical tiles, dissipate sound energy.

10. Briefly describe how acoustical materials are installed.
11. Discuss how suspended ceilings are used to reduce the amount of sound transmission.

Installation of Acoustical Materials
1. Emphasize that the manufacturer's installation recommendations should be followed to ensure acoustical materials work properly.
2. Describe the preparation necessary before painting perforated boards or acoustical tile. Point out that these materials can be painted so long as the pores are not clogged with paint.

Chapter Review

1. Review the chapter objectives. Be sure that the students fully understand each objective.
2. Assign *Technical Vocabulary, Test Your Knowledge* questions, *Curricular Connections,* and *Outside Assignments* for Chapter 15 of the text. Review the answers in class.
3. Assign Chapter 15 in the workbook. Review the answers in class.

Evaluation

This chapter provides three methods for evaluating student performance. Students should complete the *Test Your Knowledge* section using the book as reference. Students should also be allowed to use the book for reference when completing the workbook material. Use the Chapter 15 Quiz in the instructor's resources for in-class evaluation. Correct the quizzes, return them to the students, and review the quiz questions in group discussion.

Procedure Checklist

Using the procedure checklist *Installing Batts and Blankets,* have students evaluate the techniques used to perform these tasks.

Answers to Test Your Knowledge
Text Page 528

1. False.
2. conduction
3. radiation
4. low
5. The product of one day and the number of °F that the mean temperature is below 65°F.
6. Rigid, flexible, loose fill, reflective.
7. dewpoint
8. warm
9. 12″
10. blown
11. rigid
12. infiltration
13. decibel
14. 35
15. Sound transmission class or STC
16. cane
17. stud space
18. Noises from activities such as walking, moving furniture, or operating vacuum cleaners and other equipment.
19. Noise reduction coefficient
20. The thinner mixture is less likely to clog the pores of the material.

Answers to Workbook Questions
Pages 87–96

1. heating
2. resistance
3. conduction
4. A. Radiation.
   B. Convection.
   C. Conduction
5. *(any order)*
   Glass fibers.
   Glass foam.
   Mineral fiber.
   Organic fiber.
   Foamed plastic.
6. A. hour
   B. 1″
7. 1056 Btu.
8. B. U = 0.05
9. D. R-19
10. 0.087
11. R-22.6
12. 65°F
13. reflective
14. A. Blanket.
    B. Batt.
    C. Loose fill.
15. B. Rigid insulation

16. B. 3/4″
17. D. 55 lb.
18. A. Siding.
    B. Flashing.
    C. Extruded polystyrene.
19. dewpoint
20. C. between the inside wall covering and wall frame
21. C. Both the insulation and vapor barrier should be continuous under the entire floor.
22. D. 1/1600
23. B. 12″
24. C. polystyrene
25. A. pouring
    B. blowing
26. Walls: 840
    Ceiling: 1100
27. Long-sleeved shirts or blouses, long trousers, gloves.
28. decibel
29. second
30. C. Noise reduction coefficient
31. 39 dB
32. D. Sound transmission class
33. A. 33
    B. 39
    C. 45
    D. 50
34. stud space
35. A. 20–25 dB
36. C. 70%
37. A. spray gun

Answers to Chapter Quiz

1. True.
2. True.
3. True.
4. False.
5. True.
6. D. All of the above.
7. B. Btu
8. D. Either B or C.
9. A. Impact
10. C. sprayed
11. C. dewpoint
12. D.
13. B.
14. C.
15. E.
16. A.

Typical Insulating Values

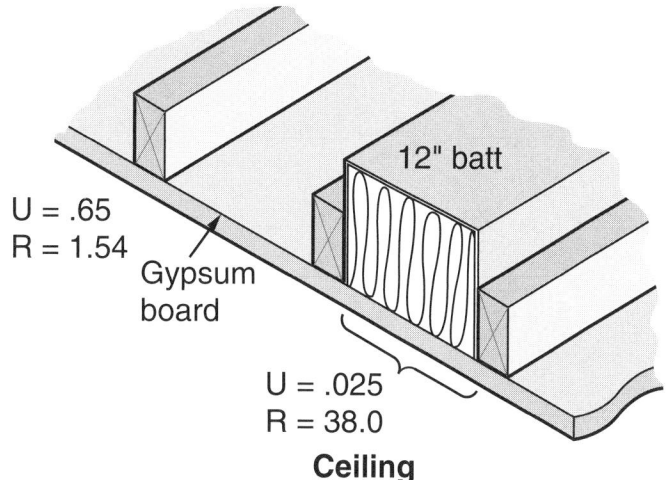

Ceiling

U = .65
R = 1.54
Gypsum board

12" batt

U = .025
R = 38.0

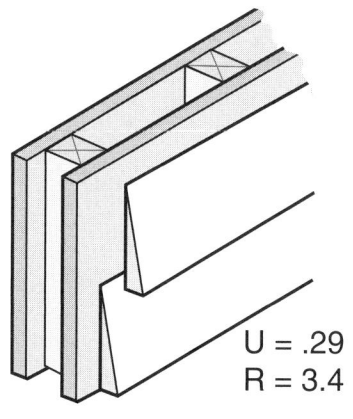

U = .29
R = 3.4

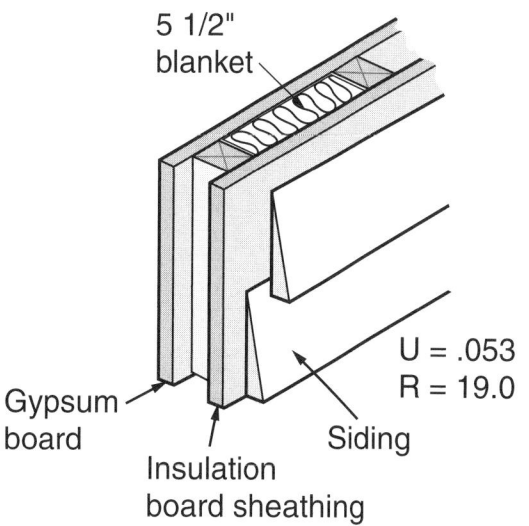

5 1/2" blanket

U = .053
R = 19.0

Gypsum board
Insulation board sheathing
Siding

Wall

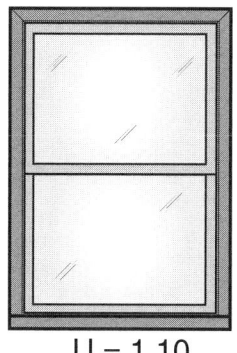

U = 1.10
R = .91

Single-glazed window

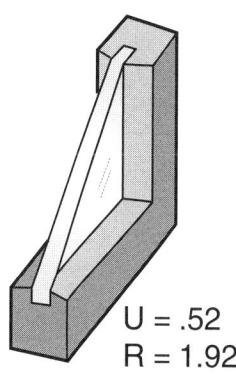

U = .52
R = 1.92

Sealed double-glazing or storm panel

RM 15-1

Insulating Band Joists at Sills

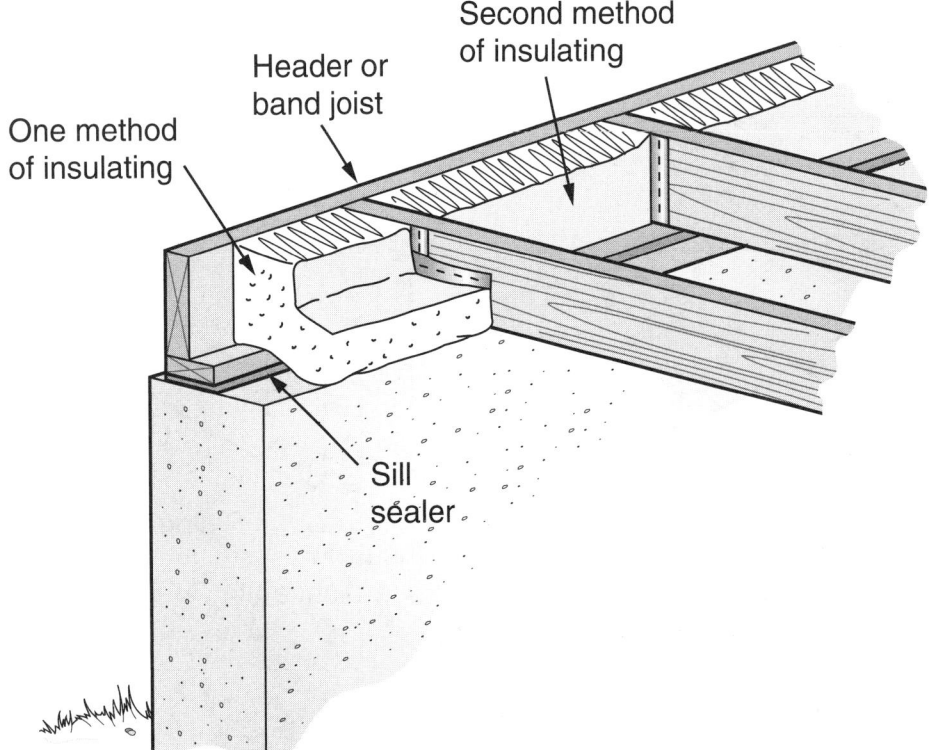

Insulating Band Joists at Ceilings

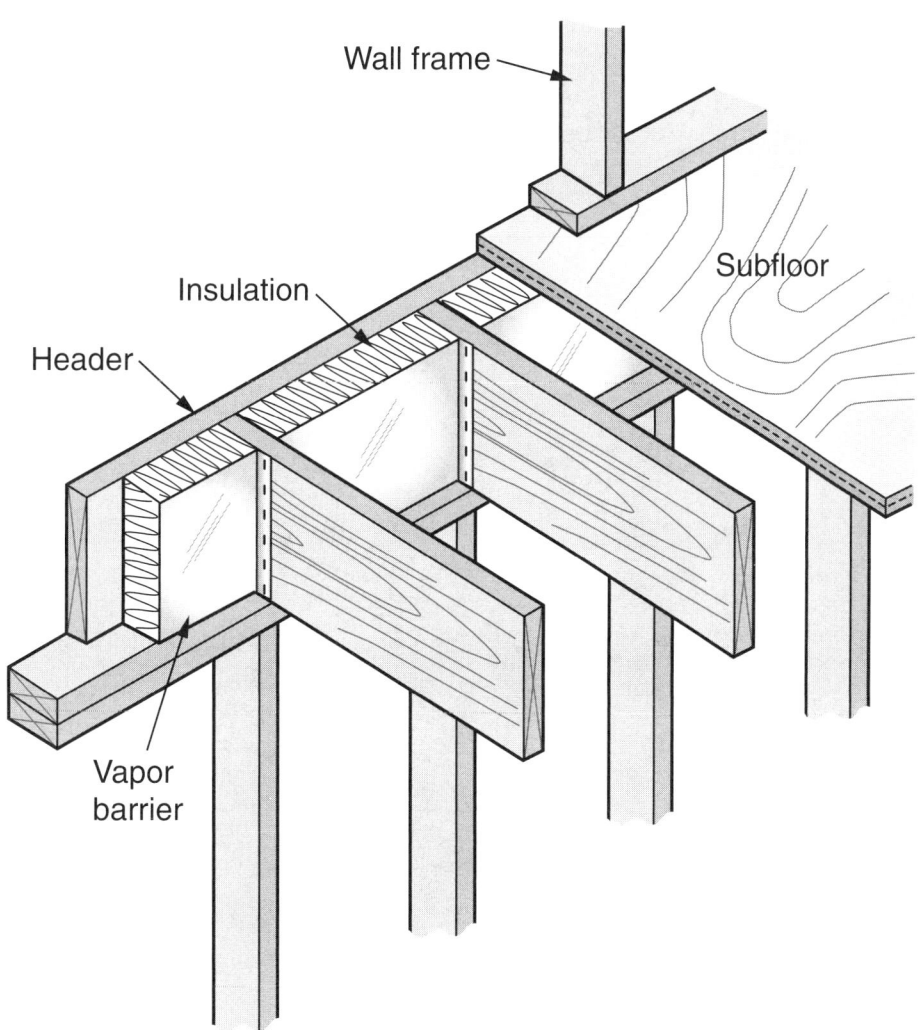

RM 15-3

Insulating to Prevent Ice Dams

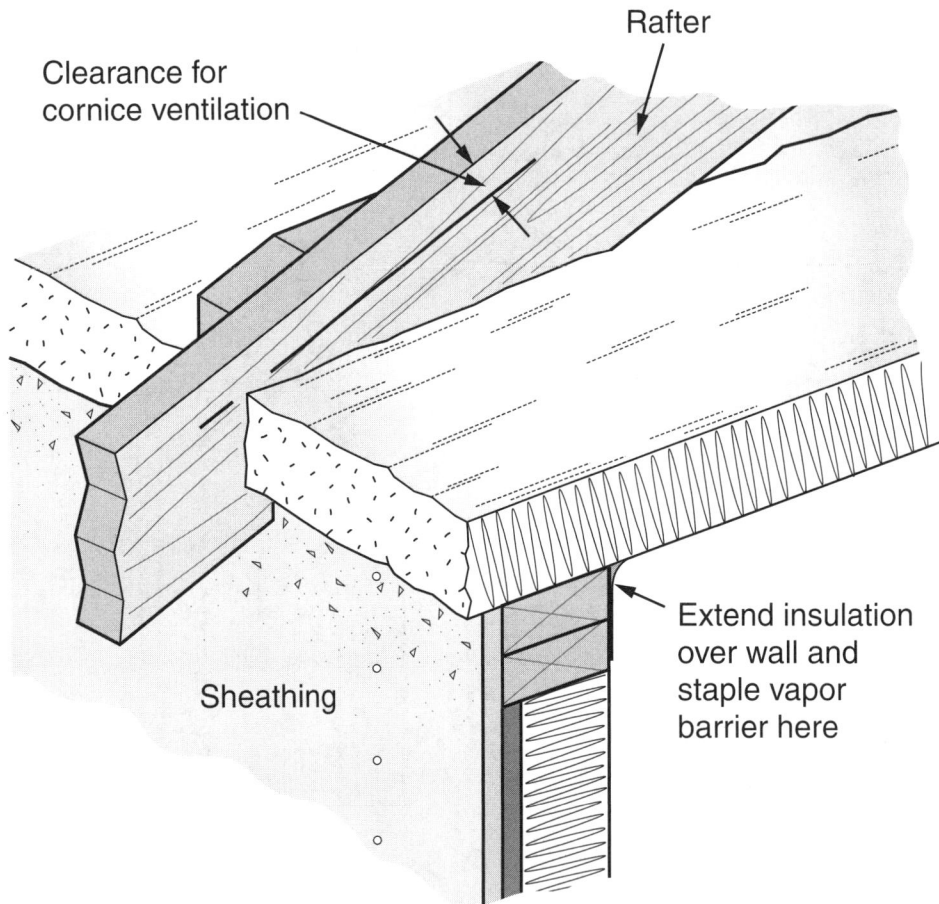

RM 15-4

Chapter 15 Procedure Checklist
Installing Batts and Blankets

Name _____ Total _____

❏	Wears proper protective equipment.	5	4	3	2	1	Neglects to wear protective equipment.
❏	Carefully measures and cuts batts or blankets.	5	4	3	2	1	Incorrectly measures batt or blanket length; carelessly cuts insulation resulting in wasted material.
❏	Properly installs batts by starting from the bottom and working up and at the top and working down; overlaps vapor barrier.	5	4	3	2	1	Incorrectly installs insulation; vapor barrier facing toward the exterior of the structure.
❏	Secures flanges in place (if necessary); applies separate vapor barrier (if required).	5	4	3	2	1	Neglects to secure flanges into place; forgets to apply separate vapor barrier (if required).

Chapter 15 Quiz
Thermal and Sound Insulation

Name _____ Date _____ Score _____

True-False
Circle T if the answer is True or F if the answer is False.

T F 1. Radiation is the process of heat transfer by means of wave motion.

T F 2. More insulation is required in a climate with a high number of degree days.

T F 3. A vapor barrier must be located on the warm side of an insulated wall.

T F 4. Frequency is the unit of measure used to indicate the loudness of a sound.

T F 5. A good insulation material has a high R-value.

Multiple Choice
Choose the answer that correctly completes the statement. Write the corresponding letter in the space provided.

_____ 6. Heat transfer takes place by means of _____.
   A. convection
   B. conduction
   C. radiation
   D. All of the above.

_____ 7. A(n) _____ is the amount of heat needed to raise the temperature of 1 lb. of water 1° F.
   A. calorie
   B. Btu
   C. R-value
   D. degree day

_____ 8. Moisture coming up through the ground can be controlled by covering the area with _____.
   A. loose fill insulation
   B. heavy roll roofing
   C. 6 mil polyethylene plastic film
   D. Either B or C.

_____ 9. _____ sounds are carried throughout a building by the vibrations of the structural materials.
   A. Impact
   B. Reverberation
   C. Masking
   D. None of the above.

_____ 10. Acoustical plaster should be ____ onto the surface.
   A. troweled
   B. spread
   C. sprayed
   D. Either A or B.

_____ 11. The ____ is the temperature at which the air is completely saturated with moisture.
   A. R-value
   B. U-value
   C. dewpoint
   D. saturation point

Identification
Identify the types of insulation in the illustration below.

_____ 12. Loose fill.

_____ 13. Batt.

_____ 14. Blanket.

_____ 15. Reflective.

_____ 16. Rigid.

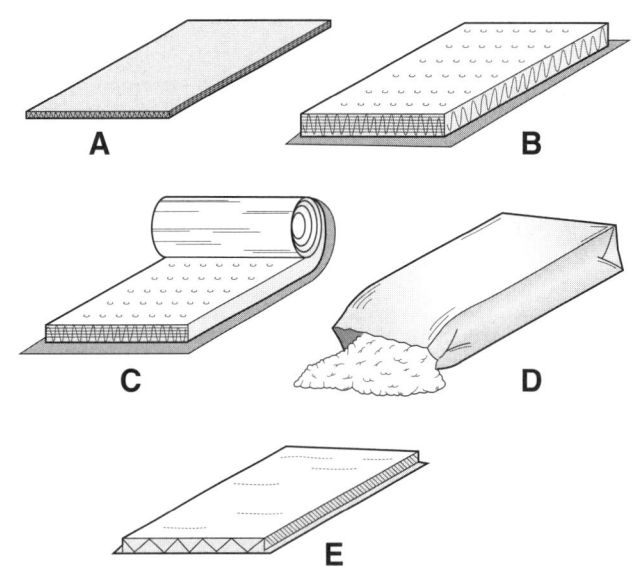

16 Interior Wall and Ceiling Finish

Objectives

After studying this chapter, students will be able to:
- Explain wall and ceiling covering materials.
- Describe wallboard cutting, nailing, and adhesive techniques.
- Describe the characteristics of gypsum plaster.
- Explain how gypsum and metal lath are applied.
- Illustrate the use of plaster grounds.
- Describe plastering methods.
- Illustrate how double layer and predecorated wallboard are applied.
- List the procedures for installing wood paneling.
- Lay out ceiling tile and install furring strips.
- Describe methods for leveling and installing a suspended ceiling.
- Estimate quantities of lath, wallboard, and ceiling tiles for a specific interior.

Instructional Materials

Text: Pages 531–570
- *Technical Vocabulary*, page 531
- *Test Your Knowledge*, page 569
- *Curricular Connections*, page 570
- *Outside Assignments*, page 570

Workbook: Pages 99–106

Instructor's Resource:
- Reproducible masters:
  - RM 16-1A *Drywall Application*
  - RM 16-1B *Drywall Application—Fasteners*
  - RM 16-1C *Double-Layer Drywall Application*
  - RM 16-2 *Suspended Ceiling System*
- Procedure Checklist: *Installing Drywall Using Single Layer-Construction*
- Chapter Quiz

Trade-Related Math

Plasterers usually base their prices and estimates on the number of square yards to be covered. Square yards can be determined by dividing the number of square feet by 9. For example, to determine the number of square yards contained in a wall measuring 8′ × 24′, the following calculations provide the answer:

Square feet = height × width
= 8′ × 24′
= 192 sq. ft.

Square yards = square feet ÷ 9
= 192 ÷ 9
= 21.3 sq. yd.

Instructional Concepts and Student Learning Experiences

Drywall Installation

1. Have the students list the types of materials used to cover interior walls. Have as many of these materials on hand as possible for student inspection. Discuss the common sizes of each type of material.
2. Discuss the advantages and disadvantages of both drywall and plaster as interior wall finish materials. Mention that drywall is the most prominent type of interior wall finish material used today.
3. Identify types of gypsum wallboard that are not suitable as interior wall finish materials.
4. Describe the difference between single-layer and double-layer drywall construction. Cite advantages and disadvantages of each type of construction.
5. Using reproducible master RM 16-1A *Drywall Application*, describe the two methods of installing drywall sheets. Note advantages of each method.

6. Discuss the techniques used to lay out and make straight drywall cuts. Stress the importance of using a sharp knife.
7. Demonstrate the proper techniques for cutting drywall. Show students how to make straight cuts as well as curved cuts.
8. Using reproducible master RM 16-1B *Drywall Application—Fasteners,* identify the various types of nails and screws that can be used to attach drywall and gypsum lath to studs or other framing. If available, show samples of all fasteners.
9. Discuss the nailing pattern and spacing that should be used for drywall. Emphasize the importance of drawing the drywall tight against the framing.
10. Demonstrate the correct methods used to install sheets of drywall on walls and on any surfaces to be tiled.
11. Show the correct methods for installing drywall with screws. If one is available, demonstrate the use of a power drywall driver with adjustable screw depth.
12. Demonstrate the correct methods of installing drywall on a ceiling. Discuss possible problems that could be encountered when installing drywall overhead.
13. Discuss the procedure for installing drywall with an adhesive. Cite applications of such an installation.
14. Discuss how joint compound and reinforcing tape are applied over seams and fasteners. Demonstrate the proper procedure in detail.
15. Describe the use of pressure-sensitive, glass-fiber tape to cover the seams of drywall.
16. Discuss the use of a banjo (taping tool) to simultaneously apply both reinforcing tape and drywall compound. Cite advantages over the other method of applying tape.
17. Identify the materials used to reinforce inside and outside corners of drywall. Demonstrate the proper procedure for installing corner beads and paper flanges.

Double-Layer Construction
1. Using reproducible master RM 16-1C *Double-Layer Drywall Application,* discuss double-layer application. Cite advantages of this method over the single-layer application.
2. Discuss the means of attaching the base layer to the framing and finish layer to the base layer. Emphasize that the joints of the finish layer should be offset from those of the base layer by at least 10″.

Finishing Double-Layer Wallboard
1. Compare the finishing of double-layer wallboard to that of single-layer construction.

Moisture-Resistant (MR) Wallboard and Cement Board
1. Distinguish between common drywall, MR wallboard, and cement board. Explain where MR wallboard and cement board should be used.
2. Referring to Figures 16-20 through 16-23, discuss the installation of MR wallboard or cement board around the perimeter of a bathtub. Stress the importance of avoiding application of regular joint compound on any surfaces to be tiled.
3. Referring to Figure 16-24, discuss tools and methods used when working with cement board.
4. Suggest that the correct placement of holes for stub-outs in bathrooms can be assured by first laying out the dimensions on a large piece of cardboard. Then, using the cardboard as a template, lay out the openings on the MR wallboard or cement board.

Veneer Plaster
1. Describe the application of veneer plaster. Emphasize that the manufacturer's directions should be carefully followed for the specific type of gypsum plaster being used.

Predecorated Wallboard
1. Discuss the use of predecorated wallboard. Mention that the wallboard is usually installed vertically because of the difficulty in matching and finishing butt joints.
2. Stress the importance of using a plastic-headed hammer, rawhide mallet, or a special cover placed over the face of a regular hammer when installing colored nails that match the surface.
3. Explain how edges and joints are covered when using predecorated wallboard.

Wallboard on Masonry Walls
1. Describe the installation of wallboard over metal or wood furring strips attached to masonry walls, such as in a basement.
2. Explain how insulation should be installed on interior masonry walls prior to installing wallboard.

Installing Plywood Paneling
1. Discuss the preparation and storage methods that should be used for interior plywood.
2. Stress the importance of carefully planning the panel arrangement. Discuss the application designs shown in Figure 16-30.
3. Review portable saw safety. Mention that the cutting should be performed from the back side of the panels to avoid splintering of the face.
4. Describe the installation of plywood panels over a masonry wall.
5. Explain the purpose of installing 1/4″ plywood over a base of 1/2″ drywall.

Hardboard
1. Discuss the special preparation that should be used for hardboard panels. Cite problems that may occur if the panels have not been allowed to acclimate to the humidity level of the living space.

Plastic Laminates
1. Explain why plastic laminates are generally bonded to backer material before installation on a wall.

Solid Lumber Paneling
1. Identify the types of softwood lumber that are commonly used as wall paneling. List the dimensions in which they are usually available.
2. Explain that furring strips are usually not required when wood paneling is applied horizontally.
3. Discuss how narrow widths of tongue-and-groove paneling are blind-nailed to conceal the nail heads. Stress that the paneling should be allowed to attain a humidity level close to the humidity of the room in which it will be installed *before* installation.

Plaster
1. List the wall and ceiling qualities that can be obtained from using plaster.
2. Identify the types of plaster bases used in residential construction. State the thicknesses that should be used for different stud spacing.
3. Describe the installation of plaster bases. Emphasize that the end joints should be staggered when installing plaster bases.

Metal Lath
1. Cite the applications of metal lath in residential construction.
2. Describe the installation of metal lath and waterproof felt paper in areas subjected to moisture.

Reinforcing
1. Identify places where expanded metal lath is used to minimize cracking. Stress that the lath should be lightly tacked into position so it becomes a part of the plaster base.
2. Identify the type of reinforcement used for outside corners. Describe the purpose of corner beads.

Plaster Grounds
1. Discuss the purpose of plaster grounds. Identify the types of materials commonly used as plaster grounds.

Plaster Base on Masonry Walls
1. List the methods that can be used to attach furring strips to a masonry surface.
2. Discuss why furring strips would be used on a masonry surface when applying plaster. Describe the installation of insulation before applying plaster.

Plastering Materials and Methods
1. Discuss the composition of plaster.
2. Distinguish between *two-coat work* and *three-coat work*.
3. Describe the procedure for applying the scratch coat. Emphasize the thickness of the coat that should be obtained.
4. Describe the application of the brown coat. Emphasize the thickness of the coat that should be obtained.

5. Describe the application of the finish coat in three-coat work. Stress that the finish coat should only be about 1/16" thick.
6. Demonstrate the application of plaster using the three-coat method.

Ceiling Tile
1. List the types of ceiling tiles that are commonly used in residential work.
2. Discuss the layout procedure used for ceiling tile. Emphasize that the border courses along opposite walls should be the same width.
3. Discuss the reason for installing furring strips for ceiling tiles. Indicate where the strips should be placed. Explain how to level the furring strips.
4. Describe *sheet furring* and how it can be used in place of furring strips.
5. Emphasize the importance of checking the placement and levelness of furring strips prior to installing tile.
6. Describe the installation procedure for tile. Stress to students that they should keep their hands clean while installing the tile to avoid soiling the tile. Demonstrate the installation procedure for ceiling tile.
7. Discuss how a metal track system can be used for the installation of ceiling tiles.

Suspended Ceilings
1. Using reproducible master RM 16-2 *Suspended Ceiling System*, identify the parts of a suspended ceiling system. List advantages of using this type of system.
2. Describe the installation procedure for suspended ceilings. If possible, demonstrate the procedure.

Estimating Materials
1. Describe the method for estimating the amount of wall or ceiling materials.
2. Describe the method for estimating the amount of gypsum lath used on a residential project.

Chapter Review
1. Review the chapter objectives. Be sure that the students fully understand each objective.
2. Assign *Technical Vocabulary, Test Your Knowledge* questions, *Curricular Connections,* and *Outside Assignments* for Chapter 16 of the text. Review the answers in class.
3. Assign Chapter 16 in the workbook. Review the answers in class.

Evaluation
This chapter provides three methods for evaluating student performance. Students should complete the *Test Your Knowledge* section using the book as reference. Students should also be allowed to use the book for reference when completing the workbook material. Use the Chapter 16 Quiz in the instructor's resources for in-class evaluation. Correct the quizzes, return them to the students, and review the quiz questions in group discussion.

Procedure Checklist
Using the procedure checklist *Installing Drywall Using Single Layer-Construction*, have students evaluate the techniques used to perform these tasks.

Answers to Test Your Knowledge
Text Page 569
1. Gypsum wallboard, gypsum lath for plaster veneering, predecorated gypsum paneling, plywood and particleboard, hardboard and fiberboard, solid wood paneling, plaster, and cement board.
2. A. Store it inside and flat on a clean floor in the center of the largest room.
   C. Lay it flat with the ceiling drywall on top.
3. 1/2
4. Parallel—long edges of panels run in the same direction as studs and joists. Perpendicular—long edges of panels are at right angles to studs and joists.
5. ceilings
6. 12", 16"
7. 10
8. False.
9. 1/4", 7/16", 1/2"
10. floors, ceilings
11. True.

12. Diagonal, chevron, and herringbone.
13. 8, 10
14. grounds
15. 48
16. expanded metal lath
17. 1/2
18. 12″ × 12″
19. 2
20. wires

Answers to Workbook Questions Pages 99–106

1. A. 4′
   B. 14′
2. A. Tapered edge.
   B. Beveled edge.
   C. Round edge.
   D. Square edge.
   E. T&G.
3. A. 12″
   B. 16″
4. A. 7″
   B. 8″
5. Cement board
6. B. 10″
7. C. green
8. B. 24
9. A. 1/16″
10. 48 hours
11. B. 8% to 10%
12. A. Eliminates need for vapor barrier.
13. A. 1/32″ or 1/16″
14. D. 48″
15. D. 16 × 48
16. C. 1/2″
17. B. Use a No. 13 GA nail with a minimum length of 1″.
18. grounds
19. A. Metal lath.
    B. Cornerite.
    C. Corner bead.
20. furring strips
21. A. Does not withstand moisture well.
22. A. scratch coat
    B. brown coat
23. A. In most residential plastering, the first two coats are applied almost simultaneously.
24. True.
25. B. unit weight
26. A. Tongue.
    B. Stapling flange.
    C. Groove.
27. C. cut notches in lower edge of low joists
28. 232 bd. ft.
29. A. in any one of the corners
30. metal track
31. No. of panels: 6
    Sq. ft. of plywood: 192
32. Sq. ft.: 4036
    Bundles of lath: 64
33. sq. yd.: 449
34. No. of tiles: 294
    No. of cartons: 5
35. A. Plaster.
    B. Plaster base.
    C. Plaster grounds.

Answers to Chapter Quiz

1. False.
2. False.
3. True.
4. False.
5. True.
6. False.
7. True.
8. B. knife
9. C. Moisture-resistant
10. D. All of the above.
11. C. fiberboard
12. D. Either A or B.

Drywall Application

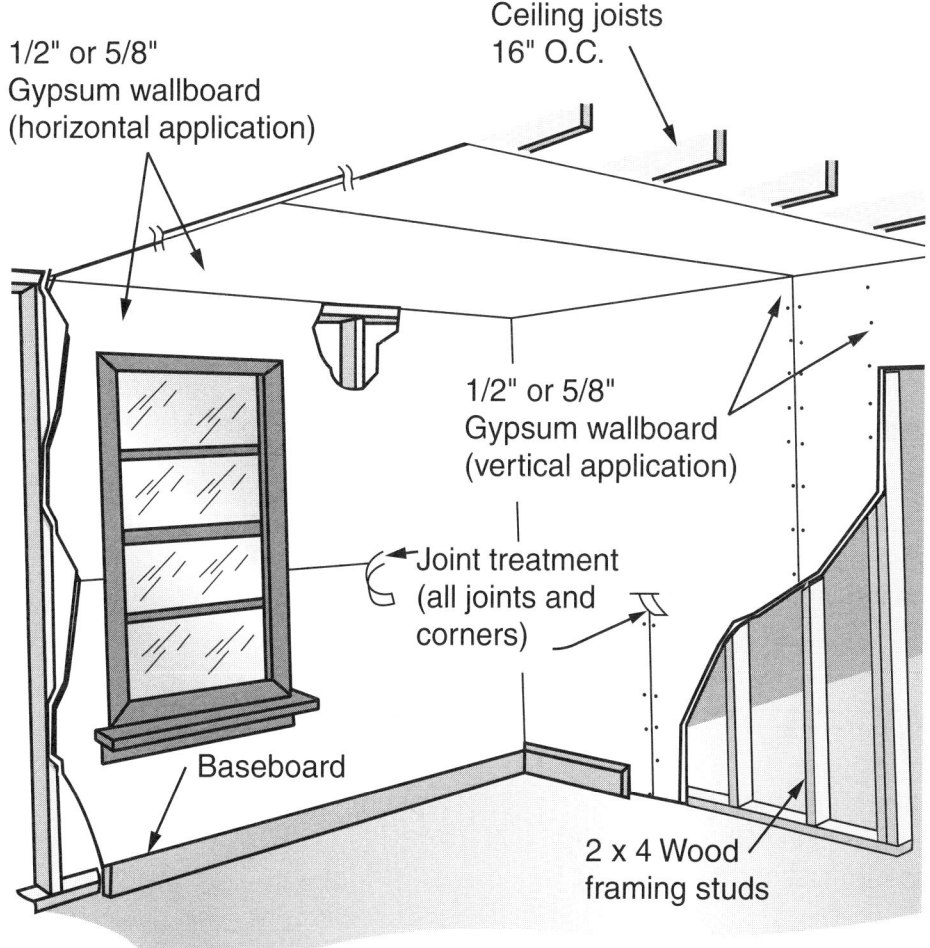

RM 16-1A

Drywall Application—Fasteners

Annular ring nail attaches drywall directly to wood frame.

Type W screw attaches drywall directly to wood frame.

6d cement-coated nail attaches drywall over existing wall materials.

Type S screw attaches drywall to metal studs.

Nail with matching color head for use with prefinished gypsum wallboard.

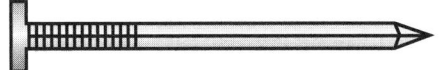

Gypsum lathing nail

RM 16-1B

Double-Layer Drywall Application

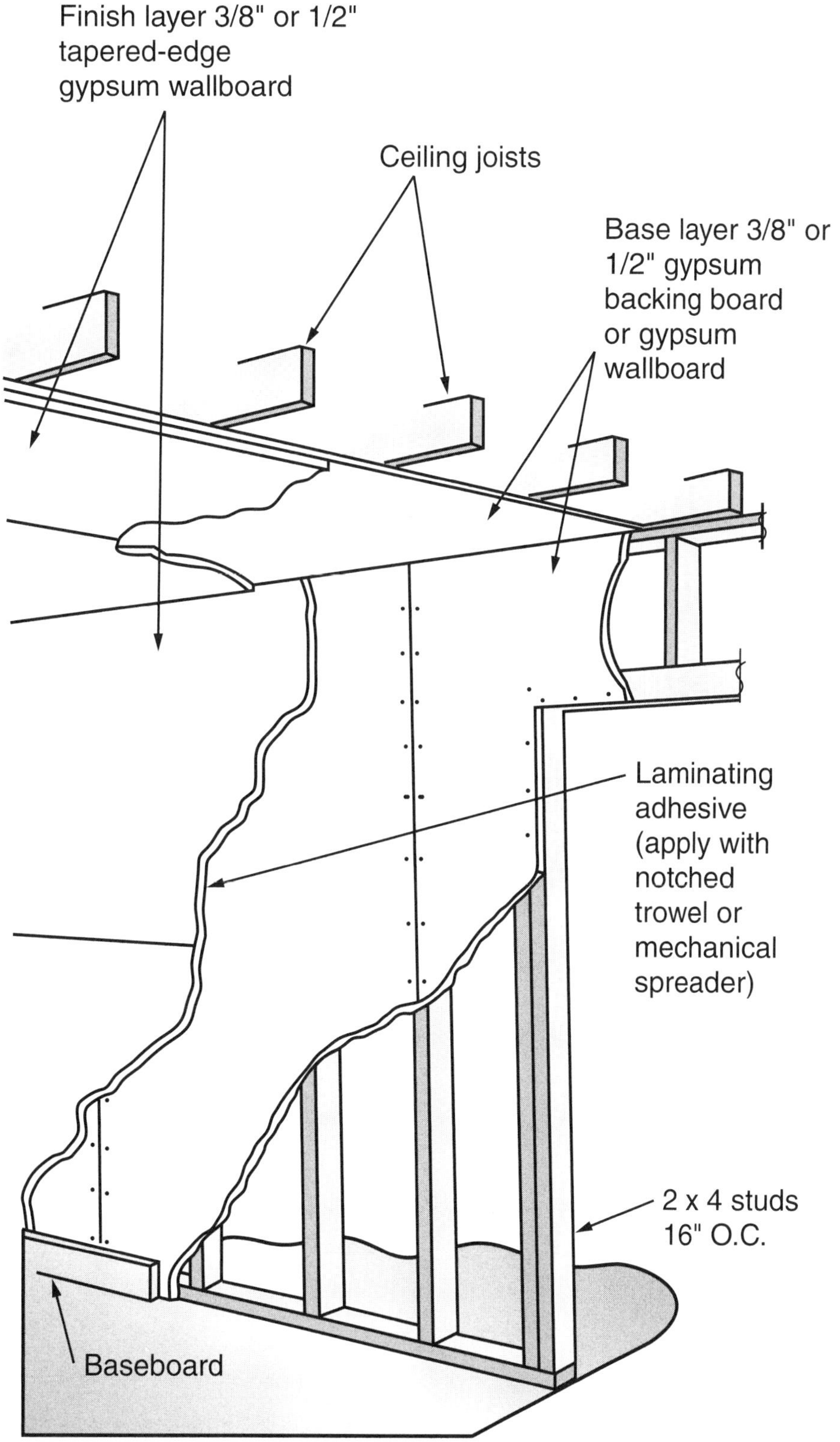

Finish layer 3/8" or 1/2" tapered-edge gypsum wallboard

Ceiling joists

Base layer 3/8" or 1/2" gypsum backing board or gypsum wallboard

Laminating adhesive (apply with notched trowel or mechanical spreader)

2 x 4 studs 16" O.C.

Baseboard

RM 16-1C

Permission granted to reproduce for educational use only.   Copyright by Goodheart-Willcox Co., Inc.

Suspended Ceiling System

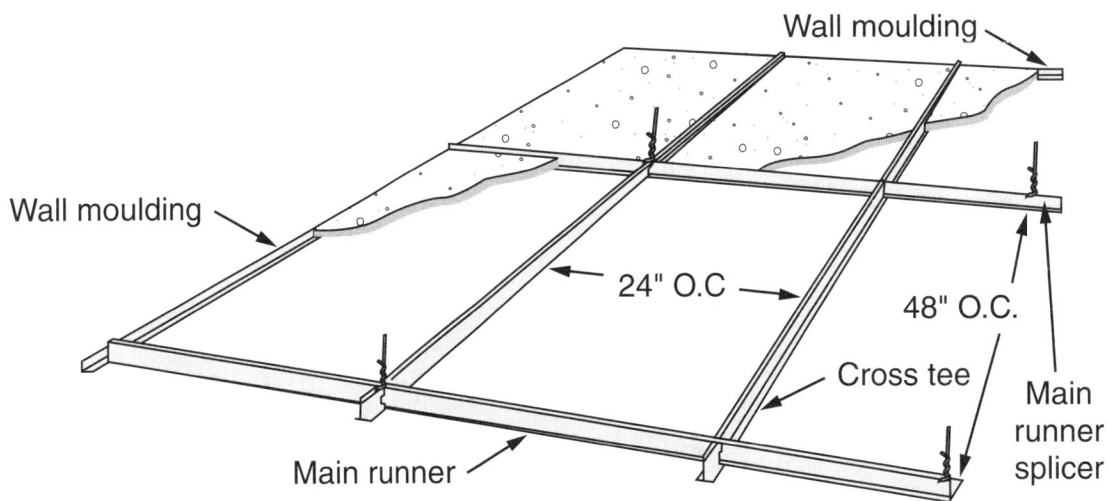

Grid system designed for 24" x 48" panels

Chapter 16 Procedure Checklist
Installing Drywall Using Single-Layer Construction

Name _____ Total _____

❏	Determines whether long edges will be parallel or perpendicular to the studs; carefully makes measurements, taking a reading for each side of the panel.	5	4	3	2	1	Disregards application direction for panels; takes only one measurement when laying out each panel.
❏	Accurately cuts panels using a knife; snaps panel by pressing down on the overhang; smoothes cut if necessary.	5	4	3	2	1	Uses handsaw or power saw to cut panel; produces uneven, inaccurate cut.
❏	Determines proper type of fastener; draws panels tight against studs; affixes panel straight and true.	5	4	3	2	1	Uses common nails for drywall; loosely fits panel against studs.
❏	Applies bedding coat of joint compound to joints; embeds reinforcing tape into joint; applies skim coat over bedding coat; applies joint compound to fastener heads.	5	4	3	2	1	Neglects to apply bedding coat and reinforcing tape; forgets to cover fasteners.
❏	Applies another coat of joint compound after skim coat is completely dry, feathering the edges; applies final coat if necessary; sands all joints and fasteners.	5	4	3	2	1	Neglects to apply final coat of joint compound; does not feather the edges; forgets to sand joints and fasteners.

Permission granted to reproduce for educational use only.   Copyright by Goodheart-Willcox Co., Inc.

Chapter 16 Quiz
Interior Wall and Ceiling Finish

Name _____ Date _____ Score _____

True-False
Circle T if the answer is True or F if the answer is False.

T F 1. Particleboard is commonly referred to as drywall.

T F 2. When nailing drywall to studs, use a nail set to drive the heads of the nails below the surface.

T F 3. Drywall can be glued and/or nailed into position.

T F 4. It is not necessary to allow plywood to adjust to room temperature before using it since it is a manufactured product.

T F 5. When cutting plywood, cut from the back side of the panel.

T F 6. Cement board or backerboard is used only as floor underlayment.

T F 7. In three-coat plaster work, the first coat is the scratch coat, the second coat is the brown coat, and the final coat is the finish coat.

Multiple Choice
Choose the answer that correctly completes the statement. Write the corresponding letter in the space provided.

_____ 8. Straight cuts should be made in drywall with a ____.
   A. reciprocating saw
   B. knife
   C. circular saw
   D. crosscut handsaw

_____ 9. ____ wallboard should be used as a base under ceramic tile in a shower.
   A. Backing
   B. Predecorated
   C. Moisture-resistent
   D. Gypsum

_____ 10. Why is it recommended to install 1/4" plywood over a 1/2" drywall base?
   A. To bring studs into alignment.
   B. To provide a rigid finished surface.
   C. To improve the fire-resistant qualities.
   D. All of the above.

Permission granted to reproduce for educational use only. Copyright by Goodheart-Willcox Co., Inc.

_____ 11. Hardboard is also referred to as ____.
   A. drywall
   B. gypsum wallboard
   C. fiberboard
   D. particleboard

_____ 12. In most residential construction, ____ is used as a base for plaster.
   A. gypsum lath
   B. expanded metal lath
   C. wood lath
   D. Either A or B.

17 Finish Flooring

Objectives

After studying this chapter, students will be able to:
- Describe strip, plank, and unit block wood flooring.
- Lay out and install strip flooring on concrete or plywood subfloors.
- Describe the procedure for applying hardboard, particleboard, waferboard, and plywood underlayment.
- Outline the basic steps for installing resilient flooring.

Instructional Materials

Text: Pages 571–596
  Technical Vocabulary, page 571
  Test Your Knowledge, page 595
  Curricular Connections, page 596
  Outside Assignments, page 596
Workbook: Pages 107–112
Instructor's Resource:
  Reproducible masters:
    RM 17-1A *Installing Strip Flooring*
    RM 17-1B *Nailing Strip Flooring*
    RM 17-1C *Laying Strip Flooring around Barriers*
    RM 17-2 *Strip Flooring Sequence*
    RM 17-3 *Laying Out Parquet Flooring*
  Procedure Checklist: *Installing Wood Strip Flooring*
  Procedure Checklist: *Installing Resilient Flooring*
  Chapter Quiz

Trade-Related Math

To determine the board feet of strip flooring needed to cover a given area, first calculate the area in square feet. Then add a percentage (shown in Figure 17-12) for the particular size being used. For example, if the floor dimensions are 20′ × 20′ and 3/4″ × 2″ wood strip flooring is used, the calculations are:

Total area = width × length
           = 20 × 20
Total area = 400 sq. ft.

Bd. ft. of flooring = floor area + (floor area × percentage)
                   = 400 + (400 × .425)
                   = 400 + 170
Bd. ft. of flooring = 570

Instructional Concepts and Student Learning Experiences

Wood Flooring

1. List the types of hardwoods and softwoods used for wood flooring. Explain why these woods are selected as flooring materials.
2. Have the students identify the four general types of wood flooring used in residential construction, including strip, plank, block, and laminated wood.
3. Identify the common sizes and standard thicknesses of hardwood strip flooring. Mention that random widths are available for hardwood strip flooring.
4. List the range of widths available for hardwood plank flooring.
5. Discuss the factors that are considered when grading wood flooring, including appearance, knots, streaks, color, pinworm holes, and sapwood. Have the students refer to Appendix B in the textbook for additional information regarding the grading of wood flooring.
6. Discuss the purpose of having wood flooring delivered a few days before actual installation.
7. Describe the subflooring that is required for a wood flooring installation.
8. Describe the features of strip flooring, such as the tongue and groove sides and ends

Copyright by Goodheart-Willcox Co., Inc.

and the undercut. Discuss the purpose of these features.
9. Using reproducible master RM 17-1A *Installing Strip Flooring,* describe the preparation necessary before installing wood strip flooring.
10. Explain that strip flooring should be laid at right angles to the floor joists, which is generally the longest dimension of a rectangular room.
11. Referring to Figure 17-6, discuss the size of nails that should be used to nail strip flooring. Mention that the nails should go through the subflooring and into the joists, when possible, to reduce squeaking.
12. Using reproducible master RM 17-1B *Nailing Strip Flooring,* discuss the nailing technique used for wood strip flooring. Emphasize the importance of making certain the first strip is perfectly aligned with a chalk line to ensure that the remainder of the strips will be square.
13. Use reproducible master RM 17-1C *Laying Strip Flooring Around Barriers* as you describe the procedure for laying strip flooring around projections such as walls or partitions.
14. Using reproducible master RM 17-2 *Strip Flooring Sequence,* explain how strip flooring is installed throughout several rooms. Using a corner or portion of a room, demonstrate the procedure for installing wood strip flooring. Double-sided carpet tape can be used to hold the flooring, yet allow it to be disassembled and used another time.
15. Discuss the procedure used to estimate the amount of strip flooring needed for a given area.
16. Describe the steps necessary to prepare a concrete slab for wood strip flooring installation.
17. Explain how the presence of moisture in a concrete slab can be tested.
18. Describe the two procedures that can be used to prepare a slab-on-grade for wood strip flooring installation. Emphasize the importance of preventing moisture from coming into contact with wood strip flooring.

Wood Block (Parquet) Flooring
1. Explain the two methods used to manufacture wood block flooring.
2. Discuss the similarities between preparation of the subfloor for installation of strip flooring and wood block flooring.
3. Using reproducible master RM 17-3 *Laying Out Parquet Flooring,* explain the steps for laying out parquet flooring. Stress the importance of locating the center of the room in both directions and then putting down chalk lines as guides for laying the first blocks. Explain that the same procedure can be used for laying down resilient tile.

Prefinished Wood Flooring
1. Cite advantages and disadvantages of using prefinished wood flooring.
2. Since installation of prefinished flooring is the last step in interior finishing, explain how this affects installation of door jambs and casing.

Laminated Wood Strip Flooring
1. Describe the fabrication of laminated wood strip flooring. Secure one or more samples and show them during your explanation of its history and features.
2. Explain that this flooring type is intended to float on a foam underlayment and should not be fastened to the subflooring.
3. Stress the need to follow the manufacturer's instructions when installing.
4. Secure a copy of a manufacturer's installation manual and have students study it.

Underlayment for Nonwood Floors
1. Identify the types of underlayment that are used for vinyl and linoleum. Describe the type of underlayment that might be required on concrete floors.
2. Discuss the preparation necessary before installing hardboard or particleboard as underlayment.
3. Describe the procedure for installing underlayment (hardboard, particleboard, or cement board). Point out the importance, when using hardboard, of leaving spacing at the perimeter for expansion. Point out that hardboard also requires 1/32″ space between panels, but that particleboard and cement board can be butted at joints.
4. Discuss nail spacing for installing hardboard, particleboard, and cement board.

Note also that nailing patterns may be printed on some types of underlayment.
5. Have students list reasons why carpenters prefer plywood underlayment to hardboard or particleboard.
6. Describe the procedure for installing plywood underlayment. Discuss the nailing pattern used.
7. Use a small scale model with 1″ = 1′-0″ or 1 1/2″ = 1′-0″ scale. Form the layout of a room by nailing or screwing plywood walls (approximately 8″–12″ high) on three sides of another sheet of plywood representing the floor. Mark the direction and position of the joists, and possibly lay out cabinets or other obstacles. Using 1/8″ plywood or hardboard panels cut to scale, demonstrate the layout of the panels. Emphasize the direction of the panels and how they can be positioned to conserve materials.

Resilient Floor Tile
1. Discuss the steps that should be taken after the underlayment has been laid and before the floor tile is installed. Emphasize the importance of having a smooth surface for pliable materials such as vinyl, rubber, and linoleum. Suggest that a layer of felt be applied before the linoleum.
2. Describe the procedure for laying out resilient tile. Discuss the purpose of a trial layout to avoid installing border tiles that are too narrow.
3. Discuss the procedure for spreading adhesives. Stress the importance of spreading the correct amount of adhesive.
4. Explain the procedure used to set the tile in place. Caution students to avoid *sliding* tiles into position. Emphasize the importance of following the manufacturer's recommendations regarding the rolling of the tile after installation.
5. Describe the finishing touches that can be used for resilient tile, including a feature strip, border strip, and/or cove base.

Self-Adhering Tiles
1. Discuss the procedure for installing self-adhering tiles.

Sheet Vinyl Flooring
1. Discuss the procedure for installing sheet vinyl floor covering.
2. Explain the methods used to adhere the covering to the floor.

Chapter Review
1. Review the chapter objectives. Be sure that the students fully understand each objective.
2. Assign *Technical Vocabulary*, *Test Your Knowledge* questions, *Curricular Connections*, and *Outside Assignments* for Chapter 17 of the text. Review the answers in class.
3. Assign Chapter 17 in the workbook. Review the answers in class.

Evaluation
This chapter provides three methods for evaluating student performance. Students should complete the *Test Your Knowledge* section using the book as reference. Students should also be allowed to use the book for reference when completing the workbook material. Use the Chapter 17 Quiz in the instructor's resources for in-class evaluation. Correct the quizzes, return them to the students, and review the quiz questions in group discussion.

Procedure Checklist
Using the procedure checklists *Installing Wood Strip Flooring* and *Installing Resilient Flooring*, have students evaluate the techniques used to perform these tasks.

Answers to Test Your Knowledge
Text Page 595
1. Any material used as the final surface of a floor.
2. Strip, laminated strip, plank, and block.
3. 1/2″
4. False.
5. spline
6. 24
7. laminated

8. False.
9. glueless, glued
10. It is dimensionally stable, impervious to water, and suited for use under ceramic tile floors.
11. linoleum
12. center
13. Same procedure as for standard tiles, except adhesive is not spread on the underlayment.
14. Impervious tile would be preferable since it does not absorb water.
15. sanded grout

Answers to Workbook Questions
Pages 107–112
1. Finish
2. C. 3/4"
3. B. clear
4. D. 16"
5. Portable nailer.
6. A. 1/2"
   B. Face nail.
   C. Blind nail.
   D. 50°
7. B. 8"
8. spline
9. Bd. ft.: 614
   Bundles: 26
10. Bd. ft.: 489
    Bundles: 21
11. A. 3/4" strip flooring.
    B. 1 × 2 strip.
    C. Polyethylene film.
    D. Lap.
    E. Polyethylene film.
12. B. laying out several rows of strip flooring prior to toenailing them in place.
13. C. Time is saved since prefinished units can be butted directly against baseboards.
14. Fiberboard
15. Using a tapping block to drive tongues into grooves.
16. A. 24
17. A. 6"
    B. 3"
18. telegraphing
19. 1/32"
20. C. 5'
21. B. one-fourth
22. wax
23. D. 12'

Answers to Chapter Quiz
1. True.
2. False.
3. True.
4. True.
5. False.
6. True.
7. True.
8. C. plywood
9. B. at the center
10. A. along one sidewall
11. A. 1/4"
12. C.
13. B.
14. D.
15. A.

Installing Strip Flooring

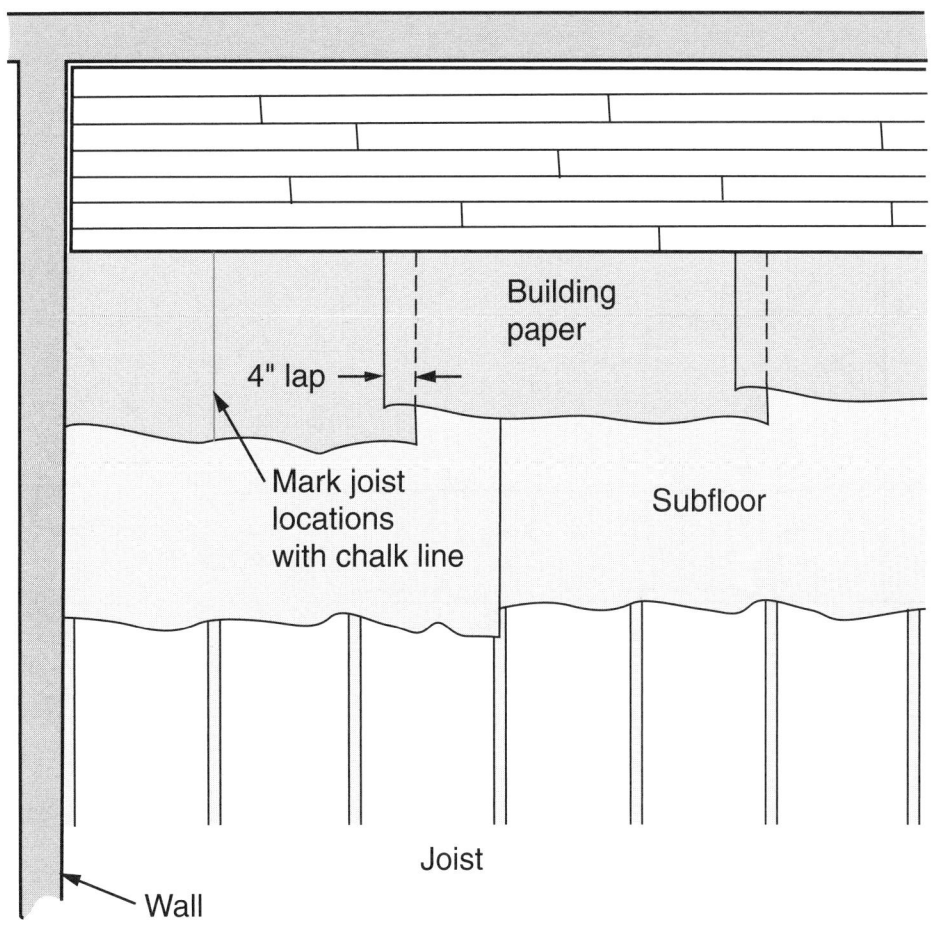

RM 17-1A

Nailing Strip Flooring

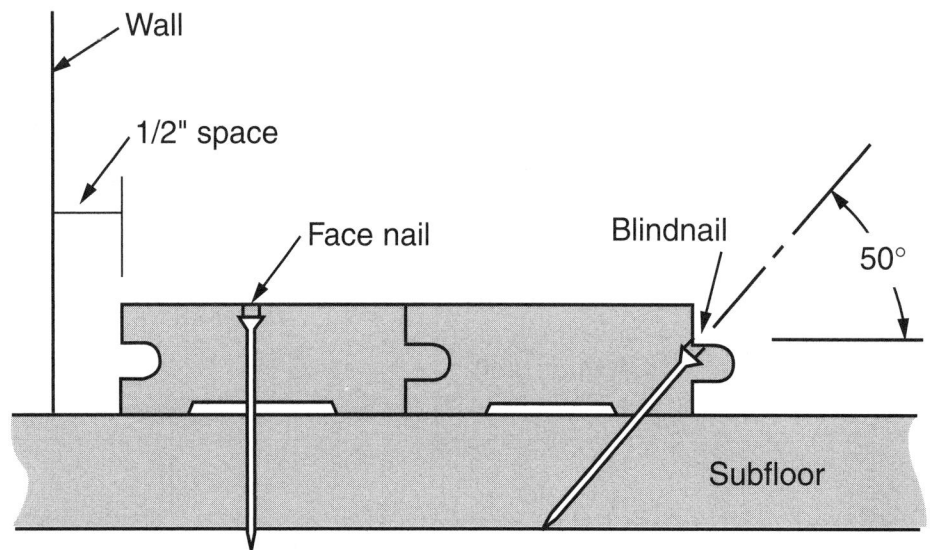

RM 17-1B

Laying Strip Flooring around Barriers

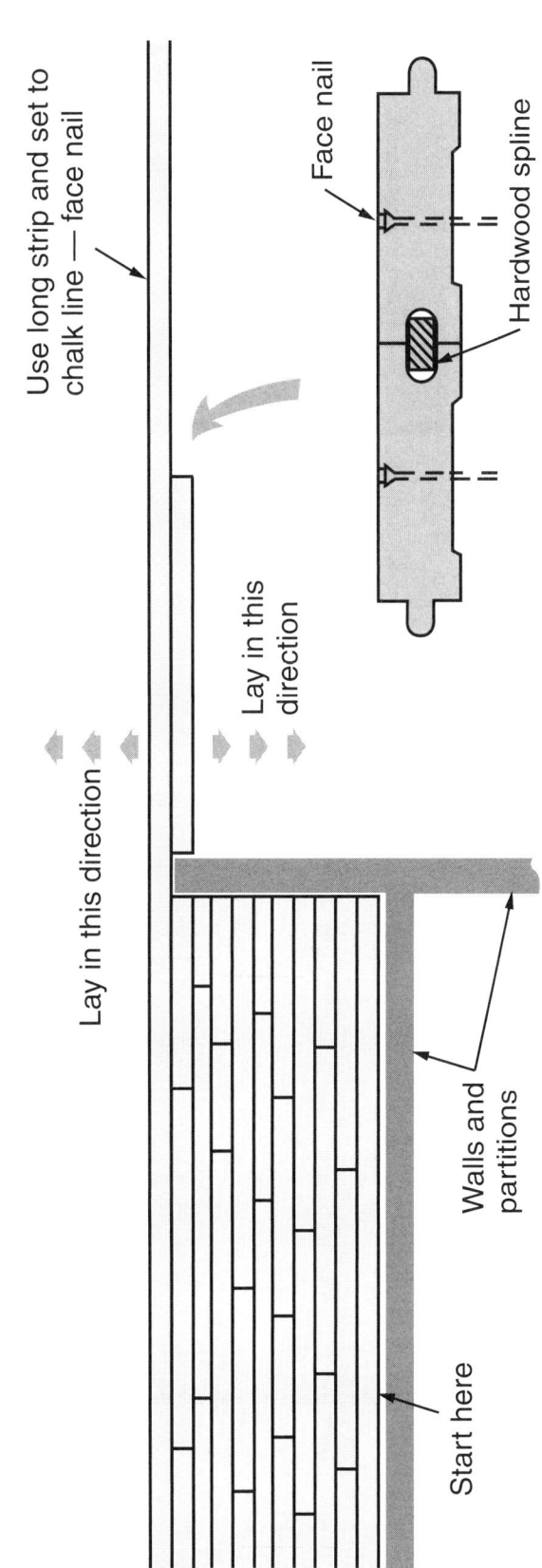

RM 17-1C

336

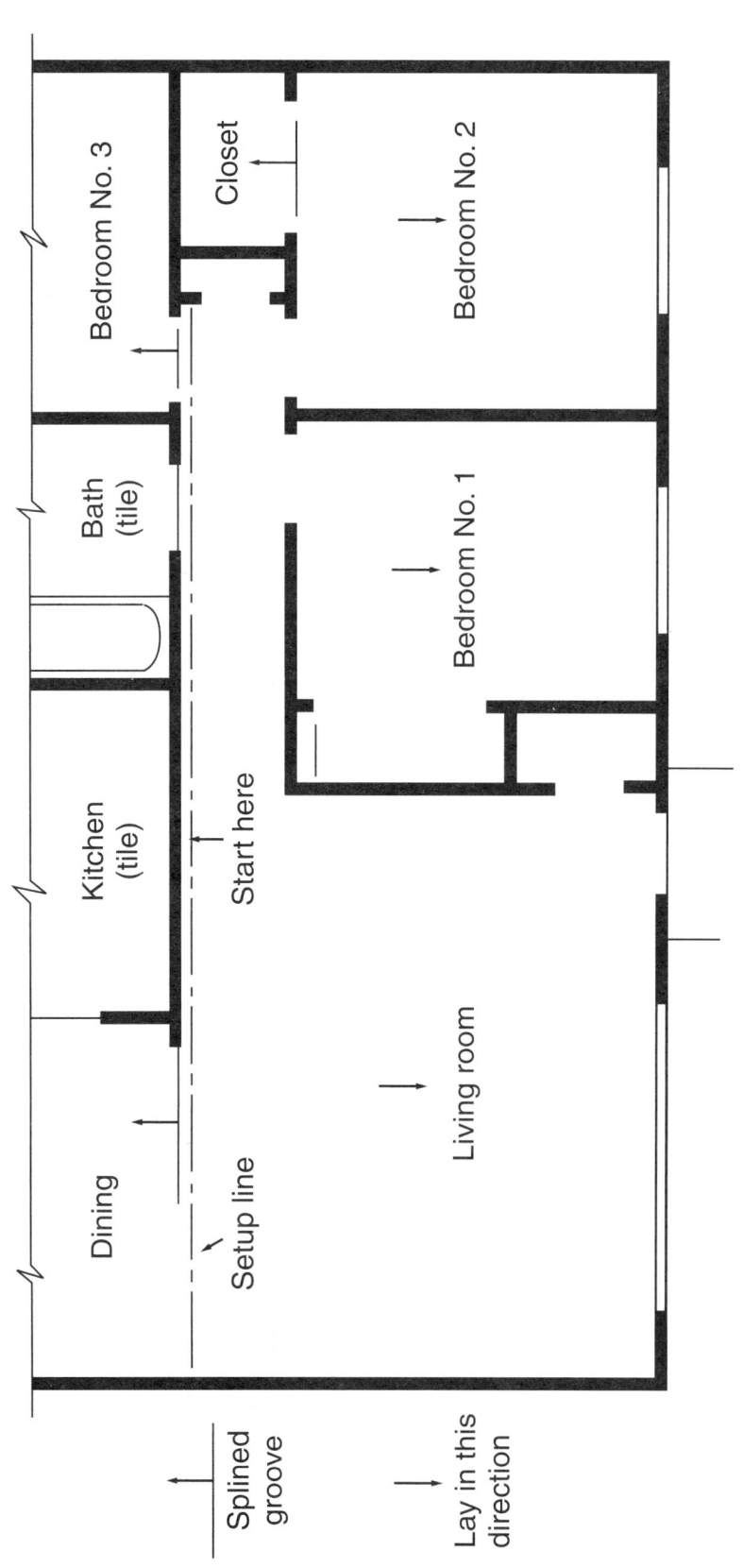

RM 17-2

Laying Out Parquet Flooring

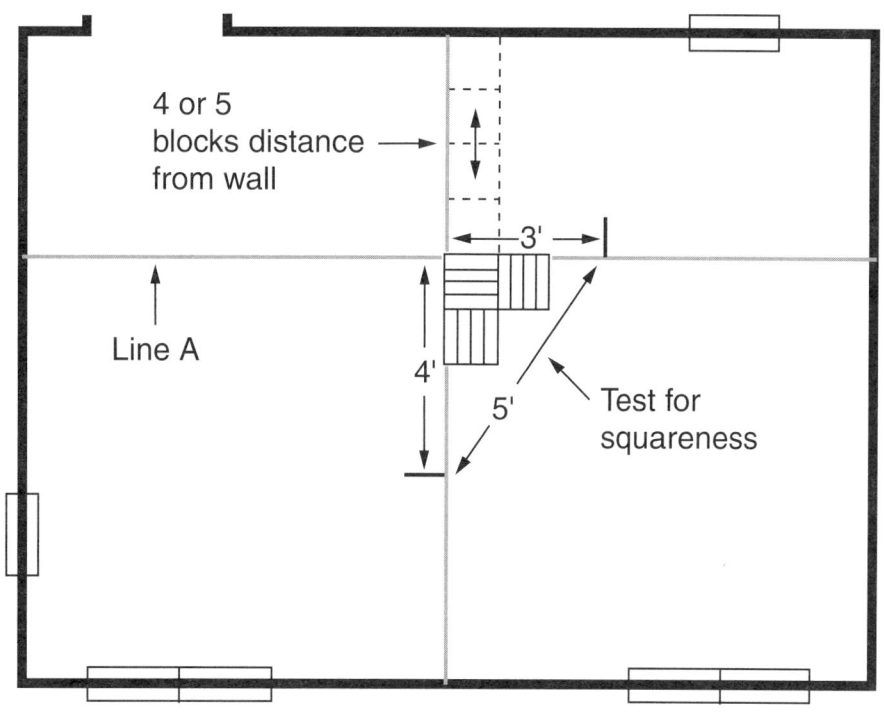

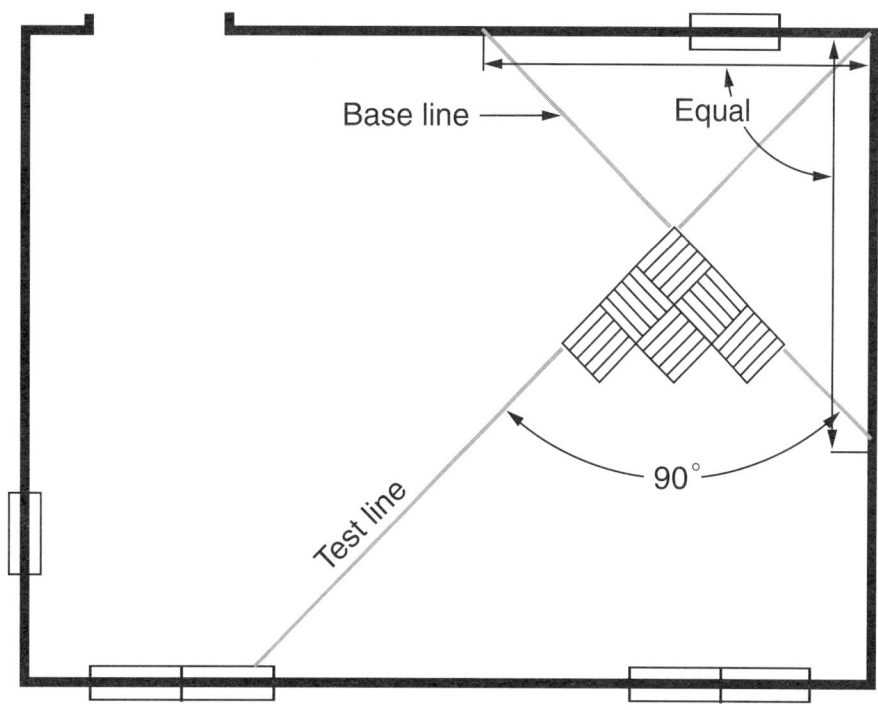

RM 17-3

Chapter 17 Procedure Checklist
Installing Wood Strip Flooring

Name _____ Total _____

❏	Checks subfloor to make sure it is clean and that nail patterns are complete; lays down good-quality building paper, lapping it properly; snaps chalk lines on paper indicating floor joists; applies building paper over ductwork that projects through floor.	5	4	3	2	1	Disregards the condition of subfloor; neglects to lay down building paper; does not snap chalk lines; does not apply building paper over ductwork.
❏	Determines the best direction for strip flooring; selects appropriate type of nails for flooring installation.	5	4	3	2	1	Does not consider joist direction when determining direction for strip flooring; does not select proper type of flooring nail.
❏	Lays the first strip along a sidewall, allowing 1/2" space along edge; makes sure the first strip is accurately aligned; properly nails the first strip.	5	4	3	2	1	Starts laying wood strips in the center of floor; neglects to check alignment of strip.
❏	Blind nails succeeding strips; uses a nail set to finish nailing; tightly fits succeeding strips; does not align joints in flooring.	5	4	3	2	1	Face nails all strips; does not blind nail strip flooring; aligns joints in adjacent pieces.

Permission granted to reproduce for educational use only. Copyright by Goodheart-Willcox Co., Inc.

Chapter 17 Procedure Checklist
Installing Resilient Flooring

Name _____ Total _____

❏	Installs appropriate underlayment; sweeps and vacuums surface carefully; checks to make sure surfaces are smooth and joints are level; installs base material (if necessary).	5	4	3	2	1	Neglects to install proper underlayment; forgets to sweep and/or vacuum surface; disregards smoothness of surface and joints; neglects to install base material (if needed).
❏	Locates center of tile layout and snaps a chalk line; lays out a second centerline at a right angle to the main one and snaps a chalk line; makes trial layout of tiles in both directions.	5	4	3	2	1	Neglects to lay out the center of room with chalk lines; does not make trial layout.
❏	Removes loose tiles; cleans floor surface; spreads adhesive over one-quarter of room; allows initial set before tile is laid.	5	4	3	2	1	Neglects to clean floor; spreads adhesive over most of room; begins laying tiles as soon as adhesive is spread.
❏	Starts laying tile at the center of the room, making sure edges align with the chalk line; butts adjacent tiles and carefully lays them into place.	5	4	3	2	1	Starts laying tiles along sidewall, disregarding chalk lines; sloppily places tile into position.
❏	Carefully cuts border tiles and sets into position; rolls tile (if necessary).	5	4	3	2	1	Neglects to install border tiles; forgets to roll tile (if required).

Permission granted to reproduce for educational use only. Copyright by Goodheart-Willcox Co., Inc.

Chapter 17 Quiz
Finish Flooring

Name _____ Date _____ Score _____

True-False
Circle T if the answer is True or F if the answer is False.

T F 1. Grading of wood flooring is based on the appearance of the material.

T F 2. Strip flooring should be laid parallel to the floor joists when possible.

T F 3. Conventional subflooring can also be used as underlayment.

T F 4. When laying linoleum, a base layer of felt is recommended.

T F 5. When installing wood strip flooring, carefully align the joints in successive courses.

T F 6. Perimeter-bonded flooring is fastened down only around the edges and at seams.

T F 7. Wood strip flooring can be installed directly over a concrete floor if the floor is suspended with an air space below.

Multiple Choice
Choose the answer that correctly completes the statement. Write the corresponding letter in the space provided.

_____ 8. In construction, _____ is commonly used as a subfloor.
   A. good-quality lumber
   B. gypsum wallboard
   C. plywood
   D. planks

_____ 9. When installing resilient tile, start _____ of the room.
   A. along one sidewall
   B. at the center
   C. at opposite ends
   D. None of the above.

_____ 10. When installing wood strip flooring, start _____ of the room.
   A. along one sidewall
   B. at the center
   C. at opposite ends
   D. None of the above.

_____ 11. Use _____ hardboard for underlayment.
   A. 1/4"
   B. 1/2"
   C. 3/4"
   D. 1"

Permission granted to reproduce for educational use only. Copyright by Goodheart-Willcox Co., Inc.

Identification

Identify the parts of the following section of strip flooring.

_____ 12. Undercut.

_____ 13. Tongue

_____ 14. Groove.

_____ 15. Face width.

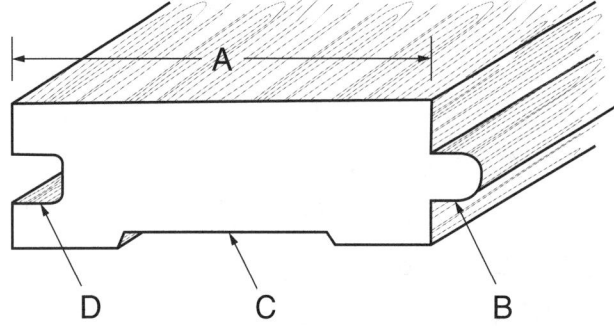

18 Stair Construction

Objectives

After studying this chapter, students will be able to:
- Identify the various types of stairs.
- Define basic stair parts and terms.
- Calculate the rise-run ratio, number and size of risers, and stairwell length.
- Prepare sketches of the types of stringers.
- Lay out stringers for a given stair rise and run.
- List prefabricated stair parts that are commonly available.

Instructional Materials

Text: Pages 597–618
  Technical Vocabulary, page 597
  Test Your Knowledge, page 616
  Curricular Connections, page 616
  Outside Assignments, page 616
Workbook: Pages 113-118
Instructor's Resource:
  Reproducible masters:
    RM 18-1A *Stair Terminology*
    RM 18-1B *Stair Designs*
    RM 18-2 *Calculating Sizes of Stair Treads and Risers and Laying Out Stringers*
    RM 18-3 *Stringer Types*
  Transparencies (binder/CD only):
    CT 18-1 *Stair Terminology*
    CT 18-2 *Sizing Stairwells and Determining Rise and Run*
  Chapter Quiz

Trade-Related Math

To calculate the number and size of risers and treads (less the nosing) for a given stair run, first divide the total rise by 7. For example, if the total rise for a basement stairway is 8′-4″ or 100″, the answer is 14.29″. Since there must be a whole number of risers, select the one closest to 14.29″ and divide it into the total rise.

$100″ \div 14 = 7.14″$ or $7\ 1/64″$
Number of risers = 14
Riser height = $7\ 1/64″$

In any stairway, the number of treads is always one less than the number of risers. A 10 1/2″ tread is correct for the example and the total run can be calculated as follows:

Number of treads = 13
Total run = $10\ 1/2 \times 13$
= 136.5″
Total run = 11′-4 1/2″

Instructional Concepts and Student Learning Experiences

Types of Stairs
1. Describe how the construction of stairways has evolved over the years. Explain when stairways are typically installed in a construction project.
2. Identify the two main types of stairs—main stairs and service stairs. Explain that these two types can be open, closed, or a combination of open and closed. Ask students to identify the type of stairs, if any, in their homes.

Stair Parts
1. Using reproducible master RM 18-1A *Stair Terminology*, discuss components and terms related to stair construction. Be sure that students can distinguish between unit run and rise and total run and rise.
2. Stress the importance of accurate layout and construction of any stairway. Describe the types of trimmers and headers that should be used and where framing anchors should be installed.

3. Referring to reproducible master RM 18-1B *Stair Designs*, discuss the various stairway designs.

Stair Design
1. Identify the three generally accepted rules for calculating the rise-run or riser-tread ratio. Give the students hypothetical riser and/or tread dimensions and have them determine the other dimension using the three rules.
2. Discuss problems that may occur if an incorrect riser-tread ratio is used in stair construction. Emphasize the importance of making all risers the same height and all treads the same width when constructing a stairway.
3. Identify the stairway and handrail dimensions that are recommended by some of the model building codes. Have the students refer to the local building code to determine the recommended dimensions for stairways and handrails in your area.
4. Review the stair details included in a set of stock plans or other available residential plans. Point out the dimensions that will be used for the stair construction, including the riser height, tread width, stringer size, and rough opening.

Stair Calculations
1. Describe the procedure for calculating stair dimensions. Given a hypothetical total run and total rise, have the students calculate number of treads and risers, as well as the dimensions of each. As they begin this exercise, display the procedure in reproducible master RM 18-2 *Calculating Sizes of Stair Treads and Risers and Laying Out Stringers*.

Stringer Layout
1. Explain how the riser height is determined using a story pole. Describe how these dimensions are transferred to a stringer and laid out with a framing square. Once again, stress the importance of accuracy.

Treads and Risers
1. Identify the materials that are commonly used for treads and risers of main stairs.
2. Using Figure 18-18, define the term *nosing* and discuss the various designs.
3. Describe the basic stair riser shapes: vertical, sloping, and open.

Types of Stringers
1. Using reproducible master RM 18-3 *Stringer Types*, identify the three main types of construction used for stringers, open riser, semihoused, and housed. Also describe or show examples of a cleated stringer. Describe the method of construction used in each.
2. Discuss how a housed stringer stairway is constructed.

Winder Stairs
1. Discuss the complaints that are commonly associated with winder stairs.
2. Describe how the wider tread width is determined for winder stairs.

Open Stairs
1. Using Figure 18-25, identify the parts of an open stair. Stress the importance of securely anchoring the starting newel post to the starting step or carrying it down through the floor and attaching it to the floor framing.

Spiral Stairways
1. Describe the advantages offered by spiral stairways in residential construction.

Disappearing Stair Units
1. Define *disappearing stairs* and how they are used in residential construction.

Chapter Review
1. Review the chapter objectives. Be sure that the students fully understand each objective.
2. Assign *Technical Vocabulary, Test Your Knowledge* questions, *Curricular Connections*, and *Outside Assignments* for Chapter 18 of the text. Review the answers in class.
3. Assign Chapter 18 in the workbook. Review the answers in class.

Evaluation
This chapter provides three methods for evaluating student performance. Students should complete the *Test Your Knowledge* section using the book as reference. Students should also be allowed to use the book for reference when completing the workbook material. Use

the Chapter 18 Quiz in the instructor's resources for in-class evaluation. Correct the quizzes, return them to the students, and review the quiz questions in group discussion.

Answers to Test Your Knowledge
Text Page 616
1. landings
2. 6'-8"
3. 24"–25"
4. nosing
5. 5'-6" (66")
6. False.
7. cut-out
8. Wedges
9. balusters
10. regular

Answers to Workbook Questions
Pages 113-118
1. underlayment
2. 3'
3. A. Open.
   B. Open.
   C. Closed.
   D. Combination.
4. A. 4'
5. A. Tread.
   B. Riser.
   C. Unit run.
   D. Unit rise.
   E. Total run.
   F. Total rise.
   G. Headroom.
6. C. 30°–35°
7. C. 24–25
8. B. 11 1/2"–12 1/2"
9. B. 2'-8"
10. A. 36"
    B. 30"
    C. 34"
    D. 42"
11. No. of risers: 15
    Riser height: 7 1/8"
    No. of treads: 14
    Tread width: 10 3/4"
12. 12'-6 1/2"
13. story pole
14. C. shortening the bottom riser by an amount equal to tread thickness
15. A. 1 1/2"
    B. decreased
16. A. Vertical.
    B. Sloping.
    C. Open.
17. B. one-third
18. semi-housed
19. D. 3/4"
20. outside
21. A. Newel post.
    B. Baluster.
    C. Handrail.
    D. Nosing.
    E. Stringer.
22. screwdriver, nail set and hammer
23. C. Newel
24. millwork

Answers to Chapter Quiz
1. True.
2. False.
3. True.
4. True.
5. E.
6. F.
7. C.
8. D.
9. B.
10. H.
11. J.
12. I.
13. G.
14. A.
15. B. headroom
16. C. 17"–18"
17. B. 3'-0"
18. D. stringers
19. A. balustrade

Stair Terminology

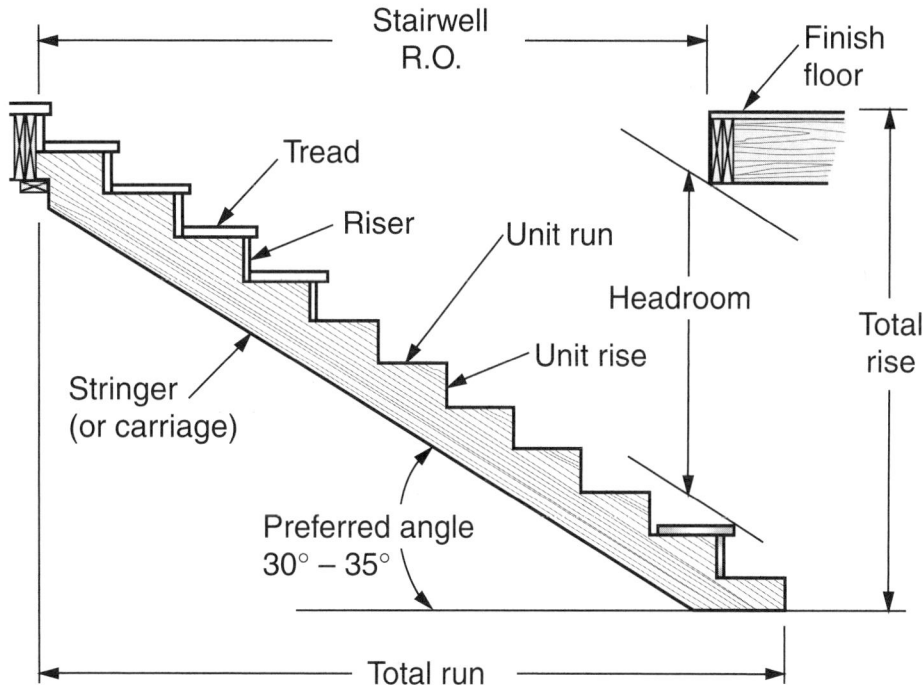

RM 18-1A

Stair Designs

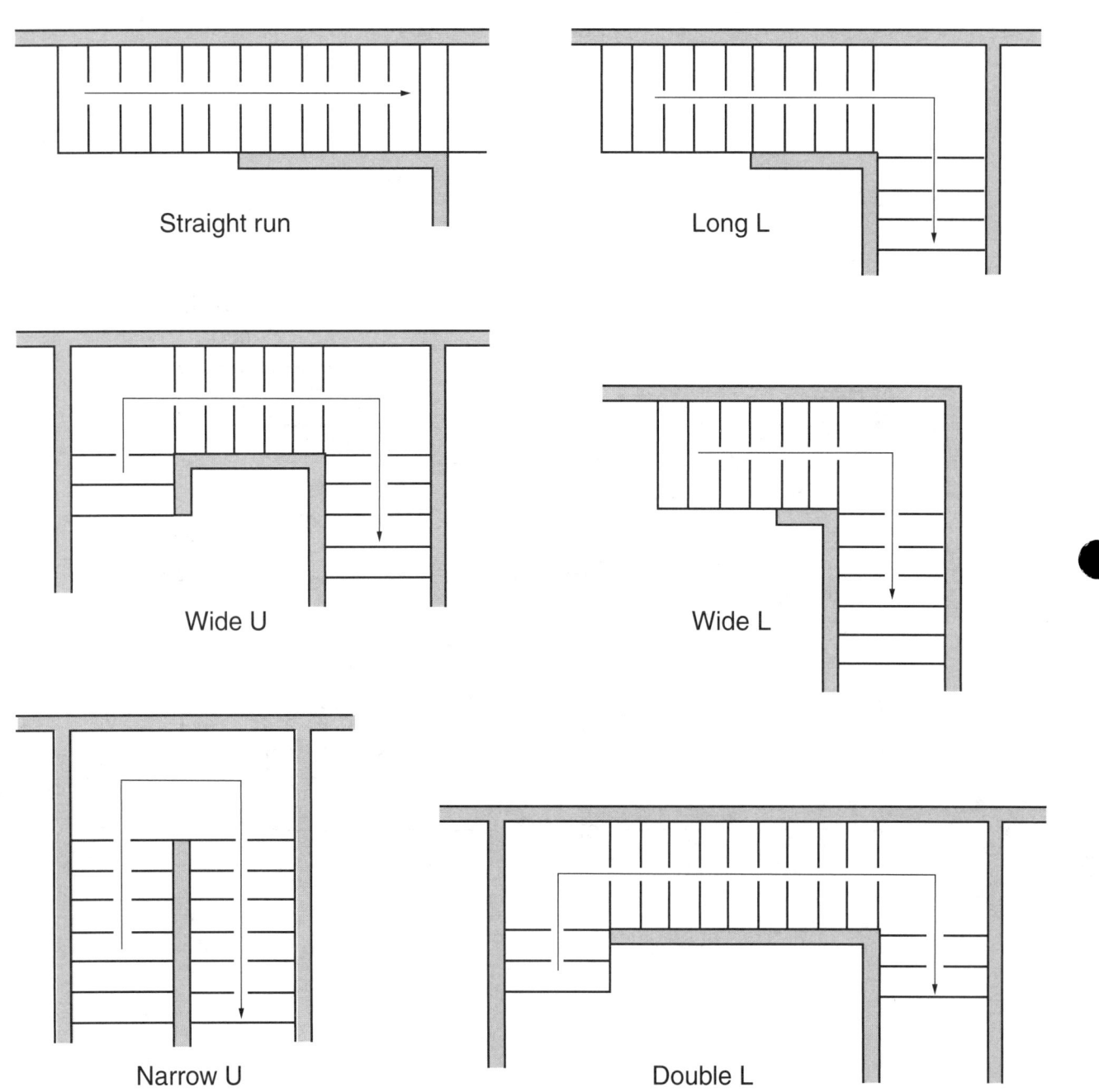

RM 18-1B

Calculating Sizes of Stair Treads and Risers and Laying Out Stringers

Note: These calculations must be made during framing of the upper floor to find the size of the stairwell.

1. Measure the total rise (finish floor to finish floor).

2. Divide rise by 7 or 8 to find the number of risers needed.

3. If the result is a whole number and a fraction, go to the nearest whole number.

4. There will always be one less tread than risers.

5. Choose a tread width and multiply by the number of treads to get the run.

6. Use the run to frame in the stair opening in the floor frame.

7. Lay out the first stringer.

    a. On a story pole, mark off the total rise. Measure from the top of the finish floor above to the top of the finish floor below.

    b. Set a pair of dividers to a single riser height and step off each rise distance on the story pole. If these results are more or less than the total rise on the story pole, adjust the dividers until the step off comes out even.

    c. Set up the rise and run on a carpenter's square and use the step-off method to mark the stringer for treads and risers.

8. Lay out one or more stringers in the same manner.

RM 18-2

Stringer Types

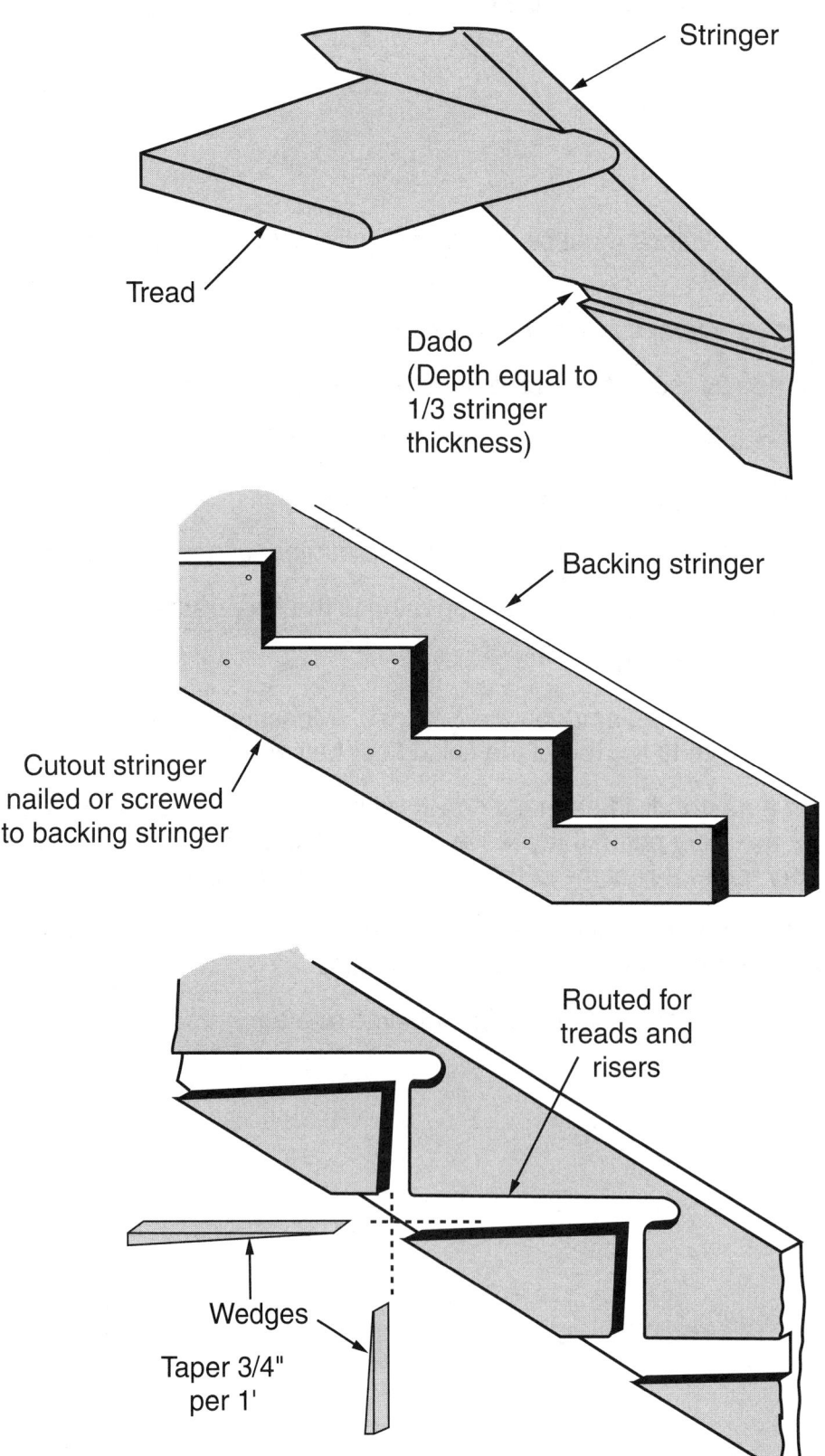

RM 18-3

Chapter 18 Quiz
Stair Construction

Name _____ Date _____ Score _____

True-False
Circle T if the answer is True or F if the answer is False.

T F 1. Along with the revival of traditional home styles, split level and multilevel designs have made stair construction an important skill.

T F 2. The carriage is a vertical support for stairs and is attached to the stairs at their highest point.

T F 3. A carpenter can calculate the size of a rough opening of a stairwell if it is not shown in the architectural drawing.

T F 4. Simple dados are often cut for stair stringers where risers will not be used.

Identification
Identify the basic stair parts and related terms.
5. Unit run.
6. Unit rise.
7. Tread.
8. Riser.
9. Finish floor.
10. Total rise.
11. Total run.
12. Stringer.
13. Headroom.
14. Stairwell rough opening.

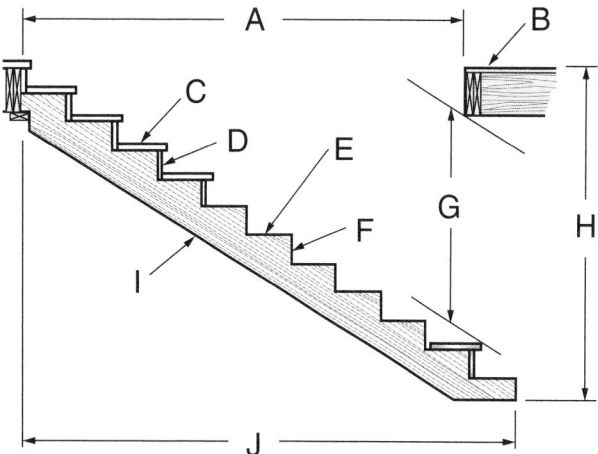

Multiple Choice

Choose the answer that correctly completes the statement. Write the corresponding letter in the space provided.

15. The vertical space above the stair is the ____.
    A. total rise
    B. headroom
    C. unit rise
    D. None of the above.
16. The sum of one riser and one tread should equal ____.
    A. 9"–10"
    B. 13"–14"
    C. 17"–18"
    D. 21"–22"
17. A minimum width of ____ is generally recommended for main stairs.
    A. 2'-6"
    B. 3'-0"
    C. 3'-6"
    D. 4'-0"
18. Treads and risers are supported by the ____.
    A. finish floor
    B. tail joists
    C. headers
    D. stringers
19. The principal members of a(n) ____ are the newel, baluster, and handrail.
    A. balustrade
    B. open stringer
    C. closed stringer
    D. winding stair

19 Doors and Interior Trim

Objectives

After studying this chapter, students will be able to:
- Describe how door frames and casings are installed.
- Explain the difference between panel- and flush-type doors.
- List the steps for hanging a door.
- Name lock parts and describe typical installation procedures.
- Compare the pocket and bypass types of sliding doors.
- Outline the order in which window trim members should be applied.
- Cut, fit, and nail baseboard trim.

Instructional Materials

Text: Pages 619–646
  Technical Vocabulary, page 619
  Test Your Knowledge, page 645
  Curricular Connections, page 645
  Outside Assignments, page 646
Workbook: Pages 119–126
Instructor's Resource:
  Reproducible masters:
    RM 19-1A *Typical Mouldings*
    RM 19-1B *Typical Mouldings*
    RM 19-2 *Casing Interior Doors*
    RM 19-3A *Installing Baseboard and Base Shoe*
    RM 19-3B *Installing Baseboard and Base Shoe*
  Procedure Checklist: *Installing Baseboards and Base Shoe*
  Chapter Quiz

Trade-Related Math

The amount of base trim required is determined by calculating the perimeter of the room and adding 5% for waste. The perimeter of a room is determined by adding the overall dimensions. When the room is square or rectangular, twice the width can be added to twice the length of the room. For example, if the room dimensions are 8′ × 14′, determine the perimeter:

Perimeter = 2W + 2L
          = (2 × 8′) + (2 × 14′)
Perimeter = 44′

Five percent waste is then calculated as follows:

Total linear feet = perimeter + (perimeter × 5%)
                  = 44′ + (44′ × .05)
                  = 44′ + 2.2′
Total linear feet = 46.2′

Or save a step and multiply (1.05 × 44′) = 46.2′

Instructional Concepts and Student Learning Experiences

Mouldings
1. Describe the purpose of mouldings and identify the mouldings shown in reproducible masters RM 19-1A and 19-1B *Typical Mouldings*.

Interior Door Frames
1. Identify the components of a door frame. Discuss the types of materials used for door frames. Explain why the back sides of jambs are usually kerfed.
2. Secure an adjustable doorjamb and describe how it can be adjusted to accommodate different wall thicknesses.

Installing Door Frames
1. Describe the installation procedure used for interior door frames. Explain the purpose of the spreader that is commonly used between the side jambs. Demonstrate the techniques used for installing door frames.

2. Using reproducible master RM 19-2 *Casing Interior Doors*, explain the purpose of a door casing. Have the students note that the casing covers the blocking and is attached to the jamb and wall surface.
3. Describe how the side pieces are laid out and cut. List the types of nails used to attach them to the jamb and studs and how they are attached.

Panel Doors
1. Identify the two general types of doors: panel and flush. Cite characteristics of each.
2. Identify the parts of a panel door, and list some of the materials used for these parts.

Flush Doors
1. Describe the construction of flush doors by referring to Figure 19-13. Identify the types of materials used in their construction.
2. List the standard sizes for interior and exterior doors used in residential construction.
3. Identify the interior door designs shown in Figure 19-14.

Door Installation
1. List the two pieces of information regarding doors that can be determined from the architectural drawings and door schedule.
2. Cite reasons why doors should not be cut to fit smaller openings.
3. Discuss the storage methods that should be used for doors. Have the students explain why doors should be conditioned a few days before installation.
4. Identify the recommended clearances for interior doors. Describe how doors can be trimmed to exact size. Explain the purpose of beveling the edge on the lock side and rounding all edges of the door.
5. Demonstrate the use of a door-and-jamb template, if one is available. Emphasize the importance of accuracy when cutting gains.
6. Discuss the procedure used to mount the hinges on a door and jamb. Demonstrate this procedure as well.
7. Explain the purpose of a doorstop. Describe how one is installed.
8. Using Figure 19-20, identify the types of lock sets that are used in residential construction. Have the students rate the locks based on security and ease of installation.
9. Using Figure 19-15, discuss how to determine the hand of the door. Determine the hand of the door for doors in your classroom or on working drawings.
10. Discuss the purpose of a deadbolt.

Door Locks
1. Describe how locks are installed. Explain that the locks are commonly installed 36″ to 38″ from the floor.
2. Identify the various tools that can be used to drill the holes for locks and make the mortise for the faceplate.

Thresholds and Door Sweeps
1. Explain the purpose of a threshold and list the materials that are used to make them.
2. Discuss materials and methods for sealing the space at door bottoms.

Prehung Door Unit
1. Identify the advantages of using prehung door units.
2. Describe the procedure for installing prehung doors.

Pocket Doors
1. Identify the primary advantage of pocket-type bypass doors. Describe the installation procedure required for this type of bypass door.

Sliding Bypass Doors
1. Discuss the procedure for installing sliding bypass doors.
2. Identify the hardware components used for sliding bypass doors.

Bifold Doors
1. Using Figure 19-31, describe the hardware components that are commonly used for folding doors.

Multifold Doors
1. Have the students list applications for multi-panel folding doors. In addition, have them identify advantages of this type of door.

Window Trim
1. Using Figure 19-35, identify the trim members used for a double-hung window.
2. Describe the procedure for installing trim around a window.
3. Demonstrate the procedure for cutting a returned end. Discuss the purpose of a returned end.

Baseboard and Base Shoe
1. Discuss the installation of the baseboard and base shoe using reproducible master RM 19-3A *Installing Baseboard and Base Shoe*. Mention that even though the baseboard and base shoe are fitted at the same time, the base shoe usually is not nailed into position until after the floor surface finishes are applied.
2. Using reproducible master RM 19-3B *Installing Baseboard and Base Shoe,* identify where coped joints and miter joints will be used. Demonstrate the procedure for cutting coped and mitered joints for baseboard trim members.

Chapter Review
1. Review the chapter objectives. Be sure that the students fully understand each objective.
2. Assign *Technical Vocabulary, Test Your Knowledge* questions, *Curricular Connections,* and *Outside Assignments* for Chapter 19 of the text. Review the answers in class.
3. Assign Chapter 19 in the workbook. Review the answers in class.

Evaluation
This chapter provides three methods for evaluating student performance. Students should complete the *Test Your Knowledge* section using the book as reference. Students should also be allowed to use the book for reference when completing the workbook material. Use the Chapter 19 Quiz in the instructor's resources for in-class evaluation. Correct the quizzes, return them to the students, and review the quiz questions in group discussion.

Procedure Checklist
Using the procedure checklist *Installing Baseboards and Base Shoe,* have students evaluate the techniques used to perform these tasks.

Copyright by Goodheart-Willcox Co., Inc.

Answers to Test Your Knowledge
Text Page 645
1. shape
2. 5 1/4
3. prehung door unit
4. door casing or trim
5. A setback from the edge of the frame of about 1/8" or 3/16" that allows room for hinges and strike plate while improving the appearance of the trim.
6. A plinth block is a decorative corner trim used on door frames and window frames. It eliminates mitered corners.
7. False.
8. stiles
9. skins
10. solid, hollow
11. 2'-6"
12. 1/16"
13. tubular
14. Double-cylinder
15. To seal the space between the bottom of the door and the sill.
16. pocket door
17. bifold door
18. stool, apron
19. mitered-lap or scarf
20. coped

Answers to Workbook Questions
Pages 119–126
1. A. Base shoe.
   B. Bed moulds.
   C. Quarter round.
   D. Cove moulds.
   E. Door/window stops.
   F. Mullion casing.
   G. Apron.
   H. Stool.
2. C. 5 1/4"
3. A. Lug.
   B. Head jamb.
   C. Side jamb.
4. 6'-9"
5. C. 8d
6. A. 1 3/4"
   B. 1 3/8"

7. A. 3/16″
   B. Side jamb.
   C. Blocking.
   D. Casing.
8. D. Use 8d casing or finish nails to secure the casing to the jamb and space them about 10″ apart.
9. B. horizontal
   A. vertical
10. A. Stiles.
    B. Rails.
    C. Panels.
11. A Top rail.
    B. Mullion.
    C. Panel.
    D. Lock or intermediate rail.
    E. Stile.
    F. Bottom rail.
12. B. 40%
13. A 3/32″
    B. 1/16″
    C. 1/16″
    D. 5/8″
14. D. 3 1/2°
15. B. 1/16″
16. A. Cylindrical.
    B. Mortise.
    C. Unit lock set.
    D. Tubular.
17. deadbolt or deadlock
18. A. LH.
    B. RH.
    C. LHR.
    D. RHR.
19. 38″
20. A. templates
21. pocket door
22. bifold
23. bypass
24. D. stack
25. A. Miter.
    B. Head casing.
    C. Mullion trim.
    D. Side casing.
    E. Stool.
    F. Apron.

Answers to Chapter Quiz

1. C. 36″–38″
2. D. left-hand
3. B. baseboard
4. D.
5. B.
6. A.
7. E.
8. C.
9. D.
10. C.
11. G.
12. A.
13. B.
14. E.
15. F.

Typical Mouldings

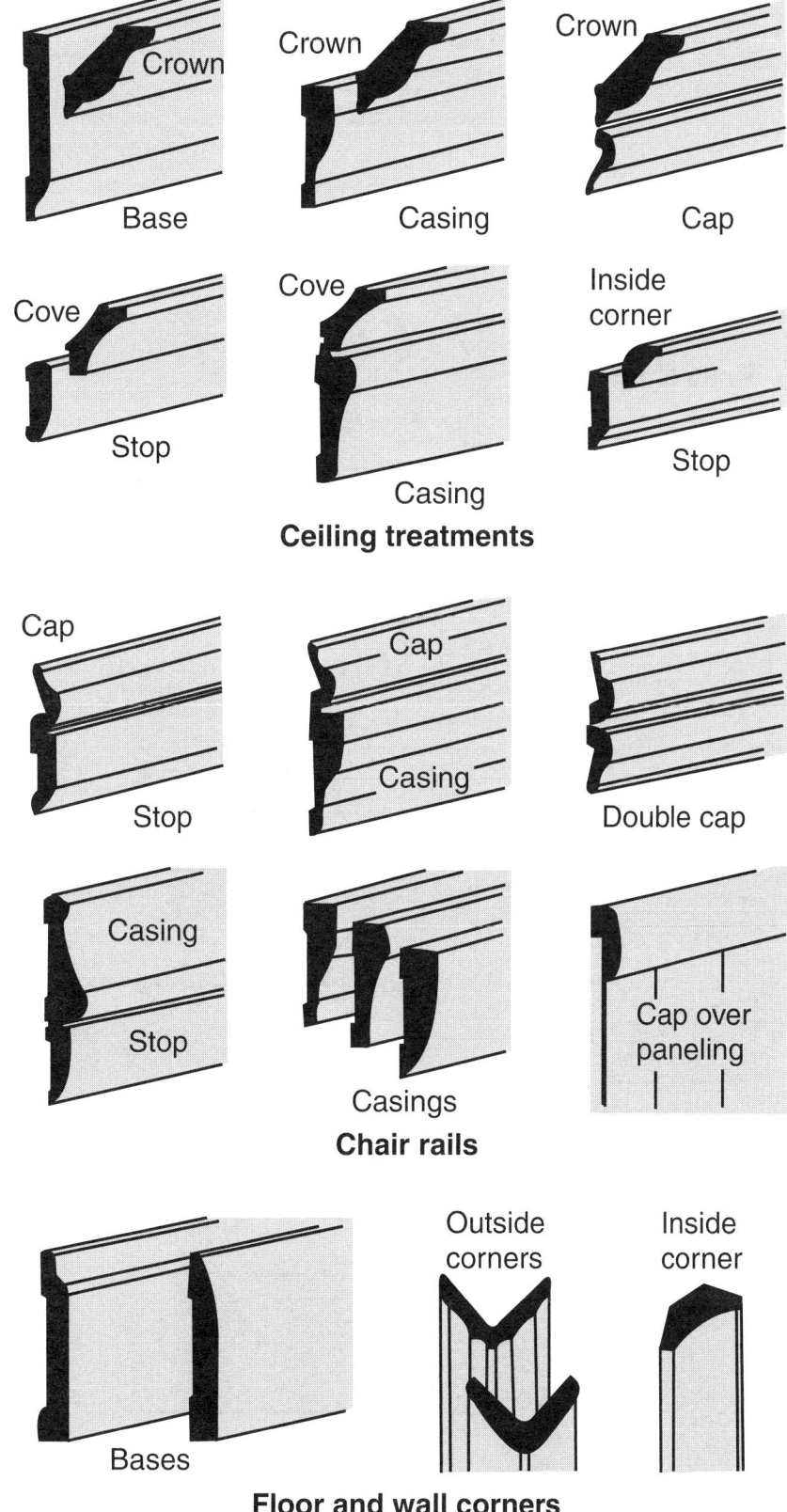

RM 19-1A

Typical Mouldings

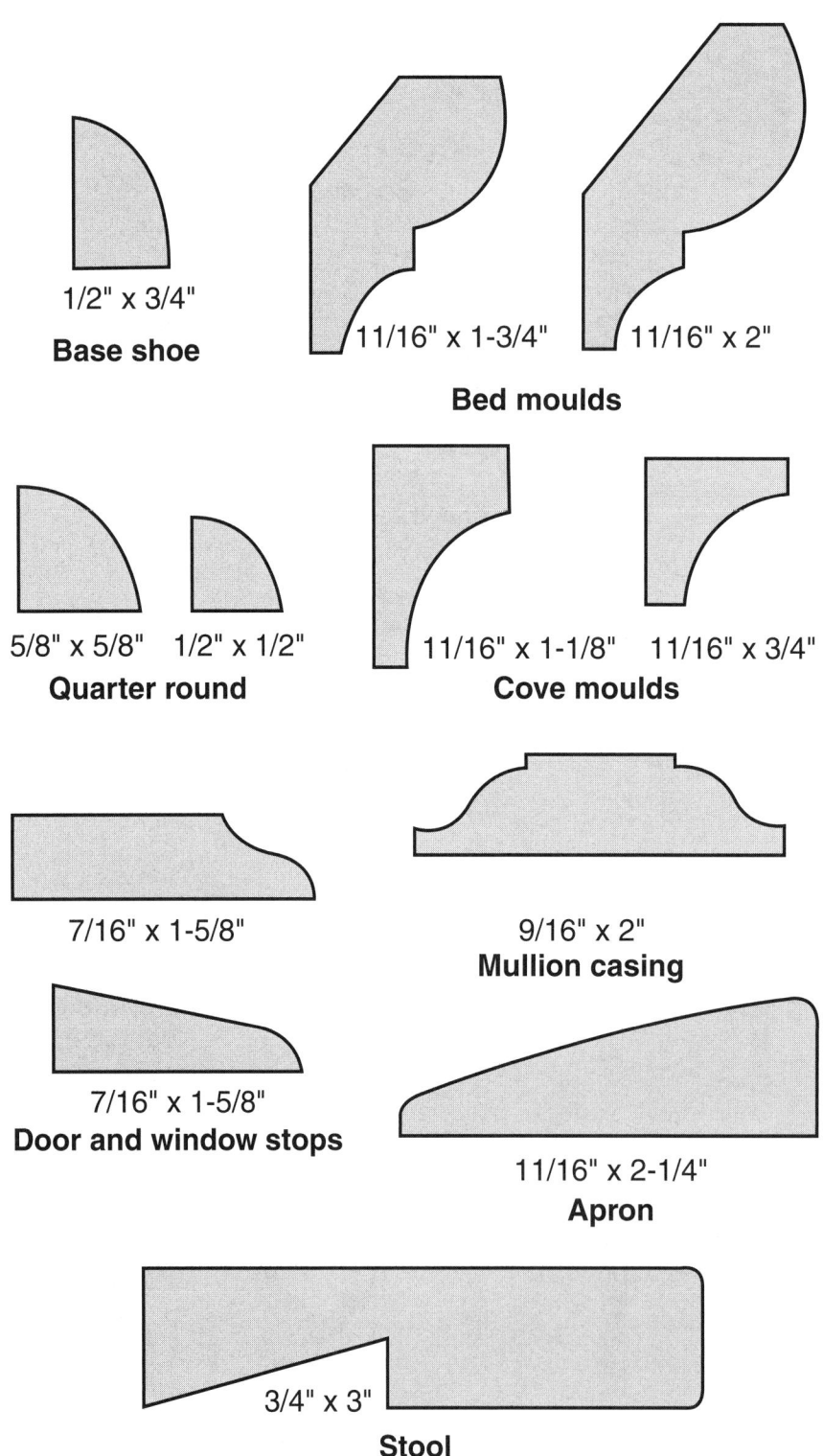

Casing Interior Doors

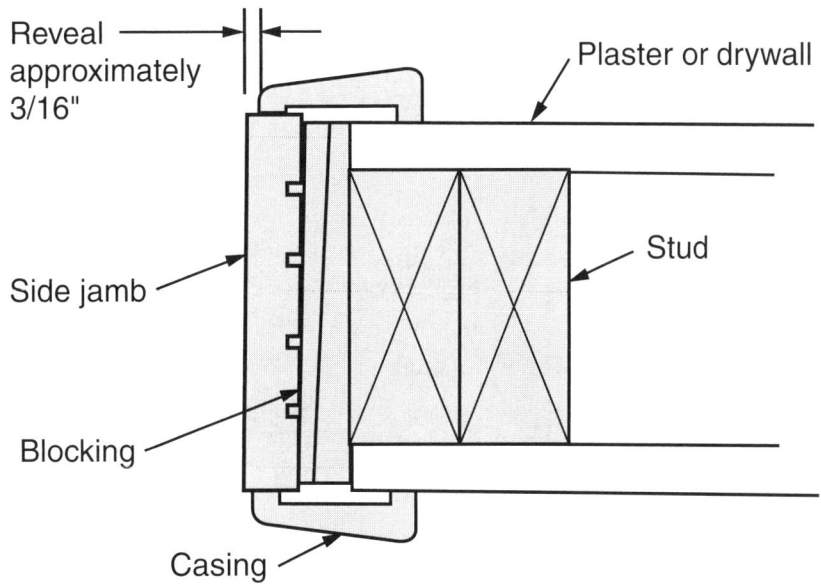

RM 19-2

Installing Baseboard and Base Shoe

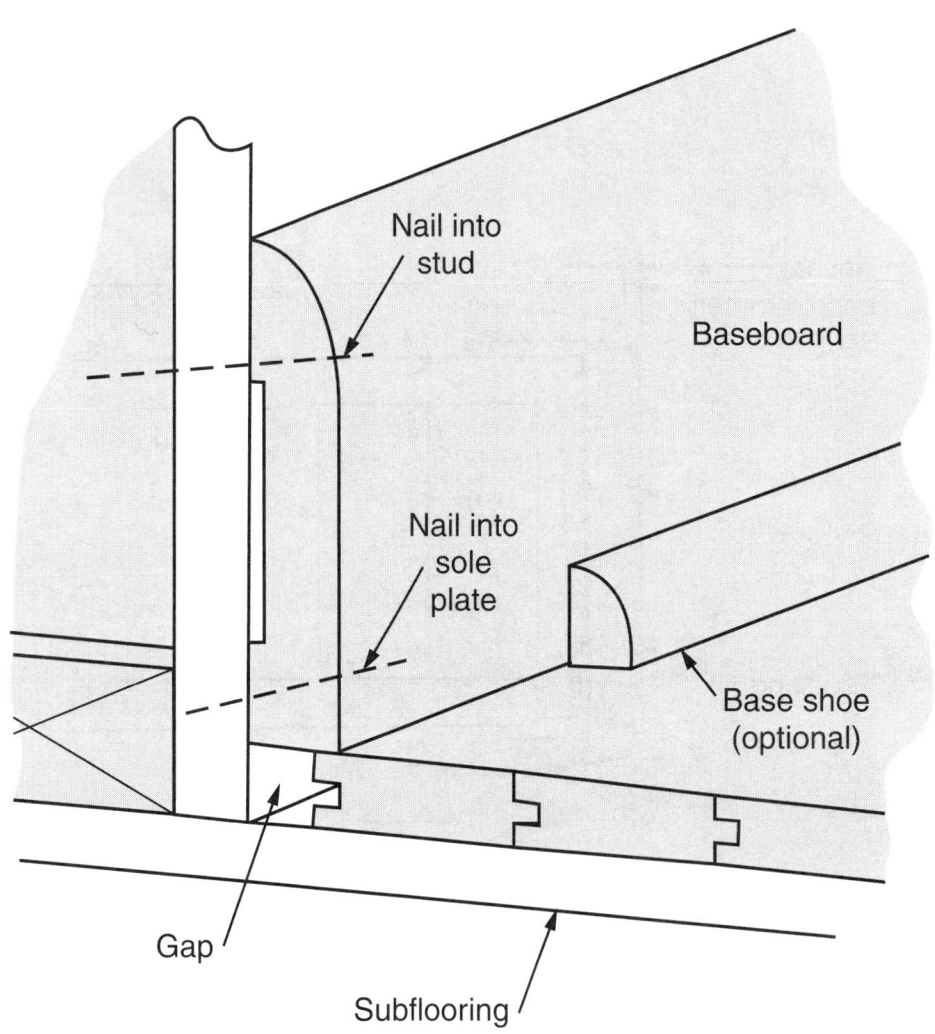

RM 19-3A

Installing Baseboard and Base Shoe

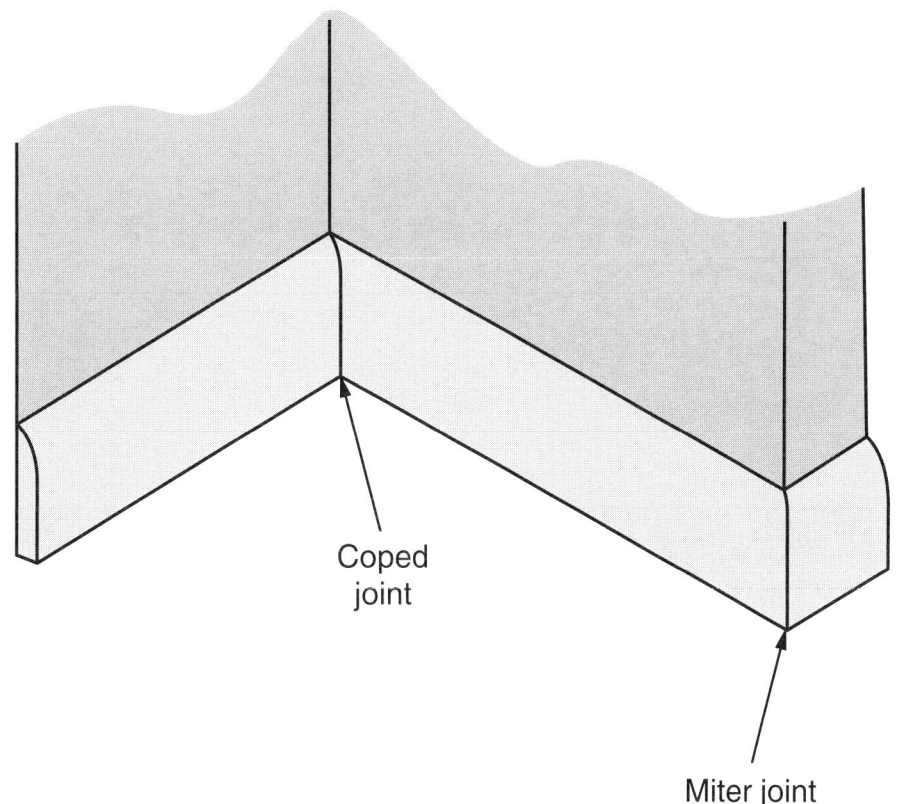

Coped joint

Miter joint

RM 19-3B

Chapter 19 Procedure Checklist
Installing Baseboards and Base Shoe

Name _____ Total _____

❏ Determines where baseboard material will be located; sorts pieces to reduce amount of waste.	5	4	3	2	1	Cannot determine where baseboard material is to be located; disregards lengths of baseboard materials when determining where cuts are to be made.
❏ Locates wall studs; marks wall for nailing of baseboard.	5	4	3	2	1	Forgets to mark positions of wall studs.
❏ Carefully cuts and fits first piece of baseboard; uses scarf joints when connecting lengths of baseboard.	5	4	3	2	1	Miscalculates length of first piece of baseboard; uses butt joints when connecting lengths of baseboard.
❏ Creates coped joints for inside corners; uses miter joints on exterior corners; properly nails baseboard into position.	5	4	3	2	1	Uses butt joints for inside and exterior corners; misses studs when nailing baseboard.
❏ Installs base shoe after floor finish has been applied.	5	4	3	2	1	Installs base shoe immediately after baseboard, disregarding whether floor finish is to be applied.

Permission granted to reproduce for educational use only.   Copyright by Goodheart-Willcox Co., Inc.

Chapter 19 Quiz
Doors and Interior Trim

Name _____ Date _____ Score _____

Multiple Choice
Choose the answer that correctly completes the statement. Write the corresponding letter in the space provided.

_____ 1. Lock sets are usually installed _____ from the floor.
  A. 24″–26″
  B. 30″–32″
  C. 36″–38″
  D. 42″–44″

_____ 2. A door that is hinged on the left and opens inward is referred to as a _____ door.
  A. right-hand reverse
  B. left-hand reverse
  C. right-hand
  D. left-hand

_____ 3. The _____ covers the joint between the wall surface and finish flooring.
  A. base shoe
  B. baseboard
  C. crown moulding
  D. stool

Identification
Identify the parts of the inside passage door frame.

_____ 4. Casing.

_____ 5. Door stop.

_____ 6. Head jamb.

_____ 7. Door.

_____ 8. Side jamb.

Identify the various types of mouldings.

_____ 9. Cove mould.
_____ 10. Quarter round.
_____ 11. Stool.
_____ 12. Base shoe.
_____ 13. Bed mould.
_____ 14. Mullion casing.
_____ 15. Apron.

20 Cabinetry

Objectives

After studying this chapter, students will be able to:
- Select prefabricated cabinets for a specific floor plan.
- Install prefabricated base and wall cabinets.
- Compare the common alternative procedures for building cabinets on the job.
- Lay out and frame a cabinet from drawings.
- Describe the three types of drawer guides.
- List the steps in cutting and assembling drawers.
- Describe material choices for cabinet shelves and doors.
- Explain how to install a plastic laminate surface.

Instructional Materials

Text: Pages 647–675
  Technical Vocabulary, page 647
  Test Your Knowledge, page 674
  Curricular Connections, page 674
  Outside Assignments, page 675
Workbook: Pages 127–134
Instructor's Resource:
  Reproducible masters:
    RM 20-1 *Standard Cabinet Dimensions*
    RM 20-2 *Cabinet Styles*
    RM 20-3 *Installing Factory-Built Cabinets*
  Transparencies (binder/CD only):
    CT 20-1 *Preparing to Install Kitchen Cabinets*
  Procedure Checklist: *Installing Factory-Built Cabinets*
  Chapter Quiz

Trade-Related Math

Many times a carpenter will be required to find the middle of a dimension or divide fractional amounts by 2. To divide a fraction by 2, simply multiply the bottom number (denominator) by 2. For example:

$1/2 \div 2 = 1/2 \times 2 = 1/4$
$1/2 \div 2 = 1/4$

A mixed number (number containing both a whole number and a fraction) can be divided by 2 using three steps. First, divide the whole number by 2. The answer will always be a whole number (2, 4, 6, etc.) or a whole number and one-half (2 1/2, 3 1/2, 5 1/2, etc.). Next, divide the fraction by 2 using the method shown in the previous example. Finally, add the two parts together. You may need to find a common denominator before adding, however.

$8\ 1/2 \div 2$
$8 \div 2 = 4$
$1/2 \div 2 = 1/4$
$4 + 1/4 = 4\ 1/4$
$8\ 1/2 \div 2 = 4\ 1/4$

Instructional Concepts and Student Learning Experiences

Drawings for Cabinetwork
1. List the drawings that commonly show information related to cabinetwork. Using a stock plan that includes cabinet layout and details (or other comparable set of plans), show the students these drawings and describe the primary dimensions that will be needed in the construction.

Standard Sizes
1. Explain that the overall heights and other dimensions of built-in cabinets are standardized. Using reproducible master RM 20-1 *Standard Cabinet Dimensions*, identify the common dimensions of cabinetwork. List other pieces of furniture and appliances that usually have standard dimensions.

Factory-Built Cabinets

1. Point out that most builders today use factory-built cabinets, although occasionally they may be built on site. Discuss the three forms in which factory-built cabinets may be delivered: disassembled; assembled, but not finished; and assembled and finished. Discuss the advantages and disadvantages of each.
2. Using reproducible master RM 20-2 *Cabinet Styles*, review the different styles in which cabinets are made: frame with cover (face-frame) and frameless.
3. Ask your students to secure literature and information about standard cabinet units from local building supply stores. Have them compare features and dimensions of the various cabinets to see if there are similarities among cabinets built by different manufacturers.
4. Identify and discuss the types of natural or manufactured materials used in factory-built cabinets. Compare qualities of various materials.
5. Discuss joinery and other fastening techniques and compare quality. Recognizing the marks of quality in construction is important.
6. Using reproducible master RM 20-3 *Installing Factory-Built Cabinets*, review the standard procedure for installing cabinets. Note that some builders prefer to install the wall cabinets before the base cabinets. Discuss the advantages of this practice.
7. If a set of base and wall cabinets is available, demonstrate the correct procedure for installation. Involve your students in this task.
8. Describe the steps for fitting and installing countertops.

Building Cabinets

1. Discuss the approaches used for building cabinets on the job. List advantages and disadvantages for each approach.
2. Describe how a master layout is made for a cabinet and discuss its use. Group the students in pairs and provide each with a set of drawings for cabinetwork. Have each pair prepare a master layout for cabinets. When all groups have completed their work, rotate the groups and have them check another group's layout. Have the students mark any discrepancies.
3. Describe the basic framing of base cabinets. Using a scale model, demonstrate how the base cabinets are framed in.
4. Identify the materials that are commonly used for cabinet facings. Add the facing materials to the scale model of the cabinet.
5. Referring to Figure 20-29, identify the different styles of drawer guides that may be used. Emphasize that many cabinetmakers use manufactured drawer guides.
6. Describe the two general types of drawers. Show the students the construction techniques used for manufactured drawers, citing good and poor techniques.
7. Review the use of the table saw, emphasizing the safety rules. Demonstrate the construction of lip and flush doors and point out the main differences in construction. Stress the importance of squaring the drawer up before gluing or nailing it together. Have the pairs of students construct one drawer for their cabinet. Make sure that the drawer fits their cabinet.
9. Identify the different means of supporting shelves in cabinetwork. List the advantages and disadvantages of each type.
10. Discuss the maximum spacing that should be used for shelves. Explain that the function of the cabinet dictates what type of spacing and shelf support is used.
11. Identify the types of doors—flush, overlay, and lip—that are used in cabinet construction. Have the students discuss the major differences.
12. Demonstrate the construction techniques used for flush, lip, and overlay doors.
13. Have the pairs of students construct a door for their cabinet.
14. Identify the types of hinges that are used for flush cabinet doors as shown in Figure 20-37.
15. Discuss applications for sliding doors in cabinetry. Describe the different types of tracks or door designs that are used for sliding doors.
16. Identify the types of materials that are used for cabinet tops. Emphasize the importance of using a backing material that is dimensionally stable and suitable for lamination.

Chapter 20 Cabinetry

17. Demonstrate how laminates are laid out and cut. Stress the proper cutting side to avoid splintering and cracking.
18. Emphasize the precautions that should be taken when using contact cement for bonding laminates to a backing material. Using a cabinet top sized for your scale model, demonstrate the preparation of the base material. When the base has been properly prepared, show the students how to apply the contact cement, and then apply the plastic laminate.
19. When the adhesive has properly set, demonstrate the procedure for trimming the edges using a laminate trimmer or router.
20. Have each pair of students construct a top for their cabinet.
21. Identify various types of hardware that can be used for cabinetry.

Other Built-In Units
1. Review advantages and disadvantages of built-in cabinets.
2. Ask students to list the built-in cabinets they have in their homes, the location of the cabinets, and the purpose of the cabinets.

Sequence of Interior Finish
1. Discuss the sequence of events that occur in finishing the interior of a house. Stress that good communication with other tradespeople is vital to avoid bottlenecks and interference with other workers.

Chapter Review

1. Review the chapter objectives. Be sure that the students fully understand each objective.
2. Assign *Technical Vocabulary, Test Your Knowledge* questions, *Curricular Connections,* and *Outside Assignments* for Chapter 20 of the text. Review the answers in class.
3. Assign Chapter 20 in the workbook. Review the answers in class.

Evaluation

This chapter provides three methods for evaluating student performance. Students should complete the *Test Your Knowledge* section using the book as reference. Students should also be allowed to use the book for reference when completing the workbook material. Use the Chapter 20 Quiz in the instructor's resources for in-class evaluation. Correct the quizzes, return them to the students, and review the quiz questions in group discussion.

Procedure Checklist

Using the procedure checklist *Installing Factory-Built Cabinets,* have students evaluate the techniques used to perform these tasks.

Answers to Test Your Knowledge
Text Page 674
1. A. Built on the job.
   B. Custom-built in local cabinet shop.
   C. Mass-produced from cabinet factory.
2. architectural plans
3. 36
4. frameless
5. False.
6. story pole
7. master layout
8. After the bottom panels have been cut and nailed in place on the base.
9. stiles
10. center guides
11. 42
12. before
13. Where the swing of regular doors would be awkward or cause interference.
14. backing sheet
15. Above the centerline of the drawer front.

Answers to Workbook Questions
Pages 127–134
1. attached
2. D. carpenter
3. B. 24″
4. C. assembled but not finished
5. A. Magnetic.
   B. Friction.
   C. Ball/bullet.
   D. Magnetic.
6. A. Face frame.
   B. Frameless.

Copyright by Goodheart-Willcox Co., Inc.

7. A. 30"
   B. 7'-0"
   C. 36"
   D. 6'-0"
   E. 31"
   F. 5'-4"
   G. 2'-0"
8. No. 3012: 30" × 12" × 12 1/2"
   No. 27303: 27" × 30" × 12 1/2"
9. toggle
10. shims, blocking
11. master layout
12. A. Faceplate/face frame.
    B. End panel.
    C. Rabbet.
    D. Web frame.
13. rails
14. B. End panels are installed after the bottom is attached to the base.
15. C. A marked piece should not be used to lay out duplicate parts.
16. C. 3/8"
17. A. Corner.
    B. Side.
    C. Center.
18. A. kicker
19. D. front and sides
20. D. top and sides
21. A. front
22. before
23. D. 42"
24. A. Flush.
    B. Overlay.
    C. Lipped.
25. C. gain
26. B. raising the door and pulling the lower edge outward
27. B. 1/16"
28. B. contact bond cement
29. C. 4 sq. ft.
30. above
31. A. 2
    B. 4
    C. 5
    D. 1
    E. 3
32. Narrow wood pieces that are used to attach the countertop to the base cabinets.

Answers to Chapter Quiz

1. True.
2. False.
3. True.
4. True.
5. C. 36"
6. B. stiles
7. A. 42"
8. B. width
9. C. lipped
10. C. Fir plywood.
11. D. All of the above.

Standard Cabinet Dimensions

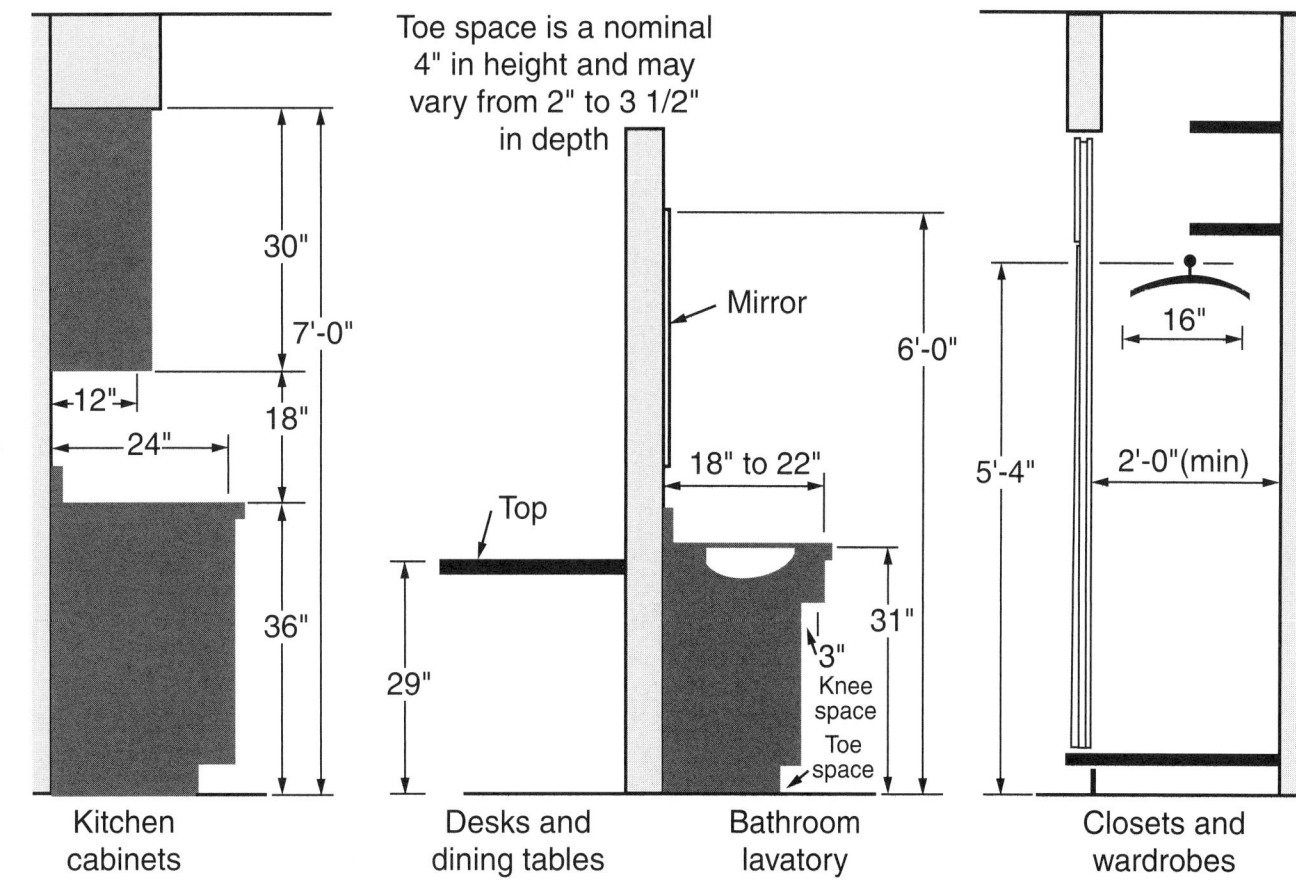

RM 20-1

Cabinet Styles

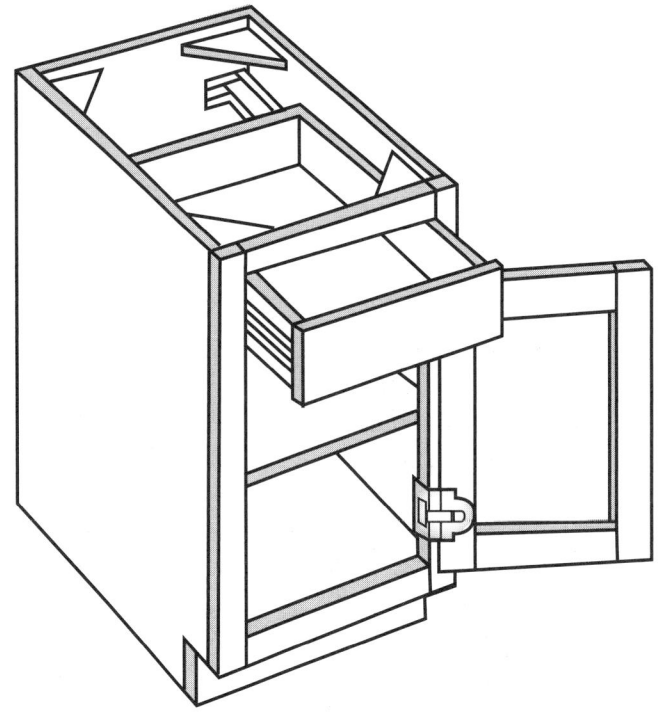

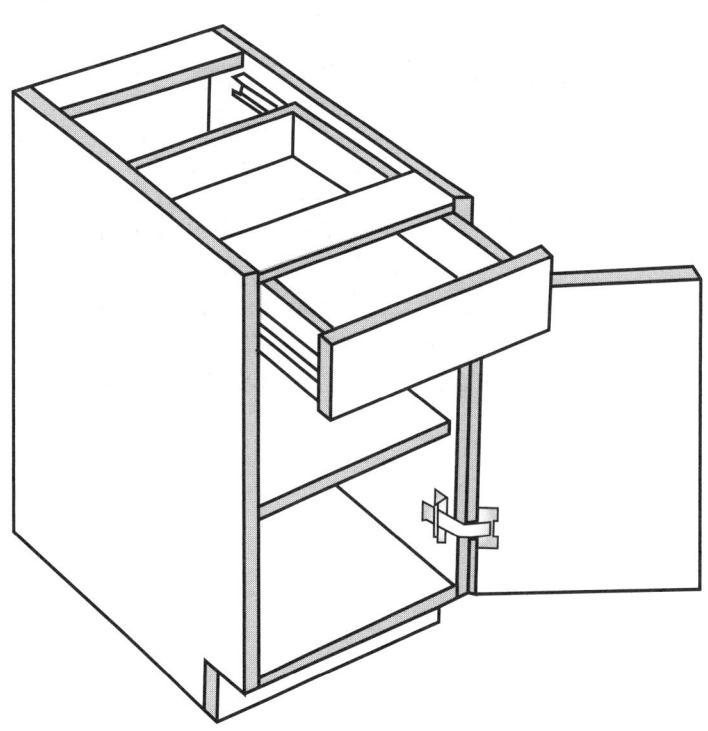

RM 20-2

Installing Factory-Built Cabinets

1.
Locate the position of all wall studs where cabinets are to hang by tapping with a hammer. Mark their position where the marks can easily be seen when the cabinets are in position.

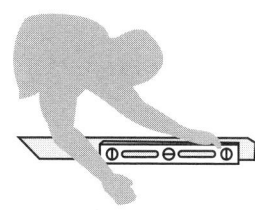

2.
Find the highest point on the floor with a level. This is important for both base and wall cabinet installation later. Remove the baseboard from all walls where cabinets are to be installed. This will allow them to go flush against the walls.

3.
Start the installation with the corner or end unit. Slide it into place then continue to slide the other base cabinets into the proper position.

4.
When all base cabinets are in position, fasten the cabinets together. This is done by drilling a 1/4" diameter hole through the face frames, and using the 3" screws and T-nuts provided. To get maximum holding power from the screw, one hole should be close to the top of the end stile and one should be close to the bottom.

5.
Check the position of each cabinet with a spirit level, going from the front of the cabinet to the back of the cabinet. Next shim between the cabinet and the wall for a perfect base cabinet installation.

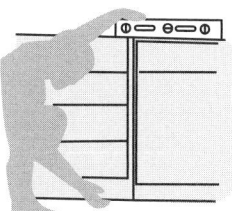

6.
Starting at the high point in the floor, level the leading edges of the cabinets. Continue to shim between the cabinets and the floor until all the base cabinets have been brought to level.

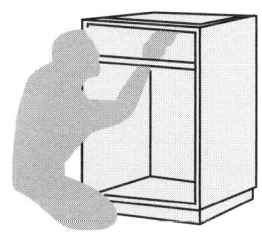

7.
After the cabinets have been leveled, both front to back and across the front, fasten the cabinets to the wall at the stud locations. This is done by drilling a 3/32" diameter hole 2 1/4" deep through both the hanging strips for the 2 1/2" x 8 screws that are provided.

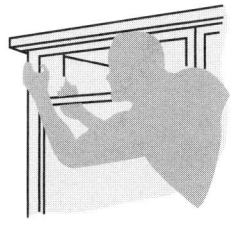

8.
Fit the counter top into position and attach it to the base cabinets by predrilling and screwing through the front corner blocks into the top. Use caution not to drill through the top. Cover the counter top for protection while all the cabinets are being installed.

9.
Position the bottom of the 30" wall cabinets 19" from the top of the base cabinet, unless the cabinets are to be installed against a soffit. A brace can be made to help hold the wall cabinets in place while they are being fastened. Start the wall cabinet installation with a corner end cabinet. Use care in getting this cabinet installed plumb and level.

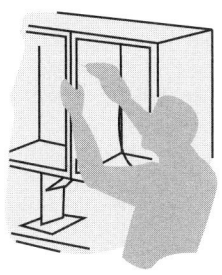

10.
Temporarily secure the adjoining wall cabinets so that the leveling may be done without removing them. Drill through the end stiles of the cabinets and fasten them together as was done with the base cabinets.

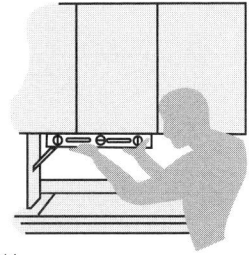

11.
Use a spirit level to check the horizontal surfaces. Shim between the cabinet and the wall until the cabinet is level. This is necessary if doors are to fit properly.

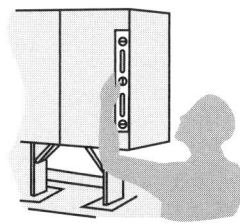

12.
Check the perpendicular surface of each frame at the front. When the cabinets are level, both front to back and across the front, permanently attach the cabinets to the wall. This is done by predrilling a 3/32" diameter hole 2 1/4" deep through the hanging strip inside the top and below the bottom of the cabinets at the stud location. Enough number 8 screws should be used to fasten the cabinets securely to the wall.

RM 20-3

Permission granted to reproduce for educational use only.   Copyright by Goodheart-Willcox Co., Inc.

Chapter 20 Procedure Checklist
Installing Factory-Built Cabinets

Name _____ Total _____

❏	Locates wall studs where cabinets are to be placed and marks their positions; finds highest point on the floor with a level; removes baseboard where base cabinets are to be placed.	5	4	3	2	1	Neglects to find studs or highest point on floor; forgets to remove baseboard where base cabinets will be installed, or removes baseboard where cabinets are not to be installed.
❏	Starts base cabinet installation in corner; slides remainder of base cabinets against adjacent cabinet; fastens all cabinets together.	5	4	3	2	1	Starts base cabinet installation in middle; neglects to fasten cabinets together.
❏	Checks position of cabinets with level; shims between cabinets and wall; levels leading edges of cabinets, shimming between the cabinets and floor.	5	4	3	2	1	Neglects to check position of cabinets.
❏	Fastens cabinets to wall at stud locations.	5	4	3	2	1	Neglects to securely fasten cabinets to wall.
❏	Correctly installs build-up strips to base cabinets.	5	4	3	2	1	Neglects to install build-up strips to base cabinets.
❏	Fits countertop to base cabinets.	5	4	3	2	1	Neglects to fit countertop to base cabinet build-up strips.

Permission granted to reproduce for educational use only. Copyright by Goodheart-Willcox Co., Inc.

Chapter 20 Procedure Checklist Installing Factory-Built Cabinets (continued)

- ❏ Positions wall cabinets and uses brace to hold in position; starts installation with corner or end cabinet.   5   4   3   2   1   Tries to hold wall cabinets in position while marking position; starts installation in middle of wall.

- ❏ Temporarily secures adjacent cabinets; checks level of wall cabinets, shimming between the cabinet and wall; checks the plumb of the cabinet using a level.   5   4   3   2   1   Neglects to check level and plumb of cabinets.

Chapter 20 Quiz
Cabinetry

Name _____ Date _____ Score _____

True-False
Circle T if the answer is True or F if the answer is False.

T F 1. Horizontal members of a face frame are called rails.

T F 2. A kicker is placed along the bottom of a base cabinet to provide clearance for a person's toes.

T F 3. Plywood should not be used for drawer sides and backs.

T F 4. Plastic laminates can be cut to rough size with a handsaw, table saw, portable saw, or portable router.

Multiple Choice
Choose the answer that correctly completes the statement. Write the corresponding letter in the space provided.

_____ 5. Base kitchen cabinets are usually _____ high.
    A. 30″
    B. 33″
    C. 36″
    D. 39″

_____ 6. The vertical members of a face frame are called _____.
    A. rails
    B. stiles
    C. facing strips
    D. mullions

_____ 7. Standard 3/4″ shelving should be supported every _____ or closer.
    A. 42″
    B. 48″
    C. 54″
    D. 60″

_____ 8. When specifying the size of the opening of a cabinet door, always list the _____ first.
    A. thickness
    B. width
    C. height

_____ 9. A(n) _____ cabinet door is rabbetted along all edges so that part of the door is inside the door frame.
   A. flush
   B. overlay
   C. lipped

_____ 10. Which of the following is *not* satisfactory as a base for plastic laminates?
   A. Particleboard.
   B. Hardboard.
   C. Fir plywood.
   D. Waferboard.

_____ 11. Which of the following can be used to apply contact cement to a base material?
   A. Brush.
   B. Roller.
   C. Spreader.
   D. All of the above.

21 Painting, Finishing, and Decorating

Objectives

After studying this chapter, students will be able to:
- Cite safety rules that apply to painting and finishing.
- List tools and equipment and demonstrate their use.
- Select proper materials for various painting, finishing and decorating jobs.
- Prepare exterior and interior surfaces for painting.
- Explain proper procedures for painting, finishing and wallpaper hanging.

Instructional Materials

Text: Pages 677–703
 Technical Vocabulary, page 677
 Test Your Knowledge, page 702
 Curricular Connections, page 702
 Outside Assignments, page 703
Workbook: Pages 135–138
Instructor's Resource:
 Reproducible masters:
  RM 21-1 *Safety Rules for Painting and Finishing*
  RM 21-2 *Parts of a Paintbrush*
  RM 21-3 *Types of Brushes*
  RM 21-4 *Parts of a Spray Gun*
  RM 21-5 *Identifying Sprayer Heads*
  RM 21-6 *Efficient Method of Painting a Paneled Door*
  RM 21-7 *Wallpapering Tools*
 Transparencies (binder/CD only):
  CT 21-1 *Interior Paint: Types and Uses*
 Chapter Quiz

Trade-Related Math

Simple multiplication and division are used to determine the amount of paint needed to cover areas to be finished. In the first step, the dimensions of the wall or ceiling are measured. Then, the two dimensions are multiplied to determine the square footage. Finally, long division is used to determine the amount of paint required.

For example, how much paint is needed to paint a wall that is 8' high and 14' long if the coverage is 400 sq. ft./gal.?

wall height × wall length = sq. ft.
14' × 8' = 112 sq. ft.
Number of sq. ft. ÷ Coverage/gal. = Quantity of paint needed

112 sq. ft. ÷ 400 sq. ft./gal. = 0.28 gal.

Instructional Concepts and Student Learning Experiences

Safety with Paints and Finishes

1. Review the safety rules at the beginning of this chapter and emphasize the need to take precautions when working with coatings. Distribute reproducible master RM 21-1 *Safety Rules for Painting and Finishing* for additional emphasis.
2. Explain that paints, stains, and varnishes contain ingredients that could cause serious health problems if splashed into eyes or onto skin.
3. Caution students about the health hazards connected with the inhaling of toxic fumes. Stress the need for adequate ventilation when working in enclosed areas.
4. Call special attention to the danger of ignition sources around flammable liquids or in situations with heavy airborne dust.
5. Review the procedures for testing for the presence of lead in old paint when preparing older structures for repainting.

Brushes

1. Using reproducible master RM 21-2 *Parts of a Paintbrush,* identify the parts of a paintbrush.

Mention that quality brushes have flagged bristles so that they can hold more paint and provide better coverage.
2. Discuss both natural bristles and synthetic bristles. Inform the students that synthetics are best for water-based paints and finishes.
3. Discuss the various types of brushes and the special uses of each. During this presentation, use reproducible master RM 21-3 *Types of Brushes*, to illustrate the various types. If possible, have several types of brushes available to pass among the students.
4. Display and demonstrate the use of wire brushes.

Rollers, Pans, and Pads
1. Refer to Figures 21-5 and 21-6 as you introduce these painting tools. Explain why roller covers are made in both long and short naps. Also, discuss the wide range of uses for rollers.
2. Compare paint pads to brushes and rollers. Explain the advantages and disadvantages and discuss the uses of paint pads.
3. Demonstrate the proper use of the paintbrush (how to hold it for painting various surfaces, etc.).
4. Demonstrate the proper use of the pan to hold paint and evenly distribute paint on the roller.
5. Demonstrate the proper use of the pan and paint pad.

Mechanical Spraying Equipment
1. Using reproducible master RM 21-4 *Parts of a Spray Gun*, name the various parts of a spray gun and explain the principle of operation.
2. Note that there are two different types of spray guns: suction type and pressure type. Explain how each works.
3. Have students examine the parts of a spray gun as you disassemble it. Note the difference between an internal mix and an external mix spraying head using reproducible master RM 21-5 *Identifying Sprayer Heads*. Refer also to Figure 21-9.
4. Have students observe proper cleaning of the spray gun. Stress the importance of this step in maintaining the unit in proper working condition.

Ladders and Scaffolds
1. Refer to Chapter 31 while introducing students to the safe use of scaffolds and ladders.

Electric Sanders
1. Refer to Chapter 5 as you review with students the types of electric sanders and the special uses of each.
2. Demonstrate the proper use of each type.
3. Demonstrate the proper technique for installing sandpaper on the sander.

Hand Sanders
1. Discuss the various types of abrasives available and show samples of sandpaper, explaining the uses of each.
2. Demonstrate the procedure for attaching sandpaper to various types of hand sanders used in your program.

Paints, Varnishes, and Stains
1. Define and compare these coatings and explain their differences.
2. Define the terms *paint* and *coatings* and explain their differences.
3. Name and explain the role of each ingredient in paint.
4. Introduce clear coatings and their relationship to stains.
5. Discuss fillers and their uses.
6. Explain the purpose of stains and demonstrate their effect on various types of woods.
7. Compare the three types of stains: spirit stains, oil stains, and water-based stains.

Color Selection
1. Define the nine color selection terms and their relationship to the color wheel.
2. Explain that paints may be selected ready-mixed from the factory or mixed to the customer's specifications at the paint store.

Preparing Surfaces for Coatings
1. Stress the need to properly prepare surfaces before applying a finish.
2. Discuss various surface conditions that must be corrected before finishes can be applied.

Painting Wood Exteriors
1. Have students prepare new wood for painting. Stress the need to properly prepare the new

surfaces. Knots and pitch-containing areas must be covered with a shellac or knot sealer.
2. Discuss problems that may be encountered when working with previously painted surfaces. Refer to Figure 21-20 as you discuss causes of paint failure.
3. Have students prepare previously painted surfaces using tools available in your shop. Demonstrate the use of various tools in removing deteriorated surfaces.
4. Demonstrate the proper use of brushes, rollers, and pads in applying paint. Discuss the differences in application methods between oil paints and water-based paints.
5. If spray equipment is available, demonstrate the proper procedures for preparing paint and for spraying.

Problems with Coatings
1. Collect photos or samples of defects in old coatings. Have students determine the type of failure, its cause, and how it could have been avoided.
2. In a similar manner, collect examples of problems in clear finishes. Have students study them and suggest their causes.

Working with Stains and Clear Finishes
1. Discuss surface preparation, including lifting of dents, filling of holes, repair of minor defects, and sanding. Stress the importance of proper sanding to the appearance of the finished surface.
2. Explain the purpose and practice of bleaching wood.
3. Demonstrate the application of stains and clear finishes. Have students apply finishes to prepared surfaces.

Estimating
1. Have students measure a shop wall and compute the area.
2. Next, have them read the label on a paint container to find the coverage of the paint.
3. Finally, have students estimate the amount of paint needed to coat the wall.

Interior Painting
1. Explain the importance of protecting surfaces that are *not* being painted. List the various ways of providing protection.
2. Detail the steps that must be taken to prepare surfaces, such as removing grease and soil, deglossing surfaces, etc. Note that deglossing can be done with chemical preparations.
3. Review with students the proper order for painting an entire room, trim, doors, and windows.
4. Using reproducible master RM 21-6 *Efficient Method of Painting a Paneled Door,* discuss the appropriate sequence for painting paneled doors.

Hanging Wallcoverings
1. Review the types of wallpaper and list their important characteristics.
2. Using reproducible master RM 21-7 *Wallpapering Tools,* discuss the use of each tool.
3. Explain that wallpaper is measured by the roll with a single roll varying from 27 to 29 square feet.
4. Have students take room measurements and, using the chart in Figure 21-28, determine the number of rolls needed for coverage.
5. Discuss the tools and other materials needed for wallpapering and explain their use.
6. Describe the wall preparations needed before hanging paper. Include the following areas in your discussion: stripping of old coverings, use of sizing on new plaster or drywall, drawing a plumb line as a guide to hanging the first strip of wallpaper.
6. Describe the procedure of preparing a strip of wallpaper for hanging.
7. Explain the term *booking* and demonstrate the technique.
8. Demonstrate the technique for hanging the strips.

Chapter Review
1. Review the chapter objectives. Be sure that the students fully understand each objective.

2. Assign *Technical Vocabulary, Test Your Knowledge* questions, *Curricular Connections,* and *Outside Assignments* for Chapter 21 of the text. Review the answers in class.
3. Assign Chapter 21 in the workbook. Review the answers in class.

Evaluation

This chapter provides three methods for evaluating student performance. Students should complete the *Test Your Knowledge* section using the book as reference. Students should also be allowed to use the book for reference when completing the workbook material. Use the Chapter 21 Quiz in the instructor's resources for in-class evaluation. Correct the quizzes, return them to the students, and review the quiz questions in group discussion.

Answers to Test Your Knowledge
Text Page 702

1. exposure to ultraviolet light, moisture, and microscopic organisms
2. False.
3. Bristle or stock, ferrule, handle, setting, plug
4. longer
5. fast-drying
6. External mix.
7. Pigment
8. Filler
9. primary
10. To prevent the dry wood from drawing the vehicle out of the paint.
11. Intermix the paint from different containers. To achieve uniform color and texture.
12. elasticity
13. Paint the ceiling, then the walls, and then the wood trim and doors.
14. cutting in
15. Apply a drop of warm water under the spot which causes the grain to swell and rise to or above the surface, let it dry, and then sand smooth.
16. 3
17. Cotton, linen, hemp, wood, and waste paper.
18. False.
19. False.
20. After trimming each strip.

Answers to Workbook Questions
Pages 135–138

1. Respirator or air mask.
2. A. Bristle or stock.
   B. Ferrule.
   C. Plug.
   D. Setting.
   E. Handle.
3. B. create a void that will hold a supply of paint
4. suction
5. A. orbital
   B. vibrating
6. A. alcohol
   B. acetone
7. B. Provide a slightly roughened surface for better adhesion of the next coat.
8. Value
9. B. provide a place to strike off excess paint from a brush or roller
10. True.
11. False.
12. A. water
13. B. water under the coating is pushing paint film away from wood surface
14. D. hard finishing coat applied over a softer primer
15. 2 gal.

Answers to Chapter Quiz

1. True.
2. False.
3. True.
4. True.
5. internal mix
6. Vehicles
7. Fillers
8. primary
9. primer, sealer
10. bleaching
11. holiday
12. C.
13. E.
14. B.
15. D.
16. A.

Safety Rules for Painting and Finishing

Follow these safety rules when working with paints and finishes:

- Wear safety glasses when applying finishing materials.

- Wear rubber gloves, goggles, and a rubber apron when working with bleaches and acids.

- When working with or spraying thinners and reducers (such as naphtha, lacquer thinner, and enamel reducer), keep the work area well ventilated. The fumes are highly toxic.

- Store chemicals and soiled rags in safe containers.

- Wear an approved respirator when using toxic chemicals.

- Never smoke while sanding or applying finishes. Not only will mixtures of sanding dust and smoke create a breathing hazard, but the combination could cause a fire or explosion.

- Wear a respirator or mask and protective clothing when operating a paint sprayer.

- Thoroughly wash your hands after applying finishes to remove any toxic materials.

- Locate the nearest sink, shower, or eyewash station in case of a splash or spill that lands on your skin or in your eyes.

- Keep a fire extinguisher handy in the finishing area.

- When preparing older structures for repainting, be sure to test for lead in the old paint before sanding or scraping. Lead can cause serious health problems. Sanding of lead-containing paints requires special precautions to prevent breathing in the lead particles that would be released. Removal of lead-containing paint should be done only by trained professionals.

RM 21-1

Parts of a Paintbrush

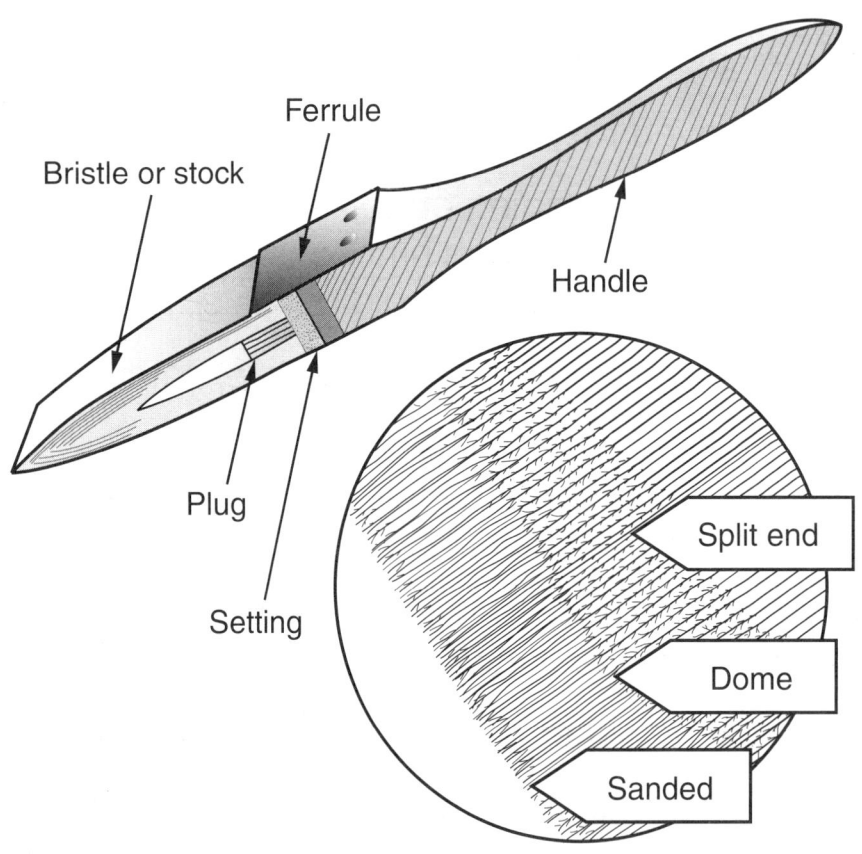

RM 21-2

Types of Brushes

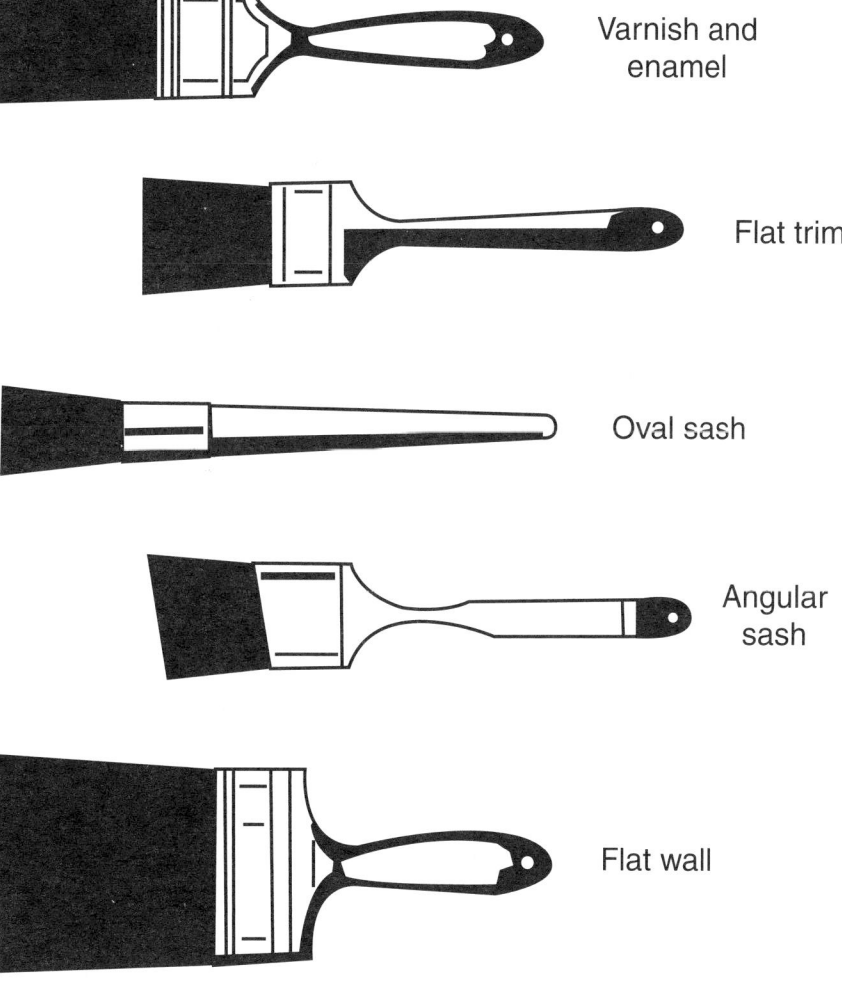

Parts of a Spray Gun

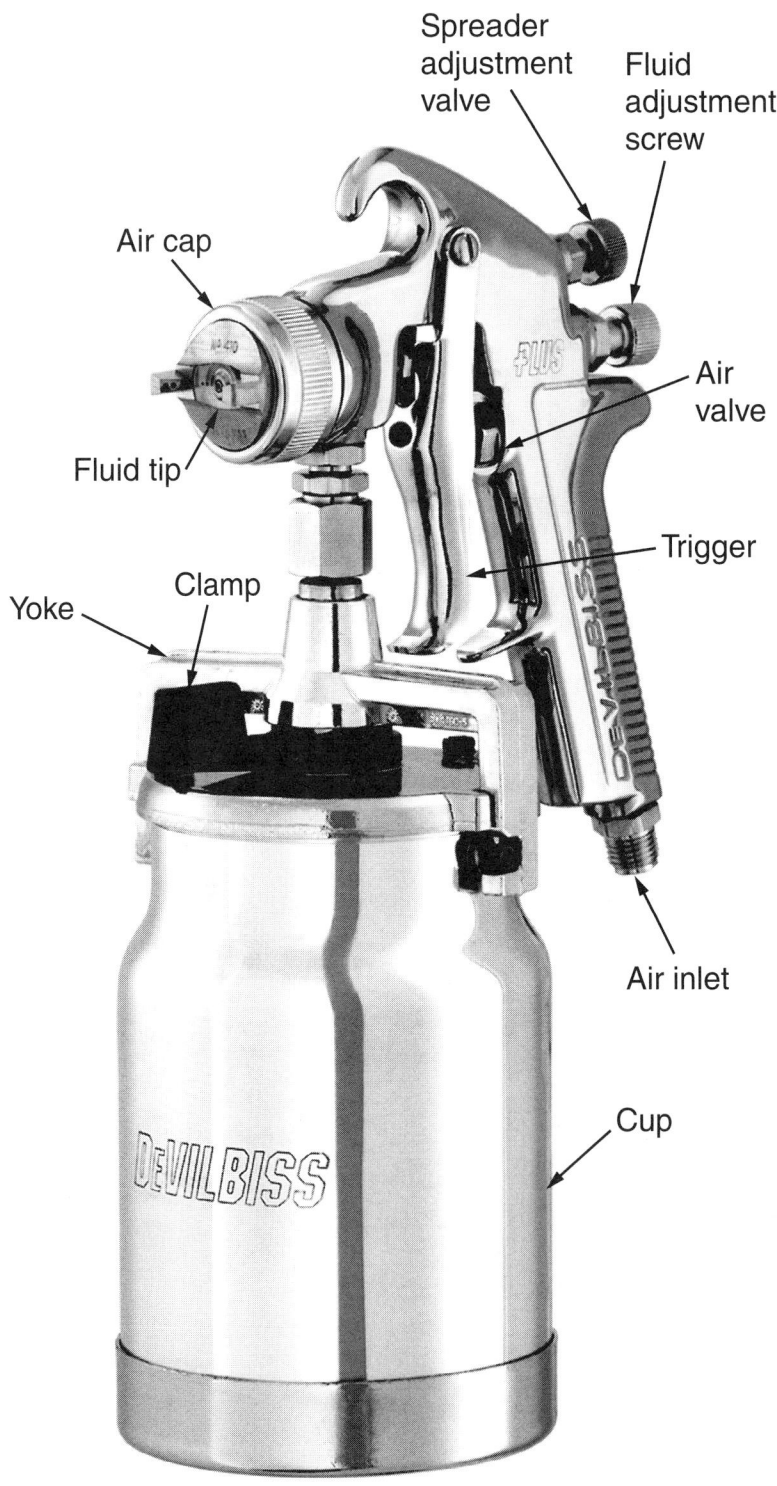

RM 21-4

Identifying Sprayer Heads

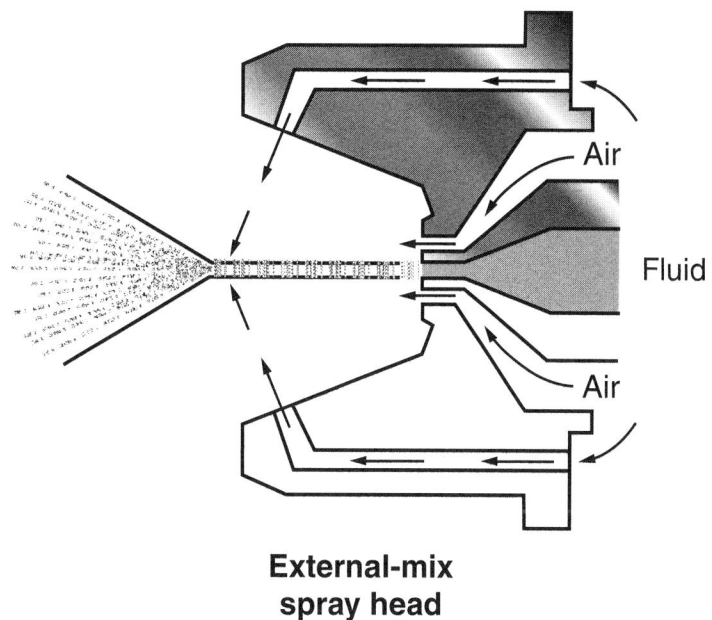

External-mix spray head

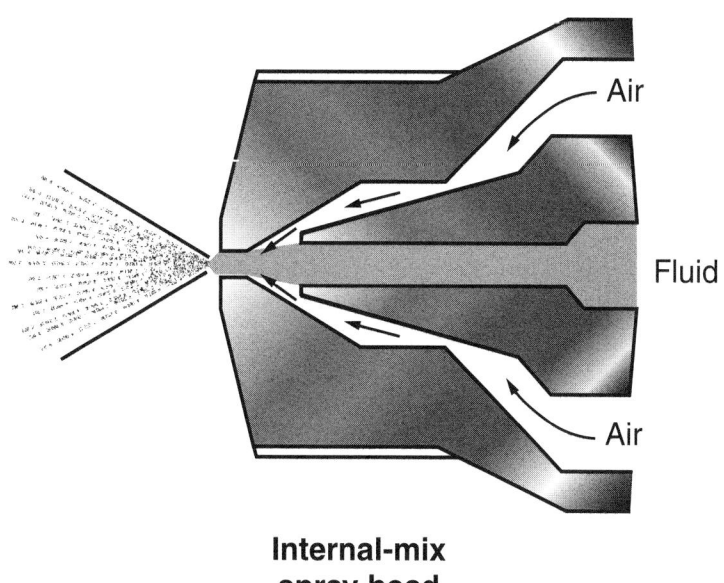

Internal-mix spray head

RM 21-5

Efficient Method of Painting a Paneled Door

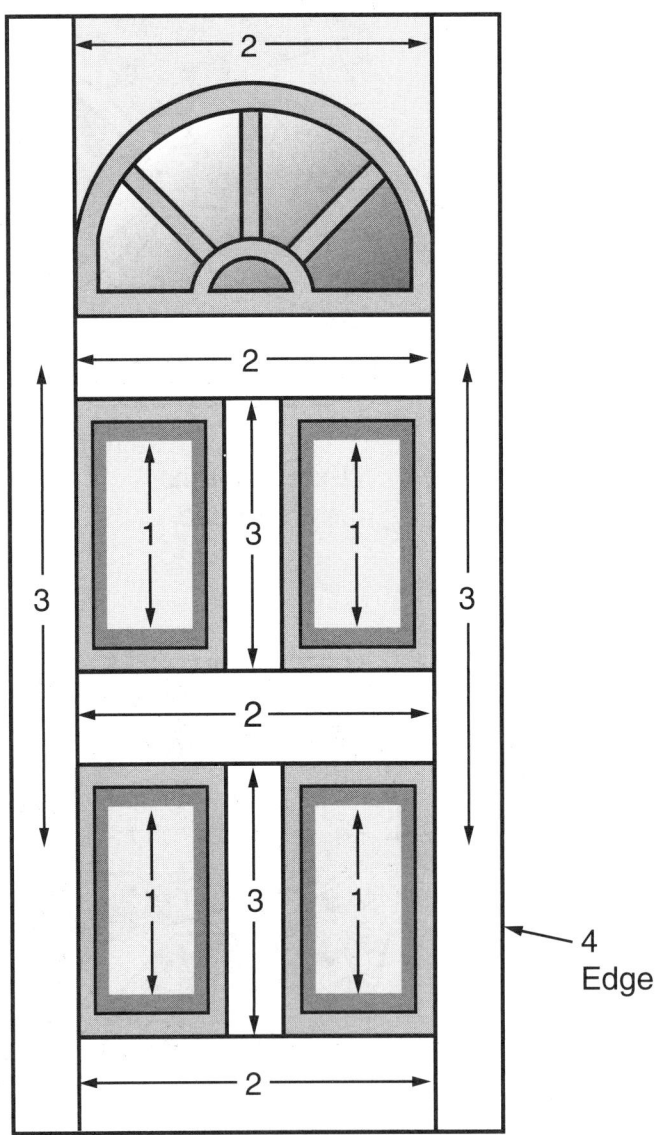

RM 21-6

Wallpapering Tools

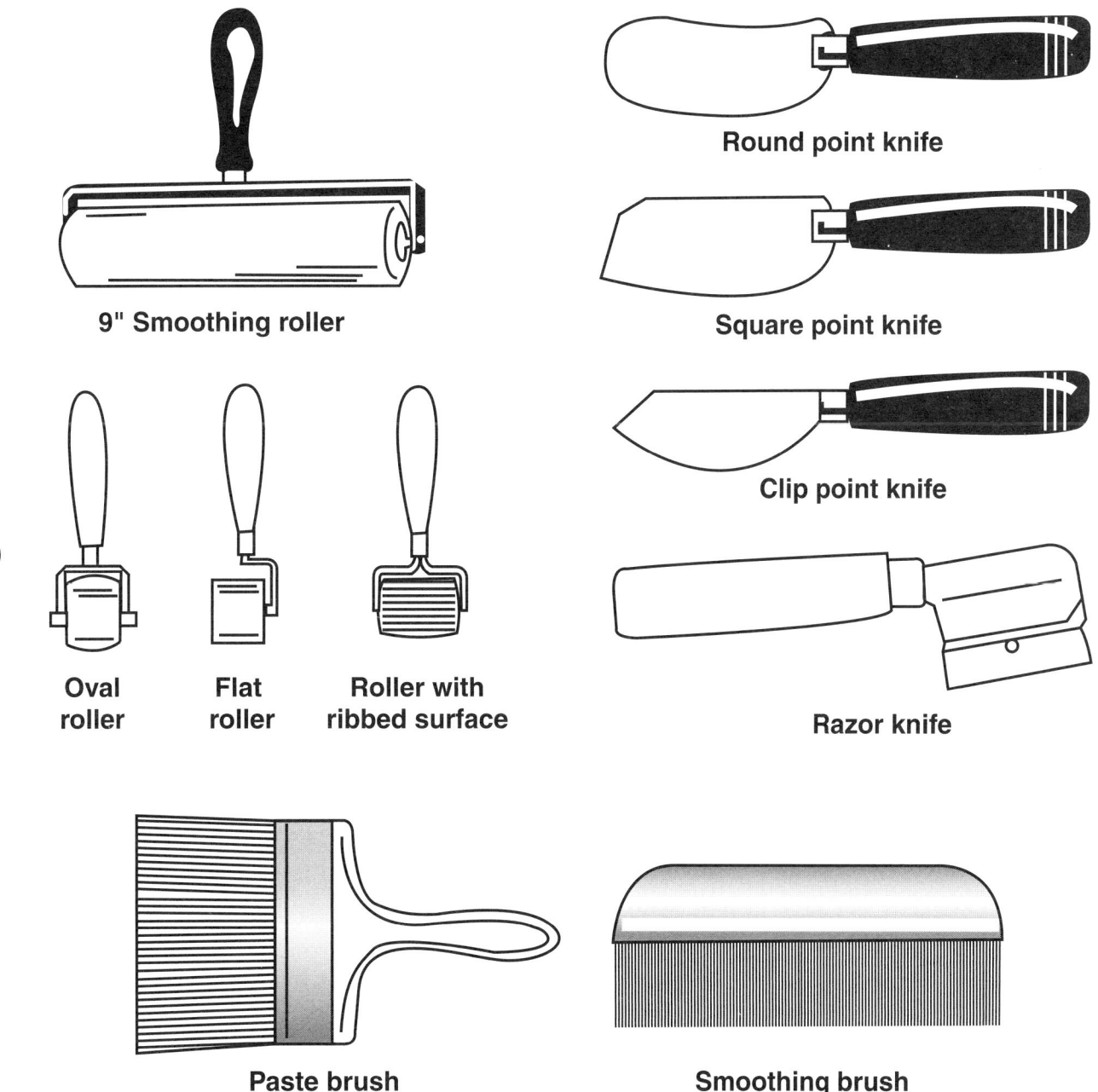

Chapter 21 Quiz
Painting, Finishing, and Decorating

Name _____ Date _____ Score _____

True-False
Circle T if the answer is True or F if the answer is False.

T   F   1. Coatings is a term used to describe all types of finishes.

T   F   2. It is safe for anyone wearing a respirator to remove paint containing lead.

T   F   3. Quality paintbrushes taper from the ferrule to the tip of the stock.

T   F   4. A suction-feed spray gun works best with light-bodied coating materials.

Completion
Fill in the correct word(s) that best completes the sentence.

_____ 5. A(n) _____ spray gun works best when air pressures are low.

_____ 6. _____ are the oils or resins that make a paint fluid.

_____ 7. _____ are heavy-bodied liquids that fill the depressions of an open-grain wood.

_____ 8. Red, blue, and yellow are known as the _____ colors.

_____ 9. On new exterior wood, the first coat of finish should be a(n) _____ or a(n) _____.

_____ 10. Wood _____ is the removal of some of a wood's color.

_____ 11. A(n) _____ is a bare spot in a clear finish.

Identification

Identify the parts of the paintbrush.

_____ 12. Handle.

_____ 13. Plug.

_____ 14. Ferrule.

_____ 15. Setting.

_____ 16. Bristle or stock.

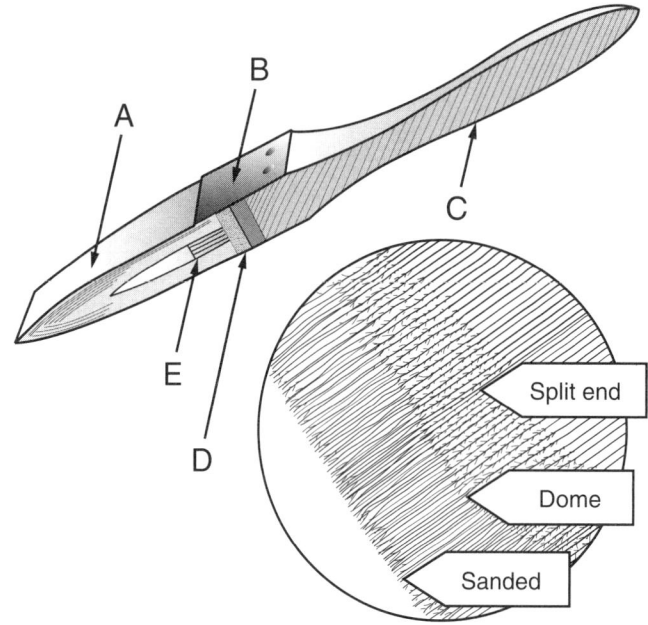

Section 4 Exam
Finishing

Name _____ Date _____ Score _____

True-False
Circle T if the answer is True or F if the answer is False.

T F 1. Insulation with a higher R-value provides better insulating qualities than insulation with a lower value.

T F 2. A vapor barrier should be applied to the cold side of a wall.

T F 3. A portable circular saw must be used to cut drywall.

T F 4. Veneer plaster should be applied in thin layers, less than 1/8" thick.

T F 5. In three-coat plaster work, the first coat is called the brown coat.

T F 6. When installing wood strip flooring, nails for the finish flooring should go through the subfloor and into the joists when possible.

T F 7. Underlayment is not required for flooring materials such as vinyl and linoleum.

T F 8. In stair construction, the number of treads is always one less than the number of risers.

T F 9. The interior door frame covers the unfinished edges of the door opening and provides support for the door and its hardware.

T F 10. Gains are recesses used for hinges.

T F 11. The standard height for base kitchen cabinets is 30".

T F 12. The facing is finished strips applied to the front of the cabinet frame.

T F 13. Flush drawers have a rabbet along the top and sides of the front.

Multiple Choice
Choose the answer that correctly completes the statement. Write the corresponding letter in the space provided.

_____ 14. A(n) ____ is the product of one day and the number of degrees Fahrenheit that the mean temperature is below 65°F.
   A. R-value
   B. Btu
   C. degree day
   D. U-value

Permission granted to reproduce for educational use only.   Copyright by Goodheart-Willcox Co., Inc.

_____ 15. The temperature at which moisture is released as condensation when warm air is cooled is called the ____.
   A. degree day
   B. dewpoint
   C. R-value
   D. None of the above.

_____ 16. ____ insulation is a rigid insulation commonly used for the perimeter of structures.
   A. Polyethylene
   B. Polyurethane
   C. Polyester
   D. Polystyrene

_____ 17. The unit of measure used to indicate the intensity or loudness of sound is called a(n) ____.
   A. impact sound
   B. masking sound
   C. decibel
   D. STC

_____ 18. When cabinets are constructed on the job, the ____ is responsible for determining the kinds and sizes of joints.
   A. carpenter
   B. architect
   C. owner
   D. contractor

_____ 19. In drawer construction, a ____ is used to prevent the drawer from tilting forward when it is opened.
   A. leveler
   B. kicker
   C. baluster
   D. guide

Matching

Select the correct answer from the list on the right and place the corresponding letter in the blank on the left.

_____ 20. Conduction.   A. Transfer of heat by another agent, usually air.

_____ 21. Convection.   B. Transfer of heat through wave motion.

_____ 22. Radiation.   C. Transfer of heat from one molecule to another within a material or from one material to another when they are held in direct contact with one another.

Name _____

_____ 23. Btu.
_____ 24. k.
_____ 25. C.
_____ 26. R.
_____ 27. U.

A. Represents the total heat transmission.
B. Reciprocal of conductivity.
C. Conductance of a material.
D. Amount of heat needed to raise one pound of water one degree Fahrenheit.
E. Amount of heat transferred in one hour through one square foot of a given material that is 1″ thick and has a temperature difference between its surfaces of one degree Fahrenheit.

_____ 28. Unit rise.
_____ 29. Unit run.
_____ 30. Headroom.
_____ 31. Nosing.
_____ 32. Stringer.

A. Support for a stairway.
B. Part of the tread that overhangs the riser.
C. Line measurement along the front edges of the treads to the header above.
D. Height of a riser.
E. Width of a tread.

Identification
Identify the parts of the door.

_____ 33. Stiles.
_____ 34. Panels.
_____ 35. Rails.

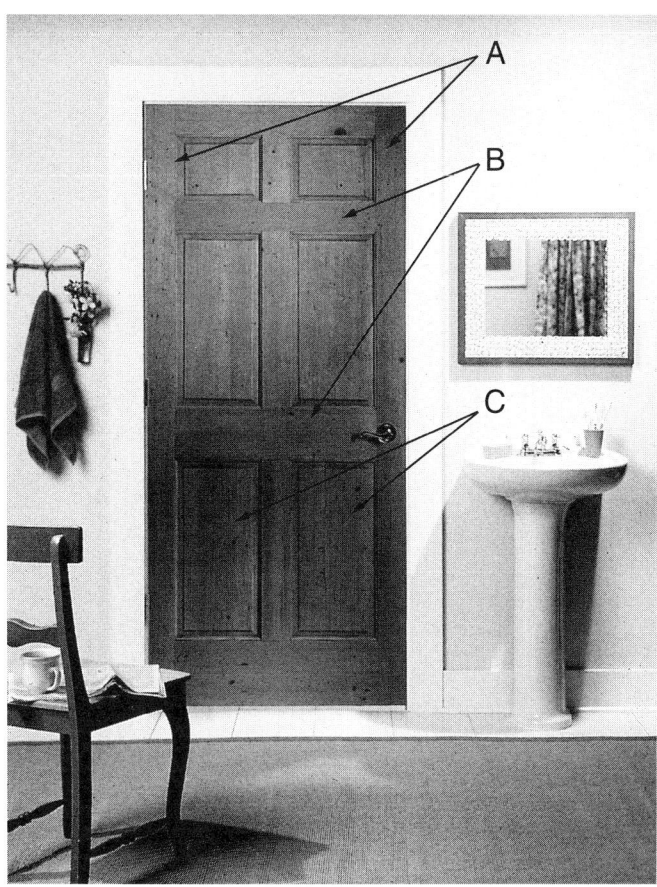

Identify the parts of the open stair.

_____ 36. Baluster.

_____ 37. Handrail.

_____ 38. Newel post.

_____ 39. Stringer.

_____ 40. Nosing.

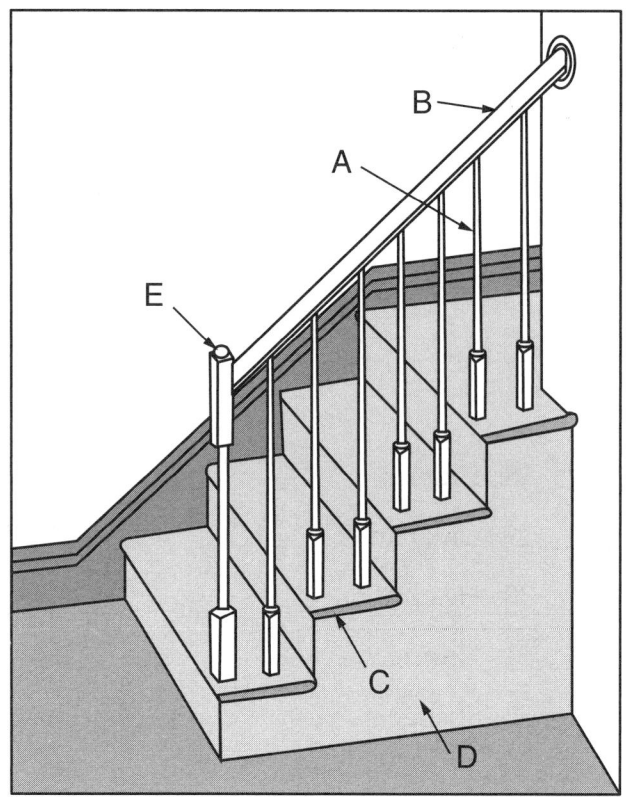

Identify the types of spray heads.

_____ 41. Internal mix.

_____ 42. External mix.

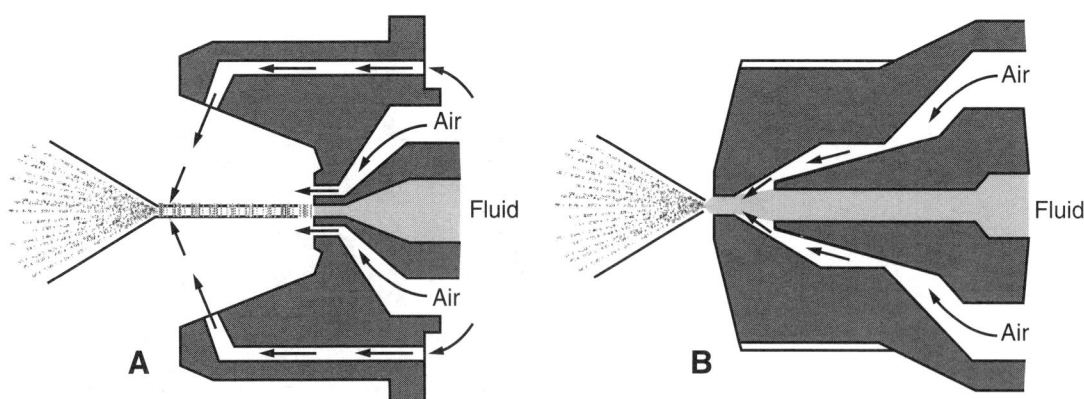

Name _____

Completion
Place the answer that correctly completes the statement in the space provided.

_____ 43. Sounds that are carried through a building by the vibrations of the materials themselves are called ____.

_____ 44. The reduction of the intensity of sound as it moves through a wall is called ____.

_____ 45. The best grade of plain-sawed oak flooring is ____.

_____ 46. A(n) ____ is a decorative structure that supports the handrail for open main stairways.

_____ 47. A(n) ____ covers the joints between the wall surface and the floor.

_____ 48. Plastic laminates are commonly adhered to a base material with ____.

_____ 49. ____ refers to air that leaks into buildings through cracks.

_____ 50. ____ is a gypsum board with a gray liner paper on both sides.

_____ 51. A(n) ____ is thin sheet material laid down to provide a smooth, even surface for the finish flooring.

_____ 52. The sum of one riser and one tread should equal ____ inches.

_____ 53. When constructing open stairways, the ____ must be securely anchored to the starter step or carried down through the floor and attached to a floor joist.

22 Chimneys and Fireplaces

Objectives

After studying this chapter, students will be able to:
- Explain how masonry chimneys are constructed around flue linings.
- Name the parts of a typical masonry fireplace.
- Describe procedures for the construction of the chimney, hearth, walls, and throat.
- Define the functions of the damper and smoke shelf.
- Calculate the flue area for a given fireplace.
- Describe the common types of factory-built fireplaces.
- List special considerations for installing factory-built fireplace units.
- Install a prefabricated flue.

Instructional Materials

Text: Pages 705–720
    Technical Vocabulary, page 705
    Test Your Knowledge, page 720
    Curricular Connections, page 720
    Outside Assignments, page 720
Workbook: Pages 139–144
Instructor's Resource:
    Reproducible Masters:
        RM 22-1 *Masonry Fireplace Components*
        RM 22-2 *Parts of a Prefabricated Chimney*
    Transparencies (binder/CD only):
        CT 22-1 *Major Components of a Masonry Fireplace*
    Chapter Quiz

Trade-Related Math

Ratios can be used to compare relationships between numbers. For example, one method of sizing flues for fireplaces is to allow 13 square inches of flue area for every 1 square foot of fireplace opening. If you want to determine the flue size that is appropriate for a fireplace with a 9 square foot opening, the ratio can be set up as follows:

$$\text{Flue size} = 13 \text{ sq. in.} / 1 \text{ sq. ft.} \times 9 \text{ sq. ft.}$$
$$= 13 \text{ sq. in.} \times 9$$
$$= 117 \text{ sq. in.}$$

Instructional Concepts and Student Learning Experiences

Masonry Chimneys

1. Explain that masonry chimneys do not receive support *from* or give support *to* the building frame.
2. Discuss the factors that determine the size of a chimney.
3. Cite reasons for extending chimneys above the roofline of a structure. Refer to Figure 22-1 for examples of the minimum requirements for chimney heights above rooflines. Have the students refer to the local building code to determine if these heights are similar to those required in your locality.
4. Explain that combustible materials such as wood framing should be located at least 2″ away from the chimney wall. List the types of materials that can be used to fill this open space.
5. Discuss the purpose of the flue lining.
6. Have the students identify the basic shapes of flue linings. Explain that there are different methods of measurement for the three types.
7. Describe the procedure typically used for constructing a masonry chimney. Mention that the chimney wall is usually constructed around the flue lining.
8. Discuss the reasons for corbelling a chimney.
9. Review the type of flashing that is commonly used around a chimney. Mention that one part of the flashing is built into the chimney

while the other part is attached to the surface of the roof.

Masonry Fireplaces

1. Using reproducible master RM 22-1 *Masonry Fireplace Components,* identify the primary parts. Describe the purpose of each part as it is identified.
2. Refer to Figure 22-6 or to a stock plan and point out the fireplace details that are important for a carpenter to notice.
3. Discuss the criteria that can be used to determine the appropriate size of a fireplace for a given structure. Refer to Figure 22-7 for dimensions that are commonly used for fireplaces.
4. Describe the construction of a hearth. Discuss variations of the basic design for slab-on-grade structures.
5. Illustrate the design of the side and back walls. Mention that the total thickness of the walls, including the firebrick, should not be less than 8″.
6. Define *splay* and describe its purpose.
7. Identify the two parts of the damper. Discuss how the damper affects the downdraft.
8. Review the purposes of the smoke shelf and smoke chamber. Describe possible scenarios that may occur if a gust of wind passes over the flue or if the smoke shelf and chamber were omitted from a design.
9. Discuss the methods used to determine the cross-sectional area of a flue. Mention that for chimneys over 20′ tall, the flue size should be increased.
10. Discuss a typical construction sequence for masonry fireplaces.
11. Using photographs from architectural magazines, show the students fireplace designs. Discuss how the flue area is determined for these types of fireplaces.
12. Discuss the advantages of built-in circulators. Describe the construction of a fireplace around a circulator.

Prefabricated Chimneys

1. Using reproducible master RM 22-2 *Parts of a Prefabricated Chimney,* discuss the construction of prefabricated chimneys. Explain the tasks of a carpenter when installing these types of chimneys.
2. Stress the importance of installing prefabricated chimneys that are approved by the Underwriters Laboratories (UL) or other recognized associations.
3. Explain how the construction of the chimney prevents superheating of its outside facing.

Prefabricated Fireplaces

1. Compare the operation of a prefabricated fireplace to that of a built-in circulator.
2. Define the term *zero clearance* and how it applies to prefabricated fireplaces.
3. Describe the frame construction around a prefabricated fireplace. Stress that the manufacturer's recommendations should be followed when constructing the framing.
4. Refer to Figure 22-20 to illustrate the type of chimney system commonly used for prefabricated fireplaces.
5. Define *chase* and describe how it can be framed and constructed.

Glass Enclosures

1. Explain the purpose of glass enclosures for fireplaces.

Chapter Review

1. Review the chapter objectives. Be sure that the students fully understand each objective.
2. Assign *Technical Vocabulary, Test Your Knowledge questions,, Curricular Connections, and Outside Assignments* for Chapter 22 of the text. Review the answers in class.
3. Assign Chapter 22 in the workbook. Review the answers in class.

Evaluation

This chapter provides three methods for evaluating student performance. Students should complete the *Test Your Knowledge* section using the book as reference. Students should also be allowed to use the book for reference when completing the workbook material. Use the Chapter 22 Quiz in the instructor's resources for in-class evaluation. Correct the quizzes, return them to the students, and review the quiz questions in group discussion.

Answers to Test Your Knowledge
Text Page 720

1. flues
2. 2″
3. 60
4. damper
5. width
6. 1/10
7. triple
8. stainless steel
9. rest directly on wood floor and touch wood framing members
10. chase

Answers to Workbook Questions
Pages 139–144

1. D. 6″
   C. 4″
2. A. 2′-6″
   B. 2′-0″
   C. 3′-0″
3. 2″, 7″
4. B. 5/8″
5. C. 15″ dia.
6. D. 60″
7. C. 6″
8. A. Flue.
   B. Damper.
   C. Smoke shelf.
   D. Firebrick.
   E. Hearth.
   F. Lintel.
   G. Smoke chamber.
9. ash pit
10. B. lintel
11. A. damper
    B. 8″
12. C. 5″ per foot
13. B. size
14. D. expansion
15. B. 1/2″
16. D. 13 sq. in.
17. larger
18. A. 4″
19. smoke chamber
20. A. 3 1/2″
21. A. Warm air is fed into the room from grillwork along the bottom edge.
22. A. single-walled
23. chase

Answers to Chapter Quiz

1. B. damper
2. D. 2′-0″
3. A. 4″
4. C. smoke chamber
5. B. 3 1/2″
6. J.
7. I.
8. F.
9. G.
10. A.
11. D.
12. C.
13. H.
14. B.
15. E.

Masonry Fireplace Components

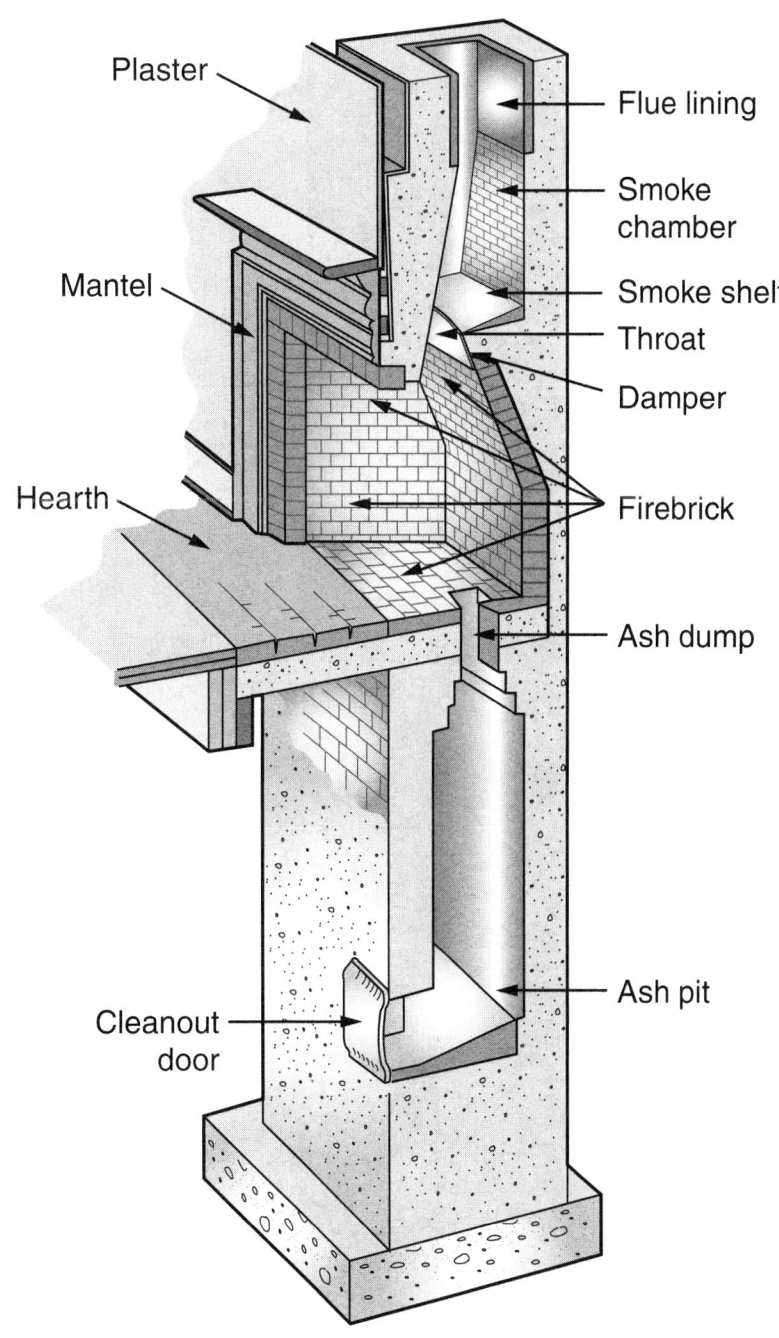

RM 22-1

Parts of a Prefabricated Chimney

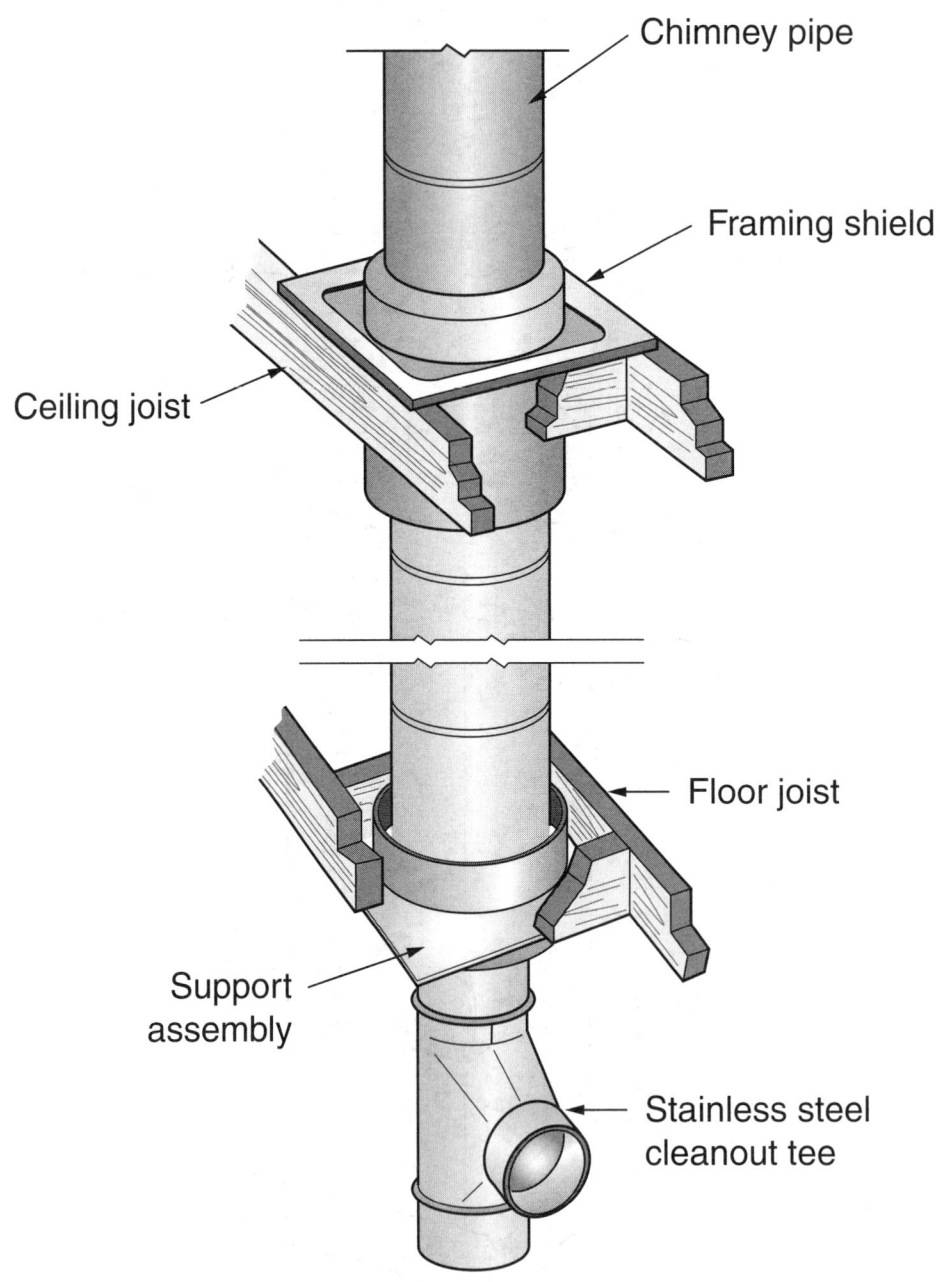

RM 22-2

Chapter 22 Quiz
Chimneys and Fireplaces

Name _____ Date _____ Score _____

Multiple Choice
Choose the answer that correctly completes the statement. Write the corresponding letter in the space provided.

_____ 1. The _____ is used to control a fire and also prevent loss of heat from a room when the fireplace is not being used.
  A. smoke shelf
  B. damper
  C. throat
  D. cleanout door

_____ 2. A chimney should extend _____ above any roof ridge that is within a 10-foot horizontal distance.
  A. 6"
  B. 1'-0"
  C. 1'-6"
  D. 2'-0"

_____ 3. The flue lining should project at least _____ above the top brick course or cap.
  A. 4"
  B. 8"
  C. 11"
  D. 1'-4"

_____ 4. The _____ is the space extending from the top of the throat to the bottom of the flue.
  A. flue lining
  B. hearth
  C. smoke chamber
  D. smoke shelf

_____ 5. According to FHA specifications, wooden parts of a prefabricated chimney should not be placed closer than _____ from the edge of the opening.
  A. 1 1/2"
  B. 3 1/2"
  C. 5 1/2"
  D. 7 1/2"

Identification

Identify the parts of a masonry fireplace.

_____ 6. Mantel.

_____ 7. Hearth.

_____ 8. Ash dump.

_____ 9. Ash pit.

_____ 10. Flue lining.

_____ 11. Throat.

_____ 12. Smoke shelf.

_____ 13. Cleanout door.

_____ 14. Smoke chamber.

_____ 15. Damper.

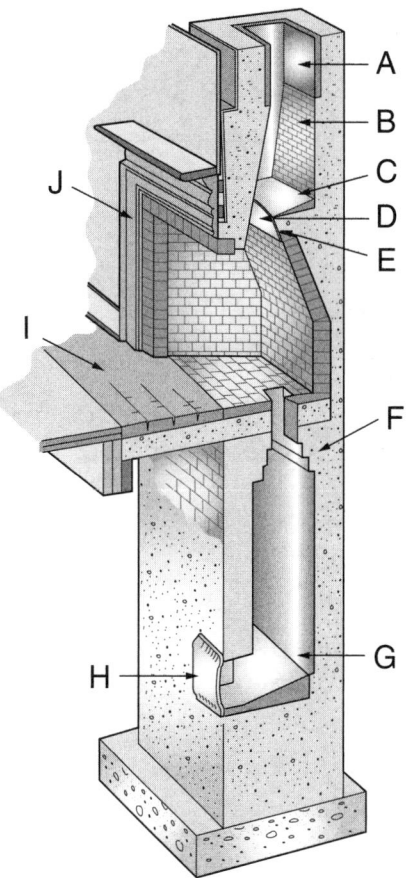

23 Post-and-Beam Construction

Objectives

After studying this chapter, students will be able to:
- List the advantages and disadvantages of post-and-beam construction.
- Describe general specifications for supporting posts.
- Compare transverse and longitudinal beams.
- Describe how roof and floor planks should be selected and installed.
- Sketch basic construction details of stressed skin panels and box beams.

Instructional Materials

Text: Pages 721–740
  Technical Vocabulary, page 721
  Test Your Knowledge, page 738
  Curricular Connections, page 738
  Outside Assignments, page 739
Workbook: Pages 145–150
Instructor's Resource:
  Reproducible Masters:
    RM 23-1A *Post-and-Beam Framing Details*
    RM 23-1B *Post-and-Beam Framing Details*
    RM 23-2 *Plank-and-Beam Roof Construction*
  Transparencies (binder/CD only):
    CT 23-1, *Post-and-Beam Construction*
  Chapter Quiz

Trade-Related Math

In many cases, a carpenter is required to read tables and charts. Span tables can be used to determine the size of beams required for a given span.

Instructional Concepts and Student Learning Experiences

Advantages
1. Compare typical post-and-beam construction with conventional framing. Have students list the advantages of post-and-beam construction. Also cite limitations of this construction method.

Foundations and Posts
1. Discuss the two basic types of foundations that can be used for post-and-beam construction: continuous walls or piers under each post.
2. Identify the minimum size posts that are required. Emphasize that these posts must not only be able to support the load, but also must provide bearing surfaces for the ends of the beams. Mention that as the post height increases, the cross-sectional area must also increase.
3. Using reproducible master RM 23-1A *Post-and-Beam Framing Details,* discuss the purpose of bearing blocks in post-and-beam construction.
4. Using reproducible master RM 23-1B *Post-and-Beam Framing Details,* compare the use of plates in post-and-beam framing construction to that of plates in conventional framing.

Floor Beams
1. Describe the type of floor beams that can be used for post-and-beam construction.
2. Explain how the silhouette of the structure can be kept low by forming beam pockets in the foundation walls.

Beam Descriptions
1. Discuss techniques that can be used to improve the appearance of exposed beams.

Roof Beams
1. Using reproducible master RM 23-2 *Plank-and-Beam Roof Construction,* identify the two types of beams used to support roof systems. Discuss the purpose of each type.

2. Describe the techniques used to secure transverse and ridge beams into position.

Fasteners
1. Stress that conventional nailing patterns *cannot* be used for post-and-beam construction. Identify the types of metal fasteners that can be used.

Partitions
1. Discuss the problems that may be encountered when trying to erect partitions in post-and-beam construction. Mention that it is best to erect these partitions after the beams and planks are in position.
2. Describe methods for installing partitions that run parallel to transverse beams.

Planks
1. Identify the plank patterns that are commonly used. Note that when end-matched planks are used, they need not meet over beams.
2. Stress the importance of selecting materials (floor planks, roof planks, beams, and posts) that will correspond closely to the moisture content of the interior of the structure. Have the students identify problems that may occur if the moisture content varies a great deal.
3. Describe how insulation and a vapor barrier are installed for plank roof structures.

Stressed Skin Panels
1. Explain the construction of stressed skin panels.
2. Discuss advantages of using these panels.

Box Beams
1. Discuss advantages of box beams in residential construction.
2. Describe the construction of box beams.

Laminated Beams and Arches
1. Identify the basic types of laminated wood arches shown in Figure 23-27. Have the students note the support and lateral thrust that must be provided.

Chapter Review
1. Review the chapter objectives. Be sure that the students fully understand each objective.

2. Assign *Technical Vocabulary, Test Your Knowledge questions, Curricular Connections*, and *Outside Assignments* for Chapter 23 of the text. Review the answers in class.
3. Assign Chapter 23 in the workbook. Review the answers in class.

Evaluation
This chapter provides three methods for evaluating student performance. Students should complete the *Test Your Knowledge* section using the book as reference. Students should also be allowed to use the book for reference when completing the workbook material. Use the Chapter 23 Quiz in the instructor's resources for in-class evaluation. Correct the quizzes, return them to the students, and review the quiz questions in group discussion.

Answers to Test Your Knowledge
Text Page 738
1. posts, beams, planks
2. Distinctive architectural effect created by the exposed beams in the ceiling and added ceiling height; the underside of the roof planks may serve as the ceiling surface, thus providing savings in materials; savings in labor
3. 4, 4
4. smallest
5. transverse
6. mortise-and-tenon
7. 4″
8. sheets of plywood (skins)
9. 120
10. False.

Answers to Workbook Questions
Pages 145–150
1. A. Planks.
   B. Beam.
   C. Plate.
   D. Transverse beam.
   E. Post.
2. fire resistance
3. C. bearing blocks
4. 30

5. 28
6. A. Solid.
   B. Vertical laminated.
   C. Horizontal laminated.
   D. Spaced with wood blocking.
7. A. 16″
8. A. Sole plate.
   B. Post or stud.
   C. Plank.
   D. Beam.
   E. Sill.
   F. Band joist.
9. longitudinal
10. lag screws
11. D. sloping
12. is
13. C. 2″ to 4″
14. A. Vapor barrier.
   B. Rigid insulation.
   C. Built-up roof.
   D. Gravel stop.
15. A. Transverse Beam
   B. Longitudinal Beam
16. sandwich
17. D. 120′
18. softwood
19. A. Radial.
   B. Gothic.
   C. A-frame.
   D. Tudor.
   E. Three-centered.
   F. Parabolic.
20. B. 24″

Answers to Chapter Quiz

1. B. 4×4
2. D. All of the above.
3. D. Both B and C.
4. C. Stressed skin
5. D.
6. E.
7. F.
8. A.
9. B.
10. C.
11. G.
12. D.
13. F.
14. A.
15. B.
16. E.
17. C.

Post-and-Beam Framing Details

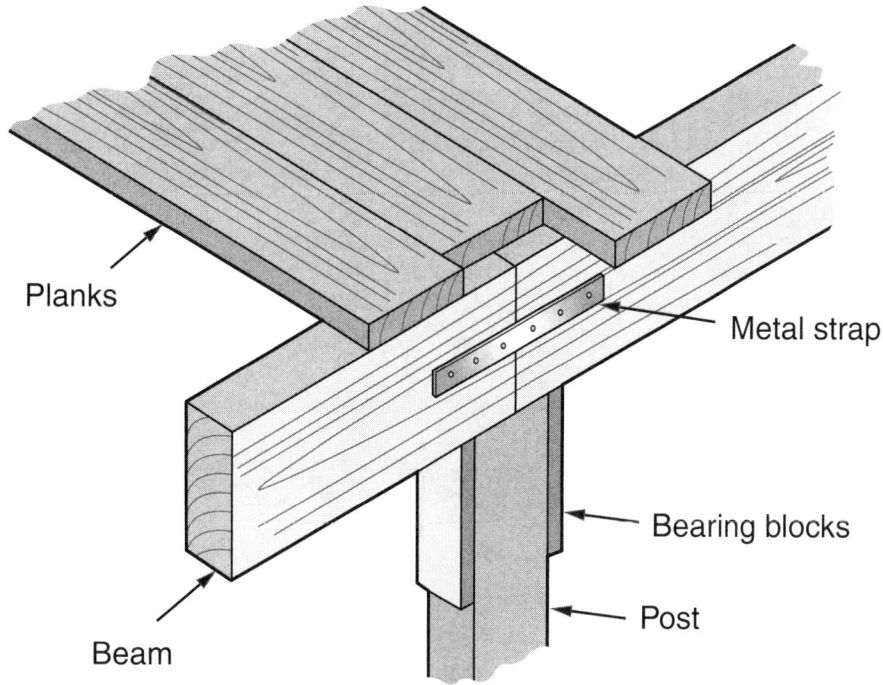

RM 23-1A

Post-and-Beam Framing Details

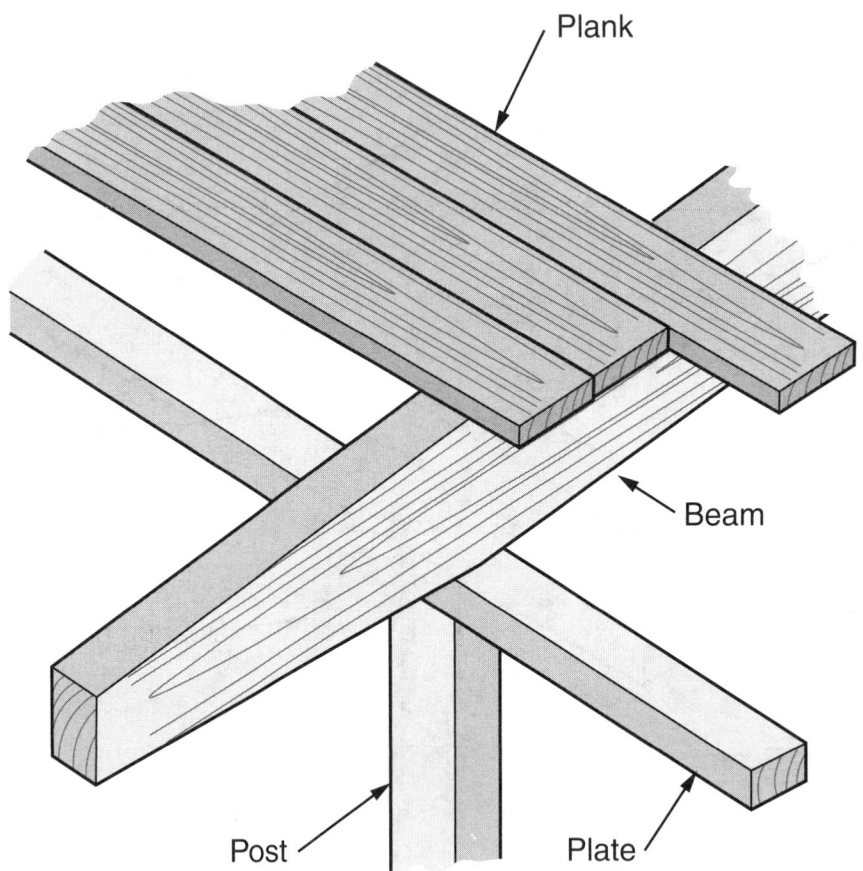

RM 23-1B

Plank-and-Beam Roof Construction

Transverse beam

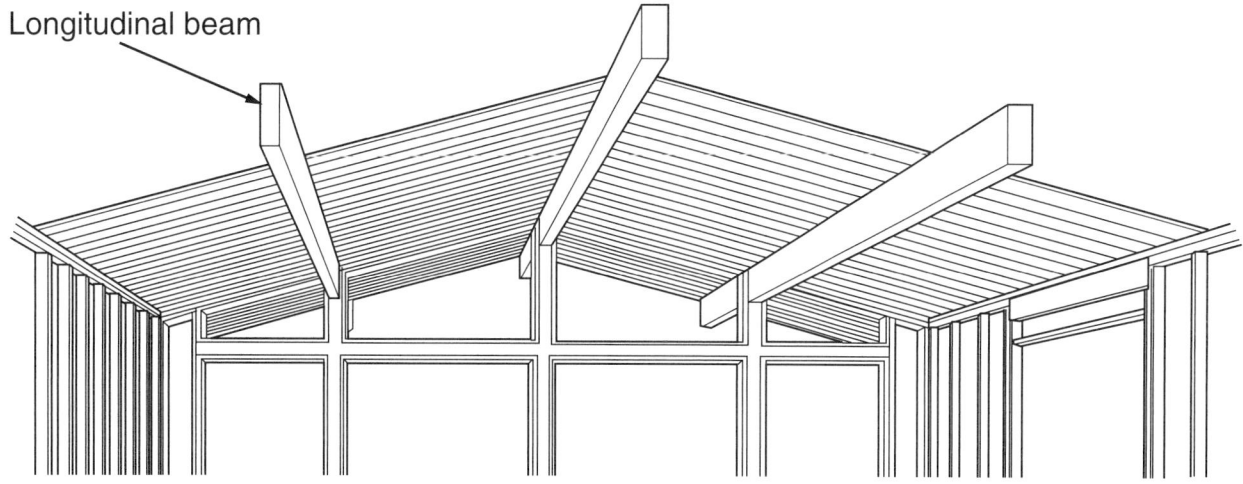

Longitudinal beam

RM 23-2

Chapter 23 Quiz
Post-and-Beam Construction

Name _____ Date _____ Score _____

Multiple Choice
Choose the answer that correctly completes the statement. Write the corresponding letter in the space provided.

_____ 1. In general, posts should not have a nominal size less than ____.
  A. 2 × 4
  B. 4 × 4
  C. 8 × 8

_____ 2. Beams for floor structures may be ____.
  A. solid
  B. glue-laminated
  C. built-up
  D. All of the above.

_____ 3. ____ beams run parallel to the supporting side walls and ridge beam.
  A. Transverse
  B. Longitudinal
  C. Purlin
  D. Both B and C.

_____ 4. ____ panels are made by gluing sheets of plywood to longitudinal frame members.
  A. Solid-core plywood
  B. Particle board
  C. Stressed skin

Identification
Identify the parts of the typical sill construction for the post-and-beam frame.

_____ 5. Sill.

_____ 6. Foundation.

_____ 7. Band joist.

_____ 8. Post.

_____ 9. Plank.

_____ 10. Beam.

_____ 11. Sole plate.

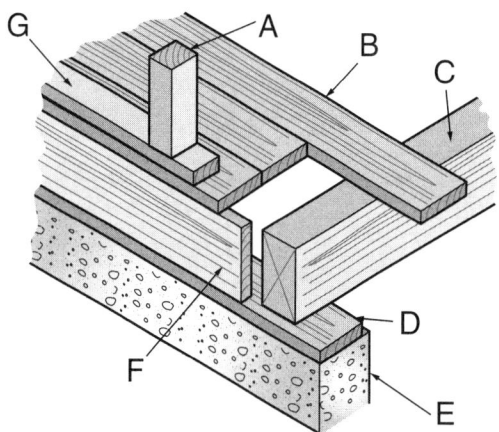

Identify the types of laminated wood arches.

_____ 12. Tudor.

_____ 13. Parabolic.

_____ 14. Radial.

_____ 15. Gothic.

_____ 16. Three-centered.

_____ 17. A-frame.

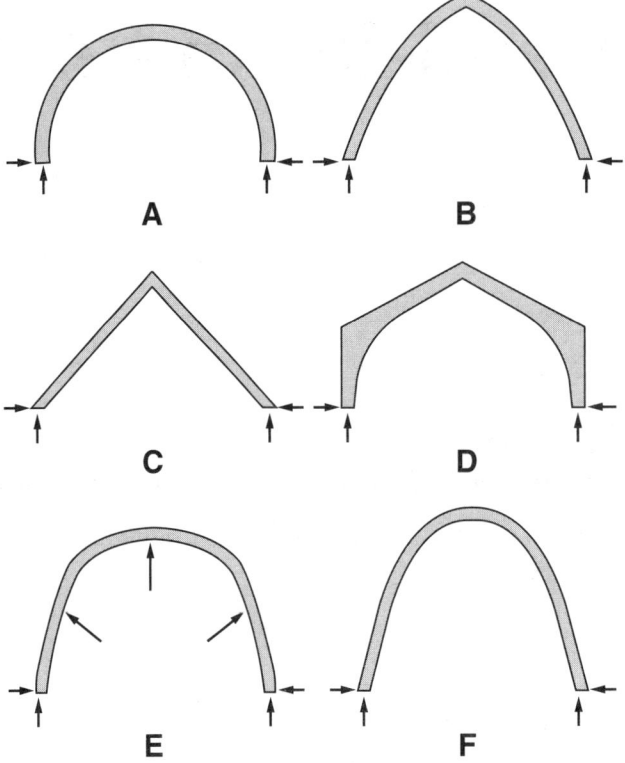

24 Systems-Built Housing

Objectives
After studying this chapter, students will be able to:
- Describe the changes that have taken place in the technology of systems-built housing.
- Identify the variety of factory-built components that are utilized in a systems-built home.
- List and differentiate between the basic types of systems-built structures.
- Explain the erection sequence of a panelized home.
- Define terms used in the systems-built housing industry.

Instructional Materials
Text: Pages 741–756
 Technical Vocabulary, page 741
 Test Your Knowledge, page 756
 Curricular Connections, page 756
 Outside Assignments, page 756
Workbook: Pages 151–154
Instructor's Resource:
 Reproducible masters:
  RM 24-1 *Panelized Construction*
  RM 24-2 *Typical Closed Panels for Systems-Built Housing*
 Chapter Quiz

Instructional Concepts and Student Learning Experiences

Introduction
1. Define the term *systems-built housing*.
2. Describe the technological changes that have occurred in the factory-built housing industry.

Transporting
1. Describe the method of moving systems-built housing from the factory to the building site.
2. List types of buildings that are assembled or partially assembled in the factory setup.

Components
1. List the components commonly used in prefabricated construction. Cite reasons why these components are factory built, while others are not.
2. Explain the advantages gained through prefabrication of building components.

Types of Systems-Built Homes
1. Identify the five basic types of systems-built homes and briefly describe the construction of each.
2. Briefly discuss the four qualities offered by factory-built homes.
3. Review the factory cutting and assembly of a panelized home.
4. List the characteristics of a precut house.
5. Using reproducible master RM 24-1 *Panelized Construction*, list the characteristics of a panelized prefabrication and explain how it differs from precut prefabrication.
6. List the characteristics of sectionalized (modular) prefabrication and explain how it differs from panelized construction. Refer to reproducible master RM 24-2 *Typical Closed Panels for Systems-Built Housing*. Discuss the advantages that this type of construction offers over other prefabrication methods. Describe any limitations or disadvantages of sectionalized prefabrication.
7. List the characteristics of manufactured home construction. Discuss advantages and disadvantages of this type of prefabrication.

On-site Building Erection
1. Describe the general procedure for on-site construction of a modular prefabricated house.
2. Discuss disadvantages of prefabricated construction that may occur on the building site.

Chapter Review

1. Review the chapter objectives. Be sure that the students fully understand each objective.
2. Assign *Technical Vocabulary, Test Your Knowledge* questions, *Curricular Connections,* and *Outside Assignments* for Chapter 24 of the text. Review the answers in class.
3. Assign Chapter 24 in the workbook. Review the answers in class.

Evaluation

This chapter provides three methods for evaluating student performance. Students should complete the *Test Your Knowledge* section using the book as reference. Students should also be allowed to use the book for reference when completing the workbook material. Use the Chapter 24 Quiz in the instructor's resources for in-class evaluation. Correct the quizzes, return them to the students, and review the quiz questions in group discussion.

Answers to Test Your Knowledge
Text Page 756

1. Systems-built housing
2. Roof truss.
3. Modular homes (or mods or modules)
4. mechanical
5. panelized
6. precut
7. Foundation or slab has already been constructed and the systems-built house is on trailers.
8. False.
9. 5 to 20 hours.
10. foundation

Answers to Workbook Questions
Pages 151–154

1. building site
2. modules
3. C. high-production
4. Modular: C
   Precut: B
   Manufactured home: D
   Log home: E
   Panelized: A
5. Floor truss.
6. B. gang-nail
7. panelized
8. jigs
9. channels, chases
10. A. power nailers
11. C. Plumbing fixtures are seldom installed until erection is completed on the building site.
12. mechanical core
13. B. 4500 lb.
14. A. Roof panel.
    B. Ceiling joist.
    C. THA joist hanger.
    D. Wall panel.
    E. Glue/sealant.
15. True.

Answers to Chapter Quiz

1. True.
2. False.
3. False.
4. F. All of the above.
5. C. modular
6. C. mechanical
7. A. closed panels

Panelized Construction

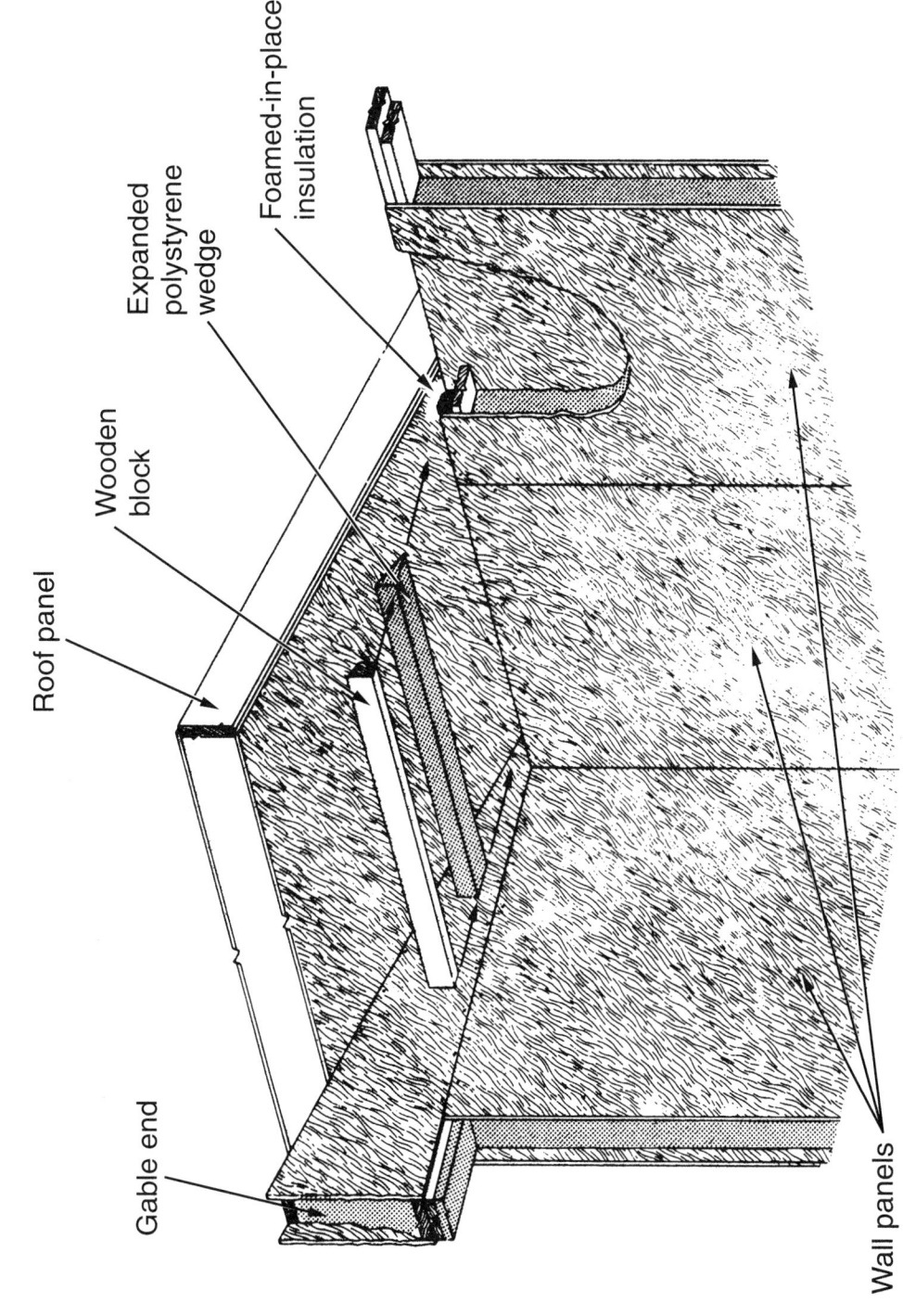

RM 24-1

Typical Closed Panels for Systems-Built Housing

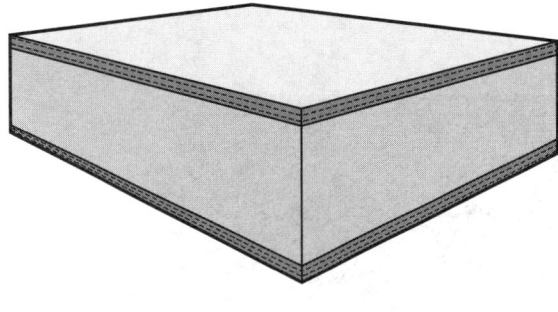

Structural pannel with rigid polystyrene center and facings of OSB. Center may be up to 11 3/8″ thick.

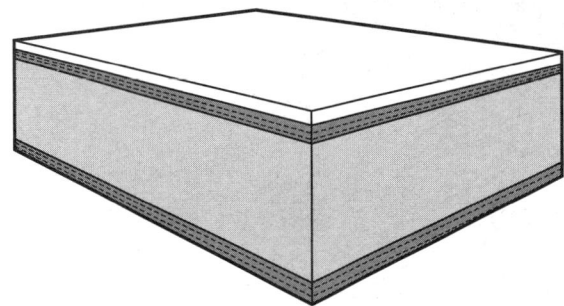

Sandwich panel with a drywall interior facing over OSB.

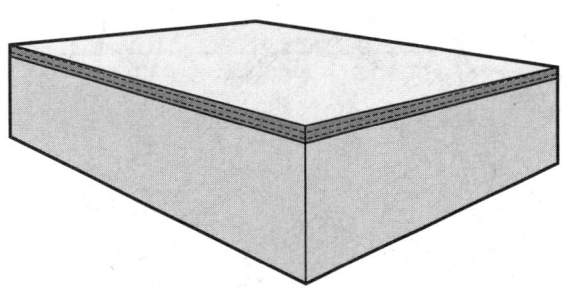

Nail-base panel designed to add a thick layer of insulation over a completed roof deck or wall.

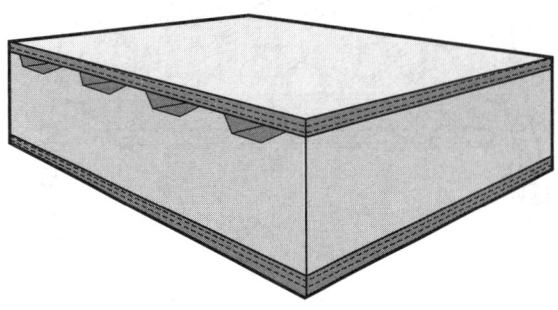

Vented panel designed to provide roof ventilation when desired (Insulspan).

RM 24-2

Chapter 24 Quiz
Systems-Built Housing

Name _____ Date _____ Score _____

True-False
Circle T if the answer is True or F if the answer is False.

T F 1. A systems-built house consists of components, panels, or modules cut and assembled in a factory.

T F 2. Firms producing systems-built structures do not offer custom designing.

T F 3. Modular units are easily lifted by hand onto their foundation.

Multiple Choice
Choose the answer that correctly completes the statement. Write the corresponding letter in the space provided.

_____ 4. A ____ home is a basic type of factory-built construction.
   A. precut
   B. panelized
   C. modular
   D. log
   E. manufactured
   F. All of the above.

_____ 5. In ____ systems construction, entire sections of the structure are built and finished in manufacturing plants.
   A. precut
   B. panelized
   C. modular
   D. log
   E. All of the above.

_____ 6. A modular section that has a group of plumbing and heating facilities is often called a(n) ____ core.
   A. electrical
   B. modular
   C. mechanical
   D. facilities

_____ 7. Prefabricated panels finished on both inside and outside are called ____.
   A. closed panels
   B. open panels
   C. stressed skin panels
   D. mechanical cores

25 Passive Solar Construction

Objectives

After studying this chapter, students will be able to:
- Define conduction, convection, radiation, and thermosiphoning.
- Explain the difference between passive and active solar construction.
- List and describe the three types of passive solar construction.
- Calculate the amount of glazing and storage needed for a passive solar system.
- Locate a dwelling on a lot for maximum solar gain.
- Design and install various passive solar.

Instructional Materials

Text: Pages 757–776
 Technical Vocabulary, page 757
 Test Your Knowledge, page 775
 Curricular Connections, page 775
 Outside Assignments, page 776
Workbook: Pages 155–158
Instructor's Resource:
 Reproducible masters:
  RM 25-1 *Trombe Wall Section*
  RM 25-2 *Cross Section of a Well-Insulated Dwelling*
 Transparencies (binder/CD only):
  CT 25-1 *Storing and Moving Solar-Generated Heat*
 Chapter Quiz

Trade-Related Math

The width of the overhang is important when designing a solar structure. Three factors are used to determine the overhang distance: height of the window or collector, height difference between the header and the window or collector, and latitude of the building site. For example, the window height might be 6'-8", the header height 7'-6", and the building site in southern Minnesota. The formula, used with the chart in Figure 25-15, is as follows:

$$\text{Projection} = \frac{(\text{window height} + \text{height difference})}{\text{factor}}$$

$$\text{Projection} = \frac{(6'\text{-}8'' + (7'\text{-}6'' - 6'\text{-}8''))}{2.1}$$

$$= \frac{(6'\text{-}8'' + 10'')}{2.1}$$

$$= \frac{90''}{2.1}$$

$$= 42.85''$$

$$= 42\frac{27}{32}''$$

$$\text{Projection} = 3'\text{-}6\frac{27}{32}''$$

Instructional Concepts and Student Learning Experiences

How Radiation and Heat Act

1. Define the term *greenhouse effect*. Discuss its effect on solar construction.
2. Identify the three heat transfer methods—conduction, convection, and radiation.
3. Describe the concept of conduction as it relates to building materials.
4. Describe the concept of convection, stressing that this type of heat transfer only occurs in fluids or gases.
5. Describe the concept of radiation as it relates to building components.
6. Define *thermosiphoning* and how this concept is applied to both passive and active solar heating.

Types of Energy Systems

1. Identify the two approaches used in solar construction—active and passive.

2. Describe an active solar energy system used in residential construction. Explain why it is called active.
3. Using Figure 25-6, identify the typical components of an active solar energy system.

Passive Solar Construction
1. Describe the difference between an active solar energy system and a passive solar energy system.
2. Define the term *gain* as it relates to solar construction.
3. Identify the three basic types of passive solar construction—direct gain, indirect gain, and isolated gain.
4. Ask the students to list the architectural styles that work best with passive solar construction.
5. Discuss how a simple direct-gain solar system works. Be sure to include the terms *radiation* and *convection* in the discussion. List disadvantages of this type of system.
6. Explain the difference between a direct gain and an indirect gain system.
7. Discuss the purpose of a Trombe wall and describe its operation. Explain how the radiation and convection principles are used to distribute the heat.
8. Describe how a water storage wall works. Discuss the use of phase change materials instead of water.
9. Explain how an isolated gain system works. Have students list its advantages over other types of solar systems.

Passive Solar Advantages/Disadvantages
1. Discuss the advantages of passive solar energy systems over active solar energy systems.
2. Discuss the disadvantages of passive solar systems.

Solar Heat Control
1. Identify methods used to control solar heat for passive solar systems. These might include: structural features of the solar house, movable insulation, and natural shade obtained from trees and other surroundings.
2. List the three factors that are used to determine the width of the overhang for a solar structure.
3. Use the formula shown in section 25.6.1 Overhangs in the text to determine the overhang projection that is required in your area of the country.
4. Discuss the advantages of using movable insulation for solar structures.
5. Identify various types of movable insulation that can be used and cite advantages or disadvantages of each type.
6. Explain the purpose of adequate venting in indirect and isolated gain systems.
7. Discuss the proper orientation of a solar structure for taking maximum advantage of the solar system.
8. Identify the three sources of energy that supply heat to a structure on a winter day.
9. Discuss the appropriate location of appliances in a solar structure to balance internal heat gain.

Building Passive Solar Structures
1. Identify the materials commonly used to store heat in a solar structure. Cite advantages and disadvantages of each type.
2. Discuss how thermal storage systems are sized for solar structures.
3. Explain how the thickness and color of the storage walls also affect the temperature inside a solar structure.
4. Using reproducible master RM 25-1 *Trombe Wall Section*, discuss the construction of a Trombe wall. Have the students note the use of the insulation in the hollow header and joist spaces. Explain the types of adjustments that must be made to the footing and foundation on which a Trombe wall is located.

Special Concerns
1. Mention that thermal glazing should be constructed so that the glass panels can be removed for cleaning. Emphasize that double glazing is the most efficient type of glazing used in a solar structure.

Designing an Isolated Gain System
1. Discuss the design of an isolated gain system. Based on the sketch shown in Figure 25-11, have the students determine the most inexpensive, yet effective, design.

Passive Thermosiphon System
1. Have the students determine the volume of the storage area required for a given size solar collector. Stress that the rock bins for thermal storage must be well insulated. Also explain that dampers should be used in the ductwork leading to the storage bin so that heat is not released back to the bin at night.

Insulating Passive Solar Buildings
1. Using reproducible master RM 25-2 *Cross Section of a Well-Insulated Dwelling,* emphasize the importance of placing thermal barriers anywhere heat could exit the structure.

Chapter Review
1. Review the chapter objectives. Be sure that the students fully understand each objective.
2. Assign *Technical Vocabulary, Test Your Knowledge* questions, *Curricular Connections,* and *Outside Assignments* for Chapter 25 of the text. Review the answers in class.
3. Assign Chapter 25 in the workbook. Review the answers in class.

Evaluation
This chapter provides three methods for evaluating student performance. Students should complete the *Test Your Knowledge* section using the book as reference. Students should also be allowed to use the book for reference when completing the workbook material. Use the Chapter 25 Quiz in the instructor's resources for in-class evaluation. Correct the quizzes, return them to the students, and review the quiz questions in group discussion.

Answers to Test Your Knowledge
Text Page 775
1. greenhouse
2. Conduction, convection, and radiation.
3. Thermosiphoning
4. A. It has few, if any, moving parts.
   B. It is usually a stationary, structural part of the house.
   D. Collection, storage, and transporting of heat is naturally done by the materials used in construction.
5. A. Control of the heat is not as responsive as either conventional heat systems or active solar systems.
   B. It is not a simple matter to control heat and heat distribution.
6. The height of the window or collector. The height of the header above the window or collector. The latitude of the building.
7. appliances, occupants
8. 150 lb.
9. False.
10. B. 520 to 800 cu. ft.

Answers to Workbook Questions
Pages 155–158
1. heat
2. A. Heat from solar radiation cannot pass through glass.
3. C. System is expensive to maintain.
   D. System will not work during a power outage.
4. A. Trees/natural shade.
   B. Constructed protection/outdoor structures.
   C. Movable insulation.
5. B. Direct gain.
6. active
7. A. Thermal storage wall.
   B. Nighttime insulation.
   C. Vertical south glazing.
   D. Additional thermal storage.
   E. Circulation vents.
8. 5'-3"
9. C. 5.6
10. Movable insulation.
11. E. locate the structure so one wall will catch the sun's rays all day long
12. B. orientation
13. windows/glazing
14. north
15. C. 10"–14"
16. A. 10
    B. 20

Answers to Chapter Quiz
1. True.
2. False.

3. False.
4. True.
5. False.
6. False.
7. True.
8. D. All of the above.
9. B. indirect
10. B. south
11. C. isolated
12. D. All of the above.

Trombe Wall Section

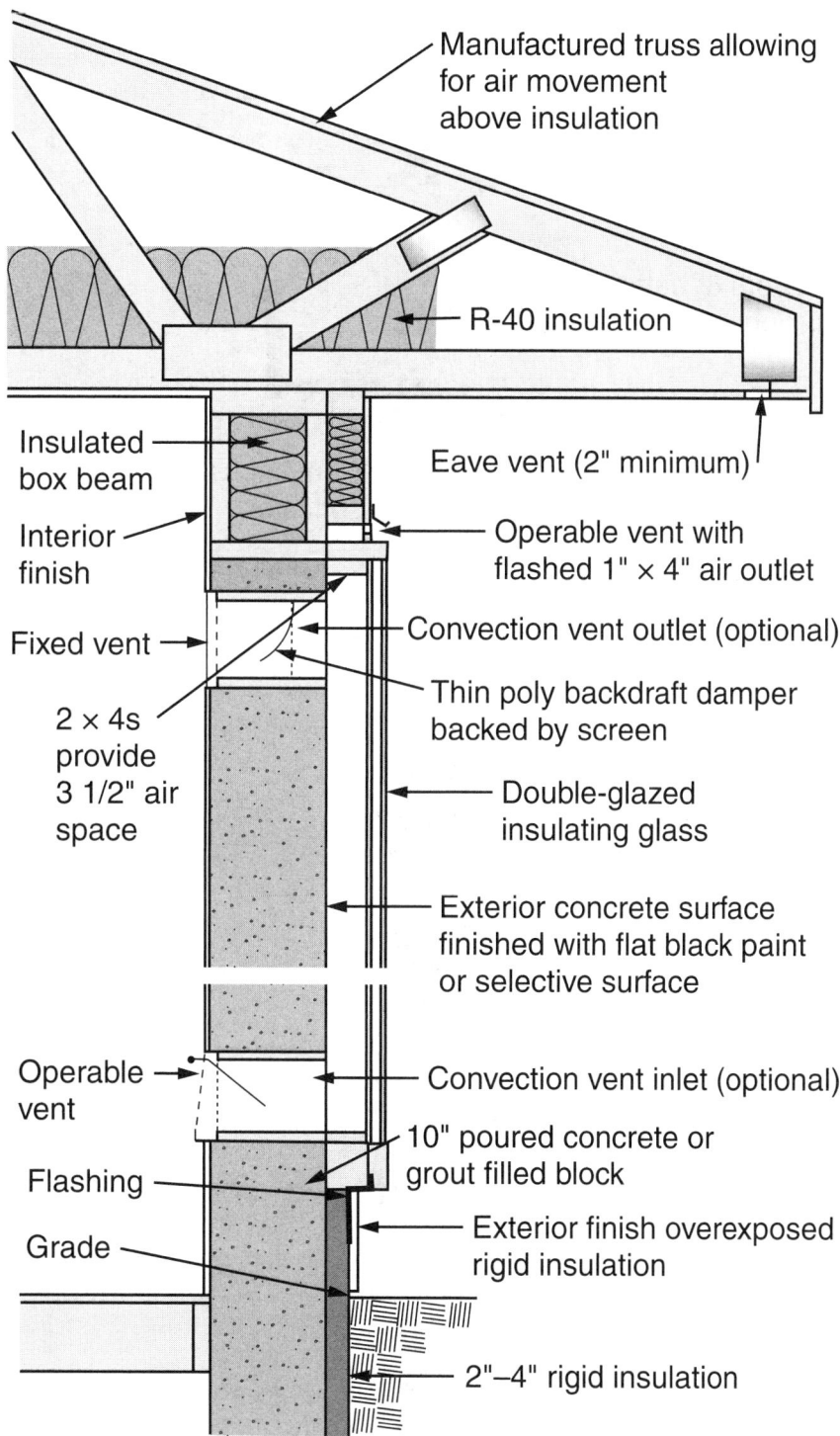

RM 25-1

Cross Section of a Well-Insulated Dwelling

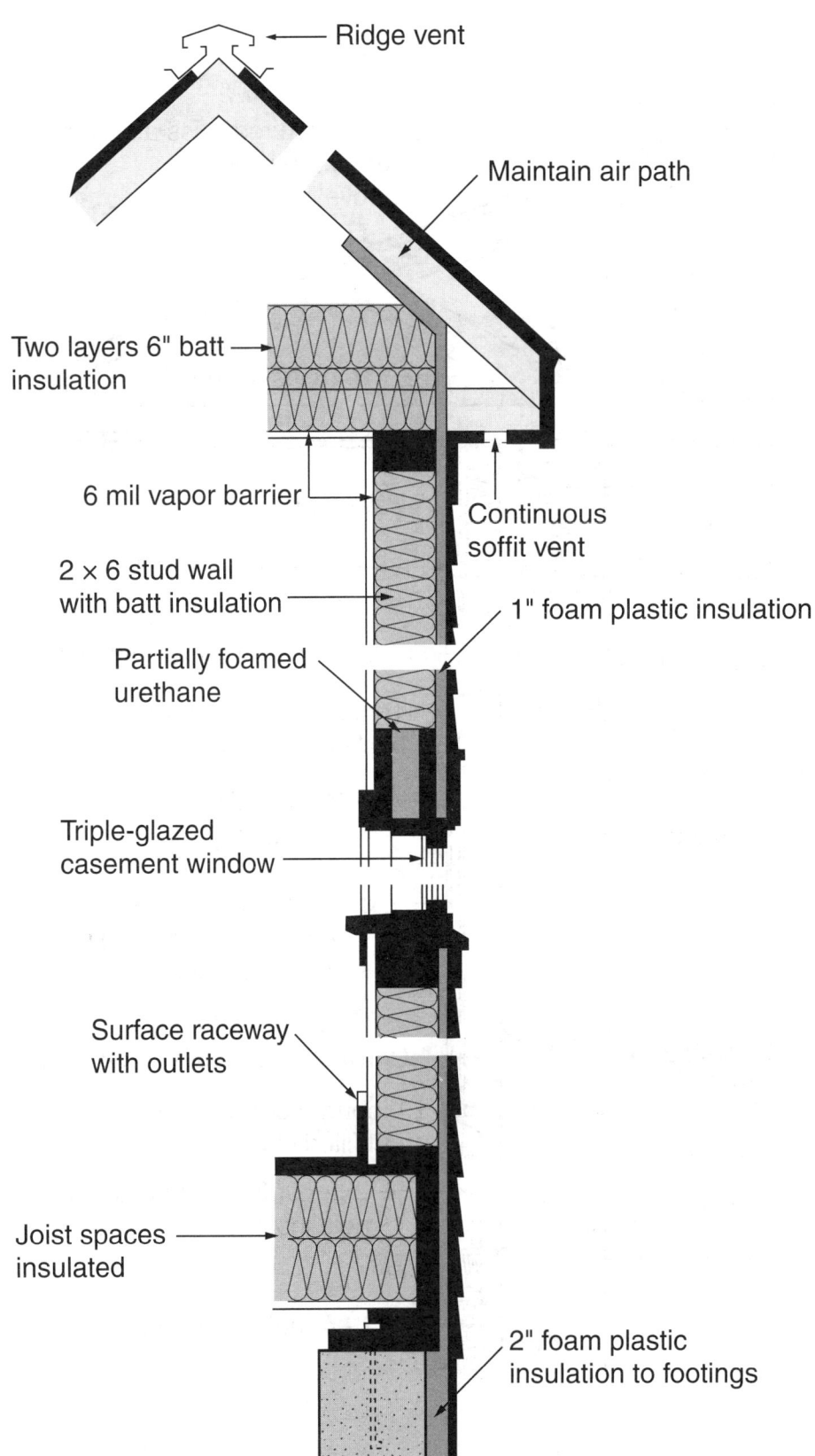

RM 25-2

Chapter 25 Quiz
Passive Solar Construction

Name _____ Date _____ Score _____

True-False
Circle T if the answer is True or F if the answer is False.

T   F   1. Convection occurs only in fluids or gases.

T   F   2. Heat gained from appliances or occupants of a home is referred to as residential heat.

T   F   3. Passive solar systems require pumps or blowers to carry heated air or fluid to the place where it will be used or stored.

T   F   4. A major disadvantage of direct gain systems is the wide range of heat fluctuation.

T   F   5. A Trombe wall is a nonbearing wall.

T   F   6. In a direct gain system, the sun's rays enter directly through the glazing and heat up a thermal mass.

T   F   7. Water is an effective material for the storage of solar heat.

Multiple Choice
Choose the answer that correctly completes the statement. Write the corresponding letter in the space provided.

_____ 8. Heat can travel by _____.
   A. radiation
   B. convection
   C. conduction
   D. All of the above.

_____ 9. The Trombe wall is an example of a(n) _____ gain solar system.
   A. direct
   B. indirect
   C. isolated
   D. transferred

_____ 10. Most of the windows in solar construction are placed in the _____-facing wall.
   A. north
   B. south
   C. east
   D. west

_____ 11. In the _____ gain system, the solar heat is collected and stored in an area away from the living or working space.
   A. direct
   B. indirect
   C. isolated
   D. transferred

_____ 12. A material commonly used for thermal storage wall construction is _____.
   A. water
   B. concrete
   C. brick
   D. All of the above.

26 Remodeling, Renovating, and Repairing

Objectives

After studying this chapter, students will be able to:
- Identify different types of residential construction by visual inspection.
- Set up a proper sequence of renovation or repair for the interior and exterior of a house.
- Repair and replace deteriorated components and systems.
- Remove parts of the structure without damaging the total structure.
- List steps for removal of wall sections prior to remodeling.
- Identify bearing walls.
- Determine loads and calculate the correct header size for the span.
- Install and support headers, concealed headers, and saddle beams.
- Follow accepted methods in replacing all types of doors.
- Make repairs to wood and asphalt shingles.
- Make a solar retrofit on an older home.

Instructional Materials

Text: Pages 777–802
  Technical Vocabulary, page 777
  Test Your Knowledge, page 801
  Curricular Connections, page 801
  Outside Assignments, page 802
Workbook: Pages 159–162
Instructor's Resource:
  Reproducible masters:
    RM 26-1 *Remodeling Post-and-Beam Construction*
    RM 26-2 *Replacing Rotted Sills*
    RM 26-3 *Guidelines for Sizing Headers*
  Transparencies (binder/CD only):
    CT 26-1 *Sizing Headers*
    CT 26-2 *Calculating Loads*
  Chapter Quiz

Trade-Related Math

The method used to compute the load on a header is shown in Figure 26-25. Instruct students that the number of square feet must be determined first. The length of the span needed is then multiplied by half of the distance between load-bearing walls. Any other loads that the header must support are added to find the total load.

Instructional Concepts and Student Learning Experiences

Exterior Renovation

1. Instruct students about the importance of making structural repairs before attempting any other exterior or interior renovation projects. Jacking of a sagging frame may affect fit of doors and windows; other repairs may be needed to ensure personal safety.
2. Review the sequence of tasks for exterior renovation listed under heading 26.1.1.
3. If you have "live" renovation work, have students examine the structure from the outside and prepare a list of the work that needs to be done. Have a class discussion during which students compare their lists and prepare a final work order for the renovation.
4. If live work is not available, secure photos of local structures and have students study them and list needed repairs and/or renovation tasks.

Interior Renovation

1. Explain why interior renovations may coincide with exterior work.
2. Discuss ways of doing interior renovation while the dwelling is still occupied. Review zone-by-zone and room-by-room renovation methods.
3. Review interior renovation details under heading 26.1.2.

4. If live work is available, have students prepare a sequence for the work to be done. Review in class and finalize the list before beginning the renovation.
5. If live work is not available, give students a simulated work order for interior renovation and have them prepare a sequence of tasks.

Replacing Rotted Sills
1. Review Figure 26-11 with students. Using reproducible master RM 26-2 *Replacing Rotted Sills*, discuss the method of supporting a building frame while a rotted member is replaced.
2. Explain sistering to support rotting vertical framing pieces.

Design of Old Structures
1. Explain that many older structures have balloon framing or post-and-beam construction. Using Figure 26-9, review the characteristics of balloon framing. Include the building height studs, firestops, and let-in bracing.
2. Using reproducible master RM 26-1 *Remodeling Post-and-Beam Construction*, review the components of this type of structure. Emphasize to the students that they should be aware of the components and type of construction so they can anticipate possible problems.

Hidden Structural Details
1. Discuss the type of inspection that should take place before any remodeling work begins. Have students identify the types of utilities they should be looking for, including gas or fuel lines, electrical circuits, and plumbing service. Stress that the utility companies should be notified if interruption to any of these services is anticipated.
2. Explain why an exterior inspection is necessary and what they should be looking for when making an exterior inspection.

Removing Old Walls
1. Review the tools that are commonly used in remodeling work.
2. Discuss the preliminary steps in remodeling work, including the removal of trim and wall covering. Mention that in many cases trim members may need to be reused, so care should be taken in removing these items as well as the fasteners used.
3. Stress the importance of safe work habits in remodeling work. Suggest that a large dumpster should normally be rented for major remodeling projects.

Recognizing Bearing Walls
1. Identify the characteristics of bearing walls. Stress that framing supported by bearing walls needs temporary shoring if changes are being made.

Providing Shoring
1. Identify two types of temporary shoring that can be used for a remodeling project. Emphasize that shoring should be placed on both sides of an interior bearing wall to prevent sagging.
2. Describe the construction of a short wall consisting of 2×4 plates and studs. Demonstrate how this short wall is constructed.
3. Discuss the use of adjustable steel posts for temporary shoring. Stress that the shoring must rest on adequate support and that it should be positioned across several joists to distribute the load. Mention that if the shoring is running parallel to the floor joists that planking should be laid down to distribute the load.

Framing Openings in a Bearing Wall
1. Discuss the procedure used to frame openings in a bearing wall. Suggest possible methods of construction for the header.
2. Describe how a header is installed and supported.
3. Have students refer to and study the local building code to determine the size of the header needed for a remodeling project.
4. Show the students how to compute the load on a header by using Figure 26-35 or reproducible master RM 26-3 *Guidelines for Sizing Headers*. Emphasize that the load calculations should be checked (or specified) by an architect or structural engineer.
5. Use actual drawings of a residence and have students determine the loads on one or more headers.

Concealed Headers and Saddle Beams
1. Refer to Chapter 9 for a discussion of flush beams and strongbacks as you explain the construction of concealed headers and saddle beams.
2. Discuss the use of concealed headers and saddle beams in remodeling. Describe the construction of each.

Replacing an Outside Door
1. Refer to Figure 26-28 as you discuss replacement of a worn outside door with a steel unit.
2. Explain step by step how to install the door. Have students study Figure 26-29.
3. If live work is available, have students replace an outside door under your supervision.

Replacing or Repairing an Interior Door
1. Have students review Chapter 9 for the procedure on framing a door opening and Chapter 19 for the procedure on hanging an interior door.
2. Review steps for correcting problems such as binding or sagging doors.
3. Demonstrate the method for trimming the bottom of an existing door to accommodate new flooring materials.

Installing New Windows
1. Demonstrate steps for removing a window that is to be replaced. Explain that removal of trim must be done carefully, since it may be necessary to use the trim again.
2. Demonstrate installation and fastening of a replacement window. Explain how to reframe the rough opening if the new window is not the same size.

Repairing Wood and Asphalt Shingles
1. Explain and demonstrate the method for removing and replacing damaged wood shingles.
2. Explain and demonstrate methods for replacing damaged asphalt shingles.

Building Additions onto Older Homes
1. Discuss the items that should be checked when building additions onto older homes. Stress that dressed dimensions for framing members, ceiling heights, and standard foundation thicknesses may have been different when the structure was originally built than they are now. Explain what should be done if the dimensions vary a great deal.

Solar Retrofitting
1. Review the three passive solar designs—direct gain, indirect gain, and isolated gain.
2. Describe the work involved in installing a direct gain system in an existing structure.
3. Discuss two methods of installing a thermosiphon (solar furnace).

Responsible Renovation
1. Explain the concept of recycling old building materials where possible.
2. Have students study the interior and exterior of a remodeling project to see what might be recyclable.
3. Visit a recycling center to see what might be done with recycled building materials.

Fall Protection
1. Procure a copy of OSHA guidelines on fall protection from a local builder and discuss them with your students.
2. Review photos of scaffolding or study on-site scaffolding to see what measures are taken to prevent falls.

Chapter Review
1. Review the chapter objectives. Be sure that the students fully understand each objective.
2. Assign *Technical Vocabulary*, *Test Your Knowledge* questions, *Curricular Connections*, and *Outside Assignments* for Chapter 26 of the text. Review the answers in class.
3. Assign Chapter 26 in the workbook. Review the answers in class.

Evaluation
This chapter provides three methods for evaluating student performance. Students should complete the *Test Your Knowledge* section using the book as reference. Students should also be allowed to use the book for reference when completing the workbook material. Use the Chapter 26 Quiz in the instructor's resources

for in-class evaluation. Correct the quizzes, return them to the students, and review the quiz questions in group discussion.

Answers to Test Your Knowledge
Text Page 801
1. D. Repairing any leaks found.
2. List what needs to be done.
3. paint
4. B. Building must be supported some way to remove load from sills.
5. Nailing another stud alongside a rotted member to reinforce it.
6. This will make removal of structural elements much easier and safer.
7. underground
8. A. The wall runs down the middle of the length of the house.
   B. Ceiling joists run perpendicular to the wall.
   C. Overhead joists are spliced over the wall, indicating they depend on the wall for support.
   D. The wall runs at right angles to overhead joists and breaks up a long span.
   E. Wall is directly below a parallel wall on the upper level.
9. Shoring
10. 8"
11. Saddle beam, concealed header.
12. Adding some form of solar heating or electricity generation to a structure.
13. True.
14. thermosiphon
15. Major remodeling of a building

Answers to Workbook Questions
Pages 159–162
1. B. Demolish construction that is to be changed and dispose of the debris.
   D. Perform all structural work, proceeding from the ground up.
   H. Re-grade site and provide drainage away from house.
   C. Repair or replace the roof
   A. Repair or replace windows.
   E. Stain or prime wood siding.
   G. Caulk, glaze, and putty.
   F. Paint.
2. Jacks have been placed to raise and support the house frame in preparation for replacing a rotten sill.
3. visualize
4. A. Ribbon.
   B. Joist.
   C. Firestop.
   D. Sill.
   E. Firestop.
   F. Stud.
5. underground
6. B. garden spade
7. B. The wall runs parallel to an outside wall.
8. A. 20 lbs.
   B. 30 lbs.
9. trimmer studs
10. A. Rafter.
    B. Joist.
    C. Firestop.
    D. Subflooring.
    E. Sill.
    F. (Let-in) brace.
    G. Stud.
11. joist hangers
12. B. Fasten clips to doorjamb and then install the assembly in the rough opening.
13. C. 150 lbs.
14. thermosiphon
15. True.

Answers to Chapter Quiz
1. B. doing temporary repairs to stop further deterioration
2. D. demolish what is being eliminated and remove the debris
3. A. remove all trim
4. C. trimmers
5. B. solar furnace
6. H.
7. E.
8. I.
9. G.
10. F.
11. B.
12. D.
13. J.
14. C.
15. A.

Remodeling Post-and-Beam Construction

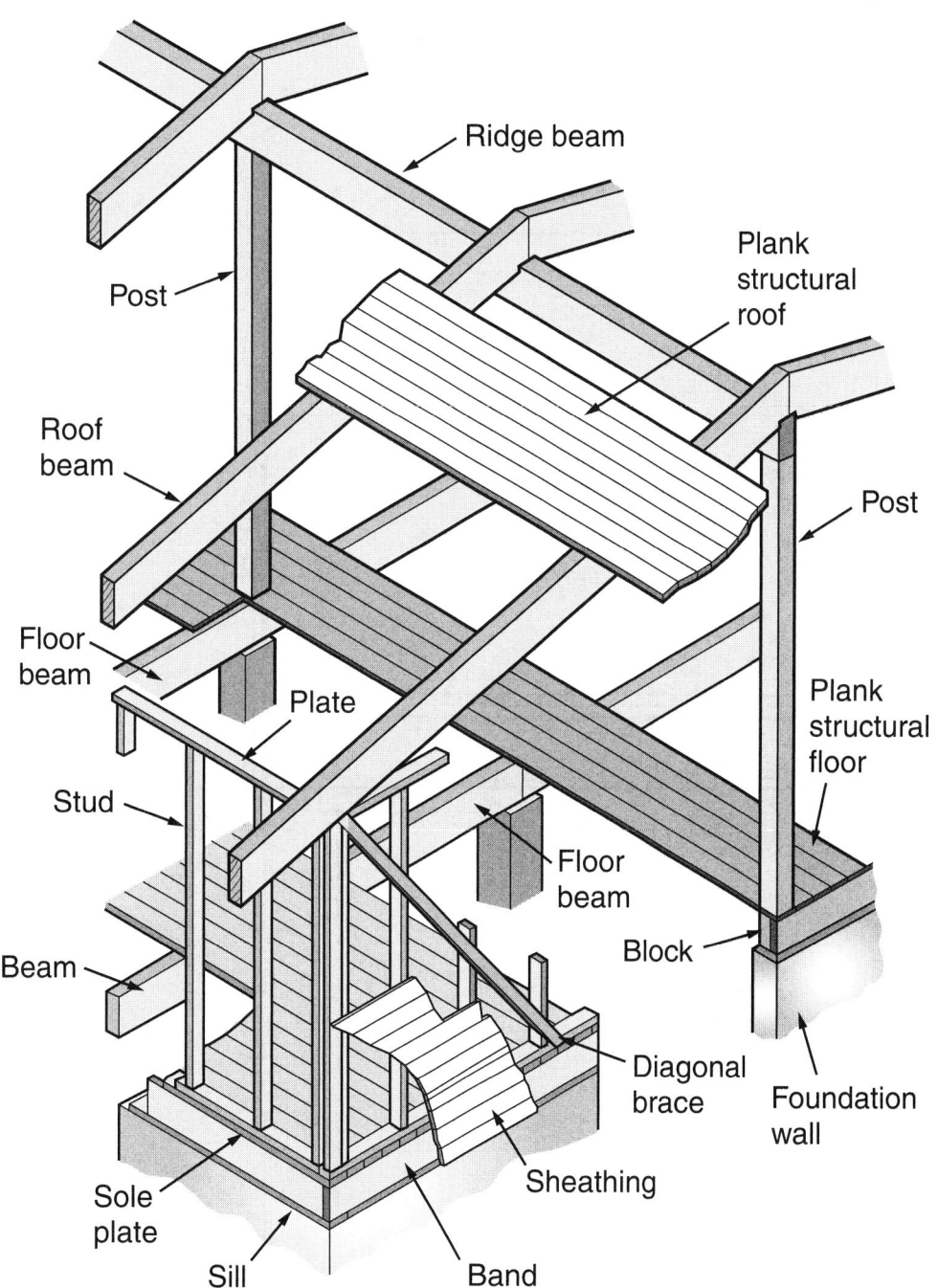

RM 26-1

Replacing Rotted Sills

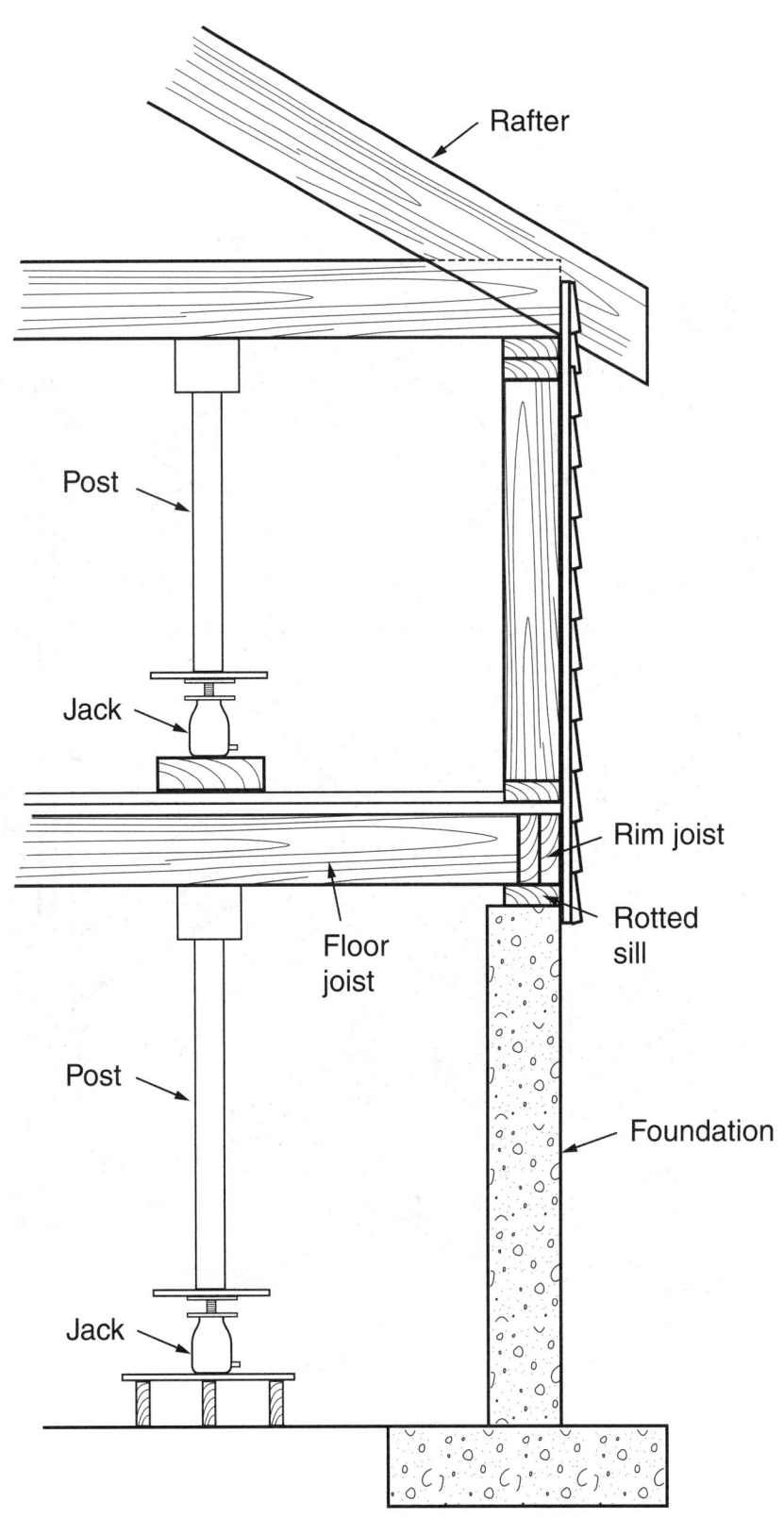

RM 26-2

Guidelines for Sizing Headers

Average weight of house by area	
Unit	Load/square foot
Roof	40 lb.
Attic (low)	20 lb.
Attic (full)	30 lb.
Second floor	30 lb.
First floor	40 lb.
Wall	12 lb.

Built-up wood header (double or triple on two 4" x 4" posts)								
Span (in feet)	Weight (in pounds) safely supported by:								
	Two 2 x 6	Two 2 x 8	Two 2 x 10	Two 2 x 12	Three 2 x 6	Three 2 x 8	Three 2 x 10	Three 2 x 12
4	2250	4688	5000	5980	3780	5850	7410	8970
6	1680	3126	5000	5980	2520	4689	7410	8970
8	—	2657	3761	5511	—	3985	5641	8266
10	—	2125	3008	4409	—	3187	4512	6613
12	—	—	2507	3674	—	—	3760	5511
14	—	—	—	3149	—	—	—	4723

Steel plate header (on two 4" x 4" posts)								
Plate \ Span (in feet)	Weight (in pounds) safely supported by wood sides and plate								
	Two 2 x 8 + 7 1/2" by			Two 2 x 10 + 9 1/2" by			Two 2 x 12 + 11 1/2" by		
	3/8"	7/16"	1/2"	3/8"	7/16"	1/2"	3/8"	7/16"	1/2"
10	6754	7538	8242	10,973	12,199	13,418	15,933	17,729	19,604
12	5585	6216	6827	9095	10,131	11,106	13,224	14,517	16,265
14	4756	5293	5811	7751	8623	9463	11,295	12,561	13,876
16	—	4481	5036	6746	7494	8221	9815	10,953	12,086
18	—	—	—	5942	6606	7158	8675	9652	10,647
20	—	—	—	—	—	6466	7746	8618	9408

RM 26-3

Chapter 26 Quiz
Remodeling, Renovating, and Repairing

Name _____ Date _____ Score _____

Multiple Choice

Choose the answer that correctly completes the statement. Write the corresponding letter in the space provided.

_____ 1. The first step in repairing, remodeling, or renovating a long-neglected house should be ____.
  A. painting the exterior
  B. doing temporary repairs to stop further deterioration
  C. demolishing "add-ons" that are to be removed
  D. making needed foundation repairs

_____ 2. When making interior renovations, first ____.
  A. make alterations affecting walls, especially bearing walls
  B. rough-in plumbing and electrical changes
  C. insulate exterior walls
  D. demolish what is being eliminated and remove the debris

_____ 3. The first step in opening up a wall is to ____.
  A. remove all trim
  B. remove headers
  C. cut studs using a reciprocating saw
  D. remove the wall covering

_____ 4. Headers are supported by resting them on top of short studs called ____.
  A. joists
  B. girders
  C. trimmers
  D. supporters

_____ 5. A thermosiphon is also referred to as a ____.
  A. direct gain system
  B. solar furnace
  C. thermostat
  D. heat pump

Identification

Identify the parts of the balloon-framed structure.

_____ 6. Sill.

_____ 7. Girder.

_____ 8. Sheathing.

_____ 9. Subflooring.

_____ 10. Ledger.

_____ 11. Firestops.

_____ 12. 1×4 Let-in brace.

_____ 13. Ribbon.

_____ 14. Stud.

_____ 15. Joist.

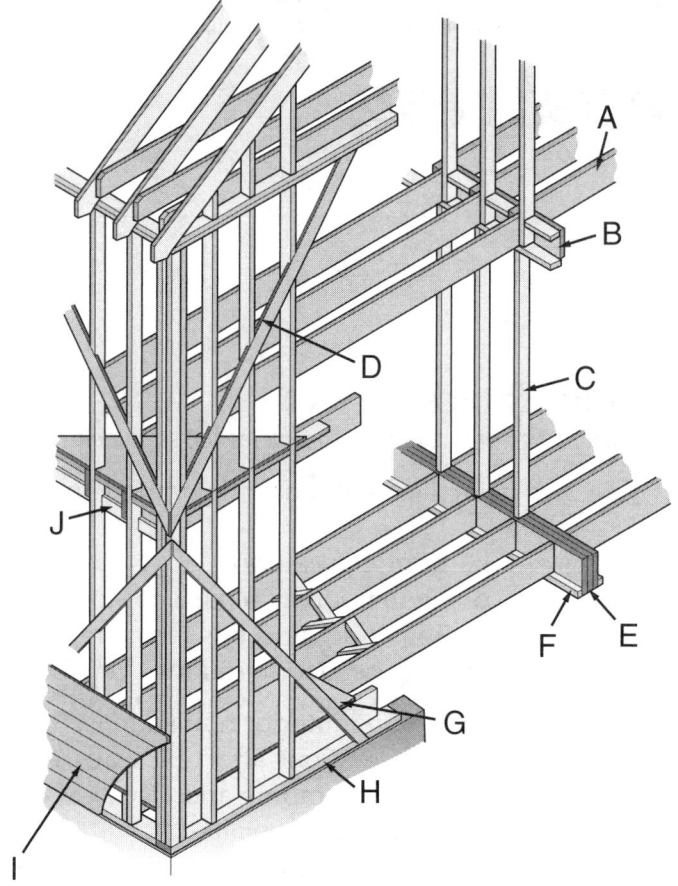

27 Building Decks and Porches

Objectives

After studying this chapter, students will be able to:
- Identify the different types of decks and porches.
- Describe the advantages and disadvantages of various structural and decking materials.
- Select and install the appropriate types of fasteners for deck construction.
- Prepare the site, then layout and construct a deck.
- Describe the differences between deck and porch construction.

Instructional Materials

Text: Pages 803–819
Technical Vocabulary, page 803
Test Your Knowledge, page 819
Curricular Connections, page 819
Outside Assignments, page 819

Workbook: Pages 163–164

Instructor's Resource:
Reproducible masters:
RM 27-1 *Softwoods Suited for Decks*
RM 27-2 *Deck Fasteners and Connectors*
RM 27-3 *Cutting Dadoes for Treads*
Transparencies (binder/CD only):
CT 27-1 *Softwoods Suited for Decks*
Chapter Quiz

Trade-Related Math

A deck measuring 12′ by 20′ is to be covered with 2″ by 6″ by 12′ deck boards. Boards will be spaced 1/2″ apart. How many board feet of lumber are required?

Convert 20′ (length of deck) to inches = 12″ × 20′
= 240″ ÷ 6
= 40 bds

Thus, 40 × 2 × 6 × 12 ÷ 12 = 480 bd.ft.

Instructional Concepts and Student Learning Experiences

Types of Decks
1. Point out that there are three basic types of decks and describe the features of each.
2. Describe how soil characteristics of the site affect how excavation for footings are dug.

Structural Materials
1. Explain that there are choices to be made about grades, species, and sizes of wooden structural materials.
2. Point out that the most important is the ability of the materials to resist decay and withstand the stress of being exposed to the elements.
3. Using reproducible master RM 27-1 *Softwoods Suited for Decks,* discuss the suitability of different woods to resist decay.
4. Mention that treated woods are often selected because they are less expensive than redwood or cedar.
5. Discuss the EPA order that phased out CCA as an acceptable preservative for wood and phasing in ACQ.
6. List the engineered woods suitable for outdoor construction.
7. Describe the manufacturing process for each.

Composite Decking
1. Explain that composite boards are a blend of plastic and wood fibers.
2. Discuss the features of a composite that make it a suitable alternative to wood.
3. Note the standard widths and thicknesses of composite boards.
4. Stress that composites are suitable for deck or porch boards, but that they are not intended for use as beams or joists (framing members).
5. Point out that composite scrap is not biodegradable and must be disposed of according to EPA recommendations.

6. Discuss the suitability of vinyls for deck boards, railings, spindles, and facia.

Fasteners and Connectors
1. Using reproducible master RM 27-2 *Deck Fasteners and Connectors,* show the different types of fasteners and connectors available for decks and porches.
2. Stress that these metals must be either stainless steel or double-dipped, zinc-coated steel.

Using Concealed Fasteners
1. Draw students' attention to Figures 27-9 and 27-10 and discuss the use of concealed fasteners to secure deck boards.
2. Encourage discussion on the merits of concealed fasteners.

Planning and Layout
1. Before beginning a deck plan, tell students to study local codes regarding deck building. Explain the consequences of ignoring this step.
2. Explain the need of a building permit and that it must be prominently displayed on the site.

Site Preparation
1. Explain what site preparation means and the several steps that may be involved.
2. Describe process of laying out a deck using either instruments or measuring tapes.
3. Tell students how to prove that corners are square using diagonal measurements.
4. Discuss the use and installation of a ledger for an attached deck.
5. Remind students that a previous chapter explained how to locate piers and establish batter boards. Then, review the process with students.
6. Go over the 3–4–5 method of double-checking a corner for squareness.

Installing Piers
1. Explain why it is necessary to rest posts on concrete piers or pads that assist the soil in supporting deck loads.
2. Stress that footings must be located below the frostline in cold climates.

Installing Posts
1. Explain the installation process of posts, stressing the use of bracing to keep posts plumb.
2. Since it is preferable that posts rest on concrete above ground, describe the use of Sonotube® forms to hold concrete until cured.
3. Discuss embedding of connectors in wet concrete piers to secure posts.

Placing Beams and Joists
1. Refer students to span tables for beams and joists. Emphasize the importance of sizing beams and joists to carry loads without sagging or breaking.
2. Discuss the use of connectors and hangers to secure beams and joists.
3. Show students how to find the crown of joists and explain why joists should be installed crown up.

Installing Wood Deck Boards
1. Explain why deck installation begins at the outer edge and ends against the building.
2. Describe the use of a chalk line to detect and correct deck boards that are warped.
3. Describe how warped boards can be straightened and nailed.
4. Explain cupping in boards and how such boards must be fastened.
5. Discuss proper (1/4") spacing of deck boards to avoid edge decay. Explain that treated lumber should be installed without spacing since shrinkage provides sufficient spacing.
6. Discuss the practice of drilling pilot holes and how it avoids problems.

Installing Composite Deck Boards
1. Explain that spans are essentially the same for composites as for wood boards.
2. Review once more the use of concealed fasteners, but explain that using face nailing or screws is also accepted practice.

Installing Stairs
1. Stress once again the need to conform to local codes when designing and building railings.
2. Explain that standard railing height is usually 36", although local code requirements take precedence.

3. Discuss proper attachment of posts to deck framing.
4. Obtain ads or brochures showing prefabricated rails and show them, explaining alternatives to site-built railings.

Stairs
1. Observe that most decks not at ground level require steps.
2. Review the principal parts of stairs and their purpose.
3. Ask students to review the information in Chapter 18 on design and construction of stairs.
4. Using reproducible master RM 27-3 *Cutting Dadoes for Treads*, explain how to produce dado cuts in carriages to receive treads.
5. Show students brochures of ready-built steps offered by manufacturers.

Porches
1. Explain the similarities between decks and porches.
2. Describe the various types of porches and how they differ.
3. Note that porch floors slope away from the building to allow for water to drain away from the building.
4. Stress the importance of painting all sides of porch flooring before installation.

Chapter Review
1. Review the chapter objectives. Be sure that the students fully understand each objective.
2. Assign *Technical Vocabulary, Test Your Knowledge* questions, *Curricular Connections*, and *Outside Assignments* for Chapter 27 of the text. Review the answers in class.
3. Assign Chapter 27 in the workbook. Review the answers in class.

Evaluation
This chapter provides three methods for evaluating student performance. Students should complete the *Test Your Knowledge* section using the book as reference. Students should also be allowed to use the book for reference when completing the workbook material. Use the Chapter 27 Quiz in the instructor's resources for in-class evaluation. Correct the quizzes, return them to the students, and review the quiz questions in group discussion.

Answers to Test Your Knowledge
Text Page 819
1. Attached, freestanding
2. Freestanding
3. False.
4. heartwood
5. Plastic with wood fibers or sawdust.
6. Corrosion resistant.
7. False
8. In cold climates, or unstable soils.
9. pergola
10. Open, semi-enclosed, closed.

Answers to Workbook Questions
Pages 163–164
1. attached, elevated
2. True.
3. decay
4. Studies show that arsenic, a toxic substance, could leach out of the wood and contaminate the soil and groundwater.
5. B.
6. Stacked finger-jointed layers of standard lumber and adhered layers.
7. Composite decking
8. Fasteners should be galvanized steel with a G-185 rating and electrogalvanized items should have a class rating of 40 or higher.
9. A. 4'
   B. 5'
10. Level the ground; provide drainage; remove sod or lay down sheet material to eliminate weed growth; excavate and install piers.
11. pier
12. Two sloping boards supported at the top by the deck's rim joist or fascia.
13. Porches are narrower than decks (8' is the norm).
14. porch

Answers to Chapter Quiz
1. False.
2. False.
3. False.
4. True.
5. C.
6. A.
7. B.
8. E.
9. D.
10. C, D
11. B
12. C, D, E
13. C.

Softwoods Suited for Decks

Western Red Cedar	Highly resistant to warping and weathering; like redwood, though coarser; the heartwood resists decay but not termite attacks; easy to work though weak and brittle; moderate ability to hold nails.
Douglas Fir **Western Larch**	Heavy, strong, stiff, holds nails well; not easily worked with hand tools; when pressure treated, resists decay and termites.
True Fir **Eastern and Western Hemlock**	While firs are mostly lightweight and moderately soft, hemlocks are moderately strong and stiff; firs are easy to work, but hemlocks more difficult; shrinkage could be a problem; resistant to termites and decay only when pressure treated.
Ponderosa Pine	Somewhat strong and stiff, but not as strong as southern pine; very resistant to warping; holds nails well; when pressure treated, resists termites and decay.
Red Pine	Strong and stiff, but not to degree of southern pine; easier to work and holds nails well; resistant to termites and decay when pressure treated.
Southern Yellow Pine	Hard, very stiff, and strong with good nail-holding quality; moderately easy-working; decay and termite resistant when pressure treated.
Redwood	Heartwood famous for durability and resistance to decay and termites; moderately light, but limited in structural strength; workable, but brittle; moderate ability to hold nails.

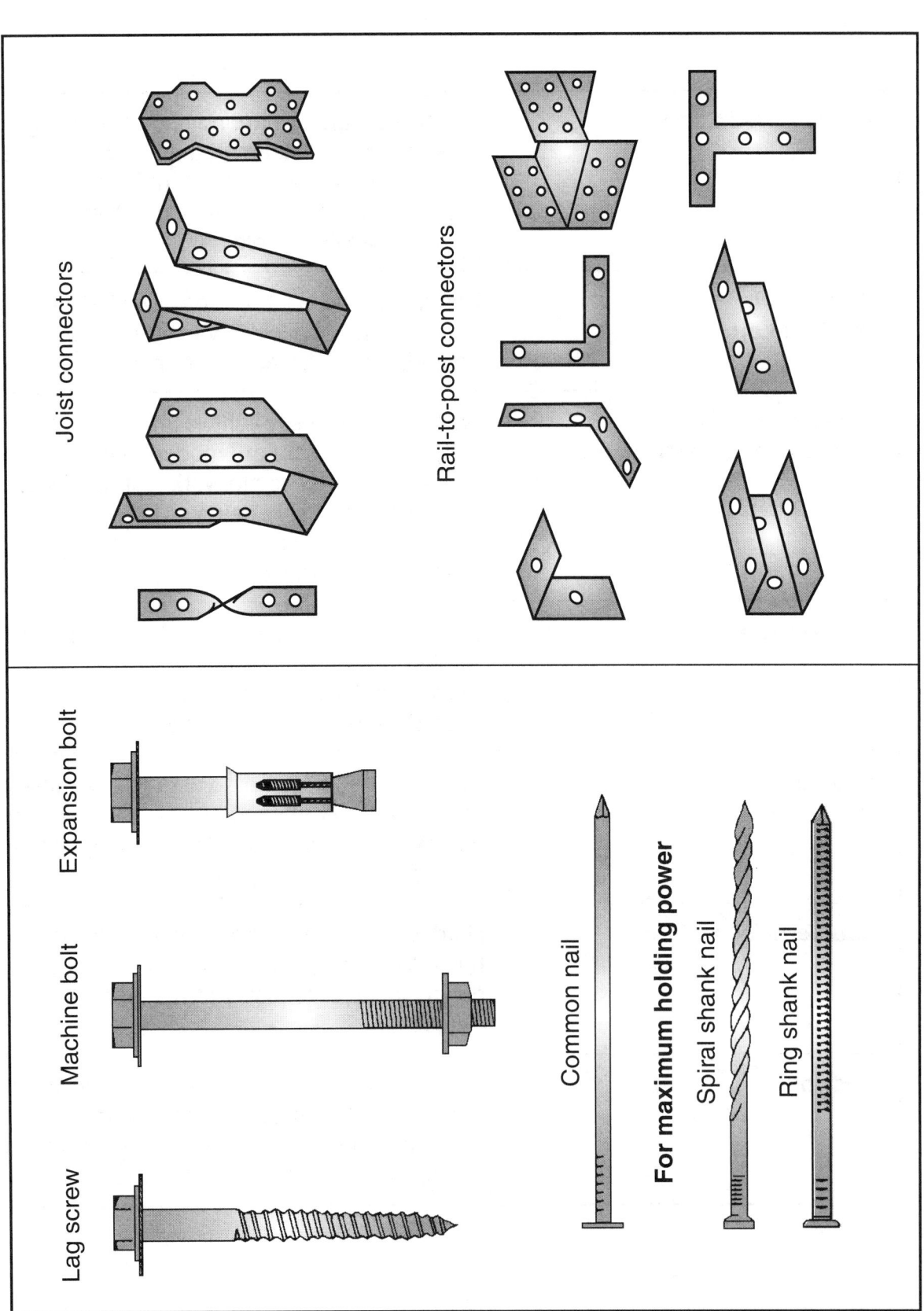

Cutting Dadoes for Treads

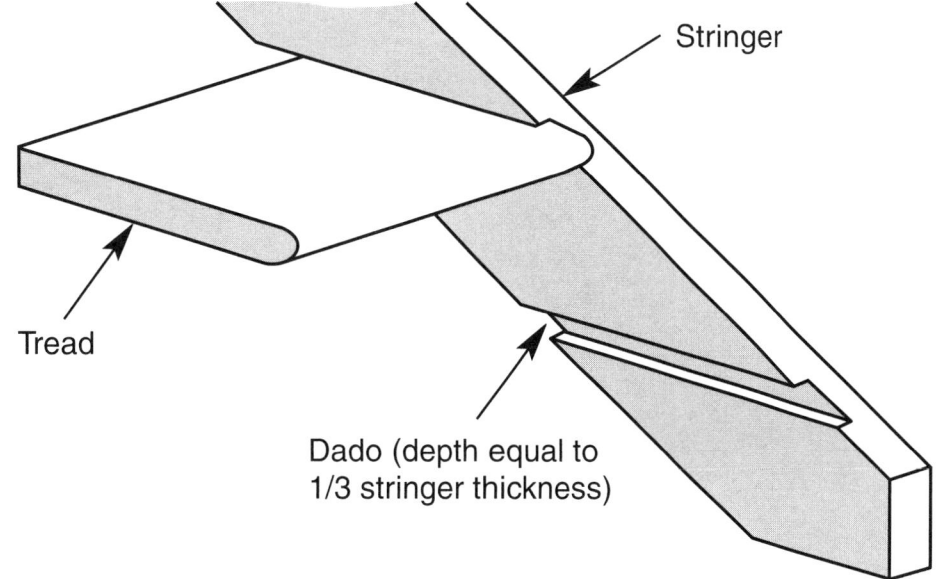

Stringer

Tread

Dado (depth equal to 1/3 stringer thickness)

RM 27-3

Chapter 27 Quiz
Building Decks and Porches

Name _____ Date _____ Score _____

True-False
Circle T if the answer is True or F if the answer is False.

T   F   1. There are two types of decks: one is attached to a building, while the other stands alone.

T   F   2. Only treated wood resists decay or insect infestation.

T   F   3. The EPA considers CCA an environmentally safe wood treatment.

T   F   4. Glulams are manufactured from strips of standard lumber held together by an adhesive.

Identification
Identify the five types of fasteners shown in the illustration.

_____ 5. Expansion bolt.

_____ 6. Lag screw.

_____ 7. Machine bolt.

_____ 8. Rail-to-post connector.

_____ 9. Joist connector.

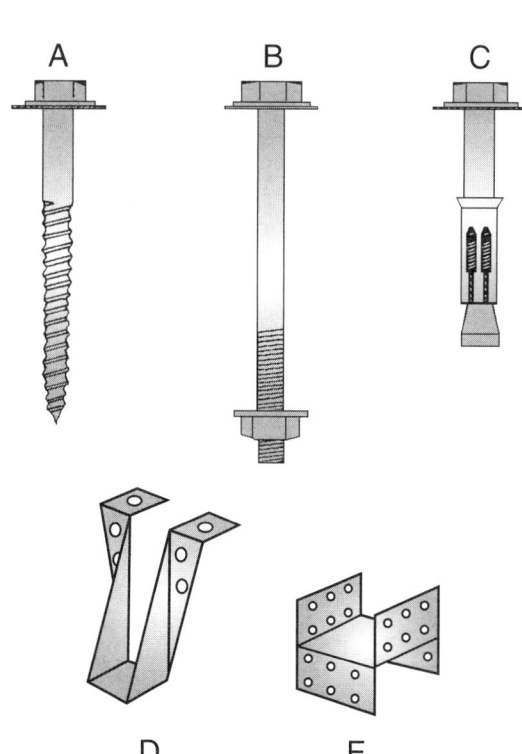

Permission granted to reproduce for educational use only. Copyright by Goodheart-Willcox Co., Inc.

Multiple Choice

Choose the answer(s) that correctly complete each statement.

_____ 10. To prevent decay on wood used in deck construction, it is best to:
   A. apply paint immediately after construction.
   B. make sure that wood is not in contact with the soil.
   C. use lumber that is naturally resistant to decay.
   D. use lumber that has been treated with a preservative such as ACQ.

_____ 11. Before designing a deck, the first step is to:
   A. do a soil test to determine size of footings needed.
   B. check local code requirements.
   C. consult a structural engineer for size of beams and joists.
   D. determine if there is a drainage problem.

_____ 12. Composites are a good choice for deck boards because:
   A. they can be painted before application.
   B. spacing between boards is not necessary.
   C. they are easily maintained.
   D. they are easy to cut.
   E. they will last many years.

_____ 13. Porch floor boards should be sloped _____ to provide proper drainage.
   A. 1 1/2" in 8'
   B. 1" in 10'
   C. 1" in 8'
   D. 2" in 10'

Section 5 Exam
Special Construction

Name _____ Date _____ Score _____

True-False
Circle T if the answer is True or F if the answer is False.

T F 1. Footings that are 2″ thick are sufficient for masonry chimneys.

T F 2. Longitudinal beams are also called purlin beams.

T F 3. In panelized prefabrication, entire sections of the structure are built and finished in manufacturing plants.

T F 4. Heat always travels from an area of higher temperature to one of lower temperature.

T F 5. One major disadvantage of direct gain solar systems is the wide range of heat fluctuations.

T F 6. The amount of overhang used for solar structures in the southern United States should be greater than the amount used in northern parts of the country.

T F 7. Thicker storage walls in a passive solar structure store more heat than thinner walls.

T F 8. When remodeling a structure, shoring need only be placed on one side of a bearing wall.

Multiple Choice
Choose the answer that correctly completes the statement. Write the corresponding letter in the space provided.

_____ 9. ____ beams run parallel to the supporting sidewalls and ridge beam in post-and-beam construction.
   A. Transverse
   B. Steel
   C. Longitudinal
   D. Horizontal

_____ 10. ____ are made by gluing sheets of plywood to longitudinal framing members or other core materials.
   A. Longitudinal beams
   B. Stressed skin panels
   C. Transverse beams
   D. Box beams

_____ 11. The basic type(s) of passive solar systems is/are _____.
   A. indirect gain
   B. direct gain
   C. isolated gain
   D. All of the above.

_____ 12. Heat that is gained from household appliances and occupants is called _____.
   A. internal heat
   B. radiation
   C. solar energy
   D. generated heat

_____ 13. Which of the following usually indicates a bearing wall?
   A. The wall runs down the middle of the length of the house.
   B. Overhead joists are spliced over the wall.
   C. The wall runs at right angles to overhead joists and breaks up a long span.
   D. All of the above.

_____ 14. Beam sizes for post-and-beam construction are based on the _____.
   A. span
   B. permitted deflection
   C. load they must carry
   D. All of the above.

Matching

Select the correct answer from the list on the right and place the corresponding letter in the blank on the left.

_____ 15. Hearth.

_____ 16. Damper.

_____ 17. Smoke shelf.

_____ 18. Smoke chamber.

_____ 19. Flue.

A. Space extending from the top of the throat to the bottom of the flue.

B. Consists of two parts: one located in the front and the other under the fire area.

C. Passage in a chimney through which smoke, gases, and fumes rise.

D. Helps to change the flow direction of the downdraft.

E. Used to control combustion and prevent loss of heat from the room.

Name _____

Completion
Write the answer that correctly completes the statement in the space provided.

_____ 20. A(n) _____ is also referred to as a solar furnace.

_____ 21. In a(n) _____ solar system, there are separate spaces that have solar storage systems for collecting and distributing heat to other parts of the structure.

_____ 22. Headers are supported on top of short studs called _____ studs.

_____ 23. _____ are adjustable steel posts used in place of studs for shoring.

_____ 24. A(n) _____ is a thick masonry wall placed next to the exterior glazing to store solar energy in passive solar construction.

_____ 25. Most of the windows in a solar structure should be placed in the _____-facing wall so that solar radiation can be collected.

_____ 26. _____ is the transfer of heat by another agent, such as air or water.

_____ 27. Planks for floor and roof decking in post-and-beam construction may range in size from _____ to _____ inches thick, depending on the span.

_____ 28. A(n) _____ is a wood frame which supports a prefabricated chimney extending from an outside wall.

_____ 29. A prefabricated chimney should have a label that indicates it has been tested by the _____ or another recognized testing organization.

Identification
Identify the parts of the sill construction for post-and-beam framing.

_____ 30. Sole plate.

_____ 31. Post.

_____ 32. Beam.

_____ 33. Foundation.

_____ 34. Band joist.

_____ 35. Plank.

_____ 36. Sill.

Identification

Identify the indicated parts of the fireplace cross section.

_____ 37. Throat.

_____ 38. Chimney flue.

_____ 39. Smoke shelf.

_____ 40. Smoke chamber.

_____ 41. Fireplace.

_____ 42. Flue lining.

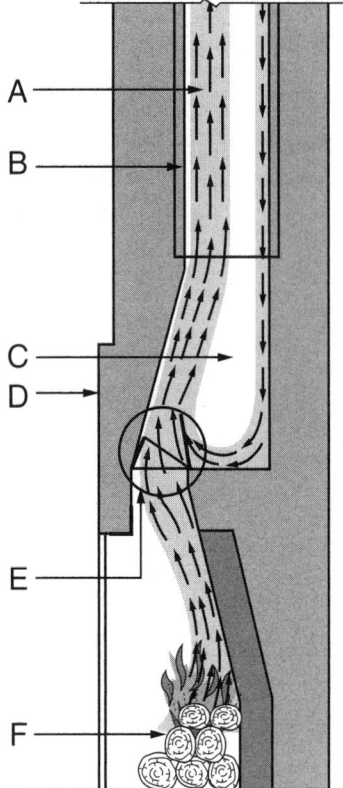

28 Electrical Wiring

Objectives

After studying this chapter, students will be able to:
- Define basic electrical terms.
- Explain what is included in an electrical wiring system.
- List the tools, devices, and materials required to do electrical wiring in a residential building.
- Demonstrate the proper use of tools and handling of materials.
- Demonstrate an understanding of basic circuit theory.
- Use approved methods for simple wiring installation tasks.
- Perform simple electrical troubleshooting.
- Describe the components of a home security alarm system.

Instructional Materials

Text: Pages 821–842
  Technical Vocabulary, page 821
  Test Your Knowledge, page 842
  Curricular Connections, page 842
  Outside Assignments, page 842
Workbook: Pages 165–166
Instructor's Resource:
  Reproducible masters:
    RM 28-1 *Basic Tool List for Electricians*
    RM 28-2 *Electrical Symbols*
  Transparencies (binder/CD only):
    CT 28-1 *Symbols for Most Commonly Used Electrical Devices*
    CT 28-2 *Basic Electrical Plan*
  Chapter Quiz

Instructional Concepts and Student Learning Experiences

Introduction
1. Define *electrical wiring* and explain what is included in a residential electrical service and its circuitry.
2. Explain the term *current* and the laws governing its functional principles and characteristics.
3. Introduce the National Electrical Code and explain its importance in terms of safety to the electrical trades.

Tools and Equipment
1. Using reproducible master RM 28-1 *Basic Tool List for Electricians,* discuss the tools used in the electrical trade and explain their purposes.
2. If possible, demonstrate the use of each tool.
3. Show conductors, boxes, fuses, circuit breakers, switches, receptacles, conduit, and connectors. If individual examples are not available, point them out in the shop or classroom. Explain the purpose of each as well as correct installation methods.

Basic Electrical Wiring Theory
1. Explain the theory of electron flow through conducting material.
2. Note the difference between alternating current and direct current.
3. Discuss transformers, explaining their purpose and construction.
4. Detail the difference between a step-up transformer and a step-down transformer.
5. Explain the two levels of voltage used in residential wiring and how it is provided.

Installing the Service
1. Define the terms *service* and *distribution panel*.
2. Explain where the service is found, where it begins, and where it ends.
3. List all of the devices found inside a distribution panel and explain their functions.

Reading Prints
1. Using reproducible master RM 28-2 *Electrical Symbols*, go over the symbols commonly found in an electrical plan. Explain that these symbols are placed on house plans to show where each device is to be located.
2. Wherever possible, show each device along with its symbol.
3. Obtain a drawing from a house plan containing an electrical plan and pass it among the students for study.
4. Discuss the electrician's use of the plan in installing an electrical system in a residence.

Running Branch Circuits
1. Define *branch circuitry*.
2. Refer to the definition of a circuit as you explain it is a path along which electric current may travel.
3. Discuss the types of control devices and current-using devices that are part of a branch circuit.
4. Review the types and principles of operation of devices designed to protect electrical conductors from damage.

Device Wiring
1. Demonstrate the proper technique for making electrical connections between two conductors or conductors and devices.
2. Demonstrate stripping of insulation from the ends of conductors.
3. Wire a simple circuit and demonstrate that it works when plugged into a power source.
4. Referring to Figure 28-32, explain the operation of a three-way switch.

Electrical Troubleshooting
1. Refer to Figures 28-34 through 28-36 as you demonstrate the procedures for testing receptacles, switches, and fixtures.

Chapter Review
1. Review the chapter objectives. Be sure that the students fully understand each objective.
2. Assign *Technical Vocabulary, Test Your Knowledge* questions, *Curricular Connections*, and *Outside Assignments* for Chapter 28 of the text. Review the answers in class.
3. Assign Chapter 28 in the workbook. Review the answers in class.

Evaluation
This chapter provides three methods for evaluating student performance. Students should complete the *Test Your Knowledge* section using the book as reference. Students should also be allowed to use the book for reference when completing the workbook material. Use the Chapter 28 Quiz in the instructor's resources for in-class evaluation. Correct the quizzes, return them to the students, and review the quiz questions in group discussion.

Answers to Test Your Knowledge
Text Page 842
1. Conductors (wires), boxes, and various devices that control the distribution and use of electricity in the building.
2. Current is the flow of electrons through a conducting material.
3. National Electrical Code
4. Switches
5. alternating
6. True.
7. transformer
8. short circuit
9. False.
10. A continuous loop along which electric current can travel.
11. wire nut
12. The problem is in the circuit. Sometimes an open neutral is a problem.
13. True.
14. Installation of home automation systems.
15. Coaxial

Answers to Workbook Questions
Pages 165–166
1. before
2. False.
3. A fish tape. It is used to pull individual wires through conduit or cable through a wall that is otherwise inaccessible.
4. wires, current
5. A. Conductor.
   B. Load.
   C. Switch.
   D. To power source.
6. fuses, circuit breakers
7. False.
8. service
9. A. Ceiling outlet.
   B. Wall outlet.
   C. Floor outlet.
10. A. hot or black wire
11. It is a test to see if the circuit is live.
12. False. (It could also mean that the circuit breaker is tripped or that one of the circuits is at fault.)

Answers to Chapter Quiz
1. False.
2. False.
3. True.
4. False.
5. D.
6. B.
7. E.
8. A.
9. C.
10. D. switch
11. A. voltage
12. C. entrance panel

Basic Tool List for Electricians

Striking tools Claw hammer Lineman's or electrician's hammer	**Cutting and sawing tools** Files Crosscut saw Keyhole saw Hacksaw Circular saw, 7″ Compound miter saw Reciprocating saw Pocketknife or electrician's knife Cable cutters Wood chisel Wire strippers Cable strippers

Drilling tools
Cordless drill, 1/2″ chuck
Cordless drill, 3/8″ chuck
Cordless drill, 1/4″ chuck
Drill bits, various sizes
    wood twist
    metal
    masonry
    spade
    bit extenders	

	Pliers Slip joint pliers Lineman's pliers Side cutting pliers Diagonal pliers Long nose pliers End cutting pliers Curved jaw pliers
Soldering and wire-joining tools Soldering iron Soldering gun Propane torch Solder, rosin core Soldering paste Blow torch Crimping tool	
	Special and miscellaneous tools Fish tape wire puller Wire pulling lubricant Conduit or pipe cutter Reamer Conduit bender (hickey) Fuse puller Tap and die set Flashlight Plumb bob Test light, continuity tester Level Conduit threader Trouble light Gas generator, about 1500 W Portable space heater Assorted wood or fiberglass ladders Wire grips Chalk line Tool pouch
Fastening tools Standard screwdriver Phillips screwdriver Offset screwdriver Torque head screwdriver Adjustable wrench Allen wrenches Socket/ratchet wrenches Box end wrenches	
Measuring tools Folding ruler Carpenter's extension ruler Steel tape 12″ ruler or meter stick Wire gage VOM	

RM 28-1

Electrical Symbols

Outlets, general		
Ceiling	**Wall**	
○	−○	Outlet
Ⓔ	−Ⓔ	Electrical outlet—used only when circle alone might be confused with other symbols.
Ⓕ	−Ⓕ	Fan
Ⓙ	−Ⓙ	Junction box
Ⓛ	−Ⓛ	Lamp holder
Ⓛ$_{PS}$	−Ⓛ$_{PS}$	Lamp holder, pull switch
Ⓢ	−Ⓢ	Pull switch
Ⓥ	−Ⓥ	Vapor discharge lamp
Ⓒ	−Ⓒ	Clock (indicate voltage)

Outlets, convenience	
⊕	Duplex
⊕$_{1.3}$	Convenience outlet other than duplex
⊕$_{WP}$	Weatherproof
⊕$_{R}$	Range
⊕$_{S}$	Switch and convenience outlet
⊕Ⓡ	Radio and convenience outlet
⊕$_{GFCI}$	Ground-fault circuit interrupter Receptacle outlet
▲	Special purpose outlet (designated in specifications)
⦿	Floor outlet

Outlets, switch	
S	Single pole switch
S$_2$	Double pole switch
S$_3$	Three-way switch
S$_4$	Four-way switch
S$_D$	Automatic door switch
S$_E$	Electrolier switch
S$_K$	Key-operated switch
S$_P$	Switch and pilot lamp
S$_{CB}$	Circuit breaker

Chapter 28 Quiz
Electrical Wiring

Name _____ Date _____ Score _____

True-False
Circle T if the answer is True or F if the answer is False.

T   F   1. The National Electrical Code is a collection of laws on how electrical systems must be installed.

T   F   2. Wire connectors are slowly being replaced by soldered electrical connections.

T   F   3. Fiberglass ladders are recommended for electrical work because they are not conductors of electricity.

T   F   4. Most homes use direct current instead of alternating current.

Identification
Identify the electrical symbols.

_____ 5. Single pole switch.

_____ 6. Duplex outlet.

_____ 7. Double pole switch.

_____ 8. Wall outlet.

_____ 9. Floor outlet.

      A   B   C   D   E

Multiple Choice
Choose the answer that correctly completes the statement. Write the corresponding letter in the space provided

_____ 10. Manual control of circuits is possible through installation of a _____ in the hot conductor.
    A. fuse
    B. circuit breaker
    C. receptacle
    D. switch

_____ 11. A transformer changes _____ in an electrical system utilizing principles of induced magnetism.
   A. voltage
   B. current
   C. resistance
   D. power

_____ 12. The box that houses a main breaker and circuit breakers or fuses for all house circuits is called a(n) _____.
   A. fuse box
   B. breaker box
   C. entrance panel
   D. service

29 Plumbing Systems

Objectives

After studying this chapter, students will be able to:
- Cite codes that govern the installation of plumbing systems.
- List necessary plumbing tools and explain how to use them.
- Describe the different types of materials used in plumbing systems.
- Name and recognize devices and fixtures that are part of the plumbing system.
- Explain the proper design and installation of plumbing systems.
- Read plumbing prints.
- Demonstrate a basic understanding of well and pump systems.
- Unplug drains using chemicals and the special tools designed to clear out clogs.
- Cite safety measures that plumbers must observe.

Instructional Materials

Text: Pages 843–870
  Technical Vocabulary, page 843
  Test Your Knowledge, page 870
  Curricular Connections, page 870
  Outside Assignments, page 870
Workbook: Pages 167–170
Instructor's Resource:
  Reproducible masters:
    RM 29-1 *Typical Plumbing System*
    RM 29-2 *Parts of a Globe Valve*
    RM 29-3 *Components of a Toilet*
  Transparencies (binder/CD only):
    CT 29-1 *Plumbing System*
    CT 29-2 *Plumbing Symbols*
  Chapter Quiz

Trade-Related Math

Often, plumbers must compute the lengths of pipe offsets. One method is to use a formula designed to find one side of a right-angle triangle. The theory behind the formula is that the square of the hypotenuse of a right-angle triangle (side opposite the 90° angle) is equal to the sum of the squares of the other two sides. For example, suppose that the two pipes to be joined are 10″ apart and one is 12″ above the other:

$$10^2 + 12^2 = H^2$$
$$100 + 144 = 244$$
$$\sqrt{244} = 15.62″$$

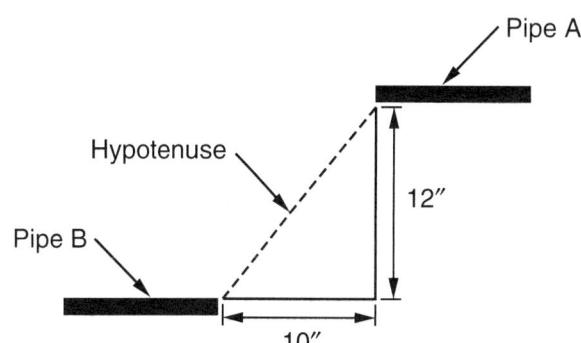

Instructional Concepts and Student Learning Experiences

Plumbing Codes
1. Discuss the necessity of adhering to plumbing code standards and the possible repercussions if these standards are not followed.
2. Secure and distribute copies of your community's plumbing code to your students. Discuss and compare the code with that of another community.

Two Separate Systems
1. Using reproducible master RM 29-1 *Typical Plumbing System,* compare the design and functions of the two separate parts of a plumbing system.
2. Explain why one is pressurized and the other works by gravity flow.
3. Stress the importance of making both systems watertight.
4. Discuss the purpose of venting and explain how it is designed.

Tools
1. Display a full kit of plumbing tools, if available, and explain how to use each.

Materials
1. List the various types of materials that make up the plumbing system. Explain where they might appropriately be used.
2. Demonstrate how to make watertight connections with each type of material.
3. Have students practice making all types of connections.

Valves
1. Discuss the function of a valve in a pressurized supply system.
2. Using reproducible master RM 29-2 *Parts of a Globe Valve,* review the construction and parts of a globe valve. Remind students that there are other designs for valves that are in common use.

Faucets
1. Compare the function and construction of faucets with those of valves.

Fixtures
1. Define the term *fixture*.
2. Have students list the different types of fixtures found in a residence.
3. Using reproducible master RM 29-3 *Components of a Toilet,* explain and demonstrate how to replace worn or deteriorated parts.

Reading Prints
1. Have students review Chapter 3.
2. Discuss the use of symbols to represent plumbing devices and fixtures. Refer the class to Figures 29-17 and 29-18 and have them study the symbols shown.
3. Have students draw a plumbing system for a small house. Discuss and critique the designs in class.

Installing Plumbing
1. Point out that plumbing is usually done by specialists, but that a skilled homeowner can do simple installations or remodeling.
2. Demonstrate the cutting of pipes and tubing with both saws and cutters.
3. Have students practice cutting and reaming operations.

Sweat Soldering
1. Demonstrate the proper procedure for sweat soldering. Impress on your students the necessity for starting with a clean surface that has been brightened with steel wool.
2. Explain the role of flux in producing a leak-free joint.
3. If time permits, allow students to practice sweat soldering joints.

Making Compression Joints
1. Explain the principle of compression joints.
2. Demonstrate the procedure for completing a compression joint.

Bending and Unrolling Copper Tubing
1. Explain the method of bending and unrolling copper tubing to prevent tubing damage.

Making Plastic Pipe Connections
1. Demonstrate cleaning, applying adhesive, and making the fitting connection.
2. Caution students that speed and accuracy are extremely important because the adhesive will set up in seconds, making any further adjustment impossible.

Making Galvanized Pipe Connections
1. Mention that galvanized pipe is one of the easiest connections to make and change.
2. Explain that these pipe connections should always be made using either pipe compound or Teflon® tape on the threads.

3. Demonstrate the procedure and then have students practice making connections.

● **Fixing Sink Drain Problems**
1. Demonstrate the use of various tools commonly used to unplug drains.
2. Have students practice repairs common to sinks and toilets.
3. Explain what parts of a toilet system might cause leaking and what repairs are then required.

Wells and Pumps
1. Discuss the different types of wells. Mention that most wells today are drilled or bored.
2. List the various essential parts of the system and explain the role of each.
3. Discuss common system failures and repair methods to correct them.

Safety
1. Discuss safety rules and proper attire.
2. Discuss good practices that avoid the potential for fires from use of certain tools and equipment.

● Chapter Review

1. Review the chapter objectives. Be sure that the students fully understand each objective.
2. Assign *Technical Vocabulary, Test Your Knowledge* questions, *Curricular Connections,* and *Outside Assignments* for Chapter 29 of the text. Review the answers in class.
3. Assign Chapter 29 in the workbook. Review the answers in class.

Evaluation

This chapter provides three methods for evaluating student performance. Students should complete the *Test Your Knowledge* section using the book as reference. Students should also be allowed to use the book for reference when completing the workbook material. Use the Chapter 29 Quiz in the instructor's resources for in-class evaluation. Correct the quizzes, return them to the students, and review the quiz questions in group discussion.

Answers to Test Your Knowledge
Text Page 870

1. To be sure that the holes will not weaken joists and studs.
2. C
3. A) An improperly installed system will not pass inspection and will need to be redone.
   B) A poorly designed system will not perform well.
   C) A poorly designed system could be unhealthy because it may allow wastewater to contaminate potable water.
4. water supply
5. The drainage, waste, and venting system (DMV); venting permits air to circulate in pipes, prevents backpressure and siphoning of water from traps, and may under certain conditions prevent introduction of wastewater into the potable water supply.
6. (*select two*) K, L, or M
7. Chlorinated polyvinyl chloride; 180° F
8. hand sling
9. rough-in
10. Copper pipe.
11. The fittings slide over the outside of the pipe and are secured with quick-curing solvent cement.
12. It prevents sewer gases from entering the building.
13. Chemical cleaners, plungers, snakes, and closet augers.
14. Pumps and pressure tanks.
15. Dug, driven, drilled, bored.

Answers to Workbook Questions
Pages 167–170

1. Building Officials and Code Administrators International, Inc. (BOCA), International Conference of Building Officials (ICBO), and Southern Building Code Congress International, Inc. (SBCCI).
2. See Figure 29-2B in the text.
3. Venting
4. C. malleable iron
5. ABC, PVC

Copyright by Goodheart-Willcox Co., Inc.

6. A. Hub and spigot.
   B. No-hub.
7. A. Packing nut.
   B. Bonnet.
   C. Valve seat.
   D. Stem.
8. fixtures
9. False.
10. True.
11. tubing spring
12. Drilled
    Bored
13. (*any two*) Seals harden and leak, check valves wear out, pumps wear and lose efficiency, galvanized pipes rust and leak.
14. Molten lead is poured into the hub after it has been sealed with an oakum packing. The solidified lead is then stamped to form a seal against the bell. The joint formed by a hub and a spigot is sealed with a neoprene gasket. Joints of the no-hub type of soil pipe are also sealed with neoprene held in place by a stainless steel clamp.
15. A) Seat.
    B) Drain body.
    C) Tailpiece.

Answers to Chapter Quiz

1. False.
2. False.
3. True.
4. False.
5. A.
6. C.
7. B.
8. C. sweat soldering
9. E. All of the above.
10. B. pressure tank

Typical Plumbing System

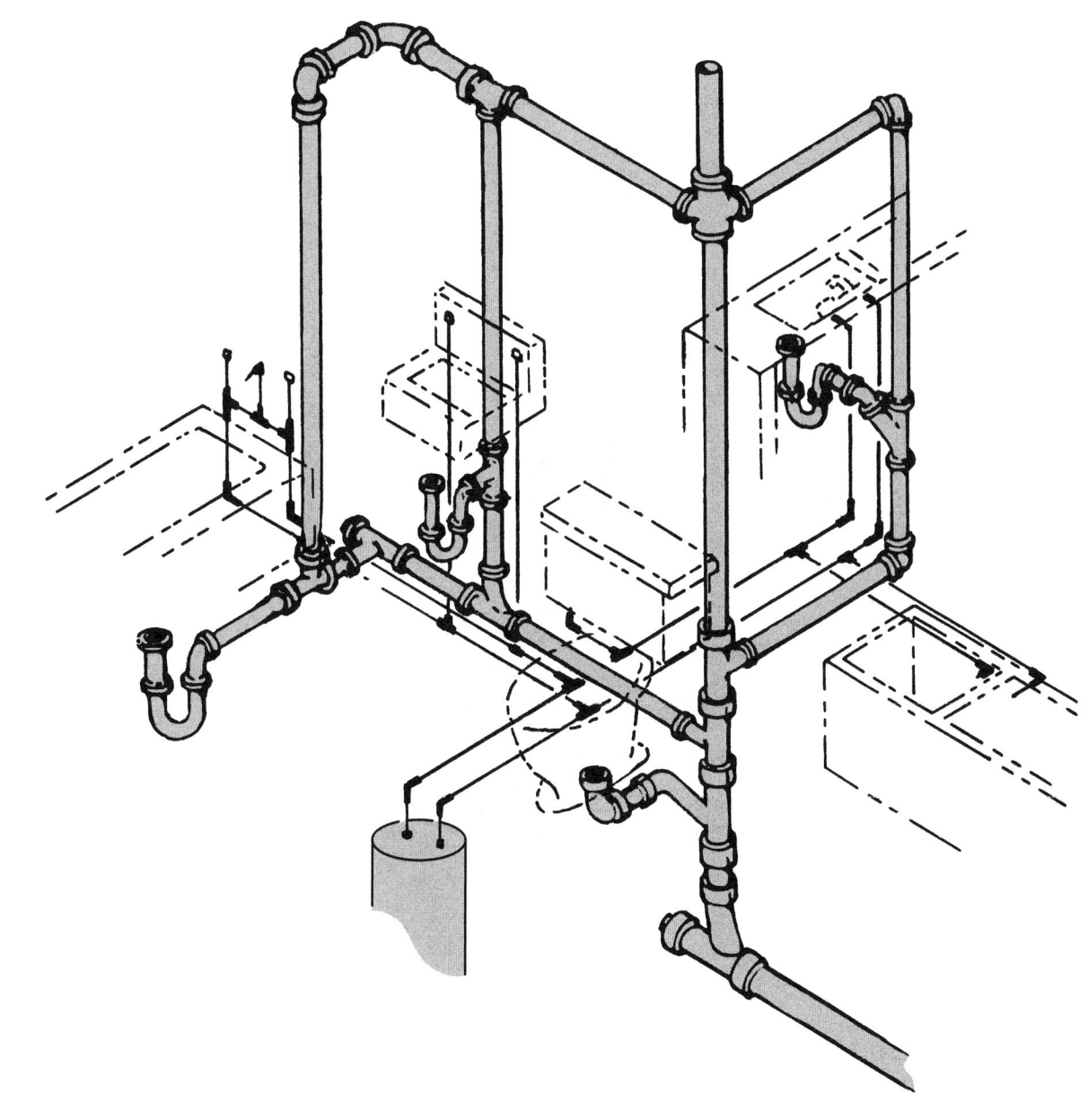

RM 29-1

Parts of a Globe Valve

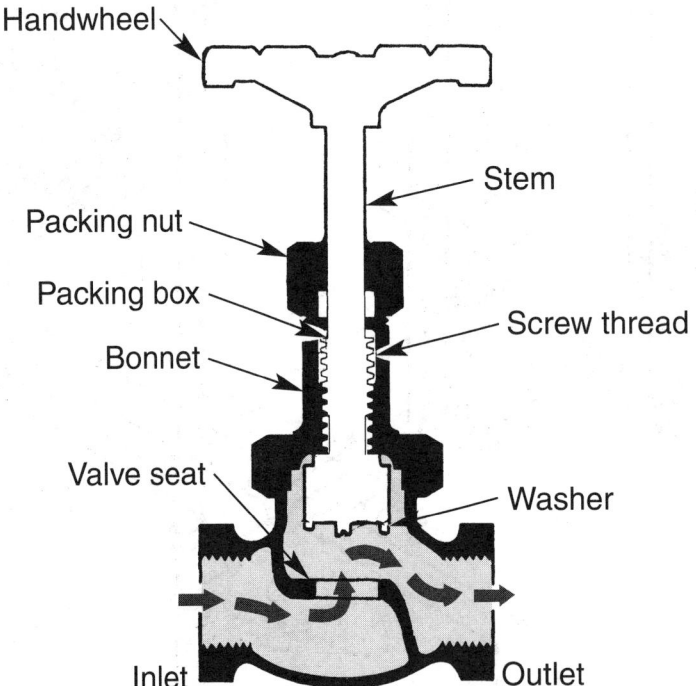

Components of a Toilet

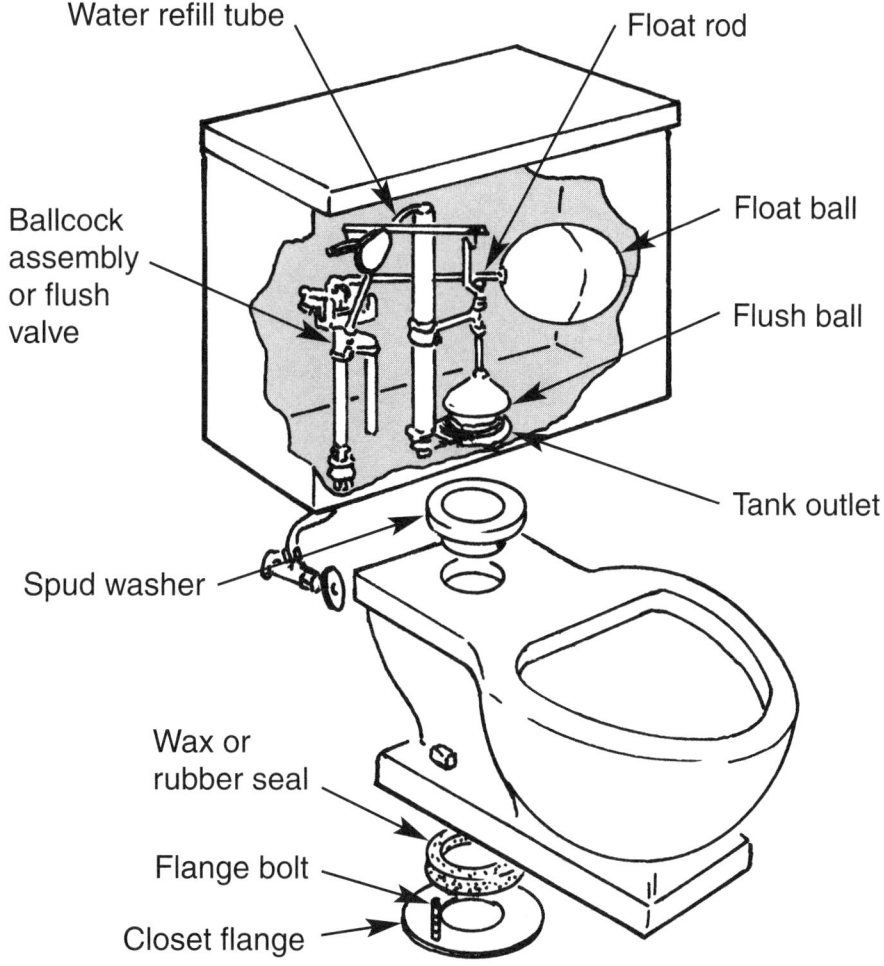

RM 29-3

Chapter 29 Quiz
Plumbing Systems

Name _____ Date _____ Score _____

True-False
Circle T if the answer is True or F if the answer is False.

T   F   1. Plumbers are not allowed to cut or notch framing members; they must have carpenters perform these tasks.

T   F   2. Since leveling of plumbing is not necessary, a level is not an important plumbing tool.

T   F   3. CPVC connections can be threaded or solvent welded.

T   F   4. A tubing spring is permanently installed at bends in copper tubing.

Identification
Identify the types of plumbing sketches in the illustrations.

_____ 5. Plan view.

_____ 6. Isometric sketch.

_____ 7. Riser diagram.

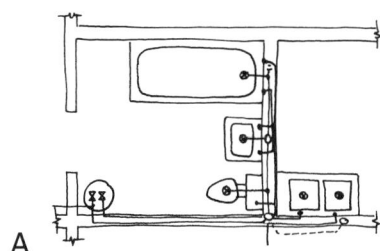

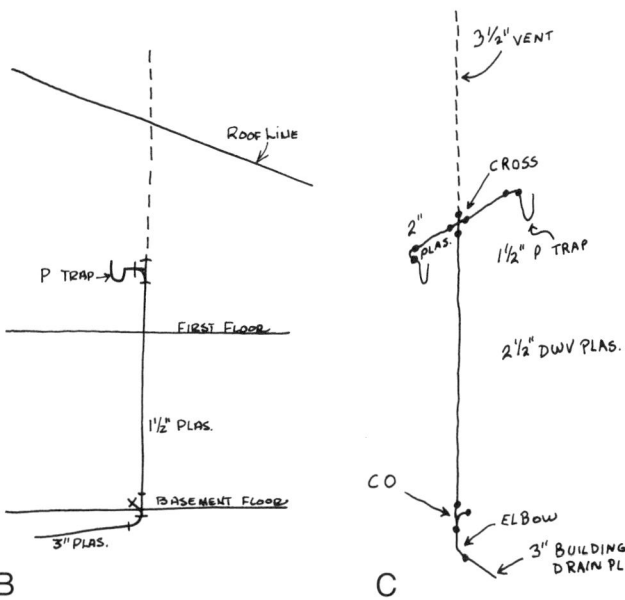

Multiple Choice

Choose the answer that correctly completes the statement. Write the corresponding letter(s) in the space provided.

_____ 8. Copper plumbing connections are made by ____.
  A. solvent bonding
  B. welding
  C. sweat soldering
  D. threaded couplings

_____ 9. A ____ is used for unclogging a drain.
  A. chemical cleaner
  B. plunger
  C. snake
  D. closet auger
  E. All of the above.

_____ 10. A well system uses a ____ to store water under pressure so it will be available on demand.
  A. well casing
  B. pressure tank
  C. submersible pump
  D. check valve

30 Heating, Ventilation, and Air Conditioning

Objectives

After studying this chapter, students will be able to:
- Identify ways to conserve energy in housing.
- Define EER ratings and list the appliances to which they are applied.
- List the characteristics of different central air conditioning systems.
- Describe the functions of HVAC system components.
- Explain the design and operation of HVAC systems.
- Describe automatic controls for heating and cooling systems.

Instructional Materials

Text: Pages 871–889
  Technical Vocabulary, page 871
  Test Your Knowledge, page 888
  Curricular Connections, page 888
  Outside Assignments, page 888
Workbook: Pages 171–174
Instructor's Resource:
  Reproducible masters:
    RM 30-1 *Fundamentals of a Gas Furnace*
    RM 30-2 *Basic Hydronic Heating System*
  Transparencies (binder/CD only):
    CT 30-1 *Central Air-Conditioning System*
    CT 30-2 *Heat Pump Operation*
  Chapter Quiz

Trade-Related Math

Basic math skills are essential to the person installing heating and cooling appliances. These skills are needed for making accurate measurements, properly replacing parts, and completing work orders and time sheets. Example: A part-time, hourly technician worked six hours on Monday and eight hours on Tuesday. At a pay rate of $15.00 per hour, what amount will the technician be paid for this work?

  6 hours + 8 hours = 14 hours
  14 hours × $15.00/hr. = $210.00

Instructional Concepts and Student Learning Experiences

Conservation Measures
1. Review the three ways by which heat is transported from one point to another.
2. Relate these physical principles to measures that will conserve heat energy in a building.
3. Point out to students that cost-effectiveness of any conservation measure is directly related to the costs of conservation measures and the cost of energy used to heat or cool a building. As fuel and energy costs rise, conservation becomes more cost effective.
4. Discuss the meaning of an EER and its significance in choosing one brand of appliance over another.

Heating Systems
1. Explain to students that heating systems make use of the physical principles governing the movement of heat from one location to another.
2. List and describe the four types of central heating systems.
3. Discuss the method of heat transfer used by each system.
4. Describe the role of the components of each system in controlling and moving heat.
5. Use reproducible master RM 30-1 *Fundamentals of a Gas Furnace* to explain the sequence of events in a gas furnace. Begin with the thermostat calling for heat and note each step, ending with the signal from the thermostat to stop sending heat.

6. Use reproducible master RM 30-2 *Basic Hydronic Heating System* as you identify the parts of this system and explain how it operates.

Air Cooling Systems
1. Discuss the type of transfer medium used by air conditioning systems.
2. Remind students that the principles of heat transfer also apply to appliances that cool air.
3. Compare the air conditioner to a refrigeration unit.
4. Explain the roles of the cooling coil and the condenser.

Controls
1. Explain that controls react to sensing devices or electric signals that cause them to regulate operation of furnaces and air conditioners.
2. Explain the terms *cut-in point*, *cut-out point*, and *differential*.
3. Explain the difference between series connection and parallel connection of the thermostat in the control circuit.

Air Exchangers
1. Explain the purpose of an air exchanger.
2. Discuss its operation.
3. Explain that with airtight homes, an air exchanger may be necessary to maintain sufficient fresh air in the building.

Chapter Review
1. Review the chapter objectives. Be sure that the students fully understand each objective.
2. Assign *Technical Vocabulary*, *Test Your Knowledge* questions, *Curricular Connections*, and *Outside Assignments* for Chapter 30 of the text. Review the answers in class.
3. Assign Chapter 30 in the workbook. Review the answers in class.

Evaluation
This chapter provides three methods for evaluating student performance. Students should complete the *Test Your Knowledge* section using the book as reference. Students should also be allowed to use the book for reference when completing the workbook material. Use the Chapter 30 Quiz in the instructor's resources for in-class evaluation. Correct the quizzes, return them to the students, and review the quiz questions in group discussion.

Answers to Test Your Knowledge
Text Page 888
1. Radiation, conduction, and convection
2. A) Sealing of cracks at joints with caulk and housewrap. B) Increasing the amount of insulation in walls, ceilings, and floors. C) Using an air exchanger to wring heat out of air being exhausted. D) Replacing heating and cooling appliances with newer ones having higher efficiency ratings. E) Installing insulated ductwork for forced-air heating systems.
3. True.
4. An EER is an energy efficiency rating; it indicates how well an appliance uses energy. This rating covers furnaces, central and room air conditioners, water heaters, and other major appliances.
5. A) Forced-air perimeter heating. B) Hydronic perimeter heating. C) Hydronic radiant heating.
6. forced air
7. Air is the medium in a forced-air system, while water is the medium in a hydronic system.
8. Two-pipe hydronic system.
9. It has high operating costs.
10. False.
11. thermostat
12. It can be set to automatically change temperatures at different times of the day to save fuel costs.
13. True.
14. heat pump
15. Refrigerant.

Answers to Workbook Questions
Pages 171–174
1. True.
2. True.
3. A. Power vent blower.
   B. Furnace blower.
4. A. Boiler.

5. air return
6. (*any two*) sheet metal, vitrified tile, concrete pipe, plastic pipe.
7. A. Return air intake.
   B. Feeder ducts.
   C. Perimeter ducts.
   D. Register.
   E. Concrete floor slab.
8. D. the building has zone heating
9. A. Baseboard units.
   B. Return pipe.
   C. Pump.
   D. Supply pipe.
10. A. cooling coil
    B. condenser
11. Air exchanger.
12. C. every two to three hours

Answers to Chapter Quiz
1. True.
2. False.
3. True.
4. False.
5. Ducts
6. heating season
7. E.
8. C.
9. A.
10. B.
11. D.

Fundamentals of a Gas Furnace

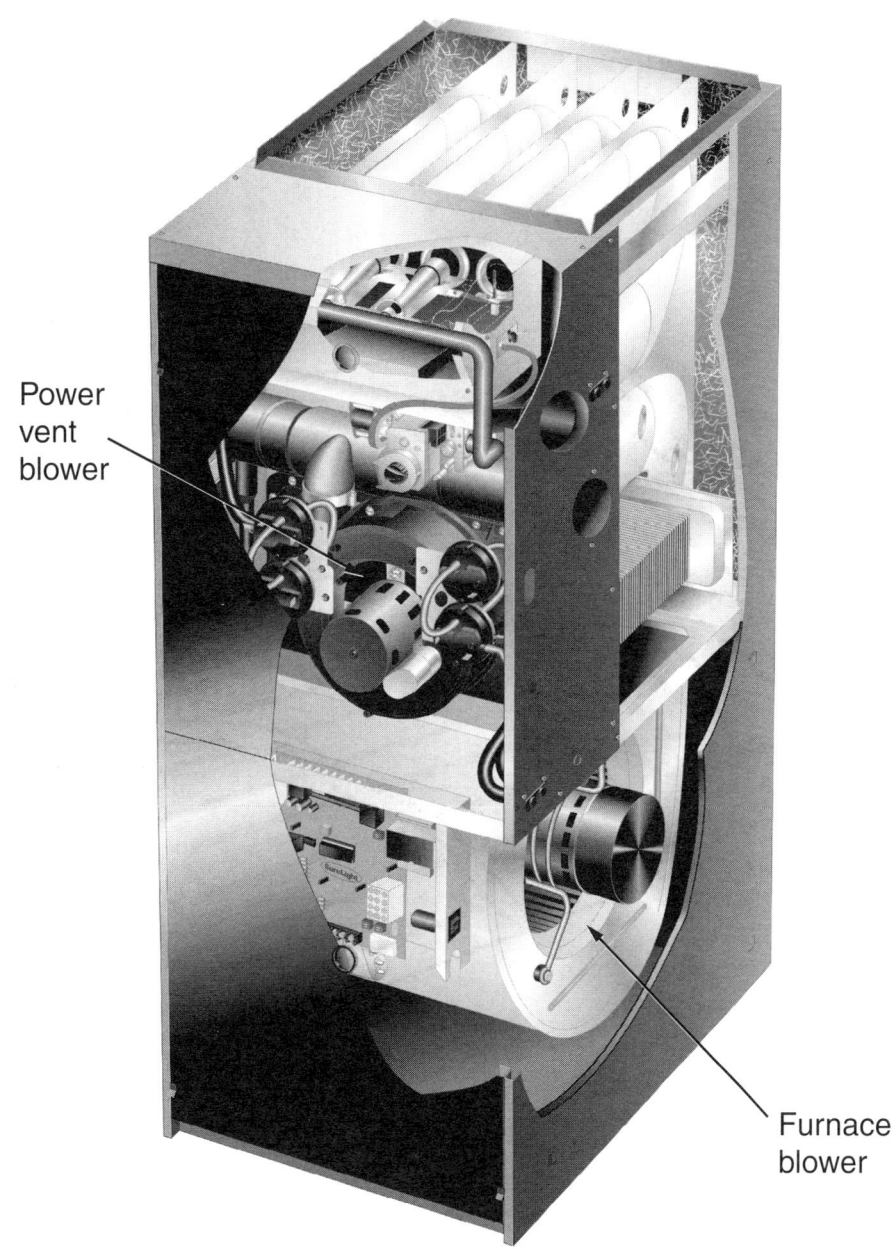

Power vent blower

Furnace blower

RM 30-1

Basic Hydronic Heating System

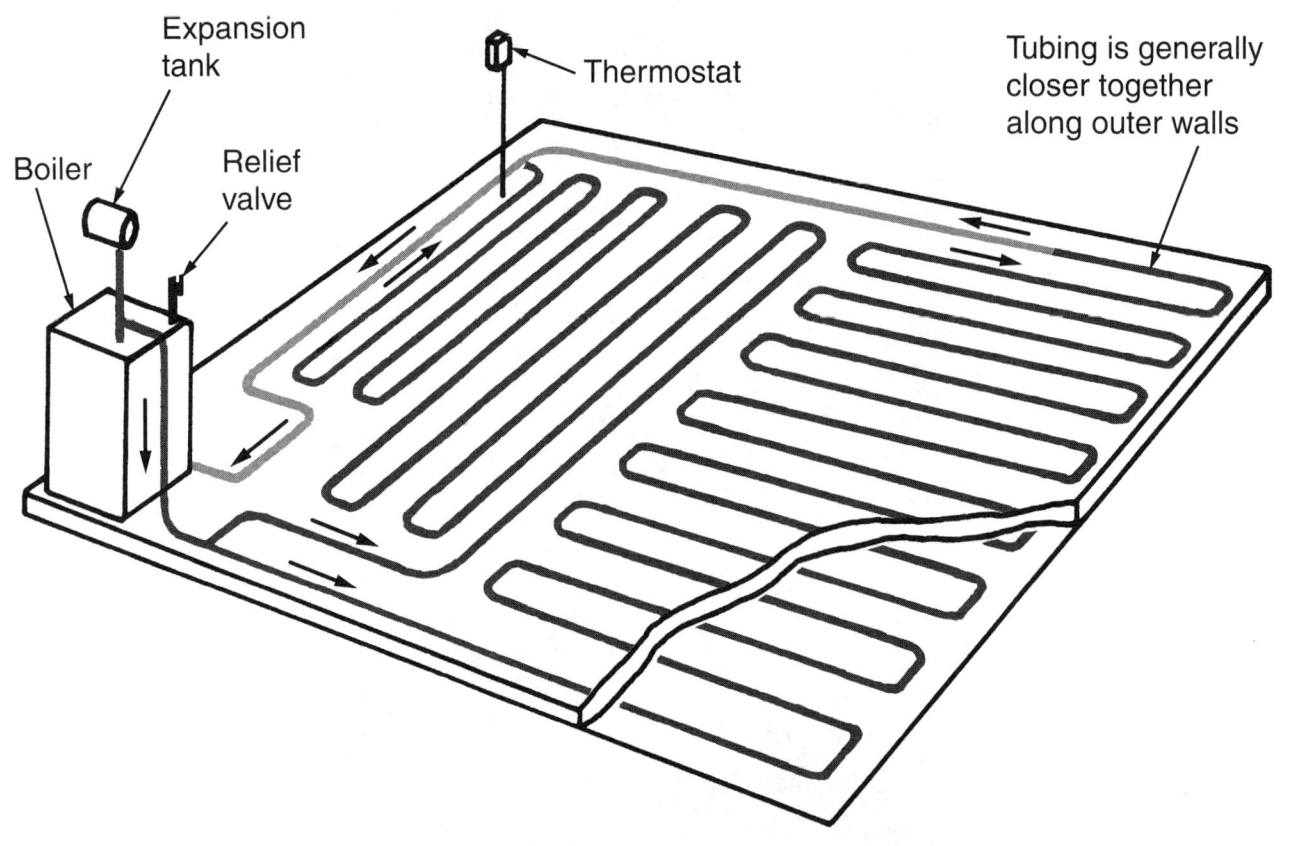

RM 30-2

Chapter 30 Quiz
Heating, Ventilation, and Air Conditioning

Name _____ Date _____ Score _____

True-False
Circle T if the answer is True or F if the answer is False.

T   F   1. Four factors are involved in energy efficient homes: sealing cracks, insulation levels, wringing heat out of warm air before exhausting it, and efficient appliances.

T   F   2. New furnaces can achieve efficiencies up to 80%.

T   F   3. Among other items, an EER label compares an appliance's efficiency with that of comparable products on the market.

T   F   4. A heat exchanger wrings heat from exhausted warmed air.

Sentence Completion
Complete each sentence with the correct word or phrase.

_____ 5. _____ are passageways that carry conditioned air from a heating or cooling appliance and distributes it to various rooms of a building.

_____ 6. Blower belts on a forced-air system should be inspected before every _____.

Identification
Identify the indicated parts.

_____ 7. Supply pipe.

_____ 8. Pump.

_____ 9. Baseboard units.

_____ 10. Return pipe.

_____ 11. Boiler

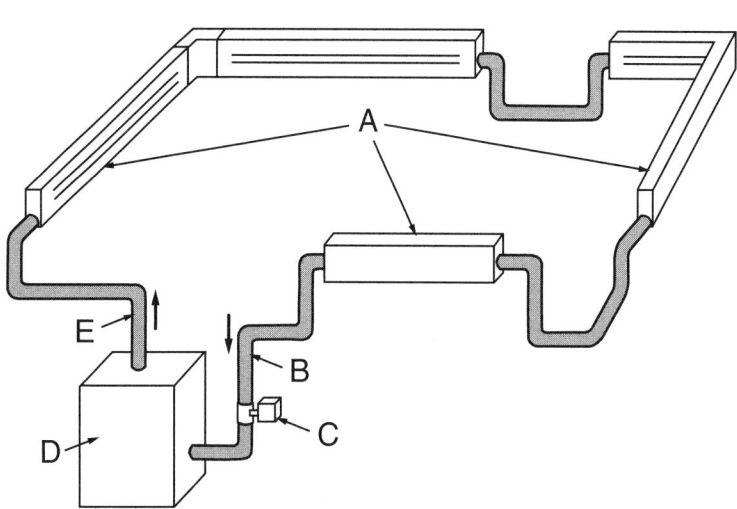

Section 6 Exam
Mechanical Systems

Name _____ Date _____ Score _____

True-False
Circle T if the answer is True or F if the answer is False.

T F 1. Electricity is the only mechanical system used in a house.

T F 2. Electric current results when a conductor is passed through a magnetic field.

T F 3. Notches for plumbing should be square or rectangular and then reinforced with metal strapping.

T F 4. A plumber may choose to follow any of the five plumbing codes.

T F 5. It is not possible to operate furnaces without chimneys.

T F 6. The lower the EER rating of an appliance, the greater its efficiency.

Multiple Choice
Choose the answer that correctly completes the statement. Write the corresponding letter in the space provided.

_____ 7. The purpose of an electrical box is to _____.
   A. hold devices such as switches and receptacles
   B. enclose connections between conductors
   C. protect connections between two or more conductors
   D. All of the above.

_____ 8. Venting is a part of a plumbing system that _____.
   A. permits air to circulate in the pipes
   B. prevents introduction of wastewater into the potable water supply
   C. prevents backpressure and siphoning of water from traps
   D. All of the above.

_____ 9. A _____ heating system heats a building with a boiler and pipes buried in the floor.
   A. forced-air
   B. hydronic perimeter
   C. hydronic radiant
   D. resistance radiant

Completion
Place the answer that correctly completes the statement in the space provided.

_____ 10. ____ are the wires that carry electric current from one part of a house wiring system to another.

_____ 11. A hydronic ____ or radiant heating system use water as a medium for moving heat from the unit.

_____ 12. ____ is a ropelike, tarred material used to seal lead joints in DWV systems.

_____ 13. Copper tubing comes in rolls and must be carefully unrolled to prevent ____.

_____ 14. Furnaces and ____ are major users of energy in a home.

_____ 15. ____ cover the ends of forced air ducts and distribute warmed air into rooms.

Matching
Select the correct answer from the list on the right and place the corresponding letter in the blank on the left.

_____ 16. Transformer.

_____ 17. Coil.

_____ 18. Direct current.

_____ 19. Alternating current.

_____ 20. Induction.

A. Process by which a magnetic field from one coil causes a current in a nearby coil.

B. Device that can increase or decrease electrical voltage.

C. Electrons flow to and fro in a conductor.

D. Electrons flow in only one direction.

E. Several wrappings of a conductor around an iron core.

_____ 21. Compression fitting.

_____ 22. CPVC.

_____ 23. ABS.

_____ 24. Neoprene.

A. Inexpensive plastic pipe that resists effects of chemicals.

B. Used to make connections in copper tubing.

C. Used as gasket material to seal plumbing joints.

D. A buff-colored thermoplastic used for hot water piping.

_____ 25. Cooling coil.

_____ 26. Condenser.

_____ 27. Thermostat.

_____ 28. Cut-in point.

A. Signals air conditioner to provide cooled air.

B. Coil in a furnace receiving cooled refrigerant from an air conditioner.

C. Exhausts heat from heated refrigerant to the air.

D. Temperature setting that causes a thermostat to call for heat or cooled air.

Name _____

Identification
Identify the parts of the air conditioning system pictured below.

_____ 29. Fan.

_____ 30. Condenser.

_____ 31. Register.

_____ 32. Orifice.

_____ 33. Blower.

_____ 34. Furnace.

_____ 35. Filter.

_____ 36. Compressor.

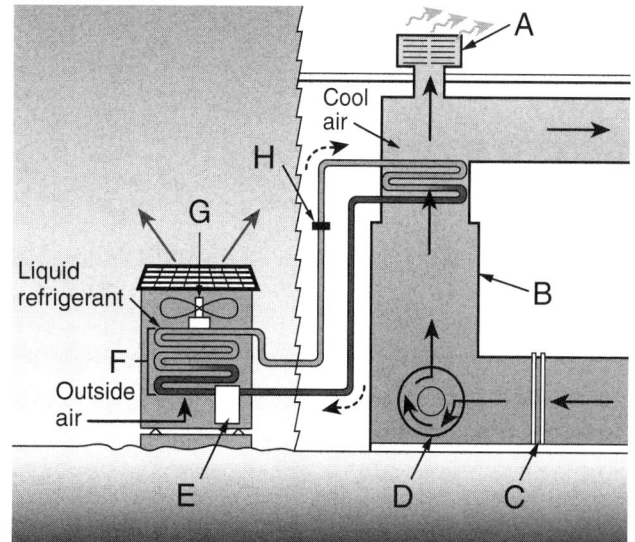

31 Scaffolds and Ladders

Objectives

After studying this chapter, students will be able to:
- Explain typical designs and construction of manufactured and site-built scaffolding.
- Discuss the types and uses of brackets and jacks.
- List ladder types and maintenance techniques.
- Apply ladder and scaffolding safety rules.

Instructional Materials

Text: Pages 891–901
  Technical Vocabulary, page 891
  Test Your Knowledge, page 901
  Curricular Connections, page 901
  Outside Assignments, page 901
Workbook: Pages 175–178
Instructor's Resource:
  Reproducible masters:
    RM 31-1A *Wooden Scaffold Designs*
    RM 31-1B *Wooden Scaffold Designs*
    RM 31-2 *Metal Scaffold Assembly*
    RM 31-3 *Ladder Handling and Care*
  Transparencies (binder/CD only):
    CT 31-1 *Safe Scaffolding Design*
  Chapter Quiz

Trade-Related Math

The feet of a ladder should be placed away from the building one-fourth of the distance to the top support. In other words, if the distance from the ground to the eaves trough is 20′, the feet of the ladder should be placed 5′ away from the building to assure adequate support.

$20 \div 4 = 5$

Instructional Concepts and Student Learning Experiences

Types of Scaffolding

1. Identify the designs of wooden scaffolds—double-pole and single-pole. Using reproducible masters RM 31-1A and 31-1B *Wooden Scaffold Designs*, discuss the construction of both designs. Stress the importance of selecting straight-grain lumber that is free of large knots. Also, emphasize that the edge grain of the lumber should be parallel to the surface.
2. Identify the components of a scaffold assembly using reproducible master RM 31-2 *Metal Scaffold Assembly*. Stress the importance of setting up the scaffold on a solid base plate, ensuring that the legs will not sink into the ground.
3. Discuss the advantages of using wall brackets when it is necessary to reach high elevations. Emphasize the importance of securely attaching the wall brackets to walls using plenty of bolts or 16d or 20d nails.
4. Describe the use of roof brackets when working on steep slopes.
5. Explain the use of ladder jacks to support simple scaffolds for repair projects. Stress that a lifeline should be used when moving the scaffold, as well as when seated and working on the scaffold.
6. Discuss the use of trestle jacks for interior work. Stress the importance of using good-quality, sound stock for the platform and ledger.
7. Review the safety rules for scaffolding found under heading 31.2 in the text. Emphasize the importance of adhering to the safety rules when working on the job.

Ladders

1. Have the students identify the types of ladders commonly used in the construction

trade—safety rolling ladders, stepladders, extension ladders, and one-piece (single-straight) ladders.
2. Review the safety rules for ladders found under heading 31.3 in the text. Using reproducible master RM 31-3 *Ladder Handling and Care*, emphasize the importance of adhering to the safety rules when working on the job.
3. Discuss the proper means of maintaining a ladder for safe use.
4. Demonstrate the correct, safe procedure for erecting one-piece ladders and extension ladders.

Chapter Review

1. Review the chapter objectives. Be sure that the students fully understand each objective.
2. Assign *Technical Vocabulary, Test Your Knowledge* questions, *Curricular Connections*, and *Outside Assignments* for Chapter 31 of the text. Review the answers in class.
3. Assign Chapter 31 in the workbook. Review the answers in class.

Evaluation

This chapter provides three methods for evaluating student performance. Students should complete the *Test Your Knowledge* section using the book as reference. Students should also be allowed to use the book for reference when completing the workbook material. Use the Chapter 31 Quiz in the instructor's resources for in-class evaluation. Correct the quizzes, return them to the students, and review the quiz questions in group discussion.

Answers to Test Your Knowledge
Text Page 901

1. To allow carpenters to work in areas that are out of reach while standing on the ground or floor deck and to help workers avoid stooping and reaching.
2. False.
3. It can be moved from place to place without disassembly.
4. 2 × 6
5. A board horizontally fastened to scaffolding slightly above the planking to keep tools and materials from falling on workers below.
6. 8
7. four
8. 26
9. rails
10. 3

Answers to Workbook Questions
Pages 175–178

1. safety
2. reaching
   A. Pole.
   B. Guard rails.
   C. Ribbon.
   D. Brace.
   E. Bearer.
   F. Brace.
   G. Footing plank.
4. C. 2 × 6
5. B. 10′
6. diagonal braces
7. A. Roofing bracket.
   B. Ladder jack.
   C. Wall bracket.
8. C. four
9. trestle jacks
10. A. Safety rolling.
    B. Stepladder.
    C. Extension ladder.
    D. One-piece (single-straight) ladder.
11. C. 25%
12. B. 3′
13. C. equip the bottom end of the rails with safety shoes
14. B. At least three legs should rest on solid support.
15. electrical current

Answers to Chapter Quiz

1. True.
2. True.
3. False.
4. False.
5. D. 2 × 10
6. C. Swinging
7. B. 12″
8. C. one-fourth
9. B. 3′

Wooden Scaffold Designs

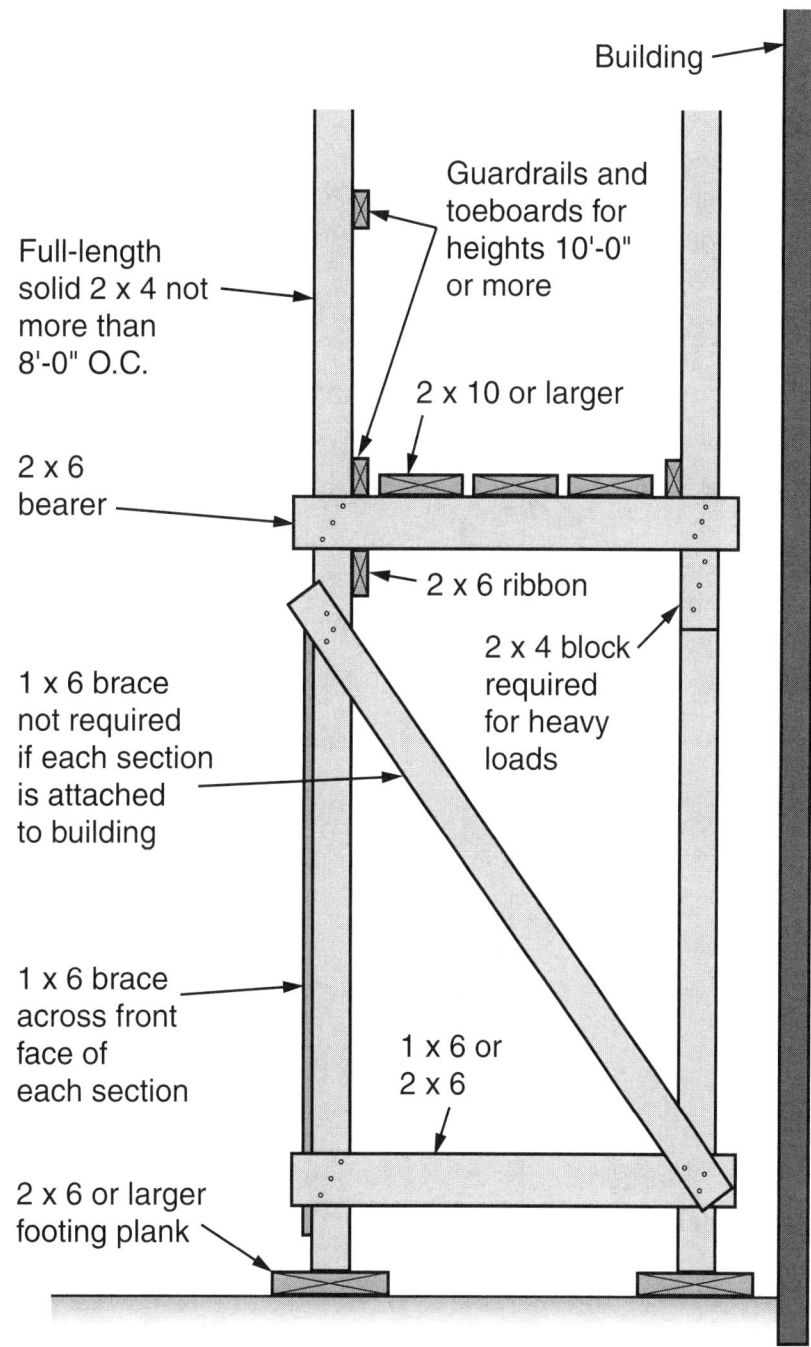

RM 31-1A

Wooden Scaffold Designs

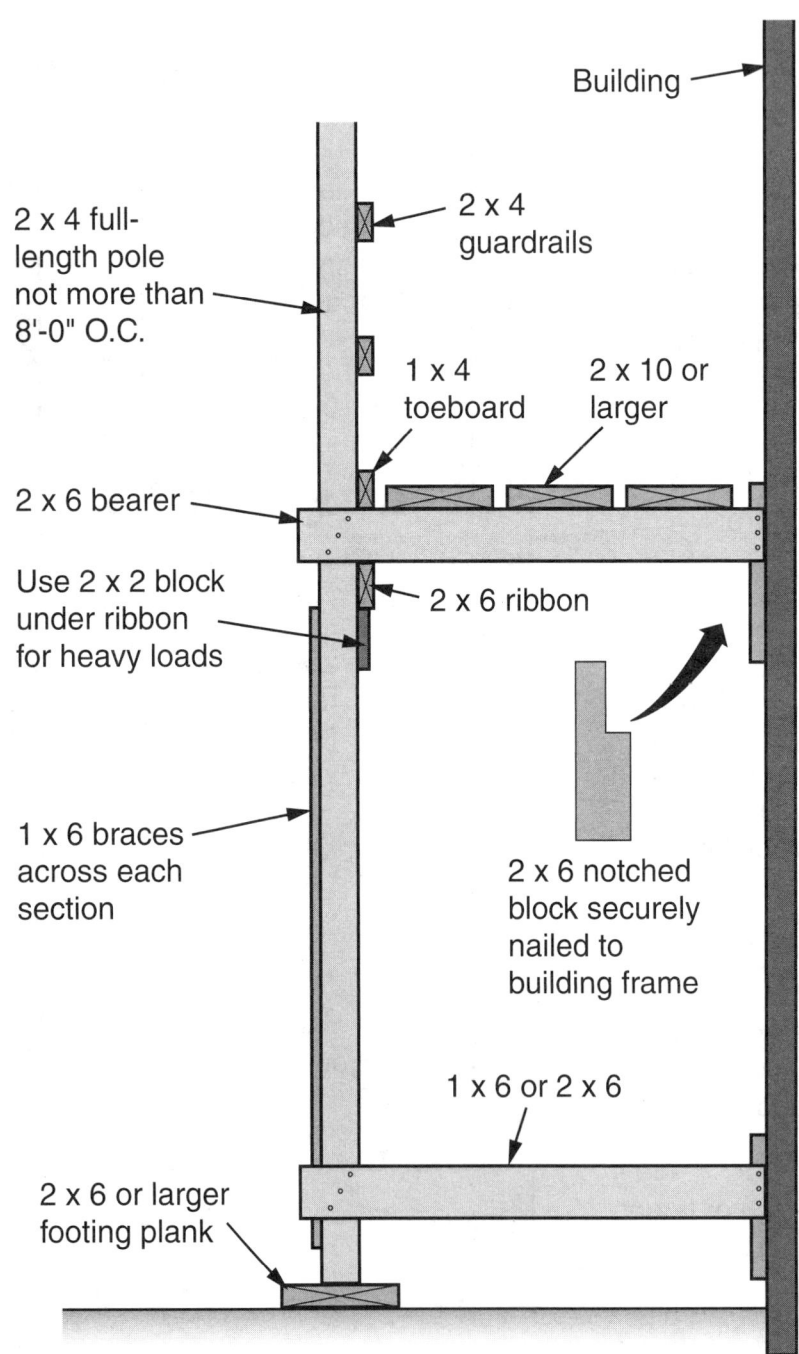

Metal Scaffold Assembly

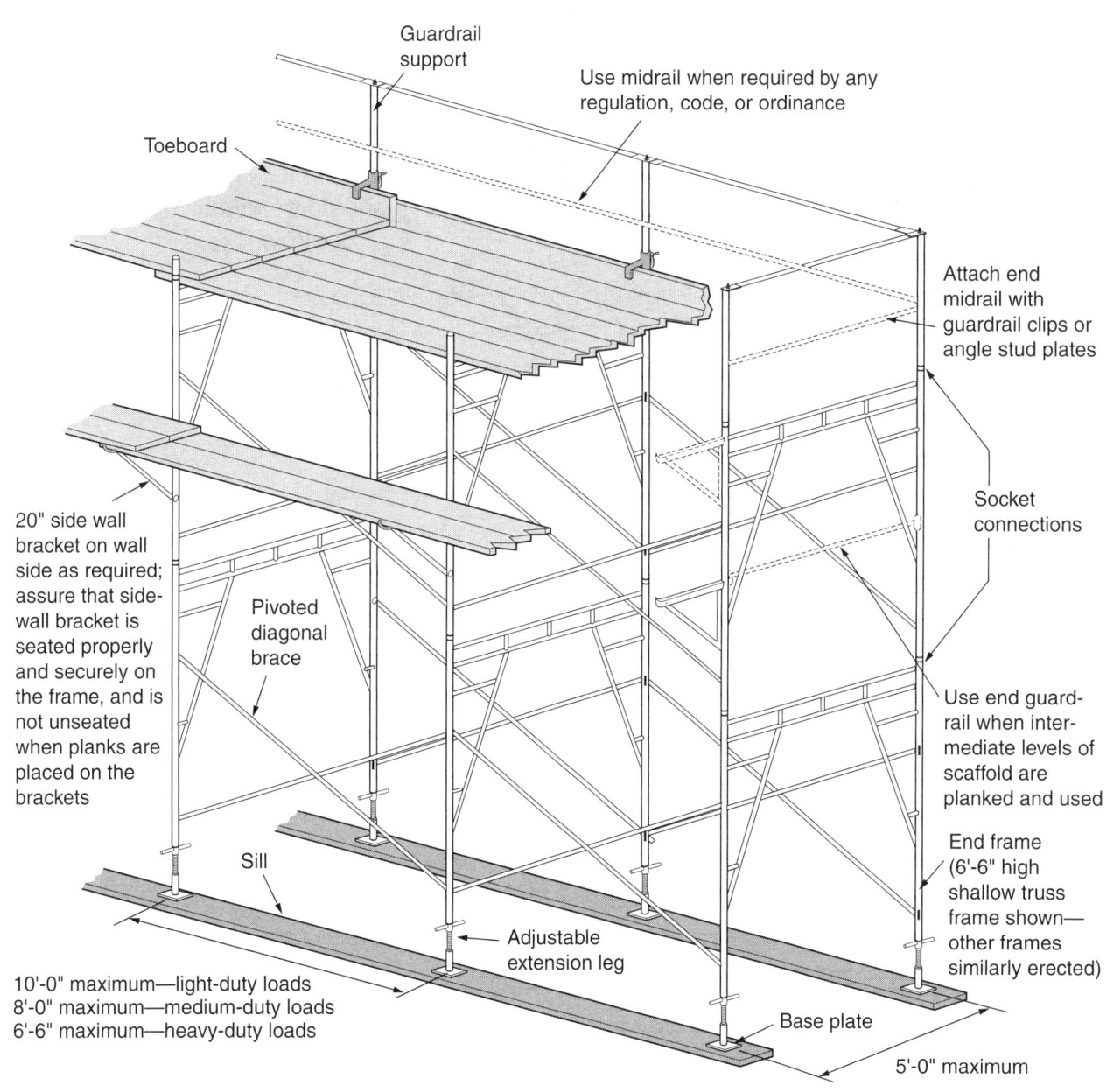

RM 31-2

Ladder Handling and Care

Inspection

Ladders should be inspected frequently. Those with defects should be either repaired or destroyed.

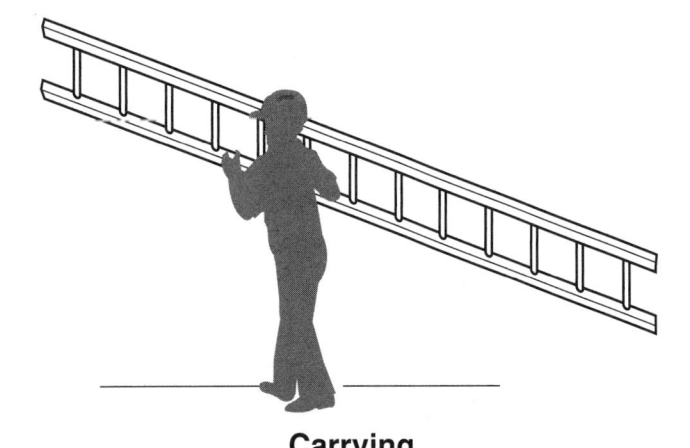

Carrying

Always carry a ladder over your shoulder with the front end elevated. Be sure not to drop it or let it fall. Such an impact weakens a ladder.

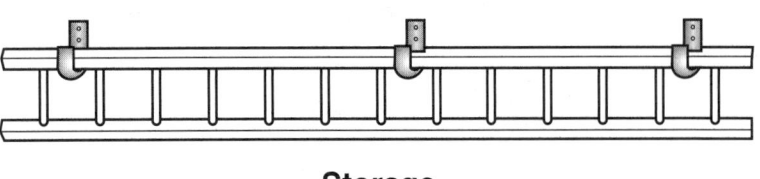

Storage

Store horizontally on supports to prevent sagging. Do not store near heat or out in the weather.

RM 31-3

Chapter 31 Quiz
Scaffolds and Ladders

Name _____ Date _____ Score _____

True-False
Circle T if the answer is True or F if the answer is False.

T   F   1. Some manufactured scaffolding allows the height of the platform to be adjusted.

T   F   2. For wooden scaffolds, choose lumber in which the edge grain runs parallel to the surface.

T   F   3. Ladder rungs should be painted with a high-visibility color.

T   F   4. Safety shoes must be used for ladders on all types of bearing surfaces.

Multiple Choice
Choose the answer that correctly completes the statement. Write the corresponding letter in the space provided.

_____ 5. Planking for wooden scaffolds must be _____ or larger.
   A. 1 × 6
   B. 2 × 4
   C. 2 × 6
   D. 2 × 10

_____ 6. _____ scaffolds are suspended from the roof or other overhead structures.
   A. Double-pole
   B. Single-pole
   C. Swinging
   D. Jack-type

_____ 7. Scaffold planking should be lapped _____ and extend 6" beyond all supports.
   A. 6"
   B. 12"
   C. 18"
   D. 24"

_____ 8. Place a ladder so the horizontal distance from the lower end to the vertical wall is _____ the length of the ladder.
   A. one-half
   B. one-third
   C. one-fourth
   D. one-eighth

_____ 9. A 36′ extension ladder should lap at least _____.
   A. 2′
   B. 3′
   C. 4′
   D. 6′

32 Carpentry—A Career Path

Objectives

After studying this chapter, students will be able to:
- Cite the projected demand for carpenters in coming years.
- List job possibilities for the trained carpenter.
- Describe the sequence of carpentry training and apprenticeship.
- Discuss abilities and characteristics needed by those in the carpentry field.

Instructional Materials

Text: Pages 903–916
  Technical Vocabulary, page 903
  Test Your Knowledge, page 916
  Curricular Connections, page 916
  Outside Assignments, page 916
Workbook: Pages 179–182
Instructor's Resource:
  Reproducible masters:
    RM 32-1 *Apprenticeship Training and Related Groups*
  Transparencies (binder/CD only):
    CT 32-1 *Apprentice and Training System for Carpentry Trade*
  Chapter Quiz

Instructional Concepts and Student Learning Experiences

Economic Outlook
1. Using a current edition of the *Occupational Outlook Handbook*, prepare a handout for students on the economic outlook for construction.
2. Emphasize that a share of the nation's economic growth is in construction of buildings.
3. Note that there are other areas of construction that also offer opportunities for individuals with carpentry skills.

Employment Outlook
1. Discuss the size of the current workforce in carpentry (an estimated 850,000). Note that the demand for carpenters is the highest of any of the trades.
2. Have students look at the cyclical nature of layoffs.
3. Suggest that for those interested in a carpentry career, careful budgeting of finances is necessary to bridge layoffs.

Job Opportunities
1. Discuss the types of job opportunities available for a carpenter.
2. Have the students list factors that should be considered when selecting the type of work they would like to do.

Training
1. List the types of courses that students should take in high school to enhance their career in carpentry. Be prepared to explain why courses such as English or social studies are important in their training.
2. Describe the "roads" that can be taken after graduating from high school to prepare for a career in the carpentry profession.

Apprenticeship
1. Discuss the historic background of the apprenticeship training program and how it has developed into today's program.

Apprenticeship Stages
1. Describe the basic requirements for a carpentry apprentice.

2. Explain the stages that a person must typically go through when involved in an apprenticeship program. Discuss such things as responsibilities, courses they will be required to take, and wages.
3. Using reproducible master RM 32-1 *Apprenticeship Training and Related Groups,* explain that industry and unions are supportive of apprenticeship programs and offer important learning opportunities for apprentice carpenters.

Personal Qualifications
1. Have the students list the personal qualifications necessary to become a successful carpenter. These should include not only work-related traits, but also character traits and interpersonal skills.

Chapter Review
1. Review the chapter objectives. Be sure that the students fully understand each objective.
2. Assign *Technical Vocabulary, Test Your Knowledge* questions, *Curricular Connections,* and *Outside Assignments* for Chapter 32 of the text. Review the answers in class.
3. Assign Chapter 32 in the workbook. Review the answers in class.

Evaluation
This chapter provides three methods for evaluating student performance. Students should complete the *Test Your Knowledge* section using the book as reference. Students should also be allowed to use the book for reference when completing the workbook material. Use the Chapter 32 Quiz in the instructor's resources for in-class evaluation. Correct the quizzes, return them to the students, and review the quiz questions in group discussion.

Answers to Test Your Knowledge
Text Page 916
1. West, South
2. C. 850,000
3. B. one-third.
4. heat, freezing temperatures
5. ten
6. (*any nine*) Woodworking; building construction; drafting; print reading; career education; concrete work; bricklaying; plumbing; sheet metal; electric wiring.
7. four
8. A tradesperson who is fully qualified to perform all tasks of the trade.
9. starts and operates a business
10. An organization that promotes development of excellence in construction and holds state and national competitions to encourage students in a variety of occupations, including building trades.

Answers to Workbook Questions
Pages 179–182
1. Colorado
2. C. Heating, plumbing, and electrical maintenance in commercial buildings.
3. D. All the above.
4. C. child-parent
5. D. seven years
6. journeyman
7. management
8. C. Associated General Contractors of America, Inc.
9. B. 17 years
10. C. four
11. D. 144
12. C. 50%
13. journeyman
14. Manual dexterity

Answers to Chapter Quiz
1. True.
2. False.
3. False.
4. False.
5. B. 10
6. C. journeyman
7. B. 4

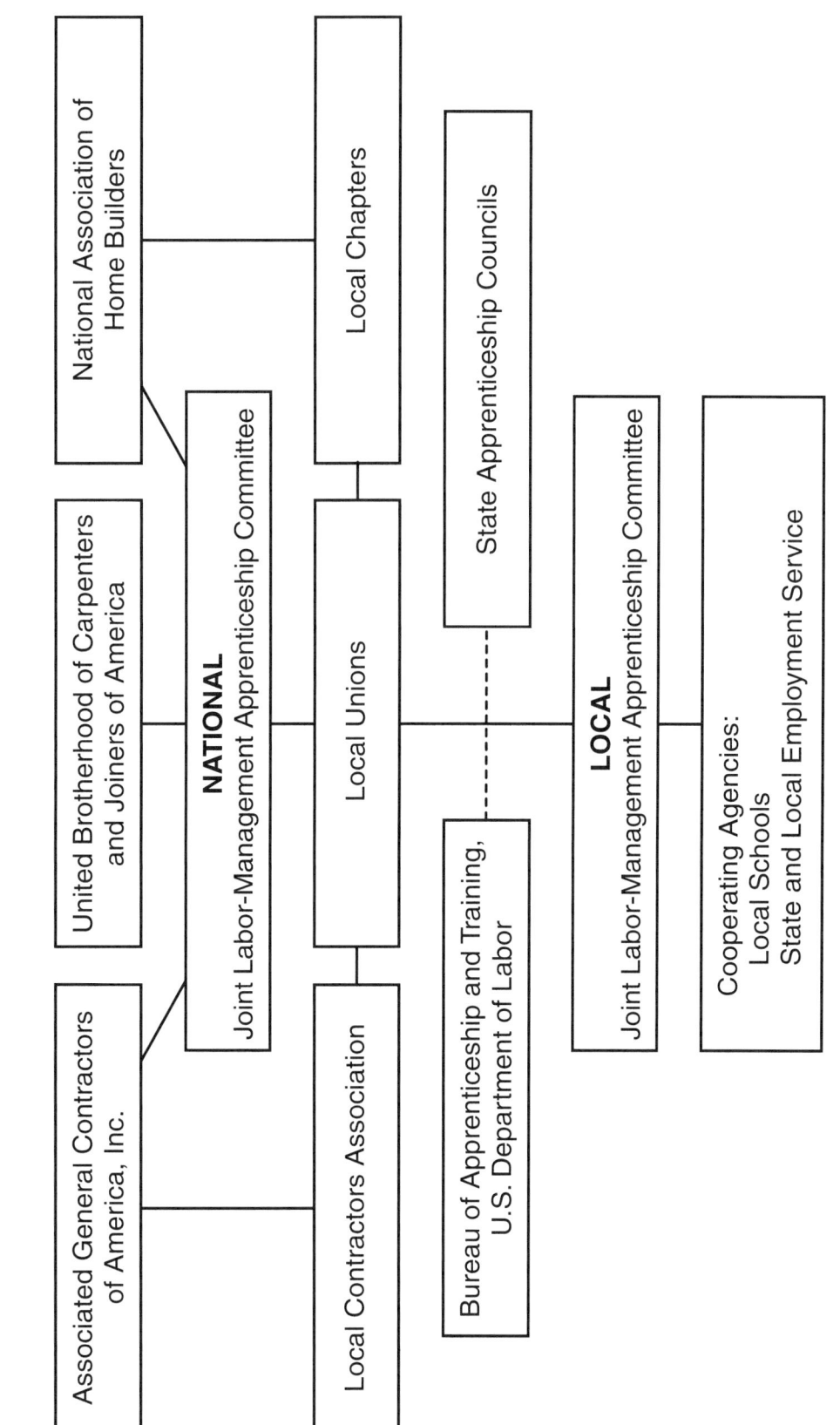

Chapter 32 Quiz
Carpentry—A Career Path

Name _____ Date _____ Score _____

True-False
Circle T if the answer is True or F if the answer is False.

T   F   1. Interpersonal skills are important to being a successful carpenter.

T   F   2. Math and science have little impact on the carpentry trade and are therefore not important aspects of training.

T   F   3. Apprenticeship training is a recently developed concept.

T   F   4. In modern apprenticeship programs, the apprentices are generally not paid.

Multiple Choice
Choose the answer that correctly completes the statement. Write the corresponding letter in the space provided.

_____ 5. Four out of _____ carpenters is self-employed.
    A. 8
    B. 10
    C. 12
    D. 15

_____ 6. A(n) _____ is a person who is fully qualified in a trade.
    A. apprentice
    B. laborer
    C. journeyman
    D. traveler

_____ 7. The term of an apprentice carpenter is _____ years under normal conditions.
    A. 2
    B. 4
    C. 5
    D. 6

Section 7 Exam
Scaffolds and Careers

Name _____ Date _____ Score _____

True-False
Circle T if the answer is True or F if the answer is False.

T F 1. Guardrails and toeboards are required for scaffolds only at heights greater than 25′.

T F 2. Carpenter apprentices must be at least 25 years old.

T F 3. The term of a carpentry apprenticeship is four years.

T F 4. Courses such as science and math are not really necessary to understand the technical aspects of modern plumbing.

T F 5. A journeyman is a person learning a trade or craft.

T F 6. Apprenticeship training consists of on-the-job, as well as classroom-training.

Multiple Choice
Choose the answer that correctly completes the statement. Write the corresponding letter in the space provided.

_____ 7. The sides of a ladder are called _____.
   A. rungs
   B. stiles
   C. rails
   D. stretchers

_____ 8. When a ladder is used to climb onto a roof, it should extend at least _____ above the roof edge.
   A. 2′
   B. 3′
   C. 4′
   D. 5′

_____ 9. Scaffold planking should lap at least _____.
   A. 3″
   B. 6″
   C. 9″
   D. 12″

_____ 10. The height of a rolling scaffold platform should not exceed ____ times the smallest base dimension.
A. two
B. three
C. four
D. five

_____ 11. A 48′ ladder should lap at least ____ between sections.
A. 2′
B. 3′
C. 4′
D. 5′

_____ 12. The initial wage scale for an apprentice is about ____ of a journeyman.
A. 15%
B. 25%
C. 40%
D. 50%

Identification
Identify the parts of the double-pole scaffold.

_____ 13. Footing plank.

_____ 14. Guardrail and toeboard.

_____ 15. Brace.

_____ 16. Ribbon.

_____ 17. Bearer.

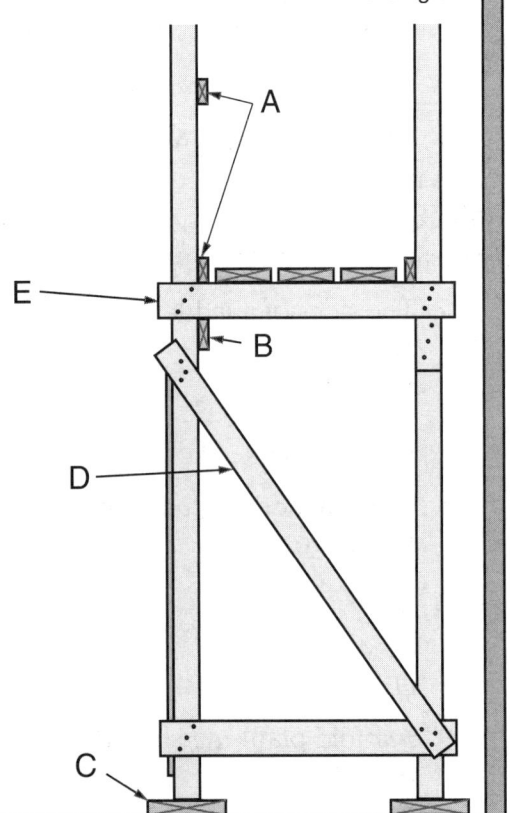

Answers to Section Exams

Answers to Section 1 Exam
1. False.
2. True.
3. False.
4. True.
5. True.
6. False.
7. True.
8. False
9. C. studs, joists, rafters, and wall plates
10. D. 12.5%
11. B. face
12. A. width of the belt
13. B. 6"
14. D. 12"
15. D. cambium layer
16. E
17. A
18. C
19. B
20. D
21. F
22. Eight
23. plot
24. 90
25. line of sight
26. benchmark or datum
27. 1 1/2" × 3 1/2"
28. 120
29. contact cement
30. 10
31. diameter
32. D.
33. B.
34. A.
35. G.
36. E.
37. F.
38. C.
39. E.
40. A.
41. C.
42. F.
43. B.
44. D.

Answers to Section 2 Exam
1. False.
2. False.
3. False.
4. False.
5. True.
6. True.
7. False.
8. True.
9. True.
10. True.
11. B. hydration
12. C. areaway
13. D. 3/8"
14. C. 9.5
15. A. 4"
16. D. All of the above are admixtures.
17. D. All of the above.
18. B. Trimmer studs
19. B. ceiling joists
20. B.
21. C.
22. A.
23. B.
24. C.
25. D.
26. E.
27. A.
28. A.
29. E.
30. B.
31. D.
32. C.
33. ledger board
34. 8
35. sixth
36. sump pit
37. 4

38. 1/2
39. P.E.T.
40. self-tapping screws, welds
41. A.
42. B.
43. D.
44. E.
45. C.
46. F.
47. A.
48. D.
49. B.
50. C.
51. F.
52. E.

Answers to Section 3 Exam
1. True.
2. False.
3. False.
4. True.
5. True.
6. True.
7. True.
8. True.
9. True.
10. False.
11. C. fascia
12. A. square
13. B. centerline
14. A. saddle
15. B. Exterior Insulation Finishing System
16. B. 3'-0"
17. D. All of the above.
18. C. 4
19. B. Sheet metal
20. C.
21. B.
22. D.
23. E.
24. A.
25. C.
26. A.
27. B.
28. E.
29. D.
30. Step
31. 4
32. 5.8
    10.25
33. float glass
34. 6'-8"
35. F.
36. D.
37. A.
38. E.
39. B.
40. C.

Answers to Section 4 Exam
1. True.
2. False.
3. False.
4. True.
5. False.
6. True.
7. False.
8. True.
9. True.
10. True.
11. False.
12. True.
13. False.
14. C. degree day
15. B. dewpoint
16. D. Polystyrene
17. C. decibel
18. A. carpenter
19. B. kicker
20. C.
21. A.
22. B.
23. D.
24. E.
25. C.
26. B.
27. A.
28. D.
29. E.
30. C.
31. B.
32. A.
33. A.
34. C.
35. B.
36. A.
37. B.
38. E.
39. D.
40. C.
41. B.
42. A.

43. impact sounds
44. Sound Transmission Loss (STL)
45. clear
46. balustrade
47. baseboard
48. contact cement
49. Infiltration
50. Backing board
51. underlayment
52. 17–18
53. starting newel

Answers to Section 5 Exam
1. False.
2. True.
3. False.
4. True.
5. True.
6. False.
7. True.
8. False.
9. C. Longitudinal
10. B. Stressed skin panels
11. D. All of the above.
12. A. internal heat
13. D. All of the above.
14. D. All of the above.
15. B.
16. E.
17. D.
18. A.
19. C.
20. thermosiphon
21. isolated
22. trimmer
23. Jack posts
24. Trombe wall
25. south
26. Convection
27. 2,4
28. chase
29. Underwriters' Laboratories
30. G.
31. A.
32. C.
33. E.
34. F.
35. B.
36. D.
37. E.
38. A.
39. D.
40. C.
41. F.
42. B.

Answers to Section 6 Exam
1. False.
2. True.
3. True.
4. False.
5. False.
6. False.
7. D. All of the above.
8. D. All of the above.
9. C. hydronic radiant
10. Conductors
11. perimeter
12. Oakum
13. kinks
14. air conditioners
15. Registers
16. B.
17. E.
18. D.
19. C.
20. A.
21. B.
22. D.
23. A.
24. C.
25. B.
26. C.
27. A.
28. D.
29. G.
30. F.
31. A.
32. H.
33. D.
34. B.
35. C.
36. E.

Answers to Section 7 Exam
1. False.
2. False.
3. True.
4. False.
5. False.
6. True.
7. C. rails

8. B. 3'
9. D. 12"
10. C. four
11. C. 4'
12. D. 50%
13. C.
14. A.
15. D.
16. B.
17. E.

Transparency Captions

The transparency package is intended to be used as an additional resource when teaching from **Modern Carpentry.** The transparencies are designed to assist your carpentry students in understanding principles and practices of carpentry. They can be used to help illustrate uses of carpentry products, show details of construction, and build additional interest in the subject. They may be coordinated with and worked into your daily lesson plans.

Additionally, the transparencies may also be used as reproducible handouts and as worksheets or quizzes (with the callouts covered and replaced with letters or numbers).

The identification number found at the bottom of each transparency indicates the unit and its position. For example, transparency CT 1-1 is the first transparency in Chapter 1, CT 1-2 is the second, etc. The captions below coincide with the transparencies. The captions offer a brief description and offer useful suggestions for using the transparencies.

CT 1-1 Reading a Typical Plywood Trademark
Transparency 1-1 shows a typical plywood trademark with callouts indicating the different parts of the stamp. The transparency may be used while discussing different types of plywood. If possible, have samples on hand to pass around to the students. Obtain samples with different stamps to show the students.

CT 2-1 Top Employer Expectations for Beginning Carpenters
Use this transparency with a class discussion on employable skills. Emphasize that most of these expectations are not related to carpentry skills. While specific job skills are important, appropriate behavior is equally important.

CT 2-2 General Safety Rules
Use this transparency to review some general safety rules. This can be used as an introduction to safety information specific to your specific shop and equipment.

CT 2-3 Fire Extinguishers and Fire Classifications
Use this transparency when discussing proper selection of fire extinguishers. Emphasize the four classes of fires and associated symbols. Also, point out that not all fire extinguishers are appropriate to use on all fires.

CT 3-1 Getting Measurements from Scaled Drawings
Transparency 3-1 shows an architect's scale and examples of scaling measurements from drawings. For the scaled drawing measurements, you can mark each foot mark on each illustration. You can also show the students how to calculate these measurements using mathematics.

CT 4-1 Parts of a Plane
Transparency 4-1 shows a bench plane with callouts indicating the various parts. Use the transparency while discussing the use of hand tools and their care.

Copyright by Goodheart-Willcox Co., Inc.

CT 4-2 Parts of a Claw Hammer
Transparency 4-2 shows a claw hammer with callouts indicating the various parts. Use the transparency while discussing the use of hand tools and their care.

CT 5-1 Parts of a Table Saw
Transparency 5-1 shows a table saw with callouts indicating the various parts. Regardless of size, all table saws have the same basic parts. Callouts are used to aid students in identifying and remembering them. Use the transparency as an aid to help students remember the nomenclature and as a point of departure in explaining the role of each part.

CT 5-2 Parts of a Radial Arm Saw
Transparency 5-2 shows a photo of a radial arm saw with callouts indicating the various parts. Use the transparency to introduce stationary power tools and while discussing the safe use of power tools.

CT 5-3 Parts of a Circular Saw
Transparency 5-3 shows a photo of a circular saw with callouts indicating the various parts. Use the transparency while discussing the safe use of power tools.

CT 6-1 Laser Leveling Unit
Transparency 6-1 shows a laser leveling unit with callouts indicating the various parts. Use the transparency when introducing leveling instruments in Chapter 6 of the text.

CT 6-2 Parts of a Builder's Level
Use this transparency to introduce the components and operation of a builder's level.

CT 6-3 Parts of a Transit
Use this transparency to introduce the components and operation of a transit. Discuss the differences between a builder's level and a transit.

CT 7-1 Forming Up for a Slab-on-Grade Foundation in a Warm Climate
Transparency 7-1 shows an Alabama building site with preparations completed for pouring a slab-on-grade foundation and callouts indicating the various parts. Use the transparency when introducing the different types of foundations.

CT 7-2 Proper Bracing of a Poured Basement
Transparency 7-2 shows proper bracing of a poured basement with callouts indicating the various parts. Use the transparency when discussing the need for bracing (due to pressure from exterior forces) until the floor is framed on top of it.

CT 7-3 Pile Foundation
Transparency 7-3 shows a pile foundation on a barrier island. Callouts indicate the various parts. Use the transparency when discussing the different types of foundations.

Copyright by Goodheart-Willcox Co., Inc.

CT 7-4 Prefabricated Plastic Footing Form
Transparency 7-4 shows the details of a plastic footing form. Callouts indicate the various parts. The forming system pictured is left in place and provides drainage of ground water away from the foundation. Since it is hollow, the system receives water through perforations in the outer edges and carries the water away from the footing area.

CT 7-5 Preparing to Pour a Footing for a Foundation
Transparency 7-5 is a photo detailing the preparation for pouring a footing for a foundation. Callouts indicate the various parts.

CT 7-6 Traditional Foundation Form
Transparency 7-6 shows a traditional foundation form made of plywood sides held together with ties. Use the transparency when discussing foundation forms including traditional forms and alternative forms.

CT 7-7 New Types of Foundation Forms
Transparency 7-7 shows two alternative types of foundation forms.
Top:
- Typical of the new forms are these rigid foam forms that are stacked on top of each other as needed.
- Reinforcing can be placed in the cavities, both horizontally and vertically.
- The form may be allowed to remain (in some types of foundations) where it provides excellent insulating quantities or it can be removed.

Bottom:
- Another example of expanded polystyrene concrete forms called "Smartblock."
- Forms come standard width or variable in nominal widths of 8", 10", and 12". Forms are 40" long and 12" high.

CT 8-1 Basic Components of a House
Transparency 8-1 is a cutaway drawing of a residential structure. Callouts indicate the basic parts of a home. The transparency may be used to introduce an individual component or to cover all of the components in a general discussion.

CT 8-2 Second-Story Floor Framing
Transparency 8-2 shows second-floor framing using proper technique for platform framing whether it is for a second floor or a ceiling frame.

CT 9-1 Using Metal Strapping to Strengthen Joists
Many types of strapping are available to secure framing joists against stresses from high winds and earthquakes.

CT 10-1 Rafter Layout Terminology
Use this transparency to introduce rafter terminology.

CT 10-2 Allowable Rafter Spans
Make sure students know that these tables are found in the Technical Information section of the textbook. Work through a few examples with students to show them how to read the tables.

CT 10-3 Length of Common Rafters
Make sure students know that these tables are found in the Technical Information section of the textbook. Work through a few examples with students to show them how to read the tables.

CT 10-4 Standard Fink Truss
Transparency 10-4 illustrates a standard Fink truss with callouts indicating standard parts.

CT 10-5 Truss Rafter Designs
Transparency 10-5 illustrates twelve roof truss designs used in residential and light commercial construction.

CT 10-6 Bracing Truss Rafters
Transparency 10-6 illustrates both temporary and permanent bracing. Roof trusses must be carefully aligned and braced and temporary bracing must be kept in place until sheathing is applied. Stress to students that workers should never leave the job at night until all necessary bracing is in place.

CT 11-1 Framing with Steel
Many residential builders have turned to steel as an alternative to wood framing. Here is a close-up view of a wall and rafter construction in steel.

CT 11-2 Steel Framing Assembly Details
This transparency shows details of how to assemble and secure steel framing for floors and walls.

CT 12-1 Opening Up Attics for Proper Ventilation
Transparency 12-1 shows one system of ridge venting. Ventilating attic space at the soffit and at the ridge allows air to circulate continuously. This action clears away super-heated air and humidity, saving energy and prolonging the life of the roof.

CT 13-1 Wall Framing for Windows
Transparency 13-1 shows a detailed drawing with callouts indicating the parts of the wall framing for a window.

CT 13-2 Window Design
Transparency 13-2 shows detailed drawings with callouts indicating the parts of modern window design. The drawings show the relation of the parts to both the interior and exterior side of the window.

CT 14-1 Stucco Exterior Finish
This transparency is a cutaway drawing with callouts showing appropriate substrates for a traditional stucco siding.

CT 14-2 Exterior Insulated Finish System (EIFS)
Transparency 14-2 uses callouts to indicate each layer of a synthetic stucco exterior siding system.

CT 14-3 Brick Veneer Construction
Transparency 14-3 shows details of typical brick veneer exterior finish.

CT 15-1 Where to Insulate
Important areas for insulation application in a residential structure. Insulating basement and crawl space walls is desirable in most climates, as well.

CT 18-1 Stair Terminology
This transparency shows basic terminology for stair design. Use it when introducing stair construction.

CT 18-2 Sizing Stairwells and Determining Rise and Run
In using this transparency, always stress the importance of following the basic rules:
- Always keep risers and runs the same dimensions to avoid falls.
- The sum of two risers and one tread should be 24" or 25".
- The sum of one riser and one tread should equal 17" or 18".
- The height of the riser times the width of the tread should be between 70" and 75".

CT 20-1 Preparing to Install Kitchen Cabinets
Transparency 20-1 details installation steps that must be taken so that cabinets are made to be level and plumb. Discuss each item with your students.

CT 21-1 Interior Paint: Types and Uses
Transparency 21-1 lists four types of interior paints and their recommended uses.

CT 22-1 Major Components of a Masonry Fireplace
Transparency 22-1 is a cutaway view showing the components of a masonry fireplace.

CT 23-1 Post-and-Beam Construction
In post-and-beam construction, headers can be eliminated, which simplifies framing around windows and doors.

CT 25-1 Storing and Moving Solar-Generated Heat
Solar heat can enter dwelling space directly from sunshine. Other methods, both active and passive, move heat from sun space or storage. Passive systems use convection currents or radiation to cause air exchange. An active system uses an electric fan to pull heated air into living areas.

CT 26-1 Sizing Headers
When using this transparency, describe the use of each table and work through a few examples of reading the table.

CT 26-2 Calculating Loads
Use this transparency to work through examples of calculating the load on a header or post. Provide additional examples, and have the students calculate a load on their own.

CT 27-1 Softwoods Suited for Decks
Transparency 27-1 is a chart that presents the characteristics of each of the major softwoods species suited for use in deck construction.

Copyright by Goodheart-Willcox Co., Inc.

CT 28-1 Symbols for Most Commonly Used Electrical Devices
Transparency 28-1 is a chart that may be used for teaching students the symbols of the most important devices in a home's electrical system. The transparency may also be used when discussing drawings and plans.

CT 28-2 Basic Electrical Plan
Use this transparency to introduce the residential electrical system and also as an example for reading electrical prints.

CT 29-1 Plumbing System
Use this transparency to introduce the water supply systems, plumbing fixtures, and DWV system.

CT 29-2 Plumbing Symbols
Plumbers use (and must understand) these symbols to know what pipe and fittings to use. Symbols apply to all materials: copper, galvanized steel, and plastic.

CT 30-1 Central Air-Conditioning System
Transparency 30-1 shows the primary components and refrigeration flow in a typical central air-conditioning system.

CT 30-2 Heat Pump Operation
Transparency 30-2 shows a simplified drawing that may be used to explain to students how a heat pump functions.

CT 31-1 Safe Scaffolding Design
Scaffolding must safeguard workers and protect them from falls. Call students' attention to toeboards, guardrails, and adjustable feet.

CT 32-1 Apprentice and Training System for Carpentry Trade
This diagram shows the various apprenticeship and training programs for carpenters.